5000431220

D1434009

Texts in Theoretical Computer Science
An EATCS Series

Jörg Rothe

Complexity Theory and Cryptology

An Introduction to Cryptocomplexity

With 63 Figures and 56 Tables

 Springer

Author

Prof. Dr. Jörg Rothe
Universität Düsseldorf
Institut für Informatik
Universitätsstr. 1
40225 Düsseldorf, Germany
rothe@cs.uni-duesseldorf.de

Series Editors

Prof. Dr. Wilfried Brauer
Institut für Informatik der TUM
Boltzmannstrasse 3
85748 Garching, Germany
Brauer@informatik.tu-muenchen.de

Prof. Dr. Grzegorz Rozenberg
Leiden Institute of Advanced Computer Science
University of Leiden
Niels Bohrweg 1
2333 CA Leiden, The Netherlands
rozenber@liacs.nl

Prof. Dr. Arto Salomaa
Turku Centre for Computer Science
Lemminkäisenkatu 14 A
20520 Turku, Finland
asalomaa@utu.fi

Library of Congress Control Number: 2005928704

ACM Computing Classification (1998): E.3, F. 1.3, F.2.2

ISBN-10 3-540-22147-6 Springer Berlin Heidelberg New York

ISBN-13 978-3-540-22147-0 Springer Berlin Heidelberg New York

Springer is a part of Springer Science+Business Media
springeronline.com

© Springer-Verlag Berlin Heidelberg 2005
Printed in Germany

Cover design: KünkelLopka, Heidelberg
Typesetting: Camera ready by author
Production: LE-TeX Jelonek, Schmidt & Vöckler GbR, Leipzig
Printed on acid-free paper   45/3142/YL - 5 4 3 2 1 0

To Irene, Paula, and Ella

Preface

This book is an accessible introduction to complexity theory and cryptology, two closely related areas in theoretical computer science. Based on courses taught at Heinrich-Heine-Universität Düsseldorf and Friedrich-Schiller-Universität Jena since 1996, this textbook is written mainly for undergraduate and graduate students in computer science, mathematics, and engineering. Researchers, teachers, and practitioners working in these fields will also find this book a comprehensive, up-to-date, research-focused guide to central topics in cryptocomplexity.

Chapter 1 provides more details about this book, including suggestions for how to use it and a brief outline of its chapters.

Acknowledgments

I am deeply indebted to Gerd Wechsung who encouraged me to write this book. I am also much indebted to Tobias Riege, Holger Spakowski, and Gerd Wechsung for carefully proofreading parts of the book and for their invaluable help, corrections, and suggestions. The remaining errors are my responsibility because I couldn't persuade any of the proofreaders to take responsibility for them.

For their generous advice, help, and support over the past decade and for hosting numerous wonderful, inspiring, and prolific research visits at the University of Rochester and the Rochester Institute of Technology, I am deeply indebted to Lane A. Hemaspaandra and Edith Hemaspaandra. I also thank all my fellow researchers, coauthors, and colleagues: Lane and Edith Hemaspaandra, Alina Beygelzimer, Bernd Borchert, Judy Goldsmith, André Große, Christopher M. Homan, Zhigen Jiang, Mitsunori Ogihara, Kari Pasanen, Rajesh P. N. Rao, Tobias Riege, Amitabh Saxena, Holger Spakowski, Jörg Vogel, Osamu Watanabe, and Gerd Wechsung. Some of the research described in this book has been done jointly with them.

I very much appreciate the help and advice of my friends in Rochester, NY, and Atlanta, GA, who had to read some of the stories in this book. I am grateful to Kathleen and Charles Landers-Appell, Mette Stromnes and Dave Lutz, Narin Hassan and Mark Leibert, and, last but not least, Jodi Beckwith and Stefan Cohen.

I gratefully acknowledge inspiring discussions with Klaus Ambos-Spies, Sigurd Assing, Harald Hempel, Uwe Schöning, Andreas Stelzer, Dietrich Stoyan, Klaus W. Wagner, and Gerd Wechsung. For providing a pleasant work environment, I thank my colleagues at the Computer Science departments in Düsseldorf and Jena: Volker Aurich, Stefan Conrad, Gabor Erdélyi, André Große, Arndt von Haeseler, Harald Hempel, Maren Hinrichs, Dieter Kratsch, Gerhard Lischke, Martin Mauve, Haiko Müller, Tobias Riege, Holger Spakowski, Jörg Vogel, Egon Wanke, and Gerd Wechsung. The support of the technical and secretarial staff in Düsseldorf is also gratefully acknowledged. Thanks to Claudia Forstinger, Claudia Kiometzis, Guido Königstein, Berthold Nöckel, Marga Potthoff, Janus Tomaschewski, and Lutz Voigt.

I thank Claude Crépeau for his kind permission to use his original Alice and Bob design in Figure 1.1.

For generous advice and professional support, I am grateful to the Springer series editors and staff, in particular to Wilfried Brauer, Grzegorz Rozenberg, Arto Salomaa, Alfred Hofmann, Ingeborg Mayer, and Ronan Nugent, and to Julia Merz for the cover design. The support of the DFG under grant RO 1202/9-1 and of the DAAD and the NSF under grant NSF-INT-9815095/DAAD-315-PPP-gü-ab, which funded my research projects during the planning and writing of this book, is also gratefully acknowledged.

Above all, I thank my wife, Irene, and my daughters, Paula and Ella, for their love, advice, encouragement, and support. In particular, I thank Irene for her little dragon, ring, and grail, and I thank Paula and Ella for starring in some of the stories told in this book.

Düsseldorf, December 2004   *Jörg Rothe*

Contents

Preface VII

1   Introduction to Cryptocomplexity   1

2   Foundations of Computer Science and Mathematics   9
   2.1   Algorithmics   9
   2.2   Formal Languages and Recursive Function Theory 16
   2.3   Logic 29
      2.3.1   Propositional Logic 29
      2.3.2   Predicate Logic 34
   2.4   Algebra, Number Theory, and Graph Theory 37
      2.4.1   Algebra and Number Theory 37
      2.4.2   Permutation Groups 41
      2.4.3   Graph Theory 43
   2.5   Probability Theory 46
   2.6   Exercises and Problems 47
   2.7   Summary and Bibliographic Remarks 51

3   Foundations of Complexity Theory 53
   3.1   Tasks and Aims of Complexity Theory 53
   3.2   Complexity Measures and Classes 56
   3.3   Speed-Up, Compression, and Hierarchy Theorems 63
   3.4   Between Logarithmic and Polynomial Space 72
   3.5   Reducibilities and Completeness 77
      3.5.1   Many-One Reducibilities, Hardness, and Completeness 77
      3.5.2   NL-Completeness 81
      3.5.3   NP-Completeness 88
   3.6   Inside NP 106
      3.6.1   P versus NP and the Graph Isomorphism Problem 106
      3.6.2   The Berman–Hartmanis Isomorphism Conjecture and
            One-Way Functions 108

3.7   Exercises and Problems 114
3.8   Summary and Bibliographic Remarks 118

4   Foundations of Cryptology................................... 127
4.1   Tasks and Aims of Cryptology.............................. 127
4.2   Some Classical Cryptosystems and Their Cryptanalysis........... 130
    4.2.1   Substitution and Permutation Ciphers 130
    4.2.2   Affine Linear Block Ciphers 135
    4.2.3   Block and Stream Ciphers 145
4.3   Perfect Secrecy 151
    4.3.1   Shannon's Theorem and Vernam's One-Time Pad 151
    4.3.2   Entropy and Key Equivocation 155
4.4   Exercises and Problems 161
4.5   Summary and Bibliographic Remarks 168

5   Hierarchies Based on NP 171
5.1   Boolean Hierarchy over NP 172
5.2   Polynomial Hierarchy 190
5.3   Parallel Access to NP 201
    5.3.1   A Brief Digression to Social Choice Theory 206
    5.3.2   Determining Young Winners Is Complete for Parallel
        Access to NP... 208
5.4   Query Hierarchies over NP 212
5.5   The Boolean Hierarchy Collapsing the Polynomial Hierarchy...... 217
5.6   Alternating Turing Machines 221
5.7   The Low and the High Hierarchy within NP 232
5.8   Exercises and Problems 241
5.9   Summary and Bibliographic Remarks 248

6   Randomized Algorithms and Complexity Classes 261
6.1   The Satisfiability Problem of Propositional Logic 262
    6.1.1   Deterministic Time Complexity 263
    6.1.2   Probabilistic Time Complexity 265
6.2   Probabilistic Polynomial-Time Classes........................ 268
    6.2.1   PP, RP, and ZPP: Monte Carlo and Las Vegas Algorithms .. 268
    6.2.2   BPP: Bounded-Error Probabilistic Polynomial Time 275
6.3   Quantifiers and Arthur-Merlin Games 279
    6.3.1   Quantifiers and BPP 279
    6.3.2   Arthur-Merlin Hierarchy 286
6.4   Counting Classes 290
6.5   Graph Isomorphism and Lowness 294
    6.5.1   Graph Isomorphism Is in the Low Hierarchy 294
    6.5.2   Graph Isomorphism Is in SPP 298
6.6   Exercises and Problems 302
6.7   Summary and Bibliographic Remarks 306

7   RSA Cryptosystem, Primality, and Factoring 311
  7.1   RSA 312
     7.1.1   RSA Public-Key Cryptosystem....................... 312
     7.1.2   RSA Digital Signature Scheme...................... 316
  7.2   Primality Tests 317
     7.2.1   Fermat Test 319
     7.2.2   Miller–Rabin Test 323
     7.2.3   Solovay–Strassen Test 329
     7.2.4   Primality Is in P 335
  7.3   Factoring 335
     7.3.1   Trial Division 336
     7.3.2   Pollard's Algorithm 337
     7.3.3   Quadratic Sieve.............................. 338
     7.3.4   Other Factoring Methods........................ 343
  7.4   Security of RSA: Possible Attacks and Countermeasures.......... 345
  7.5   Exercises and Problems 353
  7.6   Summary and Bibliographic Remarks 357

8   Other Public-Key Cryptosystems and Protocols 361
  8.1   Diffie–Hellman and the Discrete Logarithm Problem 362
     8.1.1   Diffie and Hellman's Secret-Key Agreement Protocol 362
     8.1.2   Discrete Logarithm and the Diffie–Hellman Problem 366
  8.2   ElGamal's Protocols 369
     8.2.1   ElGamal's Public-Key Cryptosystem 369
     8.2.2   ElGamal's Digital Signature Scheme 371
     8.2.3   Security of ElGamal's Protocols 373
  8.3   Rabin's Public-Key Cryptosystem........................ 380
     8.3.1   Rabin's Cryptosystem 381
     8.3.2   Security of Rabin's System 383
  8.4   Arthur-Merlin Games and Zero-Knowledge 386
  8.5   Merkle and Hellman's Public-Key Cryptosystem 393
  8.6   Rabi, Rivest, and Sherman's Protocols 396
  8.7   Exercises and Problems 402
  8.8   Summary and Bibliographic Remarks 408

List of Figures 413

List of Tables 415

References 417

Index 444

1

Introduction to Cryptocomplexity

About This Book

This book is an introduction to two areas, *complexity theory* and *cryptology*, which are closely related but have developed rather independently of each other. Modern cryptology employs mathematically rigorous concepts and methods of complexity theory. Conversely, current research in complexity theory is often motivated by questions and problems arising in cryptology. This book takes account of this trend, and therefore its subject is what may be dubbed "*cryptocomplexity*," some kind of symbiosis of these two areas.

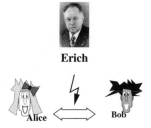

Erich

Fig. 1.1. A typical cryptographic scenario (the design of Alice and Bob is due to Crépeau)

Figure 1.1 shows a typical scenario in cryptography. Alice and Bob wish to exchange messages over an insecure channel such as a public telephone line on which Erich is an eavesdropper. That is why Alice encrypts her messages to Bob in such a way that Bob can easily decrypt them, but Erich cannot. Cryptography is the art and science of designing secure cryptosystems. Alice and Bob use cryptosystems and cryptographic techniques to protect their private data and keep it secret, to electronically sign their messages so that their signatures cannot be forged, for authentication, for the protection of copyrights, to make secure use of computer networks, to exchange information and do business over the internet in a secure way.

Their adversary is Erich, angry that he can intercept or eavesdrop their messages alright, but to no avail for himself. He aims at unauthorized decryption of their ciphertexts, he wants to get his hands at their decryption keys to break their cryptosystem. Cryptanalysis is the art and science of breaking cryptosystems. Cryptology comprises both these fields, cryptography and cryptanalysis.

Cryptography and cryptanalysis have fought an ongoing war against each other since ancient times. When our ancestors learned to think and speak and write, they not only sought to convey their thoughts and messages but also to protect them from unauthorized recipients, i.e., to keep them secret. Even Gaius Julius Caesar, dictator perpetuus of Rome, made use of a simple (and easy-to-break) cryptosystem.

Battle after battle has been fought between these two opposing worlds ever since: As soon as the cryptographers have designed a new cryptosystem, the cryptanalysts do not rest before they have broken it, whereupon better cryptosystems are developed, and so forth. The phrases "war" and "battle" can be taken literally here. During World War II, the struggle of the Allied codebreakers against the infamous encryption machine *Enigma* used by the Deutsche Wehrmacht was a matter of life and death. The *Enigma*, considered unbreakable at first, was eventually broken by the British codebreakers from Bletchley Park, aided by previous work of Polish mathematicians and the cooperation of a German spy. Their achievement was decisive—if not for the war then for a number of battles, especially for the big sea battles and the destruction of the German submarine fleet. Singh [Sin99] and Bauer [Bau00a] elaborately tell the thrilling story of this struggle between the German cryptographers and the Allied cryptanalysts. The success of breaking the *Enigma* is attributed to Alan Turing among others. His brilliance as a cryptanalyst is surpassed only by his ingenious, fundamental achievements in theoretical computer science. By inventing the Turing machine, which is named after him, Turing laid the foundations of recursive function and computability theory, the mother of complexity theory.

That efficient algorithms have useful applications in practice is obvious. In contrast, complexity theory aims at proving that certain problems are not efficiently solvable. It provides the means and methods for classifying problems with respect to their inherent computational complexity. It also provides useful tools and techniques for comparing the relative complexity of two given problems via reductions.

In cryptographic settings, provable inefficiency means security: The security of current cryptosystems is based on the assumption that certain problems cannot be solved efficiently. The problem of breaking a cryptosystem can be linked via reductions to suitable problems widely believed to be intractable. Cryptography thus requires and utilizes the computational intractability of problems. In short, cryptography needs and motivates complexity-theoretic notions, models, methods, and results. In particular, the notions of one-way functions, interactive proof systems, and zero-knowledge protocols are central both in cryptology and in complexity theory, which demonstrates the mutual pervasion of these two fields. This book introduces both cryptology and complexity theory, with a particular focus on their interrelation.

How to Use This Book

This book is based on the author's lectures held at Heinrich-Heine-Universität Düsseldorf and Friedrich-Schiller-Universität Jena since 1996. Written mainly for undergraduate and graduate students in computer science, mathematics, and engineering, it is a valuable source also for researchers, university teachers, and practitioners working in these fields.

This textbook can be used for teaching in more ways than one. On the one hand, it can be used for introductory courses in cryptology from a complexity-theoretic perspective. On the other hand, it can be used for introductory courses in complexity theory, emphasizing potential applications in cryptology. In both regards, this book provides a comprehensive, up-to-date, research-focused guide to the state of the art in these two fields, stressing their connections and choosing a unified approach.

Ideally, however, this book should be used for a series of interrelated courses introducing both these areas jointly. For example, based on the material presented in this book, a series of four one-semester courses for undergraduate students was test-driven by the author in Düsseldorf. The students' positive feedback suggests that the approach of focusing on the interrelations between complexity theory and cryptology is more profitable for them than teaching these fields separately and independently. A typical course series consists of the following four modules on cryptocomplexity:

Cryptocomplexity I: gives an introduction to complexity theory based on material selected from Chapter 2, Chapter 3, Chapter 5 (e.g., Sections 5.1, 5.2, and 5.6), and Chapter 6 (e.g., Sections 6.1, 6.2, and 6.3).

Cryptocomplexity II: presents more advanced topics from complexity theory based on material selected from Chapter 5 (e.g., Sections 5.3, 5.4, 5.5, and 5.7) and Chapter 6 (e.g., Sections 6.4 and 6.5).

Cryptocomplexity III: gives an introduction to cryptology based on material selected from Chapters 2, 4, and 7.

Cryptocomplexity IV: presents more advanced topics from cryptology based on material selected from Chapters 7 and 8.

Of course, the topics presented in this book can be supplemented by current original research results and other material of interest. Detailed descriptions of these modules can be found at http://wwwold.cs.uni-duesseldorf.de/~rothe.

Much care has been taken to motivate and explain the notions and results presented. Numerous examples, figures, and tables are provided to make the text comprehensible, easy-to-read, and hopefully even entertaining at times. Occasionally, before presenting some notion or result in abstract, formal, mathematical terms, it is first introduced and explained using a short story.

Reading this book is not only fun, though, it is also hard work: Every chapter has a set of exercises and problems, with hints at possible solutions or pointers to the original literature. The degree of difficulty of the exercises varies in a broad range; there are rather easy exercises and there are hard ones. Many of the problems are most challenging. Some of them are research problems that were solved only recently in the literature, and they sometimes require deep insights or clever ideas. Even if they turn out to be too difficult, it is worth trying to solve them.

Due to its comprehensive bibliography (with 516 entries) and subject index (with 1466 main entries), this textbook is also a valuable source for researchers working in complexity theory and cryptology. Starting from scratch and seeking a unified approach, it works its way to the frontiers of current research in selected topics from these two fields. Every chapter concludes with a summary that describes the historical development of the notions and results presented, explains related notions and ideas, and provides comprehensive, detailed bibliographic remarks.

The subject index has an abundance of entries and cross-references because a textbook is only as useful as its index is.[1] Every catchword can have several entries, a boldfaced main entry pointing to its definition, and a number of other entries pointing to theorems containing the catchword. A textbook without an index, or with a poorly or sloppily made index, is of no more help to the reader than a library lacking a classified catalog and having all its books huddled together unsorted. You may stand in front of this huge heap of books, knowing that they contain all the knowledge and the wisdom of the universe, and still you won't be able to find that particular piece of information you are looking for so desperately. This point has been eloquently made by Borges [Bor89] in his short story, "The Library of Babel." By the way, each of the catchwords mentioned in Footnote 1 can indeed be found in the index. Check it out.

Admittedly, this book has a clear focus on theory. Practical aspects of security engineering, such as the creation of secure public-key infrastructures, cannot be found here. A recommendable reference for this topic is Buchmann [Buc01].

In 2003 and 2004, a group of University of Düsseldorf students developed a system that implements a number of cryptosystems, which are also treated in this book. Acknowledgments are due to Tobias Riege, who supervised the students, and to Yves Jerschow, Claudia Lindner, Tim Schlüter, David Schneider, Andreas Stelzer, Philipp Stöcker, Alexander Tchernin, Pavel Tenenbaum, Oleg Umanski, Oliver Wollermann, and Isabel Wolters. The source code in Java can be downloaded from `http://wwwold.cs.uni-duesseldorf.de/~riege/praktikum`.

Overview of the Book Chapters

Chapter 2 provides some background from those fields of computer science and mathematics that are relevant to the topics from complexity theory and cryptology covered in this book. The concepts used are explained with mathematical rigor and in as short a way as possible but to the extent necessary to understand them. In particular, it provides some of the elementary foundations of algorithmics, the theory of formal languages, recursive function theory, logic, algebra, number theory, graph

---

[1] Suppose you are looking for each occurrence of the phrase *baby cloning* in this book. Or you are interested in a particular tool, say a *chain-saw* or a *Turing machine*. Or you may want to know what this book has to say about *polygamy*, the wizard *Merlin*, the *Ruling Ring*, the *Holy Grail*, or *DNA tests*. Or you may want to learn everything about its *dogmas*.

theory, and probability theory. Although each field is explained from scratch and not much mathematical background is assumed from the reader, some familiarity with the foundations of mathematics and theoretical computer science might be helpful.

In Chapters 3 and 4, the foundations of complexity theory and cryptology are laid, and their historical development is briefly sketched. In Chapter 3, complexity measures and classes are defined in the traditional worst-case model. (The average-case complexity model is not treated here; a useful reference is Wang's excellent survey [Wan97].) Fundamental properties of worst-case complexity are studied, including linear tape-compression and speed-up and the hierarchy theorems for time and space. The relations between the most central complexity classes between logarithmic and polynomial space are explored. Most notable among them are the classes P and NP, deterministic and nondeterministic polynomial time.

P is thought of as a complexity class capturing the intuitive notion of efficient computation, whereas the hardest problems in NP, the NP-complete problems, are thought of as a collection of intractable problems, assuming $P \neq NP$. The P versus NP question, which asks whether or not these two classes differ, is one of the most important open questions in theoretical computer science, and it has kept annoying complexity theorists for more than thirty years now. If $P \neq NP$ then no NP-complete problem can have efficient (i.e., polynomial-time computable) algorithms. On the other hand, if $P = NP$ then all problems in NP are polynomial-time solvable and, in particular, most of the cryptosystems currently in use can be broken.

Particular attention is paid in Chapter 3 to complexity-bounded reducibilities, such as the polynomial-time many-one reducibility, and to the related notions of hardness and completeness. Reducibilities are powerful tools for comparing the complexity of two given problems, and completeness captures the hardest problems in a complexity class with respect to a given reducibility. In particular, the complete problems in the classes NL (nondeterministic logarithmic space) and NP are intensely investigated, and a host of specific examples of natural complete problems in these classes are given. These include various variants of the satisfiability problem, which asks whether or not a given boolean formula is satisfiable. The list of problems shown to be NP-complete in this chapter includes certain graph problems, such as the graph three-colorability problem, and certain variants of the knapsack problem. Chapter 8 presents a cryptosystem based on such a knapsack-type problem.

There are problems in NP that seem to be neither NP-complete nor to have efficient algorithms. One such example is the graph isomorphism problem, introduced in Chapter 2 and more deeply studied in Chapters 3, 6, and 8. Another example of a problem that can be solved in nondeterministic polynomial time but is not known to be solvable in deterministic polynomial time is the factoring problem, which will be carefully investigated in Chapter 7. Many cryptosystems, including the famous RSA public-key cryptosystem, are based on the hardness of the factoring problem.

Chapter 3 also introduces an interesting complexity class that seems to lack complete problems: UP, "unambiguous polynomial time," contains exactly those NP problems that never have more than one solution. The complexity class UP is useful for characterizing the existence of certain types of one-way functions in the worst-case model. A function is one-way if it is easy to compute but hard to invert. In complexity theory, such functions are closely related to Berman and Hartmanis' isomorphism conjecture. One-way functions (in an adequate model of complexity) are also important in cryptography; such functions are discussed in Chapter 8.

Chapter 4 introduces the basic notions of cryptology, such as symmetric (a.k.a. private-key) and asymmetric (a.k.a. public-key) cryptosystems. This chapter presents some classical symmetric cryptosystems, including the substitution, affine, and permutation ciphers, affine linear block ciphers, stream ciphers, the Vigenère, and the Hill cipher. Cryptanalytic attacks on these cryptosystems are provided by example. Moreover, based on the notion of entropy from Shannon's information and coding theory, the notion of perfect secrecy for cryptosystems is introduced and Shannon's result is presented, which provides necessary and sufficient conditions for a cryptosystem to achieve perfect secrecy.

Chapter 5 turns to complexity theory again and introduces hierarchies based on NP, including the boolean hierarchy over NP and the polynomial hierarchy. Relatedly, various polynomial-time Turing reducibilities are defined. Both these hierarchies contain NP as their first level and are very useful to classify important problems that seem to be harder than NP-complete problems. Examples of problems complete in the higher levels of the boolean hierarchy are the "exact" variants of NP-complete optimization problems, facet problems, and critical graph problems. Examples of problems complete in the higher levels of the polynomial hierarchy are certain variants of NP-complete problems that can be represented by a bounded number of alternating polynomially length-bounded quantifiers. The canonical example of such problems is the quantified boolean formula problem with a bounded number of alternating quantifiers, which generalizes the satisfiability problem.

Relatedly, the notion of alternating Turing machines is introduced in Chapter 5, and P and PSPACE are characterized in terms of such machines: Deterministic polynomial time equals alternating logarithmic space, and deterministic polynomial space equals alternating polynomial time. The former result shows that alternating Turing machines are a reasonable model of parallel computation, since they satisfy Cook's criterion that parallel time is roughly the same as sequential (i.e., deterministic) space. The latter result shows that the quantified boolean formula problem with an unbounded number of alternating quantifiers is complete for PSPACE.

There is a remarkable connection between the polynomial hierarchy and the boolean hierarchy over NP: If the boolean hierarchy collapses to a finite level, then so does the polynomial hierarchy. Chapter 5 further introduces the query hierarchies over NP with a bounded number of queries, and the low and high hierarchies within NP. The low hierarchy can be used to measure the complexity of NP problems that seem to be neither in P nor NP-complete.

Chapter 6 is concerned with randomized algorithms and probabilistic complexity classes. In particular, a randomized algorithm for the NP-complete satisfiability problem is introduced, which still runs in exponential time but is faster than the naive deterministic algorithm for this problem. Moreover, Monte Carlo and Las Vegas algorithms and the probabilistic complexity classes PP (probabilistic polynomial time), RP (random polynomial time), ZPP (zero-error probabilistic polynomial time), and BPP (bounded-error probabilistic polynomial time) are introduced and thoroughly studied in Chapter 6. Bounding the error away from one half yields a very useful probability amplification by which the error in the computation can be made exponentially small in the input size. Such a small error probability can be safely neglected for most practical applications. Again, some of the probabilistic complexity classes (e.g., PP) do have complete problems, whereas others (e.g., BPP) are unlikely to have complete problems.

Chapter 6 also studies the Arthur-Merlin games introduced by Babai and Moran. Arthur-Merlin games can be regarded as interactive proof systems with public coin tosses, and they can be used to define a hierarchy of complexity classes. The main results about the Arthur-Merlin hierarchy in Chapter 6 are, first, that this hierarchy collapses to a finite level, and, second, that the graph isomorphism problem is contained in the second level of this hierarchy. Consequently, the graph isomorphism problem is contained in the low hierarchy and thus is unlikely to be NP-complete.

Chapter 7 introduces the RSA cryptosystem, the first public-key cryptosystem developed in the public sector, which is still widely used in practice today. The RSA digital signature scheme, which is based on the RSA public-key cryptosystem, is also presented. A digital signature protocol enables Alice to sign her messages to Bob so that Bob can verify that indeed she was the sender, and without Erich being able to forge Alice's signature. In addition, numerous cryptanalytic attacks on the RSA system are surveyed and thoroughly discussed, and for each attack on RSA presented, possible countermeasures are suggested.

Related to the RSA system, Chapter 7 investigates the factoring problem and the primality problem in depth. On the one hand, the security of RSA crucially depends on the presumed hardness of factoring large integers. On the other hand, the RSA cryptosystem and digital signature scheme both require the efficient generation of large primes, as do many other cryptosystems. The complexity of the most prominent factoring methods known, such as the quadratic sieve, is discussed in Chapter 7. Note that the factoring problem is currently known neither to have an efficient algorithm nor to have a rigorous proof of its hardness.

Chapter 7 further presents a number of efficient primality tests that are used in practice, including the Fermat test, the Miller–Rabin test, and the Solovay–Strassen test. These are randomized algorithms, and some of them are of the Monte Carlo type. A recent result showing that the primality problem can be solved in deterministic polynomial time is also discussed.

Chapter 8 surveys further important public-key cryptosystems and cryptographic protocols, including the Diffie–Hellman secret-key agreement protocol and the El-Gamal digital signature protocol. The latter protocol, with appropriate modifications, has been adopted as the United States digital signature standard. Relatedly, the discrete logarithm problem is carefully studied in this chapter. The security of many important protocols, such as the two just mentioned, relies on the presumed hardness of the discrete logarithm problem.

Revisiting the graph isomorphism problem and the notion of Arthur-Merlin games that were studied in previous chapters, Chapter 8 introduces the notion of zero-knowledge protocols, which is related to the cryptographic task of authentication.

There have been attempts in the past to base cryptosystems on NP-hard problems; in particular, on variants of the knapsack problem. Some of those cryptosystems were broken, whereas others are still unbroken. One such cryptosystem is presented and critically discussed in Chapter 8. Relatedly, the notion of a trapdoor one-way function, which is important in public-key cryptography, is discussed. Finally, this chapter introduces protocols for secret-key agreement and digital signatures that are based on associative, strongly noninvertible one-way functions (in the worst-case model).

Obviously, there are many interesting topics and results in complexity theory and cryptology that could not be covered in this book. Here are some recommendable references. For example, approximation and nonapproximation results, which are of both theoretical and practical importance, are not covered here; see, for example, Ausiello et al. [ACG+03], Vazirani [Vaz03], and the comprehensive, up-to-date compendium of NP optimization problems edited by Crescenzi, Kann, Halldórsson, Karpinski, and Woeginger:

http://www.nada.kth.se/~viggo/problemlist/compendium.html.

For a variety of further important topics of complexity theory, see the books by Balcázar, Díaz, and Gabarró [BDG95, BDG90], Bovet and Crescenzi [BC93], Du and Ko [DK00], Garey and Johnson [GJ79], L. Hemaspaandra and Ogihara [HO02], Papadimitriou [Pap94], Reischuk [Rei90], Vollmer [Vol99], Wagner and Wechsung [WW86, Wec00], and Wegener [Weg87, Weg03], and the collections edited by Selman and L. Hemaspaandra [Sel90, HS97] and Ambos-Spies, Homer, and Schöning [AHS93]. For topics of cryptology not covered here, see, for example, Goldreich [Gol99, Gol01], Luby [Lub96], Micciancio and Goldwasser [MG02], Salomaa [Sal96], Schneier [Sch96], Stinson [Sti02], and Welsh [Wel98].

2

Foundations of Computer Science and Mathematics

The language of the Netherlands is Dutch. The language of life is the genetic code. And the language of nature and science is mathematics. Just as with most fields of science, the language of mathematics describes the notions, results, and methods of computational complexity and cryptology in the most precise and most elegant way.

This chapter provides an introductory course to those fields of computer science and mathematics that are relevant to the topics from complexity theory and cryptology covered in this book. The concepts used are explained with mathematical rigor and in as short a way as possible but to the extent necessary to understand them. In particular, we provide some basic background from algorithmics, formal languages, recursive function theory, logic, algebra, number theory, graph theory, and probability theory. One may as well skip this chapter and return to it whenever necessary.

2.1 Algorithmics

What is an algorithm? This question, which in a certain sense has also a philosophical dimension, is to be treated merely pragmatically and informally for now. Everyone surely has an intuitive idea of what an algorithm is. A mathematically precise, formal model of the notion of an algorithm, the Turing machine, is introduced later on in Section 2.2, see Definitions 2.15 and 2.16. Turing machines and other, equivalent algorithmic models can be used to formalize the notions of computability of functions and of decidability of problems.

The term "algorithm" has developed by language transformation from the name of the Persian-Arabian scientist Muhammed Ibn Musa Abu Djáfar al Choresmi (773 until 850),[1] the court mathematician of the caliphate in Baghdad. In 820, he wrote the highly influential book "On the Indian Numbers" in which the decimal system (including the number zero) is introduced.

---

[1] Other spellings of his name are known as well, such as Abu Ja'far Mohammed Ibn Musa Al-Khowarizmi [Sch02a]. His name has transformed into "algorithm" via the Latin phrase "*dixit algorizmi*," which might be translated as "Thus spoke al Choresmi" and which was meant to approve the correctness of a calculation with some kind of quality seal.

Intuitively, an algorithm is a finite set of rules or procedures that must be followed in solving some problem. The process of applying these rules on some input may terminate after a finite number of steps either successfully, thereby transforming the input into an output solving the given problem instance, or unsuccessfully, thereby rejecting the input. It may also happen that this process never terminates and the algorithm runs forever. Telling the latter case apart from the first two cases in which the algorithm does terminate is more difficult than one may suspect at first glance. This problem, which is known as the halting problem, asks whether or not a given algorithm (encoded as a string) on a given input ever halts. A fundamental result of recursive function theory says that the halting problem is not decidable algorithmically [Tur36], which means that there is provably no algorithm that solves the halting problem. This result is the first in a long list of so-called undecidability results that show the limitations of algorithms and computers.

$\text{EUCLID}(n, m)$ {
    if $(m = 0)$ return n;
       else return $\text{EUCLID}(m, n \bmod m)$;
}

Fig. 2.1. Euclidian Algorithm

Let us consider an example. One of the most simple and most profound algorithms has been known since ancient times and is mentioned in the book "Elements" by Euclid of Alexandria (about 325 until 265 B.C.). Despite its age, Euclid's algorithm is still very useful, for example in Chapter 7 that introduces the popular public-key cryptosystem RSA.

Let $\mathbb{N} = \{0, 1, 2, \ldots\}$ be the set of natural numbers, and let $\mathbb{Z} = \{0, \pm1, \pm2, \ldots\}$ be the set of integers. The Euclidian Algorithm determines the greatest common divisor of two given integers m and n with $m \leq n$, i.e., the greatest number $k \in \mathbb{N}$ for which there are numbers $a, b \in \mathbb{Z}$ with $m = a \cdot k$ and $n = b \cdot k$. This k is denoted by $\gcd(n, m)$, and is output by the algorithm shown in pseudocode in Figure 2.1.

The Euclidean Algorithm successively modifies the numbers given, n and m, by calling itself recursively with the new numbers m (instead of n) and $n \bmod m$ (instead of m); the notation "$n \bmod m$" and the arithmetics modulo m are explained in Problem 2.1 at the end of this chapter. EUCLID keeps performing this recursion until the break condition ($m = 0$) is reached. By this time, the current value of n is the greatest common divisor $\gcd(n, m)$ of the original input n and m, see (2.1).

There is no doubt that this recursive representation of the Euclidean Algorithm is elegant. It can, however, as well be implemented iteratively. This means that there are no recursive calls, but the intermediate values of the computation are stored explicitly on a stack. Table 2.1 shows a test run for the Euclidean Algorithm on input $n = 170$ and $m = 102$. In this particular case, the algorithm indeed computes the correct solution, since $\gcd(170, 102) = 34$. However, already Edsger Dijkstra (1930 until

n	m	$n \bmod m$
170	102	68
102	68	34
68	34	0
34	0	

Table 2.1. Test run of the Euclidean Algorithm

2002) knew that such tests for particular inputs can display merely the presence of errors, yet not their absence. To prove the correctness of Euclid's algorithm, it is enough to show the following equation:

$$\gcd(n, m) = \gcd(m, n \bmod m). \tag{2.1}$$

For the number $r = n \bmod m$ and an appropriate number $s \in \mathbb{Z}$, we have $n = s \cdot m + r$, where $0 \leq r < m$. In order to prove (2.1), we show that every common divisor of n and m is also a common divisor of m and $r = n \bmod m$, and vice versa. Let k be any common divisor of m and n. Then, there are numbers $a, b \in \mathbb{Z}$ with $m = a \cdot k$ and $n = b \cdot k$. Substituting these values, we obtain $b \cdot k = s \cdot m + r = s \cdot a \cdot k + r$, which implies $r = (b - s \cdot a)k$. Thus, k is also a divisor of $r = n \bmod m$. Conversely, let k now be any common divisor of m and $r = n \bmod m$. Then, there are numbers $c, d \in \mathbb{Z}$ with $m = c \cdot k$ and $r = d \cdot k$. Substituting these values now gives $n = s \cdot m + r = s \cdot c \cdot k + d \cdot k = (s \cdot c + d)k$. Hence, k is also a divisor of n, and (2.1) is proven. Thus, the Euclidean Algorithm is correct.

As mentioned above, the Euclidian Algorithm follows a recursive divide-and-conquer strategy, since the numbers considered become strictly smaller with each recursive call. The general scheme of divide-and-conquer algorithms is given by:

1. **Divide** the problem into pairwise disjoint subproblems of the same type and of smaller size.
2. **Conquer** the problem by solving these smaller subproblems recursively.
3. **Merge** the solutions of the subproblems to a solution of the original problem.

Unlike most other applications of divide-and-conquer algorithms, the Euclidean Algorithm does not require the merge step, since merging the solutions of the smaller subproblems is not necessary here to obtain a solution of the given problem.

However, in the extended version of Euclid's algorithm displayed in Figure 2.2, the merge step is not omitted. This extended Euclidean Algorithm computes a linear combination of the given two numbers, m and n, by determining numbers x and y such that $\gcd(n, m) = x \cdot n + y \cdot m$. This algorithm again is very useful in various applications such as the RSA cryptosystem in Chapter 7. The merge step here consists of computing the values x and y from the recursively computed values x' und y'. The notation "$\lfloor \frac{n}{m} \rfloor$" in Figure 2.2 denotes the greatest integer not exceeding n/m. Similarly, "$\lceil \frac{n}{m} \rceil$" denotes the least integer not dropping below n/m.

Table 2.2 shows a test run of the extended algorithm of Euclid for $n = 170$ and $m = 102$. The two leftmost columns of the table are filled top-down as with the Euclidean Algorithm, thereby calling the algorithm EXTENDED-EUCLID recursively

```
EXTENDED-EUCLID(n, m) {
    if (m = 0) return (n, 1, 0);
        else {
            (g, x', y') := EXTENDED-EUCLID(m, n mod m);
            x := y';
            y := x' − y' * ⌊n/m⌋;
            return (g, x, y);
        }
}
```

Fig. 2.2. Extended Euclidean Algorithm

for new values of n and m in each loop. In the last row of the table, the break condition is reached with $n = 34$ and $m = 0$. No further recursive call is initiated, but the algorithm now sets $(g, x, y) := (34, 1, 0)$, and while EXTENDED-EUCLID is returning from its recursive calls one after the other, the three rightmost columns are filled bottom-up. Finally, EXTENDED-EUCLID$(170, 102)$ returns the triple $(34, -1, 2)$ in the first row of the table. This result indeed is correct in this particular case, since

$$(-1) \cdot 170 + 2 \cdot 102 = 34 = \gcd(170, 102).$$

Exercise 2.1 asks you to prove the correctness of EXTENDED-EUCLID.

n	m	g	x	y
170	102	34	−1	2
102	68	34	1	−1
68	34	34	0	1
34	0	34	1	0

Table 2.2. Test run of the extended Euclidean Algorithm

Another important feature of an algorithm besides its correctness is its running time. Is the algorithm efficient? Or does it require, for certain "hard" problem instances or even on average, an exorbitantly long running time until it yields the result? The running times of the Euclidean Algorithm and of its extended version are essentially the same; therefore, only the former is to be analyzed now. Obviously, it is crucial to estimate the number of recursive calls of the Euclidean Algorithm in order to analyze its running time. To this end, some preliminaries are in order.

Definition 2.1 (Fibonacci Numbers).
The sequence $\mathfrak{F} = \{f_n\}_{n \geq 0}$ of Fibonacci numbers is defined inductively by:

$$f_0 = 0,$$
$$f_1 = 1,$$
$$f_n = f_{n-1} + f_{n-2} \quad \text{for } n \geq 2.$$

Mathematically speaking, the Fibonacci numbers are defined by a homogeneous linear recurrence equation of second degree. That is, the elements of the sequence $\mathfrak{F}$ are of the form:

$$
\begin{aligned}
T(0) &= r, \\
T(1) &= s, \\
T(n) &= p \cdot T(n-1) + q \cdot T(n-2) \quad \text{for } n \geq 2,
\end{aligned}
\tag{2.2}
$$

where p, q, r, and s are real constants with $p \neq 0$ and $q \neq 0$.

Theorem 2.2. *The solution of the recurrence equation (2.2) has the form:*

$$
T(n) = \begin{cases} A \cdot \alpha^n - B \cdot \beta^n & \text{if } \alpha \neq \beta \\ (A \cdot n + B)\alpha^n & \text{if } \alpha = \beta, \end{cases}
$$

where α and β are the two real solutions to the quadratic equation $a^2 - p \cdot a - q = 0$, and where the numbers A and B are defined as follows:

$$
A = \begin{cases} \frac{s - r \cdot \beta}{\alpha - \beta} & \text{if } \alpha \neq \beta \\ \frac{s - r \cdot \alpha}{\alpha} & \text{if } \alpha = \beta \end{cases} \quad \text{and} \quad B = \begin{cases} \frac{s - r \cdot \alpha}{\alpha - \beta} & \text{if } \alpha \neq \beta \\ r & \text{if } \alpha = \beta. \end{cases}
$$

The proof of Theorem 2.2 is left to the reader as Exercise 2.2. In the case of the Fibonacci numbers, the constants satisfy $p = q = s = 1$ and $r = 0$. The first twenty values of the sequence $\mathfrak{F}$ are given in Table 2.3.

n	0	1	2	3	4	5	6	7	8	9	10	11	12	13	14	15	16	17	18	19
f_n	0	1	1	2	3	5	8	13	21	34	55	89	144	233	377	610	987	1597	2584	4181

Table 2.3. The first twenty Fibonacci numbers

The rapid growth of the first Fibonacci numbers in Table 2.3 suggests that the sequence $\mathfrak{F} = \{f_n\}_{n \geq 0}$ grows exponentially. Before proving this conjecture, we look at an illustrative example. When one thinks of exponential growth, the breeding of rabbits might come to mind. And this was indeed the original motivation for the investigations of Leonardo Pisano (1170 until 1250) whose nickname was Fibonacci. The sequence that now carries his name provides a mathematical description of rabbit reproduction, under certain simplifying assumptions. In Fibonacci's model, every rabbit gives birth to one new rabbit each month, except for the first two months of its lifetime. Furthermore, in abstraction of reality, it is assumed that all rabbits are of the same gender and immortal, and they do not have any natural enemies. Starting your rabbit breeding with just one rabbit makes you the proud owner of a population with exactly f_n rabbits after n months. Table 2.4 displays this process for the initial part of the sequence $\mathfrak{F}$.

0th month		$f_0 = 0$
1st month		$f_1 = 1$
2nd month		$f_2 = 1$
3rd month		$f_3 = 2$
4th month		$f_4 = 3$
5th month		$f_5 = 5$
6th month		$f_6 = 8$
7th month		$f_7 = 13$
8th month		$f_8 = 21$
9th month		$f_9 = 34$
10th month		$f_{10} = 55$

Table 2.4. The Fibonacci numbers proliferate like rabbits and vice versa

We now prove our conjecture that the sequence $\mathfrak{F} = \{f_n\}_{n \geq 0}$ grows exponentially in n. We show by induction on n that for suitable constants a and c and for all sufficiently large n:

$$f_n \geq c \cdot a^n. \tag{2.3}$$

The induction base is trivial. Now, substituting the induction hypothesis into the recurrence equation for f_n gives:

$$f_n = f_{n-1} + f_{n-2} \geq c \cdot a^{n-1} + c \cdot a^{n-2} = c \cdot a^n \cdot \frac{a+1}{a^2} \geq c \cdot a^n.$$

The induction is completed if we can show the latter inequality above, which is equivalent to $a^2 - a - 1 \leq 0$. A quadratic equation of the form $a^2 + p \cdot a + q = 0$ has the two real-valued solutions $-p/2 \pm \sqrt{p^2/4 - q}$. In our case ($a^2 - a - 1 = 0$), we have $p = -1 = q$ and obtain the following solutions:

$$\alpha = \frac{1}{2} + \sqrt{\frac{1}{4} + 1} = \frac{1 + \sqrt{1+4}}{2} = \frac{1 + \sqrt{5}}{2},$$

$$\beta = \frac{1}{2} - \sqrt{\frac{1}{4} + 1} = \frac{1 - \sqrt{1+4}}{2} = \frac{1 - \sqrt{5}}{2}.$$

Hence, the induction step is shown for all $a \leq \alpha = \left(1 + \sqrt{5}\right)/2 \approx 1.618$. The number $\alpha = \left(1 + \sqrt{5}\right)/2$ occurs in various contexts in mathematics and computer science. In geometry, for example, this number occurs in subdividing a rectangle into a square and a smaller rectangle such that the side lengths of the two rectangles have the same ratio. This subdivision is called the "golden cut" and is described in detail in Exercise 2.3.

By Theorem 2.2, the numbers α and β yield $A = 1/\sqrt{5}$ and $B = 1/\sqrt{5}$, which implies for the nth Fibonacci number that

$$f_n = \frac{1}{\sqrt{5}} \left(\frac{1 + \sqrt{5}}{2} \right)^n - \frac{1}{\sqrt{5}} \left(\frac{1 - \sqrt{5}}{2} \right)^n. \tag{2.4}$$

The second term in (2.4), $-1/\sqrt{5} \left((1 - \sqrt{5})/2 \right)^n$, can be neglected, since $\beta = \left(1 - \sqrt{5} \right)/2$ has an absolute value smaller than 1, and $1/\sqrt{5} \left((1 - \sqrt{5})/2 \right)^n$ thus goes to zero for increasing n. Analogously, one can show that for suitable constants d and y and for all sufficiently large n,

$$f_n \leq d \cdot y^n.$$

Next, we show that the sequence $\mathfrak{F} = \{f_n\}_{n \geq 0}$ of Fibonacci numbers is closely related to the number of calls of the Euclidean Algorithm. Theorem 2.3 determines numbers giving the worst running time of the Euclidean Algorithm.

Theorem 2.3. *For each $k \geq 1$, the following two statements hold.*

1. *The computation of* EUCLID(f_{k+3}, f_{k+2}) *requires exactly k recursive calls.*
2. *If the computation of* EUCLID(n, m) *makes at least k recursive calls, then $|n| \geq f_{k+3}$ and $|m| \geq f_{k+2}$.*

Proof. Without loss of generality, we may assume that the inputs n and m in the second assertion are from $\mathbb{N}$, so we do not have to consider negative values and may drop the absolute values. Both assertions of the theorem are shown by induction on k.

Induction base: $k = 1$. Then, $f_{k+3} = f_4 = 3$ and $f_{k+2} = f_3 = 2$. Since EUCLID$(3, 2)$ triggers the recursive call of EUCLID$(2, 1)$, which in turn terminates without any further recursive call, the first assertion is true for $k = 1$. The second assertion is also true for $k = 1$, since EUCLID$(2, 1)$, EUCLID$(2, 2)$, and EUCLID$(n, 1)$ terminate without any further recursive calls for all $n \geq 1$.

Induction step: $(k - 1) \mapsto k$. Let $k \geq 2$. By definition of the f_n, we have $f_n \geq 1$ for all $n \geq 1$, and thus $f_n > f_{n-1}$ for each $n \geq 3$. Hence, for $n \geq 1$,

$$f_{n+2} < f_{n+3} = f_{n+2} + f_{n+1} < 2f_{n+2},$$

which implies that f_{k+3} is not divisible by f_{k+2} for $k \geq 2$.

Since $f_{k+3} \bmod f_{k+2} = f_{k+1}$, the computation of EUCLID(f_{k+3}, f_{k+2}) recursively calls EUCLID(f_{k+2}, f_{k+1}). By the induction hypothesis, the computation of EUCLID(f_{k+2}, f_{k+1}) requires exactly $k - 1$ further recursive calls. Altogether, EUCLID(f_{k+3}, f_{k+2}) requires exactly k calls, which proves the first assertion.

To prove the second assertion, we assume that the computation of EUCLID(n, m) requires at least $k \geq 2$ recursive calls. The first call is EUCLID$(m, n \bmod m)$. By the induction hypothesis, we have $m \geq f_{k+2}$ and $(n \bmod m) \geq f_{k+1}$. It remains to prove that $n \geq f_{k+3}$. Since $n \geq m$ and m is no divisor of n (for otherwise, EUCLID(n, m) had not been called), it follows that

$$n \geq m + (n \bmod m) \geq f_{k+2} + f_{k+1} = f_{k+3},$$

which proves the theorem.   ∎

For any given function $g : \mathbb{N} \to \mathbb{N}$, define the function class $\mathcal{O}(g)$ by

$$\mathcal{O}(g) = \{f : \mathbb{N} \to \mathbb{N} \mid (\exists c > 0)\,(\exists n_0 \in \mathbb{N})\,(\forall n \geq n_0)\,[f(n) \leq c \cdot g(n)]\}.$$

(If you are not familiar with notation such as the $\exists$ and $\forall$ quantifiers, see Section 2.3.)

A function $f \in \mathcal{O}(g)$ grows no faster than g asymptotically. The $\mathcal{O}$ notation ne-
glects additive constants, constant factors, and finitely many exceptions. That is why
it is so useful for analyzing the running times of algorithms. In particular, the base of
logarithms is irrelevant in the $\mathcal{O}$ notation, see Exercise 2.4. Therefore, we agree by
convention that the logarithm log is always base 2, dropping the subscript. Additional
asymptotic rate-of-growth notation is provided in Section 3.2, see Definition 3.5.

Returning to the analysis of EUCLID, Theorem 2.3 says that the number of recursive calls of EUCLID(n, m) is bounded by $\max\{k \mid f_{k+3} \leq n\}$. We know from (2.3)
that $f_{k+3} \geq c \cdot \alpha^{k+3}$ for $\alpha = \frac{1+\sqrt{5}}{2} \approx 1.618$ and a suitable constant c. Taking
logarithms to the base α in the inequality $c \cdot \alpha^{k+3} \leq f_{k+3} \leq n$ then gives:

$$\log_\alpha c + \log_\alpha \alpha^{k+3} = \log_\alpha c + k + 3 \leq \log_\alpha n.$$

It follows from the above considerations that the number k of recursive calls
of EUCLID(n, m) is in $\mathcal{O}(\log n)$. The input numbers n and m can be represented in
binary by $b = \lfloor \log n \rfloor + 1$ bits; see the paragraph right after Definition 2.4. Noting that
one iteration of EUCLID has the bit complexity $\mathcal{O}(b^2)$, which is due to one division
when computing $\gcd(n, m)$, we obtain a bit complexity of $\mathcal{O}(\log n) \cdot \mathcal{O}(b^2) = \mathcal{O}(b^3)$
for the entire computation. In fact, the bit complexity of EUCLID can even be shown
to be in $\mathcal{O}(b^2)$, see [CLRS01, Sch01]. Hence, EUCLID is an efficient algorithm.

2.2 Formal Languages and Recursive Function Theory

In this section, the foundations of the theory of formal languages and automata are
laid, and recursive function theory is introduced. Proofs are omitted in this section.

Definition 2.4 (Alphabet, String, and Language).
An alphabet *is a finite, nonempty set Σ of letters (or symbols). A string over Σ is a
finite sequence of elements from Σ. The set of all strings over Σ is denoted by Σ^*.*

The length *of any string $w \in \Sigma^*$, denoted by $|w|$, is the number of symbols
occurring in w. The* empty string, *denoted by ε, is the uniquely determined string of
length zero. Every subset of Σ^* is a (formal)* language *(over Σ). The* cardinality *of a
language $L \subseteq \Sigma^*$ is the number of its strings, and is denoted by $\|L\|$.*

Problems are encoded as languages over some fixed alphabet; typically, we are
working with the binary alphabet $\Sigma = \{0, 1\}$. Numbers are encoded as strings over

some fixed alphabet. In particular, $\mathtt{bin}(n)$ denotes the *binary representation* of a number $n \in \mathbb{N}$ without leading zeros. For example, $\mathtt{bin}(19) = 10011$.

In addition to the usual set-theoretic operations such as union, intersection, and complementation that can be performed on languages, we now define some further basic operations on strings and languages.

Definition 2.5 (Operations on Strings and Languages).

- *Let A and B be any languages over some alphabet Σ. Define the* intersection *of A and B by $A \cap B = \{x \in \Sigma^* \mid x \in A \text{ and } x \in B\}$, the* union *of A and B by $A \cup B = \{x \in \Sigma^* \mid x \in A \text{ or } x \in B\}$, and the* complement *of A by $\overline{A} = \{x \in \Sigma^* \mid x \notin A\}$.*
- *Let $u = u_1 u_2 \cdots u_m$ and $v = v_1 v_2 \cdots v_n$ be two strings over some alphabet Σ. The* concatenation *of u and v is defined by $uv = u_1 u_2 \cdots u_m v_1 v_2 \cdots v_n$.*
- *The* concatenation *of two languages $A \subseteq \Sigma^*$ and $B \subseteq \Sigma^*$ is defined by*

$$AB = \{ab \mid a \in A \text{ and } b \in B\}.$$

- *The* iteration *of a language $A \subseteq \Sigma^*$ (a.k.a. the* Kleene closure *of A) is the language A^*, which is inductively defined by*

$$A^0 = \{\varepsilon\}, \quad A^n = AA^{n-1}, \quad A^* = \bigcup_{n \geq 0} A^n.$$

Define the ε-free iteration of A by $A^+ = \bigcup_{n \geq 1} A^n$. Note that $A^+ = A^* - \{\varepsilon\}$.

If you start learning a new language, such as Dutch, you first need to learn the language's vocabulary and its grammar. The vocabulary is just the set of all words in this language. The grammar is a list of rules that specifies how to combine words and word groups, along with the appropriate punctuation, so as to form syntactically correct sentences. Later on, you will learn how to form semantically correct (or even meaningful) sentences. For now, let us focus on the syntax of languages. Consider, for example, the language $L = \{a^n b^n \mid n \in \mathbb{N}\}$, which consists of all strings that start with n symbols a followed by n symbols b, for any $n \geq 0$. Note that also the empty string ε belongs to L, due to the case $n = 0$.

A formal language such as L has one thing in common with a natural language such as Dutch: They both need a grammar specifying their syntax.

Definition 2.6 (Grammar).   *A* grammar *is a quadruple $G = (\Sigma, \Gamma, S, R)$, where Σ and Γ are disjoint alphabets (i.e., $\Sigma \cap \Gamma = \emptyset$), $S \in \Gamma$ is the* start symbol, *and $R \subseteq (\Sigma \cup \Gamma)^+ \times (\Sigma \cup \Gamma)^*$ is the finite set of* rules *(or* productions*). The symbols in Σ are called* terminals; *they are indicated by lower-case letters. The symbols in Γ are called* nonterminals *(or* variables*); they are indicated by capital letters. Rules (p, q) in R are also written as $p \rightarrow q$.*

Next, we explain how to derive strings by applying the rules of a grammar, and we define the language generated by a grammar. Such languages contain only strings over the terminal alphabet.

Definition 2.7. *Let $G = (\Sigma, \Gamma, S, R)$ be a grammar, and let $u, v \in (\Sigma \cup \Gamma)^*$.*

- *Define the* (immediate) *derivation relation with respect to G, denoted by $\vdash_G$, by:*

$$u \vdash_G v \iff u = xpy \text{ and } v = xqy \text{ for some } x, y \in (\Sigma \cup \Gamma)^*$$
$$\text{and for some rule } p \rightarrow q \text{ in } R.$$

We write $u \vdash_G^n v$ if and only if $u = x_0 \vdash_G x_1 \vdash_G \cdots \vdash_G x_n = v$ for $n \geq 0$ and for some $x_0, x_1, \ldots, x_n \in (\Sigma \cup \Gamma)^*$. In particular, $u \vdash_G^0 u$.

- *Define $\vdash_G^* = \bigcup_{n \geq 0} \vdash_G^n$ to be the reflexive and transitive closure of $\vdash_G$, i.e., $\vdash_G^*$ is the smallest reflexive, transitive binary relation on $(\Sigma \cup \Gamma)^*$ containing $\vdash_G$.*
- *Strings of terminal letters are called* words. *The* language of G *is defined by*

$$L(G) = \{w \in \Sigma^* \mid S \vdash_G^* w\}.$$

Example 2.8 (Grammar).   Consider the following two simple grammars.

1. Let $G_1 = (\Sigma_1, \Gamma_1, S_1, R_1)$ be the following grammar: the terminal alphabet is $\Sigma_1 = \{a, b\}$, the nonterminal alphabet is $\Gamma_1 = \{S_1\}$, and the set of rules is given by $R_1 = \{S_1 \rightarrow aS_1b, \ S_1 \rightarrow \varepsilon\}$. It is not hard to see that G_1 generates the language $L = \{a^n b^n \mid n \in \mathbb{N}\}$, i.e., $L(G_1) = L$; see Exercise 2.5.
2. Now, let $G_2 = (\Sigma_2, \Gamma_2, S_2, R_2)$ be the following grammar: the terminal alphabet is $\Sigma_2 = \{\text{by, eaten, fox, rabbit, the, was}\}$, the nonterminal alphabet is $\Gamma_2 = \{S_2, P_n, P_v, V_a, V, N, P, A\}$, and the set of rules is given by

$$R_2 = \left\{ \begin{array}{l} S_2 \rightarrow P_n P_v, \quad P_n \rightarrow AN, \quad P_v \rightarrow V_a V P P_n, \quad V_a \rightarrow \text{was,} \\ V \rightarrow \text{eaten,} \quad N \rightarrow \text{fox,} \quad N \rightarrow \text{rabbit,} \quad P \rightarrow \text{by,} \quad A \rightarrow \text{the} \end{array} \right\}.$$

Note that English words such as "fox" are considered as only one terminal symbol here. The nonterminals have the following intuitive meaning: S_2 for "sentence," P_n for "noun phrase," P_v for "verb phrase," V_a for "auxiliary verb," V for "verb," N for "noun," P for "preposition," and A for "article."

Obviously, by applying appropriate rules of the grammar, one can derive from the start symbol S_2 the following English sentence:

the rabbit was eaten by the fox

which is a sequence of terminal letters and thus a word in $L(G_2)$, the language of G_2. Figure 2.3 displays the syntax tree for this derivation. Note that also

the fox was eaten by the rabbit

can be derived from S_2 and is thus a word in $L(G_2)$; see Exercise 2.5. Whether this word, which represents an English sentence, expresses a true statement or not is of no concern here; we are merely interested in the syntax of languages.

The process of deriving words is inherently nondeterministic, since more than one rule may be applied in one derivation step. Syntax trees can be used to visualize one concrete derivation, see Figure 2.3. Distinct grammars can generate the same

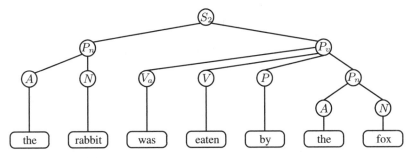

Fig. 2.3. Syntax tree for the grammar G_2 from Example 2.8

language; in fact, for every language L, there are infinitely many distinct grammars generating L. Two grammars are said to be *equivalent* if and only if they generate the same language. That is, a grammar is a syntactical object that specifies via the notions given in Definition 2.7 a semantical object, namely its language.

Grammars are classified according to certain restrictions imposed on their rules. This gives rise to the Chomsky hierarchy, a hierarchy of classes of languages to be defined now.

Definition 2.9 (Chomsky Hierarchy).   *Let $G = (\Sigma, \Gamma, S, R)$ be a grammar.*

- *G is a* grammar of type 0 *if there are no restrictions imposed on R.*
- *G is a* grammar of type 1 *(or a "context-sensitive" grammar) if all rules $p \to q$ in R satisfy $|p| \leq |q|$.*
- *G is a* grammar of type 2 *(or a "context-free" grammar) if all rules $p \to q$ in R satisfy $p \in \Gamma$.*
- *G is a* grammar of type 3 *(or a "regular" grammar) if all rules $p \to q$ in R satisfy $p \in \Gamma$ and $q \in \Sigma \cup \Sigma\Gamma$.*
- *A language $L \subseteq \Sigma^*$ is of type $i \in \{0, 1, 2, 3\}$ if and only if there exists a grammar G of type i such that $L(G) = L$.*
- *For each $i \in \{0, 1, 2, 3\}$, define the language class*

$$\mathfrak{L}_i = \{L(G) \mid G \text{ is a grammar of type } i\}.$$

The Chomsky hierarchy *consists of these four language classes, which are commonly referred to as follows:*
- *$\mathfrak{L}_0$ is the class of all languages that can be generated by some grammar;*
- *$\mathfrak{L}_1 = CS$ is the class of all context-sensitive languages;*
- *$\mathfrak{L}_2 = CF$ is the class of all context-free languages;*
- *$\mathfrak{L}_3 = REG$ is the class of all regular languages.*

Obviously, both grammars from Example 2.8 are context-free. The term "context-free" for type 2 grammars accounts for the fact that applying rules of the form $A \to q$, where A is a nonterminal, replaces A by q regardless of the context of A. Similarly, the term "context-sensitive" for type 1 grammars accounts for the fact that any grammar whose rules have the form $p \rightarrow q$ with $|p| \leq |q|$ can be transformed into an equivalent grammar $G = (\Sigma, \Gamma, S, R)$ whose rules are of the form $uAv \rightarrow uwv$ with $A \in \Gamma$, $u, v, w \in (\Sigma \cup \Gamma)^*$, and $w \neq \varepsilon$. That is, the nonterminal A can be replaced only in the context of u and v when applying such a rule of G.

It is not difficult to see that the Chomsky hierarchy has the inclusion structure stated in Fact 2.10. One can show that all these inclusions are strict, see Theorem 2.21. In particular, the context-free language $L = \{a^n b^n \mid n \in \mathbb{N}\}$ defined in Example 2.8 is not regular, which proves that REG $\neq$ CF; see Problem 2.2.

Fact 2.10 REG $\subseteq$ CF $\subseteq$ CS $\subseteq \mathfrak{L}_0$.

Among the classes of the Chomsky hierarchy, the context-free languages are particularly important in computer science, e.g., in building compilers for programming languages. However, this theme is not to be pursued here. Rather, we now turn to automata theory and recursive function theory both of which are closely related to the theory of formal languages. In particular, each class of the Chomsky hierarchy can be characterized by some suitable type of automata. For example, for the lowest class in the hierarchy, $\mathfrak{L}_3 = $ REG, it is known that every regular language can be recognized by a finite automaton, and every language recognizable by some finite automaton is regular. We start by introducing the notion of a deterministic finite automaton.

Definition 2.11 (Deterministic Finite Automaton).   *A deterministic finite automaton (a DFA, for short) is a quintuple $M = (\Sigma, Z, \delta, z_0, F)$, where Σ is an alphabet, Z is a finite, nonempty set of states with $\Sigma \cap Z = \emptyset$, $\delta : Z \times \Sigma \rightarrow Z$ is the transition function, $z_0 \in Z$ is the initial state, and $F \subseteq Z$ is the set of final states.*
The extended transition function $\widehat{\delta} : Z \times \Sigma^* \rightarrow Z$ of M is inductively defined by

$$\widehat{\delta}(z, \varepsilon) = z \quad \text{for each } z \in Z;$$
$$\widehat{\delta}(z, ax) = \widehat{\delta}(\delta(z, a), x) \quad \text{for each } z \in Z, a \in \Sigma, \text{ and } x \in \Sigma^*.$$

The language accepted by M is defined by $L(M) = \{x \in \Sigma^* \mid \widehat{\delta}(z_0, x) \in F\}$.

A finite automaton M can be represented by a graph whose vertices are the states of M and whose edges indicate a transition according to M's transition function δ. If $\delta(z, a) = z'$ for some symbol $a \in \Sigma$ and for two states $z, z' \in Z$, then the directed edge from z to z' is labeled by a. The distinguished initial state z_0 is marked by an arrow pointing to it, and the final states are marked by two circles, see Figure 2.4. As noted in Definition 2.11, DFAs can recognize languages. Given an input string $x \in \Sigma^*$, DFA M executes $|x|$ steps after which it either accepts or rejects x. Starting at the initial state z_0, M reads its input x symbol by symbol, one in each step, moving from state to state according to its transition function δ: If M currently is in state z and reads the symbol $a \in \Sigma$ and $\delta(z, a) = z'$, then M's state changes into z'. The computation halts after the last symbol of x is read. If M is in a final state then, it accepts x; otherwise, it rejects x. The extended transition function formally expresses the process just described: $\widehat{\delta}(z_0, x) \in F$ if and only if M accepts x.

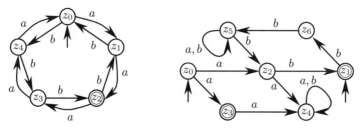

Fig. 2.4. A deterministic and a nondeterministic finite automaton

We now introduce the notion of nondeterminism, a very powerful concept that is crucial in many areas of computer science and in particular in the upcoming chapters of this book. The DFA shown on the left-hand side in Figure 2.4 is deterministic, since every move it can make is uniquely determined by its transition function; see also the left table in Table 2.5. The right-hand side in Figure 2.4 and in Table 2.5 displays a nondeterministic finite automaton whose transition function maps pairs (z, a) of states and symbols to a subset of the states. Thus, computation paths of this automaton are not uniquely determined. An input is accepted by such a nondeterministic finite automaton if and only if there exists at least one path from one of the initial states to one of the final states. The question of which languages are accepted by the DFA and the NFA in Figure 2.4 is left to the reader as Exercise 2.6.

δ	z_0	z_1	z_2	z_3	z_4
a	z_1	z_2	z_3	z_4	z_0
b	z_4	z_0	z_1	z_2	z_3

δ	z_0	z_1	z_2	z_3	z_4	z_5	z_6
a	$\{z_2, z_3\}$	$\emptyset$	$\{z_4\}$	$\{z_4\}$	$\{z_4\}$	$\{z_5\}$	$\emptyset$
b	$\emptyset$	$\{z_6\}$	$\{z_1\}$	$\emptyset$	$\{z_4\}$	$\{z_2, z_5\}$	$\{z_5\}$

Table 2.5. Transition functions of the DFA and the NFA from Figure 2.4

Definition 2.12 (Nondeterministic Finite Automaton).   *A nondeterministic finite automaton (an NFA, for short) is a quintuple $M = (\Sigma, Z, \delta, S, F)$, where Σ is an alphabet, Z is a finite, nonempty set of states with $\Sigma \cap Z = \emptyset$, $\delta : Z \times \Sigma \to \mathfrak{P}(Z)$ is the transition function, $S \subseteq Z$ is the set of initial states, and $F \subseteq Z$ is the set of final states. Here, $\mathfrak{P}(Z)$ denotes the power set of Z, i.e., the set of all subsets of Z.*

The extended transition function $\widehat{\delta} : \mathfrak{P}(Z) \times \Sigma^* \to \mathfrak{P}(Z)$ of M is inductively defined by

$$\widehat{\delta}(Z', \varepsilon) = Z' \quad \text{for each } Z' \subseteq Z;$$
$$\widehat{\delta}(Z', ax) = \bigcup_{z \in Z'} \widehat{\delta}(\delta(z, a), x) \quad \text{for each } Z' \subseteq Z, a \in \Sigma, \text{ and } x \in \Sigma^*.$$

The language accepted by M is defined by $L(M) = \{x \in \Sigma^* \mid \widehat{\delta}(S, x) \cap F \neq \emptyset\}$.

Every language can be recognized by an NFA if and only if it can be generated by a regular grammar, see Exercise 2.7. By definition, every DFA is a particular NFA whose transition function δ maps each pair (z, a) to a set containing exactly one state, and whose set of initial states is also a singleton. Conversely, for every NFA there is an equivalent DFA; the proof of Theorem 2.13 is left to the reader as Exercise 2.8. Thus, regular grammars and deterministic and nondeterministic finite automata are pairwise equivalent concepts; they all characterize the class of regular languages.

Theorem 2.13 (Rabin and Scott). *Every language that can be recognized by some NFA can also be recognized by some DFA.*

Corollary 2.14. $\mathfrak{L}_3 = \text{REG} = \{L(M) \mid M \text{ is a DFA}\} = \{L(M) \mid M \text{ is an NFA}\}.$

Similar characterizations by suitable types of automata are known for the other classes of the Chomsky hierarchy as well. For instance, the class $\mathfrak{L}_2 = \text{CF}$ of context-free languages is characterized by push-down automata, the class $\mathfrak{L}_1 = \text{CS}$ of context-sensitive languages is characterized by linear bounded automata, and the class $\mathfrak{L}_0$ is characterized by Turing machines, see Definitions 2.15 and 2.16 below. This theme is not to be pursued any further here.

Complexity theory, one of the main topics of this book, is in particular concerned with proving "lower bounds" on the computational complexity of problems. The difficulty here is that it does not suffice to analyze the running time of one concrete algorithm solving a given problem. Rather, one has to prove that no algorithm whatsoever that solves this problem has a running time better than the bound to be shown. Among the algorithms that must be considered in proving lower bounds for some problem are even those algorithms that have not been designed as yet. Consequently, one first has to formalize the notion of algorithms in a mathematically rigorous way, for otherwise one could not speak about the set of algorithms in its totality.

Since the 1930s, various attempts have been made to propose a formal model of algorithms. Any two of the models proposed are equivalent in the sense that either one can be transformed into the other one. Loosely speaking, such a transformation might be seen as some kind of compilation between distinct programming languages. Due to the equivalence of all these models of computation, Church's Thesis postulates that each one of these algorithmic models captures precisely the notion of what intuitively is considered to be computable, an inherently somewhat vague notion.

The algorithmic model adopted here is the Turing machine, introduced in 1936 by Alan Turing (1912 until 1954) in his groundbreaking paper [Tur36]. The Turing machine is a quite simple, abstract model of a computer. We now define this model by giving its syntax and its semantics. As with finite automata, one can distinguish deterministic and nondeterministic Turing machines. It is convenient to start by introducing the latter model first. Deterministic Turing machines then result immediately as a special case of nondeterministic Turing machines.

First, we give some technical details and describe the working method of Turing machines. A Turing machine is equipped with k working tapes that are infinite in both directions and subdivided into cells. For each tape, there is a head accessing exactly one cell at a time. Each cell may contain one symbol. The absence of a symbol in a cell is indicated by a special symbol, the blank □, belonging to the working alphabet of the machine, but not to its input alphabet. The actual computation is performed on the working tapes, and it starts with the input string being written on the input tape and with all other tape cells being blank. If the computation is completed, the machine halts with the resulting output string being written on the output tape. It may be determined that the input tape is a read-only tape and that the output tape is a write-only tape, but such a convention is not necessary and the input and output tapes may as well be regular read-write working tapes. One may also agree by convention on various further variations of the technical details and constraints. For example, one may define tapes to be infinite in only one direction, or that the tape heads are allowed to move in just one direction, or that the number of tapes is restricted, etc.

One step in the computation of a Turing machine consists of the following actions: Each head reads the symbol written on the cell it is accessing currently and possibly overwrites it with another symbol, and then the head moves either one cell to the left, or one cell to the right, or it does not move at all. At the same time, the machine may change its current state that is stored in its finite control. Figure 2.5 displays a Turing machine with two tapes.

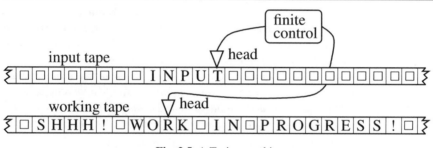

Fig. 2.5. A Turing machine

Definition 2.15 (Syntax of Turing Machines).
A (nondeterministic) Turing machine with k tapes (an NTM with k tapes, for short) is a septuple $M = (\Sigma, \Gamma, Z, \delta, z_0, \square, F)$, where Σ is the input alphabet, Γ is the working alphabet with $\Sigma \subseteq \Gamma$, Z is a finite, nonempty set of states with $Z \cap \Gamma = \emptyset$, $\delta : Z \times \Gamma^k \to \mathfrak{P}(Z \times \Gamma^k \times \{L, R, N\}^k)$ is the transition function, $z_0 \in Z$ is the initial state, $\square \in \Gamma - \Sigma$ is the blank symbol, and F is the set of final states with $F \subseteq Z$. Recall that $\mathfrak{P}(Z)$ denotes the power set of Z, the set of all subsets of Z.

In place of $(z', \mathbf{b}, \mathbf{x}) \in \delta(z, \mathbf{a})$ with $z, z' \in Z$, $\mathbf{a}, \mathbf{b} \in \Gamma^k$, and $\mathbf{x} \in \{L, R, N\}^k$, we also write $(z, \mathbf{a}) \mapsto (z', \mathbf{b}, \mathbf{x})$. Such a Turing instruction has the following meaning. If z is the current state of M and, for each i with $1 \leq i \leq k$, if the ith head of M scanning the ith tape of M currently reads a cell on which the symbol a_i is written, where $\mathbf{a} = (a_1, a_2, \ldots, a_k)$, then:

- a_i is replaced by b_i, where $\mathbf{b} = (b_1, b_2, \ldots, b_k)$,
- z' is the new state of M, and
- M moves its ith head according to $x_i \in \{L, R, N\}$, where $\mathbf{x} = (x_1, x_2, \ldots, x_k)$, i.e., the ith head moves one cell to the left if $x_i = L$, or one cell to the right if $x_i = R$, or it does not move at all if $x_i = N$.

The special case of a deterministic Turing machine with k tapes *(a DTM with k tapes, for short) is obtained by letting the transition function δ map from $Z \times \Gamma^k$ to $Z \times \Gamma^k \times \{L, R, N\}^k$.*

For $k = 1$, we obtain the one-tape Turing machine for which we simply use NTM or DTM as a shorthand. Every k-tape NTM and k-tape DTM can be simulated by an equivalent one-tape Turing machine, with only doubling the running time. If efficiency is important, it can be sensible to have more than one tape.

Turing machines can be used as acceptors, which accept languages, or they can be used as transducers, which compute functions. This difference is taken into account when we now define the semantics of Turing machines. For convenience, we restrict ourselves here to the case of one-tape Turing machines; the generalization to the case of k-tape Turing machines is straightforward.

Definition 2.16 (Semantics of Turing Machines).

Let $M = (\Sigma, \Gamma, Z, \delta, z_0, \Box, F)$ be a one-tape NTM. A configuration of M is a string $k \in \Gamma^* Z \Gamma^*$. Here, $k = \alpha z \beta$ means that $\alpha\beta$ is the current tape inscription (i.e., the string whose letters are written on the already visited part of the tape), that the head currently scans the first symbol of β, and that z is the current state of M.

On the set $\mathfrak{K}_M = \Gamma^* Z \Gamma^*$ of all configurations of M, we define a binary relation $\vdash_M$ describing the transition from a configuration $k \in \mathfrak{K}_M$ to another configuration $k' \in \mathfrak{K}_M$ by applying the transition function δ. For all strings $\alpha = a_1 a_2 \cdots a_m$ and $\beta = b_1 b_2 \cdots b_n$ in Γ^*, where $m \geq 0$ and $n \geq 1$, and for all states $z \in Z$, define

$$\alpha z \beta \vdash_M \begin{cases} a_1 a_2 \cdots a_m z' c b_2 \cdots b_n & \text{if } (z, b_1) \mapsto (z', c, N),\, m \geq 0,\, \text{and } n \geq 1 \\ a_1 a_2 \cdots a_m c z' b_2 \cdots b_n & \text{if } (z, b_1) \mapsto (z', c, R),\, m \geq 0,\, \text{and } n \geq 2 \\ a_1 a_2 \cdots a_{m-1} z' a_m c b_2 \cdots b_n & \text{if } (z, b_1) \mapsto (z', c, L),\, m \geq 1,\, \text{and } n \geq 1. \end{cases}$$

Two special cases are to be considered separately:

1. *If $n = 1$ and $(z, b_1) \mapsto (z', c, R)$ (i.e., M's head moves to the right and encounters a $\Box$ symbol), then $a_1 a_2 \cdots a_m z b_1 \vdash_M a_1 a_2 \cdots a_m c z' \Box$.*
2. *If $m = 0$ and $(z, b_1) \mapsto (z', c, L)$ (i.e., M's head moves to the left and encounters a $\Box$ symbol), then $z b_1 b_2 \cdots b_n \vdash_M z' \Box c b_2 \cdots b_n$.*

The initial configuration of M on input x is always $z_0 x$. The final configurations of M on input x have the form $\alpha z \beta$ with $z \in F$ and $\alpha, \beta \in \Gamma^*$.

Let $\vdash_M^*$ be the reflexive, transitive closure of $\vdash_M$. That is, for any two configurations $k, k' \in \mathfrak{K}_M$, we have $k \vdash_M^* k'$ if and only if there exists a finite sequence $k_0, k_1, \ldots, k_t$ of configurations in $\mathfrak{K}_M$ such that

$$k = k_0 \vdash_M k_1 \vdash_M \cdots \vdash_M k_t = k',$$

where $k = k_0 = k_t = k'$ *is possible. If* $k_0 = z_0 x$ *is the initial configuration of* M *on input* x, *then this sequence of configurations is called a* finite computation *of* $M(x)$. *If in addition* k_t *is a final configuration (i.e., the state in* k_t *is a final state), we say that* M halts *on input* x. The *language accepted by* M *is defined as*

$$L(M) = \{x \in \Sigma^* \mid z_0 x \vdash^*_M \alpha z \beta \text{ with } z \in F \text{ and } \alpha, \beta \in \Gamma^*\}.$$

The set F *of* M's *final states can also be partitioned into the set* F_a *of* accepting *final states and the set* F_r *of* rejecting *final states, where* $F = F_a \cup F_r$ *and* $F_a \cap F_r = \emptyset$. *In this case, the language accepted by* M *is defined by*

$$L(M) = \{x \in \Sigma^* \mid z_0 x \vdash^*_M \alpha z \beta \text{ with } z \in F_a \text{ and } \alpha, \beta \in \Gamma^*\}.$$

Let Σ *and* Δ *be alphabets. A Turing machine* M computes *a* word function $f : \Sigma^* \to \Delta^*$ *if and only if for each* $x \in \Sigma^*$ *and for each* $y \in \Delta^*$,

- $x \in D_f$ *if and only if* M *halts on input* x *after finitely many steps, and*
- *for each* $x \in D_f$, $f(x) = y \iff z_0 x \vdash^*_M zy$ *for some* $z \in F$,

where D_f *denotes the* domain *of* f. *A word function is said to be* computable *if and only if there is a Turing machine computing it.*

A function $f : \mathbb{N}^k \to \mathbb{N}$ *is said to be* computable *if and only if the word function* $g : \{0, 1, \#\}^* \to \{0, 1\}^*$ *is computable, which is defined by*

$$g(\text{bin}(x_1)\#\text{bin}(x_2)\# \cdots \#\text{bin}(x_k)) = \text{bin}(f(x_1, x_2, \dots, x_k)).$$

In the case of NTMs, configurations can have more than one successor configuration. Thus, we obtain a *computation tree* whose root is the initial configuration and whose leaves are the final configurations. Trees are special graphs (see Definition 2.49 and Problem 2.3) and thus they consist of vertices and edges. The vertices of the computation tree of $M(x)$ are the configurations of M on input x. For any two configurations k and k' from $\mathfrak{K}_M$, there exists a directed edge from k to k' exactly if $k \vdash_M k'$. A *computation path* in the tree of $M(x)$ is a sequence of configurations $k_0 \vdash_M k_1 \vdash_M \cdots \vdash_M k_t \vdash_M \cdots$. The computation tree of an NTM can have infinite paths. In the case of a DTM, every configuration (except the initial configuration, of course) is uniquely determined by its immediate predecessor configuration. That is why the computation tree of a DTM degenerates into a linear chain, starting with the initial configuration and ending with some final configuration if the machine halts on the given input; otherwise, the computation chain goes to infinity.

Definition 2.16 introduced the notion of computable functions that is central to recursive function theory. Note that "computable function" and "recursive function" are used synonymously here. For languages, the notion corresponding to the computability of functions is called "decidability."

Definition 2.17 (Computability and Decidability).   *Let* $\mathbb{P}$ *denote the class of all partial recursive (i.e., computable) functions, and let* $\mathbb{R} = \{f \mid f \in \mathbb{P} \text{ and } f \text{ is total}\}$ *denote the class of all total (i.e., everywhere defined) recursive functions. The characteristic function of a language* L *is defined by*

$$c_L(x) = \begin{cases} 1 & \text{if } x \in L \\ 0 & \text{if } x \notin L. \end{cases}$$

A language L is said to be decidable *if and only if $c_L \in \mathbb{R}$. Let* REC *denote the class of all decidable languages.*

It can be shown that every context-sensitive language is decidable: CS $\subseteq$ REC. Moreover, this inclusion is strict: CS $\neq$ REC.

Example 2.18. Consider the language $L = \{a^n b^n c^n \mid n \geq 1\}$. A Turing machine accepting L is defined by

$$M = (\{a, b, c\}, \{a, b, c, \$, \square\}, \{z_0, z_1, \ldots, z_6\}, \delta, z_0, \square, \{z_6\}),$$

where the list of M's Turing instructions according to the transition function δ is given in Table 2.6. Table 2.7 gives the meaning of the single states of M as well as the intention behind each state of M. Since $c_L \in \mathbb{R}$ via M, L is decidable. Note that M has the property that it never leaves the range of its tape on which the input is written. Such a Turing machine is called a *linear bounded automaton*. Since the class CS can be characterized by linear bounded automata, L is even context-sensitive. However, L is not context-free, which proves that CF $\neq$ CS; see Problem 2.2.

$(z_0, a) \mapsto (z_1, \$, R)$	$(z_2, \$) \mapsto (z_2, \$, R)$	$(z_5, c) \mapsto (z_5, c, L)$
$(z_1, a) \mapsto (z_1, a, R)$	$(z_3, c) \mapsto (z_3, c, R)$	$(z_5, \$) \mapsto (z_5, \$, L)$
$(z_1, b) \mapsto (z_2, \$, R)$	$(z_3, \square) \mapsto (z_4, \square, L)$	$(z_5, b) \mapsto (z_5, b, L)$
$(z_1 \$) \mapsto (z_1, \$, R)$	$(z_4, \$) \mapsto (z_4, \$, L)$	$(z_5, a) \mapsto (z_5, a, L)$
$(z_2, b) \mapsto (z_2, b, R)$	$(z_4, \square) \mapsto (z_6, \square, R)$	$(z_5, \square) \mapsto (z_0, \square, R)$
$(z_2, c) \mapsto (z_3, \$, R)$	$(z_4, c) \mapsto (z_5, c, L)$	$(z_0, \$) \mapsto (z_0, \$, R)$

Table 2.6. M's transition function δ for $L = \{a^n b^n c^n \mid n \geq 1\}$

state	meaning	intention
z_0	initial state	start a new cycle
z_1	one a stored	search for the next b
z_2	one a and one b stored	search for the next c
z_3	one a, one b, and one c deleted	search for the right boundary
z_4	right boundary reached	move back and test whether all a, b, c are deleted
z_5	test not successful	move back and start a new cycle
z_6	test successful	accept

Table 2.7. Interpretation of the states of M

Another notion central to recursive function theory is the notion of recursively enumerable sets. Synonymously, such sets are called "semi-decidable," since they can be defined equivalently as follows: A language L is *semi-decidable* if and only if $\hat{c}_L \in \mathbb{P}$, where the partial characteristic function $\hat{c}_L$ of L is defined by $\hat{c}_L(x) = 1$ if $x \in L$, and $\hat{c}_L(x)$ is undefined if $x \notin L$. In other words, a semi-decision for L means that some algorithm (implemented, for example, by a Turing machine) gives the answer "yes" for each input x in L, but never halts on inputs not in L. Below, we define the equivalent notion of recursively enumerable sets.

Definition 2.19 (Recursive Enumerability).

A language A is said to be recursively enumerable *if and only if either A is the empty set, or A is the image of some total recursive function f. This function f enumerates A recursively in the sense that $A = \{y \mid f(x) = y \text{ for some } x\}$. Let* RE *denote the class of all recursively enumerable sets.*

Much is known about the recursively enumerable sets. Here, we state just a few results without proof. Many such proofs apply the proof method of "*diagonalization.*" An important ingredient needed for this method to work is the notion of a "*Gödelization of Turing machines,*" which is not defined formally here. We merely give a rough outline, leaving the somewhat cumbersome task of filling in the formal details to the reader as Exercise 2.9.

Informally speaking, the objective is to systematically enumerate all algorithms from a given class of algorithms; for example, one wants to enumerate all Turing machines. The point is that (syntactically correct) Turing machines are encoded by strings over some suitable alphabet. Such code words can be lexicographically ordered, provided that an ordering of the underlying alphabet is given. Strings that do not encode syntactically correct Turing machines are dropped. In the remaining ordered sequence, every Turing machine imaginable occurs. If the underlying alphabet has k symbols, code words for Turing machines can be identified with numbers in k-adic representation. Thus, we obtain an enumeration of Turing machines; the number assigned to a machine is called its *Gödel number*, named after the famous mathematician Kurt Gödel (1906 until 1978). The crucial point to observe here is that one can *effectively* (i.e., via an algorithm) determine the Gödel number of a given Turing machine, and vice versa.

To a given Gödelization $M_0, M_1, M_2, \ldots$ of Turing machines that are transducers, there corresponds an enumeration $\varphi_0, \varphi_1, \varphi_2, \ldots$ of functions in $\mathbb{P}$, where for each i, M_i computes φ_i. Similarly, to a given Gödelization $N_0, N_1, N_2, \ldots$ of Turing machines that are acceptors, there corresponds an enumeration $L_0, L_1, L_2, \ldots$ of languages, where for each i, N_i accepts L_i, i.e., $L(N_i) = L_i$. Of course, distinct Turing machines can compute the same function or can accept the same language, respectively. Thus, infinitely many machines (to which distinct Gödel numbers are assigned) compute one and the same function or accept one and the same language, respectively.

The totality of all languages corresponding to any fixed Gödelization of Turing machine acceptors equals RE, the class of recursively enumerable sets. Below, we list without proof a number of conditions equivalent to being recursively enumerable, and further basic properties of the classes RE and REC.

Theorem 2.20.   *1. $A \in$ REC if and only if $A \in$ RE and $\overline{A} \in$ RE. Thus, REC $\subseteq$ RE.*

   2. $A \in$ RE if and only if A is the projection of some decidable set B, i.e., if and only if there is a set $B \in$ REC such that $(\forall x)\, [x \in A \iff (\exists y)\, [(x, y) \in B]]$.

   3. Let $\varphi_0, \varphi_1, \ldots$ be a fixed Gödelization of $\mathbb{P}$, and let $D_i = D_{\varphi_i}$ and $R_i = R_{\varphi_i}$ denote the domain and range, respectively, of the ith function φ_i in $\mathbb{P}$. Then,

$$\text{RE} = \{ D_i \mid i \in \mathbb{N} \} = \{ R_i \mid i \in \mathbb{N} \}.$$

   4. The halting problem, which is defined by $H = \{ i \in \mathbb{N} \mid i \in D_i \}$, is recursively enumerable, yet not decidable. Thus, REC $\neq$ RE.

   5. RE $= \mathfrak{L}_0$.

   6. $A \in$ RE if and only if $\hat{c}_A \in \mathbb{P}$.

To summarize, Fact 2.10 can be expanded and strengthened to the following claim, where for classes $\mathcal{C}$ and $\mathcal{D}$ of sets, we denote *strict inclusion* by $\mathcal{C} \subset \mathcal{D}$, i.e., $\mathcal{C} \subset \mathcal{D} \iff (\mathcal{C} \subseteq \mathcal{D} \text{ and } \mathcal{C} \neq \mathcal{D})$.

Theorem 2.21. $\mathfrak{L}_3 = \text{REG} \subset \mathfrak{L}_2 = \text{CF} \subset \mathfrak{L}_1 = \text{CS} \subset \text{REC} \subset \mathfrak{L}_0 = \text{RE}$.

Finally, we define the notion of oracle Turing machines.

Definition 2.22 (Oracle Turing Machine).

An oracle set (or an oracle, for short) is a set of strings. An oracle Turing machine M, say with oracle B, is a Turing machine that is equipped with a special working tape, the so-called oracle tape or query tape, and whose set of states contains a special query state, $z_?$, and the two answer states z_{yes} and z_{no}. As long as M is not in the query state $z_?$, it works just like a regular Turing machine. However, when M reaches the query state $z_?$ during its computation, it interrupts its computation and queries its oracle about the string q that currently is written on the oracle tape. The oracle B can be imagined as some kind of "black box": B answers the query of whether it contains q or not within one step of M's computation, regardless of how difficult it is to decide the set B. If $q \in B$, then M changes its current state into the new state z_{yes} and continues its computation. Otherwise (if $q \notin B$), M continues its computation in the new state z_{no}. We then say that the computation of M on input x is performed relative to the oracle B, and we write $M^B(x)$.

Let $L(M^B)$ be the language accepted by M^B. A class $\mathcal{C}$ of languages is said to be relativizable *if and only if it can be represented in this way by oracle Turing machines relative to the empty oracle. A language $L \in \mathcal{C}$ is said to be* represented by *an oracle Turing machine M if and only if $L = L(M^\emptyset)$. For any relativizable class $\mathcal{C}$ and for any oracle B, define the class $\mathcal{C}$ relative to B by*

$$\mathcal{C}^B = \{ L(M^B) \mid M \text{ is an oracle Turing machine representing some set in } \mathcal{C} \}.$$

For any class $\mathcal{B}$ of oracle sets, define $\mathcal{C}^{\mathcal{B}} = \bigcup_{B \in \mathcal{B}} \mathcal{C}^B$.

Clearly, $\mathcal{C}^\emptyset = \mathcal{C}$, and the superscript can be dropped if the oracle is empty. We use the shorthand DOTM and NOTM, respectively, for *deterministic* and for *nondeterministic oracle Turing machine*. If the running time of a DOTM or an NOTM, respectively, is bounded by some polynomial, we write DPOTM and NPOTM; see also Section 3.2.

2.3 Logic

2.3.1 Propositional Logic

"*I did not have sex with that woman*," a former U.S. president is quoted as saying. Did he make a true statement? Logic cannot answer this question. However, what logic *can* do is evaluate the truth of complicated, involved propositions composed of several atomic statements that are connected by logical operations such as *and*, *or*, and *not*. The truth value of such a composed statement, which is called a (boolean) formula, can be determined from the given truth values of the formula's atomic statements. For example, consider the following proposition:

"I did not have sex with that woman, or if I ever did have sex with that woman and I'm not a liar, then I was just telling you the plain truth."

One can safely make this statement, even under oath, simply because it is always true, provided that we choose to interpret its contents textually. To analyze the truth value of the formula S representing the sentence quoted above, decompose it into its atomic parts and consider its logical structure.

What are the atomic parts of S? Let A denote the statement "*I did not have sex with that woman.*" The statement "*I ever did have sex with that woman*" is the logical negation of A and is written as $\neg A$. Further, let B denote the statement "*I'm a liar*," whose negation $\neg B$ is "*I'm not a liar.*" Finally, let C denote the statement "*I was just telling you the plain truth.*"

We use the symbols $\neg$, $\vee$, $\wedge$, $\Longrightarrow$, and $\Longleftrightarrow$ for the logical operations *negation* ("not"), *disjunction* ("or"), *conjunction* ("and"), *implication* ("if...then..."), and *equivalence* ("if and only if"). In this notation, the logical structure of S is

$$S = A \vee ((\neg A \wedge \neg B) \Longrightarrow C). \tag{2.5}$$

Boolean operations are defined by their truth tables. For example, the negation $\neg$ flips the truth value of its argument: If A is true then $\neg A$ is false, and if A is false then $\neg A$ is true. For convenience, we represent the constant truth values *true* and *false* by 1 and 0, respectively. Table 2.8 gives the truth tables for the remaining boolean operations mentioned above, under every possible truth assignment of their two arguments. Altogether, there are exactly $2^4 = 16$ distinct binary boolean operations.

x	y	$x \vee y$	$x \wedge y$	$x \Longrightarrow y$	$x \Longleftrightarrow y$
0	0	0	0	1	1
0	1	1	0	1	0
1	0	1	0	0	0
1	1	1	1	1	1

Table 2.8. Truth tables for various boolean operations

Suppose that the person making the statement S tells the truth. Clearly, S is true in this case. Now suppose that the person making the statement S is lying, i.e., S is false. By the definition of "$\vee$" in Table 2.8, both the statement A ("*I did not have sex with that woman*") and the statement $(\neg A \wedge \neg B) \implies C$ must be false. Since A is false, we know that $\neg A$ is true. However, B ("*I'm a liar*") is also true in this case, which implies that $\neg B$ is false. Hence, the hypothesis $\neg A \wedge \neg B$ of the implication in (2.5) is false. Thus, by the definition of "$\implies$" in Table 2.8, the implication $(\neg A \wedge \neg B) \implies C$ is true, no matter whether or not its conclusion C is true. Contradiction. It follows that the current case cannot occur: S is true regardless of whether or not the person making the statement S was telling the plain truth.

The above argument shows that the notion of "truth" and the definition of a "liar" are somewhat vague and elastic in real life, and especially so in politics. Therefore, in the rigorous and abstract field of logic, we usually do not interpret the contents of statements textually. In logical terms, S is not a "*tautology*," i.e., S is not a boolean formula that is true for each possible truth assignment to its variables. If we abstract from its contents and regard its atomic subformulas A, B, and C merely as boolean variables that are either true or false, then S is not always true because we obtain a truth assignment that makes S false by setting each of A, B, and C to false.

Definition 2.23 (Syntax of Boolean Formulas).

* *The boolean constants* true *and* false, *respectively, are represented by* 1 *and* 0. *Let* $x_1, x_2, \ldots$ *be boolean variables, i.e.,* $x_i \in \{0, 1\}$ *for each* i. *Boolean variables and constants are also called* atomic formulas. *Variables and their negations are called* literals. *We agree by convention that the subscripts of variables may be dropped, and we may sometimes write* $x, y, z, \ldots$ *in place of* $x_1, x_2, x_3, \ldots$
* Boolean formulas (formulas, *for short) are inductively defined as follows:*
    1. *Every atomic formula is a formula.*
    2. *If* φ *is a formula, then* $\neg \varphi$ *is a formula.*
    3. *If* φ *and* ψ *are formulas, then* $\varphi \vee \psi$ *and* $\varphi \wedge \psi$ *are formulas.*
* *As a shorthand, we use*
    - $\varphi \implies \psi$ *to denote* $\neg \varphi \vee \psi$,
    - $\varphi \iff \psi$ *to denote* $(\varphi \wedge \psi) \vee (\neg \varphi \wedge \neg \psi)$,
    - $\bigvee_{i=1}^{n} \varphi_i$ *to denote* $\varphi_1 \vee \varphi_2 \vee \cdots \vee \varphi_n$, *and*
    - $\bigwedge_{i=1}^{n} \varphi_i$ *to denote* $\varphi_1 \wedge \varphi_2 \wedge \cdots \wedge \varphi_n$.
* *A boolean formula* φ *is in* conjunctive normal form *(CNF, for short) if and only if* φ *is of the form*

$$\varphi(x_1, x_2, \ldots, x_n) = \bigwedge_{i=1}^{m} \left(\bigvee_{j=1}^{k_i} \ell_{i,j} \right)$$
$$= (\ell_{1,1} \vee \cdots \vee \ell_{1,k_1}) \wedge \cdots \wedge (\ell_{m,1} \vee \cdots \vee \ell_{m,k_m}),$$

where the $\ell_{i,j}$ *are literals over* $\{x_1, x_2, \ldots, x_n\}$, *and the disjuncts* $\left(\bigvee_{j=1}^{k_i} \ell_{i,j} \right)$ *of literals are said to be the* clauses *of* φ.

- *A boolean formula φ is in k-CNF if and only if φ is in CNF and each clause of φ has at most k literals.*

Analogously to the notion of CNF defined above one can define the *disjunctive normal form* (*DNF*, for short) of boolean formulas, see Exercise 2.10.

Definition 2.24 (Semantics of Boolean Formulas).

- *Given a boolean formula $\varphi(x_1, x_2, \ldots, x_n)$, a truth assignment of φ is a mapping $\alpha : \{x_1, x_2, \ldots, x_n\} \rightarrow \{0, 1\}$ assigning truth values to each variable of φ. By evaluating φ according to α, a truth value $\alpha(\varphi) \in \{0, 1\}$ is assigned to φ.*
- *A truth assignment α satisfies a boolean formula φ if and only if α makes φ true, i.e., $\alpha(\varphi) = 1$. A satisfying truth assignment α of a formula φ is also called a* model *of φ. A boolean formula is* satisfiable *if and only if there exists a satisfying truth assignment for it. A boolean formula φ is said to be* valid *(or a* tautology*) if and only if every truth assignment of φ makes φ true.*
- *Any two formulas φ and ψ (with the same variables) are said to be* (semantically) equivalent *(denoted by $\varphi \equiv \psi$) if and only if for each truth assignment α, we have $\alpha(\varphi) = \alpha(\psi)$.*

Note that formulas with distinct variables may as well be semantically equivalent. For example, every tautology is equivalent to the constant *true*. Table 2.9 gives a number of equivalences that can be used to simplify boolean formulas. The proof of the equivalences stated in Table 2.9 is deferred to Exercise 2.12.

Name	Rule	Name	Rule
idempotence	$\varphi \vee \varphi \equiv \varphi$	associativity	$(\varphi \vee \psi) \vee \rho \equiv \varphi \vee (\psi \vee \rho)$
	$\varphi \wedge \varphi \equiv \varphi$		$(\varphi \wedge \psi) \wedge \rho \equiv \varphi \wedge (\psi \wedge \rho)$
commutativity	$\varphi \vee \psi \equiv \psi \vee \varphi$	distributivity	$\varphi \vee (\psi \wedge \rho) \equiv (\varphi \vee \psi) \wedge (\varphi \vee \rho)$
	$\varphi \wedge \psi \equiv \psi \wedge \varphi$		$\varphi \wedge (\psi \vee \rho) \equiv (\varphi \wedge \psi) \vee (\varphi \wedge \rho)$
tautology rule	$1 \vee \varphi \equiv 1$	absorption	$\varphi \vee (\varphi \wedge \psi) \equiv \varphi$
	$1 \wedge \varphi \equiv \varphi$		$\varphi \wedge (\varphi \vee \psi) \equiv \varphi$
unsatisfiability rule	$0 \vee \varphi \equiv \varphi$	deMorgan's rule	$\neg(\varphi \vee \psi) \equiv \neg\varphi \wedge \neg\psi$
	$0 \wedge \varphi \equiv 0$		$\neg(\varphi \wedge \psi) \equiv \neg\varphi \vee \neg\psi$
double negation	$\neg\neg\varphi \equiv \varphi$		

Table 2.9. Equivalences between boolean formulas

Example 2.25 (Boolean Formula).

1. The boolean formulas φ and ψ defined by

$$\varphi(w, x, y, z) = (x \vee y \vee \neg z) \wedge (x \vee \neg y \vee \neg z) \wedge (w \vee \neg y \vee z) \wedge (\neg w \vee z);$$
$$\psi(w, x, y, z) = (\neg w \vee x \vee \neg y \vee z) \wedge (x \vee y \vee \neg z) \wedge (\neg w \vee y \vee z)$$

are both satisfiable, see also Exercise 2.11. Here, φ is a formula in 3-CNF. In contrast, ψ is not in 3-CNF, since its first clause contains four literals.

2. Exercise 2.11 asks you to prove that the formula $\varphi = ((\neg x \wedge \neg y) \implies \neg y)$ is a tautology. Note that any formula φ is valid if and only if $\neg\varphi$ is not satisfiable.

In Chapter 3, variations of the satisfiability problem for boolean formulas are studied, see Definition 3.44 in Section 3.5. Chapter 5 investigates the complexity of certain problems for *quantified boolean formulas*, see in particular Definition 5.34 in Section 5.2 and also Section 5.6. The set of quantified boolean formulas is obtained by adding *existential* and *universal quantifiers* to the boolean formulas introduced in Definition 2.23.

Definition 2.26 (Quantified Boolean Formulas).
Extending the set of boolean formulas, the set of quantified boolean formulas *(QBFs, for short) is defined as the closure of the set of boolean constants, 0 and 1, and boolean variables, $x_1, x_2, \ldots$, under the following boolean operations:*

- $\neg$ *(negation), $\vee$ (disjunction), and $\wedge$ (conjunction);*
- $\exists x_i$ *(existential quantification) and $\forall x_i$ (universal quantification).*

Occasionally, we write $\bigvee$ for $\exists$, and $\bigwedge$ for $\forall$.

Every occurrence of a variable is either bound by a quantifier or free. An occurrence of a variable x in a QBF F is said to be *bound* (or *quantified*) if x occurs in a subformula of F that is of the form $(\exists x)\, G$ or $(\forall x)\, G$; otherwise, this occurrence of x is *free*. A QBF F is said to be *closed* if all variables occurring in F are quantified. Otherwise (i.e., if there occur free variables in F), F is said to be *open*.

The semantics of QBFs is defined in the obvious way, see Definitions 2.24 and 2.32. The details are left to the reader as Exercise 2.12(b). The notions of satisfiability, validity, and semantic equivalence introduced in Definition 2.24 straightforwardly extend to quantified boolean formulas.

Note that every closed QBF F evaluates to either true or false. In contrast, an open QBF F is a boolean function of its $k \geq 1$ free (i.e., not quantified) variables, which maps from $\{0,1\}^k$ to $\{0,1\}$. In Chapter 5, we will focus on closed QBFs.

Note further that the equivalences stated in Table 2.9 for boolean formulas can as well be proven for quantified boolean formulas, see Exercise 2.12. Due to the addition of quantifiers in QBFs, additional equivalences can be shown. In particular, deMorgan's rule can be generalized to:

$$\neg(\exists x)\,[F(x)] \equiv (\forall x)\,[\neg F(x)] \quad \text{and} \quad \neg(\forall x)\,[F(x)] \equiv (\exists x)\,[\neg F(x)]. \quad (2.6)$$

Example 2.27 (Quantified Boolean Formulas).   Consider the open QBF

$$F = (\forall x)\,(\exists y)\,[(x \wedge y) \vee \neg z] \vee \neg(\forall x)\,[x \vee \neg y]. \quad (2.7)$$

The free variables of F are z and the rightmost occurrence of y; all other variables are quantified. Note that one and the same variable can occur both free and quantified in a formula. Example 2.29 shows that F is satisfiable. Now consider the closed QBF

$$G = (\forall x)\,[x \wedge (\exists y)\,[(x \wedge y) \implies \neg x]].$$

To evaluate G, consider the subformula $H(x) = (\exists y)\,[(x \wedge y) \implies \neg x]$ of G first. The variable y is existentially quantified; assigning the truth value 0 to y thus simplifies $H(x)$ to $H(x) \equiv ((x \wedge 0) \implies \neg x) \equiv (0 \implies \neg x) \equiv 1$. Hence,

$$G \equiv (\forall x)\,[x \wedge H(x)] \equiv (\forall x)\,[x \wedge 1] \equiv (\forall x)\,[x] \equiv 0 \wedge 1 \equiv 0.$$

Thus, G is false.

Every QBF can be transformed into an equivalent QBF in prenex form, i.e., all quantifiers appear in a leftmost prefix of the formula. Moreover, one can combine contiguous equal quantifiers to one quantifier of the same type, which thus quantifies a set of variables; we write them here as sets but use an encoding by a standard pairing function when dealing with computational problems for QBFs in Chapter 5. By renaming the quantified variables, the variable sets after each quantifier can be made pairwise disjoint.

Definition 2.28 (Prenex Form of a QBF).
A QBF F is said to be in prenex form *if and only if F is of the form:*

$$F(x_1, \ldots, x_k) = (\mathfrak{Q}_1 y_1) \cdots (\mathfrak{Q}_n y_n)\, \varphi(x_1, \ldots, x_k, y_1, \ldots, y_n),$$

where $\mathfrak{Q}_i \in \{\exists, \forall\}$ for each i with $1 \leq i \leq n$, φ is a boolean formula without quantifiers, and $x_1, \ldots, x_k$ are the free variables occurring in F.

Example 2.29 (Prenex Form of a QBF).   Consider the open QBF F from (2.7):

$$F(y, z) = (\forall x)\,(\exists y)\,[(x \wedge y) \vee \neg z] \vee \neg(\forall x)\,[x \vee \neg y].$$

F is transformed into an equivalent QBF in prenex form as follows:

Step 1: Rename the quantified variables to transform F into an equivalent formula F_1 in which no variable occurs both free and quantified and in which all quantified variables are disjoint:

$$F_1(y, z) = (\forall x)\,(\exists u)\,[(x \wedge u) \vee \neg z] \vee \neg(\forall v)\,[v \vee \neg y].$$

Step 2: Transform F_1 into an equivalent formula F_2 in prenex form:

$$F_2(y, z) = (\forall x)\,(\exists u)\,(\exists v)\,[(x \wedge u) \vee \neg z \vee (\neg v \wedge y)].$$

Step 3: Combine contiguous equal quantifiers in F_2 to one quantifier of the same type, which thus quantifies a set of variables:

$$F_3(y, z) = (\forall x)\,(\exists\{u, v\})\,[(x \wedge u) \vee \neg z \vee (\neg v \wedge y)].$$

Note that F_3 and F are equivalent QBFs. To see that F_3 (and thus F) is satisfiable, choose the assignment that makes the free variables y and z true. Evaluating F_3 under this assignment then yields a closed QBF that can be simplified to

$$(\forall x)\,(\exists\{u, v\})\,[(x \wedge u) \vee \neg v]$$

by applying the tautology rule and the unsatisfiability rule from Table 2.9. Since for each truth assignment to x, there exist truth assignments to u and v such that the subformula $(x \wedge u) \vee \neg v$ evaluates to true, F_3 (and thus F) is satisfiable.

2.3.2 Predicate Logic

Not everything one may wish to express can be formulated in terms of propositional logic. For example, consider the statement: "There exists an apple tree all apples of which are red." To formalize this sentence in logical terms, we need to formally express properties of objects, such as the color of apples. Such properties are called *predicates*. In addition, one often wants to express a certain functional relationship between objects. Recall, for example, the definition of the $\mathcal{O}$ notation:

$$\mathcal{O}(g) = \{f : \mathbb{N} \to \mathbb{N} \mid (\exists c > 0)\,(\exists n_0 \in \mathbb{N})\,(\forall n \geq n_0)\,[f(n) \leq c \cdot g(n)]\}.$$

Written verbosely, this definition reads: "$\mathcal{O}(g)$ consists of those functions f mapping from $\mathbb{N}$ to $\mathbb{N}$ for which there exist constants $c > 0$ and $n_0 \in \mathbb{N}$ such that for all $n \geq n_0$, $f(n) \leq c \cdot g(n)$." This statement uses existential and universal quantifiers, the functions f, g, and multiplication and the relation $\leq$. (A binary relation such as $\leq$ is a set of pairs of elements from the universe, and is thus a two-ary predicate.)

Predicate logic expands propositional logic by adding predicate symbols and function symbols to quantified boolean formulas. Again, we define both the syntax and the semantics of predicate logic. To introduce formulas in predicate logic, we first need to define the notion of terms, of which these formulas are composed.

Definition 2.30 (Syntax of Predicate Logic).

- *Let $x_1, x_2, \ldots$ be variables. A* predicate symbol *is of the form P_i^k and a* function symbol *is of the form f_i^k, where the superscript $k \in \mathbb{N}$ denotes the arity of these symbols and the subscript $i \in \{1, 2, \ldots\}$ is used to distinguish them from each other. Function symbols of arity zero are also called* constants.
- Terms *are inductively defined as follows:*
  1. *Every variable is a term.*
  2. *If f_i^k is a k-ary function symbol and $t_1, \ldots, t_k$ are terms, then $f_i^k(t_1, \ldots, t_k)$ is a term. Note that for $k = 0$, f_i^0 is a constant, i.e., an element in the universe.*
- *In predicate logic,* formulas *are inductively defined as follows:*
  1. *If P_i^k is a k-ary predicate symbol and $t_1, \ldots, t_k$ are terms, then $P_i^k(t_1, \ldots, t_k)$ is an (atomic) formula.*
  2. *If F is a formula, then $\neg F$ is a formula.*
  3. *If F and G are formulas, then $F \vee G$ and $F \wedge G$ are formulas.*
  4. *If x is a variable and F is a formula, then $(\exists x)F$ and $(\forall x)F$ are formulas.*

Example 2.31 (Syntax of Predicate Logic).   Consider the formula F defined by

$$F = (\forall x)\,[Q(a(x, 1), s(x)) \wedge (\exists y)\,[P(y) \wedge P(s(y))$$
$$\wedge((\neg Q(x, y) \wedge P(x)) \implies \neg P(s(x)))]],$$

with the predicate symbols P and Q and the function symbols a and s.

To give meaning to the syntax of formulas in predicate logic, we define the notion of a *structure* consisting of a universe of objects and a mapping that interprets the predicate symbols (namely, P and Q in F above) and the terms (namely, x, y, 1, a, and s in F) of the formula, which are its syntactic building blocks. Based on this interpretation, the truth value of such a formula can be defined.

Definition 2.32 (Semantics of Formulas in Predicate Logic).

- A structure *is a pair* $\mathfrak{A} = (U_{\mathfrak{A}}, I_{\mathfrak{A}})$, *where* $U_{\mathfrak{A}}$ *is a nonempty set called the universe, and* $I_{\mathfrak{A}}$ *is a mapping from the set* $\{x_i, P_i^k, f_i^k \mid i, k \in \mathbb{N} \text{ and } i \geq 1\}$ *to the set* $U_{\mathfrak{A}} \cup \{P \mid P \text{ is a predicate on } U_{\mathfrak{A}}\} \cup \{f \mid f \text{ is a function on } U_{\mathfrak{A}}\}$. *That is,* $I_{\mathfrak{A}}$ *interprets every variable* x_i, *every predicate symbol* P_i^k, *and every function symbol* f_i^k *on which it is defined by mapping it to an element of* $U_{\mathfrak{A}}$, *to a* k-*ary predicate on* $U_{\mathfrak{A}}$, *and to a* k-*ary function on* $U_{\mathfrak{A}}$, *respectively. Again, subscripts and superscripts of* x_i, P_i^k *and* f_i^k *may be dropped. We use the shorthand* $x^{\mathfrak{A}}$ *for* $I_{\mathfrak{A}}(x)$, $P^{\mathfrak{A}}$ *for* $I_{\mathfrak{A}}(P)$, *and* $f^{\mathfrak{A}}$ *for* $I_{\mathfrak{A}}(f)$.
- *A structure* $\mathfrak{A} = (U_{\mathfrak{A}}, I_{\mathfrak{A}})$ *is* suitable *for a formula* F *if and only if* $I_{\mathfrak{A}}$ *is defined on all free variables, predicate symbols, and function symbols occurring in* F.
- *Let* F *be a formula, and let* $\mathfrak{A} = (U_{\mathfrak{A}}, I_{\mathfrak{A}})$ *be a structure suitable for* F. *For each term* t *occurring in* F, *we define the* value *of* t *in* $\mathfrak{A}$, *denoted by* $\mathfrak{A}(t)$, *inductively as follows:*
  1. *If* $t = x$ *is a variable, then* $\mathfrak{A}(t) = x^{\mathfrak{A}}$.
  2. *If* $t = f(t_1, \ldots, t_k)$, *where* f *is a* k-*ary function symbol and* $t_1, \ldots, t_k$ *are terms, then* $\mathfrak{A}(t) = f^{\mathfrak{A}}(\mathfrak{A}(t_1), \ldots, \mathfrak{A}(t_k))$.
- *The* truth value *of the formula* F *in the structure* $\mathfrak{A}$, *denoted by* $\mathfrak{A}(F)$, *is inductively defined as follows:*
  1. *If* $F = P(t_1, \ldots, t_k)$, *where* P *is a* k-*ary predicate symbol and* $t_1, \ldots, t_k$ *are terms, then*
  $$\mathfrak{A}(F) = \begin{cases} 1 & \text{if } (\mathfrak{A}(t_1), \ldots, \mathfrak{A}(t_k)) \in P^{\mathfrak{A}} \\ 0 & \text{otherwise.} \end{cases}$$
  2. *If* $F = \neg G$, *then*
  $$\mathfrak{A}(F) = \begin{cases} 1 & \text{if } \mathfrak{A}(G) = 0 \\ 0 & \text{otherwise.} \end{cases}$$
  3. *If* $F = G \vee H$, *then*
  $$\mathfrak{A}(F) = \begin{cases} 1 & \text{if } \mathfrak{A}(G) = 1 \text{ or } \mathfrak{A}(H) = 1 \\ 0 & \text{otherwise.} \end{cases}$$
  4. *If* $F = G \wedge H$, *then*
  $$\mathfrak{A}(F) = \begin{cases} 1 & \text{if } \mathfrak{A}(G) = 1 \text{ and } \mathfrak{A}(H) = 1 \\ 0 & \text{otherwise.} \end{cases}$$
  5. *For any variable* x *and for any element* $a \in U_{\mathfrak{A}}$, *let* $\mathfrak{A}_{(x:a)} = (U_{\mathfrak{A}}, I_{\mathfrak{A}_{(x:a)}})$ *denote the structure that coincides with* $\mathfrak{A}$ *except that* $x^{\mathfrak{A}_{(x:a)}} = a$, *regardless of whether or not* $I_{\mathfrak{A}}$ *is defined on* x. *If* $F = (\exists x) G$, *then*
  $$\mathfrak{A}(F) = \begin{cases} 1 & \text{if there exists some } a \in U_{\mathfrak{A}} \text{ such that } \mathfrak{A}_{(x:a)}(G) = 1 \\ 0 & \text{otherwise.} \end{cases}$$

6. If $F = (\forall x)\, G$, then

$$\mathfrak{A}(F) = \begin{cases} 1 & \text{if for all } a \in U_{\mathfrak{A}},\ \mathfrak{A}_{(x:a)}(G) = 1 \\ 0 & \text{otherwise.} \end{cases}$$

- *A structure $\mathfrak{A}$ suitable for a formula F satisfies F (or is a model of F) if and only if $\mathfrak{A}(F) = 1$. A formula F is satisfiable if and only if there exists a model for it. F is said to be valid if and only if every structure suitable for F is a model of F.*
- *Any two formulas F and G are said to be* (semantically) equivalent *(denoted by $F \equiv G$) if and only if for each structure $\mathfrak{A}$ suitable for F and G, we have $\mathfrak{A}(F) = \mathfrak{A}(G)$.*

Example 2.33 (Semantics of Predicate Logic).   Consider the formula

$$G = (\forall x)\, [Q(a(x, 1), s(x)) \wedge (P(x) \implies \neg P(s(x)))].$$

A structure $\mathfrak{A} = (U_{\mathfrak{A}}, I_{\mathfrak{A}})$ suitable for G is given by:

- $U_{\mathfrak{A}} = \mathbb{N}$, the set of nonnegative integers,
- $I_{\mathfrak{A}}(P) = P^{\mathfrak{A}} = \{n \in U_{\mathfrak{A}} \mid n \text{ is a prime number}\}$,
- $I_{\mathfrak{A}}(Q) = Q^{\mathfrak{A}} = \{(m, n) \mid m, n \in U_{\mathfrak{A}} \text{ and } m = n\}$,
- $I_{\mathfrak{A}}(a) = a^{\mathfrak{A}}$ is the addition function on $U_{\mathfrak{A}}$, i.e., $a^{\mathfrak{A}}(m, n) = m + n$,
- $I_{\mathfrak{A}}(s) = s^{\mathfrak{A}}$ is the successor function on $U_{\mathfrak{A}}$, i.e., $s^{\mathfrak{A}}(n) = n + 1$, and
- $I_{\mathfrak{A}}(1) = 1^{\mathfrak{A}}$ is the constant $1 \in U_{\mathfrak{A}}$.

Clearly, the predicate $Q(a(x, 1), s(x))$ is true for each x in $\mathbb{N}$. However, the implication $(P(x) \implies \neg P(s(x)))$, which says that the successor of every prime is not a prime, is false: There exists a prime number (namely, $2 \in \mathbb{N}$) whose successor, 3, is also a prime number. Thus, the closed formula G is false in the given structure $\mathfrak{A}$. Can you think of a different structure in which G is true?

In contrast, the closed formula

$$F = (\forall x)\, [Q(a(x, 1), s(x)) \wedge (\exists y)\, [P(y) \wedge P(s(y))$$
$$\wedge ((\neg Q(x, y) \wedge P(x)) \implies \neg P(s(x)))]]$$

from Example 2.31 is true in the above structure $\mathfrak{A}$, since the variable y can be interpreted as $2 \in U_{\mathfrak{A}}$. Thus, both $y = 2$ and $s(y) = 3$ are prime numbers, and the successor of each odd prime number is not prime. Can you think of a different structure suitable for F in which F is false?

It is important to realize the interplay between the syntax and the semantics of formulas in predicate logic, and in particular between the syntactical objects of a structure $\mathfrak{A}$ and the semantical interpretation of variables, predicate symbols, and function symbols by $x^{\mathfrak{A}}$, $P^{\mathfrak{A}}$, and $f^{\mathfrak{A}}$. By defining distinct structures for a given formula F, one may obtain distinct interpretations of F.

Observe that the assertions we have seen to hold for (quantified) boolean formulas in propositional logic straightforwardly transfer to formulas in predicate logic. For instance, any formula is valid if and only if its negation is unsatisfiable.

As noted above, predicate logic expands propositional logic. Indeed, one obtains propositional logic from predicate logic by requiring all predicate symbols to be of arity zero. Then, the notions of terms, variables, and quantifiers are superfluous and the predicate symbols of arity zero play the role of atomic formulas from propositional logic. In fact, it is enough to exclude variables (and thus quantifiers) from predicate logic in order to degenerate it to propositional logic (without quantifiers).

To avoid confusion, we stress here that we distinguish the boolean variables and constants used in propositional logic from the variables and constants in predicate logic. The former ones are interpreted simply as truth values, whereas the latter ones are interpreted as objects (or individuals) of the universe in a given structure.

Although predicate logic has more expressive power than propositional logic, one still cannot formulate everything one may wish to express in predicate logic. The type of predicate logic introduced here is called first-order logic. Crucially, only quantification of variables is allowed in first-order logic. By allowing quantification of predicate and function symbols in addition, the expressive power of first-order predicate logic can be increased even further to second-order predicate logic. This theme is not to be pursued any further here.

2.4 Algebra, Number Theory, and Graph Theory

The algorithms and problems to be dealt with in subsequent chapters require some foundations of algebra and in particular from group theory, number theory, and graph theory. The current section may as well be skipped for now, and the definitions and results can be looked up later on when they are needed. Again, most of the proofs are omitted here.

2.4.1 Algebra and Number Theory

We start by introducing some fundamental algebraic structures.

Definition 2.34 (Group, Ring, and Field).

- A group $\mathfrak{G} = (S, \circ)$ is defined by a nonempty set S and a binary operation $\circ$ on S satisfying the following axioms:
  - **Closure:** $(\forall x \in S)(\forall y \in S)[x \circ y \in S]$.
  - **Associativity:** $(\forall x \in S)(\forall y \in S)(\forall z \in S)[(x \circ y) \circ z = x \circ (y \circ z)]$.
  - **Neutral element:** $(\exists e \in S)(\forall x \in S)[e \circ x = x \circ e = x]$.
  - **Inverse element:** $(\forall x \in S)(\exists x^{-1} \in S)[x \circ x^{-1} = x^{-1} \circ x = e]$.

  The element e is called the neutral element of the group $\mathfrak{G}$. The element x^{-1} is called the inverse element of x. Define the order of an element x of $\mathfrak{G}$ to be the smallest positive integer k such that $x^k = \underbrace{x \circ x \circ \cdots \circ x}_{k \ times} = e$.

- $\mathfrak{M} = (S, \circ)$ is a monoid if and only if it satisfies associativity and closure under $\circ$. Note that a monoid $\mathfrak{M}$ may have no neutral element, and not every element in $\mathfrak{M}$ may have an inverse.

- A group $\mathfrak{G} = (S, \circ)$ *(respectively, a monoid $\mathfrak{M} = (S, \circ)$) is said to be* commutative *(or* abelian*) if and only if for each $x, y \in S$, $x \circ y = y \circ x$. The number of elements of a finite group $\mathfrak{G}$ is said to be the* order *of $\mathfrak{G}$ and is denoted by $||\mathfrak{G}||$.*
- *Let $\mathfrak{G} = (S, \circ)$ be a group. $\mathfrak{H} = (T, \circ)$ is said to be a* subgroup *of $\mathfrak{G}$ (denoted by $\mathfrak{H} \leq \mathfrak{G}$) if and only if $T \subseteq S$ and $\mathfrak{H}$ satisfies the group axioms.*
- *A* ring *is a triple $\mathfrak{R} = (S, +, \cdot)$ such that $(S, +)$ is an abelian group, $(S, \cdot)$ is a monoid, and the distributive laws are satisfied for all x, y, and z in S:*

$$x \cdot (y + z) = (x \cdot y) + (x \cdot z);$$
$$(x + y) \cdot z = (x \cdot z) + (y \cdot z).$$

- *A ring $\mathfrak{R} = (S, +, \cdot)$ is said to be* commutative *if and only if the monoid $(S, \cdot)$ is commutative.*
- *Let $\mathfrak{R} = (S, +, \cdot)$ be a ring. The neutral element of the group $(S, +)$ is said to be the* zero element *(the* zero, *for short) of $\mathfrak{R}$. The neutral element of the monoid $(S, \cdot)$, if it exists, is said to be the* one element *(the* one, *for short) of $\mathfrak{R}$.*
- *Let $\mathfrak{R} = (S, +, \cdot)$ be a ring with one. An element x of $\mathfrak{R}$ is* invertible *if and only if it is invertible in the monoid $(S, \cdot)$.*
- *A* field *is a commutative ring with one in which each element distinct from zero is invertible.*

Note that the neutral element and the inverse elements defined above are uniquely determined if they exist. Consider the following simple examples.

Example 2.35 (Group, Ring, and Field).

1. Let $k \in \mathbb{N}$. The set $\mathbb{Z}_k = \{0, 1, \ldots, k - 1\}$ is a finite group with respect to addition modulo k, and with the neutral element 0. The arithmetics modulo an integer is explained in Problem 2.1 at the end of this chapter. With respect to addition and multiplication modulo k, $\mathbb{Z}_k$ is a commutative ring with one, see also Problem 2.1. If p is a *prime number* (i.e., $p \geq 2$ is divisible by 1 and by p only), then $\mathbb{Z}_p$ is a field with respect to addition and multiplication modulo p.
2. The greatest common divisor $\gcd(n, m)$ of two integers m and n is defined in Section 2.1. For any fixed $k \in \mathbb{N}$, define the set

$$\mathbb{Z}_k^* = \{i \mid 1 \leq i \leq k - 1 \text{ and } \gcd(i, k) = 1\}.$$

With respect to multiplication modulo k, $\mathbb{Z}_k^*$ is a finite group with the neutral element 1.

If the operation $\circ$ of a group $\mathfrak{G} = (S, \circ)$ is clear from the context, we omit stating it explicitly. The group $\mathbb{Z}_k^*$ from Example 2.35 is particularly important in Section 7.1, which introduces the RSA cryptosystem.

Definition 2.36 (Euler Function).
The Euler function *φ gives the order of the group $\mathbb{Z}_k^*$, i.e., $\varphi(k) = ||\mathbb{Z}_k^*||$.*

The following properties of φ follow from the definition:

- $\varphi(m \cdot n) = \varphi(m) \cdot \varphi(n)$ for each $m, n \in \mathbb{N}$ with $\gcd(m, n) = 1$, and
- $\varphi(p) = p - 1$ for each prime p.

The proof of these properties is left to the reader as Exercise 2.14. In particular, these properties immediately imply the following fact that we need in Section 7.1.

Fact 2.37 *If $n = p \cdot q$ for prime numbers p and q, then $\varphi(n) = (p - 1)(q - 1)$.*

Euler's theorem below is a special case of Lagrange's theorem, which states that for every finite group $\mathfrak{G}$ of order k, the order of each subgroup of $\mathfrak{G}$ divides k. Since the order of any group element a is the order of the subgroup generated by a, it follows that the order of a divides k. Letting e denote the neutral element of $\mathfrak{G}$, we have $a^k = e$. Since $\mathbb{Z}_n^*$ is a finite multiplicative group of order $\varphi(n)$, we have proven Euler's theorem.

Theorem 2.38 (Euler).   *For each $a \in \mathbb{Z}_n^*$, $a^{\varphi(n)} \equiv 1 \bmod n$.*

The special case of Euler's theorem with a prime number n coprime with a is known as Fermat's Little Theorem.

Corollary 2.39 (Fermat's Little Theorem).
If p is prime and $a \in \mathbb{Z}_p^*$, then $a^{p-1} \equiv 1 \bmod p$.

We now define several number-theoretic notions that are central for the cryptographic protocols in subsequent chapters.

Definition 2.40 (Primitive Element).   *A primitive element of a number $n \in \mathbb{N}$ is an element $r \in \mathbb{Z}_n^*$ satisfying $r^d \not\equiv 1 \bmod n$ for each d with $1 \leq d < \varphi(n)$.*

A primitive element r of n is a generator of the entire group $\mathbb{Z}_n^*$. That is, we have $\mathbb{Z}_n^* = \{r^i \mid 0 \leq i < \varphi(n)\}$. Recall that $\mathbb{Z}_p^*$ is a group of order $\varphi(p) = p - 1$, for each prime p. Note that $\mathbb{Z}_p^*$ has exactly $\varphi(p-1)$ primitive elements, see also Exercise 2.15.

Example 2.41 (Primitive Element).   Consider $\mathbb{Z}_5^* = \{1, 2, 3, 4\}$. Since $\mathbb{Z}_4^* = \{1, 3\}$, we have $\varphi(4) = 2$, and the two primitive elements of 5 are 2 and 3. Both 2 and 3 generate all of $\mathbb{Z}_5^*$, since

$$2^0 = 1; \ 2^1 = 2; \ 2^2 = 4; \qquad 2^3 \equiv 3 \bmod 5;$$
$$3^0 = 1; \ 3^1 = 3; \ 3^2 \equiv 4 \bmod 5; \ 3^3 \equiv 2 \bmod 5.$$

Not every integer has a primitive element; the number 8 is the smallest such example. It is known from elementary number theory that a number n has a primitive element if and only if n either is in $\{1, 2, 4\}$, or is of the form $n = q^k$ or $n = 2q^k$ for some odd prime q.

Definition 2.42 (Discrete Logarithm).   *Let p be a prime, and let r be a primitive element of p. The modular exponential function with base r and modulus p is the function $\exp_{r,p}$ mapping from $\mathbb{Z}_{p-1}$ into $\mathbb{Z}_p^*$ and defined by $\exp_{r,p}(a) = r^a \bmod p$. Its inverse function is called the discrete logarithm and maps, for fixed p and r, the value $\alpha = \exp_{r,p}(a)$ to a. If $\alpha = \exp_{r,p}(a)$, we write $a = \log_r \alpha \bmod p$.*

Definition 2.43 (Quadratic Residue and Nonresidue).

- *For $n \in \mathbb{N}$, an element $x \in \mathbb{Z}_n^*$ is said to be a* quadratic residue modulo n *if and only if there exists some $w \in \mathbb{Z}_n$ such that $x \equiv w^2 \bmod n$. Otherwise, x is said to be a* quadratic nonresidue modulo n.
- *Define the decision problems*

$$\mathtt{QR} = \{(x, n) \mid x \in \mathbb{Z}_n^*, n \in \mathbb{N}, \text{ and } x \text{ is a quadratic residue modulo } n\};$$

$$\mathtt{QNR} = \{(x, n) \mid x \in \mathbb{Z}_n^*, n \in \mathbb{N}, \text{ and } x \text{ is a quadratic nonresidue modulo } n\},$$

where x and n are represented in binary.

The notions of quadratic residues and nonresidues defined above and the related decision problems $\mathtt{QR}$ and $\mathtt{QNR}$ are important for various cryptosystems to be introduced in subsequent chapters. Euler's criterion below can be used to design a deterministic polynomial-time algorithm for $\mathtt{QR}$ if the modulus is an odd prime number.

Theorem 2.44 (Euler Criterion).   *Let p be an odd prime number. Then, x is a quadratic residue modulo p if and only if*

$$x^{(p-1)/2} \equiv 1 \bmod p.$$

Proof.   Suppose that x is a quadratic residue modulo p, i.e., $x \equiv w^2 \bmod p$ for some $w \in \mathbb{Z}_p^*$. By Fermat's Little Theorem (see Corollary 2.39), $w^{p-1} \equiv 1 \bmod p$. Thus,

$$x^{(p-1)/2} \equiv \left(w^2\right)^{(p-1)/2} \equiv w^{p-1} \equiv 1 \bmod p.$$

Conversely, suppose that $x^{(p-1)/2} \equiv 1 \bmod p$. Let r be a primitive element modulo p. Then, we have $x \equiv r^i \bmod p$ for some i. It follows that

$$x^{(p-1)/2} \equiv \left(r^i\right)^{(p-1)/2} \equiv r^{i(p-1)/2} \equiv 1 \bmod p.$$

Since r has the order $p - 1$, it follows that $p - 1$ divides $i(p - 1)/2$. Hence, i is even, and the two square roots of x are $\pm r^{i/2}$.   ∎

For future reference, we next define the Legendre and Jacobi symbols.

Definition 2.45 (Legendre Symbol and Jacobi Symbol).

- *For $m \in \mathbb{N}$ and a prime number p, the* Legendre symbol $\left(\frac{m}{p}\right)$ *is defined by*

$$\left(\frac{m}{p}\right) = \begin{cases} 0 & \text{if } m \equiv 0 \bmod p \\ 1 & \text{if } m \text{ is a quadratic residue modulo } p \\ -1 & \text{if } m \text{ is a quadratic nonresidue modulo } p. \end{cases}$$

- *Let $m \in \mathbb{N}$, and let $n > 2$ be an odd number whose prime factorization is $n = p_1^{e_1} \cdots p_k^{e_k}$. The* Jacobi symbol $\left(\frac{m}{n}\right)$ *generalizes the Legendre symbol to composite "denominators" n and is defined by*

$$\left(\frac{m}{n}\right) = \prod_{i=1}^{k} \left(\frac{m}{p_i}\right)^{e_i}.$$

By Euler's criterion (see Theorem 2.44), one can efficiently compute the Legendre symbol, since for any odd prime p, we have

$$\left(\frac{x}{p}\right) \equiv x^{(p-1)/2} \bmod p. \tag{2.8}$$

By using certain number-theoretic facts, also the Jacobi symbol $\left(\frac{m}{n}\right)$ can be computed in polynomial time without knowing the prime factorization of n.

Finally, we state one more useful number-theoretic fact without proof.

Theorem 2.46 (Chinese Remainder Theorem). *Let $m_1, m_2, \ldots, m_k$ be k positive integers that are pairwise relatively prime (i.e., $\gcd(m_i, m_j) = 1$ for $i \neq j$), let*

$$M = \prod_{i=1}^{k} m_i,$$

and let $a_1, a_2, \ldots, a_k$ be any integers. For each i with $1 \leq i \leq k$, define $q_i = M/m_i$, and let q_i^{-1} denote the inverse element of q_i in $\mathbb{Z}_{m_i}^*$. Then, the system of k congruences $x \equiv a_i \bmod m_i$, where $1 \leq i \leq k$, has the unique solution

$$x = \sum_{i=1}^{k} a_i q_i q_i^{-1} \bmod M.$$

2.4.2 Permutation Groups

Section 6.5 will be concerned with algorithms for the graph isomorphism problem, and Section 8.4 will present a zero-knowledge protocol for the graph isomorphism problem. This problem can be considered to be a special case of certain group-theoretic problems. In particular, permutation groups are important here. We start by defining them, and give illustrating examples later on in Section 2.4.3.

Definition 2.47 (Permutation Group).

- *A permutation is a bijective mapping of a set onto itself. For any natural number $n \geq 1$, let $[n]$ denote the set $\{1, 2, \ldots, n\}$. The set of all permutations of $[n]$ is denoted by $\mathfrak{S}_n$. For algorithmic purposes, we represent permutations $\pi \in \mathfrak{S}_n$ as lists of n ordered pairs $(i, \pi(i))$ from $[n] \times [n]$.*
- *For permutations π and τ in $\mathfrak{S}_n$, define their composition $\pi\tau$ to be the permutation in $\mathfrak{S}_n$ that results from first applying π and then applying τ to the elements from $[n]$, i.e., $(\pi\tau)(i) = \tau(\pi(i))$ for each $i \in [n]$. $\mathfrak{S}_n$ is said to be a permutation group with respect to the composition of permutations. Its neutral element is the identical permutation, defined as $\mathrm{id}(i) = i$ for each $i \in [n]$. The subgroup of $\mathfrak{S}_n$ that contains id as its only element is denoted by $\mathbf{id}$.*

- *For any subset $\mathfrak{T}$ of $\mathfrak{S}_n$, define the* permutation group $\langle \mathfrak{T} \rangle$ *generated by* $\mathfrak{T}$ *to be the smallest subgroup of* $\mathfrak{S}_n$ *containing* $\mathfrak{T}$. *Subgroups* $\mathfrak{G}$ *of* $\mathfrak{S}_n$ *are represented by their generators. In* $\mathfrak{G}$, *the* orbit *of any element* $i \in [n]$ *is defined by*

$$\mathfrak{G}(i) = \{\pi(i) \mid \pi \in \mathfrak{G}\}.$$

- *For any subset T of $[n]$, let $\mathfrak{S}_n^T$ denote the subgroup of $\mathfrak{S}_n$ that maps each element of T onto itself. In particular, for $i \leq n$ and any subgroup $\mathfrak{G}$ of $\mathfrak{S}_n$, the* (pointwise) stabilizer *of $[i]$ in $\mathfrak{G}$ is defined by*

$$\mathfrak{G}^{(i)} = \{\pi \in \mathfrak{G} \mid \pi(j) = j \text{ for each } j \in [i]\}.$$

Note that $\mathfrak{G}^{(n)} = \mathbf{id}$ and $\mathfrak{G}^{(0)} = \mathfrak{G}$.

- *Let $\mathfrak{G}$ and $\mathfrak{H}$ be permutation groups with $\mathfrak{H} \leq \mathfrak{G}$. For $\tau \in \mathfrak{G}$, the* right co-set of *$\mathfrak{H}$ in $\mathfrak{G}$ is defined by*

$$\mathfrak{H}\tau = \{\pi\tau \mid \pi \in \mathfrak{H}\}.$$

Any two right co-sets of $\mathfrak{H}$ in $\mathfrak{G}$ are either identical or disjoint. Thus, the permutation group $\mathfrak{G}$ can be partitioned into right co-sets of $\mathfrak{H}$ in $\mathfrak{G}$:

$$\mathfrak{G} = \mathfrak{H}\tau_1 \cup \mathfrak{H}\tau_2 \cup \cdots \cup \mathfrak{H}\tau_k. \tag{2.9}$$

Every right co-set $\mathfrak{H}$ in $\mathfrak{G}$ has the cardinality $\|\mathfrak{H}\|$. The set $\{\tau_1, \tau_2, \ldots, \tau_k\}$ from (2.9) is called the *complete right transversal of $\mathfrak{H}$ in $\mathfrak{G}$*.

The notion of pointwise stabilizers is in particular important for designing algorithms for problems on permutation groups. The decisive structure employed here is the so-called "*tower of stabilizers*" of a given permutation group $\mathfrak{G}$:

$$\mathbf{id} = \mathfrak{G}^{(n)} \leq \mathfrak{G}^{(n-1)} \leq \cdots \leq \mathfrak{G}^{(1)} \leq \mathfrak{G}^{(0)} = \mathfrak{G}.$$

For each i with $1 \leq i \leq n$, let $\mathfrak{T}_i$ be a complete right transversal of $\mathfrak{G}^{(i)}$ in $\mathfrak{G}^{(i-1)}$. Then, $\mathfrak{T} = \bigcup_{i=1}^{n-1} \mathfrak{T}_i$ is said to be a *strong generator of $\mathfrak{G}$*. Note that $\mathfrak{G} = \langle \mathfrak{T} \rangle$. Every $\pi \in \mathfrak{G}$ has a unique factorization $\pi = \tau_1 \tau_2 \cdots \tau_n$, where $\tau_i \in \mathfrak{T}_i$.

The following basic algorithmic results about permutation groups will be useful later on in Sections 6.5.1 and 6.5.2. The proof of Theorem 2.48 is omitted.

Theorem 2.48. *Let a permutation group $\mathfrak{G} \leq \mathfrak{S}_n$ be given by its generating set. Then, we have the following two assertions.*

1. *For each $i \in [n]$, the orbit $\mathfrak{G}(i)$ of i in $\mathfrak{G}$ can be computed in polynomial time.*
2. *The tower of stabilizers $\mathbf{id} = \mathfrak{G}^{(n)} \leq \mathfrak{G}^{(n-1)} \leq \cdots \leq \mathfrak{G}^{(1)} \leq \mathfrak{G}^{(0)} = \mathfrak{G}$ can be computed in time polynomially in n. That is, there is a polynomial-time algorithm that determines the complete right transversals $\mathfrak{T}_i$ of $\mathfrak{G}^{(i)}$ in $\mathfrak{G}^{(i-1)}$ for each i with $1 \leq i \leq n$, and thus a strong generator of $\mathfrak{G}$.*

2.4.3 Graph Theory

The notions introduced in Definition 2.47 are now explained for concrete examples from graph theory. In particular, we consider the automorphism group of a given graph, and the set of isomorphisms between two given graphs. To this end, we need some basic notions from graph theory.

Definition 2.49 (Graph Isomorphism and Graph Automorphism).
A graph G consists of a finite set of vertices, $V(G)$, and a finite set of edges, $E(G)$, connecting some of the vertices. G is said to be a directed graph *(respectively, an* undirected graph*) if the edges are ordered (respectively, unordered) pairs of vertices. We assume that there are no multiple or reflexive edges. That is, there is at most one edge connecting any two vertices, and there is no edge connecting any vertex with itself. The graphs we consider need not be connected in general, i.e., they may have more than one component. In this section, we focus on undirected graphs, the corresponding notions for directed graphs can be defined analogously.*

Let G and H be two given graphs. The disjoint union *of G and H, denoted by $G \cup H$, is defined to be the graph with vertex set $V(G) \cup V(H)$, where $V(G)$ and $V(H)$ are made disjoint by renaming if necessary, and edge set $E(G) \cup E(H)$.*

Assume that G and H are graphs with the same number of vertices. An isomorphism *between G and H is an edge-preserving bijection from $V(G)$ onto $V(H)$. That is, if we agree by convention that $V(G) = \{1, 2, \ldots, n\} = V(H)$, then G and H are isomorphic ($G \cong H$, for short) if and only if there exists a permutation $\pi \in \mathfrak{S}_n$ such that for any two vertices $i, j \in V(G)$,*

$$\{i, j\} \in E(G) \iff \{\pi(i), \pi(j)\} \in E(H). \tag{2.10}$$

An automorphism *of G is an edge-preserving bijection from $V(G)$ onto itself. Every graph contains the trivial automorphism* id.
Denote the set of all isomorphisms between G und H by ISO(G, H), *and denote the set of all automorphisms of G by* Aut(G). *Define the* graph isomorphism problem *(GI, for short) and the* graph automorphism problem *(GA, for short) by*

$$\text{GI} = \{\langle G, H \rangle \mid G \text{ and } H \text{ are isomorphic graphs}\};$$
$$\text{GA} = \{G \mid G \text{ contains a nontrivial automorphism}\}.$$

For algorithmic purposes, graphs are represented either by their vertex and edge lists or by their adjacency matrix, which has the entry 1 at position (i, j) if $\{i, j\}$ is an edge, and the entry 0 otherwise. This representation of graphs is suitably encoded over the alphabet $\Sigma = \{0, 1\}$. Pairs of graphs are represented using a standard bijective pairing function $\langle \cdot, \cdot \rangle$ that maps from $\Sigma^* \times \Sigma^*$ onto Σ^*, is computable in polynomial time, and has polynomial-time computable inverses. This pairing function can be extended to encode k-tuples of strings from

$$(\Sigma^*)^k = \underbrace{\Sigma^* \times \Sigma^* \times \cdots \times \Sigma^*}_{k \text{ times}}.$$

Example 2.50 (Graph Isomorphism and Graph Automorphism).
The graphs G and H in Figure 2.6 are isomorphic. An isomorphism π between G and H preserving the adjacency of the vertices according to (2.10) is given by $\pi = \left(\begin{smallmatrix} 1 & 2 & 3 & 4 & 5 \\ 3 & 4 & 1 & 5 & 2 \end{smallmatrix}\right)$ or, in cyclic notation, by $\pi = (1\,3)(2\,4\,5)$. There are three more isomorphisms between G and H, i.e., $\|\mathrm{ISO}(G, H)\| = 4$, see Exercise 2.16. However, neither G nor H is isomorphic to F. This is immediately clear if one looks at the sequence of *vertex degrees* (i.e., the number of edges incident to the single vertices) of G and H, respectively, which is distinct from the sequence of vertex degrees of F: For G and H, this sequence is $(2, 3, 3, 4, 4)$, whereas it is $(3, 3, 3, 3, 4)$ for F.

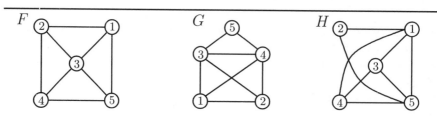

Fig. 2.6. Three graphs: G is isomorphic to H, but not to F

A nontrivial automorphism $\varphi : V(G) \to V(G)$ of G is given by $\varphi = \left(\begin{smallmatrix} 1 & 2 & 3 & 4 & 5 \\ 2 & 1 & 4 & 3 & 5 \end{smallmatrix}\right)$ or, in cyclic notation, by $\varphi = (1\,2)(3\,4)(5)$; another one is given by $\tau = \left(\begin{smallmatrix} 1 & 2 & 3 & 4 & 5 \\ 1 & 2 & 4 & 3 & 5 \end{smallmatrix}\right)$ or $\tau = (1)(2)(3\,4)(5)$. There are two more automorphisms of G, i.e., $\|\mathrm{Aut}(G)\| = 4$, see Exercise 2.16.

The permutation groups $\mathrm{Aut}(F)$, $\mathrm{Aut}(G)$, and $\mathrm{Aut}(H)$ are subgroups of $\mathfrak{S}_5$. The tower $\mathrm{Aut}(G)^{(5)} \leq \mathrm{Aut}(G)^{(4)} \leq \cdots \leq \mathrm{Aut}(G)^{(1)} \leq \mathrm{Aut}(G)^{(0)}$ of stabilizers of $\mathrm{Aut}(G)$ consists of the subgroups $\mathrm{Aut}(G)^{(5)} = \mathrm{Aut}(G)^{(4)} = \mathrm{Aut}(G)^{(3)} = \mathbf{id}$, $\mathrm{Aut}(G)^{(2)} = \mathrm{Aut}(G)^{(1)} = \langle\{\mathtt{id}, \tau\}\rangle$, and $\mathrm{Aut}(G)^{(0)} = \mathrm{Aut}(G)$. In the automorphism group $\mathrm{Aut}(G)$ of G, the vertices 1 and 2 have the orbit $\{1, 2\}$, the vertices 3 and 4 have the orbit $\{3, 4\}$, and the vertex 5 has the orbit $\{5\}$.

We now prove a useful lemma that will be needed later on in Section 6.5.1.

Lemma 2.51. *For any two given graphs G and H, we have:*

$$\|\mathrm{ISO}(G, H)\| = \begin{cases} \|\mathrm{Aut}(G)\| = \|\mathrm{Aut}(H)\| & \text{if } G \cong H \\ 0 & \text{if } G \not\cong H; \end{cases} \qquad (2.11)$$

$$\|\mathrm{Aut}(G \cup H)\| = \begin{cases} 2 \cdot \|\mathrm{Aut}(G)\| \cdot \|\mathrm{Aut}(H)\| & \text{if } G \cong H \\ \|\mathrm{Aut}(G)\| \cdot \|\mathrm{Aut}(H)\| & \text{if } G \not\cong H. \end{cases} \qquad (2.12)$$

Proof. $\mathrm{ISO}(G, H)$ and $\mathrm{Aut}(G)$ have equal size if and only if G and H are isomorphic. This is true, since if G and H are isomorphic, then $\mathrm{Aut}(G) = \mathrm{ISO}(G, G)$ implies $\|\mathrm{ISO}(G, H)\| = \|\mathrm{Aut}(G)\|$. Otherwise, if $G \not\cong H$, then $\mathrm{ISO}(G, H)$ is empty, whereas $\mathrm{Aut}(G)$ always contains the trivial automorphism $\mathtt{id}$. This implies the assertion (2.11) from Lemma 2.51.

For proving the assertion (2.12), we assume that G and H are connected; otherwise, we consider the co-graphs $\overline{G}$ and $\overline{H}$ in place of G and H, see Exercise 2.17. An automorphism of $G \cup H$ exchanging the vertices of G and H is composed of an isomorphism in $\mathrm{ISO}(G, H)$ and an isomorphism in $\mathrm{ISO}(H, G)$. Thus, $\|\mathrm{Aut}(G \cup H)\| = \|\mathrm{Aut}(G)\| \cdot \|\mathrm{Aut}(H)\| + \|\mathrm{ISO}(G, H)\|^2$, which implies the assertion (2.12) via (2.11). ∎

If G and H are isomorphic graphs and τ is an isomorphism in $\mathrm{ISO}(G, H)$, then $\mathrm{ISO}(G, H) = \mathrm{Aut}(G)\tau$. That is, $\mathrm{ISO}(G, H)$ is a right co-set of $\mathrm{Aut}(G)$ in $\mathfrak{S}_n$. Since any two right co-sets are either disjoint or equal, $\mathfrak{S}_n$ can be partitioned into right co-sets of $\mathrm{Aut}(G)$ according to (2.9):

$$\mathfrak{S}_n = \mathrm{Aut}(G)\tau_1 \cup \mathrm{Aut}(G)\tau_2 \cup \cdots \cup \mathrm{Aut}(G)\tau_k, \tag{2.13}$$

where $\|\mathrm{Aut}(G)\tau_i\| = \|\mathrm{Aut}(G)\|$ for each i, $1 \leq i \leq k$. Thus, the set $\{\tau_1, \tau_2, \ldots, \tau_k\}$ of permutations in $\mathfrak{S}_n$ is a complete right transversal of $\mathrm{Aut}(G)$ in $\mathfrak{S}_n$. Denoting by $\pi(G)$ the graph H that is obtained by applying the permutation $\pi \in \mathfrak{S}_n$ to the vertices of G, and noting that $H \cong G$, it follows that

$$\{\tau_i(G) \mid 1 \leq i \leq k\} = \{H \mid H \cong G\}.$$

Since there are exactly $n! = n(n-1)\cdots 2 \cdot 1$ many permutations in $\mathfrak{S}_n$,

$$\|\{H \mid H \cong G\}\| = k = \frac{\|\mathfrak{S}_n\|}{\|\mathrm{Aut}(G)\|} = \frac{n!}{\|\mathrm{Aut}(G)\|}$$

follows from (2.13). This proves the following corollary.

Corollary 2.52. *To any graph G with n vertices, $\frac{n!}{\|\mathrm{Aut}(G)\|}$ graphs are isomorphic.*

For example, exactly $5!/4 = 30$ graphs are isomorphic to the graph G from Figure 2.6 in Example 2.50.

The following lemma will be needed later on in Section 6.5.1. Let G and H be two given graphs with n vertices each. Define the set

$$A(G, H) = \{\langle F, \varphi \rangle \mid F \cong G \wedge \varphi \in \mathrm{Aut}(F)\} \cup \{\langle F, \varphi \rangle \mid F \cong H \wedge \varphi \in \mathrm{Aut}(F)\}.$$

Lemma 2.53. *For any two given graphs G and H with n vertices each, we have*

$$\|A(G, H)\| = \begin{cases} n! & \text{if } G \cong H \\ 2n! & \text{if } G \not\cong H. \end{cases}$$

Proof. If F and G are isomorphic, then $\|\mathrm{Aut}(F)\| = \|\mathrm{Aut}(G)\|$ implies

$$\|\{\langle F, \varphi \rangle \mid F \cong G \wedge \varphi \in \mathrm{Aut}(F)\}\| = \frac{n!}{\|\mathrm{Aut}(F)\|} \cdot \|\mathrm{Aut}(F)\| = n!$$

by Corollary 2.52. Analogously, $\|\{\langle F, \varphi \rangle \mid F \cong H \wedge \varphi \in \mathrm{Aut}(F)\}\| = n!$.

If G and H are isomorphic, then the sets $\{\langle F, \varphi \rangle \mid F \cong G \wedge \varphi \in \mathrm{Aut}(F)\}$ and $\{\langle F, \varphi \rangle \mid F \cong H \wedge \varphi \in \mathrm{Aut}(F)\}$ are equal, which implies $\|A(G, H)\| = n!$.

If G and H are nonisomorphic, then the sets $\{\langle F, \varphi \rangle \mid F \cong G \wedge \varphi \in \mathrm{Aut}(F)\}$ and $\{\langle F, \varphi \rangle \mid F \cong H \wedge \varphi \in \mathrm{Aut}(F)\}$ are disjoint. Hence, $\|A(G, H)\| = 2n!$. ∎

2.5 Probability Theory

Randomness is a crucial concept in algorithmics, complexity theory, and cryptology. To discuss the perfect secrecy of cryptosystems in Chapter 4 and to introduce randomized algorithms and probabilistic complexity classes in Chapter 6 in mathematical terms, we need some notions from elementary probability theory.

We are concerned with finite probability spaces only, which are specified by a finite set $\mathcal{E} = \{e_1, e_2, \ldots, e_k\}$ of elementary events each of which is assigned a probability $p_i = \Pr(e_i)$ such that $\sum_{i=1}^{k} p_i = 1$. The idea is that each e_i is one of the possible results of a stochastic experiment. For example, a randomized algorithm can make random choices that affect the result of the computation.

The assignment of probabilities to the elementary events is called a *probability distribution*. If all events occur with the same probability (i.e., $p_i = 1/k$ for each i with $1 \leq i \leq k$), we obtain the *uniform distribution*. The assignment of probabilities can be extended from the elementary events e_i to any subset $E \subseteq \mathcal{E}$ by defining $\Pr(E) = \sum_{e_i \in E} p_i$. Such a subset E is said to be an *event*. If we have the uniform distribution on $\mathcal{E}$, then $\Pr(E) = ||E||/||\mathcal{E}||$ is simply the ratio of the number of "good" cases and the number of "all" cases. The following basic properties of the probability function $\Pr(\cdot)$ are easy to see:

1. $0 \leq \Pr(E) \leq 1$, where $\Pr(\emptyset) = 0$ and $\Pr(\mathcal{E}) = 1$.
2. $\Pr(\overline{E}) = 1 - \Pr(E)$, where $\overline{E} = \mathcal{E} - E$ is the complementary event for E.
3. $\Pr(E \cup F) = \Pr(E) + \Pr(F) - \Pr(E \cap F)$.

We now define the notion of conditional probability and (stochastic) independence of events.

Definition 2.54. *Let A and B be events with $\Pr(B) > 0$.*

- *The* probability that A occurs under the condition that B occurs *is defined by*

$$\Pr(A \mid B) = \frac{\Pr(A \cap B)}{\Pr(B)}.$$

- *A and B are said to be* independent *if and only if $\Pr(A \cap B) = \Pr(A) \cdot \Pr(B)$; equivalently, if and only if $\Pr(A \mid B) = \Pr(A)$.*

Lemma 2.55 (Bayes).
Let A and B be events with $\Pr(A) > 0$ and $\Pr(B) > 0$. Then,

$$\Pr(B) \cdot \Pr(A \mid B) = \Pr(A) \cdot \Pr(B \mid A).$$

Proof.   By definition, we have

$$\Pr(B) \cdot \Pr(A \mid B) = \Pr(A \cap B) = \Pr(B \cap A) = \Pr(A) \cdot \Pr(B \mid A),$$

which proves the lemma.   ∎

Moreover, if A and B are independent, we have:

$$Pr(A) = Pr(A \mid B) \cdot Pr(B) + Pr(A \mid \overline{B}) \cdot (1 - Pr(B)).$$

A *random variable* is a function mapping from $\mathcal{E}$ to $\mathbb{R}$ (or to $\mathbb{Z}$). For example, if every elementary event e_i is the input of a randomized algorithm A, then one might define the random variable $\mathbf{X}(e_i)$ to be the running time of A on input e_i.

If $\mathbf{X} : \mathcal{E} \rightarrow \mathbb{R}$ is a random variable on a probability space $\mathcal{E}$, then "$\mathbf{X} = x$" denotes the event E that $\mathbf{X}$ takes on the value $x \in \mathbb{R}$, i.e., $E = \{e_i \in \mathcal{E} \mid \mathbf{X}(e_i) = x\}$. The *expectation value* and the *variance* of a random variable $\mathbf{X}$ are defined by:

$$E(\mathbf{X}) = \sum_{e_i \in \mathcal{E}} \mathbf{X}(e_i) \cdot Pr(e_i);$$

$$V(\mathbf{X}) = E((\mathbf{X} - E(\mathbf{X}))^2) = E(\mathbf{X}^2) - (E(\mathbf{X}))^2.$$

Intuitively, the expectation value $E(\mathbf{X})$ gives the value taken on by $\mathbf{X}$ on the average, with respect to the underlying probability distribution. The variance is a measure of how far the values of $\mathbf{X}$ deviate from $E(\mathbf{X})$.

Let p denote the probability that a certain event E occurs, and let $\mathbf{X}$ be a random variable that gives the number of independent trials until E occurs for the first time. Let μ denote the number of independent trials *on the average* until E occurs for the first time, i.e., $\mu = E(\mathbf{X})$. With probability p, E occurs with the first trial already (which is thus successful), and with probability $1 - p$ one still needs on the average μ trials after this first (unsuccessful) trial. Hence,

$$\mu = p \cdot 1 + (1 - p)(1 + \mu),$$

which implies $E(\mathbf{X}) = \mu = 1/p$. For example, if a randomized algorithm provides some desired result with probability p, then this algorithm has to be simulated $1/p$ times on the average until this desired result is obtained.

2.6 Exercises and Problems

Exercise 2.1 Prove that the extended algorithm of Euclid in Figure 2.2 is correct.

Exercise 2.2 Prove Theorem 2.2 by induction.

Exercise 2.3 Golden Cut: Consider a rectangle with the side lengths a and b, where $a < b$. If one cuts a square of side length a out of this rectangle, one obtains another rectangle with the side lengths $b - a$ and a. The question is for which numbers of a and b the ratio of the side lengths of these two rectangles is equal: $a/b = (b - a)/a$.
(a) Prove that the ratio $(1 + \sqrt{5})/2$ satisfies this equation.
(b) By which other (negative) ratio is this equation also satisfied?

Exercise 2.4 Prove that the base of the logarithm is irrelevant in the $\mathcal{O}$ notation: If $a, b > 1$ are two distinct bases, then $\log_b n = (\log_b a)(\log_a n)$, which implies that $\log_b n \in \mathcal{O}(\log_a n)$.

Exercise 2.5 Consider the grammars G_1 and G_2 from Example 2.8.

(a) Draw the syntax tree for the derivation $S_1 \vdash_{G_1} aS_1 b \vdash_{G_1} aaS_1 bb \vdash_{G_1} aabb$. Prove that $L(G_1) = \{a^n b^n \mid n \in \mathbb{N}\}$.

(b) Determine the language $L(G_2)$ generated by G_2. To this end, guess what $L(G_2)$ might be, and then verify your guess by proving that *exactly* the words you guessed to be in $L(G_2)$ can be derived from the start symbol S_2.

Exercise 2.6 Let M be the DFA displayed on the left-hand side of Figure 2.4, and let N be the NFA displayed on the right-hand side of Figure 2.4.

(a) Determine the language $L(M)$ accepted by M.

(b) Determine the language $L(N)$ accepted by N.

Exercise 2.7 Prove that every language can be recognized by an NFA if and only if it can be generated by a regular grammar.

Exercise 2.8 Prove Theorem 2.13.

Hint: Given an NFA M, define a DFA whose states are the subsets of M's set of states, and modify the transition function of M and its initial and final states appropriately.

Exercise 2.9 **(a)** Give a formal definition of the notion of a Gödelization of Turing machines. In particular, specify the underlying alphabet Σ and explain how to encode syntactically correct Turing machines by strings over Σ.

(b) Give a detailed definition of the notion of a Gödelization of deterministic finite automata.

Exercise 2.10 Define the *disjunctive normal form* (*DNF*, for short) of boolean formulas dually to the conjunctive normal form from Definition 2.23 by exchanging $\wedge$ and $\vee$. That is, a boolean formula φ is in DNF if and only if it is a disjunction of conjuncts:

$$\varphi(x_1, x_2, \ldots, x_n) = \bigvee_{i=1}^{m} \left(\bigwedge_{j=1}^{k_i} \ell_{i,j} \right),$$

where the $\ell_{i,j}$ are literals over $\{x_1, x_2, \ldots, x_n\}$. Define the satisfiability problem for boolean formulas in disjunctive normal form by

$$\text{DNF-SAT} = \{\varphi \mid \varphi \text{ is a satisfiable boolean formula in DNF}\}.$$

Design a deterministic polynomial-time algorithm for testing whether or not a given formula in DNF is satisfiable.

Exercise 2.11 Consider the boolean formulas φ and ψ defined in Example 2.25.

(a) Find all satisfying assignments of both φ and ψ.

(b) Using appropriate rules from Table 2.9, turn both φ and ψ into an equivalent formula in DNF.

(c) Prove that the formula $\varphi = ((\neg x \wedge \neg y) \implies \neg y)$ is a tautology by looking at its truth table. Prove that $\neg \varphi$ is unsatisfiable.

Exercise 2.12 (a) Prove the equivalences stated in Table 2.9 by looking at the corresponding truth tables.

(b) Define the the semantics of QBFs analogously to Definition 2.24.

(c) Prove the generalization of deMorgan's rule for quantified boolean formulas stated in (2.6).

(d) Generalize the distributive laws from Table 2.9 to quantified boolean formulas.

Exercise 2.13 (a) Prove that $\mathbb{Z}$ is a ring with respect to addition and multiplication.

(b) Is $\mathbb{Z}$ a field?

(c) What can be said about the properties of the algebraic structures $(\mathbb{N}, +)$, $(\mathbb{N}, \cdot)$, $(\mathbb{N}, +, \cdot)$, $(\mathbb{Q}, +, \cdot)$, and $(\mathbb{R}, +, \cdot)$? Here, $+$ and $\cdot$ denote ordinary addition and multiplication, $\mathbb{Q}$ denotes the set of rational numbers, and $\mathbb{R}$ denotes the set of real numbers.

Exercise 2.14 (a) Prove the following properties of Euler's φ function:

- $\varphi(m \cdot n) = \varphi(m) \cdot \varphi(n)$ for all $m, n \in \mathbb{N}$ with $\gcd(m, n) = 1$, and
- $\varphi(p) = p - 1$ for each prime p.

(b) Using these properties, prove Fact 2.37.

Exercise 2.15 (a) How many primitive elements do $\mathbb{Z}_{13}^*$ and $\mathbb{Z}_{14}^*$ have?

(b) Which one (if any) of the two rings $\mathbb{Z}_{13}$ and $\mathbb{Z}_{14}$ is a field? Find all primitive elements of $\mathbb{Z}_{13}^*$ and $\mathbb{Z}_{14}^*$ and prove that they indeed are primitive elements.

(c) For each of the primitive elements of 13 and 14, respectively, prove that it generates all of $\mathbb{Z}_{13}^*$ and $\mathbb{Z}_{14}^*$.

Exercise 2.16 Consider the graphs F, G, and H from Figure 2.6 in Example 2.50.

(a) Determine all isomorphisms between G and H.

(b) Determine all automorphisms of F, G, and H.

(c) For which isomorphism between G and H is $\mathrm{ISO}(G, H)$ a right co-set of $\mathrm{Aut}(G)$ in $\mathfrak{S}_5$, i.e., for which $\tau \in \mathrm{ISO}(G, H)$ does $\mathrm{ISO}(G, H)$ equal $\mathrm{Aut}(G)\tau$? Determine the complete right transversals of $\mathrm{Aut}(F)$, $\mathrm{Aut}(G)$, and $\mathrm{Aut}(H)$ in $\mathfrak{S}_5$.

(d) Determine the orbit of all vertices of F in $\mathrm{Aut}(F)$ and the orbit of all vertices of H in $\mathrm{Aut}(H)$.

(e) For the subgroups $\mathrm{Aut}(F) \leq \mathfrak{S}_5$ and $\mathrm{Aut}(H) \leq \mathfrak{S}_5$, respectively, determine the tower of stabilizers.

(f) How many graphs with five vertices are isomorphic to F?

Exercise 2.17 The *co-graph* $\overline{G}$ of a given graph G is defined by the vertex set $V(\overline{G}) = V(G)$ and the edge set $E(\overline{G}) = \{\{i, j\} \mid i, j \in V(\overline{G}) \text{ and } \{i, j\} \notin E(G)\}$. Prove that

(a) $\mathrm{Aut}(G) = \mathrm{Aut}(\overline{G})$;

(b) $\mathrm{ISO}(G, H) = \mathrm{ISO}(\overline{G}, \overline{H})$;

(c) $\overline{G}$ is connected if G is not connected.

Problem 2.1 (Arithmetics in $\mathbb{Z}_k$)

Let $k \in \mathbb{N}$ and $x, y, z \in \mathbb{Z}$. The number x *is congruent to* y *modulo* k ($x \equiv y \bmod k$, for short) if and only if k divides the difference $y - x$. For example, $-3 \equiv 16 \bmod 19$ and $8 \equiv 0 \bmod 2$. The congruence $\equiv$ modulo k defines an *equivalence relation* on $\mathbb{Z}$, i.e., it is *reflexive* ($x \equiv x \bmod k$), *symmetric* ($x \equiv y \bmod k$ implies $y \equiv x \bmod k$), and *transitive* (if $x \equiv y \bmod k$ and $y \equiv z \bmod k$, then $x \equiv z \bmod k$).

The set $x + k\mathbb{Z} = \{y \in \mathbb{Z} \mid y \equiv x \bmod k\}$ is said to be the *remainder class of* $x \bmod k$. For example, the remainder class of $3 \bmod 7$ is the set

$$3 + 7\mathbb{Z} = \{3, 3 \pm 7, 3 \pm 2 \cdot 7, \ldots\} = \{3, 10, -4, 17, -11, \ldots\}.$$

We always choose the smallest natural number in $x + k\mathbb{Z}$ to *represent* the remainder class of $x \bmod k$; e.g., 3 represents the class $3 \bmod 7$. The set of all remainder classes modulo k is $\mathbb{Z}_k = \{0, 1, \ldots, k - 1\}$. On $\mathbb{Z}_k$, define the *addition modulo* k by $(x + k\mathbb{Z}) + (y + k\mathbb{Z}) = (x + y) + k\mathbb{Z}$ and the *multiplication modulo* k by $(x + k\mathbb{Z}) \cdot (y + k\mathbb{Z}) = (x \cdot y) + k\mathbb{Z}$. For example, in the arithmetics modulo 7, we have $(3 + 7\mathbb{Z}) + (6 + 7\mathbb{Z}) = (3 + 6) + 7\mathbb{Z} = 2 + 7\mathbb{Z}$ and $(3 + 7\mathbb{Z}) \cdot (4 + 7\mathbb{Z}) = (3 \cdot 4) + 7\mathbb{Z} = 5 + 7\mathbb{Z}$.

Prove that in the arithmetics modulo k:

(a) $(\mathbb{Z}_k, +, \cdot)$ is a commutative ring with one;

(b) the set $\mathbb{Z}_k^*$ defined in Example 2.35 is a multiplicative group;

(c) for each prime number p, $(\mathbb{Z}_p, +, \cdot)$ is a field.

(d) Prove that in any group, the neutral element and the inverse elements are always unique.

(e) Prove that the invertible elements in a commutative ring $\mathfrak{R}$ with one form a group, which is called the *unity group of* $\mathfrak{R}$. What is the unity group of the ring $\mathbb{Z}_k$?

Problem 2.2 (Pumping Lemma)

There are two versions of the Pumping Lemma that can be used as a tool to prove that certain languages are not regular and are not context-free, respectively.

Lemma 2.56 (Pumping Lemma for Regular Languages).

Let L be any language in REG. *Then, there exists an integer $n \geq 1$ (depending on L) such that each string $x \in L$ with $|x| \geq n$ can be written in the form $x = uvw$, where $|v| \geq 1$, $|uv| \leq n$, and for each $i \geq 0$, $uv^i w \in L$.*

Using Lemma 2.56, prove that the context-free language $L = \{a^n b^n \mid n \in \mathbb{N}\}$ defined in Example 2.8 is not regular.

Lemma 2.57 (Pumping Lemma for Context-Free Languages).

Let L be any language in CF. *Then, there exists an integer $n \geq 1$ (depending on L) such that each string $z \in L$ with $|z| \geq n$ can be written in the form $z = uvwxy$, where $|vx| \geq 1$, $|vwx| \leq n$, and for each $i \geq 0$, $uv^i wx^i y \in L$.*

Using Lemma 2.57, prove that the context-sensitive language $L = \{a^n b^n c^n \mid n \geq 1\}$ defined in Example 2.18 is not context-free.

Problem 2.3 (Tree Isomorphism)

The graph isomorphism problem GI is efficiently solvable on certain special graph classes, for instance, on the class of trees. An (undirected) *tree* is a connected, cycle-free graph, where a *cycle* is a sequence of pairwise incident edges that returns to the point of origin. The *leaves of a tree* are the vertices with degree one. Design an efficient algorithm for the *tree isomorphism problem*, which is defined by

$$\texttt{TI} = \{\langle G, H \rangle \mid G \text{ and } H \text{ are isomorphic trees}\}.$$

Hint: Label the vertices of the given two trees successively by suitable number sequences, and compare the resulting sequences of labels in the single loops of the algorithm. Starting from the leaves of the trees and working step by step towards the center of the trees, the algorithm halts when all vertices are labeled; see also [KST93].

2.7 Summary and Bibliographic Remarks

General Remarks: As a preparation for the subsequent chapters, this chapter introduced the elementary foundations of a variety of fields from computer science and mathematics. For each such field, there are many good books some of which are mentioned here.

A wonderful introduction to algorithmics is due to Cormen, Leiserson, Rivest, and Stein [CLRS01]. The books by Schöning [Sch01] and by Ottmann and Widmayer [OW02] are also very recommendable. Among the classics in the theory of formal languages and automata are the books by Hopcroft, Motwani, and Ullman [HMU01] and by Salomaa [Sal73]. Closely related to these fields is the theory of recursive functions and computability, which builds on the early work by Turing [Tur36] and others. Among the classics here are the books by Kleene [Kle52], H. Rogers [Rog67], Odifreddi [Odi89], and Homer and Selman [HS01]. The fields mentioned in this paragraph are covered in Sections 2.1 and 2.2; they provide the fundament of theoretical computer science.

Sections 2.3, 2.4, and 2.5 introduced to various mathematical fields. At least one reference per field is given. Shoenfield [Sho67] presents the foundations of logic from a mathematical point of view. For the computer scientist, also the very readable book by Schöning [Sch95a] and Part II of Papadimitriou's book [Pap94] are recommendable. An introduction to number theory can be found in the books by Hardy and Wright [HW79] and Rosen [Ros99]. For graph theory, the reader is referred to the books by Harary [Har69], Golumbic [Gol80], and Brandstädt et al. [BLS99]. More background on algebra can be found in the books by Anton [Ant00] and Jacobson [Jac74], and for an introduction to probability theory, we refer to Feller's book [Fel68].

Specific Remarks: The idea of nondeterministic machines was introduced by Rabin and Scott who received the Turing Award in 1976 for their joint paper [RS59] that studies nondeterministic finite automata. Nondeterminism proved to be an enormously valuable concept, and their classic paper has been a continuous source of inspiration for subsequent work in this field. One particularly important instance of this research is the study of the class NP and the development of the theory of NP-completeness, see Section 3.5.3.

3

Foundations of Complexity Theory

3.1 Tasks and Aims of Complexity Theory

The first and most central task of complexity theory is to determine the computational complexity or "hardness" of problems as precisely as possible. Consider the set S defined by $S = \{x2^{|x|}x \mid x \in \{0,1\}^*\}$, whose elements are strings over the alphabet $\{0,1,2\}$. How "hard" is S? That is, how hard is it to algorithmically decide whether or not a given input string belongs to S? The first answer is: Well, it depends!

First, one has to formally specify the notion of "algorithm"; second, one has to formally specify what type of "complexity" is to be measured and in which way. Throughout this book, *algorithms* are represented by *Turing machines*, a simple mathematical model of a computer that is formally described in Section 2.2. An algorithmic device such as a Turing machine can be equipped with varying technical abilities that affect its computational power and efficiency. In fact, the observation that distinct algorithms for one and the same problem can have distinct running times and distinct memory requirements marks the beginning of complexity theory. So, the second and more specific answer to the above question is in fact at least four answers:

1. Turing machines with one read-only input tape and one read-write working tape can solve S in real-time, i.e., the number of steps in the computation equals the length of the input; see also Problem 3.1 at the end of this chapter.
2. Turing machines with only one working tape and no separate input tape require time at least quadratic in the input size to solve S; see also Problem 3.1.
3. Alternating Turing machines (a model to be introduced in Section 5.6) need time no more than logarithmic in the input size to solve S.
4. Finite automata cannot solve S at all. Note that finite automata can be considered to be very restricted Turing machines, which are equipped only with a one-way read-only input tape (i.e., the head is allowed to go only from left to right in each step), have no working tape, and must finish their work in real-time.

This observation is well known from everyday life. If one faces the problem of cutting down a tree of two yards in diameter, it does make a difference with which tools or devices one is equipped to solve the problem. A worker equipped with only an axe certainly will need much more time for this task than a worker using a chain-saw. A worker equipped with some inappropriate tool such as a nail file may take forever or, frustrated, he may just give up. Thus, depending on the devices used to solve a given task or problem, one can assign a certain complexity to this problem. In the example of the tree, one could measure the time needed to cut it down and take this value to be the problem's complexity. One could also measure the physical power or energy that it takes to do the job, thus obtaining another value for the same problem's complexity; that is, one would measure a different kind of complexity in this case. For a different problem though, the chain-saw, which at first glance appears to be more powerful a tool than the axe, may turn out to be actually less suitable and thus less efficient. For example, if you are facing the problem of chopping fifty logs up into firewood, you should use the axe, not the chain-saw, and you'll be done with it much faster. These observations suggest that the *computational* complexity of a problem is determined by the following three characteristics:

- the *computational model* or *algorithmic device* used—e.g., the two-way, multi-tape Turing machine defined in Section 2.2;
- the *computational paradigm* or *acceptance mode* of this computational model—e.g., deterministic or nondeterministic or probabilistic or alternating or unambiguous, etc. Turing machines;
- the *complexity measure* or *resource* used—e.g., the time (i.e., the number of steps executed in the computation) or the space (i.e., the number of tape cells used in the computation), etc. that is needed to solve the problem.

Frankly speaking, the set S mentioned in the first paragraph of this section is not an earthshakingly interesting problem. Complexity theory studies important, interesting, natural problems from almost every field of sciences, including areas as diverse as logic, graph theory, algebra and number theory, algorithmics, cryptography, coding and information theory, data compression, formal languages and automata, circuit theory, genome sequencing, social choice theory, and many more. Classifying such problems according to their computational complexity is one of the main tasks of complexity theory.

Another important task of complexity theory is to compare the computational power of various algorithmic devices and computational paradigms with each other, and to determine trade-offs between various complexity measures. For example, the time versus space question and the determinism versus nondeterminism question are investigated in Sections 3.2, 3.3, and 3.4. In particular, Section 3.2 defines the complexity measures time and space in the worst-case complexity model and introduces the corresponding complexity classes. A complexity class is a set of problems that, according to a given computational model and paradigm, can be solved by algorithms using at most a specified amount of a given complexity resource. In Section 3.3, the linear speed-up and tape-compression theorems and the hierarchy theorems for time and space will be proven. These results answer the question of how much a complexity resource must be increased such that strictly more problems can be solved using algorithms bounded by this resource. Section 3.4 then explores the realm between logarithmic and polynomial space.

As mentioned above, complexity classes are suitable to describe, or to *classify*, the complexity of a problem by providing an upper bound and a matching lower bound. For any complexity class C and any problem A, proving C to be an *upper bound* for A requires "merely" the design of an algorithm solving the problem and using at most as much of the complexity resource considered as C provides. That is, one and only one appropriate algorithm is enough to establish an upper bound. Proving C to be a *lower bound* for A usually is much harder. One has to show that *every* algorithm solving the problem necessarily uses *at least* as much of the complexity resource considered as C provides. In other words, one has to argue that *no algorithm whatsoever* can solve the problem with less resources than that of C.

To compare two problems according to their computational complexity, *complexity-bounded reducibilities* are introduced in Section 3.5. Reducing a problem A to a problem B means that A is at most as hard as B. In particular, the polynomial-time and logarithmic-space many-one reducibilities are investigated. Relatedly, the notions of *hardness* and of *completeness* of a problem for a complexity class are introduced. The complete problems in a complexity class are the hardest problems in this class, with respect to the reducibility considered. That is, *every* problem in the class can be reduced to any problem complete for the class. In this sense, every C-complete problem represents the entire class C. Note, however, that not all complexity classes are known to have complete problems. For example, so-called "promise classes" are unlikely to have complete problems; see Sections 6.2.1 and 6.5.2.

In particular, the important notions of NL-*completeness* and NP-*completeness* are investigated. Problems complete for NL and NP include variations of the satisfiability problem for boolean formulas and certain graph problems. An example of an NL-complete problem is the graph accessibility problem: Given a directed graph G and two designated vertices s and t of G, is there a path in G from s to t? Another example of an NL-complete problem is 2-SAT: Given a boolean formula φ with two literals per clause, does there exist a truth assignment to the variables of φ that makes φ true? In contrast, the general satisfiability problem (with no restriction on the number of literals per clause) is a standard NP-complete problem by Cook's Theorem. His breakthrough result shows that the computation of any given NP machine on any given input can be encoded into a boolean formula such that the formula is satisfiable exactly if the computation accepts its input. By finding suitable reductions from the satisfiability problem, many other important problems can be shown to be NP-complete, including 3-SAT (the satisfiability problem restricted to three literals per clause), the graph three-colorability problem, and thousands of other problems.

Section 3.6 studies the important classes P and NP, deterministic and nondeterministic polynomial time. For the P versus NP question, which is one of the most important open questions in theoretical computer science, the notion of NP-completeness from Section 3.5 is particularly useful. In contrast, there are subclasses of NP that are very unlikely to have complete problems. For example, the class UP ("*unambiguous polynomial time*") is the class of those NP problems that either have no solution at all or a unique solution. Also, the graph isomorphism problem currently is the most prominent candidate for a problem in NP that is neither in P nor NP-complete. On the one hand, despite considerable efforts in the past, no efficient algorithm for solving this problem could be designed as yet. On the other hand, it is very unlikely to be NP-complete, for reasons to be explained later on in Section 5.7.

3.2 Complexity Measures and Classes

In this section, the complexity measures time and space are introduced in the worst-case complexity model. Intuitively, the *time complexity* of a computation is the number of steps an algorithm performs on a given input, and the *space complexity* of a computation is the memory size an algorithm uses on a given input. The time and space complexity functions depend on the input size. *Worst-case complexity* means that, for an algorithm M and for each input size n, the value of the complexity function of M at length n is the *maximum* complexity of the computations of M, taken over all inputs of length n.

Turing machines, which are our model of an algorithm, and the notions of a Turing machine's configuration and computation are formally defined in Section 2.2. Let M be any Turing machine with input alphabet $\Sigma = \{0,1\}$, and let $x \in \Sigma^*$ be any input string. $M(x)$ denotes the *computation of M on input x*. Recall that if M is a deterministic Turing machine (DTM, for short), then its computation is a sequence of configurations. If M is a nondeterministic Turing machine (NTM, for short), then its computation is a tree whose vertices are configurations, whose root is the start configuration, and whose leaves are the final configurations. It is reasonable to require that a computation has a complexity exactly if it terminates in finitely many steps. For the case of a nondeterministic Turing machine, it is enough that at least one path in the computation tree terminates. The *language of M*, denoted by $L(M)$, is the set of all inputs x that M accepts, i.e., for which $M(x)$ has at least one accepting computation path. (DTMs never have more than one computation path.)

Definition 3.1 (Deterministic Time and Space Complexity Measures).
Let M be any DTM with $L(M) \subseteq \Sigma^*$, and let $x \in \Sigma^*$ be any input. For the computation $M(x)$, define the time function *and the* space function*, denoted respectively by* Time_M *and* Space_M*, both of which map from Σ^* to $\mathbb{N}$, as follows:*

$$\mathrm{Time}_M(x) = \begin{cases} m & \text{if } M(x) \text{ has exactly } m+1 \text{ configurations} \\ \text{undefined} & \text{otherwise;} \end{cases}$$

$$\mathrm{Space}_M(x) = \begin{cases} \text{number of tape cells in a largest} & \\ \quad \text{configuration of } M(x) & \text{if } M(x) \text{ terminates} \\ \text{undefined} & \text{otherwise.} \end{cases}$$

Define the functions $\mathrm{time}_M : \mathbb{N} \to \mathbb{N}$ *and* $\mathrm{space}_M : \mathbb{N} \to \mathbb{N}$ *by:*

$$\mathrm{time}_M(n) = \begin{cases} \max_{x:|x|=n} \mathrm{Time}_M(x) & \text{if } \mathrm{Time}_M(x) \text{ is defined for} \\ & \text{each } x \text{ with } |x| = n \\ \text{undefined} & \text{otherwise;} \end{cases}$$

$$\mathrm{space}_M(n) = \begin{cases} \max_{x:|x|=n} \mathrm{Space}_M(x) & \text{if } \mathrm{Space}_M(x) \text{ is defined for} \\ & \text{each } x \text{ with } |x| = n \\ \text{undefined} & \text{otherwise.} \end{cases}$$

That the time complexity function should be undefined whenever the computation does not terminate is immediately clear. That the space complexity function, too, should be undefined in this case may need some more thought. After all, a nonterminating, infinite computation can occur in a limited amount of space. For example, a Turing machine that never moves its heads needs only one tape cell for its computation, but it is not guaranteed to terminate. The question of whether such an infinite computation occurring in limited space should nonetheless be assigned a specific space complexity is, in fact, a philosophical (or an axiomatic) matter. In this book, we take the point of view that any computation should have a complexity if and only if it yields a result, i.e., if and only if it terminates. In fact, this assumption is exactly the first of two conditions, which are enough to axiomatically introduce an abstract notion of complexity measure. The second condition says that there exists an algorithm that, given any algorithm M, any input $x \in \Sigma^*$, and any value $m \in \mathbb{N}$, decides whether or not the computation of $M(x)$ has exactly the complexity m. These two conditions are known as Blum's axioms. The time and space functions from Definition 3.1 are Blum complexity measures; see Exercise 3.3. Throughout this book, only these two complexity measures are considered. Note, however, that many other measures satisfy Blum's axioms, including rather pathological ones.

Blum's Axioms

Some elementary notions from recursive function theory were introduced in Section 2.2. In particular, $\mathbb{P}$ is the class of all partial recursive (i.e., computable) functions, and $\mathbb{R}$ is the class of all total recursive functions, see Definition 2.17. Recall that the domain of any function f is denoted by D_f.

Let $\varphi_0, \varphi_1, \varphi_2, \ldots$ be a fixed Gödelization (i.e., an effective enumeration) of all one-argument functions in $\mathbb{P}$. Let $\Phi \in \mathbb{P}$ be a function mapping from $\mathbb{N} \times \Sigma^*$ to $\mathbb{N}$, and write $\Phi_i(x)$ as a shorthand for $\Phi(i, x)$. We say that Φ is a *Blum complexity measure* if and only if the following two axioms are satisfied:

Axiom 1:   For each $i \in \mathbb{N}$, $D_{\Phi_i} = D_{\varphi_i}$.
Axiom 2:   The set $\{(i, x, m) \mid \Phi_i(x) = m\}$ is decidable.

Deterministic Time and Space Complexity Classes

Definition 3.2 (Deterministic Time and Space).   *Let t and s be functions in $\mathbb{R}$ mapping from $\mathbb{N}$ to $\mathbb{N}$. Define the following deterministic complexity classes with resource function t and s, respectively:*

$$\text{DTIME}(t) = \left\{ A \left| \begin{array}{l} A = L(M) \text{ for some DTM } M \text{ and,} \\ \text{for each } n \in \mathbb{N}, \text{time}_M(n) \leq t(n) \end{array} \right. \right\};$$

$$\text{DSPACE}(s) = \left\{ A \left| \begin{array}{l} A = L(M) \text{ for some DTM } M \text{ and,} \\ \text{for each } n \in \mathbb{N}, \text{space}_M(n) \leq s(n) \end{array} \right. \right\}.$$

Note that a deterministic Turing machine M *decides* its language. If $A = L(M)$ then both time$_M(n)$ and space$_M(n)$ are defined for each $n \in \mathbb{N}$. In contrast, a nondeterministic Turing machine *accepts* its language. Thus, the nondeterministic case is treated slightly differently in Definitions 3.3 and 3.4 below.

The resource functions t and s in Definition 3.1 are called the *names* of DTIME(t) and DSPACE(s), respectively. If M is a Turing machine with more than one tape, then Space$_M(x)$, the size of "a largest configuration of $M(x)$," is defined to be the maximum number of tape cells, where the maximum is taken both over all tapes and over all configurations in the computation. If there is a separate read-only input tape, then only the space used on the working tapes is to be taken into account. This assumption is reasonable, since one may also want to consider sublinear space functions such as logarithmic space, and the $\log n$ space bound is trivially exceeded by the n input symbols written on the input tape. For time complexity classes, it is reasonable to consider only resource functions $t \geq$ id, where $\text{id}(n) = n$ denotes the identity function, since in less than n steps one could not even scan each of the n input bits. However, for "alternating Turing machines," introduced in Section 5.6, it does make sense to consider "logarithmic time."

Nondeterministic Time and Space Complexity Classes

In order to introduce nondeterministic complexity measures and complexity classes, let $M(x)$ be the computation tree of any nondeterministic Turing machine M on input x, and let α be any fixed path in $M(x)$. Note that the computation of $M(x)$ along α is nothing else than a deterministic computation: it is a sequence of configurations. Define the time and space functions for each path α in $M(x)$ analogously to Definition 3.1 and denote them by Time$_M(x, \alpha)$ and Space$_M(x, \alpha)$, respectively.

Definition 3.3 (Nondeterministic Time and Space Complexity Measures).
Let M be any NTM with $L(M) \subseteq \Sigma^*$, and let $x \in \Sigma^*$ be any input. For the computation $M(x)$, define the time function *and the* space function, *denoted respectively by* NTime$_M$ *and* NSpace$_M$, *both of which map from Σ^* to $\mathbb{N}$, as follows:*

$$\text{NTime}_M(x) = \begin{cases} \min\{\text{Time}_M(x, \alpha) \mid M(x) \text{ accepts on path } \alpha\} & \text{if } x \in L(M) \\ \text{undefined} & \text{otherwise;} \end{cases}$$

$$\text{NSpace}_M(x) = \begin{cases} \min\{\text{Space}_M(x, \alpha) \mid M(x) \text{ accepts on path } \alpha\} & \text{if } x \in L(M) \\ \text{undefined} & \text{otherwise.} \end{cases}$$

Definition 3.4 (Nondeterministic Time and Space).   *Let t and s be functions in $\mathbb{R}$ mapping from $\mathbb{N}$ to $\mathbb{N}$. We say that M accepts a set A in time t if and only if*

- *for each $x \in A$, we have* NTime$_M(x) \leq t(|x|)$, *and*
- *for each $x \notin A$, M does not accept x.*

We say that M accepts a set A in space s if and only if

- *for each $x \in A$, we have* NSpace$_M(x) \leq s(|x|)$, *and*
- *for each $x \notin A$, M does not accept x.*

Define the following nondeterministic complexity classes with resource function t *and* s, *respectively:*

$$\text{NTIME}(t) = \left\{ A \,\middle|\, \begin{array}{l} A = L(M) \text{ for some NTM } M \\ \text{that accepts } A \text{ in time } t(n) \end{array} \right\};$$

$$\text{NSPACE}(s) = \left\{ A \,\middle|\, \begin{array}{l} A = L(M) \text{ for some NTM } M \\ \text{that accepts } A \text{ in space } s(n) \end{array} \right\}.$$

Of course, one does not want to view, say, $\text{DTIME}(n^2)$ and $\text{DTIME}(n^2 + 1)$ as being two properly distinct complexity classes.[1] Instead, it is reasonable to consider collections $\mathcal{F}$ of "similar" resource functions and to define the complexity class corresponding to $\mathcal{F}$ by $\text{DTIME}(\mathcal{F}) = \bigcup_{f \in \mathcal{F}} \text{DTIME}(f)$. Such a collection $\mathcal{F}$ contains all resource functions with a similar rate of growth. For example, consider the following collections of functions mapping from $\mathbb{N}$ to $\mathbb{N}$ each:

- $\mathbb{L}\text{in}$ containing all linear functions,
- $\mathbb{P}\text{ol}$ containing all polynomials,
- $2^{\mathbb{L}\text{in}}$ containing all exponential functions whose exponent is linear in n, and
- $2^{\mathbb{P}\text{ol}}$ containing all exponential functions whose exponent is polynomial in n.

More generally, for any function $t : \mathbb{N} \to \mathbb{N}$, define the collection of all functions linear in t (respectively, polynomial in t) by:

$$\mathbb{L}\text{in}(t) = \{f \mid f = \ell \circ t \text{ and } \ell \in \mathbb{L}\text{in}\};$$
$$\mathbb{P}\text{ol}(t) = \{f \mid f = p \circ t \text{ and } p \in \mathbb{P}\text{ol}\},$$

where the composition of any two functions, g and h, is the function defined by $g \circ h(n) = g(h(n))$. Similarly, define the collections $2^{\mathbb{L}\text{in}(t)}$ and $2^{\mathbb{P}\text{ol}(t)}$. Note that $\mathbb{L}\text{in} = \mathbb{L}\text{in}(\text{id})$, $\mathbb{P}\text{ol} = \mathbb{P}\text{ol}(\text{id})$, $2^{\mathbb{L}\text{in}} = 2^{\mathbb{L}\text{in}(\text{id})}$, and $2^{\mathbb{P}\text{ol}} = 2^{\mathbb{P}\text{ol}(\text{id})}$.

The time and space complexity measures as well as the resulting complexity classes are clearly invariant under finite variations, since a finite number of exceptions can always be handled by table-lookup, where the table of exceptions can be hard-wired into the program of a Turing machine. The $\mathcal{O}$ and o notations take account of this fact. Definition 3.5 below defines these and other rate-of-growth notations.

Definition 3.5 (Asymptotic Rate-of-Growth Notation).
For functions f and g mapping from $\mathbb{N}$ to $\mathbb{N}$, define the following notation:

- $f(n) \leq_{\text{ae}} g(n)$ *to mean that* $f(n) \leq g(n)$ *is true for all but finitely many* $n \in \mathbb{N}$. *Analogously, the notations* $<_{\text{ae}}$, $\geq_{\text{ae}}$, *and* $>_{\text{ae}}$ *are defined. The index "ae" of* "$\leq_{\text{ae}}$," *etc. stands for "almost everywhere."*
- *Similarly, the notation* $f(n) \leq_{\text{io}} g(n)$ *means that* $f(n) \leq g(n)$ *is true for infinitely many* $n \in \mathbb{N}$. *Analogously, the notations* $<_{\text{io}}$, $\geq_{\text{io}}$, *and* $>_{\text{io}}$ *are defined. The index "io" of* "$\leq_{\text{io}}$," *etc. stands for "infinitely often."*
- $f \in \mathcal{O}(g) \iff$ *there is a real constant $c > 0$ such that* $f(n) + 1 \leq_{\text{ae}} c \cdot (g(n) + 1)$.

---

[1] In fact, the linear speed-up theorem in Section 3.3 shows that they are not distinct.

- $f \in o(g) \iff$ *for all real constants* $c > 0$, $f(n) + 1 <_{\text{ae}} c \cdot (g(n) + 1)$.
- $f \preceq g \iff \limsup_{n \to \infty} \frac{f(n)+1}{g(n)+1} < \infty$. *Note that* $f \in \mathcal{O}(g) \iff f \preceq g$.
  Intuitively, $f \preceq g$ *means that, by order of magnitude,* f *does not grow faster than* g, *with at most finitely many exceptions allowed.*
- $f \prec g \iff \limsup_{n \to \infty} \frac{f(n)+1}{g(n)+1} = 0$. *Note that* $f \in o(g) \iff f \prec g$.
  Intuitively, $f \prec g$ *means that, by order of magnitude,* g *does grow strictly faster than* f, *with at most finitely many exceptions allowed.*
- $f \preceq_{\text{io}} g \iff \liminf_{n \to \infty} \frac{f(n)+1}{g(n)+1} < \infty$.
  Intuitively, $f \preceq_{\text{io}} g$ *means that, by order of magnitude,* f *does not grow faster than* g, *at least not for infinitely many arguments.*
- $f \prec_{\text{io}} g \iff \liminf_{n \to \infty} \frac{f(n)+1}{g(n)+1} = 0$.
  Intuitively, $f \prec_{\text{io}} g$ *means that, by order of magnitude,* g *does grow strictly faster than* f, *at least for infinitely many arguments.*

Write $f \succeq g$ *for* $g \preceq f$, $f \succ g$ *for* $g \prec f$, $f \succeq_{\text{io}} g$ *for* $g \preceq_{\text{io}} f$, *and* $f \succ_{\text{io}} g$ *for* $g \prec_{\text{io}} f$.

The additive constant 1 in the denominators of the limit expressions above merely ensures that the denominator is distinct from zero, so the quotient is well-defined. For expressions such as $\limsup_{n \to \infty}(f(n)+1)/(g(n)+1)$, the additive constant 1 in the enumerator prevents it from going to zero without g growing strictly faster than f. For example, the constant functions 0 and 2, which do not grow at all, should satisfy $0 \preceq 2 \preceq 0$. Without the additive 1, however, we had $0 \prec 2$, which is not desirable.

Theorem 3.6. *1.* DTIME$(t) \subseteq$ DSPACE(t).
2. If $s \geq \log$, *then* DSPACE$(s) \subseteq$ DTIME$(2^{\mathbf{Lin}(s)})$.

Proof. The first statement is immediately clear, since in time t any Turing machine can move its heads by at most t tape cells.

To prove the second statement, let M be a DTM working in space $s(n)$ and in time $t(n)$. Suppose M has q states, k working tapes and one input tape, and a working alphabet with ℓ symbols. For each input x of length n, M's time bound $t(n)$ is bounded above by the number of distinct configurations of $M(x)$. To see why, note that if there were one configuration occurring twice in the computation of $M(x)$, then since M works deterministically, it would loop forever and would never halt, a contradiction.

How many distinct configurations can $M(x)$ have? There are q possible states, n possible head positions on the input tape, $(s(n))^k$ possible head positions on the k working tapes, and $\ell^{k \cdot s(n)}$ possible tape inscriptions. Hence, there exist suitable positive constants a, b, and c such that:

$$t(n) \leq q \cdot n \cdot (s(n))^k \cdot \ell^{k \cdot s(n)} \leq q \cdot 2^{\log n} \cdot 2^{a \cdot s(n)}$$
$$\leq q \cdot 2^{b \cdot s(n)} \leq 2^{c \cdot s(n)},$$

where the third inequality uses the assumption that $s \geq \log$. Thus, t is in $2^{\mathbf{Lin}(s)}$. ∎

Space classes	Time classes
L = DSPACE(log)	REALTIME = DTIME(id)
NL = NSPACE(log)	LINTIME = DTIME($\mathbb{L}$in)
LINSPACE = DSPACE($\mathbb{L}$in)	P = DTIME($\mathbb{P}$ol)
NLINSPACE = NSPACE($\mathbb{L}$in)	NP = NTIME($\mathbb{P}$ol)
PSPACE = DSPACE($\mathbb{P}$ol)	E = DTIME($2^{\mathbb{L}in}$)
NPSPACE = NSPACE($\mathbb{P}$ol)	NE = NTIME($2^{\mathbb{L}in}$)
EXPSPACE = DSPACE($2^{\mathbb{P}ol}$)	EXP = DTIME($2^{\mathbb{P}ol}$)
NEXPSPACE = NSPACE($2^{\mathbb{P}ol}$)	NEXP = NTIME($2^{\mathbb{P}ol}$)

Table 3.1. Some central worst-case complexity classes

Table 3.1 shows some of the most important deterministic and nondeterministic complexity classes. As mentioned above, the logarithmic resource function makes sense only for the space complexity classes, not for the time classes. It will turn out later on that PSPACE = NPSPACE, see Corollary 3.31 below. However, all other pairs of complexity classes in Table 3.1 are either two provably distinct classes, or it is not known whether or not they are equal.

It is no coincidence that the polynomial and exponential functions are considered the most important resource functions for complexity classes. For practical purposes, it is common to view algorithms running in polynomial time as being "feasible," whereas algorithms with an exponential-time lower bound are viewed as being "intractable."

Dogma 3.7 *Polynomial time captures the intuitive notion of efficiency, and exponential time captures the intuitive notion of inefficiency.*

Dogma 3.7 is supported by the observation that polynomial and exponential functions differ significantly in their asymptotical rate of growth. Table 3.2 compares the growth rates for certain typical polynomial and exponential time functions $t(n)$, assuming a computer that executes one million instructions per second and runs a $t(n)$ time-bounded algorithm on certain practice-relevant input sizes n up to $n = 60$. Observe that all polynomials have a feasible execution time up to $n = 60$, whereas a 3^n time-bounded algorithm needs years to solve the problem for instances of size $n = 30$ already, it needs centuries for inputs of size $n = 40$, and for $n = 50$ and $n = 60$ its execution time is truly astronomical.

Table 3.3 is even more revealing: The dramatic development in computer technology, which has been accomplished during the last few decades and can be expected to continue, does not help at all in order to significantly reduce the absolute execution time of an exponential-time algorithm on input sizes that are relevant in practice. Table 3.3 shows what happens if we had a computer that runs 100 times or 1000 times faster than the computers in use today. For the function $t_i(n)$, where $i \in \{1, 2, \ldots, 6\}$, N_i is the largest input size that can be solved by a $t_i(n)$ time-bounded algorithm within one hour. Observe that a one-thousand-fold increase in computing speed only adds about 10 to the size of the largest problem instance solvable by a 2^n time-bounded algorithm within one hour. In contrast, within one hour

$t(n)$	$n = 10$	$n = 20$	$n = 30$	$n = 40$	$n = 50$	$n = 60$
n	.00001 sec	.00002 sec	.00003 sec	.00004 sec	.00005 sec	.00006 sec
n^2	.0001 sec	.0004 sec	.0009 sec	.0016 sec	.0025 sec	.0036 sec
n^3	.001 sec	.008 sec	.027 sec	.064 sec	.125 sec	.256 sec
n^5	.1 sec	3.2 sec	24.3 sec	1.7 min	5.2 min	13.0 min
2^n	.001 sec	1.0 sec	17.9 min	12.7 days	35.7 years	366 centuries
3^n	.059 sec	58 min	6.5 years	3855 centuries	$2 \cdot 10^8$ centuries	$1.3 \cdot 10^{13}$ centuries

Table 3.2. Comparing some polynomial and exponential functions

an n^5 time-bounded algorithm can handle input sizes about four times larger with the same increase in computing power. The data in both tables is quoted from Garey and Johnson [GJ79].

$t_i(n)$	Computer today	100 times faster	1000 times faster
$t_1(n) = n$	N_1	$100 \cdot N_1$	$1000 \cdot N_1$
$t_2(n) = n^2$	N_2	$10 \cdot N_2$	$31.6 \cdot N_2$
$t_3(n) = n^3$	N_3	$4.64 \cdot N_3$	$10 \cdot N_3$
$t_4(n) = n^5$	N_4	$2.5 \cdot N_4$	$3.98 \cdot N_4$
$t_5(n) = 2^n$	N_5	$N_5 + 6.64$	$N_5 + 9.97$
$t_6(n) = 3^n$	N_6	$N_6 + 4.19$	$N_6 + 6.29$

Table 3.3. What if the computers get faster?

Of course, a dogma is just a dogma, a matter of faith, and as such Dogma 3.7 should be critically disputed. Obviously, an algorithm running in $n^{10^{77}}$ steps, which formally is a polynomial whose exponent happens to be roughly the current estimate of the number of atoms in the visible universe, is impractical and inefficient and not even useful for trivial input sizes such as $n = 2$. Moreover, one may argue that even a polynomial of degree, say, 10 is far from being practical or efficient, and it may not even be useful for modest input sizes. On the other hand, an exponential time bound such as $2^{0.0001 \cdot n}$ may be considered feasible for a large fraction of practice-relevant input sizes—before the exponential rate of growth hits and the execution time has to pay its tribute. However, for the vast majority of natural problems for which a polynomial-time algorithm is known, the time bound in fact is a low-degree polynomial such as $\mathcal{O}(n^2)$ or $\mathcal{O}(n^3)$; polynomials of degree four or five or even higher occur much more rarely. Problems that provably require high-degree polynomial time do exist; L. Hemaspaandra and Ogihara mention some such results on page 264 of [HO02]. In Section 7.2.4, a pathbreaking algorithm for the primality problem that runs in time $\mathcal{O}(n^{12})$ will be presented. These results notwithstanding, we follow Dogma 3.7 throughout this book.

3.3 Speed-Up, Compression, and Hierarchy Theorems

The central question in this section is: *How much must a resource be increased in order to be able to compute strictly more?* Consider, for example, the deterministic time class DTIME(t_1), for some resource function t_1. How much stronger than t_1 must another function, t_2, grow in order to ensure that DTIME(t_1) $\neq$ DTIME(t_2)? The linear tape-compression and speed-up theorems (see Theorems 3.10 and 3.11 below) say that a linear increase of the given resource function does *not* suffice to get a strictly bigger complexity class.

Before turning to the linear tape-compression and speed-up theorems, note that it is possible to construct arbitrarily complex problems, i.e., problems that defeat any given complexity bound.

Fact 3.8 *For each $t \in \mathbb{R}$, there exists a problem A_t such that $A_t \notin$ DTIME(t).*

Proof.   The proof is by diagonalization. Let $M_0, M_1, M_2, \ldots$ be a Gödelization (i.e., an effective enumeration) of all DTMs. Define

$$A_t = \{0^i \mid M_i \text{ does not accept } 0^i \text{ within } t(i) \text{ steps}\}.$$

Suppose $A_t \in$ DTIME(t). Then, there exists a j such that $L(M_j) = A_t$ and $\text{time}_{M_j}(n) \leq t(n)$ for each $n \in \mathbb{N}$. Hence,

$$0^j \in A_t \iff M_j \text{ does not accept } 0^j \text{ within } t(j) \text{ steps}$$
$$\iff 0^j \notin L(M_j) = A_t,$$

which is a contradiction. It follows that $A_t \notin$ DTIME(t). ∎

Since complexity classes such as DTIME(t) are closed under finite invariance (see Exercise 3.2), "$A_t \in$ DTIME(t)" means: "For some DTM M, $L(M) = A_t$ and $\text{time}_M(n) \leq_{\text{ae}} t(n)$." (Recall notations such as "$\leq_{\text{ae}}$" from Definition 3.5.) Hence, "$A_t \notin$ DTIME(t)" above means: "For each DTM M with $L(M) = A_t$, $\text{time}_M(n) >_{\text{io}} t(n)$." However, "$A_t \notin$ DTIME(t)" does not exclude that, for infinitely many other $n \in \mathbb{N}$, $\text{time}_M(n) \leq_{\text{io}} t(n)$ may nonetheless be true. In this sense, Rabin's Theorem [Rab60] below is much stronger than Fact 3.8. The proof of Rabin's Theorem, which uses a clever priority argument in its diagonalization, is omitted.

Theorem 3.9 (Rabin's Theorem).
For each $t \in \mathbb{R}$, there exists a decidable set D_t such that for each DTM M deciding D_t, it holds that $\text{time}_M(n) >_{\text{ae}} t(n)$.

Now, we turn to the linear tape-compression and speed-up theorems.

Theorem 3.10 (Linear Tape-Compression Theorem).
For each function $s \in \mathbb{R}$, DSPACE(s) = DSPACE($\mathbb{L}\text{in}(s)$).

Proof. It is enough to show that DSPACE$(2s) \subseteq$ DSPACE(s). Let M be a DTM working, on any input x of length n, in space $2s(n)$. It is convenient to make, without loss of generality, the following assumptions about M: (a) M has only one tape that (b) is infinite in just one direction, (c) the tape cells are enumerated by 1, 2, etc., and (d) M's head makes a left turn only on even-numbered cells. (If the given machine does not have these properties, it is not difficult to replace it by an equivalent one that does have the desired properties; see Exercise 3.4.) Suppose further that Γ is the working alphabet of M.

The goal is to construct a new DTM N that, on input x of length n, simulates the computation of $M(x)$ but works in space $s(n)$. The idea is that N, which has more states than M and whose working alphabet is $\Gamma \times \Gamma$, "delays" the simulation of M: it will wait and see what M is going to do next before actually doing it. To this end, view M's tape as being subdivided into blocks of two adjacent cells each, i.e., the blocks are the pairs of cells with numbers $(2i - 1, 2i)$, for $i \geq 1$. Each such block is now considered to be *one* tape cell of N, and every ordered pair of symbols $(a, b) \in \Gamma \times \Gamma$ is now considered to be *one* symbol of N. Then, $N(x)$ simulates the computation of $M(x)$, except that N moves its head to the left or to the right only when M's head crosses a boundary between two blocks to the left or to the right. All steps of M within any one block can be simulated by N's finite control. That is why N needs more states than M. Clearly, $N(x)$ performs the exact same computation as $M(x)$ and needs only space $s(n)$.   ∎

The linear speed-up theorem below makes a similar statement about the complexity resource time. Its proof is slightly more complicated, and the theorem's statement is slightly more restrictive: Linear speed-up can be achieved only for resource functions that, except for finitely many exceptions, grow strictly stronger than the identity function. This is not a severe restriction, though, since for deterministic classes it does not make sense to consider time resource functions below the identity.

Theorem 3.11 (Linear Speed-Up Theorem).
For each function $t \in \mathbb{R}$ with id $\prec t$, DTIME$(t) =$ DTIME$(\mathbb{L}in(t))$.

Proof. Let A be any set in DTIME(t), and let M be a DTM such that $L(M) = A$ and M works in time $t(n)$ on inputs of length n. The goal is to construct a DTM N with $L(N) = A$ but at least m times as fast as M, for some constant $m > 1$. That is, m steps of M are to be simulated within just one step of N. Again, the idea is that patience will pay off: N will "delay" the simulation of M, i.e., N will wait and see what M is going to do within the next m steps, then doing it all at once within a single step of its own. Again, N will compress the input using a larger alphabet and more states. However, N can use its compressed encoding not before it has scanned every input bit and has transformed the input into the compressed encoding to be used later on. In other words, the head moves on the input tape cannot be speeded up. Thus, the computation of N, on input x of length n, is done in two phases:

Phase 1: Preparation. Let $m > 1$ be a fixed integer whose value will be specified below. In this phase, N copies the input $x \in \Sigma^*$ onto a working tape, thereby

erasing the input tape, and it encodes the input as follows. Subdivide the input string $x = x_1 x_2 \cdots x_n$ of length n into blocks of length m, where the ith block, $i \geq 1$, is represented by the string $\beta_i = x_{1+(i-1)m} x_{2+(i-1)m} \cdots x_{im}$.
Thus, x can be written as $x = \beta_1 \beta_2 \cdots \beta_{k+1}$, with $k = \lfloor n/m \rfloor$ and $|\beta_{k+1}| < m$. Here, for each real number r, $\lfloor r \rfloor$ denotes the largest integer s with $s \leq r$. Note that β_{k+1} is empty if and only if m divides n. Since a nonempty β_{k+1} can be handled by N's finite control, it may conveniently be assumed that m indeed does divide n and, thus, $k = n/m$ and β_{k+1} is empty. Then, N writes on its working tape the following redundant encoding of the input string:[2]

$$(\square^m, \beta_1, \beta_2) \, (\beta_1, \beta_2, \beta_3) \, (\beta_2, \beta_3, \beta_4) \, \cdots \, (\beta_{k-2}, \beta_{k-1}, \beta_k) \, (\beta_{k-1}, \beta_k, \square^m).$$

Every triple of the form $(\beta_{i-1}, \beta_i, \beta_{i+1})$, where $1 < i < k$, or $(\square^m, \beta_1, \beta_2)$ or $(\beta_{k-1}, \beta_k, \square^m)$ is considered to be just *one* symbol of N. After N has copied the input in this compressed (and somewhat redundant) form onto the working tape and has moved the head back to the leftmost symbol, $(\square^m, \beta_1, \beta_2)$, this working tape will henceforth be used as the input tape. The original input tape, which has been erased during Phase 1, will henceforth be used as a working tape.
Phase 1 requires $n + k = (1 + 1/m) \, n$ steps.

Phase 2: Simulation.   The above compressed (and somewhat redundant) encoding is also used for all working tapes of N during Phase 2. It is enough to describe the simulation for just one tape. Suppose the current content of this tape in the computation of $M(x)$ is a string a of length ℓ. As described above, N's encoding of $a = a_1 a_2 \cdots a_\ell$ is of the form

$$(\square^m, \alpha_1, \alpha_2) \, (\alpha_1, \alpha_2, \alpha_3) \, (\alpha_2, \alpha_3, \alpha_4) \, \cdots \, (\alpha_{z-2}, \alpha_{z-1}, \alpha_z) \, (\alpha_{z-1}, \alpha_z, \square^m),$$

where (1) a is subdivided into $z + 1$ blocks, $a = \alpha_1 \alpha_2 \cdots \alpha_{z+1}$, (2) for each i with $1 \leq i \leq z$, block $\alpha_i = a_{1+(i-1)m} a_{2+(i-1)m} \cdots a_{im}$ has length m, and (3) block α_{z+1} with $|\alpha_{z+1}| < m$ is handled by N's finite control.
Now, $N(x)$ simulates m steps of $M(x)$ as follows. If M's head is currently scanning a tape cell contained in some block α_j, then N's head is currently scanning the symbol $(\alpha_{j-1}, \alpha_j, \alpha_{j+1})$.[3] After m steps, M's head has moved by at most m tape cells. Hence, it must scan a tape cell corresponding to either one of the blocks α_{j-1}, α_j, or α_{j+1}, and none of the other blocks has been changed by M. Since N's head is currently scanning $(\alpha_{j-1}, \alpha_j, \alpha_{j+1})$, it can do all of M's changes within a single step of its own, and it moves its head to the symbol:
$(\alpha_{j-2}, \alpha_{j-1}, \alpha_j)$ if M scans a tape cell in block α_{j-1} after these m steps;[3]
$(\alpha_{j-1}, \alpha_j, \alpha_{j+1})$ if M scans a tape cell in block α_j after these m steps;
$(\alpha_j, \alpha_{j+1}, \alpha_{j+2})$ if M scans a tape cell in block α_{j+1} after these m steps.[3]
If M accepts or rejects x within these m steps, then so does N. Hence, $L(N) = L(M)$. Phase 2 requires at most $\lceil t(n)/m \rceil$ steps, i.e., in the simulation phase,

---

[2] This redundancy of the encoding is necessary, since without it no speed-up would be possible when the head frequently moves back and forth between two adjacent blocks.

[3] The case of $\square^m$ being the first or the third component of this triple is treated analogously.

$N(x)$ is roughly m times as fast as $M(x)$. Here, for each real number r, $\lceil r \rceil$ denotes the smallest integer s with $s \geq r$.

To estimate the total time of $N(x)$, recall that $\text{id} \prec t$, i.e., $n \in o(t(n))$. Thus,

$$(\forall c > 0) \, [n <_{\text{ae}} c \cdot t(n)], \tag{3.1}$$

where the notation "$f(n) <_{\text{ae}} g(n)$" for any two functions f and g is explained in Definition 3.5. Summing up the time spent in both phases, $N(x)$ needs no more than

$$\left(1 + \frac{1}{m}\right) n + \left\lceil \frac{t(n)}{m} \right\rceil <_{\text{ae}} \left(1 + \frac{1}{m}\right) \frac{1}{m\left(1 + \frac{1}{m}\right)} t(n) + \left\lceil \frac{t(n)}{m} \right\rceil \leq \left\lceil \frac{2t(n)}{m} \right\rceil + 1$$

steps, where the first inequality follows from (3.1) for the specific constant

$$\hat{c} = \frac{1}{m\left(1 + \frac{1}{m}\right)} = \frac{1}{m+1}.$$

The finitely many exceptions allowed in the $\leq_{\text{ae}}$-notation can be handled by table-lookup. Thus, an arbitrary linear speed-up is possible by suitably choosing m. ∎

By way of illustration, suppose that $t(n) = d \cdot n$, for some constant $d > 1$, and $N(x)$ has running time

$$T(n) = \left(1 + \frac{1}{m}\right) n + \frac{t(n)}{m} = \left(1 + \frac{1}{m}\right) n + \frac{d \cdot n}{m} = \left(1 + \frac{d+1}{m}\right) n,$$

where we assume for convenience that m divides both n and $t(n)$. Since $d > 1$, choosing $m > (d+1)/(d-1)$ implies $T(n) < d \cdot n = t(n)$ and thus a genuine speed-up. Since the function $t(n) = d \cdot n$, where $d > 1$, does not grow strictly stronger than the identity function, the example above shows that the hypothesis $\text{id} \prec t$ in Theorem 3.11 is slightly stronger than necessary. This example also suggests that the above proof does not work for $d = 1$, i.e., it does not work for $t = \text{id}$. In fact, Rosenberg [Ros67] showed that $\text{DTIME}(t) \neq \text{DTIME}(\mathbb{L}\text{in}(t))$ for $t = \text{id}$:

Theorem 3.12 (Rosenberg).   REALTIME $\neq$ LINTIME.

Linear tape-compression and speed-up are also known for nondeterministic complexity classes. Interestingly, for nondeterministic classes linear speed-up can be achieved even for the time resource $t = \text{id}$. The proof of this strong result, which is due to Book and Greibach [BG70], is omitted here.

Theorem 3.13.   *1. For each function $s \in \mathbb{R}$, $\text{NSPACE}(s) = \text{NSPACE}(\mathbb{L}\text{in}(s))$.*
2. For each function $t \in \mathbb{R}$ with $t \geq \text{id}$, $\text{NTIME}(t) = \text{NTIME}(\mathbb{L}\text{in}(t))$.

Recall the question raised in the first paragraph of this section: *How much must a resource be increased in order to be able to compute strictly more?* We know from Theorems 3.10 and 3.11 that a linear increase of the given resource function does not suffice to get a strictly bigger complexity class. For example, if s_1 and s_2 are space resource functions with

$$s_2 \preceq s_1 \iff (\exists c > 0)\, [s_2(n) \leq_{\text{ae}} c \cdot s_1(n)], \tag{3.2}$$

then by Theorem 3.10, s_2 does not grow strongly enough to outperform s_1. Thus, the least one has to require is that $s_2 \preceq s_1$ is not true. Negating Equation (3.2) gives:

$$s_2 \succ_{\text{io}} s_1 \iff (\forall c > 0)\, [s_2(n) >_{\text{io}} c \cdot s_1(n)].$$

The space hierarchy theorem (Theorem 3.15 below) says that requiring $s_2 \succ_{\text{io}} s_1$ indeed suffices to obtain a strictly larger complexity class. Thus, Theorems 3.10 and 3.15 complement each other and they are both optimal.[4] The time hierarchy theorem (Theorem 3.19 below) makes a similar assertion, although it requires a stronger hypothesis: the two given functions must differ by at least a logarithmic factor.

For the proofs of the hierarchy theorems for space and time to work, a technical property of resource functions is needed: they must be *space-constructible* and *time-constructible*, respectively. All common resource functions, such as the logarithm function, the polynomials in $\mathbb{P}\text{ol}$, the exponential functions in $2^{\mathbb{L}\text{in}}$ and in $2^{\mathbb{P}\text{ol}}$, etc. are space-constructible, and all those functions except the logarithm function are time-constructible; see Exercise 3.6.

Definition 3.14 (Space- and Time-Constructibility).
Let f, s, and t be functions in $\mathbb{R}$ mapping from $\mathbb{N}$ to $\mathbb{N}$.

- *We say that s is* space-constructible *if and only if there exists a DTM M such that, for each n, M on any input of length n uses no more than $s(n)$ tape cells and prints the string $\#1^{s(n)-2}\$$ on one of its tapes, where $\#$ and $\$$ are special symbols marking the left and right boundaries. We then say that M has* marked *the space $s(n)$.*
- *We say that f is* constructible in time t *if and only if there exists a DTM M such that, for each n, M on any input of length n runs for exactly $t(n)$ steps and prints the string $\#1^{f(n)-2}\$$ on its tape, where $\#$ and $\$$ are special symbols marking the left and right boundaries. We say that t is* time-constructible *if and only if t is constructible in time t.*

Theorem 3.15 (Space Hierarchy Theorem).
If $s_1 \prec_{\text{io}} s_2$ and s_2 is space-constructible, then $\text{DSPACE}(s_2) \not\subseteq \text{DSPACE}(s_1)$.

Proof.   We prove the theorem only for the case of $s_1 \geq \log$. Using a result of Sipser [Sip80], one can get rid of this simplifying assumption.

---

[4] Some textbooks state the space hierarchy theorem by using the stronger hypothesis that $s_1 \in o(s_2)$, i.e., $s_1 \prec s_2$. Note that $s_1 \prec s_2$ implies $s_1 \prec_{\text{io}} s_2$, but $s_1 \prec_{\text{io}} s_2$ does not imply $s_1 \prec s_2$. Using this unnecessarily strong assumption does not give the strongest result possible and leaves an unnecessary gap between the hypotheses of the space hierarchy theorem and the linear tape-compression theorem.

To construct a set A in the difference $\mathrm{DSPACE}(s_2) - \mathrm{DSPACE}(s_1)$ by diagonalization, fix a Gödelization $M_0, M_1, M_2, \ldots$ of all DTMs having one working tape; see Exercise 3.8 for why it is enough to consider, without loss of generality, only one-tape DTMs. Define a DTM N with an input tape and three working tapes. On input $x \in \{0, 1\}^*$ of length n, DTM N works as follows:

1. N marks the space $s_2(n)$ on all three working tapes.
2. Suppose x is of the form $x = 1^i y$, where $0 \le i \le n$ and $y \in \{\varepsilon\} \cup 0\{0, 1\}^*$. That is, x starts with a (possibly empty) prefix of i ones followed either by the empty string (in which case $x = 1^n$), or followed by a zero and a (possibly empty) string from $\{0, 1\}^*$. DTM N interprets i as a machine number, and it writes the suitably encoded program of M_i onto its first working tape. If this is not possible, since M_i's program is too large to fit in the marked space $s_2(n)$, then N aborts the computation and rejects x. Otherwise, N proceeds by simulating the computation of $M_i(x)$ on the second working tape, using the program of M_i on its first working tape and reading the symbols of x from its own input tape.
3. The third working tape contains a binary counter that is initially set to zero and is incremented by one in each step of the simulation of $M_i(x)$. If the simulation of $M_i(x)$ succeeds on N's second working tape before the counter on N's third working tape overflows, then $N(x)$ accepts if and only if $M_i(x)$ rejects. Otherwise, N rejects x.

Some technical explanations are in order:

- The counter on N's third working tape guarantees that $N(x)$ halts, even if $M_i(x)$ would never terminate.
- There exists a constant c_i such that the simulation of $M_i(x)$ on N's second working tape can be done in space at most $c_i \cdot \mathrm{space}_{M_i}(n)$. Why? DTM N must be able to simulate *every* DTM M_i, $i \in \mathbb{N}$. If for some i, M_i has z_i states and ℓ_i symbols in its working alphabet, then N can encode these states and symbols in binary, i.e., by strings over $\{0, 1\}$ of length $\lceil z_i \rceil$ and $\lceil \ell_i \rceil$, respectively. This encoding causes a constant space overhead for the simulating machine N, where the constant, call it c_i, depends only on M_i.

Define $A = L(N)$. Clearly, $A \in \mathrm{DSPACE}(s_2)$. To prove that $A \notin \mathrm{DSPACE}(s_1)$, suppose for a contradiction that $A \in \mathrm{DSPACE}(s_1)$. Thus, there exists some i such that $A = L(M_i)$ and $\mathrm{space}_{M_i}(n) \le s_1(n) \prec_{\mathrm{io}} s_2(n)$. Recall what $s_1 \prec_{\mathrm{io}} s_2$ means:

$$(\forall c > 0) \, [s_2(n) >_{\mathrm{io}} c \cdot s_1(n)]. \tag{3.3}$$

Hence, for each real constant $c > 0$, there exist infinitely many arguments $n_0, n_1, n_2, \ldots$ in $\mathbb{N}$ such that $s_2(n_k) > c \cdot s_1(n_k)$ for each k. From this infinite sequence of arguments, choose n_j large enough such that the following three conditions hold:

(a) M_i's program can be computed and written onto N's second working tape in space $s_2(n_j)$;
(b) the simulation of $M_i(1^i 0^{n_j - i})$ succeeds in space $s_2(n_j)$;
(c) $\mathrm{time}_{M_i}(n_j) \le 2^{s_2(n_j)}$.

Condition (a) can be satisfied for a large enough n_j, since the size of the program of M_i is a constant not depending on the machine's input.

Condition (b) can be satisfied for a large enough n_j, since the simulation of $M_i(1^i0^{n_j-i})$ succeeds in space:

$$c_i \cdot \text{space}_{M_i}(n_j) \le c_i \cdot s_1(n_j) < s_2(n_j),$$

where c_i is the above constant that is due to N having to encode M_i's states and symbols, and where the last inequality follows from Equation (3.3).

Condition (c) can be satisfied for a large enough n_j, since Theorem 3.6 implies for $s_1 \ge \log$:

$$\begin{aligned}
\text{time}_{M_i}(n_j) &\le 2^{d \cdot \text{space}_{M_i}(n_j)} \quad \text{for a suitable constant } d \\
&\le 2^{d \cdot s_1(n_j)} \\
&< 2^{s_2(n_j)},
\end{aligned}$$

where the last inequality again follows from Equation (3.3). Hence, the simulation of $M_i(1^i0^{n_j-i})$ succeeds before the binary counter of length $s_2(n_j)$ on N's third working tape is full. Conditions (a), (b), and (c) and the construction of N imply that for the string $x = 1^i0^{n_j-i}$,

$$\begin{aligned}
x \in A &\iff N \text{ accepts } x \\
&\iff M_i \text{ rejects } x.
\end{aligned}$$

Thus, $A \ne L(M_i)$, contradicting our supposition. Hence, $A \notin \text{DSPACE}(s_1)$. ∎

The proof of Theorem 3.15 in fact gives a stronger result than that stated in the theorem.

Corollary 3.16. *For each space-constructible function s_2,*

$$\text{DSPACE}(s_2) \not\subseteq \bigcup_{s_1 \prec_{io} s_2} \text{DSPACE}(s_1).$$

Theorem 3.15 immediately implies Corollary 3.17 below. Note that for sets A and B, $A \subset B$ denotes *strict inclusion*, i.e., $A \subseteq B$ and $A \ne B$.

Corollary 3.17. *If $s_1 \le s_2$, $s_1 \prec_{io} s_2$, and s_2 is space-constructible, then*

$$\text{DSPACE}(s_1) \subset \text{DSPACE}(s_2).$$

Define POLYLOGSPACE $= \bigcup_{k \ge 1} \text{DSPACE}((\log n)^k)$. Corollary 3.17 implies the following strict hierarchy of deterministic space classes. The proof of Corollary 3.18 is left to the reader as Exercise 3.7(a).

Corollary 3.18. L $\subset$ POLYLOGSPACE $\subset$ LINSPACE $\subset$ PSPACE $\subset$ EXPSPACE.

Theorem 3.19 (Time Hierarchy Theorem).
If $t_2 \geq$ id and $t_1 \prec_{io} t_2$ and t_2 is constructible in time $t_2 \log t_2$, then

$$\text{DTIME}(t_2 \log t_2) \not\subseteq \text{DTIME}(t_1).$$

Here is an outline of the proof idea of Theorem 3.19. The proof of this theorem is based on a similar diagonalization as that given in the proof of Theorem 3.15. Given a fixed Gödelization $M_0, M_1, M_2, \ldots$ of all DTMs, the diagonalizing DTM N working in time $t_2 \log t_2$ must "defeat" every M_i, i.e., the construction must ensure that if M_i works in time t_1, then the languages of N and M_i differ. Since N must be able to simulate every multitape DTM M_i, the issue arises of how N, which has a fixed number of tapes, can do so. While the number of tapes does not matter for the space used in N's simulation of M_i, it does matter for the resource time. Every k-tape DTM working in space s can be simulated by a one-tape DTM using the same number s of tape cells, see Exercise 3.8. Thus, in the proof of Theorem 3.15, it was enough to consider only one-tape DTMs M_i. In contrast, simulating a k-tape DTM M working in time t exacts its price: a one-tape DTM simulating M will need time t^2, and a two-tape DTM simulating M will need time $t \log t$. The latter result is due to Hennie and Stearns [HS66] and explains the occurrence of "$t_2 \log t_2$" in Theorem 3.19. Using this result, it is enough to show that N "defeats" every two-tape DTM M_i, and this can be achieved by a four-tape DTM N.

Corollary 3.20. If $t_1 \leq t_2 \log t_2$ and $t_2 \geq$ id and $t_1 \prec_{io} t_2$ and t_2 is constructible in time $t_2 \log t_2$, then $\text{DTIME}(t_1) \subset \text{DTIME}(t_2 \log t_2)$.

Corollary 3.21. For each constant $k > 0$, $\text{DTIME}(n^k) \subset \text{DTIME}(n^{k+1})$ and $\text{DTIME}(2^{k \cdot n}) \subset \text{DTIME}(2^{(k+1)n})$.

Corollary 3.22. $P \subset E \subset \text{EXP}$.

Story 3.23 *We conclude this section with the story about two sisters, Paula and Ella, and their best friends, Ann Paula and Ann Ella, who are sisters, too. Four-year-old Paula loves to play with Ann P., who just turned five. Their big sisters Ella and Ann E., eight and nine years of age, respectively, are also close friends. One day, Paula and Ann P. fight with each other for Paula's favorite toy, a dancing hamster, who looks like an old hippie, plays cool, funky music like the 1974 song "Jungle Boogie" from a built-in tape, and dances like crazy. Ann P. is bigger and stronger than Paula, so she takes her dancing hamster away. From that day on, the two little girls are separated.*

Paula's big sister, Ella, has got the same music as Paula, not on a tape within a hamster but nicely compressed on CD. Watching the fight, she is upset and translates her anger towards Ann P.'s big sister, Ann E. In fury, Ella throws her "Jungle Boogie" CD at Ann E. and yells at her. From that day on, the two big girls are separated as well.

What has this story to do with complexity theory? Well, what happened to the children can also happen to complexity classes. We present Book's "upward separation" result, which says that a separation via tally sets between two small complexity classes "translates upward" to separate two related, much bigger classes. "Upward separation" is sometimes dubbed "downward collapse," which means that if two large complexity classes coincide, then so do their "little sisters" on the tally sets. This alternative view gives a happy end to the sad story above: The next day, after Ann E. gave Ella's CD back to Ella, so did Ann P. with Paula's dancing hamster. Sharing their toys, the four of them were best friends again.

To the two pairs of siblings in the above story correspond the following two pairs of exponentially related complexity classes: the deterministic time classes P and E, and their nondeterministic counterparts, NP and NE. Ella's music, compressed on CD in the above story, corresponds to any given language L succinctly represented in binary, and Paula's dancing hamster corresponds to the tally encoding of L.

Definition 3.24 (Tally Encoding of a Language).

- *A tally language is any subset of $\{1\}^*$, the set of strings over the one-letter alphabet $\{1\}$. Let TALLY denote the set of all tally languages.*
- *Let $\Sigma = \{0, 1\}$ be a two-letter alphabet, and let $L \subseteq \Sigma^*$ be any set of strings over Σ. Prefix every string $x \in L$ by a 1 and then interpret $1x$ as a natural number $\mathrm{bin}(1x)$ in binary representation. The tally encoding of L is defined by $\mathrm{Tally}(L) = \{1^{\mathrm{bin}(1x)} \mid x \in L\}$.*
- *Conversely, every tally language $T \subseteq \{1\}^+$ can be transformed into a set over Σ, which is defined by $\mathrm{Bin}(T) = \{x \in \Sigma^* \mid 1^{\mathrm{bin}(1x)} \in T\}$, where the empty string has been dropped from T for technical reasons.*

Clearly, for each set $L \subseteq \Sigma^*$, $\mathrm{Bin}(\mathrm{Tally}(L)) = L$, and for each tally language $T \subseteq \{1\}^+$, $\mathrm{Tally}(\mathrm{Bin}(T)) = T$. Note that $\mathrm{Tally}(L)$ is an "exponentially verbose" representation of L, and that $\mathrm{Bin}(T)$ contains the same information as $T \in$ TALLY in "logarithmically compressed" form. This observation is stated in the following lemma whose proof is left to the reader as Exercise 3.9.

Lemma 3.25. *For each set $L \subseteq \Sigma^*$,*

1. *$L \in \mathrm{E} \iff \mathrm{Tally}(L) \in \mathrm{P}$, and*
2. *$L \in \mathrm{NE} \iff \mathrm{Tally}(L) \in \mathrm{NP}$.*

Using Lemma 3.25, one can prove the following upward separation result, which links the separation of NP and P by a tally language to the separation of their exponential-time analogs.

Theorem 3.26. NE = E *if and only if every tally language in NP is in P.*

Proof.   To prove the implication from left to right, suppose NE = E. Let $T \subseteq \{1\}^+$ be any tally language in NP. By part 2 of Lemma 3.25, $\mathrm{Bin}(T)$ is in NE. Since NE = E, it follows that $\mathrm{Bin}(T)$ is in E. By part 1 of Lemma 3.25, T is in P.

Conversely, to prove the implication from right to left, let L be any given set in NE. By part 2 of Lemma 3.25, $\mathrm{Tally}(L)$ is in NP. Since every tally language in NP is in P, it follows that $\mathrm{Tally}(L)$ is in P. Part 1 of Lemma 3.25 then implies that L is in E. Thus, NE $\subseteq$ E, so NE = E.   ∎

3.4 Between Logarithmic and Polynomial Space

Theorem 3.27 below explores the inclusion relationships among those complexity classes from Table 3.1 that are between logarithmic and polynomial space. None of the inclusions stated is known to be proper, although it is widely conjectured that they all are. Complexity theory has yielded many important and beautiful results, and as many important and interesting open questions. One of the most famous questions in complexity theory is the question of whether or not P equals NP.

Theorem 3.27. $L \subseteq NL \subseteq P \subseteq NP \subseteq PSPACE$.

Proof.   The inclusions $L \subseteq NL$ and $P \subseteq NP$ are immediately clear, since every DTM, by definition, is a special NTM.

To prove that $NP \subseteq PSPACE$, let M be any NTM running in time $p(n)$ for some $p \in \mathbb{P}ol$. To define a DTM N that decides $L(M)$ in polynomial space, we take advantage of an important property of the complexity resource space: Unlike the time resource, *space is reusable*. Using the same space on its working tape again and again, DTM N performs a depth-first search through the computation tree of $M(x)$, traversing path after path in search of an accepting configuration.

Construct DTM N, running on input x of length n, as follows. In addition to its input tape, N has one working tape subdivided into three tracks. Recall that every polynomial is space-constructible. N first marks the space $p(n)$ on its working tape, i.e., N marks exactly $p(n)$ cells. Then, N systematically traverses the computation tree of $M(x)$ by a depth-first search. To keep track of the current position in the search, N writes the name of the path of $M(x)$ currently being traversed on track 1 of the working tape. A path name can be encoded in binary[5] by a length $p(n)$ string $s \in \{0, 1\}^*$, where the ith bit of s represents the ith branching of $M(x)$. The bits of s may be marked by a hat as needed, indicating that the marked bits of s correspond to the initial part of the path that has already been processed.

Initially, N writes the path name $0^{p(n)}$ on track 1 and it writes the start configuration of $M(x)$ on track 2. Then, N starts the search by simulating the computation of $M(x)$ along the path whose name, say s, is currently written on track 1. N writes two successive configurations occurring along this path alternately on the tracks 2 and 3. Let $C_0 \vdash_M C_1 \vdash_M \cdots \vdash_M C_{p(n)}$ be the sequence of configurations corresponding to s. For i with $1 \le i < p(n)$, consider the three successive configurations C_{i-1}, C_i, and C_{i+1}, where (a) $C_{i-1} \vdash_M C_i \vdash_M C_{i+1}$, (b) C_i is the first configuration along s as yet unvisited, (c) the first $i - 1$ bits of s are currently marked by a hat, and (d) track 2, say, currently contains C_{i-1}. Then, N writes C_i on track 3, deleting the former content of track 3 and marking the ith bit of s on track 1 by a hat. N thus proceeds, alternately switching the roles of track 2 and track 3, until the current path is completely processed and all bits of s are marked by a hat. If an accepting configuration is reached, then N halts and accepts x. If s has been processed without reaching an accepting configuration, then N adds a one in binary to the content of track 1 and keeps traversing the as yet unvisited configurations on that new path.

---

[5] Without loss of generality, we may assume that $M(x)$ is a full binary tree.

If all the paths of $M(x)$ have been processed without success, then N rejects x. It follows that $L(N) = L(M)$. Since N works deterministically in polynomial space, NP $\subseteq$ PSPACE.

To prove the remaining inclusion, NL $\subseteq$ P, let $\widehat{M}$ be any NTM operating in logarithmic space, and let x be any input of length n. Note that the above systematic search through the entire computation tree does not work here. In fact, any log-space bounded NTM can spend as much as $q(n)$ steps along each path, where $q \in$ **Pol**, which results in a total of $2^{q(n)}$ potential computation paths. Thus, a polynomial-time bounded DTM has no chance of checking every path of $\widehat{M}(x)$ up to its full length of $q(n)$ steps. Fortunately, however, an argument analogous to the proof of Theorem 3.6 shows that there exists a constant c, depending on $\widehat{M}$ only, such that the number of distinct configurations of $\widehat{M}(x)$ is bounded above by

$$2^{c \cdot \log n} = 2^{\log n^c} = n^c. \tag{3.4}$$

That is, many of the configurations in the full depth $q(n)$ computation tree of $\widehat{M}(x)$ must occur repeatedly. Hence, one can construct a DTM $\widehat{N}$ that, on input x, searches through only a polynomial-size part of the computation tree of $\widehat{M}(x)$, truncating any path as soon as some configuration is encountered twice. To this end, $\widehat{N}$ uses three working tapes. Tape 1 is again subdivided into three tracks and is used the same way the working tape of DTM N is used in the above proof of NP $\subseteq$ PSPACE. That is, track 1 again keeps track of the current position in the search, by storing the current path name and marking how much of it has already been processed. Tracks 2 and 3 again store two successive configurations, alternately producing the next one along the current path whose name is written on track 1.

In addition, DTM $\widehat{N}$ has two more tapes. Tape 2 keeps a list of every new configuration of $\widehat{M}(x)$ as yet found. Whenever a new configuration, call it C, is produced on either track 2 or track 3 of tape 1, it is compared with each configuration currently contained in tape 2 to check whether or not C indeed is new. If so, C is added to the list on tape 2; otherwise, the current path of $\widehat{M}(x)$ can safely be truncated. Tape 3 contains a binary counter of length $c \cdot \log n$, where c is the constant from Equation (3.4). This counter is incremented by one each time a new configuration is added to tape 2. If an accepting configuration of $\widehat{M}(x)$ is found in the course of this process, then N halts and accepts x. If the search through $\widehat{M}(x)$ is completed without success or if the counter on tape 3 is full, i.e., the maximum number of n^c distinct configurations is found and none of them is accepting, then N rejects x. It follows that $L(\widehat{N}) = L(\widehat{M})$.

To estimate the time needed, note that $\widehat{M}(x)$ has at most n^c configurations of length $\mathcal{O}(\log n)$ each. Thus, the number of steps needed to compare the current configuration on tape 1 with the entire content of tape 2 is in $\mathcal{O}(n^c \cdot \log n)$ and thus in $\mathcal{O}(n^{c+1})$. Hence, comparing each of the at most n^c possible configurations on tape 1 with the content of tape 2 requires altogether at most $\mathcal{O}(n^{2c+1})$ steps. Similarly, the process of producing new configurations on tape 1 and copying them onto tape 2 requires at most $\mathcal{O}(n^{c+1})$ steps. Incrementing the counter on tape 3 at most

n^c times can be done in parallel. Summing up, $\widehat{N}(x)$ needs time no more than polynomial in n. Hence, NL $\subseteq$ P.   ∎

There is nothing special about the time resource being a polynomial in the above proof of NP $\subseteq$ PSPACE, and there is nothing special about the space resource being the logarithm in the above proof of NL $\subseteq$ P. Thus, generalizing the above arguments, one obtains a stronger version of Theorem 3.6.

Corollary 3.28.   *1. If t is space-constructible, then* NTIME$(t) \subseteq$ DSPACE(t).
    2. If $s \geq \log$ is constructible in time $2^{\text{Lin}(s)}$, then NSPACE$(s) \subseteq$ DTIME$(2^{\text{Lin}(s)})$.

Corollary 3.28 immediately implies that:

$$\text{NTIME}(t) \subseteq \text{DTIME}(2^{\text{Lin}(t)}) \quad \text{and} \quad \text{NSPACE}(s) \subseteq \text{DSPACE}(2^{\text{Lin}(s)}),$$

which upperbounds, for both time and space, the costs of trading nondeterminism for determinism. What about the lower bounds? Is an exponential increase in the resources really necessary in order to deterministically simulate nondeterminism? For the time resource, the answer to this question is not known. For the space resource, the answer is no! Theorem 3.29 shows that for the resource space, already a quadratic increase is enough to deterministically simulate nondeterminism.

Theorem 3.29 (Savitch's Theorem).
If $s \geq \log$ is space-constructible, then NSPACE$(s) \subseteq$ DSPACE(s^2).

Proof.   Let A be any set in NSPACE(s), and let M be some NTM accepting A and working in space $s(n)$ on inputs of length n. We want to construct a DTM N deciding A in space $\mathcal{O}(s^2)$; by Theorem 3.10, the constant implicit in the $\mathcal{O}$ notation can safely be neglected.
    Since $s \geq \log$, Theorem 3.6 implies that M accepts A in time $t(n) \leq 2^{c \cdot s(n)}$, for some constant c. Note that the constant c depends on the program of M only and can be easily determined according to the proof of Theorem 3.6. We make the following simplifying assumptions:

- ACCEPT$_M$ is the uniquely determined accepting configuration of M on any input,[6] and START$_M(x)$ is the uniquely determined start configuration of M on input x.
- Let $k = c \cdot s(n)$, where we assume that $2^{k-1} < t(n) \leq 2^k$, which implies $\lceil \log t(n) \rceil = k$.
- Suppose that the configurations of $M(x)$ are suitably encoded by strings over a fixed alphabet, and that all such strings have the exact same length $d \cdot s(n)$, for some constant d. Enumerate all strings of length $d \cdot s(n)$ as $C_1, C_2, \ldots, C_m$ in the lexicographical ordering. Note that not all strings C_i may encode syntactically correct configurations of $M(x)$.

---

[6] Convince yourself that it is possible to make this assumption without loss of generality. For example, one can require that M, before it accepts, always erases its working tape and moves the input head back to the leftmost input symbol.

The main idea of the proof is to apply a clever divide-and-conquer strategy that is based on the simple observation that for each string $x \in \Sigma^*$:

$$x \in A \iff \text{START}_M(x) \vdash_M^{2^k} \text{ACCEPT}_M$$
$$\iff (\exists i)\,[\text{START}_M(x) \vdash_M^{2^{k-1}} C_i \text{ and } C_i \vdash_M^{2^{k-1}} \text{ACCEPT}_M]. \quad (3.5)$$

It remains to show that this idea can be realized in space $\mathcal{O}(s^2)$. On input x of length n, DTM N works as follows:

1. N constructs $s(n)$ and computes the value $k = c \cdot s(n)$, which equals $\lceil \log t(n) \rceil$.
2. N generates the following pattern on its working tape:

$$\text{START}_M(x) \underbrace{\#}_{d \cdot s(n) \text{ cells}} \overbrace{\underbrace{\Box \cdots \Box}_{d \cdot s(n) \text{ cells}} \# \underbrace{\Box \cdots \Box}_{d \cdot s(n) \text{ cells}} \# \quad \cdots \quad \# \underbrace{\Box \cdots \Box}_{d \cdot s(n) \text{ cells}}}^{k \text{ blocks}} \# \underbrace{\text{ACCEPT}_M}_{d \cdot s(n) \text{ cells}}$$

where $\#$ is a special symbol separating these $k + 2$ blocks of size $d \cdot s(n)$ each.
3. $N(x)$ simulates the computation of $M(x)$ deterministically within these $k + 2$ blocks, reusing the same space on its tape over and over again. This simulation is described in detail below; see the proof of Lemma 3.30 below.
4. N accepts x if and only if it reaches the ACCEPT_M configuration during this simulation.

To prove that N's simulation of $M(x)$ succeeds for each $x \in A$, we need the following lemma.

Lemma 3.30. *If $x \in A$, then N's simulation of* $\text{START}_M(x) \vdash_M^{2^k} \text{ACCEPT}_M$ *succeeds in the space marked above. If $x \notin A$, then N rejects x.*

Proof of Lemma 3.30.   The proof is by induction on k.

$k = 0$: N can check whether or not $\text{START}_M(x) \vdash_M^{2^0} \text{ACCEPT}_M$ by simulating $M(x)$ for one step.

$(k-1) \longmapsto k$: N systematically cycles through all strings $C_1, C_2, \ldots, C_m$ of length $d \cdot s(n)$, which potentially encode configurations of $M(x)$, searching for one C_i that satisfies (3.5). If C_i is the string currently being checked, N first checks whether or not C_i is a syntactically correct configuration of $M(x)$. If not, N proceeds by examining the next string, C_{i+1}. Otherwise (i.e., if C_i is a syntactically correct configuration of $M(x)$), N writes C_i onto the $(k+1)^{\text{st}}$ block of its working tape:

$$\text{START}_M(x) \underbrace{\#}_{d \cdot s(n) \text{ cells}} \overbrace{\underbrace{\Box \cdots \Box}_{d \cdot s(n) \text{ cells}} \# \quad \cdots \quad \# \underbrace{\Box \cdots \Box}_{d \cdot s(n) \text{ cells}}}^{k-1 \text{ blocks}} \# \underbrace{C_i}_{d \cdot s(n) \text{ cells}} \# \underbrace{\text{ACCEPT}_M}_{d \cdot s(n) \text{ cells}}$$

and checks whether or not $\text{START}_M(x) \vdash_M^{2^{k-1}} C_i$, which is possible by the induction hypothesis. If this test fails, then N erases C_i from the $(k+1)^{\text{st}}$ block and proceeds by examining the next string, C_{i+1}. Otherwise (i.e., if C_i has passed the test that $\text{START}_M(x) \vdash_M^{2^{k-1}} C_i$), N erases C_i from the $(k+1)^{\text{st}}$ block of its working tape after having it copied onto the second block of its working tape:

$$\underbrace{\text{START}_M(x)}_{d \cdot s(n) \text{ cells}} \# \underbrace{C_i}_{d \cdot s(n) \text{ cells}} \# \overbrace{\underbrace{\square \cdots \square}_{d \cdot s(n) \text{ cells}} \# \quad \cdots \quad \# \underbrace{\square \cdots \square}_{d \cdot s(n) \text{ cells}}}^{k-1 \text{ blocks}} \# \underbrace{\text{ACCEPT}_M}_{d \cdot s(n) \text{ cells}}$$

and checks whether or not $C_i \vdash_M^{2^{k-1}} \text{ACCEPT}_M$, which again is possible by the induction hypothesis. If this test fails, then N erases C_i from the second block and proceeds by examining the next string, C_{i+1}. Otherwise (i.e., if C_i has passed both tests, $\text{START}_M(x) \vdash_M^{2^{k-1}} C_i$ and $C_i \vdash_M^{2^{k-1}} \text{ACCEPT}_M$, according to (3.5)), N accepts x and halts. If none of the potential configurations C_i of $M(x)$ passes both tests, then N rejects x and halts.

This proves the lemma.

■ Lemma 3.30

By Lemma 3.30, $L(N) = A$. Since $k = c \cdot s(n)$ and there are $k + 2$ blocks of size $d \cdot s(n)$ each, $N(x)$ works in space $\mathcal{O}((s(n))^2)$. Theorem 3.10 then implies $A \in \text{DSPACE}(s^2)$, which proves the theorem.

■ Theorem 3.29

Corollary 3.31. PSPACE = NPSPACE.

Recall from the previous section that Theorem 3.15, the hierarchy theorem for deterministic space classes, implies that $L \subset \text{PSPACE}$; see Corollary 3.18. An even stronger proper inclusion is stated in Corollary 3.32 below, which follows from Theorems 3.15 and 3.29 via the following chain of inclusions some of which are proper:

$$\begin{aligned} \text{NL} &\subseteq \text{DSPACE}((\log n)^2) \subset \text{DSPACE}((\log n)^3) \subset \cdots \subset \text{DSPACE}(\text{id}) \\ &= \text{LINSPACE} \qquad\quad \subset \text{DSPACE}(n^2) \qquad \subset \cdots \subset \text{PSPACE}. \end{aligned} \tag{3.6}$$

Corollary 3.32. NL $\subset$ PSPACE.

Alternatively, Corollary 3.32 can be proven using the above Corollary 3.31 and the hierarchy theorem for *nondeterministic* space classes, which is not contained in this text but can be found in, e.g., Wagner and Wechsung's book [WW86]. Note that Exercise 3.7(b) makes a claim even stronger than Corollary 3.32, and Exercise 3.7(c) extends the above inclusion chain (3.6).

Although we know from Corollaries 3.18 and 3.32 that L and even NL are strictly contained in PSPACE, it is not known *which one* of the inclusions from Theorem 3.27 is proper. That is, it is not known which of the "$\subseteq$" relations in the inclusion chain

$$L \subseteq NL \subseteq P \subseteq NP \subseteq \text{PSPACE}$$

in fact is a "$\subset$" relation.

Corollary 3.31 suggests that nondeterminism gives much less additional computing power to the complexity resource space than it gives to the complexity resource time. This intuition is also supported by the following famous result that was independently discovered by Immerman [Imm88] and Szelepcsényi [Sze88]. For any complexity class $\mathcal{C}$, define $co\mathcal{C} = \{L \mid \overline{L} \in \mathcal{C}\}$ to be the class of complements of sets in $\mathcal{C}$.

Theorem 3.33. *If $s \geq \log$ is space-constructible, then* $\text{NSPACE}(s) = \text{coNSPACE}(s)$.

Theorem 3.33 has important corollaries for the special cases of $s = \text{id}$ and $s = \log$, respectively. In particular, the case of $s = \text{id}$ solves an open question raised by Kuroda [Kur64] in 1964: CS, the class of context-sensitive languages, is closed under complement. Note that CS is known to be equal to the complexity class NLINSPACE.

Corollary 3.34. $\text{NLINSPACE} = \text{coNLINSPACE}$ *and* $\text{NL} = \text{coNL}$.

3.5 Reducibilities and Completeness

3.5.1 Many-One Reducibilities, Hardness, and Completeness

Suppose you are given two problems, A and B, and you want to know whether or not they have distinct complexities, and if so, which one is harder to solve than the other. Perhaps you know that both belong to the same complexity class, say NP. Still, A might be very easy to solve, say in logarithmic space, whereas B is much harder. Recall that membership of some problem A in some complexity class $\mathcal{C}$ merely provides an upper bound. How can one prove lower bounds for some problem? In particular, how can one show that some given problem is one of the hardest problems of some complexity class? To prove such a result, one would have to show that *every* problem in the class is at most as hard as the given problem.

Complexity-bounded reducibilities are a powerful tool for comparing the complexity of two problems. Intuitively, if some set A reduces to some set B, then B is at least as hard as A. The notion of *hardness* for a complexity class $\mathcal{C}$, with respect to some reducibility, formalizes the intuitive notion of a lower bound: if B is hard for $\mathcal{C}$, then every set A in $\mathcal{C}$ is reducible to B. If B is not only hard for $\mathcal{C}$, but also contained in $\mathcal{C}$, then B is called $\mathcal{C}$-complete. The notion of *completeness* captures the hardest problems of a complexity class, with respect to some reducibility. That is, B is complete for $\mathcal{C}$ in the sense that all the computing power represented by the class $\mathcal{C}$ is already inherent in B. Thus, any problem complete for $\mathcal{C}$ represents $\mathcal{C}$.

Now, one of the most important reducibilities, the polynomial-time many-one reducibility, and the related notions of hardness and completeness are defined.

Definition 3.35 (Polynomial-Time Many-One Reducibility and Completeness).
Let $\Sigma = \{0, 1\}$ be a fixed alphabet, and let A and B be sets of strings over Σ. Let FP denote the set of polynomial-time computable total functions mapping from Σ^* to Σ^*. Let $\mathcal{C}$ be any complexity class.

1. *Define the* polynomial-time many-one reducibility, *denoted by* $\leq^{P}_{m}$, *as follows:* $A \leq^{P}_{m} B$ *if and only if there is a function* $f \in \mathrm{FP}$ *such that for each* $x \in \Sigma^{*}$, $x \in A \iff f(x) \in B$.
2. *A set B is* $\leq^{P}_{m}$*-hard for* C *if and only if* $A \leq^{P}_{m} B$ *for each* $A \in C$.
3. *A set B is* $\leq^{P}_{m}$*-complete for* C *if and only if B is* $\leq^{P}_{m}$*-hard for* C *and* $B \in C$.
4. C *is said to be* closed *under the* $\leq^{P}_{m}$*-reducibility (* $\leq^{P}_{m}$*-closed, for short) if and only if for any two sets A and B, if* $A \leq^{P}_{m} B$ *and* $B \in C$, *then* $A \in C$.

The term "many-one" above refers to the fact that a reduction $f \in \mathrm{FP}$ witnessing that $A \leq^{P}_{m} B$ in general can map many distinct strings to one and the same string. The above definition immediately implies the properties stated in the following lemma. The proof of Lemma 3.36 is left to the reader as Exercise 3.11.

Lemma 3.36. *1. $A \leq^{P}_{m} B$ implies $\overline{A} \leq^{P}_{m} \overline{B}$, yet in general it is not true that $A \leq^{P}_{m} \overline{A}$.*
2. The relation $\leq^{P}_{m}$ is both reflexive and transitive, yet not antisymmetric.
3. P, NP, and PSPACE are $\leq^{P}_{m}$-closed.
4. If $A \leq^{P}_{m} B$ and A is $\leq^{P}_{m}$-hard for some complexity class C, then B is $\leq^{P}_{m}$-hard for C.
5. Let C and D be any complexity classes. If C is $\leq^{P}_{m}$-closed and B is $\leq^{P}_{m}$-complete for D, then $D \subseteq C$ if and only if $B \in C$. In particular, if B is NP-complete, then $\mathrm{P} = \mathrm{NP}$ if and only if $B \in \mathrm{P}$.

The third item of Lemma 3.36, of course, is not only true for the three classes mentioned. As a matter of fact, most "reasonable" complexity classes above P are closed under $\leq^{P}_{m}$-reductions. Note also that $\leq^{P}_{m}$-closure of any class C means that, with respect to the $\leq^{P}_{m}$-reducibility, C upper bounds are inherited downward, whereas the fourth item of this lemma says that C lower bounds are inherited upward with respect to $\leq^{P}_{m}$. Finally, the last item of Lemma 3.36 is very crucial, since it ties the collapse or separation of two complexity classes to the apparently much simpler question of whether or not a single problem from one class belongs to the other. This property, as simple as its proof may be, is what makes the theory of NP-completeness so useful, important, and beautiful.

The notion of $\leq^{P}_{m}$-reducibility does not make sense for the complexity classes L, NL, and P: It is simply too "coarse" to distinguish the problems within any of these classes by their computational complexity. In particular, *every* nontrivial set in each of these classes trivially is $\leq^{P}_{m}$-complete for the class. A set B is said to be nontrivial if $\emptyset \neq B \neq \Sigma^{*}$. Lemma 3.37 illustrates this property for the case of P.

Lemma 3.37. *For each nontrivial set $B \in \mathrm{P}$ (i.e., $\emptyset \neq B \neq \Sigma^{*}$) and for each set $A \in \mathrm{P}$, $A \leq^{P}_{m} B$. Thus, every nontrivial set in P is $\leq^{P}_{m}$-complete for P.*

Proof.   Choose two strings, $b_{1} \in B$ and $b_{2} \notin B$, which is possible by the assumption that B is nontrivial. Define the $\leq^{P}_{m}$-reduction f by

$$f(x) = \begin{cases} b_{1} & \text{if } x \in A \\ b_{2} & \text{if } x \notin A. \end{cases}$$

Since A is in P, function f is in FP. By definition of f, for each $x \in \Sigma^*$, $x \in A$ if and only if $f(x) \in B$. Hence, f witnesses that $A \leq_{\mathrm{m}}^{\mathrm{P}} B$. Since A is an arbitrary set in P, it follows that B is $\leq_{\mathrm{m}}^{\mathrm{P}}$-complete for P.   ∎

In light of Lemma 3.37, a more refined reducibility than $\leq_{\mathrm{m}}^{\mathrm{P}}$ is required for P and smaller classes. Definition 3.38 below introduces the log-space many-one reducibility, $\leq_{\mathrm{m}}^{\mathrm{log}}$, and the related notions of $\leq_{\mathrm{m}}^{\mathrm{log}}$-hardness and $\leq_{\mathrm{m}}^{\mathrm{log}}$-completeness.

Note that the $\leq_{\mathrm{m}}^{\mathrm{log}}$-reducibility is still too coarse for the class L, for the same reason $\leq_{\mathrm{m}}^{\mathrm{P}}$ is too coarse for P; see Lemma 3.37. To distinguish problems in L and those in even smaller classes, reducibilities even more refined than $\leq_{\mathrm{m}}^{\mathrm{log}}$ must be used. However, such reducibilities, which are usually defined by uniform boolean circuits computing them, will not be considered in this book; the reader is referred to Vollmer's book [Vol99] instead. For NL and P, the $\leq_{\mathrm{m}}^{\mathrm{log}}$-reducibility is appropriate, and also for other classes such as NP, the $\leq_{\mathrm{m}}^{\mathrm{log}}$-reducibility yields hardness and completeness notions slightly stronger than those obtained using the $\leq_{\mathrm{m}}^{\mathrm{P}}$-reducibility.

Definition 3.38 (Log-Space Many-One Reducibility and Completeness).
Let $\Sigma = \{0, 1\}$ be a fixed alphabet, and let A and B be sets of strings over Σ. Let FL denote the set of total functions mapping from Σ^* to Σ^* that are computable in logarithmic space. Define the log-space many-one reducibility, *denoted by $\leq_{\mathrm{m}}^{\mathrm{log}}$, as follows: $A \leq_{\mathrm{m}}^{\mathrm{log}} B$ if and only if there is a function $f \in$ FL such that for each $x \in \Sigma^*$, $x \in A \iff f(x) \in B$.*

The notions of $\leq_{\mathrm{m}}^{\mathrm{log}}$-hardness, of $\leq_{\mathrm{m}}^{\mathrm{log}}$-completeness, and of $\leq_{\mathrm{m}}^{\mathrm{log}}$-closure for any complexity class $\mathcal{C}$ are defined analogously as in Definition 3.35.

Just like the $\leq_{\mathrm{m}}^{\mathrm{P}}$-reducibility, $\leq_{\mathrm{m}}^{\mathrm{log}}$ is clearly a reflexive relation. Theorem 3.39 below establishes another basic property of the $\leq_{\mathrm{m}}^{\mathrm{log}}$-reducibility that, unlike reflexivity, is not that trivial: transitivity.

Theorem 3.39. *The $\leq_{\mathrm{m}}^{\mathrm{log}}$-reducibility is a transitive relation.*

Proof.   Let A, B, and C be sets such that $A \leq_{\mathrm{m}}^{\mathrm{log}} B$ via some reduction $f \in$ FL and $B \leq_{\mathrm{m}}^{\mathrm{log}} C$ via some reduction $g \in$ FL. Let F be some DTM computing f in logarithmic space, and let G be some DTM computing g in logarithmic space. To show transitivity, construct a reduction $h \in$ FL that witnesses $A \leq_{\mathrm{m}}^{\mathrm{log}} C$. That is, construct a DTM H computing h in logarithmic space such that, for each $x \in \Sigma^*$, $x \in A$ if and only if $h(x) \in C$.

As mentioned above, showing the transitivity of the $\leq_{\mathrm{m}}^{\mathrm{log}}$-reducibility is not a trivial matter. To see why, it is useful to first consider the naive approach for defining a DTM H that computes a reduction h witnessing $A \leq_{\mathrm{m}}^{\mathrm{log}} C$, and then to see why this naive approach fails. For convenience, assume that F and G each have one read-only input tape, one read-write working tape, and one write-only output tape. In the naive approach, one would define H to have F's input tape as its own input tape, to have G's output tape as its own output tape, and to use the following three tapes as its own working tapes:

WT 1: the working tape of F,

WT 2: the output tape of F, which is identified with the input tape of G, and
WT 3: the working tape of G.

To compute $h(x) = g(f(x))$, view H on input x as the "composition" of F and G on input x. That is, $H(x)$ starts by simulating $F(x)$, using $\log |x|$ space on WT 1 and writing the value $f(x)$ on WT 2. Then, H simulates the computation of $G(f(x))$ on WT 3, writing the value $h(x) = g(f(x))$ on its output tape. The problem with this naive approach, of course, is that in light of the known result $\mathrm{DSPACE}(s) \subseteq \mathrm{DTIME}(2^{\mathrm{Lin}(s)})$ (see Theorem 3.6), the length of the output value $f(x)$ on WT 2 is not logarithmically bounded in $|x|$. In fact, there exists a constant c such that $|f(x)| \leq 2^{c \cdot \log |x|} = |x|^c$ can be as large as polynomially in $|x|$.

To overcome this problem with the naive approach, recall that the complexity resource space can be reused, and consider the following simple idea: Rather than storing the complete value of $f(x)$ during the simulation, store just one bit of $f(x)$ on WT 2, namely that bit currently scanned by G. To this end, H needs two more working tapes, WT 4 and WT 5. In particular, WT 4 is a counter that stores in binary the position i currently scanned by G's input head. Since $i \leq |x|^c$, this is possible in $\lceil c \log |x| \rceil$ space. The purpose of WT 5 will be explained below.

H on input x works as follows. Initially, the counter on WT 4 is set to one, since G's input head initially scans the leftmost symbol of its input string. All other working tapes are empty. $H(x)$ starts by simulating the computation of $F(x)$ on WT 1 until the first output bit of $f(x)$ is written on WT 2. Interrupting the simulation of $F(x)$, H now simulates the computation of $G(f(x))$ on WT 3 until G needs to scan its next input bit. Interrupting the simulation of $G(f(x))$ on WT 3, H updates the counter on WT 4 accordingly, deletes the first output bit of $f(x)$ from WT 2, continues the simulation of $F(x)$ on WT 1, and proceeds in this manner.

The general situation is the following: WT 2 contains the ith bit of $f(x)$, and WT 4 contains the number i in binary. Suppose the simulation of $G(f(x))$ has just been interrupted because H now needs to scan either the $(i-1)^{\mathrm{st}}$ or the $(i+1)^{\mathrm{st}}$ bit of $f(x)$. Consider the following two cases.

Case 1: H needs to scan the $(i+1)^{\mathrm{st}}$ bit of $f(x)$. Then, H continues the simulation of $F(x)$ on WT 1 at the point it was interrupted previously, until the $(i+1)^{\mathrm{st}}$ bit of $f(x)$ is written on WT 2. H increments the counter on WT 4 by one so that it now contains $i+1$ in binary, and proceeds with the simulation of $G(f(x))$.

Case 2: H needs to scan the $(i-1)^{\mathrm{st}}$ bit of $f(x)$. Since the $(i-1)^{\mathrm{st}}$ bit of $f(x)$ is no longer available on WT 2, the computation of $F(x)$ must be simulated anew from scratch, reusing the same space on WT 1. A second counter on WT 5 is needed for counting the number of bits of $f(x)$ up to the $(i-1)^{\mathrm{st}}$ bit. Initially, the counter on WT 5 is set to zero.

Step 1: H decrements the counter on WT 4, which currently contains the number $i > 1$ in binary, by one so that it now contains $i-1$, and it deletes the ith output bit of $f(x)$ from WT 2;

Step 2: H simulates the computation of $F(x)$ on WT 1. Whenever F attempts to write an output bit of $f(x)$ on WT 2, H does the following, according to two subcases of Step 2 in Case 2.

Subcase 2.1: WT 4 contains the number $j \neq 0$ in binary. H decrements the counter on WT 4 by one so that it now contains $j - 1$ in binary, and it increments the counter on WT 5 by one so that it now contains $i - j$ in binary. Then, H continues the simulation of $F(x)$ without writing on WT 2.

Subcase 2.2: WT 4 contains 0. Since Subcase 2.1 occurred $i - 1$ times, the counter on WT 5 currently contains $i - 1$ in binary and F currently attempts to write the $(i - 1)^{\text{st}}$ output bit of $f(x)$ on WT 2. H now writes this bit on WT 2, copies the content of WT 5 to WT 4, interrupts the simulation of $F(x)$, and proceeds with the simulation of $G(f(x))$.

Since the computation of $G(f(x))$ on WT 3 can be done in logarithmic space, $H(x)$ computes $h(x) = g(f(x))$ in logarithmic space, so $x \in A$ if and only if $h(x) \in C$. It follows that $A \leq_{\mathrm{m}}^{\log} C$ via $h \in \mathrm{FL}$. Thus, $\leq_{\mathrm{m}}^{\log}$ is transitive. ∎

Theorem 3.40 can be shown analogously to the above proof; see Exercise 3.12(a).

Theorem 3.40. L *and* NL *are* $\leq_{\mathrm{m}}^{\log}$*-closed.*

Do the reducibilities $\leq_{\mathrm{m}}^{\log}$ and $\leq_{\mathrm{m}}^{\mathrm{P}}$ coincide? Do they coincide at least on P? Viewing the relations $\leq_{\mathrm{m}}^{\log}$ and $\leq_{\mathrm{m}}^{\mathrm{P}}$ as sets of pairs, i.e., $\leq_{\mathrm{m}}^{\log} = \{(A, B) \mid A \leq_{\mathrm{m}}^{\log} B\}$ and $\leq_{\mathrm{m}}^{\mathrm{P}} = \{(A, B) \mid A \leq_{\mathrm{m}}^{\mathrm{P}} B\}$, the inclusion $\mathrm{FL} \subseteq \mathrm{FP}$ immediately implies that $\leq_{\mathrm{m}}^{\log} \subseteq \leq_{\mathrm{m}}^{\mathrm{P}}$. Whether or not the converse inclusion also is true is an open problem. However, the following result says that if L and P differ, then $\leq_{\mathrm{m}}^{\log}$ and $\leq_{\mathrm{m}}^{\mathrm{P}}$ differ on P. Define $A \not\leq_{\mathrm{m}}^{\log} B$ to mean that $A \leq_{\mathrm{m}}^{\log} B$ is not true.

Theorem 3.41. *If* $\mathrm{L} \neq \mathrm{P}$, *then there exist sets A and B in P such that $A \leq_{\mathrm{m}}^{\mathrm{P}} B$, yet* $A \not\leq_{\mathrm{m}}^{\log} B$.

Proof. To prove the contrapositive of the theorem's assertion, suppose that $\leq_{\mathrm{m}}^{\log} = \leq_{\mathrm{m}}^{\mathrm{P}}$ on P. Let B be a nontrivial set in L, i.e., $\emptyset \neq B \neq \Sigma^*$. Let A be an arbitrary set in P. By Lemma 3.37, $A \leq_{\mathrm{m}}^{\mathrm{P}} B$. Since $B \in \mathrm{L}$ and L is $\leq_{\mathrm{m}}^{\log}$-closed by Theorem 3.40, $A \in \mathrm{L}$. Since A is an arbitrary P set, $\mathrm{P} = \mathrm{L}$. ∎

3.5.2 NL-Completeness

In this section, two problems are shown to be $\leq_{\mathrm{m}}^{\log}$-complete for NL, the graph accessibility problem (GAP, for short) and the satisfiability problem for boolean formulas with (at most) two literals per clause.

The graph accessibility problem is defined for directed graphs. G is a *directed graph* if $E(G) \subseteq V(G) \times V(G)$, where $V(G)$ denotes the *vertex set of* G and $E(G)$ denotes the *edge set of* G. That is, a directed edge $e = (u, v)$ from u to v in G is an ordered pair of vertices. For any two vertices $u, v \in V(G)$ in a directed graph G, a *path from u to v* is a sequence $x_1, x_2, \ldots, x_{k+1}$ of vertices of G such that $u = x_1$ and $v = x_{k+1}$ and, for each i with $1 \leq i \leq k$, $e_i = (x_i, x_{i+1})$ is an edge of G.

Definition 3.42 (Graph Accessibility Problem).
Define the decision version of the graph accessibility problem *by*

$$\text{GAP} = \left\{ \langle G, s, t \rangle \,\middle|\, \begin{array}{l} G \text{ is a directed graph with } s, t \in V(G), \\ \text{and there is a directed path from } s \text{ to } t \text{ in } G \end{array} \right\}.$$

Theorem 3.43. GAP *is* $\leq_{\mathrm{m}}^{\log}$-*complete for* NL.

Proof.   To show that GAP is in NL, define an NTM M accepting GAP in logarithmic space as follows. Suppose that $\langle G, x_1, x_N \rangle$ is any given input, where G is a directed graph represented by the list of its edges, and $V(G) = \{x_1, x_2, \ldots, x_N\}$. Starting with x_1, M nondeterministically guesses a path in G to x_N. To this end, M stores the indices of the vertices on such a path in binary, and it always stores just two successive vertices. In more detail, if i and j are the binary numbers currently written on M's working tape, then M scans its input tape to check whether or not there is an edge (x_i, x_j) in $E(G)$. If so, M accepts the input in case $j = N$. If (x_i, x_j) is an edge in $E(G)$ and $j \neq N$, then M deletes i on its working tape and guesses a new vertex, writing its index k onto the working tape, and thus proceeds. If (x_i, x_j) is not an edge in $E(G)$, then M rejects and halts without success on this computation path.

Note that there exists a path α from x_1 to x_N in G if and only if there exists a computation path of $M(\langle G, x_1, x_N \rangle)$ on which α is guessed. Thus, M accepts $\langle G, x_1, x_N \rangle$ exactly if $\langle G, x_1, x_N \rangle \in$ GAP. Note further that M never stores more than two vertex indices simultaneously, and that the binary representation of each vertex index has length at most $\lceil \log N \rceil$. It follows that no more than $\mathcal{O}(\log n)$ tape cells on M's working tape are used if the input size is n; so M works in logarithmic space. Thus, GAP is in NL.

To prove NL-hardness of GAP, let A be any set in NL, and let M be an NTM accepting A in logarithmic space. Without loss of generality, suppose that M has one input tape and one working tape. As in the proof of Theorem 3.29, assume that $\text{START}_M(x)$ is the uniquely determined start configuration of M on input x, and ACCEPT_M is the uniquely determined accepting configuration of M on any input. For any input string of length n, define the graph $G_{M,n}$ of all potential $\log n$ space-bounded configurations of M by:

$$V(G_{M,n}) = \left\{ C \,\middle|\, \begin{array}{l} C \text{ is a potential configuration of } M \text{ for which the} \\ \text{inscription on } M\text{'s working tape has length} \leq \lceil \log n \rceil \end{array} \right\};$$
$$E(G_{M,n}) = \{(C_1, C_2) \mid C_1 \vdash_M C_2\},$$

where $\vdash_M$ denotes the immediate successor relation of M, i.e., configuration C_2 can be reached from configuration C_1 within one step of M. Note that by "potential $\log n$ space-bounded configuration" of M we mean not only the configurations in the computation tree $M(x)$ for some specific input x, but we mean *every* syntactically correct configuration of M on any input of length n with no more than $\lceil \log n \rceil$

symbols written on the working tape, even if such a configuration is not reachable from $\text{START}_M(x)$ for some x. Of course, for each fixed string $x \in \Sigma^*$ of length n, the computation tree $M(x)$ is an induced subgraph of $G_{M,n}$.

Note that every vertex of $G_{M,n}$ can be encoded by $\mathcal{O}(\log n)$ symbols:

- the current position of M's input head in binary requires $\lceil \log n \rceil$ symbols,
- the current inscription on M's working tape has at most $\lceil \log n \rceil$ symbols, and
- one symbol encoding the current state of M can be inserted into the string currently written on M's working tape to indicate the current position of the working tape head.

Thus, exactly $2(1 + \lceil \log n \rceil)$ tape cells are enough to encode every potential $\log n$ space-bounded configuration of M.

For each string $x \in \Sigma^*$ of length n, define the $\leq_m^{\log}$-reduction f from A to GAP by

$$f(x) = \langle G_{M,n}, \text{START}_M(x), \text{ACCEPT}_M \rangle.$$

It follows that, for each $x \in \Sigma^*$,

$$x \in A \iff M(x) \text{ has an accepting computation path}$$
$$\iff f(x) \in \text{GAP}.$$

To show that $f \in \text{FL}$, consider the following deterministic algorithm computing f on input x, $|x| = n$, in logarithmic space as follows:

Step 1: Mark the space $2(1 + \lceil \log n \rceil)$.

Step 2: Systematically, one after the other in lexicographic order, generate all potential $\log n$ space-bounded configurations of M whose encoding needs no more than the marked $2(1 + \lceil \log n \rceil)$ tape cells.

Step 3: For each such configuration C generated:
  1. check that C is syntactically correct;
  2. add C to the list of vertices of $G_{M,n}$;
  3. simulate M on C for one step, generating potential $\log n$ space-bounded configurations C_1 and C_2 with $C \vdash_M C_1$ and $C \vdash_M C_2$;
  4. for $i \in \{1, 2\}$, add (C, C_i) to the list of edges of $G_{M,n}$.

Step 4: When the construction of the graph $G_{M,n}$ is completed, output

$$\langle G_{M,n}, \text{START}_M(x), \text{ACCEPT}_M \rangle.$$

Thus, $f \in \text{FL}$ witnesses that $A \leq_m^{\log} \text{GAP}$. ∎

We now turn to variations of the satisfiability problem. Recall the notions of boolean formulas, truth assignments, and satisfiability of boolean formulas from Definitions 2.23 and 2.24 in Section 2.3.

Definition 3.44 (Satisfiability Problem).
Define the decision version of the satisfiability problem *by*

$$\text{SAT} = \{\varphi \mid \varphi \text{ is a satisfiable boolean formula in CNF}\}.$$

For each fixed $k \geq 1$, define the following restriction of the satisfiability problem:

$$k\text{-SAT} = \{\varphi \mid \varphi \text{ is a satisfiable boolean formula in } k\text{-CNF}\}.$$

To comprehend why the satisfiability problem above is defined for boolean formulas in CNF only, see Exercise 2.10.

Theorem 3.45. *2-SAT is $\leq_m^{\log}$-complete for NL.*

Proof. To show that 2-SAT is in NL, let any boolean formula $\varphi(x_1, x_2, \ldots, x_n)$ in 2-CNF be given; without loss of generality, suppose that φ has *exactly* two literals per clause. Construct a directed graph G_φ from φ:

$$V(G_\varphi) = \{x_1, x_2, \ldots, x_n\} \cup \{\neg x_1, \neg x_2, \ldots, \neg x_n\};$$
$$E(G_\varphi) = \{(\alpha, \beta) \mid (\neg \alpha \vee \beta) \text{ or } (\beta \vee \neg \alpha) \text{ is a clause in } \varphi\}.$$

The edges in G_φ represent the implications in φ and their contrapositives. That is, if φ contains a clause of the form $(\neg \alpha \vee \beta)$ for literals α and β, then this clause is semantically equivalent to the implication $(\alpha \Longrightarrow \beta)$, which in turn is semantically equivalent to its contrapositive $(\neg \beta \Longrightarrow \neg \alpha)$, which in turn is semantically equivalent to $(\beta \vee \neg \alpha)$. Note that, by definition, every edge in G_φ satisfies the following symmetry: If (α, β) is an edge of G_φ, then so is $(\neg \beta, \neg \alpha)$.

Consider, for example, the boolean formula $\hat{\varphi}$ with four clauses:

$$\hat{\varphi}(x_1, x_2, x_3) = (\neg x_1 \vee x_3) \wedge (\neg x_3 \vee \neg x_1) \wedge (x_1 \vee x_2) \wedge (\neg x_2 \vee x_1).$$

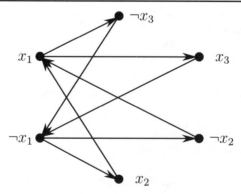

Fig. 3.1. 2-SAT is NL-complete: Graph $G_{\hat{\varphi}}$ constructed from the boolean formula $\hat{\varphi}$

Figure 3.1 displays the corresponding graph $G_{\hat{\varphi}}$ with eight edges, where two edges correspond to one clause in $\hat{\varphi}$. Note that the formula $\hat{\varphi}$ is not satisfiable.

On the other hand, loosely identifying the vertices of $G_{\hat{\varphi}}$ with the literals in $\hat{\varphi}$, there is a vertex in graph $G_{\hat{\varphi}}$ from Figure 3.1 for which there exists a path from the vertex to its negation and back to the vertex. For example, consider the cycle $(x_1, x_3, \neg x_1, x_2, x_1)$. As the following lemma shows, this property is not a coincidence.

Lemma 3.46. *Let φ be any boolean formula in 2-CNF. Then, φ is not satisfiable if and only if there exists a vertex x in G_φ for which there is a path from x to $\neg x$ and a path from $\neg x$ back to x in G_φ.*

Proof of Lemma 3.46.   To prove the direction from right to left, suppose for a contradiction that there exists a path in G_φ from x to $\neg x$ and one from $\neg x$ back to x, for some $x \in V(G_\varphi)$, and yet there exists a truth assignment t satisfying φ. Consider the following two cases.

Case 1: $t(x) = 1$.   Then $t(\neg x) = 0$. Thus, there exists an edge (α, β) on the path from x to $\neg x$ such that $t(\alpha) = 1$ and $t(\beta) = 0$. By construction of G_φ, since (α, β) is an edge, there exists a clause of the form $(\neg\alpha \vee \beta)$ or $(\beta \vee \neg\alpha)$ in φ, which is not satisfied by t. Hence, t does not satisfy φ, a contradiction.

Case 2: $t(x) = 0$.   Then $t(\neg x) = 1$. By an analogous argument, there exists an edge (α, β) on the path from $\neg x$ to x corresponding to a clause of the form $(\neg\alpha \vee \beta)$ or $(\beta \vee \neg\alpha)$ in φ that is not satisfied by t. Hence, t does not satisfy φ, which again is a contradiction.

The direction from left to right is proven by contraposition: If for no vertex x in G_φ there is a path of the form $(x, \ldots, \neg x, \ldots, x)$, then φ is satisfiable. Indeed, under the hypothesis stated, a satisfying assignment t for φ can be constructed as follows:

while (there are still variables in φ not assigned a truth value by t) {

    Step 1: Choose the first such variable x in φ and consider the corresponding vertex x in G_φ. By hypothesis, for x, there exists no path from x to $\neg x$ and back from $\neg x$ to x.

    Step 2: For each vertex γ in G_φ that is reachable from x (including x itself), set $t(\gamma) = 1$ and $t(\neg\gamma) = 0$, again loosely identifying the vertices of G_φ with the literals in φ.

}

Note that Step 2 in the while loop above is well-defined. To see why, consider the following two possibilities of what could go wrong, and convince yourself that these two bad cases in fact cannot occur.

Case 1: Suppose there exist paths from x to both γ and $\neg\gamma$ in Step 2 of the while loop above. Note that in this case we would be in trouble, since t would have to assign to both γ and $\neg\gamma$ the truth value 1, and to both $\neg\gamma$ and γ the truth value 0. However, this case cannot occur due to the symmetry in the construction of G_φ. In particular, under the above supposition, there also must exist paths from both γ and $\neg\gamma$ to $\neg x$, since a path from x to γ implies one from $\neg\gamma$ to $\neg x$ by symmetry, and hence there exists a path from x to $\neg\gamma$ and from $\neg\gamma$ to $\neg x$. Similarly, there must exist a path from x to $\neg x$ via γ. Again by symmetry, a path from x to $\neg x$ implies one from $\neg x$ to x, which is a contradiction to the choice of x.

Case 2: Suppose some vertex γ reachable from x is to be assigned the truth value 1, but it had already been assigned the truth value 0 by t in an earlier while loop. That is, suppose there exists a path from x to γ and $t(\gamma) = 0$. Then again, we would be in trouble.

However, this case cannot occur either, since in that earlier while loop also x would have been assigned the value 0: $t(\gamma) = 0$ implies $t(\neg\gamma) = 1$, which in turn implies $t(\neg x) = 1$ because of the path from $\neg\gamma$ to $\neg x$. Hence, $t(x) = 0$, which again contradicts the choice of x.

By hypothesis, for each vertex x, there exists no path from x to $\neg x$ and back from $\neg x$ to x. Hence, the above procedure for constructing a satisfying truth assignment t terminates, since in each while loop at least one variable is assigned a truth value.

It remains to show that t indeed satisfies φ. Whenever some literal is assigned a truth value of 1, then every successor of the vertex corresponding to this literal is also assigned the truth value 1. Analogously, every predecessor of a vertex for which the corresponding literal gets the truth value 0 is also assigned the truth value 0. Thus, no clause of φ yields an implication of the form $(1 \implies 0)$ under the assignment t, so t satisfies φ. The lemma is proven.   ■ Lemma 3.46

To complete the proof that 2-SAT is in NL, apply Lemma 3.46 to show that the *complement* of 2-SAT is in NL. Since NL = coNL by Corollary 3.34, this shows that 2-SAT is in NL.

On input φ, an NL machine for the complement of 2-SAT works as follows: Guess a variable x and a path in G_φ from x to $\neg x$ and from $\neg x$ back to x, and accept the input φ if and only if such a path exists. By Lemma 3.46, this nondeterministic algorithm accepts φ if and only if φ is not satisfiable.

Just as in the proof of Theorem 3.43, when such a path in G_φ is guessed, only two successive vertex indices have to be stored simultaneously. Thus, this nondeterministic algorithm works in logarithmic space. It follows that 2-SAT is in NL.

To prove that 2-SAT is NL-hard, we will provide a $\leq_m^{\log}$-reduction from the complement of a restricted version of the graph accessibility problem to 2-SAT. First, we show that this restricted version of GAP also is NL-complete.

For any graph G, a *cycle in G* is a path of the form $x = x_1, x_2, \ldots, x_n = x$ for some vertex $x \in V(G)$. A graph is said to be *acyclic* if and only if it does not contain any cycle. Define the graph accessibility problem restricted to acyclic graphs as follows: Given an acyclic graph G and two vertices s and t in G, is it true that there exists a path from s to t?

Denoting this restriction of the graph accessibility problem by $\mathrm{GAP}_{\mathrm{acyclic}}$, it is not hard to prove $\mathrm{GAP}_{\mathrm{acyclic}} \leq_m^{\log}$-complete for NL by modifying the proof of Theorem 3.43 as is explained in the proof of the following lemma.

Lemma 3.47. $\mathrm{GAP}_{\mathrm{acyclic}}$ *is* $\leq_m^{\log}$-*complete for* NL.

Proof of Lemma 3.47.   Recall the proof of Theorem 3.43. Instead of using $G_{M,n}$, the graph of all potential $\log n$ space-bounded configurations of the given NTM M

on inputs of length n, we now use the induced subgraph $M(x)$ of $G_{M,n}$ for some specifically given input string x of length n. In addition, we alter the definition of the graph $G_{M,n}$ in this proof by logging, along with each configuration C of $M(x)$, the number of steps from $\text{START}_M(x)$ to C. Define the graph $\hat{G}_{M,x}$ by:

$$V(\hat{G}_{M,x}) = \left\{ \langle C, t \rangle \left| \begin{array}{l} t \in \mathbb{N} \text{ and } C \text{ is a configuration of } M(x) \text{ for which the} \\ \text{inscription on } M\text{'s working tape has length} \leq \lceil \log n \rceil \\ \text{and exactly } t \text{ steps of } M \text{ transform } \text{START}_M(x) \text{ into } C \end{array} \right. \right\};$$

$$E(\hat{G}_{M,x}) = \{ (\langle C_1, t_1 \rangle, \langle C_2, t_2 \rangle) \mid C_1 \vdash_M C_2 \text{ and } t_2 = t_1 + 1 \}.$$

Note that $\hat{G}_{M,x}$ has no (directed) cycles. Starting from $\langle \text{START}_M(x), 0 \rangle$, $\hat{G}_{M,x}$ can be constructed deterministically by breadth-first search in logarithmic space. Moreover, for each input string x,

$$M \text{ accepts } x \iff \langle \hat{G}_{M,x}, \langle \text{START}_M(x), 0 \rangle, \langle \text{ACCEPT}_M, p(|x|) \rangle \rangle, \quad (3.7)$$

where p is a polynomial time clock such that $M(x)$ runs exactly $p(|x|)$ steps on each computation path and for each input x; cf. Corollary 3.28. Hence, (3.7) gives a $\leq_{\text{m}}^{\log}$-reduction from any given NL problem to $\text{GAP}_{\text{acyclic}}$, which proves that $\text{GAP}_{\text{acyclic}}$ is NL-hard. It is not difficult to prove that $\text{GAP}_{\text{acyclic}}$ is in NL (see Exercise 3.12(b)); thus, $\text{GAP}_{\text{acyclic}}$ is NL-complete.   ∎ Lemma 3.47

By Theorem 3.39, which says that the $\leq_{\text{m}}^{\log}$-reducibility is transitive, the proof of Theorem 3.45 is completed by proving that $\text{GAP}_{\text{acyclic}} \leq_{\text{m}}^{\log} 2\text{-SAT}$, which is stated in the following lemma. Since NL = coNL by Corollary 3.34, $\text{GAP}_{\text{acyclic}}$ is $\leq_{\text{m}}^{\log}$-complete for coNL as well. Thus, as in the above proof that 2-SAT is in NL, for proving $\text{GAP}_{\text{acyclic}} \leq_{\text{m}}^{\log} 2\text{-SAT}$ it is enough to show that the complement of $\text{GAP}_{\text{acyclic}}$, which is NL-complete by Corollary 3.34 and Lemma 3.47, $\leq_{\text{m}}^{\log}$-reduces to 2-SAT.

Lemma 3.48. $\text{GAP}_{\text{acyclic}} \leq_{\text{m}}^{\log} 2\text{-SAT}$.

Proof of Lemma 3.48.   By the above comments, it suffices to define a reduction $f \in \text{FL}$ such that, for each input x,

$$x \notin \text{GAP}_{\text{acyclic}} \iff f(x) \in 2\text{-SAT}. \quad (3.8)$$

Let $x = \langle G, v_1, v_n \rangle$ be any given instance of $\text{GAP}_{\text{acyclic}}$, where G is an acyclic directed graph with $V(G) = \{v_1, v_2, \ldots, v_n\}$. Construct the reduction f by

$$f(x) = \varphi_x(v_1, v_2, \ldots, v_n)$$
$$= v_1 \wedge \neg v_n \wedge \bigwedge_{(v_i, v_j) \in E(G)} (\neg v_i \vee v_j).$$

Clearly, $f \in \text{FL}$. Intuitively, a literal v_i in φ_x is true if and only if the vertex v_i in G is reachable from v_1. In particular, satisfying the first clause in φ_x means that v_1 is reachable from v_1. Also, satisfying the second clause in φ_x means that v_n is not reachable from v_1. Finally, satisfying each remaining clause in φ_x means that if $(v_i, v_j) \in E(G)$ and v_i is reachable from v_1, then so is v_j. Hence,

$$x \notin \text{GAP}_{\text{acyclic}} \iff \text{there exists no path from } v_1 \text{ to } v_n \text{ in } G$$
$$\iff f(x) = \varphi_x(v_1, v_2, \ldots, v_n) \in \text{2-SAT}.$$

Thus, (3.8) is true, and the lemma is proven.   ■ Lemma 3.48

Since 2-SAT is in NL by the algorithm based on Lemma 3.46, and since 2-SAT is NL-hard by Lemmas 3.47 and 3.48, the theorem is proven.   ■ Theorem 3.45

3.5.3 NP-Completeness

Historically, the first problem proven to be NP-complete is the satisfiability problem introduced in Definition 3.44 above. This pathbreaking result is due to Cook [Coo71] and, independently, to Levin [Lev73]. Thousands of further NP-completeness results followed in the sequel; see Garey and Johnson's introduction to the theory of NP-completeness [GJ79] in which several hundred of such problems are collected.

In this section, for convenience, all NP-completeness results are proven with respect to the $\leq^{\text{p}}_{\text{m}}$-reducibility only. With a little more effort, slightly stronger NP-completeness results with respect to the $\leq^{\text{log}}_{\text{m}}$-reducibility can be established as well.

Theorem 3.49 (Cook's Theorem).   SAT *is* NP-*complete.*

Proof.   To prove that SAT is in NP, consider the following NTM M accepting SAT in polynomial time as follows. Given a boolean formula $\varphi(x_1, x_2, \ldots, x_n)$, nondeterministically guess a truth assignment t of the variables $x_1, x_2, \ldots, x_n$, and for each assignment t guessed, evaluate φ according to t and accept if and only if $t(\varphi) = 1$.

To prove NP-hardness, let A be any set in NP, and let $M = (\Sigma, \Gamma, Z, \delta, \square, s_0, F)$ be an NTM accepting A in polynomial time; see Chapter 2 for the meaning of the single components in the septuple describing M. Without loss of generality, suppose that M has only one tape serving both as input and as working tape, and, on any input x of length n, M runs exactly $p(n) \geq n$ steps for some $p \in \text{Pol}$. We are going to define a reduction $f \in \text{FP}$ such that, for each x,

$$x \in A \iff f(x) = F_x \in \text{SAT}, \tag{3.9}$$

where F_x is a boolean formula whose structure and whose variables are to be described below.

Let the input string $x = x_1 x_2 \cdots x_n$ be given, where $x_i \in \Sigma$ for each i. Since M works in time $p(n)$, the tape head can move no further than $p(n)$ tape cells to the left and to the right. Enumerate the relevant tape cells from $-p(n)$ through $p(n)$. Figure 3.2 shows the tape of M at the start configuration: the input symbols $x_1 x_2 \cdots x_n$ are written onto the tape cells 0 through $n - 1$, the head currently scans the tape cell with number 0, and the start state is s_0.

We now construct the boolean formula F_x such that (3.9) is satisfied. The boolean variables of F_x, the range of their indices, and their meaning are given in Table 3.4. Intuitively, there are three types of variables:

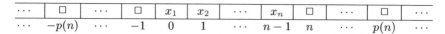

Fig. 3.2. Enumerating the tape cells of NTM M on input x in the Cook reduction

---

- $\text{state}_{t,s}$ represents the state s of M in step t;
- $\text{head}_{t,i}$ represents the number i of the tape cell that M's head scans in step t;
- $\text{tape}_{t,i,a}$ represents the symbol $a \in \Gamma$ written in the cell number i of M's tape in step t.

variable	index range	intended meaning
$\text{state}_{t,s}$	$t \in \{0, 1, \ldots, p(n)\}$ $s \in Z$	$\text{state}_{t,s}$ is true $\iff$ in step t, M is in state s
$\text{head}_{t,i}$	$t \in \{0, 1, \ldots, p(n)\}$ $i \in \{-p(n), \ldots, p(n)\}$	$\text{head}_{t,i}$ is true $\iff$ in step t, M's head scans the tape cell with number i
$\text{tape}_{t,i,a}$	$t \in \{0, 1, \ldots, p(n)\}$ $i \in \{-p(n), \ldots, p(n)\}$ $a \in \Gamma$	$\text{tape}_{t,i,a}$ is true $\iff$ in step t, the symbol a is written in the cell number i of M's tape

Table 3.4. The boolean variables of F_x and their meaning in the Cook reduction

F_x will have the following form:

$$F_x = S \wedge T_1 \wedge T_2 \wedge E \wedge C,$$

where these subformulas of F_x have the following meaning:

- S describes the correct *start* of the computation of $M(x)$;
- T_1 describes the correct *transition* from step t to step $t + 1$ for those tape cells whose contents can be altered by the head of M;
- T_2 describes the correct *transition* from step t to step $t + 1$ for those tape cells whose contents cannot be altered by the head of M;
- E describes the correct *end* of the computation of $M(x)$, i.e., E is true if and only if $M(x)$ has an accepting computation path;
- C describes the general *correctness*, i.e., C is true if and only if the following conditions hold:
  - in each step t of $M(x)$, there exists *exactly* one $s \in Z$ such that $\text{state}_{t,s}$ is true, and there exists *exactly* one i such that $\text{head}_{t,i}$ is true;
  - in each step t of $M(x)$ and for each cell number i, there exists *exactly* one $a \in \Gamma$ such that $\text{tape}_{t,i,a}$ is true.

To describe these subformulas of F_x formally, let the set of M's states be given by $Z = \{s_0, s_1, \ldots, s_k\}$, and let the working alphabet of M be given by $\Gamma = \{\square, a_1, a_2, \ldots, a_\ell\}$. Note that Γ contains the input alphabet Σ. Define the subformula C of F_x by

$$C = \bigwedge_{0 \le t \le p(n)} [D(\text{state}_{t,s_0}, \text{state}_{t,s_1}, \dots, \text{state}_{t,s_k}) \wedge$$

$$D(\text{head}_{t,-p(n)}, \text{head}_{t,-p(n)+1}, \dots, \text{head}_{t,p(n)}) \wedge \qquad (3.10)$$

$$\bigwedge_{-p(n) \le i \le p(n)} D(\text{tape}_{t,i,\square}, \text{tape}_{t,i,a_1}, \dots, \text{tape}_{t,i,a_\ell})],$$

where the structure of the three subformulas D of C in (3.10) is specified in Lemma 3.50 below. In particular, (a) D is true if and only if *exactly* one of D's variables is true, and (b) the size of D—and thus the size of C—is polynomially in n.

Lemma 3.50. *For each $m \ge 1$, there exists a boolean formula D in the variables $v_1, v_2, \dots, v_m$ such that:*

- $D(v_1, v_2, \dots, v_m)$ *is true if and only if exactly one variable v_i is true, and*
- *the size of the formula D (i.e., the number of variable occurrences in D) is in $\mathcal{O}(m^2)$.*

Proof of Lemma 3.50.   For fixed $m \ge 1$, define

$$D(v_1, v_2, \dots, v_m) = \underbrace{\left(\bigvee_{i=1}^{m} v_i \right)}_{D_\ge} \wedge \underbrace{\left(\bigwedge_{j=1}^{m-1} \bigwedge_{k=j+1}^{m} \neg(v_j \wedge v_k) \right)}_{D_\le}.$$

Note that the two subformulas $D_\ge$ and $D_\le$ of D satisfy the following properties:

$$D_\ge(v_1, v_2, \dots, v_m) \text{ is true } \iff \text{ at least one variable } v_i \text{ is true;} \quad (3.11)$$
$$D_\le(v_1, v_2, \dots, v_m) \text{ is true } \iff \text{ at most one variable } v_i \text{ is true.} \quad (3.12)$$

Equation (3.11) is obvious. To see that also (3.12) is true, observe that the formula $D_\le$ has the following structure:

$$D_\le(v_1, v_2, \dots, v_m) = (\neg v_1 \vee \neg v_2) \wedge (\neg v_1 \vee \neg v_3) \wedge \cdots \wedge (\neg v_1 \vee \neg v_m)$$
$$\wedge (\neg v_2 \vee \neg v_3) \wedge \cdots \wedge (\neg v_2 \vee \neg v_m)$$
$$\ddots \qquad \vdots$$
$$\wedge (\neg v_{m-1} \vee \neg v_m).$$

Equations (3.11) and (3.12) together imply that $D(v_1, v_2, \dots, v_m)$ is true if and only if exactly one v_i is true. Clearly, the size of D is in $\mathcal{O}(m^2)$. ∎ Lemma 3.50

To continue the proof of Theorem 3.49, define the subformula S of F_x, which for step $t = 0$ describes the correct start of the computation $M(x)$ (see Figure 3.2), by

$$S = \text{state}_{0,s_0} \wedge \text{head}_{0,0} \wedge \bigwedge_{i=-p(n)}^{-1} \text{tape}_{0,i,\square} \wedge \bigwedge_{i=0}^{n-1} \text{tape}_{0,i,x_{i+1}} \wedge \bigwedge_{i=n}^{p(n)} \text{tape}_{0,i,\square}.$$

Next, define the subformula T_1 of F_x, which describes the correct transition from step t to step $t+1$ for those tape cells whose contents can be altered by the head of M, by

$$T_1 = \bigwedge_{t,s,i,a} \left(\left(\text{state}_{t,s} \wedge \text{head}_{t,i} \wedge \text{tape}_{t,i,a} \right) \implies \right.$$

$$\left. \bigvee_{\substack{\hat{s} \in Z, \hat{a} \in \Gamma, y \in \{-1,0,1\} \\ \text{with } (\hat{s}, \hat{a}, y) \in \delta(s,a)}} \left(\text{state}_{t+1,\hat{s}} \wedge \text{head}_{t+1,i+y} \wedge \text{tape}_{t+1,i,\hat{a}} \right) \right),$$

where δ is M's transition function and $y \in \{-1, 0, 1\}$ represents the head moving by one cell to the left, not moving at all, and moving by one cell to the right, respectively.

Next, define the subformula T_2 of F_x, which describes the correct transition from step t to step $t + 1$ for those tape cells whose contents cannot be altered by the head of M, by

$$T_2 = \bigwedge_{t,i,a} \left(\left(\neg\text{head}_{t,i} \wedge \text{tape}_{t,i,a} \right) \implies \text{tape}_{t+1,i,a} \right).$$

Finally, define the subformula E of F_x, which describes the correct end of the computation of $M(x)$ and checks whether or not M accepts x:

$$E = \bigvee_{s \in F} \text{state}_{p(n),s},$$

where F is the set of accepting final states of M.

This completes the construction of the reduction f. Analyzing the structure of the formula $f(x) = F_x$ and using Lemma 3.50, it can be shown that $f \in \text{FP}$; see Exercise 3.13. So, it remains to prove (3.9): $x \in A$ if and only if the formula $f(x) = F_x$ is satisfiable.

Suppose $x \in A$. Then, there exists an accepting computation path α of $M(x)$. Assigning truth values to every variable of F_x according to α, associating with each variable its "intended meaning" according to Table 3.4, then this truth assignment satisfies each of the subformulas of F_x, and thus it satisfies F_x itself. Hence, $F_x \in$ SAT.

Conversely, suppose $F_x \in$ SAT. Then, there exists a truth assigment τ to F_x's variables satisfying F_x. According to τ, the variables $\text{state}_{t,s}$, $\text{head}_{t,i}$, and $\text{tape}_{t,i,a}$ of F_x can be sensibly interpreted as a sequence of configurations $K_0, K_1, \ldots, K_{p(n)}$ of $M(x)$ along some computation path. In particular, $\tau(S) = 1$ implies that K_0 is the start configuration of $M(x)$, $\tau(T_1) = \tau(T_2) = \tau(C) = 1$ implies that $K_{t-1} \vdash_M K_t$ for each t with $1 \leq t \leq p(n)$, and $\tau(E) = 1$ implies that $K_{p(n)}$ is an accepting final configuration of $M(x)$. Hence, $x \in A$. Equation (3.9) is proven and the proof of Theorem 3.49 is complete.   ■ Theorem 3.49

In Theorem 3.45, the restriction 2-SAT of the satisfiability problem was shown to be NL-complete. In contrast, Theorem 3.51 below shows that 3-SAT, just like the general satisfiability problem, is NP-complete. The importance of this result is due to the fact that 3-SAT is a very suitable starting point for proving further NP-completeness results.

Theorem 3.51. 3-SAT *is* NP-*complete.*

Proof.   Membership in NP for the restricted problem follows immediately from that for the general problem. To prove that SAT $\leq_m^P$ 3-SAT, define a reduction f mapping any given boolean formula φ to a boolean formula ψ in 3-CNF such that:

$$\varphi \text{ is satisfiable} \iff \psi \text{ is satisfiable.} \tag{3.13}$$

Let $\varphi(x_1, x_2, \ldots, x_n) = C_1 \wedge C_2 \wedge \cdots \wedge C_m$, where the C_j are the clauses of φ. The formula ψ is constructed from φ as follows. The variables of ψ are φ's variables $x_1, x_2, \ldots, x_n$ and, for each clause C_j of φ, the variables $y_1^j, y_2^j, \ldots, y_{h_j}^j$. Define $\psi = D_1 \wedge D_2 \wedge \cdots \wedge D_m$, where each clause D_j of ψ is constructed from the clause C_j of φ as follows. Consider the jth clause of φ, and suppose that $C_j = (z_1 \vee z_2 \vee \cdots \vee z_k)$, where each z_i is a literal over $\{x_1, x_2, \ldots, x_n\}$. Distinguish the following four cases.

Case 1: $k = 1$.   Define

$$D_j = (z_1 \vee y_1^j \vee y_2^j) \wedge (z_1 \vee \neg y_1^j \vee y_2^j) \wedge (z_1 \vee y_1^j \vee \neg y_2^j) \wedge (z_1 \vee \neg y_1^j \vee \neg y_2^j).$$

Case 2: $k = 2$.   Define $D_j = (z_1 \vee z_2 \vee y_1^j) \wedge (z_1 \vee z_2 \vee \neg y_1^j)$.
Case 3: $k = 3$.   Define $D_j = C_j = (z_1 \vee z_2 \vee z_3)$.
Case 4: $k \geq 4$.   Define

$$D_j = (z_1 \vee z_2 \vee y_1^j) \wedge (\neg y_1^j \vee z_3 \vee y_2^j) \wedge (\neg y_2^j \vee z_4 \vee y_3^j) \wedge \cdots \wedge$$
$$(\neg y_{k-4}^j \vee z_{k-2} \vee y_{k-3}^j) \wedge (\neg y_{k-3}^j \vee z_{k-1} \vee z_k).$$

Observe that the reduction f is polynomial-time computable. It remains to show that (3.13) is true.

To prove the implication from left to right in (3.13), let t be a truth assignment to the variables $x_1, x_2, \ldots, x_n$ of φ such that $t(\varphi) = 1$. Extend t to a truth assignment t' of the variables of ψ as follows. Since for $i \neq j$, the clauses D_i and D_j are disjoint with respect to the y variables, it is enough to consider all clauses of ψ separately.

Consider the clause D_j for any fixed j. In Cases 1 through 3 above, t already satisfies D_j, so t can arbitrarily be extended to t'. Consider Case 4 above. Let z_i, where $1 \leq i \leq k$ be the first literal in C_j for which $t(z_i) = 1$. Such an i must exist, since t satisfies C_j. If $i \in \{1, 2\}$, then set $t'(y_\ell^j) = 0$ for each ℓ with $1 \leq \ell \leq k - 3$. If $i \in \{k - 1, k\}$, then set $t'(y_\ell^j) = 1$ for each ℓ with $1 \leq \ell \leq k - 3$. Otherwise, set

$$t'(y_\ell^j) = \begin{cases} 1 & \text{if } 1 \leq \ell \leq i - 2 \\ 0 & \text{if } i - 1 \leq \ell \leq k - 3. \end{cases}$$

In each case, t' satisfies D_j. Hence, $t'(\psi) = 1$, so ψ is satisfiable.

Conversely, to prove the implication from right to left in (3.13), let t' be a satisfying truth assignment to ψ. Let t be the restriction of t' to the variables $x_1, x_2, \ldots, x_n$ of φ. Hence, $t(\varphi) = 1$, so φ is satisfiable, which proves (3.13) and the theorem. ∎

Note that the above proof gives a reduction from the NP-complete problem SAT not only to its restriction 3-SAT, which by definition requires that every clause has *at most* three literals, but even to the stronger restriction of SAT that requires that every clause has *exactly* three literals. This property will be useful in the proof of some further NP-completeness results.

NP-completeness results for some central graph problems are presented below. All these problems are defined for undirected graphs, i.e., graphs whose edges are unordered pairs of vertices. We consider only simple graphs, i.e., graphs without reflexive or multiple edges. Recall that $V(G)$ and $E(G)$ denote respectively the vertex set and the edge set of a given graph G.

We start by introducing some graph-theoretic notation and three well-known graph problems. For general graph-theoretic notation, see Definition 2.49 in Section 2.4.3.

Definition 3.52 (Clique, Independent Set, and Vertex Cover).
Let G be an undirected graph.

- *A* clique *of G is a subset $C \subseteq V(G)$ such that for any two vertices $x, y \in C$ with $x \neq y$, $\{x, y\} \in E(G)$.*
- *An* independent set *of G is a subset $I \subseteq V(G)$ such that for any two vertices $x, y \in I$ with $x \neq y$, $\{x, y\} \notin E(G)$.*
- *A* vertex cover *of G is a subset $C \subseteq V(G)$ such that for each edge $\{x, y\} \in E(G)$, $\{x, y\} \cap C \neq \emptyset$.*

Define the decision versions of the clique problem, *the* independent set problem, *and the* vertex cover problem *by:*

$$\text{Clique} = \{\langle G, k \rangle \mid G \text{ is a graph that has a clique of size} \geq k\};$$
$$\text{IS} = \{\langle G, k \rangle \mid G \text{ is a graph that has an independent set of size} \geq k\};$$
$$\text{VC} = \{\langle G, k \rangle \mid G \text{ is a graph that has a vertex cover of size} \leq k\}.$$

Lemma 3.53. *For each graph G and for each subset $U \subseteq V(G)$, the following are equivalent:*

1. *U is a vertex cover of G.*
2. *$\overline{U} = V(G) - U$ is an independent set of G.*
3. *$\overline{U} = V(G) - U$ is a clique of the co-graph of G, which is defined as the graph with vertex set $V(G)$ and edge set $\{\{u, v\} \mid u, v \in V(G) \text{ and } \{u, v\} \notin E(G)\}$.*

The proof of Lemma 3.53 is left to the reader as Exercise 3.14(a).

Theorem 3.54. Clique, IS, *and* VC *are NP-complete.*

Proof.   It is easy to see that each of Clique, IS, and VC belongs to NP; see Exercise 3.14(c). Lemma 3.53 implies that these three problems are pair-wise $\leq^{P}_{m}$-equivalent, i.e., for any two problems A and B chosen among Clique, IS, and VC, $A \leq^{P}_{m} B$ and $B \leq^{P}_{m} A$; see Exercise 3.14(b). Hence, it suffices to prove that 3-SAT $\leq^{P}_{m}$ IS. Let $\varphi(x_1, x_2, \dots, x_n) = C_1 \wedge C_2 \wedge \dots \wedge C_m$ be a given boolean formula with exactly three literals per clause. For each i with $1 \leq i \leq m$, let the ith clause be given by $C_i = (z_{i,1} \vee z_{i,2} \vee z_{i,3})$, where every $z_{i,j} \in \{x_1, x_2, \dots, x_n\} \cup \{\neg x_1, \neg x_2, \dots, \neg x_n\}$ is a literal.

The reduction f maps φ to the pair $\langle G, m \rangle$, where G is the graph with vertex set $V(G) = \{z_{i,j} \mid 1 \leq i \leq m \text{ and } 1 \leq j \leq 3\}$ and edge set

$$E(G) = \{\{z_{i,j}, z_{i,k}\} \mid 1 \leq i \leq m \text{ and } 1 \leq j, k \leq 3 \text{ and } j \neq k\} \cup$$
$$\{\{z_{i,j}, z_{r,s}\} \mid i \neq r \text{ and } z_{i,j} = \neg z_{r,s}\}.$$

That is, every occurrence of a literal in some clause of φ is represented by a vertex of G, the clauses of φ correspond to triangles in G, and any two vertices of distinct triangles are connected by an edge if and only if one vertex represents some literal and the other one its negation.

For example, consider the graph G in Figure 3.3, which is constructed from the formula

$$\varphi(x_1, x_2, x_3) = (x_1 \vee x_2 \vee x_3) \wedge (\neg x_1 \vee x_2 \vee x_3) \wedge (\neg x_1 \vee x_2 \vee \neg x_3) \wedge (x_1 \vee \neg x_2 \vee x_3).$$

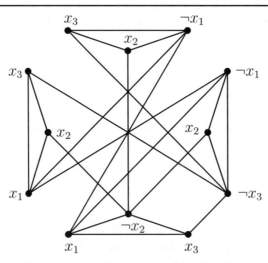

Fig. 3.3. Graph G in the reduction 3-SAT $\leq^{P}_{m}$ IS

Clearly, $f \in$ FP. The construction implies that:

$$\varphi \in 3\text{-SAT} \iff \text{there exists a truth assignment } t \text{ with } t(\varphi) = 1$$

$$\iff \text{every clause } C_i \text{ has a literal } z_{i,j_i} \text{ with } t(z_{i,j_i}) = 1$$

$$\iff \text{there exists a sequence of literals } z_{1,j_1}, z_{2,j_2}, \ldots, z_{m,j_m}$$
$$\text{such that } z_{i,j_i} \neq \neg z_{k,j_k} \text{ for } i, k \in \{1, 2, \ldots, m\} \text{ with } i \neq k$$

$$\iff \text{there exists a sequence of literals } z_{1,j_1}, z_{2,j_2}, \ldots, z_{m,j_m} \text{ such}$$
$$\text{that } \{z_{1,j_1}, z_{2,j_2}, \ldots, z_{m,j_m}\} \text{ is an independent set of size } m \text{ in } G.$$

Since G has an independent set of size at least m if and only if φ is satisfiable, the reduction f witnesses that $3\text{-SAT} \leq_m^P \text{IS}$. ∎

Next, we are concerned with graph coloring and dominating set problems, which arise in various applications and are closely related to scheduling and partitioning problems. In particular, the colorability problem asks for the minimum number of colors required to color the vertices of a given graph such that any two adjacent vertices have distinct colors.

Definition 3.55 (Chromatic Number and k-Colorability Problem).
Given an undirected graph G, a coloring of G is a mapping from $V(G)$ to the positive integers, which represent the colors. A coloring ψ of G is called legal *if for any two vertices x and y in $V(G)$, if $\{x, y\} \in E(G)$ then $\psi(x) \neq \psi(y)$.*

The chromatic number *of G, denoted by $\chi(G)$, is the minimum number of colors needed to legally color G. Given a fixed constant $k \geq 1$, graph G is said to be k-colorable if and only if there exists a legal coloring of G using no more than k colors.*

For fixed $k \geq 1$, define the decision version of the k-colorability problem by

$$k\text{-Colorability} = \{G \mid G \text{ is a graph with } \chi(G) \leq k\}.$$

It is known that 2-Colorability is polynomial-time decidable; see Exercise 3.16. In contrast, Theorem 3.56 below shows that 3-Colorability is NP-complete.

Theorem 3.56. 3-Colorability *is NP-complete.*

Proof.   Membership of 3-Colorability in NP is easy to see: Nondeterministically guess a partition of the vertex set of the given graph into three color classes, and for each partition guessed, verify deterministically that it represents a legal coloring.

The following reduction from 3-SAT to 3-Colorability will prove NP-hardness. Let $\varphi(x_1, x_2, \ldots, x_n) = C_1 \wedge C_2 \wedge \cdots \wedge C_m$ be a given 3-SAT instance with exactly three literals per clause. Define a reduction f mapping φ to the graph G constructed as follows. The vertex set of G is defined by

$$V(G) = \{v_1, v_2, v_3\} \cup \{x_i, \bar{x}_i \mid 1 \leq i \leq n\} \cup \{y_{j,k} \mid 1 \leq j \leq m \text{ and } 1 \leq k \leq 6\},$$

where the x_i and $\bar{x}_i$ are vertices representing the literals x_i and their negations $\neg x_i$, respectively. The edge set of G is defined by

$$E(G) = \{\{v_1, v_2\}, \{v_2, v_3\}, \{v_1, v_3\}\} \cup \{\{x_i, \bar{x}_i\} \mid 1 \leq i \leq n\}$$
$$\cup \{\{v_3, x_i\}, \{v_3, \bar{x}_i\} \mid 1 \leq i \leq n\}$$
$$\cup \{\{a_j, y_{j,1}\}, \{b_j, y_{j,2}\}, \{c_j, y_{j,3}\} \mid 1 \leq j \leq m\}$$
$$\cup \{\{v_2, y_{j,6}\}, \{v_3, y_{j,6}\} \mid 1 \leq j \leq m\}$$
$$\cup \{\{y_{j,1}, y_{j,2}\}, \{y_{j,1}, y_{j,4}\}, \{y_{j,2}, y_{j,4}\} \mid 1 \leq j \leq m\}$$
$$\cup \{\{y_{j,3}, y_{j,5}\}, \{y_{j,3}, y_{j,6}\}, \{y_{j,5}, y_{j,6}\} \mid 1 \leq j \leq m\}$$
$$\cup \{\{y_{j,4}, y_{j,5}\} \mid 1 \leq j \leq m\},$$

where $a_j, b_j, c_j \in \bigcup_{1 \leq i \leq n} \{x_i, \bar{x}_i\}$ are vertices representing the literals occurring in clause $C_j = (a_j \vee b_j \vee c_j)$.

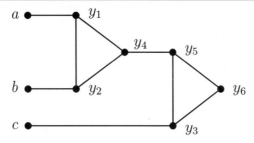

Fig. 3.4. Graph H in the reduction 3-SAT $\leq_m^P$ 3-Colorability

The graph H shown in Figure 3.4 is the key construct in this reduction, which uses m disjoint copies of H (with corresponding subscripts), one for each clause C_j of φ. The correctness of the reduction follows from the following two properties of graph H:

Any coloring of the vertices a, b, and c that assigns color 1 to   (3.14)
one of a, b, and c can be extended to a legal 3-coloring of H
that assigns color 1 to y_6.

If ψ is a legal 3-coloring of H with $\psi(a) = \psi(b) = \psi(c) = i$,   (3.15)
then $\psi(y_6) = i$.

The proof of (3.14) and (3.15) is left to the reader as Exercise 3.15. By (3.14) and (3.15), φ is satisfiable if and only if G is three-colorable. Thus, 3-Colorability is NP-complete.   ∎

We now define the notion of dominating sets in a graph and the domatic number problem. This problem, which arises in the area of computer networks, is the problem of partitioning a given graph into a maximum number of disjoint dominating sets.

Definition 3.57 (Domatic Number Problem).   *Given an undirected graph G, a dominating set of G is a subset $D \subseteq V(G)$ such that for each vertex $u \in V(G) - D$,* *there exists a vertex $v \in D$ with $\{u, v\} \in E$. The* domatic number *of G, denoted by $\delta(G)$, is the maximum number of disjoint dominating sets. Define the decision version of the* domatic number problem *by*

$$\text{DNP} = \{\langle G, k\rangle \mid G \text{ is a graph and } k \text{ is a positive integer such that } \delta(G) \geq k\}.$$

Note that $\delta(G) \leq min\text{-}deg(G) + 1$, where $min\text{-}deg(G)$ denotes the minimum degree of the vertices of graph G.

Theorem 3.58. DNP *is* NP-*complete.*

Proof. To prove that 3-Colorability $\leq_m^P$ DNP, construct a reduction f mapping any given graph G to a pair $\langle H, 3\rangle = f(G)$, where H is a graph satisfying the implications (3.16) and (3.17):

$$G \in \text{3-Colorability} \Longrightarrow \delta(H) = 3; \qquad (3.16)$$
$$G \notin \text{3-Colorability} \Longrightarrow \delta(H) = 2. \qquad (3.17)$$

Since it can be tested in polynomial time whether or not a given graph is two-colorable (see Exercise 3.16), we may assume, without loss of generality, that G is not two-colorable. We also assume that G has no isolated vertices. Note that the domatic number of any graph is always at least 2 if it has no isolated vertices; cf. [GJ79]. Graph H is constructed from G by creating $\|E(G)\|$ new vertices, one on each edge of G, and by adding new edges such that the original vertices of G form a clique. Thus, every edge of G induces a triangle in H, and every pair of nonadjacent vertices in G is connected by an edge in H.

Let $V(G) = \{v_1, v_2, \ldots, v_n\}$, and define the vertex set and the edge set of H by:

$$V(H) = V(G) \cup \{u_{i,j} \mid \{v_i, v_j\} \in E(G)\};$$
$$E(H) = \{\{v_i, u_{i,j}\} \mid \{v_i, v_j\} \in E(G)\} \cup \{\{u_{i,j}, v_j\} \mid \{v_i, v_j\} \in E(G)\}$$
$$\cup \{\{v_i, v_j\} \mid 1 \leq i, j \leq n \text{ and } i \neq j\}\}.$$

The construction of the graph H from a given graph G is illustrated by the example in Figure 3.5. Note that the example graph G in Figure 3.5 is three-colorable; for instance, color the vertices v_1 and v_4 red, color the vertex v_2 blue, and color the vertices v_3 and v_5 green. Then, the domatic number of H is 3, and the vertex set $V(H)$ can be partitioned into three dominating sets:

$$R = \{v_1, v_4, u_{2,3}, u_{2,5}\},$$
$$B = \{v_2, u_{1,5}, u_{3,4}, u_{4,5}\},$$
$$G = \{v_3, v_5, u_{1,2}, u_{2,4}\},$$

which shows (3.16) in this example.

We now prove the implications (3.16) and (3.17) in general. By construction, $min\text{-}deg(H) = 2$ and H has no isolated vertices. Thus, the inequality $\delta(H) \leq min\text{-}deg(H) + 1$ implies that $2 \leq \delta(H) \leq 3$.

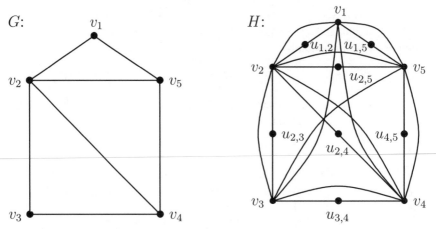

Fig. 3.5. Graph H constructed from graph G in the reduction 3-Colorability $\leq_m^P$ DNP

Suppose that G is three-colorable. Let C_1, C_2, and C_3 be the three color classes of G, i.e., $C_k = \{v_i \in V(G) \mid v_i \text{ is colored by color } k\}$, for $k \in \{1, 2, 3\}$. Form a partition of $V(H)$ by $\hat{C}_k = C_k \cup \{u_{i,j} \mid \{v_i, v_j\} \in E(G) \text{ and } v_i \notin C_k \text{ and } v_j \notin C_k\}$, for $k \in \{1, 2, 3\}$. Since $\hat{C}_k \cap V(G) \neq \emptyset$ for each k, and since $V(G)$ induces a clique in H, every $\hat{C}_k$ dominates $V(G)$ in H. Also, every triangle $\{v_i, u_{i,j}, v_j\}$ in H contains one element from each $\hat{C}_k$, so every $\hat{C}_k$ also dominates the set $\{u_{i,j} \mid \{v_i, v_j\} \in E(G)\}$ in H. Hence, $\delta(H) = 3$, which proves (3.16).

Conversely, suppose that $\delta(H) = 3$. Given a partition of $V(H)$ into three dominating sets, $\hat{C}_1$, $\hat{C}_2$, and $\hat{C}_3$, color the vertices in $\hat{C}_k$ by color k. Every triangle $\{v_i, u_{i,j}, v_j\}$ in H is three-colored, which implies that this coloring on $V(G)$ induces a legal three-coloring of G; so $G \in$ 3-Colorability. Hence, $\chi(G) = 3$ if and only if $\delta(H) = 3$. Since $2 \leq \delta(H) \leq 3$, the implication (3.17) follows. ∎

Finally, we consider certain matching, set covering, and knapsack problems. We start with the matching problem.

Definition 3.59 (Two-Dimensional Matching Problem).
A bipartite graph *is a graph with $2n$ vertices whose vertex set can be partitioned into two disjoint subsets of size n, say V_1 and V_2, that both are independent sets. That is, neither the vertices within V_1 nor the vertices within V_2 are adjacent; there are only edges connecting vertices from V_1 with vertices from V_2.*

Given a bipartite graph G with $V(G) = V_1 \cup V_2$ and $V_1 \cap V_2 = \emptyset$, a (perfect) bipartite matching *of G is a subset $M \subseteq E(G)$ of n edges such that, for any two distinct edges $\{v, w\}$ and $\{x, y\}$ in M, $v \neq x$ and $w \neq y$. The* bipartite matching problem *(a.k.a. the* two-dimensional matching problem*) asks whether or not there exists a matching in a given bipartite graph.*

Example 3.60 (Two-Dimensional Matching Problem). Consider a set V_{bride} of n brides and a set V_{groom} of n bridegrooms, who form the vertices of a bipartite graph G.

That is, the vertex set of G is partitioned into V_{bride} and V_{groom} such that $V(G) = V_{\text{bride}} \cup V_{\text{groom}}$ and $V_{\text{bride}} \cap V_{\text{groom}} = \emptyset$. An edge between two vertices indicates that the corresponding partners would be willing to marry each other. Straightforward thought reveals why there are no edges connecting the vertices within V_{bride} and no edges connecting the vertices within V_{groom}.

One may think of a matching as a way of arranging n weddings between a set of n brides and a set of n bridegrooms such that, in the words of Garey and Johnson [GJ79], "polygamy is avoided and everyone receives an acceptable spouse." The left-hand side of Figure 3.6 gives a concrete example in which four couples (f_i, m_i) can be matched according to the bold-faced edges.

The above "wedding" interpretation of bipartite matchings explains that this problem is sometimes referred to as the "marriage problem." It is known that the marriage problem can be solved in polynomial time; see Hopcroft and Karp [HK73]. In real life, their result applies as well: *To marry is easy!*

We now define the generalization of bipartite graphs and matchings to three dimensions and consider the corresponding generalized problem, which is dubbed the *three-dimensional matching problem*, a.k.a. the *tripartite matching problem*.

Definition 3.61 (Three-Dimensional Matching Problem).
Let n be a positive integer, let U, V, and W be three pairwise disjoint sets of size n, and let $R \subseteq U \times V \times W$ be a ternary relation, i.e., a set of triples (u, v, w) with $u \in U$, $v \in V$, and $w \in W$.

A tripartite matching of R is a subset $M \subseteq R$ *of size n such that, for any two distinct triples (u, v, w) and $(\hat{u}, \hat{v}, \hat{w})$ in M, we have $u \neq \hat{u}$, $v \neq \hat{v}$, and $w \neq \hat{w}$. That is, no two elements of a tripartite matching agree in any coordinate.*

Define the decision version of the three-dimensional matching problem *by*

$$
\text{3-DM} = \left\{ \langle R, U, V, W \rangle \;\middle|\; \begin{array}{l} U, V, \text{ and } W \text{ are pairwise disjoint, nonempty sets} \\ \text{of equal size, and } R \subseteq U \times V \times W \text{ is a ternary} \\ \text{relation containing a tripartite matching of size } ||U|| \end{array} \right\}.
$$

The following story continues and extends Example 3.60.

Story 3.62 *Nine months have passed. Some morning, our n happily married couples are on their way to the town hospital. A few hours of hard labor later, n babies are born, who immediately start screaming and increasing the complexity in the life of their parents considerably. To begin with, they each get rid of their name tags indicating to which pair of parents they belong, which causes a huge mess in the delivery room. Even worse, each of the new fathers—perhaps confused by the moment's excitement and intrigued by the other women's beauty—claim to have never seen before that young lady who stubbornly insists that she has just given birth to his child. Instead, the faithless father claims to be allied with the other young lady right next to her. The chaos is perfect!*

The nurse on duty thus faces a difficult problem: Which baby matches which pair of parents? In other words, to restore the n happy, harmonious, and pairwise *disjoint families, she has to find a three-dimensional matching among the n fathers, n mothers, and n babies. No wonder that, in contrast with the efficiently solvable marriage problem, the problem 3-DM turns out to be NP-complete. After all, to solve the tripartite matching problem, the nurse has to take 3n blood samples, which she then uses for certain really sophisticated DNA tests (whose description is beyond the scope of this book). Again, the result that 3-DM is NP-complete accords with common sense and worldly wisdom in real life:* With children coming along, staying a happy and harmonious family—disjoint with any other family!—occasionally tends to be quite hard a task!

Theorem 3.63. 3-DM *is NP-complete.*

Proof.   Membership of 3-DM in NP is easy to see: Given an instance $\langle R, U, V, W \rangle$ of 3-DM, where $R \subseteq U \times V \times W$ is a ternary relation over pairwise disjoint sets U, V, and W of size n each, nondeterministically guess a subset $M \subseteq R$ of size n, and for each subset M guessed, check deterministically whether or not it is a tripartite matching of R.

The intuition behind the NP-hardness proof is best understood by first looking at the approach taken by the nurse on duty in the delivery room from Story 3.62 above. How does she solve the tripartite matching problem? First, she attaches name tags to everybody in the room, making sure that they cannot be removed. Suppose the mothers are labeled $m_1, m_2, \ldots, m_n$, the fathers are labeled $f_1, f_2, \ldots, f_n$, and the babies are labeled $b_1, b_2, \ldots, b_n$. Let $\bar{b}_1, \bar{b}_2, \ldots, \bar{b}_n$ be another set of n babies, where each $\bar{b}_i$ is a clone[7] of b_i. Then, she arranges them in two circles such that the $2n$ parents form the inner circle in which fathers and mothers alternate. In the outer circle, the n babies and their n clones alternate. For $n = 4$, Figure 3.6 (right) shows these two circles in which persons standing next to each other are connected so as to form $2n$ triangles. Every father is connected with two mothers and two babies, and every mother is connected with two fathers and two babies.

For each i (modulo $n = 4$), father f_i claims to be married to mother m_{i+1} and to have the ith child together with her. Mother m_i, however, insists that *she* is the wife of f_i and that she has the ith baby together with him. These two contradictory assertions are depicted in Figure 3.6 (right). The assertion of father f_i is shown by the triangle with corners f_i, m_{i+1}, and $\bar{b}_i$, and the assertion of mother m_i is shown by the triangle with corners m_i, f_i, and b_i.

Each of the $2n$ triangles represents one potential family, and the nurse has to determine which of the triangles are the original n families and which are not. The only way to obtain n disjoint families is to choose either every triangle containing a baby b_i, or every triangle containing a cloned baby $\bar{b}_i$. By taking $3n$ blood samples and using the results of her DNA tests, the nurse can make the right choice, assigning every father to his true spouse and child and thus restoring the n original families. The remaining n babies (and this is the sad side of the nurse's approach to solving this problem—and of baby cloning in general) are sent to foster homes.

---

[7] Again, the technical details of how to clone babies—and the discussion of related ethical questions—are beyond the scope of this book.

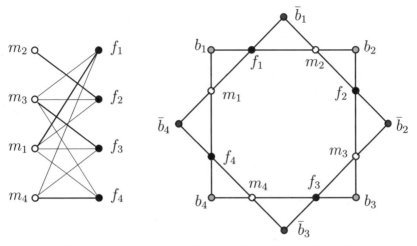

Fig. 3.6. *Left*: Marriage problem   *Right*: Truth-setting gadget

Complexity theorists do not know much about DNA testing. Fortunately, however, they are familiar with the satisfiability problem. To show NP-hardness of 3-DM, we now give a formal reduction from 3-SAT to 3-DM.

Given a boolean formula $\varphi(x_1, x_2, \ldots, x_\ell) = C_1 \wedge C_2 \wedge \cdots \wedge C_n$, where the clauses C_j of φ have exactly three literals, the goal is to construct an instance $\langle R, U, V, W \rangle$ of 3-DM such that $R \subseteq U \times V \times W$, where U, V, and W are pairwise disjoint, nonempty sets of equal size, and the following equivalence holds:

$$\varphi \text{ is satisfiable} \iff R \text{ contains a tripartite matching of size } \|U\|. \quad (3.18)$$

R consists of various types of triples, each corresponding to a certain intention. All triples of the same type are bundled into one component. The first component, call it X, contains those triples in R whose form enforces a certain truth assignment to the variables of the formula φ making sure that this assignment is consistent for all clauses of φ. That is, if some variable occurs in distinct clauses, then the same truth value is assigned to all these occurrences. That is why this component X is called the "*truth-setting*" gadget of R.

We now define the sets U, V, and W and construct the components of the relation R, beginning with X. For each variable x_i in φ, create $2n$ elements $b_1^i, b_2^i, \ldots, b_n^i$ and $\bar{b}_1^i, \bar{b}_2^i, \ldots, \bar{b}_n^i$ in U, where n is the number of clauses of φ. Here, b_j^i represents the occurrence of x_i in C_j, the jth clause of φ, and $\bar{b}_j^i$ represents the occurrence of $\neg x_i$ in C_j. Since the literals do not occur in all clauses, some b_j^i or $\bar{b}_j^i$ do not correspond to the occurrence of any literal in φ. The elements b_j^i and $\bar{b}_j^i$ form the outer circle of the graph shown in Figure 3.6 (right), for $n = 4$ and dropping the superscripts.

In addition, for each variable x_i in φ, create n elements $m_1^i, m_2^i, \ldots, m_n^i$ in V and n elements $f_1^i, f_2^i, \ldots, f_n^i$ in W, which form the inner circle of the graph shown in Figure 3.6 (right). Construct the truth-setting gadget presented in this figure by connecting the elements m_j^i, f_j^i, and b_j^i to form a triangle, and the elements f_j^i, m_{j+1}^i, and $\bar{b}_j^i$ to form another triangle.

The triangles in the gadget thus constructed correspond to triples in R. The m_j^i and f_j^i from the inner circle occur in the one gadget corresponding to the variable x_i only, whereas the b_j^i and $\bar{b}_j^i$ from the outer circle will occur in other gadgets as well. Formally, the truth-setting gadget X has the form $X = \bigcup_{i=1}^{\ell} X_i$, where for each variable x_i in φ, $X_i = F_i \cup T_i$ is defined by the following two sets of triples:

$$F_i = \{(b_j^i, m_j^i, f_j^i) \mid 1 \leq j \leq n\};$$
$$T_i = \{(\bar{b}_j^i, m_{j+1}^i, f_j^i) \mid 1 \leq j < n\} \cup \{(\bar{b}_n^i, m_1^i, f_n^i)\}.$$

Since none of the elements m_j^i and f_j^i, where $1 \leq i \leq \ell$ and $1 \leq j \leq n$, from the inner circle will occur in any triple outside of $X_i = F_i \cup T_i$, any matching M of R must contain exactly n triples from X_i, either all triples from F_i or all triples from T_i. Intuitively, this choice between triples from F_i and triples from T_i for the matching forces us to make a choice between setting the variable x_i false and setting x_i true. Since all occurrences of x_i in the formula φ are represented in the gadget X_i, this choice is consistent for the entire formula. Hence, any matching M of R specifies a truth assignment of φ such that, for each $i \in \{1, 2, \ldots, \ell\}$, the variable x_i is set to true if and only if $M \cap X_i = T_i$.

Next, we add to R the set $Y = \bigcup_{j=1}^{n} Y_j$ of triples such that each Y_j checks the satisfiability of the clause C_j in φ. That is why Y is called the "*satisfiability*" component of R. For each clause C_j, create two elements, $v_j \in V$ and $w_j \in W$, that occur only in Y_j. In addition, Y_j contains three more elements from $\bigcup_{i=1}^{\ell}\{b_j^i\} \cup \{\bar{b}_j^i\}$ corresponding to the three literals in C_j and possibly occurring also in other components of R. Formally, for each clause C_j of φ, define the satisfiability component of R by the following set of triples:

$$Y_j = \{(b_j^i, v_j, w_j) \mid x_i \text{ occurs in } C_j\} \cup \{(\bar{b}_j^i, v_j, w_j) \mid \neg x_i \text{ occurs in } C_j\}.$$

Since none of the elements v_j and w_j, $1 \leq j \leq n$, will occur in any triple of R outside of Y_j, any matching M of R must contain exactly one triple from Y_j, either (b_j^i, v_j, w_j) or $(\bar{b}_j^i, v_j, w_j)$. However, M contains a triple from Y_j with either b_j^i (if x_i occurs in C_j) or $\bar{b}_j^i$ (if $\neg x_i$ occurs in C_j) if and only if that element is not contained in the triples from $M \cap X_i$, which is the case if and only if the truth assignment chosen by M via the truth-setting gadget satisfies clause C_j.

So far, U contains $2n\ell$ elements, but both V and W contain only $n\ell + n$ elements. Adding $n(\ell - 1)$ further elements both to V and to W ensures that these three sets have the same size. In particular, add the elements $v_{n+1}, v_{n+2}, \ldots, v_{n\ell}$ to V, add the elements $w_{n+1}, w_{n+2}, \ldots, w_{n\ell}$ to W, and add the following set of triples to R:

$$Z = \{(b_j^i, v_k, w_k) \mid 1 \leq i \leq \ell \text{ and } 1 \leq j \leq n \text{ and } n + 1 \leq k \leq n\ell\}$$
$$\cup \{(\bar{b}_j^i, v_k, w_k) \mid 1 \leq i \leq \ell \text{ and } 1 \leq j \leq n \text{ and } n + 1 \leq k \leq n\ell\}.$$

The point is that whenever there exists a matching of $R - Z$ that satisfies all constraints imposed by the truth-setting gadget and the satisfiability component of R, this matching leaves exactly $n(\ell-1)$ elements from U uncovered, which can now be matched with a unique pair (v_k, w_k) occurring in Z. This extension of the matching of $R - Z$ yields a matching of R.

To summarize, the sets U, V, and W are defined by:

$$U = \{b_j^i \mid 1 \le i \le \ell \text{ and } 1 \le j \le n\} \cup \{\bar{b}_j^i \mid 1 \le i \le \ell \text{ and } 1 \le j \le n\};$$
$$V = \{m_j^i \mid 1 \le i \le \ell \text{ and } 1 \le j \le n\} \cup \{v_k \mid 1 \le k \le n\ell\};$$
$$W = \{f_j^i \mid 1 \le i \le \ell \text{ and } 1 \le j \le n\} \cup \{w_k \mid 1 \le k \le n\ell\},$$

and the relation $R \subseteq U \times V \times W$ is defined by

$$R = X \cup Y \cup Z.$$

Note that R contains exactly $2n\ell + 3n + 2n^2\ell(\ell-1)$ triples and the structure of R can be easily determined from the structure of the given formula φ. Thus, the reduction is polynomial-time computable. Equation (3.18) follows from the remarks made during the construction of R; a formal proof of (3.18) is left to the reader as Exercise 3.17. ∎

Definition 3.64 (Set Covering, Set Packing, and Exact Cover By 3-Sets).
For any set U, let $\mathfrak{P}(U)$ be the power set *of U, i.e., the set of subsets of U. Define the decision version of the* set covering problem *by*

$$\texttt{SetCovering} = \left\{ \langle \mathcal{S}, U, k \rangle \;\middle|\; \begin{array}{l} k \in \mathbb{N}, U \text{ is a finite set, } \mathcal{S} \subseteq \mathfrak{P}(U), \\ \text{and there exist } k \text{ sets } S_1, S_2, \ldots, S_k \\ \text{in } \mathcal{S} \text{ such that } U = \bigcup_{i=1}^k S_i \end{array} \right\}.$$

Given any set U and any collection $\mathcal{S} \subseteq \mathfrak{P}(U)$, let $\kappa(\mathcal{S})$ denote the maximum number of pairwise disjoint sets in $\mathcal{S}$. Define the decision version of the set packing *problem by*

$$\texttt{SetPacking} = \{\langle \mathcal{S}, U, k \rangle \mid k \in \mathbb{N}, U \text{ is a finite set}, \mathcal{S} \subseteq \mathfrak{P}(U), \text{ and } \kappa(\mathcal{S}) \ge k\}.$$

Define the decision version of the exact cover by 3-sets *problem by*

$$\texttt{X-3-Cover} = \left\{ \langle \mathcal{S}, U \rangle \;\middle|\; \begin{array}{l} U \text{ is a set with } ||U|| = 3m \text{ for some } m \in \mathbb{N}, \mathcal{S} \subseteq \mathfrak{P}(U), \\ ||S|| = 3 \text{ for each } S \in \mathcal{S}, \text{ and there exist } m \text{ pairwise} \\ \text{disjoint sets } S_1, S_2, \ldots, S_m \in \mathcal{S} \text{ such that } U = \bigcup_{i=1}^m S_i \end{array} \right\}.$$

Theorem 3.65. $\texttt{SetCovering}$, $\texttt{SetPacking}$, *and* $\texttt{X-3-Cover}$ *each are* NP-*complete.*

Proof. Again, membership in NP is easy to see for each of these problems. To prove NP-hardness, it is enough to observe that each of these problems generalizes the 3-DM problem. In particular, 3-DM is the special case of the X-3-Cover problem in which the given universe U can be partitioned into three pairwise disjoint sets of equal size, say A, B, and C, such that each set S in the given collection $\mathcal{S}$ contains exactly one element from each of A, B, and C. The problem X-3-Cover, in turn, is the special case of the SetCovering problem in which the given universe U has $3m$ elements, every set S in the given collection $\mathcal{S}$ contains exactly three elements, and the given constant k equals m. A similar argument works for the SetPacking problem; see Exercise 3.18. ∎

To conclude the section on NP-completeness, we turn to certain knapsack problems. *Knapsack problems* are single-line integer linear programming problems of the form:

$$\text{Maximize } \sum_{i=1}^{n} s_i x_i$$

$$\text{subject to } \sum_{i=1}^{n} s_i x_i \leq T, \quad \text{where } x_i \in \mathbb{Z}.$$

In general, *integer linear programming* is the problem of finding an integer solution to a given system of linear inequalities in n variables and with integer coefficients. One may thus think of a knapsack problem as an optimization problem with the objective to fill a knapsack of capacity T with items of sizes s_i such that the largest possible utilization is achieved. Theorem 3.67 below shows NP-completeness of the very special variant of the knapsack problem in which $x_i \in \{0, 1\}$, for each i, and in which equality with the target capacity T is required. It follows that the general knapsack problem (with x_i being integers and with requiring T being an upper bound only) as well as the even more general integer linear programming problem are NP-hard. Both are also NP-complete; the difficult part of the proof is showing that integer linear programming is in NP. In contrast, the *linear programming problem*, which is the same as integer linear programming except that solutions need not be integers, can be solved in polynomial time by H. Lenstra's algorithm [Len83], see also Hačijan [Hač79].

We now define the above-mentioned 0-1 restriction of the knapsack problem, which is known as the subset-of-sums problem, SOS for short. This problem has been used for certain cryptographic applications. In particular, cryptosystems were proposed whose security is based on the hardness of the SOS problem and variants thereof; see Section 8.5. Some of those systems were broken, whereas others are still in use. Moreover, the SOS problem is closely related to lattice-based cryptography, see the references in Section 8.8.

Definition 3.66 (Subset-of-Sums Problem). *The* subset-of-sums problem, SOS, *is defined as follows: Given a sequence* $s_1, s_2, \ldots, s_n, T$ *of positive integers (encoded in binary), does there exist a boolean vector* $\mathbf{x} = (x_1, x_2, \ldots, x_n)$ *in* $\{0, 1\}^n$ *such that*

$$\sum_{i=1}^{n} x_i s_i = T ?$$

The numbers s_i *are called the* sizes, *and* T *is the* target sum. *Formalized as a set of yes-instances, this decision problem has the following form:*

$$\text{SOS} = \left\{ \langle s_1, s_2, \ldots, s_n, T \rangle \;\middle|\; \begin{array}{l} s_1, s_2, \ldots, s_n, T \in \mathbb{N} - \{0\}, \text{ and there is} \\ \text{some } \mathbf{x} \in \{0,1\}^n \text{ such that } \sum_{i=1}^{n} x_i s_i = T \end{array} \right\}.$$

Theorem 3.67. SOS *is* NP-*complete*.

Proof. The proof that SOS belongs to NP is left to the reader as Exercise 3.19. To prove NP-hardness, we reduce the NP-complete problem X-3-Cover to SOS. We are given a set U of cardinality $3m$ and a collection $\mathcal{S} \subseteq \mathfrak{P}(U)$ of subsets of U such that every set in $\mathcal{S}$ has exactly three elements. Our goal is to construct an instance $\langle s_1, s_2, \ldots, s_n, T \rangle$ of the SOS problem such that some of the sizes s_i sum up to exactly T if and only if U can be partitioned into m pairwise disjoint sets from $\mathcal{S}$.

It is convenient to view the elements of the universe U as positive integers, i.e., $U = \{1, 2, \ldots, 3m\}$. Let n be the number of sets in the given collection $\mathcal{S}$, i.e., $\mathcal{S} = \{S_1, S_2, \ldots, S_n\}$. Think of each set S_i in $\mathcal{S}$ as a bit vector $\mathbf{s}_i$ of dimension $3m$. For example, let $U = \{1, 2, \ldots, 6\}$, and consider the collection $\mathcal{S} = \{S_1, S_2, S_3\}$ with three sets, where

$$\begin{aligned}
S_1 &= \{1, 3, 6\} \text{ corresponds to } \mathbf{s}_1 = (1, 0, 1, 0, 0, 1); \\
S_2 &= \{3, 4, 6\} \text{ corresponds to } \mathbf{s}_2 = (0, 0, 1, 1, 0, 1); \\
S_3 &= \{2, 4, 5\} \text{ corresponds to } \mathbf{s}_3 = (0, 1, 0, 1, 1, 0).
\end{aligned}$$

Interpret the bit vectors $\mathbf{s}_i$ as positive integers s_i in $(n+1)$-ary representation. The base $n + 1$ is chosen in order to avoid problems with the carry in the addition of the integers represented by the $\mathbf{s}_i$. That is, for each i with $1 \leq i \leq n$, the integer s_i corresponding to the set S_i is defined by

$$s_i = \sum_{j \in S_i} (n+1)^{3m-j}.$$

In the above example, we have

$$\begin{aligned}
s_1 &= 4^5 + 4^3 + 4^0 = 1089; \\
s_2 &= 4^3 + 4^2 + 4^0 = 81; \\
s_3 &= 4^4 + 4^2 + 4^1 = 276.
\end{aligned}$$

The universe U, which contains all integers j with $1 \leq j \leq 3m$, thus corresponds to the vector $\mathbf{1} = (1, 1, \ldots, 1)$ of dimension $3m$. Hence, defining the target sum T to be the integer represented by this vector in base $n + 1$:

$$T = \sum_{j=0}^{3m-1} (n+1)^j,$$

it follows that U can be partitioned into m pairwise disjoint sets from $\mathcal{S}$ if and only if $\sum_{i=1}^{n} x_i s_i = T$ for suitably chosen coefficients $x_i \in \{0, 1\}$. In particular, $x_i = 1$ if and only if S_i is one of the sets participating in the partition of U. In the above example, $U = S_1 \cup S_3$ with S_1 and S_3 being disjoint sets from $\mathcal{S}$ and, for the boolean coefficient vector $\mathbf{x} = (1, 0, 1)$, we have $s_1 + s_3 = 1365 = T$. ∎

3.6 Inside NP

3.6.1 P versus NP and the Graph Isomorphism Problem

Does P equal NP? Nobody knows. This famous question has annoyed complexity theorists since the beginnings of this field, and still no solution to this central question seems to be within reach. Given the importance of the classes P and NP, it is natural to speculate. A vast majority of complexity theorists believe that $P \neq NP$; see the $P \neq NP$ poll conducted by Gasarch in 2002 [Gas02]. If it ever turns out that $P = NP$ is true indeed, then the world of computational complexity is richer by one important insight, yet at the same time it is poorer in that it has lost much of its rich structure. For example, $P = NP$ would make Chapter 5 completely pointless (except for Section 5.6 that is concerned with alternating Turing machines). Chapter 5 studies some interesting hierarchies of complexity classes that are based on NP, and a collapse of NP to P implies that all these hierarchies also collapse to P.

The P versus NP question is also of central importance in cryptography. In particular, $P = NP$ implies that most of the cryptosystems currently in use in fact are useless, since their security is based on the assumption that certain problems such as the factoring problem are hard to solve. The factoring problem asks for the prime decomposition $p_1^{e_1} p_2^{e_2} \cdots p_k^{e_k}$ of a given integer n, along with primality certificates for its prime factors p_i. As we will see in Chapter 7, integer factoring can be done in nondeterministic polynomial time, yet there is no efficient deterministic algorithm known for solving it. However, if $P = NP$, factoring could be done in deterministic polynomial time. On the other hand, the existence of an efficient factoring algorithm does not imply $P = NP$ in any obvious way. In this regard, the factoring problem parts company with the NP-complete problems.

We know from Lemma 3.36 that $P = NP$ if and only if any one NP-complete problem is in P. Thus, if $P \neq NP$, no NP-complete problem can be in P. A natural question arises: Assuming $P \neq NP$, can there exist NP problems that are neither in P nor NP-complete? Ladner proved that the answer to this question is in the affirmative. The proof of his result is omitted here, since it will be proven later on: Theorem 3.68 is a special case of a result by Schöning stated as Theorem 5.88 in Section 5.7.

Theorem 3.68 (Ladner).
$P \neq NP$ *if and only if there exist sets in* NP *that are neither in* P *nor* NP-*complete.*

By Theorem 3.68, if $P \neq NP$, then there exist problems in NP that are neither in P nor NP-complete. However, the problems constructed in the proof of this result are not overly natural problems. Are there any *natural* NP problems that are neither in P nor NP-complete? The primality problem, which asks whether or not a given integer is prime, was considered to be one good candidate for such a problem. However, Agrawal, Kayal, and Saxena [AKS02] showed that this problem in fact is in P. Efficient primality tests are important for many cryptosystems including the RSA system; see Chapter 7.

Another good candidate is the graph isomorphism problem, see Definition 2.49 in Section 2.4. The following fact is easy to prove; see Exercise 3.20.

Fact 3.69 GI *is in* NP.

Chapter 6 will provide evidence that GI indeed is a problem in NP that seems to be not NP-complete. On the other hand, it does share many properties with the NP-complete sets. For example, just like all "natural" NP-complete problems, GI is self-reducible. Self-reducibility is a very important property and has been studied in a wide variety of contexts. For example, the results presented in Section 3.6.2, and in particular Theorem 3.75, make extensive use of the self-reducibility of NP-complete problems such as SAT; see also the remarks in Section 3.8.

Intuitively, a set A is *self-reducible* if there exists an efficient algorithm for solving A, which uses the set A itself as an oracle. If this algorithm could simply query the oracle about its input string, then every set would be self-reducible and thus this notion would be trivial. To prevent this from happening, only queries about strings that are "smaller" than the input string are allowed in a self-reduction. If simply the length of strings is meant by "smaller," then self-reductions might depend on the encoding used, which is not desirable. A variety of formal concepts capturing self-reducibility have been proposed in the literature, among which the notion proposed by A. Meyer and Paterson [MP79] has turned out to be the most useful. Their formal approach is useful to "obtain full generality and to preserve the concept under polynomially computable isomorphisms" [JY90, p. 84], see also Section 3.6.2.

Definition 3.70 (Self-Reducibility).

1. *A partial order $<_{\mathrm{pwl}}$ on Σ^* is polynomially well-founded and length-related if and only if the following two conditions hold:*
   (a) *Every strictly decreasing chain is finite, and there is a polynomial p such that every finite $<_{\mathrm{pwl}}$-decreasing chain is shorter than p of the length of its maximum element.*
   (b) *There exists a polynomial q such that for all $x, y \in \Sigma^*$, $x <_{\mathrm{pwl}} y$ implies that $|x| \leq q(|y|)$.*
2. *A set A is self-reducible if and only if there exist a polynomially well-founded and length-related order $<_{\mathrm{pwl}}$ on Σ^* and a DPOTM M such that $A = L(M^A)$ and on any input $x \in \Sigma^*$, M queries only strings y with $y <_{\mathrm{pwl}} x$.*

Theorem 3.71. *Both SAT and GI are self-reducible.*

We will not give a formal proof of Theorem 3.71 here. Rather, we merely give an intuitive outline for the satisfiability problem. Given a boolean formula φ, let φ_0 and φ_1 be the formula that results from φ when setting its first variable to false and true, respectively. Intuitively, it is clear that φ_0 and φ_1 are smaller than φ, since they have one variable fewer than φ.

Now, construct the self-reducibility tree for a given instance ψ to SAT as follows: The root is marked by ψ, and each vertex of the tree that is marked by some formula φ gets two children that are marked by φ_0 and φ_1, respectively. The depth of the tree is bounded by the number of variables, say n, and the number of its leaves is bounded by 2^n. The leaves contain formulas that can be evaluated immediately, since they don't have any variables anymore. Moreover, since for each formula φ,

$$\varphi \in \text{SAT} \iff \varphi_0 \in \text{SAT} \lor \varphi_1 \in \text{SAT},$$

the formula ψ at the root is satisfiable if and only if there exists a path from the root to some leave such that every formula on this path is satisfiable. That is why the procedure just described is called a "disjunctive" self-reduction.

3.6.2 The Berman–Hartmanis Isomorphism Conjecture and One-Way Functions

An isomorphism between any two sets, A and B, is a bijection (i.e., a one-to-one, onto mapping) between A and B. The Cantor–Bernstein Theorem in set theory says that A and B are isomorphic if and only if there is an injection from A into B and an injection from B into A. In recursive function theory, it is known that all sets many-one complete in RE are pair-wise isomorphic; see the book [Rog67] by H. Rogers. Note that "many-one complete" is here meant in the recursion-theoretic sense, i.e., the reduction must be computable, but not necessarily polynomial-time computable. The natural question arises of whether or not a polynomial-time analog of this result is true for the NP-complete sets.

Definition 3.72 (P-Isomorphism).
A function $\varphi : \Sigma^* \to \Sigma^*$ is a p-isomorphism if and only if

1. *φ is bijection on Σ^*, i.e., φ is a total, one-to-one, onto function on Σ^*, and*
2. *both $\varphi \in$ FP and $\varphi^{-1} \in$ FP.*

Any two sets A and B are p-isomorphic if and only if $A \leq_{\text{m}}^{\text{P}} B$ via some reduction φ that is a p-isomorphism.

In other words, A is p-isomorphic to B if and only if there exists a polynomial-time computable and polynomial-time invertible permutation φ on Σ^* such that $\varphi(A) = B$ and $\varphi(\overline{A}) = \overline{B}$, where $\varphi(X) = \{\varphi(x) \mid x \in X\}$ for any set X.

In 1977, Berman and Hartmanis [BH77] proved that all the then known NP-complete problems are pairwise p-isomorphic. Their results led them to the following famous conjecture.

Conjecture 3.73 (Isomorphism Conjecture of Berman and Hartmanis).
All NP-complete sets are pairwise p-isomorphic.

The Berman–Hartmanis isomorphism conjecture states that all the NP-complete problems in fact are just one problem appearing in many different guises. The importance of Conjecture 3.73 is obvious in light of the following result.

Theorem 3.74. *If all NP-complete sets are pairwise p-isomorphic, then* $P \neq NP$.

Proof.   To prove the contrapositive, suppose that $P = NP$. Then, by Lemma 3.37, all nontrivial (i.e., distinct from $\emptyset$ and Σ^*) problems in P are $\leq_{\text{m}}^{\text{P}}$-complete for NP. In particular, all nontrivial finite sets in P are $\leq_{\text{m}}^{\text{P}}$-complete in NP. However, two finite sets with a distinct number of elements cannot be isomorphic. Thus, they cannot be p-isomorphic.   ∎

Theorem 3.74 shows that any proof of the Berman–Hartmanis isomorphism conjecture would also solve the P versus NP question. Thus, a proof of Conjecture 3.73 seems to be out of reach currently. Even the weaker conjecture that if $P \neq NP$ then all NP-complete sets are pairwise p-isomorphic, which is the converse of Theorem 3.74, seems not to be within reach. Berman and Hartmanis [BH77] offered an even weaker conjecture: If $P \neq NP$, then no sparse set is $\leq_{m}^{P}$-complete in NP.

Sparse sets have been intensely studied and are central to many results in complexity theory. For any language S and any $n \in \mathbb{N}$, define the *set of strings of length up to n* by $S^{\leq n} = \{x \mid x \in S \text{ and } |x| \leq n\}$. A language S is said to be *sparse* if and only if there exists a polynomial p such that for each $n \in \mathbb{N}$, $||S^{\leq n}|| \leq p(n)$; see also Definition 5.58. Observe that none of the known NP-complete problems is sparse. Moreover, no nonsparse set can be mapped to a sparse set by a p-isomorphism. Consequently, the statement of Conjecture 3.73 implies that no sparse set is $\leq_{m}^{P}$-complete in NP.

Based on some groundwork by Berman [Ber78] and Fortune [For79] (see Section 3.8), this weaker conjecture of Berman and Hartmanis was resolved by Mahaney [Mah82]. The proof of Mahaney's result, which in particular exploits the self-reducibility of the satisfiability problem, is omitted here. Mahaney's result was strengthened later on by Ogihara and Watanabe [OW91]; see Section 5.9.

Theorem 3.75 (Mahaney).
If $P \neq NP$, *then no sparse set is* $\leq_{m}^{P}$-*complete in* NP.

An important intermediate step towards the ultimate proof of Theorem 3.75 is stated below. Theorem 3.76 provides a related result for sparse sets with an easy census function. The census function of any set L maps each number n (given in unary) to the number of elements in L up to length n; that is, $\text{census}_L(1^n) = ||S^{\leq n}||$ for each n.

Theorem 3.76. *For each sparse set S with* $\text{census}_S \in \text{FP}$, *if* $S \in NP$ *then* $\overline{S} \in NP$.

Proof.   Let M be some NPTM for S. On input x of length n, an NPTM N for $\overline{S}$ works as follows:

Step 1: Compute $k = \text{census}_S(1^n)$.

Step 2: Nondeterministically guess a sequence $\mathbf{s} = (s_1, s_2, \ldots, s_k)$ of pairwise distinct strings each having length at most n.

Step 3: For each sequence $\mathbf{s}$ guessed and successively for each string s_i in $\mathbf{s}$, nondeterministically simulate M on input s_i to verify that each s_i is in S. Reject if at least one such test fails.

Step 4: Accept if and only if x is not in $\mathbf{s}$.

Since M is an NPTM and since k is polynomially in n and can be computed in time polynomially in n, N is an NPTM. Clearly, $L(N) = \overline{S}$. Thus, $\overline{S}$ is in NP.   ∎

Let coNP $= \{L \mid \overline{L} \in \text{NP}\}$ be the class of complements of NP sets. The open question of whether or not NP equals coNP is almost as famous as the P versus NP question. Although a proof of NP $\neq$ coNP seems not to be within reach by current techniques, it is considered very unlikely that NP is closed under complementation. Thus, Corollary 3.77 says that it is very unlikely that a sparse set with an easy census function is $\leq_m^p$-complete in NP.

Corollary 3.77. *If S is a sparse $\leq_m^p$-complete set in NP with census$_S \in$ FP, then* NP $=$ coNP.

A rival view to Conjecture 3.73 was taken by Joseph and P. Young [JY85]. Based on the notion of creative sets from recursive function theory,[8] they defined the *k-creative sets for* NP by requiring that the productive functions for NP sets be one-to-one and computable (yet not necessarily invertible) in polynomial time and that the sets R_i (corresponding to the definition of creativity given in Footnote 8) need not cover all of NP but only those NP sets accepted by NTMs that run in time p for polynomials p with fixed degree k.

With this definition in hand, they proved in [JY85] that every k-creative set for NP is $\leq_m^p$-complete in NP. Furthermore, every one-to-one, polynomial-time computable, "honest" function is a productive function for some k-creative set. Here, a function $f : \Sigma^* \rightarrow \Sigma^*$ is said to be *honest* if and only if there exists a polynomial p such that for each $y \in R_f$ there exists some $x \in D_f$ such that $y = f(x)$ and $|x| \leq p(|y|)$. That is, honest functions do not shrink their inputs more than polynomially. Honesty is required to prevent the notion of non-FP-invertibility in Definition 3.78 below from being trivialized.

The following notion of a one-way function is based on the worst-case model in complexity theory. Cryptographic one-way functions require a stronger notion of noninvertibility that is based on average-case complexity and on inverters that are randomized (as opposed to deterministic) algorithms.

Definition 3.78 (One-Way Function).
Let $f : \Sigma^* \rightarrow \Sigma^*$ be any one-to-one function. Recall that R_f denotes the range of f.

1. *We say that f is FP-invertible if and only if there exists a function $g \in$ FP such that for each $y \in R_f$, $f(g(y)) = y$.*
2. *We say that f is a one-way function if and only if f is honest, $f \in$ FP, and f is not FP-invertible.*

Based on their above-mentioned results [JY85], Joseph and P. Young conjectured that if one-way functions exist, then not all k-creative sets are p-isomorphic to SAT, and hence the Berman–Hartmanis isomorphism conjecture fails. Specifically, they stated Conjecture 3.79 below.

---

[8] A recursively enumerable set A is *creative* if and only if there is a function $f \in \mathbb{R}$ such that for each recursively enumerable set R_i, $R_i \subseteq \overline{A}$ implies $f(i) \in \overline{A} - R_i$. The idea is that $\overline{A}$ cannot be recursively enumerable, since for each candidate R_i that potentially might be equal to $\overline{A}$, f produces an element $f(i)$ witnessing that $\overline{A} \not\subseteq R_i$. That is why f is called a *productive function for* $\overline{A}$.

Conjecture 3.79 (One-Way/Isomorphism Conjecture of Joseph and Young).
If there exist one-way functions, then there exist NP-complete sets that are mutually non-p-isomorphic.

In [JY85, You83], the question is raised of whether also the converse of Conjecture 3.79 holds. Kurtz, Mahaney, and Royer [KMR87] stated this converse implication as a conjecture.

Conjecture 3.80 (One-Way Conjecture of Kurtz, Mahaney, and Royer).
If there exist mutually non-p-isomorphic NP-complete sets, then there exist one-way functions.

Hartmanis and L. Hemaspaandra [HH91] established a relativized counterexample to Conjecture 3.80: There exists an oracle relative to which there are mutually non-p-isomorphic NP-complete sets, yet there exist no one-way functions. Similarly, J. Rogers [Rog97] provided a relativized counterexample to Conjecture 3.79: In some relativized world, the isomorphism conjecture holds (i.e., all NP-complete sets are pairwise p-isomorphic), and yet one-way functions do exist. We will not pursue this line of research any further here, but we refer to Section 3.8 for more details and pointers to the literature.

Closely related to the existence of one-way functions is the complexity class UP that was introduced by Valiant [Val76].

Definition 3.81 (Unambiguous Polynomial Time).
UP *is the class of sets L for which there exists an NPTM M such that:*

1. for each input x, $M(x)$ has at most one accepting computation path, and
2. $L = \{x \in \Sigma^* \mid M(x)$ has an accepting computation path$\}$.

NTMs satisfying the first of the two properties above are said to be unambiguous *Turing machines (or* categorical *Turing machines).*

It follows from the definition that $P \subseteq UP \subseteq NP$; none of the inclusions is known to be proper. The question of whether or not P equals UP can be characterized in terms of the existence of one-way functions.

Theorem 3.82. *The following three statements are pairwise equivalent:*

1. $P \neq UP$.
2. There exist one-way functions.
3. There exists a set $B \in P$ of boolean formulas such that each formula in B has at most one satisfying assignment and $B \cap SAT$ is not in P.

Proof. 1. We prove the equivalence of the first and the second statement. Suppose that $P \neq UP$. Let L be any set in $UP - P$, and let M be some unambiguous NPTM accepting L. For each string $x \in L$, let $\alpha_M(x)$ denote the unique accepting computation path of $M(x)$, encoded as a binary string. Define the function f by

$$f(x) = \begin{cases} y0 & \text{if } x = \alpha_M(y) \\ x1 & \text{otherwise.} \end{cases}$$

It is easy to check that f is total, one-to-one, honest, and polynomial-time computable. If f were FP-invertible, L could be decided in P by computing, given a string y, the value of $f^{-1}(y0)$; a contradiction. Thus, f is a one-way function.

Conversely, we prove the contrapositive: Suppose that P = UP, and let f be any total, honest, one-to-one function in FP. We have to show that f is FP-invertible. For any function g, define the *projection of g* by

$$\Pi_g = \{\langle x, y \rangle \mid x \in D_g \text{ and } y \le g(x)\},$$

where $\le$ denotes the standard lexicographic ordering on Σ^*. Note that for each function g that is polynomially length-bounded (i.e., there is some $p \in \mathbb{P}\text{ol}$ such that for each x, $|g(x)| \le p(|x|)$), it holds that $\Pi_g \in P$ if and only if $g \in FP$; see Exercise 3.21.

Consider the inverse function f^{-1}. Since f is honest and one-to-one, $\Pi_{f^{-1}}$ is in UP as witnessed by the following unambiguous NPTM: On input $\langle x, y \rangle$, unambiguously compute $f^{-1}(x)$ and accept if and only if $y \le f^{-1}(x)$. By assumption, $\Pi_{f^{-1}}$ is in P. Thus, f^{-1} is in FP. Hence, there exists no one-way function.

2. We prove the equivalence of the first and the third statement. Suppose that there exists a set B in P of boolean formulas such that each formula in B has at most one satisfying assignment and $B \cap \text{SAT}$ is not in P. Define an NPTM N as follows: On input φ, N deterministically checks that φ is a boolean formula in B, and if so, it guesses an assignment t of φ, and accepts if and only if t satisfies φ. Clearly, N is an unambiguous NPTM accepting $B \cap \text{SAT}$. Hence, $B \cap \text{SAT}$ is a set in UP $-$ P.

Conversely, suppose that P $\ne$ UP. Let L be any set in UP $-$ P, let M be some unambiguous NPTM accepting L, and let f_M be the Cook reduction constructed in Theorem 3.49. Thus, for each input x, $f_M(x) = F_{M,x}$ is a boolean formula such that:

$$x \in L \iff F_{M,x} \in \text{SAT}. \tag{3.19}$$

Since M is an unambiguous NPTM, $F_{M,x}$ has at most one satisfying assignment for each $x \in \Sigma^*$.

A careful inspection of the proof of Theorem 3.49 reveals that the Cook reduction is "parsimonious," i.e., the number of distinct accepting computation paths of $M(x)$ equals the number of distinct satisfying assignments of $F_{M,x}$. Furthermore, both the machine program of M and the input x are encoded into the formula $F_{M,x}$. Thus, given any formula φ, one can decide in polynomial time whether or not φ equals $F_{M,x}$ for some string x. Hence, the set $B = \{F_{M,x} \mid x \in \Sigma^*\}$ is in P. However, $B \cap \text{SAT}$ is not in P, since otherwise $L \in P$, a contradiction.   ∎

Corollary 3.83. UP *has* $\le^P_m$-*complete sets if and only if there exists a set $B \in P$ of boolean formulas such that each formula in B has at most one satisfying assignment and $B \cap \text{SAT}$ is* $\le^P_m$-*complete in* UP.

Proof.   The implication from right to left is immediate. Conversely, to prove the implication from left to right, let L be some complete language for UP, and let M

be some unambiguous NPTM accepting L. As in the proof of Theorem 3.82, the set $B = \{F_{M,x} \mid x \in \Sigma^*\}$ is in P, where $F_{M,x}$ is the result of the Cook reduction applied to $x \in \Sigma^*$. Since M is an unambiguous NPTM and since the Cook reduction is parsimonious, $B \cap \mathrm{SAT}$ is in UP. Moreover, (3.19) from the proof of Theorem 3.82 implies that $L \leq^P_m B \cap \mathrm{SAT}$ via the Cook reduction. Hence, $B \cap \mathrm{SAT}$ is $\leq^P_m$-complete in UP. ∎

Theorem 3.84. *The following three statements are pairwise equivalent:*

1. $P \neq UP \cap coUP$.
2. There exist onto one-way functions.
3. There exists a set $B \in P$ such that:
  a) $B \subseteq \mathrm{SAT}$,
  b) every formula in B has exactly one satisfying assignment, and
  c) no FP function can find the satisfying assignment to each $\varphi \in B$, i.e., the function f defined by

$$f(\varphi) = \begin{cases} \text{the unique satisfying assignment to } \varphi & \text{if } \varphi \in B \\ 0 & \text{if } \varphi \notin B \end{cases} \quad (3.20)$$

is not polynomial-time computable.

Proof. 1. The equivalence of the first and the second statement of this theorem can be proven analogously to the proof of Theorem 3.82; see Exercise 3.23.

2. We prove the equivalence of the first and the third statement. Let L be some set in $(UP \cap coUP) - P$, and let M and $\bar{M}$ be unambiguous NPTMs accepting L and $\bar{L}$, respectively. Define an NPTM N as follows: On input x, N nondeterministically branches for one step guessing whether $x \in L$ or $x \notin L$. On the one branch, N simulates $M(x)$; on the other branch, N simulates $\bar{M}(x)$. Hence,

$$L(N) = L(M) \cup L(\bar{M}) = L \cup \bar{L} = \Sigma^*.$$

Let $F_{N,x}$ be the result of the Cook reduction with respect to N applied to $x \in \Sigma^*$. Since both M and $\bar{M}$ are unambiguous NPTMs, N is also an unambiguous NPTM. Since the Cook reduction is parsimonious, $F_{N,x}$ has at most one satisfying assignment for each $x \in \Sigma^*$.

Define $B = \{F_{N,x} \mid x \in \Sigma^*\}$. As in the proof of Theorem 3.82, $B \in P$. Since $L(N) = \Sigma^*$, $B \subseteq \mathrm{SAT}$. Thus, the first two conditions, (3.a) and (3.b), of the third item are met by B. To prove the third condition, (3.c), note that from a given satisfying assignment to $F_{N,x}$ it is easy to determine whether $x \in L$ or $x \notin L$ was guessed in the initial nondeterministic branching of $N(x)$. Thus, if the function f defined in Equation (3.20) were polynomial-time computable, then L would be in P, a contradiction. Hence, $f \notin FP$, which proves (3.c).

Conversely, suppose that B is a set in P satisfying the three conditions, (3.a) through (3.c), in the third item of the theorem.

For any boolean formula $\varphi(x_1, x_2, \ldots, x_n)$ and for any (partial) assignment $t = (a_1, a_2, \ldots, a_k)$ to the variables of φ, let φ_t be the formula that results from plugging the a_i into φ; thus, φ_t depends only on the remaining variables. Define the set $\hat{B}$ by

$$\hat{B} = \left\{ \langle \varphi, t \rangle \, \middle| \, \begin{array}{l} \varphi \in B, \, t \text{ is a (partial) assignment to } \varphi, \text{ and} \\ \varphi_t \text{ has a unique satisfying assignment} \end{array} \right\}.$$

Clearly, $\hat{B}$ is in UP. If $\hat{B}$ were also in P, then a satisfying assignment for each formula in B could be constructed, using $\hat{B}$ and the self-reducibility of SAT. This would contradict the third condition that B satisfies. Hence, $\hat{B} \notin$ P.

To see that $\hat{B} \in$ coUP, note that

$$\langle \varphi, t \rangle \notin \hat{B} \iff \varphi \notin B \vee (\varphi \in B \wedge \bar{\varphi}_t \text{ has a unique satisfying assignment}),$$

where $\bar{\varphi}_t$ is defined to be the formula resulting from φ by picking up all assignments that contradict t. For example, if $t = (a_1, a_2, \ldots, a_k)$, then

$$\bar{\varphi}_t = \varphi_{(\neg a_1)} \vee \varphi_{(a_1, \neg a_2)} \vee \cdots \vee \varphi_{(a_1, a_2, \ldots, a_{k-1}, \neg a_k)}.$$

Thus, $\bar{\varphi}_t$ has at most one satisfying assignment. Hence, $\hat{B} \in (\mathrm{UP} \cap \mathrm{coUP}) - \mathrm{P}$. ∎

3.7 Exercises and Problems

Exercise 3.1 (a) Prove that every k-tape DTM running in time t can be simulated by an equivalent one-tape DTM running in time $\mathcal{O}(t^2)$.

(b) Prove the analogous result for nondeterministic Turing machines.

Exercise 3.2 Look at Definition 3.2. Replace the condition "$\mathrm{time}_M(n) \leq t(n)$" in the definition of the complexity class $\mathrm{DTIME}(t)$ by "$\mathrm{time}_M(n) \leq_{\mathrm{ae}} t(n)$," and replace the condition "$\mathrm{space}_M(n) \leq s(n)$" in the definition of the complexity class $\mathrm{DSPACE}(s)$ by "$\mathrm{space}_M(n) \leq_{\mathrm{ae}} s(n)$." Do these changes in the definition yield different complexity classes? What about the nondeterministic classes $\mathrm{NTIME}(t)$ and $\mathrm{NSPACE}(s)$ from Definition 3.4?

Exercise 3.3 Show that the deterministic and nondeterministic time and space functions from Definitions 3.1 and Definition 3.3 are Blum complexity measures.

Exercise 3.4 Look at the proof of Theorem 3.10. Suppose you are given a DTM M' that does not satisfy any of the conditions the DTM M in that proof is supposed to satisfy. Construct a DTM M that is equivalent to M' (i.e., $L(M) = L(M')$) and satisfies each of the following conditions: (a) M has only one tape that (b) is infinite in just one direction, (c) the tape cells are enumerated by 1, 2, etc., and (d) M's head makes a left turn only on even-numbered cells. An informal description of M suffices.

Exercise 3.5 Define the following functions:

$$c(n) = n; \quad d(n) = 5n; \quad e(n) = n \log n; \quad f(n) = n^2;$$
$$g(n) = n \left((n \bmod 2) + n((n+1) \bmod 2)\right);$$
$$h(n) = n \left(n(n \bmod 2) + (n+1) \bmod 2\right).$$

(a) Prove that $c \preceq d$ and $d \preceq c$ and $c \prec e$ and $d \prec e \prec f$.

(b) Prove that $g \prec_{io} h$ and $g \succ_{io} h$ and $g \preceq f$ and $g \prec_{io} f$ and $g \succeq_{io} f$.

Exercise 3.6 **(a)** Show that the following functions:

$$\lceil \log n \rceil, \quad n^2, \quad 2^n, \quad \text{and} \quad n!$$

are space-constructible and, except $\lceil \log n \rceil$, are time-constructible.

(b) Show that if $s_1 : \mathbb{N} \to \mathbb{N}$ and $s_2 : \mathbb{N} \to \mathbb{N}$ are space-constructible functions, then so are the functions

$$s_1(n) + s_2(n), \quad s_1(n) \cdot s_2(n), \quad 2^{s_1(n)}, \quad \text{and} \quad s_1(n)^{s_2(n)}.$$

(c) Show that if $t_1 : \mathbb{N} \to \mathbb{N}$ and $t_2 : \mathbb{N} \to \mathbb{N}$ are time-constructible functions, then so are the functions

$$t_1(n) + t_2(n), \quad t_1(n) \cdot t_2(n), \quad 2^{t_1(n)}, \quad \text{and} \quad t_1(n)^{t_2(n)}.$$

Exercise 3.7 **(a)** Prove Corollary 3.18.

(b) Use appropriate results from Sections 3.3 and 3.4 to strengthen Corollary 3.32 to:

$$\text{NLINSPACE} \subset \text{PSPACE}.$$

(c) Show that for each constant $k > 1$,

$$
\begin{aligned}
\text{L} \subset \text{DSPACE}((\log n)^k) &\subset \text{DSPACE}((\log n)^{k+1}) \\
\subset \text{POLYLOGSPACE} &\subset \text{LINSPACE} \\
\subset \text{DSPACE}(n^k) &\subset \text{DSPACE}(n^{k+1}) \\
\subset \text{PSPACE} &\subset \text{DSPACE}(2^{k \cdot n}) \\
\subset \text{DSPACE}(2^{(k+1)n}) &\subset \text{EXPSPACE}.
\end{aligned}
$$

Exercise 3.8 Let M be a DTM with k working tapes that, on inputs of length n, works in space $s(n)$ and in time $t(n)$. Construct a one-tape DTM N simulating M such that:

(a) $L(N) = L(M)$;

(b) N works in space $s(n)$;

(c) N works in time $(t(n))^2$.

Hint: Subdivide N's working tape into k tracks. If neccessary, use the linear speed-up theorem to get rid of constants.

Exercise 3.9 Prove Lemma 3.25: For each set $L \subseteq \Sigma^*$,

1. $L \in E \iff \mathtt{Tally}(L) \in P$, and
2. $L \in NE \iff \mathtt{Tally}(L) \in NP$.

Exercise 3.10 Show that $NP \subseteq E$ if and only if for each $L \in NP$, $\mathtt{Tally}(L) \in P$.

Exercise 3.11 Prove Lemma 3.36:

1. $A \leq_m^P B$ implies $\overline{A} \leq_m^P \overline{B}$, yet in general it is not true that $A \leq_m^P \overline{A}$.
2. The relation $\leq_m^P$ is both reflexive and transitive, yet not antisymmetric.

   Note: Reflexivity and transitivity are defined in Exercise 3.24. *Antisymmetry* of a relation $\leq$ means that whenever $A \leq B$ and $B \leq A$, it follows that $A = B$.
3. P, NP, and PSPACE are $\leq_m^P$-closed.
4. If $A \leq_m^P B$ and A is $\mathcal{C}$-hard for some complexity class $\mathcal{C}$, then B is $\mathcal{C}$-hard.
5. Let $\mathcal{C}$ and $\mathcal{D}$ be any complexity classes. If $\mathcal{C}$ is $\leq_m^P$-closed and B is $\leq_m^P$-complete for $\mathcal{D}$, then $\mathcal{D} \subseteq \mathcal{C}$ if and only if $B \in \mathcal{C}$. In particular, if B is NP-complete, then $P = NP$ if and only if $B \in P$.

Exercise 3.12 (a) Prove Theorem 3.40: L and NL are $\leq_m^{\log}$-closed.

(b) Prove that $\mathtt{GAP}_{\mathtt{acyclic}}$ is in NL; see Lemma 3.47.

Exercise 3.13 Look at the construction of the boolean formula $f(x) = F_x$ in the proof of Cook's Theorem; see Theorem 3.49.

(a) Argue that the Cook reduction f can be computed in polynomial time.

(b) Argue that the Cook reduction f can be computed even in logarithmic space.

Exercise 3.14 (a) Prove Lemma 3.53: For each graph G and for each subset U of $V(G)$, the following are equivalent:

1. U is a vertex cover of G.
2. $\overline{U} = V(G) - U$ is an independent set of G.
3. $\overline{U} = V(G) - U$ is a clique of the co-graph of G, which is defined as the graph with vertex set $V(G)$ and with the following set of edges: $\{\{u, v\} \mid u, v \in V(G) \text{ and } \{u, v\} \notin E(G)\}$.

(b) Apply Lemma 3.53 to prove that the problems $\mathtt{Clique}$, $\mathtt{IS}$, and $\mathtt{VC}$ are pair-wise $\leq_m^P$-equivalent, i.e., for any two problems A and B chosen among $\mathtt{Clique}$, $\mathtt{IS}$, and $\mathtt{VC}$, $A \leq_m^P B$ and $B \leq_m^P A$.

(c) Show that $\mathtt{Clique}$, $\mathtt{IS}$, and $\mathtt{VC}$ are problems in NP.

Exercise 3.15 Theorem 3.56 says that $\mathtt{3\text{-}Colorability}$ is NP-complete. Prove (3.14) and (3.15) from the proof of this theorem.

Exercise 3.16 Prove that $\mathtt{2\text{-}Colorability}$ is in P.

Exercise 3.17 Look at the proof of Theorem 3.63, which says that 3-DM is NP-complete. Argue formally that (3.18) from this proof is true:

$$\varphi \text{ is satisfiable} \iff R \text{ contains a tripartite matching } M \text{ of size } \|U\|.$$

Hint: Use the implicit remarks made during the construction of the ternary relation R in that proof.

Exercise 3.18 In the proof of Theorem 3.65, the claim is made that the 3-DM problem is a restriction of the SetPacking problem. Why is this claim true?

Exercise 3.19 Prove that SOS is in NP; see Theorem 3.67.

Exercise 3.20 Prove Fact 3.69: GI is in NP.

Exercise 3.21 Prove the claim made in the proof of Theorem 3.82: For each function g that is polynomially length-bounded (i.e., there is some $p \in$ Pol such that for each x, $|g(x)| \leq p(|x|)$), it holds that $\Pi_g \in$ P if and only if $g \in$ FP. Here, Π_g is defined by

$$\Pi_g = \{\langle x, y \rangle \mid x \in D_g \text{ and } y \leq g(x)\}.$$

Hint: The direction from right to left is trivial, and the direction from left to right employs an easy binary search algorithm. The proof can be found in [Mil76].

Exercise 3.22 Recall that coNP $= \{L \mid \overline{L} \in \text{NP}\}$ is the class of complements of NP sets.

(a) Name five problems of your choice (and define them formally) that are $\leq^p_m$-complete for coNP.

(b) Does the class NP $\cap$ coNP have $\leq^p_m$-complete sets?

(c) What about NP $\cup$ coNP?

Exercise 3.23 Prove the equivalence of the first two statements of Theorem 3.84: P $\neq$ UP $\cap$ coUP if and only if there exist onto one-way functions.

Exercise 3.24 Based on Definition 3.72, define the following relation on sets:

$$A \cong_p B \iff A \text{ is p-isomorphic to } B.$$

Prove that $\cong_p$ is an *equivalence relation*, i.e., it satisfies the following properties:
- *reflexivity*: for each A, $A \cong_p A$;
- *symmetry*: for each A and B, if $A \cong_p B$ then $B \cong_p A$;
- *transitivity*: for each A, B, and C, if both $A \cong_p B$ and $B \cong_p C$, then $A \cong_p C$.

Problem 3.1 (Lower Bound Proofs by Crossing Sequences)

(a) Design a DTM M with one input tape and one working tape that decides the set $S = \{x2^{|x|}x \mid x \in \{0,1\}^*\}$ in real-time. That is, on input z, M's input head is scanning z from left to right, the computation halts after exactly $|z|$ steps, and M accepts z if and only if $z \in S$. Describe M both informally and formally.

(b) Show that any DTM with only one working tape and no separate input tape requires time at least quadratic in the input size for solving the set S above.

Hint for (b): Let M with $L(M) = S$ be a DTM as above, and let $x = uv$ be any input string of length n.

A sequence of states of M, denoted by $cs(u|v) = (s_1, s_2, \ldots, s_n)$, is called the *crossing sequence of $M(x)$ at the cell-boundary between u and v* if and only if M's head crosses this cell-boundary exactly n times during the computation of $M(x)$ and M is in state s_i during the ith crossing.

Lemma 3.85. *If $uv \in L(M)$ and $yz \in L(M)$ and $cs(u|v) = cs(y|z)$, then $uz \in L(M)$ and $yv \in L(M)$.*

Prove Lemma 3.85. Then, using Lemma 3.85, show that $\text{time}_M(n) >_{\text{io}} c \cdot n^2$ for some constant c. To this end, use the notion of a *short crossing sequence with respect to* n, which is a crossing sequence with less than $n/\log q - 1$ states, where $q > 1$ is the number of M's states. Show that there are less short crossing sequences with respect to n than strings of length $3n$ in S.

Problem 3.2 (Primality Problem)

(a) Prove that the primality problem is in coNP.

(b) Can you also prove membership of this problem in NP?

Hint: The first known NP algorithm for the primality problem is due to Pratt, and its nontrivial proof can be found in [Pra75].

See Section 7.2 for results that improve the above assertions. In particular, note the outstanding result by Agrawal, Kayal, and Saxena [AKS02] that the primality problem even is in P, stated as Theorem 7.27; see also Problem 7.2.

3.8 Summary and Bibliographic Remarks

General Remarks: There are many very good textbooks and monographs on complexity theory. There are many very good books on cryptology. The present book is not meant to replace but to complement these books—each of which focuses on either complexity theory or cryptology—by emphasizing the interrelation between these two areas and taking a unified approach.

In complexity theory, the following books have become or are about to become classics: the books by Balcázar, Díaz, and Gabarró [BDG95, BDG90], Bovet and Crescenzi [BC93], Du and Ko [DK00], Garey and Johnson [GJ79], L. Hemaspaandra and Ogihara [HO02], Homer and Selman [HS01], Papadimitriou [Pap94] and Steiglitz [PS82], Reischuk [Rei90], Wagner and Wechsung [WW86, Wec00], and Wegener [Weg87, Weg03]. Vollmer [Vol99] has written a very useful book about circuit complexity. Brandstädt et al. [BLS99] provide a very comprehensive survey of graph classes and their algorithmic complexity, a follow-up to Golumbic's text [Gol80]. A survey of algorithms in complexity theory can be found in [Rot04a].

Specific Remarks: The beginnings of computational complexity theory are marked by the work of Hartmanis, Lewis, and Stearns. Their groundbreaking papers [HS65, SHL65, HLS65, LSH65] focus on robustness of the multitape Turing machine model, introduce the complexity measures time and space, and establish their fundamental properties. In particular, the linear tape-compression and speed-up theorems and the hierarchy theorems for time and space are due to them; Theorem 3.19, the strongest version of the time hierarchy theorem known, was obtained by Hennie and Stearns [HS66]. Originally, their result is formulated as follows (where the constructibility requirements are omitted here for better readability): If $t_1 \log t_1 \prec_{io} t_2$ then $\mathrm{DTIME}(t_2) \not\subseteq \mathrm{DTIME}(t_1)$. In contrast, Theorem 3.19 states their result as follows: If $t_1 \prec_{io} t_2$ then $\mathrm{DTIME}(t_2 \log t_2) \not\subseteq \mathrm{DTIME}(t_1)$. The two formulations are equivalent; a grateful acknowledgment for this observation is owed to Wechsung, who generously shared his personal notes with the author, see also [Wec00, WW86].

Stearns [Ste90] wrote a nice treatise on the intellectual adventures, excitement, and fascination of those early years. In recognition of their work, which established the foundations for the field of computational complexity theory, Juris Hartmanis and Richard Stearns received the prestigious Turing Award in 1993.

The elegant theory of abstract complexity measures, which are now called Blum complexity measures, was developed by Blum [Blu67]. In 1995, Manuel Blum too won the Turing Award, in recognition of his contributions to the foundations of computational complexity theory and its application to cryptography and program checking.

Book's upward separation technique [Boo74], which led to Theorem 3.26, was strengthened in two regards: with respect to the language witnessing the separation and with respect to the range of applicability to complexity classes other than NP and NE. Hartmanis, Immerman, and Sewelson [Har83b, HIS85] proved that NE = E if and only if every *sparse* language in NP is in P.[9] To this end, they developed a clever encoding of sparse sets by tally sets. Buhrman, E. Hemaspaandra, and Longpré [BHL95] discovered an even more powerful tally encoding of sparse sets. Using this stronger tally encoding, Rao, Rothe, and Watanabe [RRW94] extended the result of Hartmanis et al. [Har83b, HIS85] to several pairs of exponentially related complexity classes other than NP and NE. The main result of Rao et al. [RRW94] is a general condition sufficient to yield upward separation by sparse sets. In particular, this sufficient condition shows that FewP contains a sparse set not in P if and only if FewE $\neq$ E, where FewE and E are the exponential-time analogs of FewP and P. This result refutes a conjecture of Allender [All91], who suspected that FewP defies upward separation in suitable relativized worlds. It is still open whether the analogous result for UP is true. There is a number of results showing the limitations of the upward separation technique, including the work by Allender [All91] and by Hemaspaandra and Jha [HJ95]; see [All91, HJ95, RRW94] for related results and a more comprehensive list of references. Theorem 3.29, which establishes a quadratic

---

[9] Recall that a language is said to be *sparse* if and only if it has at most polynomially many strings at each length; see also Definition 5.58. Thus, every tally set is a sparse set, since tally sets have at most one string per length.

upper bound on the cost of trading nondeterminism for determinism, is due to Savitch [Sav70].

Complexity theory arose from the desire to understand efficient (or "feasible") computation and its limitations. Most central to complexity theory are thus the fundamental complexity classes P and NP, deterministic and nondeterministic polynomial time. Cobham [Cob64] and Edmonds [Edm65] were the first to perceive the class P as the most sensible formal embodiment of the informal term of "feasible" computation. Interestingly, Gödel addressed the issue of defining "efficient computation" already in 1956. His rediscovered letter to von Neumann stresses the importance of the number of steps that a Turing machine needs for solving some problem. Moreover, he gave two examples of polynomial time bounds, linear time and quadratic time, as instances of "efficient computation" as opposed to the exponential time bounds required by brute-force algorithms. Hartmanis [Har89] and Sipser [Sip92] surveyed the history of the P versus NP question, discussing also Gödel's letter.

Cook laid the foundations for the theory of NP-completeness by proving Theorem 3.49, which provides the first NP-completeness result. For his seminal paper [Coo71], he received the Turing Award in 1982. His result that SAT is NP-complete was independently discovered by Levin [Lev73]. Cook also established Theorem 3.51: 3-SAT is NP-complete.

Following Cook's pathbreaking result, the exploration of the boundaries and nature of the class of NP-complete problems has been one of the most active and important research areas in computer science. Most notably, Karp [Kar72] introduced the now standard methodology for proving problems NP-complete with respect to the $\leq_m^P$-reducibility, which led to the classification of thousands of problems as being NP-complete. These problems are viewed as computationally intractable. For this achievement and for his contributions to the theory of algorithms including the development of efficient algorithms for network flow and other combinatorial optimization problems, Karp received the Turing Award in 1985. Theorems 3.54, 3.63, 3.65, and 3.67 are due to him.

The proof of Theorem 3.56 is from Stockmeyer [Sto73], see also Garey, Johnson, and Stockmeyer [GJS76]. Theorem 3.58 is due to Garey, Johnson, and Tarjan (as cited in [GJ79]); the proof presented here is due to Kaplan and R. Shamir [KS94]. The literature on NP-completeness results is so extensive and this topic is covered by so many books that we do not go into further detail here. One of the best sources on the theory of NP-completeness is still the classic book by Garey and Johnson [GJ79]; see also Johnson's ongoing NP-completeness column [Joh81].

For many NP-complete problems, it is known that they can be efficiently solved for suitably restricted instances. Thus, the question arises of precisely where the boundary between easily solvable instances and hard instances lies. For illustration, we state some such results for the example of the domatic number problem:[10] By the construction given in the proof of Theorem 3.58, this problem remains NP-complete

---

[10] For graph-theoretical notions and special graph classes not defined here, we refer to the monograph by Brandstädt et al. [BLS99], a follow-up to the classic text by Golumbic [Gol80].

even if the given graph belongs to certain special classes of perfect graphs, including circular-arc graphs (see also [Bon85]), split graphs (which in particular contain the chordal and co-chordal graphs), and bipartite graphs (which in particular contain the comparability graphs). In contrast, DNP is known to be polynomial-time solvable for certain other graph classes, including strongly chordal graphs (which in particular contain the interval graphs and the path graphs) [Far84] and proper circular-arc graphs [Bon85]. Furthermore, approximability properties of virtually all important NP-complete problems have been studied in depth; see, for example, the books [ACG$^+$03, Vaz03, Pap94]. To state one such result for the domatic number problem, Feige, Halldórsson, Kortsarz, and Srinivasan [FHKS02] showed that every graph G with n vertices has a domatic partition with $(1-o(1))(min\text{-}deg(G)+1)/\ln n$ sets that can be found in polynomial time. Thus, there is a $(1+o(1))\ln n$ approximation algorithm for the domatic number $\delta(G)$. This is a tight bound, since the domatic number cannot be approximated within a factor of $(1-\varepsilon)\ln n$, where $\varepsilon > 0$ is any fixed constant, unless NP $\subseteq$ DTIME($n^{\log\log n}$).

The development of the theory of NP-completeness entailed the search for completeness results for other complexity classes as well, including the identification of $\leq_m^{\log}$-complete problems for P and NL. Theorem 3.43 was proven independently by Savitch [Sav73] and by Jones [Jon75], who thus found the first $\leq_m^{\log}$-complete problem for NL, namely GAP. Lemmas 3.46 and 3.48, which imply that 2-SAT is coNL-complete, are due to Jones, Lien, and Laaser [JLL76]. Theorem 3.45 follows from this result by virtue of the equality NL $=$ coNL, which was proven independently by Immerman [Imm88] and Szelepcsényi [Sze88]; see Theorem 3.33 and its Corollary 3.34. Problems $\leq_m^{\log}$-complete for P can be found in [Coo74, JL76]; see also Theorem 5.72 in Section 5.6. Logarithmically space-bounded reducibilities such as $\leq_m^{\log}$ were studied by Ladner and Lynch [LL76].

Theorem 3.68 is due to Ladner [Lad75]. It is the complexity-theoretic analog of the solution to Post's problem in computability theory, which asks whether there are more than two recursively enumerable Turing degrees. Post's problem was independently solved by Friedberg and Muchnik in 1956. The Friedberg–Muchnik Theorem says that there exist recursively enumerable sets that are neither decidable nor complete for RE, the class of recursively enumerable sets.

The graph isomorphism problem (see Definition 2.49) has been intensely studied in complexity theory. Still, it has eluded every attempt of classification as yet. GI is one of the most prominent candidates of a problem that is neither in P nor NP-complete, and Chapter 6 will provide some evidence in favor of this view. The best source on results and the state of the art for this problem is the book [KST93] by Köbler, Schöning, and Torán.

Self-reducibility has appeared in a variety of guises, and many different notions of self-reducibility have been introduced and intensely studied. Most notably, the still growing body of results on self-reducibility is due to the work by Schnorr [Sch76, Sch79], A. Meyer and Paterson [MP79], Balcázar [Bal90], Buhrman, van Helden, and Torenvliet [BT96, BvHT93], E. Hemaspaandra, Naik, Ogihara, and Selman [Sel88a, Sel79, Sel82a, Sel82b, HNOS96]. For an overview of results on self-reducibility, we refer to the surveys by Goldsmith, Joseph, and Young [GJY87, JY90].

One example of a topic for which the notion of self-reducibility is central is a property dubbed "search reducing to decision," see [HNOS96] and the references cited therein. This means that if a decision problem (e.g., GI) is efficiently solvable and if this decision problem is self-reducible, then an actual solution to it (an isomorphism between the given graphs in the example of GI) can be constructed efficiently.

Gál, Halevi, Lipton, and Petrank [GHLP99] did some interesting work relating the complexity of finding partial solutions of hard NP problems to that of finding complete solutions. This property might be dubbed "complete search reducing to partial search." In particular, they showed for various NP problems A that, given an instance x in A, computing a small fraction of a solution for x is no easier than computing a complete solution for x. For example, given two isomorphic graphs, computing roughly logarithmically many pairs of vertices that are mapped onto each other by a complete isomorphism φ between the graphs is as hard as computing φ itself [GHLP99]. Große, Rothe, and Wechsung [GRW02] optimally improved this result by showing that computing even a single pair of vertices that are mapped onto each other by a complete isomorphism φ between two isomorphic graphs is as hard as computing φ itself; see also Problem 5.3. The proof of this result is inspired by the proof that GI is self-reducible.

The Berman–Hartmanis isomorphism conjecture [BH77] is one of the most intensely studied questions in complexity theory. Their work on p-isomorphic sets in NP initiated various lines of research and many further results. The importance of this conjecture and of the work it has triggered can be seen from the mere number of survey and research papers on these subjects, including the papers by Mahaney [Mah86, Mah89], P. Young [You90, You92], Kurtz, Mahaney, and Royer [KMR90, KMR87, KMR88], L. Hemaspaandra, Ogihara, and Watanabe [HOW92], and Arvind et al. [AHH$^+$93]. In particular, the work on the question of whether or not NP can have sparse $\leq^P_m$-complete sets culminated in Mahaney's [Mah82] resolution of another conjecture by Berman and Hartmanis stated as Theorem 3.75. His result is based on previous work by Berman [Ber78], who proved that if P $\neq$ NP then there are no tally coNP-hard sets, and by Fortune [For79], who proved that if P $\neq$ NP then there are no sparse coNP-hard sets. Theorem 3.76 is due to Hartmanis and Mahaney [HM80]. Section 5.9 gives more details on follow-up results of Theorem 3.75, and in particular states Ogihara and Watanabe's [OW91] improvement of Theorem 3.75 to reductions more general than $\leq^P_m$.

The question of whether or not there can exist sparse complete sets was also investigated for complexity classes other than NP and for reductions other than $\leq^P_m$. For exponential time classes, A. Meyer (cf. [BH77]) proved by diagonalization that neither E nor NE have sparse $\leq^P_m$-complete sets. Based on evidence similar to the results leading to Conjecture 3.73, Hartmanis [Har78] raised the analogous question also for the classes NL and P, where the notion of p-isomorphisms has to be replaced by log-space computable isomorphisms. Building on breakthrough results by Ogihara [Ogi95], Cai and Sivakumar resolved the conjectures of Hartmanis both for P and for NL:

- If L ≠ P, then no sparse set is $\leq_{\mathrm{m}}^{\log}$-complete in P; see [CS99].
- If L ≠ NL, then no sparse set is $\leq_{\mathrm{m}}^{\log}$-complete in NL; see [CS00].

Further results related to complexity-bounded isomorphisms and the isomorphism conjecture were obtained by Allender [All88], Ganesan and Homer [GH92], Hartmanis [Har83a], Homer and Selman [HS89], Ko, Long, and Du [KLD86], Mahaney and P. Young [MY85], and Watanabe [Wat91].

The isomorphism conjecture was also intensely studied with respect to relativizations. Combining previous constructions by Kurtz (in an unpublished paper) and Rackoff [Rac82], Hartmanis and L. Hemaspaandra [HH91] provided an oracle relative to which the isomorphism conjecture fails and no one-way functions exist, thus providing a relativized counterexample to Conjecture 3.80. Kurtz, Mahaney, and Royer [KMR89] proved that the isomorphism conjecture fails relative to a random oracle, and obtained further relativized results in [KMR87]. Extending previous results by Goldsmith and Joseph [GJ86], Fenner, Fortnow, and Kurtz [FFK92] constructed an oracle relative to which the isomorphism conjecture holds. They raised the question of whether there is a relativized world in which the isomorphism conjecture holds and yet P ≠ UP, i.e., there exist one-way functions. This question was answered by J. Rogers [Rog97] who thus obtained a relativized counterexample to Conjecture 3.79.

Valiant [Val76] introduced the class UP, see Definition 3.81. In their work on P-printable sets[11] and on sparse sets in P, Allender and Rubinstein [AR88, All86] generalized UP by defining the class FewP. A language is in FewP if and only if it is accepted by an NPTM that never has more than polynomially many accepting paths. Theorem 3.82 in particular says that one-to-one one-way functions exist if and only if P ≠ UP. Analogously, Allender [All86, All85] proved that polynomial-to-one one-way functions exist if and only if P ≠ FewP; see [RH02] for a number of related results. The study of one-way functions in complexity theory was initiated by Grollmann and Selman [GS88] and others. The notion introduced in Definition 3.78 and the equivalence of the first two items in Theorems 3.82 and 3.84 are due to them and, independently, to Berman [Ber77] and Ko [Ko85]. The equivalence of the first and third items of both these theorems is due to Hartmanis and L. Hemaspaandra [HH88]; see also [RH02]. Corollary 3.83 is also from [HH88]. In addition, this paper presents an oracle relative to which UP has no complete language, and another oracle relative to which P ≠ UP ≠ NP and UP has a complete language.

That P ≠ UP ∩ coUP implies the third item of Theorem 3.84 is the UP analog of the Borodin–Demers Theorem. Borodin and Demers [BD76] proved that if P ≠ NP ∩ coNP, then there exists a set S in P of satisfiable boolean formulas such that no polynomial-time computable function can print a satisfying assignment for each formula in S. A number of related results were obtained by Fenner, Fortnow, Naik, and J. Rogers [FFNR96] and, independently, by L. Hemaspaandra, Rothe, and Wechsung [HRW97a, HRW97b, RH02]. For example, in [HRW97a], the class $\mathrm{EASY}_{\forall}^{\vee}$ is defined as the class of all NP sets L such that every NPTM accepting

---

[11] Informally speaking, a set is P-printable if all its elements up to a given length can be printed in polynomial time.

L always (i.e., for each input) has polynomial-time computable certificates. Note that $\text{EASY}_\forall^\vee \subseteq \text{P}$. Using this notation, the Borodin–Demers Theorem becomes: If $\text{P} \neq \text{NP} \cap \text{coNP}$, then $\text{P} \neq \text{EASY}_\forall^\vee$. Moreover, characterizations of $\text{EASY}_\forall^\vee$ and related classes are given in terms of Kolmogorov complexity. In [RH02], the UP and FewP analogs of $\text{EASY}_\forall^\vee$ are investigated.

Relatedly, L. Hemaspaandra and Rothe [HR00, RH02] studied the question of whether the existence of one-way permutations can be characterized by some separation of standard complexity classes, a question raised also in [GS88]. A one-way permutation is a total, one-to-one, onto one-way function. The ultimate answer to this question was given by Homan and Thakur [HT02, HT03b]: One-way permutations exist if and only if $\text{P} \neq \text{UP} \cap \text{coUP}$.

Related to the study of complexity classes of sets such as P and NP is the analogous study of complexity classes of functions. For example, FP is the function analog of P. In his seminal papers [Val79a, Val79b], Valiant introduced the function classes $\#\text{P}$ and $\#\text{P}_1$ that capture the complexity of counting the number of NP solutions: $\#\text{P}$ is the class of functions that count the number of solutions to NP problems (see also Section 6.4), and $\#\text{P}_1$ is the class of functions that count the number of solutions of tally NP sets. That is, the only difference between $\#\text{P}$ and $\#\text{P}_1$ functions is that the former have inputs in binary and the latter have inputs in unary representation.

For example, consider the problem of computing the permanent of a given matrix. Denoting the (i, j) entry of an $n \times n$ integer matrix A by $a_{i,j}$, the *permanent of A* is defined as $perm(A) = \sum_{\pi \in \mathfrak{S}_n} \prod_{i=1}^n a_{i,\pi(i)}$. Valiant [Val79a] proved that computing the permanent is $\#\text{P}$-complete, i.e., $perm \in \#\text{P}$ and $\#\text{P} \subseteq \text{FP}^{perm}$, where $perm$ is used as a function oracle. In contrast, the determinant of a matrix can be computed in polynomial time by Gaussian elimination. More recent results about the hardness of computing the permanent were obtained by Cai, Pavan, and Sivakumar [CPS99].

$\#\text{P}_1$ contains interesting natural problems as well. For example, consider the self-avoiding walk problem (see, e.g., Welsh's book [Wel93]), a classical problem of statistical physics and polymer chemistry. The self-avoiding walk problem is to compute, given an integer n in unary, the number of self-avoiding walks on the two-dimensional grid having length n and rooted at the origin. Valiant [Val79b] asked whether this problem is $\#\text{P}_1$-complete. This question is still open. Liśkiewicz, Ogihara, and Toda [OT01, LOT03] gave a partial answer to this question by proving certain variants of the self-avoiding walk problem $\#\text{P}$-complete in two-dimensional grid graphs and in hypercube graphs.

The most central question regarding $\#\text{P}$ and $\#\text{P}_1$ is whether or not they are contained in FP. Köbler [Köb89] proved that $\#\text{P} = \text{FP}$ is equivalent to $\text{P} = \text{PP}$, where PP denotes "probabilistic polynomial time," a class to be defined and studied in Chapter 6. Thus, it is very unlikely that every $\#\text{P}$ function can be computed in FP. More results about the important class $\#\text{P}$ and other functional complexity classes can be found in the excellent surveys by Selman [Sel94] and Fortnow [For97], in Chapter 9 of Wechsung's book [Wec00], and also in Chapter 6.

If $\#\text{P}_1 \subseteq \text{FP}$ then all tally NP sets are in P, which implies $\text{NE} = \text{E}$ by Book's upward separation result stated here as Theorem 3.26. Goldsmith, Ogihara, and Rothe [GOR98, GOR00] proved even more unlikely complexity class collapses from the hypothesis $\#P_1 \subseteq FP$. In particular, they proved that $\#P_1 \subseteq FP$ implies $P = BPP$ and $PH \subseteq \oplus P$, where PH is the polynomial hierarchy (see Definition 5.29 in Section 5.2) and BPP and $\oplus P$ are defined in Chapter 6. Moreover, they showed that $\#P_1 \subseteq FP$ if and only if every P set has an easy (i.e., polynomial-time computable) census function. The main result in [GOR00] is that every $\#P_1^{PH}$ function can be computed in $FP^{\#P_1^{\#P_1}}$. Consequently, every P set has an easy census function if and only if every set in the polynomial hierarchy does.

Census functions are a central notion in complexity theory and have proven useful in many contexts, including the Berman–Hartmanis isomorphism conjecture (see [BH77] and Section 3.6.2), the work on the existence of Turing-hard sparse sets for various complexity classes (see [KL80, KS85, BBS86a, HR97b] and Section 5.9), the results relating the computation times for NP sets to their densities and the results on P-printability (see [HY84, AR88, GH96]), the upward separation technique (see [Har83b, HIS85, All91, RRW94, HJ95] and Section 3.3), the results on positive relativization and relativization to sparse oracles (see [Lon85, LS86, BBS86a]), the collapse of the strong exponential-time hierarchy established by L. Hemaspaandra [Hem89], and the above-mentioned work on $\#P_1$ relating tally NP sets to easy census functions [GOR00].

4

Foundations of Cryptology

"But," said I, returning him the slip, "I am as much in the dark as ever. Were all the jewels of Golconda awaiting me upon my solution of this enigma, I am quite sure that I should be unable to earn them."
"And yet," said Legrande, "the solution is by no means so difficult as you might be led to imagine from the first hasty inspection of the characters. These characters, as any one might readily guess, form a cipher—that is to say, they convey a meaning; but then from what is known of Kidd, I could not suppose him capable of constructing any of the more abstruse cryptographs. I made up my mind, at once, that this was of a simple species—such, however, as would appear, to the crude intellect of the sailor, absolutely insoluble without the key."

(From "The Gold-Bug" by Edgar Allan Poe, Random House, Inc., 1965)

4.1 Tasks and Aims of Cryptology

Cryptography is the art and science of encrypting texts and messages such that unauthorized decryption is prevented. Cryptanalysis is the art and science of breaking existing cryptosystems, i.e., determining the encryption keys used and deciphering encrypted texts and messages without authorization. Cryptology comprises both these fields, cryptography and cryptanalysis.

Cryptography

A typical cryptographic scenario is depicted in Figure 1.1 in Chapter 1. Alice and Bob are communicating over an insecure channel such as a public telephone line or the internet. Erich is eavesdropping on their conversation. To protect themselves against eavesdropping, Alice and Bob encrypt their messages using a cryptosystem.

Definition 4.1 (Cryptosystem).

*   *A* cryptosystem *is a quintuple* $S = (M, C, K, \mathcal{E}, \mathcal{D})$ *such that:*
    1. *M, C, and K are sets, where M is the* message space *(or "plaintext space" or "cleartext space"), C is the* ciphertext space, *and K is the* key space.
    2. *$\mathcal{E} = \{E_k \mid k \in K\}$ is a family of functions $E_k : M \to C$ that are used for encryption, and $\mathcal{D} = \{D_k \mid k \in K\}$ is a family of functions $D_k : C \to M$ that are used for decryption.*

3. *For each key $e \in K$, there exists a key $d \in K$ such that for each message $m \in M$:*

$$D_d(E_e(m)) = m. \tag{4.1}$$

- A cryptosystem *is called* symmetric *(or* "private-key"*) if* $d = e$*, or if* d *can at least be "easily" computed from* e*.*
- A cryptosystem *is called* asymmetric *(or* "public-key"*) if* $d \neq e$*, and it is "practically infeasible" to compute* d *from* e*. Here,* d *is the* private key, *and* e *is the* public key*.*

One can also use different key spaces for encryption and decryption, which results in a slight modification of the above definition.

Cryptosystems usually take the form of a dialog or a conversation between the parties involved, where a "party" can be either an individual or a computer. Such a dialog is called a cryptographic protocol and consists of the messages transmitted back and forth between Alice and Bob in order to fulfill certain cryptographic tasks, such as agreeing on a joint secret key for a symmetric cryptosystem. Protocols can be viewed as algorithms the execution of which requires several (authorized) parties.

Cryptanalysis

Cryptanalysis aims at breaking ciphertexts and cryptosystems. In particular, a cryptanalyst tries to determine the keys used in a cryptographic protocol. Depending on the information available to the cryptanalyst, one can distinguish several types of attacks, which characterize certain levels of security (or vulnerability) of the cryptosystem considered:

- **Ciphertext-only attack:** The cryptanalyst knows some ciphertexts only from which he tries to determine the corresponding plaintexts or keys. This is the weakest form of an attack. A cryptosystem not resistant to it is not worth much.
- **Known-plaintext attack:** The cryptanalyst knows some pairs of ciphertexts and corresponding plaintexts from which he tries to determine the keys used or to decipher other ciphertexts.
- **Chosen-plaintext attack:** The cryptanalyst can choose plaintexts at will and learns the corresponding ciphertexts from which he tries to determine the keys.
- **Chosen-ciphertext attack:** The cryptanalyst has obtained temporary access to the decryption machinery and can choose a ciphertext to construct the corresponding plaintext.
- **Key-only attack:** This type of attack is particularly relevant to public-key cryptosystems. The cryptanalyst knows the public key only, but has not yet received any ciphertexts. He tries to determine the corresponding private key. A difference to the former types of attack is that the attacker now has as much time as he wishes to perform his computations. Therefore, public-key cryptosystems require a higher level of protection such as very large keys to be secure. Thus, public-key cryptosystems are often less efficient than symmetric cryptosystems.

Of course, this is only a very rough classification. One might wonder whether also the cryptosystem used should be kept secret. Certainly, hiding the system used might make the task of the cryptanalyst considerably harder. However, it would be silly and highly dangerous to rely on the cryptanalyst's inability to learn which cryptosystem is used. The history of cryptology is full of incidents in which somebody trusted on the secrecy of the cryptosystem used, and yet attackers were able to spy it out. That is why Kerckhoffs's principle is adopted, which was first formulated by the Dutch philologist and cryptologist Jean Guillaume Hubert Victor François Alexandre Auguste Kerckhoffs von Nieuwenhof (1835 until 1903) in his book "La cryptographie militaire."

Principle 4.2 (Kerckhoffs's Principle)   *The security of a cryptosystem must not depend on the secrecy of the system used. Rather, the security of a cryptosystem may depend only on the secrecy of the keys used.*

Crucially, cryptosystems are used to keep confidential information and data secret. Secrecy is one central task of crytography, although not the only one.

Authentication and Digital Signatures

Another important task of cryptology is authentication. For example, documents such as contracts should be signed in a way that cannot be forged; the signature thus authenticates the document. Handwritten signatures are usually very hard to forge. However, if the document is transmitted electronically, it must be authenticated by a *digital signature*: Alice wants to sign her (encrypted) messages to Bob such that

(a) Bob can verify that indeed she is the sender of the message, and
(b) also third parties (who perhaps do not trust Bob) can convince themselves of the authenticity of her signature.

Neither Erich nor any other party should be able to forge Alice's digital signature. Property (a) is already achieved by symmetric authentication codes. The specific asymmetry of digital signatures is expressed by property (b). It is this property (b) that makes digital signatures so useful and necessary for secure e-commerce, for example, since conflicts of interest between Alice and Bob are then not only possible but even to be expected.

An *authentication code* provides a method of ensuring the integrity of a message. We are now confronted not only with a passive but with an *active attacker*: In addition to eavesdropping on the conversation between Alice and Bob, Erich might now try to tamper with the messages transmitted (*substitution attack*), or he might try to introduce a message of his own into the channel, hoping it is accepted as authentic by Bob (*impersonation attack*). These types of active attacks are also known as "man-in-the-middle" or "intruder-in-the-middle" attacks. Furthermore, note that not only documents such as email messages but also *individuals* may require authentication.

Related to the above types of active attacks, one can distinguish the following authentication problems:

- **Message integrity:** How can one be sure that no intruder has tampered with the message received?
- **Message authentication:** How can one be sure that a message indeed originated from the sender asserted and was not introduced by an intruder?
- **User authentication:** How can one be sure of the identity of an individual?

In the subsequent sections and chapters, we will be concerned with a variety of methods and protocols trying to solve these problems.

4.2 Some Classical Cryptosystems and Their Cryptanalysis

In this section, some classical symmetric cryptosystems are introduced, and a very rough classification of such cryptosystems is given. Out of the huge variety of cryptosystems that have been proposed to date, only a very small number will be presented in this chapter. Modern public-key cryoposystems are introduced later on, see Chapters 7 and 8.

4.2.1 Substitution and Permutation Ciphers

Let Σ be some alphabet. Messages are elements of Σ^*, where Σ^* denotes the set of strings over Σ. In many cryptosystems, messages $m \in \Sigma^*$ are subdivided into blocks of equal length, say n, and are then encrypted block-wise. The single blocks of m are elements of Σ^n, except possibly the last block, which may be shorter. Block ciphers map from Σ^n to Σ^n. There a various methods of how to encrypt large messages block-wise, see Section 4.2.3.

Definition 4.3 (Block Cipher and Substitution Cipher).

- *A block cipher is a cryptosystem in which both the plaintext space and the ciphertext space is Σ^n, the set of length n strings over some alphabet Σ. The number n is called the* block *length (or sometimes the* period*) of the system.*
- *A substitution cipher is a block cipher with block length one.*

Since every encryption function has some corresponding decryption function, the encryption functions of a block cipher are injective. An injective function mapping from Σ^n onto Σ^n is a bijection. Hence, we have proven the following claim.

Observation 4.4 *The encryption functions of a block cipher are permutations.*

By Observation 4.4, the most general block cipher can be described as follows. Fix an alphabet Σ and a block length n, and define the message space and ciphertext space by $M = C = \Sigma^n$. Let the key space K be given by the set of all permutations of Σ^n. For each key $\pi \in K$, the encryption function E_π and the decryption function D_π, which both map from Σ^n to Σ^n, are defined by:

$$E_\pi(\mathbf{x}) = \pi(\mathbf{x});$$
$$D_\pi(\mathbf{y}) = \pi^{-1}(\mathbf{y}),$$

where π^{-1} is the inverse permutation. If Σ has m letters, then the key space contains as many as $(m^n)!$ elements. However, this cryptosystem is impracticable, since one needs the permutation π to decrypt the message. Representing $\pi \in K$ by a table containing $\pi(\mathbf{x})$ for each $\mathbf{x} \in \Sigma^n$, one obtains a table of size m^n. That is why it is more reasonable to use only those permutations that result from interchanging the position of cleartext letters. This is the *permutation cipher*, also known as the *transposition cipher*. Unlike substitution ciphers, the permutation cipher does not replace plaintext letters by other letters from the ciphertext alphabet. Rather, plaintext letters merely move to a new position in the ciphertext, but remain unchanged otherwise.

Example 4.5 (Permutation Cipher).   Let Σ be some alphabet, and let $n \in \mathbb{N}$ be the block length. Let $M = C = \Sigma^n$, and let the key space $K = \mathfrak{S}_n$ be the permutation group on n elements. For each key $\pi \in \mathfrak{S}_n$, the encryption function E_π and the decryption function D_π, which both map from Σ^n to Σ^n, are defined by:

$$E_\pi(x_1 x_2 \cdots x_n) = x_{\pi(1)} x_{\pi(2)} \cdots x_{\pi(n)};$$
$$D_\pi(y_1 y_2 \cdots y_n) = y_{\pi^{-1}(1)} y_{\pi^{-1}(2)} \cdots y_{\pi^{-1}(n)}.$$

Here, the key space has $n!$ elements, and every key can be encoded by a sequence of n numbers.

We now describe some concrete block ciphers. Consider the alphabet $\Sigma = \{A, B, \ldots, Z\}$, which in many cases will be used both for the plaintext and ciphertext space as well as for the key space. Many cryptosystems are based on simple arithmetic operations such as the arithmetics modulo some number; see Problem 2.1. To carry out these operations with letters as if they were numbers, identify Σ with the ring $\mathbb{Z}_{26} = \{0, 1, \ldots, 25\}$, see Example 2.35. The number 0 represents A, the number 1 represents B, and so on. This encoding of the plaintext alphabet by integers and the decoding of $\mathbb{Z}_{26}$ back to Σ is not part of the actual encryption and decryption, respectively.

One of the simplest block ciphers is the shift cipher, which has block length one and is thus a substitution cipher.

Example 4.6 (Shift Cipher).   The shift cipher is a monoalphabetic symmetric cryptosystem. Let $K = M = C = \mathbb{Z}_{26}$. The *shift cipher* encrypts messages by shifting (modulo 26) each character of the plaintext by the same number k of letters in the alphabet, where $k \in \mathbb{Z}_{26}$ is the key. Shifting each character of the ciphertext back using the same key k reveals the original message. That is, for each key $k \in \mathbb{Z}_{26}$, the encryption function E_k and the decryption function D_k, which both map from $\mathbb{Z}_{26}$ to $\mathbb{Z}_{26}$, are defined by:

$$E_k(x) = (x + k) \bmod 26;$$
$$D_k(y) = (y - k) \bmod 26.$$

For example, if we choose the key $k = 17 = R$, the message "BRUTUS FORCE EASILY BREAKS CAESAR" is encrypted as shown in Table 4.1.

m	B R U T U S F O R C E E A S I L Y B R E A K S C A E S A R
c	S I L K L J W F I T V V R J Z C P S I V R B J T R V J R I

Table 4.1. Example of an encryption by the shift cipher with key $k = 17$

For the special case of $k = 3$, the shift cipher is also called the *Caesar cipher*, since the Roman dictator Gaius Julius Caesar is said to have used this cipher to keep military messages secret, see Section 4.5. Shift ciphers are very simple substitution ciphers, since every plaintext letter stays at the same position in the text but is substituted by a certain letter from the ciphertext alphabet.

Since the key space is very small, shift ciphers—and in particular the Caesar cipher—can easily be broken by brute force: By simply checking each of the 26 possible keys, one can easily detect the one yielding a meaningful plaintext, provided that the ciphertext is long enough to allow a unique deciphering. Thus, the shift cipher is vulnerable by ciphertext-only attacks, the weakest form of an attack.

Another example of a substitution cipher is the *affine cipher* whose encryption functions are affine functions, i.e., mappings of the form

$$E(x) = ax + b \bmod m$$

for $a, b \in \mathbb{Z}_{26}$. The integers a and b form the key. For the special case of $a = 1$, the affine cipher degenerates to the shift cipher.

Example 4.7 (Affine Cipher).   The affine cipher is a monoalphabetic symmetric cryptosystem. Let $M = C = \mathbb{Z}_{26}$ and $K = \{(a, b) \in \mathbb{Z}_{26} \times \mathbb{Z}_{26} \mid \gcd(a, 26) = 1\}$. The *affine cipher* encrypts messages letter by letter. For each key $(a, b) \in \mathbb{Z}_{26} \times \mathbb{Z}_{26}$ with $\gcd(a, 26) = 1$, the encryption function $E_{(a,b)}$ and the decryption function $D_{(a^{-1}, b)}$, which both map from $\mathbb{Z}_{26}$ to $\mathbb{Z}_{26}$, are defined by:

$$E_{(a,b)}(x) = ax + b \bmod 26;$$
$$D_{(a^{-1}, b)}(y) = a^{-1}(y - b) \bmod 26,$$

where a^{-1} is the inverse element of a in $\mathbb{Z}_{26}$, i.e., $aa^{-1} \equiv a^{-1}a \equiv 1 \bmod 26$. Note that a^{-1} can easily be determined by the extended algorithm of Euclid; see Figure 2.2 in Chapter 2.

For example, choose the encryption key $k = (5, 7)$. Note that 21 is the inverse element of 5 modulo 26, since $5 \cdot 21 = 105 = 1 + 4 \cdot 26 \equiv 1 \bmod 26$. Hence, the decryption key is $k' = (21, 7)$. Consider the message m and its encryption c in Table 4.2. The first plaintext letter is a "T," which is encoded as 19. The corresponding first letter of the ciphertext is determined by

$$E_{(5,7)}(19) = 5 \cdot 19 + 7 \equiv 24 \bmod 26.$$

Thus, the ciphertext letter "Y," which corresponds to 24, encrypts "T."

Let us check if the decryption key $k' = (21, 7)$ correctly deciphers this letter:

$$D_{(21,7)} = 21(24 - 7) = 357 \equiv 19 \bmod 26.$$

Yes, it does. In general, if y is a ciphertext letter encrypting a plaintext letter x with key (a, b), we have

$$y \equiv ax + b \bmod 26 \iff ax \equiv y - b \bmod 26$$
$$\iff a^{-1}ax \equiv a^{-1}(y - b) \bmod 26$$
$$\iff x \equiv a^{-1}(y - b) \bmod 26,$$

which satisfies (4.1). The remaining ciphertext is given in Table 4.2.

m	T H E	E L E C T I V E	A F F I N I T I E S	B Y	G O E T H E
c	Y Q B	B K B R Y V I B	H G G V U V Y V B T	M X	L Z B Y Q B

Table 4.2. Example of an encryption by the affine cipher with key $k = (5, 7)$

Cryptanalysis of the Affine Cipher

For the alphabet $\mathbb{Z}_{26}$, the affine cipher has only $26 \cdot \varphi(26)$ keys, since the number of choices for $b \in \mathbb{Z}_{26}$ is 26 and the number of choices for $a \in \mathbb{Z}_{26}$ coprime with 26 is $\varphi(26)$, where φ is the Euler function from Definition 2.36. Thus, a ciphertext-only attack breaks the affine cipher by brute force, i.e., by an exhaustive search of the key space.

The following example demonstrates a known-plaintext attack in which two plaintext letters and their encryptions are known. The attack uses simple linear algebra, see Problem 2.1 in Chapter 2.

Example 4.8 (Known-Plaintext Attack Against the Affine Cipher).   Suppose that the cryptanalyst knows the ciphertext c from Table 4.2 in the previous example, and he also knows the first two plaintext symbols, "T" and "H," corresponding to the first two ciphertext letters, "Y" and "Q." He can then determine the keys as follows:

- Since "Y" encrypts "T" and "Q" encrypts "H," one obtains the congruences:

$$19a + b \equiv 24 \bmod 26; \tag{4.2}$$
$$7a + b \equiv 16 \bmod 26; \tag{4.3}$$

- (4.3) is equivalent to $b \equiv 16 - 7a \bmod 26$. Substituting this into (4.2) gives $19a + 16 - 7a \equiv 24 \bmod 26$ and thus $12a \equiv 8 \bmod 26$, which implies

$$6a \equiv 4 \bmod 13. \tag{4.4}$$

- Multiplying (4.4) with the inverse element 11 of 6 modulo 13 yields

$$a \equiv 44 \equiv 5 \bmod 13.$$

- It follows that $a = 5$ and $b = 7$.

Both the shift cipher and the affine cipher are monoalphabetic, since every letter in the plaintext is always replaced by the same letter in the ciphertext. The method of *frequency counts* is often useful for breaking monoalphabetic cryptosystems. It exploits the redundancy of the natural language used for encryption. In many languages, the letter "E" occurs, statistically significant, most frequently. For example, the "E" occurs with a percentage of 12.31% in English, of 15.87% in French, of 13.15% in Spanish, of 11.79% in Italian, and even of 18.46% in German texts, provided they are long and "typical" enough. Thus, if a typical German text of sufficient length is encrypted by the shift cipher and the letter "Y," which is rather rare in German, occurs with the highest frequency, then it is most likely that "Y" encrypts "E," and "U" ($k = 20$) is thus the key used.

	Letters occurring with high frequency								Total
Letter	E	T	A	O	N	I	S	R	H	
Frequency in %	12.31	9.59	8.05	7.94	7.19	7.18	6.59	6.03	5.14	**70.02%**
	Letters occurring with medium frequency									
Letter	L	D	C	U	P	F	M	W	Y	
Frequency in %	4.03	3.65	3.20	3.10	2.29	2.28	2.25	2.03	1.88	**24.71%**
	Letters occurring with low frequency									
Letter	B	G	V	K	Q	X	J	Z		
Frequency in %	1.62	1.61	0.93	0.52	0.20	0.20	0.10	0.09		**5.27%**

Table 4.3. Frequencies of letters in long, typical English texts

Some languages have other letters that occur with the highest frequency; for example, "A" is the most frequent letter in average Finnish texts, with a percentage of 12.06%, see Salomaa's textbook [Sal96]. Table 4.3 shows the frequencies of the letters in typical English texts of sufficient length; the values are taken from [Gai39]. It must be emphasized, though, that the letter frequencies compiled in different books vary from source to source. This fact is not surprising; it merely highlights the difficulty to define what a "typical" text in a natural language is. Evidently, the type of text makes a difference, be it poetry, prose, a newspaper article, a technical text, a scientific text, pidgin English, a dialect, and so on. Nonetheless, some properties of the letter distribution are common for all the frequency tables. For example, the letter "E" always tops the English frequency table and is always followed by "T"; the order of some other letters may vary from table to table.

Example 4.9 (Cryptanalysis of the Affine Cipher by Frequency Counts). Suppose that cryptanalyst Erich intercepted the ciphertext

$$c = \text{Y Q B B K B R Y V I B H G G V U V Y V B T M X L Z B Y Q B}$$

from Example 4.7, and he suspects that Alice encrypted her message by the affine cipher, which is monoalphabetic. He is smart enough to analyze c by counting the frequencies with which the single letters occur, and obtains Table 4.4.

Letter	B	Y	V	Q	G	K	R	I	H	U	T	M	X	L	Z
Frequency	7	4	4	2	2	1	1	1	1	1	1	1	1	1	1

Table 4.4. Frequencies of letters in the ciphertext from Example 4.7

Since "B" occurs with highest frequency, followed by "Y" and "V," Erich guesses that "B" encrypts "E," and that "Y" and "V" each encrypt one of the letters "T," "A," "O," "N," or "I." Checking these possibilities, he concludes that it is most likely that "Y" encrypts "T," since the first three letters "T?E" are very likely to be the common English word "THE," which gives him another letter: "Q" encrypts "H." Moreover, it is most likely that "V" encrypts "I," since "...ITIES" is a typical ending of English nouns; see Table 4.5. Continuing in this trial and error way, and using the statistical information about the frequencies of letters in typical English texts from Table 4.3, Erich finally decrypts the complete message and the keys used.

c	Y Q B	B K B R Y V I B	H G G V U V Y V B T	M X	L Z B Y Q B
V is A	T H E	E ? E ? T A ? E	? ? ? A ? A T A E ?	? ?	? ? E T H E
V is O	T H E	E ? E ? T O ? E	? ? ? O ? O T O E ?	? ?	? ? E T H E
V is N	T H E	E ? E ? T N ? E	? ? ? N ? N T N E ?	? ?	? ? E T H E
V is I	T H E	E ? E ? T I ? E	? ? ? I ? I T I E ?	? ?	? ? E T H E
m	T H E	E L E C T I V E	A F F I N I T I E S	B Y	G O E T H E

Table 4.5. Guessing in the frequency counts method: "B" is "E," "Y" is "T," and "Q" is "H"

It must be emphasized, however, that the text in the above sample message is extremely short, which means that Erich was lucky to be able to decipher the text using letter frequency tables. On the other hand, short messages can always be broken by brute force; not even a computer may be needed to do the work if they are short enough. The frequency counts method works the better the longer the message is. However, it is not guaranteed to work for each message; it only provides some statistical evidence that might help the cryptanalyst.

In addition to counting the frequency of single letters occurring in some text, one may also count the frequency of letter pairs (digrams), of letter triples (trigrams), and so on. Digrams and trigrams follow a certain probability distribution in long, typical texts of a given natural language as well, and their occurrence in a ciphertext created by a monoalphabetic cryptosystem may give additional hints for the cryptanalyst.

4.2.2 Affine Linear Block Ciphers

In contrast to monoalphabetic ciphers, *polyalphabetic ciphers* can replace plaintext letters by distinct ciphertext letters depending on their position in the text. One famous such polyalphabetic system was invented by the French diplomat and cryptographer Blaise de Vigenère (1523 until 1596). His cipher works like the shift cipher, except that the ciphertext letter encrypting any given plaintext letter X varies with the position of X in the plaintext.

Example 4.10 (Vigenère Cipher).   This symmetric polyalphabetic cryptosystem uses a so-called *Vigenère square*, a matrix consisting of 26 rows and as many columns, see Table 4.6. Every row contains the 26 letters of the alphabet, shifted (according to the arithmetics modulo 26) by one position to the left row by row. In other words, the single rows (and the single columns as well) can be viewed as the shift cipher with the keys $0, 1, \ldots, 25$. Which row of the Vigenère square is used for the encryption of a plaintext symbol depends on its position in the text.

0	A	B	C	D	E	F	G	H	I	J	K	L	M	N	O	P	Q	R	S	T	U	V	W	X	Y	Z
1	B	C	D	E	F	G	H	I	J	K	L	M	N	O	P	Q	R	S	T	U	V	W	X	Y	Z	A
2	C	D	E	F	G	H	I	J	K	L	M	N	O	P	Q	R	S	T	U	V	W	X	Y	Z	A	B
3	D	E	F	G	H	I	J	K	L	M	N	O	P	Q	R	S	T	U	V	W	X	Y	Z	A	B	C
4	E	F	G	H	I	J	K	L	M	N	O	P	Q	R	S	T	U	V	W	X	Y	Z	A	B	C	D
5	F	G	H	I	J	K	L	M	N	O	P	Q	R	S	T	U	V	W	X	Y	Z	A	B	C	D	E
6	G	H	I	J	K	L	M	N	O	P	Q	R	S	T	U	V	W	X	Y	Z	A	B	C	D	E	F
7	H	I	J	K	L	M	N	O	P	Q	R	S	T	U	V	W	X	Y	Z	A	B	C	D	E	F	G
8	I	J	K	L	M	N	O	P	Q	R	S	T	U	V	W	X	Y	Z	A	B	C	D	E	F	G	H
9	J	K	L	M	N	O	P	Q	R	S	T	U	V	W	X	Y	Z	A	B	C	D	E	F	G	H	I
10	K	L	M	N	O	P	Q	R	S	T	U	V	W	X	Y	Z	A	B	C	D	E	F	G	H	I	J
11	L	M	N	O	P	Q	R	S	T	U	V	W	X	Y	Z	A	B	C	D	E	F	G	H	I	J	K
12	M	N	O	P	Q	R	S	T	U	V	W	X	Y	Z	A	B	C	D	E	F	G	H	I	J	K	L
13	N	O	P	Q	R	S	T	U	V	W	X	Y	Z	A	B	C	D	E	F	G	H	I	J	K	L	M
14	O	P	Q	R	S	T	U	V	W	X	Y	Z	A	B	C	D	E	F	G	H	I	J	K	L	M	N
15	P	Q	R	S	T	U	V	W	X	Y	Z	A	B	C	D	E	F	G	H	I	J	K	L	M	N	O
16	Q	R	S	T	U	V	W	X	Y	Z	A	B	C	D	E	F	G	H	I	J	K	L	M	N	O	P
17	R	S	T	U	V	W	X	Y	Z	A	B	C	D	E	F	G	H	I	J	K	L	M	N	O	P	Q
18	S	T	U	V	W	X	Y	Z	A	B	C	D	E	F	G	H	I	J	K	L	M	N	O	P	Q	R
19	T	U	V	W	X	Y	Z	A	B	C	D	E	F	G	H	I	J	K	L	M	N	O	P	Q	R	S
20	U	V	W	X	Y	Z	A	B	C	D	E	F	G	H	I	J	K	L	M	N	O	P	Q	R	S	T
21	V	W	X	Y	Z	A	B	C	D	E	F	G	H	I	J	K	L	M	N	O	P	Q	R	S	T	U
22	W	X	Y	Z	A	B	C	D	E	F	G	H	I	J	K	L	M	N	O	P	Q	R	S	T	U	V
23	X	Y	Z	A	B	C	D	E	F	G	H	I	J	K	L	M	N	O	P	Q	R	S	T	U	V	W
24	Y	Z	A	B	C	D	E	F	G	H	I	J	K	L	M	N	O	P	Q	R	S	T	U	V	W	X
25	Z	A	B	C	D	E	F	G	H	I	J	K	L	M	N	O	P	Q	R	S	T	U	V	W	X	Y

Table 4.6. Vigenère square: Plaintext "H" is encrypted with key "E" as "L"

Messages are subdivided into blocks of length n, and are then encrypted block-wise. That is, $K = M = C = \mathbb{Z}_{26}^n$, where n is the block length of the system. For each key $\mathbf{k} \in \mathbb{Z}_{26}^n$, the encryption function $E_{\mathbf{k}}$ and the decryption function $D_{\mathbf{k}}$, both mapping from $\mathbb{Z}_{26}^n$ to $\mathbb{Z}_{26}^n$, are defined by:

$$E_{\mathbf{k}}(\mathbf{x}) = (\mathbf{x} + \mathbf{k}) \bmod 26$$
$$D_{\mathbf{k}}(\mathbf{y}) = (\mathbf{y} - \mathbf{k}) \bmod 26,$$

where addition and subtraction with $\mathbf{k}$ modulo 26 are carried out character-wise. More concretely, the key $\mathbf{k} \in \mathbb{Z}_{26}^n$ is written symbol by symbol above each block $\mathbf{x} \in \mathbb{Z}_{26}^n$ of the plaintext. If the last block has less than n symbols, use less symbols of the key accordingly. Let s_i denote the ith symbol of any given string $\mathbf{s}$. To encrypt the ith plaintext symbol x_i, with the ith key symbol k_i sitting on top of it, use the ith row of the Vigenère square as if it were the shift cipher with key k_i. Observe that one and the same plaintext symbol can thus be encrypted by distinct ciphertext symbols.

key	E L L A E L L A E L L A E L L A E L L A E L L A E L L A
message	H U N G A R I A N I S A L L G R E E K T O G E R M A N S
ciphertext	L F Y G E C T A R T D A P W R R I P V T S R P R Q L Y S

Table 4.7. Example of an encryption by the Vigenère cipher with key ELLA

For example, choose the period $n = 4$ and the key $\mathbf{k} = \text{ELLA}$. Table 4.7 shows the encryption of a plaintext consisting of seven blocks into a ciphertext using the Vigenère cipher with this key. The first letter of the plaintext, "H," has the key symbol "E" above it. The "H"-column intersects with the "E"-row of the Vigenère square at "L," which is thus the first symbol of the ciphertext, see Table 4.6.

Observe that the same plaintext symbol can indeed be encrypted by distinct ciphertext symbols. For example,

- the plaintext letter "A" occurs four times and is encrypted by "A" twice, by "E" once, and by "L" once;
- the plaintext letter "E" occurs three times and is encrypted by "I" once and by "P" twice;
- the plaintext letter "G" occurs three times and is encrypted by "G" once and by "R" twice;
- the plaintext letter "N" occurs three times and is encrypted by "R" once and by "Y" twice;
- the plaintext letter "R" occurs three times and is encrypted by "C" once and by "R" twice.

This observation also shows two weaknesses of the key chosen:

1. two letters of the key ELLA are equal, and
2. one letter of the key is "A," which does not alter the corresponding cleartext letters.

The Vigenère cipher is a special case of an *affine linear block cipher*, which generalizes the affine cipher. Before defining affine linear block ciphers, we recall some elementary notions from linear algebra; see also Definition 2.34 in Section 2.4. In particular, affine linear block ciphers require operations on matrices over the ring $\mathbb{Z}_m$, i.e., the matrix entries are elements of $\mathbb{Z}_m$ and the matrix operations are based on the arithmetics modulo m, see Problem 4.1 in Section 2.6.

Definition 4.11 (Inverse Matrix, Determinant, and Adjoint Matrix).

- *Let $\mathbf{u}_i = (0, \ldots, 0, 1, 0, \ldots, 0)$ denote the ith unity vector of length n, i.e., the ith coordinate of $\mathbf{u}_i$ is one, and the jth coordinate of $\mathbf{u}_i$ is zero for all $j \neq i$.*
- *The $(n \times n)$ unity matrix is defined by $U_n = (\mathbf{u}_i)_{1 \le i \le n}$, where the ith row (and column) of U_n is the ith unity vector of length n.*
- *Consider an $(n \times n)$ matrix A over the ring $\mathbb{Z}_m$. The (multiplicative) inverse of A, denoted by A^{-1}, is an $(n \times n)$ matrix satisfying that $AA^{-1} = A^{-1}A$ is the $(n \times n)$ unity matrix U_n.*
- *The determinant of A can be defined recursively:*
  - *for $n = 1$ and $A = (a)$, $\det A = a$;*
  - *for $n > 1$ and for each $i \in \{1, 2, \ldots, n\}$,*

$$\det A = \sum_{j=1}^{n} (-1)^{i+j} a_{i,j} \det A_{i,j},$$

  where $a_{i,j}$ is the (i,j)-entry of A, and the $((n-1) \times (n-1))$ matrix $A_{i,j}$ results from A by canceling out the ith row and the jth column.
- *Define the adjoint matrix of A by $A_{\texttt{adj}} = ((-1)^{i+j} \det A_{j,i})$.*

An $(n \times n)$ matrix A over the ring $\mathbb{Z}_m$ has a multiplicative inverse matrix if and only if $\gcd(\det A, m) = 1$, where $\det A$ is the determinant of A. In general, an $(n \times n)$ matrix over the reals is invertible if and only if its determinant is non-zero.

The determinant of a matrix can be computed efficiently, see Problem 4.1. It can be shown that

$$A^{-1} = (\det A)^{-1} A_{\texttt{adj}}.$$

We now define the affine linear block cipher.

Definition 4.12 (Affine Linear Block Cipher).   *A block cipher with plaintext and ciphertext space $\mathbb{Z}_m^n$ and block length n is said to be* affine linear *if and only if all its encryption functions are affine linear. That is, they all are of the following form:*

$$E_{(A,\mathbf{b})}(\mathbf{x}) = A\mathbf{x} + \mathbf{b} \bmod m, \tag{4.5}$$

where A is an $(n \times n)$ matrix with entries from $\mathbb{Z}_m$ such that $\gcd(\det A, m) = 1$, and $\mathbf{x}$, $\mathbf{y}$, and $\mathbf{b}$ are vectors in $\mathbb{Z}_m^n$; all arithmetics is done modulo m. The corresponding decryption function is

$$D_{(A^{-1},\mathbf{b})}(\mathbf{y}) = A^{-1}(\mathbf{y} - \mathbf{b}) \bmod m,$$

where A^{-1} is the inverse matrix for A.

A linear block cipher *is an affine linear block cipher for which $\mathbf{b}$ in (4.5) is the zero vector.*

As mentioned above, the Vigenère cipher is affine linear. A classical example of a linear cipher is the *Hill cipher*, invented by Lester Hill in 1929. In fact, the Hill cipher is the most general linear block cipher.

Example 4.13 (Hill Cipher).   Let Σ be an alphabet with m letters, and let n be the block length. The plaintext and cipher text space is $M = C = \mathbb{Z}_m^n$. The key space K is the set of all $(n \times n)$ matrices A with entries from $\mathbb{Z}_m$ such that $\gcd(\det A, m) = 1$. This condition ensures that the matrices are invertible, since the inverse matrix A^{-1} is used as the decryption key corresponding to the encryption key A. The encryption function E_A and the decryption function $D_{A^{-1}}$ are defined by:

$$E_A(\mathbf{x}) = A\mathbf{x} \bmod m;$$
$$D_{A^{-1}}(\mathbf{y}) = A^{-1}\mathbf{y} \bmod m.$$

The Hill cipher works best if the size m of the alphabet is a prime number. To achieve this, one usually adds the blank $\square$ (encoded as 26), the comma (encoded as 27), and the full stop (encoded as 28) to the 26 letters of the English alphabet, which are encoded by the numbers $0, 1, \ldots, 25$. Thus, $m = 29$ is a prime number and all arithmetics is done over $\mathbb{Z}_{29}$.

Choose the block length $n = 2$ and an invertible (2×2) matrix A, and compute the inverse matrix A^{-1} in the arithmetics modulo 29. For example,

$$A = \begin{pmatrix} 3 & 4 \\ 7 & 2 \end{pmatrix} \quad \text{and} \quad A^{-1} = \begin{pmatrix} 21 & 16 \\ 28 & 17 \end{pmatrix}.$$

Suppose you want to encrypt the message: "THE FOOL ON THE HILL." Table 4.8 shows the encryption of this plaintext with key A.

plaintext	T H	E $\square$	F O	O L	$\square$ O	N $\square$	T H	E $\square$	H I	L L
plaintext encoded	19 7	4 26	5 14	14 11	26 14	13 26	19 7	4 26	7 8	11 11
ciphertext encoded	27 2	0 22	13 5	28 4	18 7	27 27	27 2	0 22	24 7	19 12
ciphertext	, C	A W	N F	. E	S H	, ,	, C	A W	Y H	T M

Table 4.8. Example of an encryption by the Hill cipher

We now show that the permutation cipher introduced in Example 4.5 is linear. Thus, it is a special case of the Hill cipher.

Theorem 4.14. *The permutation cipher is linear.*

Proof.   Let $\pi \in \mathfrak{S}_n$ be a permutation. Let $U_n = (\mathbf{u}_i)_{1 \leq i \leq n}$ be the $(n \times n)$ unity matrix whose i^{th} row is $\mathbf{u}_i$, the ith unity vector of length n. Let M_π be the matrix whose i^{th} row is $\mathbf{u}_{\pi(i)}$. This matrix can be obtained from U_n by permutating its rows according to π. Hence, the jth column of M_π is $\mathbf{u}_{\pi(j)}$, and it follows that

$$(x_{\pi(1)}, x_{\pi(2)}, \ldots, x_{\pi(n)}) = M_\pi \mathbf{x}$$

for each vector $\mathbf{x} = (x_1, x_2, \ldots, x_n)$ in Σ^n.   ∎

Cryptanalysis of the Vigenère Cipher

Depending on the block length chosen, the key space of the Vigenère cipher can be rather large: it has m^n elements, where m is the number of letters in the alphabet. The method of frequency counts, which is often used to break monoalphabetic systems, is not applicable to polyalphabetic systems whose period (i.e., block length) is not known. Thus, like similar periodic cryptosystems with an unknown period, the Vigenère cipher appeared to resist the cryptanalysis by counting and analyzing the frequency of letters, digrams, and trigrams in the ciphertext.

In 1863, the German cryptanalyst Friedrich Wilhelm Kasiski found a method to break the Vigenère cipher. His achievement marks a breakthrough in the history of cryptanalysis, since previously the Vigenère cipher was considered unbreakable. In particular, Kasiski showed how to determine the period from repetitions of the same substring in the ciphertext.

Kasiski's method was independently invented by Charles Babbage, a British genius and well-known eccentric who also invented an early prototype of the computer; see Section 4.5. Before explaining the method in detail, we show how to break even polyalphabetic cryptosystems if the period is known. In that case, the problem of breaking the polyalphabetic cryptosystem can be reduced to the problem of breaking a monoalphabetic cryptosystem by the method of frequency counts.

Suppose that the period is $n = 7$. Arrange the ciphertext $C_0 C_1 C_2 \cdots C_k$, where each C_j is a letter, in seven columns such that the ith column consists of the letters C_j with subscript $j \in \{i, i + 7, i + 2 \cdot 7, \ldots\}$, where $i \in \mathbb{Z}_7$ and $j \leq k$; see Table 4.9. Since all letters in the ith column are encrypted by the same key symbol as in a monoalphabetic system, an ordinary frequency count will work to decrypt the ciphertext column by column and to determine the single key symbols. Of course, this method is the more likely to be successful the longer the ciphertext is.

C_0	C_1	C_2	C_3	C_4	C_5	C_6
C_7	C_8	C_9	C_{10}	C_{11}	C_{12}	C_{13}
C_{14}	C_{15}	C_{16}	C_{17}	C_{18}	C_{19}	C_{20}
$\vdots$	$\vdots$	$\vdots$	$\vdots$	$\vdots$	$\vdots$	$\vdots$
C_{k-8}	C_{k-7}	C_{k-6}	C_{k-5}	C_{k-4}	C_{k-3}	C_{k-2}
C_{k-1}	C_k					

Table 4.9. Cryptanalysis of a polyalphabetic system with period 7

The following example explains Kasiski's method.

Example 4.15 (Kasiski's Method).   Suppose you have intercepted the ciphertext shown in Table 4.10, and you know that it has been encrypted by the Vigenère cipher. The ciphertext has 373 letters, and you do not know the period (i.e., the length of the key) used. Analyzing the ciphertext carefully, you will find that some sequences of letters occur repeatedly in the text. Some of these repeated three-letter patterns are highlighted using different gray levels in Table 4.10.

```
L E B L D V R Y L T U U H T N H P U T N
I H U E Y T A L L N S W Y E R P V Y W L
T D U Y D L R I E E P N X S E B I H R W
P Y N Z O Z M Y E U C A Z T S W I H R A
C D C N A J G B E F D U L N A C S U Y D
L E F L U V H Y O A C D U W I R E N Z K
A A M L S Z E X X E X F C H A K I H W O
K E Q T T W G Y C T G U X P S I E C Y B
T C U F S T I B L D S E X T C P T Y O A
Q O I V O U P I P M H T I S E G E P P N
I H I F G W T B P Y L E L P T H E F T O
I S U Y D X S U T D N E M T L D V Y O H
T R V F T X T W Z U A D H P V T R Q Z R
Z B Y N A J S Y D H T W U D F P R N Z O
X N X P L A I A P N I F I C M T A H O A
A I W P T D K F L S P G L P E S A H O T
W E H H E E U N Z N H O G P B D X C Y G
V L I G E H A H O G T R N C U S E M E E
X N V C O Z E G J N D S Y
```

Table 4.10. Kasiski's method: ciphertext obtained by the Vigenère cipher

If one such pattern occurs repeatedly, this can be either due to the fact that the same plaintext string was encrypted using the same letters of the key, or it may be a pure coincidence. Suppose it is not coincidental. Hence, the distance between repeatedly occurring patterns will tell you something about the key length used. By distance, we mean the number of positions some pattern has to be shifted to coincide with another one. For example,

- the pattern "AHO" occurs three times with distances 20 and 30;
- the pattern "UYD" occurs three times with distances 55 and 125;
- the pattern "ACD" occurs twice with distance 30;
- the pattern "IHR" occurs twice with distance 20;
- the pattern "BLD" occurs twice with distance 165.

If the repeated occurrence of a pattern is no coincidence, then the key length (i.e., the period of the system) must divide all distances. For example, a distance of 20 means that the period is either 2 or 4 or 5 or 10 or 20. Since also 30 is a distance between patterns, the potential periods 4 and 20 are eliminated. Among the remaining possible periods, 2 and 5 and 10, only the period 5 divides the distances 55, 125, and 165. Thus, we have determined the key length 5.

Now we can try to find the key and to decipher the message. This can be done by the method described above: Knowing the period, we can reduce this task to the task of breaking a monoalphabetic system by frequency counts. Rearranging the ciphertext in five columns, we obtain five monoalphabetic encryptions. In particular, the second column has 75 letters, see Table 4.11.

E	R	U	P	H	A	W	V	D	R	N	I	Y	M	A	I	D	G	U	S	E	H	D	E	A
E	F	I	E	G	U	E	C	I	E	T	O	P	T	E	H	T	E	E	S	S	E	V	R	T
D	R	B	S	W	R	N	I	F	A	I	K	G	A	E	U	O	X	L	A	R	E	N	E	S

Table 4.11. Kasiski's method: second column of the ciphertext rearranged

Observe that the letter "E" occurs most frequently: 14 times, which corresponds to a percentage of 10.5%. But this means that the letters in the second column have not been encrypted at all! Analyzing the fifth column gives the same result. Thus, the second and the fifth letter of the key is an "A." In other words, whoever encrypted this message did not learn his lesson from Example 4.10, since he used the same letter twice in the key, and he used an "A."

Continuing in this way, we finally obtain the key used: "PAULA." Table 4.12 shows the complete decrypted message, a twenties memory of Woody Allen reading as follows with punctuation:

We had great fun in Spain that year and we travelled and wrote and Hemingway took me tuna fishing and I caught four cans and we laughed and Alice Toklas asked me if I was in love with Gertrude Stein because I had dedicated a book of poems to her even though they were T.S. Eliot's and I said, yes, I loved her, but it could never work because she was far too intelligent for me and Alice Toklas agreed and then we put on some boxing gloves and Gertrude Stein broke my nose.

(From "A Twenties Memory" by Woody Allen, Random House, Inc., 1971)

Cryptanalysis of Other Affine Linear Block Ciphers

Affine linear block ciphers are easy to break by known-plaintext attacks, i.e., for an attacker who knows some sample plaintexts with the corresponding encryptions, it is not too hard to find the key used to encrypt these plaintexts. They are even more vulnerable to chosen-plaintext attacks where the attacker can choose some pairs of corresponding plaintexts and encryptions, which may be useful if there are certain conjectures about the key used. We describe a known-plaintext attack.

Example 4.16 (Known-Plaintext Attack Against the Affine Linear Block Cipher). Suppose that some key $(A, \mathbf{b})$ has been fixed, that is, the plaintext $\mathbf{x} \in \mathbb{Z}_m^n$ is encrypted as $\mathbf{y} = E_{(A,\mathbf{b})}(\mathbf{x}) = A\mathbf{x} + \mathbf{b} \bmod m$, where A is an $(n \times n)$ matrix over $\mathbb{Z}_m$ with $\gcd(\det A, m) = 1$, and $\mathbf{y}$ and $\mathbf{b}$ are vectors in $\mathbb{Z}_m^n$. As usual, all arithmetics is carried out modulo m.

key	P A U L A P A U L A P A U L A P A U L A
plaintext	W E H A D G R E A T F U N I N S P A I N
ciphertext	L E B L D V R Y L T U U H T N H P U T N
plaintext	T H A T Y E A R A N D W E T R A V E L L
ciphertext	I H U E Y T A L L N S W Y E R P V Y W L
plaintext	E D A N D W R O T E A N D H E M I N G W
ciphertext	T D U Y D L R I E E P N X S E B I H R W
plaintext	A Y T O O K M E T U N A F I S H I N G A
ciphertext	P Y N Z O Z M Y E U C A Z T S W I H R A
plaintext	N D I C A U G H T F O U R C A N S A N D
ciphertext	C D C N A J G B E F D U L N A C S U Y D
plaintext	W E L A U G H E D A N D A L I C E T O K
ciphertext	L E F L U V H Y O A C D U W I R E N Z K
plaintext	L A S A S K E D M E I F I W A S I N L O
ciphertext	A A M L S Z E X X E X F C H A K I H W O
plaintext	V E W I T H G E R T R U D E S T E I N B
ciphertext	K E Q T T W G Y C T G U X P S I E C Y B
plaintext	E C A U S E I H A D D E D I C A T E D A
ciphertext	T C U F S T I B L D S E X T C P T Y O A
plaintext	B O O K O F P O E M S T O H E R E V E N
ciphertext	Q O I V O U P I P M H T I S E G E P P N
plaintext	T H O U G H T H E Y W E R E T S E L I O
ciphertext	I H I F G W T B P Y L E L P T H E F T O
plaintext	T S A N D I S A I D Y E S I L O V E D H
ciphertext	I S U Y D X S U T D N E M T L D V Y O H
plaintext	E R B U T I T C O U L D N E V E R W O R
ciphertext	T R V F T X T W Z U A D H P V T R Q Z R
plaintext	K B E C A U S E S H E W A S F A R T O O
ciphertext	Z B Y N A J S Y D H T W U D F P R N Z O
plaintext	I N T E L L I G E N T F O R M E A N D A
ciphertext	X N X P L A I A P N I F I C M T A H O A
plaintext	L I C E T O K L A S A G R E E D A N D T
ciphertext	A I W P T D K F L S P G L P E S A H O T
plaintext	H E N W E P U T O N S O M E B O X I N G
ciphertext	W E H H E E U N Z N H O G P B D X C Y G
plaintext	G L O V E S A N D G E R T R U D E S T E
ciphertext	V L I G E H A H O G T R N C U S E M E E
plaintext	I N B R O K E M Y N O S E
ciphertext	X N V C O Z E G J N D S Y

Table 4.12. Kasiski's method: Vigenère ciphertext decrypted

Suppose that the cryptanalyst knows $n + 1$ plaintexts $\mathbf{x}_0, \mathbf{x}_1, \ldots, \mathbf{x}_n$ and the corresponding ciphertexts $\mathbf{y}_0, \mathbf{y}_1, \ldots, \mathbf{y}_n$ with

$$\mathbf{y}_i = A\mathbf{x}_i + \mathbf{b} \bmod m.$$

It follows that

$$\mathbf{y}_i - \mathbf{y}_0 \equiv A(\mathbf{x}_i - \mathbf{x}_0) \bmod m. \tag{4.6}$$

Define the matrices X and Y by

$$X = (\mathbf{x}_1 - \mathbf{x}_0, \mathbf{x}_2 - \mathbf{x}_0, \dots, \mathbf{x}_n - \mathbf{x}_0) \bmod m;$$
$$Y = (\mathbf{y}_1 - \mathbf{y}_0, \mathbf{y}_2 - \mathbf{y}_0, \dots, \mathbf{y}_n - \mathbf{y}_0) \bmod m.$$

That is, the ith column of X is the difference $\mathbf{x}_i - \mathbf{x}_0 \bmod m$, and the ith column of Y is the difference $\mathbf{y}_i - \mathbf{y}_0 \bmod m$, where $1 \leq i \leq n$. It follows from (4.6) that

$$AX \equiv Y \bmod m.$$

If $\det X$ is coprime to m, then $X^{-1} = (\det X)^{-1} X_{\text{adj}}$, where $(\det X)^{-1}$ denotes the inverse of $\det X \bmod m$. Thus, we have

$$A \equiv Y((\det X)^{-1} X_{\text{adj}}) \bmod m.$$

Furthermore, since

$$\mathbf{b} = (\mathbf{y}_0 - A\mathbf{x}_0) \bmod m,$$

we have determined the key $(A, \mathbf{b})$ from $n + 1$ pairs of plaintexts and corresponding ciphertexts.

If the cryptosystem is even linear, then $\mathbf{b} = \mathbf{0}$, and we may choose $\mathbf{x}_0 = \mathbf{y}_0 = \mathbf{0}$. For example, let $n = 2$, and suppose you have intercepted two pairs of plaintexts and corresponding ciphertexts, say the first two blocks of the encryption by the Hill cipher given in Table 4.8 from Example 4.13. Table 4.13 shows these two known pairs: $\mathbf{x}_1 = (19, 7)$ and $\mathbf{y}_1 = (27, 2)$, and $\mathbf{x}_2 = (4, 26)$ and $\mathbf{y}_2 = (0, 22)$.

plaintext		T	H	E	☐
plaintext encoded		19	7	4	26
ciphertext encoded	27	2	0	22
ciphertext		,	C	A	W

Table 4.13. Breaking the Hill cipher with a known-plaintext attack

Thus, you obtain the matrices $X = \begin{pmatrix} 19 & 4 \\ 7 & 26 \end{pmatrix}$ and $Y = \begin{pmatrix} 27 & 0 \\ 2 & 22 \end{pmatrix}$. Since $\det X = 19 \cdot 26 - 4 \cdot 7 = 2$ and $m = 29$ are coprime, you further obtain $(\det X)^{-1} = 15$ and

$$X_{\text{adj}} = \begin{pmatrix} 26 & -4 \\ -7 & 19 \end{pmatrix} = \begin{pmatrix} 26 & 25 \\ 22 & 19 \end{pmatrix}.$$

Hence, the key used can be deciphered by

$$A \equiv Y((\det X)^{-1} X_{\text{adj}}) \bmod m$$
$$= \begin{pmatrix} 27 & 0 \\ 2 & 22 \end{pmatrix} \left(15 \begin{pmatrix} 26 & 25 \\ 22 & 19 \end{pmatrix} \right) = \begin{pmatrix} 27 & 0 \\ 2 & 22 \end{pmatrix} \begin{pmatrix} 13 & 27 \\ 11 & 24 \end{pmatrix}$$
$$= \begin{pmatrix} 3 & 4 \\ 7 & 2 \end{pmatrix}.$$

4.2.3 Block and Stream Ciphers

In Sections 4.2.1 and 4.2.2, various block ciphers were introduced. In this section, several ways of using block ciphers to encrypt large plaintexts are discussed. Furthermore, block ciphers are compared with stream ciphers.

Triple Encryption

The security of a block cipher can be increased by applying it repeatedly with distinct keys. This measure can increase the key space considerably. A common way of doing so is the *triple encryption*. After choosing three keys, say k_1, k_2, and k_3, a given plaintext x is encrypted by

$$y = E_{k_1}(D_{k_2}(E_{k_3}(x))),$$

where E_{k_i} are encryption functions and D_{k_i} are decryption functions for k_i. The ciphertext y can then be decrypted by

$$x = D_{k_3}(E_{k_2}(D_{k_1}(y))).$$

Electronic Codebook Mode (ECB)

Suppose we are given a block cipher with block length n. Messages are strings in Σ^*, where Σ is an alphabet, and the key space is K. For each key $k \in K$, E_k is the encryption function and D_k is the decryption function.

To encode a plaintext m in the *electronic codebook mode (ECB)*, we subdivide it into blocks of length n, where the last block may have to be padded by random letters to ensure that n divides $|m|$. If $e \in K$ is the key used for encryption, every block of length n is encrypted by e. The ciphertext is the resulting sequence of ciphertext blocks. If $d \in K$ is the decryption key corresponding to e, the ciphertext blocks are decrypted with d one after another, yielding the original plaintext m. All the examples of block ciphers given in Sections 4.2.1 and 4.2.2 have been encrypted in the ECB mode.

An obvious disadvantage of the ECB mode is that the same plaintext blocks are encrypted into the same ciphertext blocks. Thus, regularities in the plaintext yield regularities in the ciphertext. A cryptanalysist can exploit this information obtained from the ciphertext, which may be sufficient to break the cipher. For instance, look at Example 4.15 that describes Kasiski's method to break the Vigenère cipher. The highlighted patterns in the ciphertext given in Table 4.10 are a result of using the ECB mode for the Vigenère cipher. In particular, the ciphertext patterns "AHO," "UYD," and "ACD" each encrypt the plaintext "AND."

Another disadvantage of the ECB mode is that an attacker can tamper with the encrypted messages transmitted. Ciphertext blocks can be deleted or the order of the ciphertext blocks can be altered or, if the key has been determined, additional ciphertext blocks can be inserted. In each case, the authorized recipient of the message will decrypt a different message than the original one. That is why the ECB mode is not recommended for encrypting long messages. The security of the ECB mode can be increased by padding all plaintext blocks with random characters.

Example 4.17 (ECB Mode).   Consider the permutation cipher with block length 5 and alphabet $\Sigma = \{0, 1\}$. The key space is $K = \mathfrak{S}_5$. For each key $\pi \in \mathfrak{S}_5$, the encryption function $E_\pi : \Sigma^5 \to \Sigma^5$ is defined by

$$E_\pi(x_1 x_2 \cdots x_5) = x_{\pi(1)} x_{\pi(2)} \cdots x_{\pi(5)}.$$

If the message is $m = 100111010101001001$, then we subdivide it into four blocks of length five, where the last block is padded by a suffix of two zeros:

$$m = 10011\ 10101\ 01001\ 00100.$$

That is, we obtain the blocks $\mathbf{b}_1 = 10011$, $\mathbf{b}_2 = 10101$, $\mathbf{b}_3 = 01001$, and $\mathbf{b}_4 = 00100$. If the key is given by $\pi = \left(\begin{smallmatrix} 1 & 2 & 3 & 4 & 5 \\ 3 & 4 & 1 & 5 & 2 \end{smallmatrix}\right)$, the four ciphertext blocks

$$
\begin{aligned}
\mathbf{c}_1 &= E_\pi(\mathbf{b}_1) = 01110 & \mathbf{c}_2 &= E_\pi(\mathbf{b}_2) = 10110 \\
\mathbf{c}_3 &= E_\pi(\mathbf{b}_3) = 00011 & \mathbf{c}_4 &= E_\pi(\mathbf{b}_4) = 10000
\end{aligned}
$$

are obtained. Hence, the ciphertext is

$$c = 01110\ 10110\ 00011\ 10000.$$

Cipherblock Chaining Mode (CBC)

The *cipherblock chaining mode (CBC)* avoids the disadvantages of the ECB mode by working in a "context-sensitive" way; cf. the notion of context-sensitive grammars from Definition 2.9. That is, the encryption of a plaintext block in the CBC mode depends not only on the block being encrypted and the key, but also on preceding blocks. Hence, depending on their context, identical patterns in the plaintext are encrypted differently. If an attacker was tampering with the ciphertext, it can no longer be decrypted properly, which reveals that someone was trying to do something nasty. The CBC mode is explained by an example.

Example 4.18 (CBC Mode).   Let $\Sigma = \{0, 1\}$ be an alphabet, n be the block length, and $\mathfrak{S}_n$ be the key space. Consider the permutation cipher, and let E_π be the encryption function and $D_{\pi^{-1}}$ be the decryption function for key $\pi \in \mathfrak{S}_n$.

Define the logical *exclusive-or* operation $\oplus : \{0, 1\}^2 \to \{0, 1\}$ by its truth table shown in Table 4.14. Note that $\oplus$ corresponds to the bit vector addition in the field of remainder classes $\mathbb{Z}_2$. Given two vectors $\mathbf{x} = (x_1, x_2, \ldots, x_n)$ and $\mathbf{y} = (y_1, y_2, \ldots, y_n)$ in $\{0, 1\}^n$, define $\mathbf{x} \oplus \mathbf{y} = (x_1 \oplus y_1, x_2 \oplus y_2, \ldots, x_n \oplus y_n)$. For convenience, we write vectors from $\{0, 1\}^n$ as strings, dropping parentheses and commas. For example, if $\mathbf{x} = 01100$ and $\mathbf{y} = 11001$, then $\mathbf{x} \oplus \mathbf{y} = 10101$.

x	y	$x \oplus y$
0	0	0
0	1	1
1	0	1
1	1	0

Table 4.14. Truth table for the exclusive-or operation

Let $n = 5$. Consider the key $\pi = \left(\begin{smallmatrix} 1 & 2 & 3 & 4 & 5 \\ 3 & 5 & 1 & 2 & 4 \end{smallmatrix}\right) \in \mathfrak{S}_5$ and the same message as in Example 4.17:

$$m = 10011\ 10101\ 01001\ 00100$$

consisting of the blocks $\mathbf{b}_1 = 10011$, $\mathbf{b}_2 = 10101$, $\mathbf{b}_3 = 01001$, and $\mathbf{b}_4 = 00100$.

To describe the CBC mode, we choose an initial vector $\mathbf{c}_0 = 11010$ in $\{0,1\}^5$. For i with $1 \leq i \leq 4$, the ith block is encrypted by

$$\mathbf{c}_i = E_\pi(\mathbf{c}_{i-1} \oplus \mathbf{b}_i).$$

One obtains the four ciphertext blocks

$$\mathbf{c}_1 = E_\pi(\mathbf{c}_0 \oplus \mathbf{b}_1) = 01010 \qquad \mathbf{c}_2 = E_\pi(\mathbf{c}_1 \oplus \mathbf{b}_2) = 11111$$
$$\mathbf{c}_3 = E_\pi(\mathbf{c}_2 \oplus \mathbf{b}_3) = 10101 \qquad \mathbf{c}_4 = E_\pi(\mathbf{c}_3 \oplus \mathbf{b}_4) = 01100.$$

Hence, the ciphertext is

$$c = 01010\ 11111\ 10101\ 01100.$$

The inverse permutation $\pi^{-1} = \left(\begin{smallmatrix} 1 & 2 & 3 & 4 & 5 \\ 3 & 4 & 1 & 5 & 2 \end{smallmatrix}\right)$ is used as the decryption key, which satisfies $D_{\pi^{-1}}(E_\pi(\mathbf{b})) = \mathbf{b}$ for each block $\mathbf{b}$. For i with $1 \leq i \leq 4$, the ith ciphertext block is decrypted by

$$\mathbf{b}_i = \mathbf{c}_{i-1} \oplus D_{\pi^{-1}}(\mathbf{c}_i).$$

Indeed, we have

$$\mathbf{b}_1 = \mathbf{c}_0 \oplus D_{\pi^{-1}}(\mathbf{c}_1) = 11010 \oplus D_{\pi^{-1}}(01010) = 11010 \oplus 01001 = 10011,$$

and it can be shown similarly that the other blocks are decrypted correctly.

Identical messages are encrypted differently in the CBC mode by altering the initial vector. Moreover, since the encryption of plaintext blocks depends on the preceding blocks, identical plaintext blocks with a different context are encrypted differently. Attempts at tampering with the ciphertext transmitted, such as changing the order of ciphertext blocks or deleting blocks or inserting additional blocks, will be revealed because (authorized) decryption is then impossible. This is a clear advantage of the CBC mode over the ECB mode. Thus, the CBC mode is useful for encrypting large texts with a block cipher.

The disadvantage of the CBC mode is that the receiver has to wait for the next ciphertext block before starting with the decryption. These delays result in a certain inefficiency, in particular if the block length is large.

Cipher Feedback Mode (CFB)

The disadvantage of the CBC mode mentioned above can be avoided by the *cipher feedback mode (CFB)*. The idea is to subdivide the message into blocks shorter than the block length n of the block cipher used, and to not use the block cipher's own encryption function but to encrypt these shorter blocks by adding certain key blocks modulo 2. These key blocks can almost simultaneously be generated by the sender and the receiver of the ciphertext. The CFB mode is now explained by an example.

Example 4.19 (CFB Mode).   Consider the permutation cipher with alphabet $\Sigma = \{0, 1\}$, block length n, and key space $\mathfrak{S}_n$. In addition, choose some k with $1 \leq k \leq n$ and an initial vector $\mathbf{z}_0 \in \{0, 1\}^n$. However, the message m is now subdivided into $d = \lceil |m|/k \rceil$ blocks $\mathbf{b}_1, \mathbf{b}_2, \ldots, \mathbf{b}_d$ of length k. For each i with $1 \leq i \leq d$:

Step 1: Compute $\mathbf{x}_i = E_\pi(\mathbf{z}_{i-1})$.
Step 2: Let $\mathbf{y}_i$ be the string in $\{0, 1\}^k$ consisting of the first k bits of $\mathbf{x}_i \in \{0, 1\}^n$.
Step 3: Compute $\mathbf{c}_i = \mathbf{b}_i \oplus \mathbf{y}_i$.
Step 4: Compute $\mathbf{z}_i = 2^k \mathbf{z}_{i-1} + \mathbf{c}_i \bmod 2^n$, i.e., the first k bits are deleted in $\mathbf{z}_{i-1}$ and $\mathbf{c}_i$ is attached as a suffix.

The resulting ciphertext consists of the blocks $\mathbf{c}_1, \mathbf{c}_2, \ldots, \mathbf{c}_d$.

Let $n = 5$ and $k = 4$, and consider the message from Examples 4.17 and 4.18: $m = 10011\ 10101\ 01001\ 00100$. Subdivide the message into five blocks of length k: $\mathbf{b}_1 = 1001$, $\mathbf{b}_2 = 1101$, $\mathbf{b}_3 = 0101$, $\mathbf{b}_4 = 0010$, and $\mathbf{b}_5 = 0100$.

If $\pi = \left(\begin{smallmatrix} 1 & 2 & 3 & 4 & 5 \\ 3 & 5 & 1 & 2 & 4 \end{smallmatrix} \right) \in \mathfrak{S}_5$ is again our key and $\mathbf{z}_0 = 11010$ our initial vector, we encrypt these blocks as shown in Table 4.15.

i	$\mathbf{b}_i$	$\mathbf{x}_i$	$\mathbf{y}_i$	$\mathbf{c}_i$	$\mathbf{z}_i$
0	—	—	—	—	11010
1	1001	00111	0011	1010	01010
2	1101	00011	0001	1100	01100
3	0101	10010	1001	1100	01100
4	0010	10010	1001	1011	01011
5	0100	01011	0101	0001	10001

Table 4.15. Block encryption in the CFB mode

The decryption works almost like the encryption. The only difference occurs in the third step. For each i with $1 \leq i \leq d$:

Step 1: Compute $\mathbf{x}_i = E_\pi(\mathbf{z}_{i-1})$.
Step 2: Let $\mathbf{y}_i$ be the string in $\{0, 1\}^k$ consisting of the first k bits of $\mathbf{x}_i \in \{0, 1\}^n$.
Step 3: Compute $\mathbf{b}_i = \mathbf{c}_i \oplus \mathbf{y}_i$.

Step 4: Compute $z_i = 2^k z_{i-1} + c_i \bmod 2^n$, i.e., the first k bits are deleted in z_{i-1} and c_i is attached as a suffix.

The decrypted message obtained consists of the blocks $b_1, b_2, \ldots, b_d$.

Obviously, both the sender and the receiver can determine y_1 as soon as the initial vector z_0 is chosen. Then, the sender computes $c_1 = b_1 \oplus y_1$ and sends it, and the receiver computes $b_1 = c_1 \oplus y_1$. Then, they can both determine y_2, and so on. The advantage gained in comparison with the CBC mode is that the block length k can be much shorter than the actual block length n. Thus, there is much less idle time during which the receiver has to wait for the sender to complete all computations, and both can encrypt and decrypt almost simultaneously.

Output Feedback Mode (OFB)

The *output feedback mode (OFB)* is quite similar to the CFB mode. The initialization and the first three steps of both the encryption and the decryption procedure are identical. The only difference occurs in the fourth step, which determines the vector z_i for $1 \leq i \leq d$. For encryption, the OFB mode works as follows:

Step 1: Compute $x_i = E_\pi(z_{i-1})$.
Step 2: Let y_i be the string in $\{0, 1\}^k$ consisting of the first k bits of $x_i \in \{0, 1\}^n$.
Step 3: Compute $c_i = b_i \oplus y_i$.
Step 4: Compute $z_i = x_i$.

Example 4.20 (OFB Mode).   Look at the block encryption in the CFB mode shown in Table 4.15 from Example 4.19. Table 4.16 gives the corresponding block encryption in the OFB mode for the same message, key, and initial vector.

i	b_i	x_i	y_i	c_i	z_i
0	—	—	—	—	11010
1	1001	00111	0011	1010	00111
2	1101	11001	1100	0001	11001
3	0101	01110	0111	0010	01110
4	0010	10011	1001	1011	10011
5	0100	01101	0110	0010	01101

Table 4.16. Block encryption in the OFB mode

One advantage of the OFB mode over the CFB mode is that if there are transmission errors in the ciphertext of a message encrypted in the OFB mode, then this error occurs after decryption only at exactly the same position. In contrast, transmission errors in ciphertexts encrypted in the CFB mode occur after decryption as long as it takes to shift the erroneous block out of the vector z_i, which depends on the block lengths n and k.

Exercise 4.7 gives more examples for the various block cipher modes.

Stream Ciphers

Block ciphers such as the Vigenère cipher or the Hill cipher subdivide the plaintext into blocks of equal length and encrypt each block using the same key. In contrast, block ciphers can also be used to encrypt the plaintext blocks in a context-sensitive way. In the CBC mode, for example, the encryption of blocks depends on the preceding blocks. This principle is generalized by the notion of a *stream cipher*. Stream ciphers generate a continuous stream of keys such that each key may depend on the preceding keys and on the context of the plaintext already encrypted.

The next example introduces a popular stream cipher based on a linear feedback shift register, and thus explains the general idea of stream ciphers. Examples of cryptanalytic attacks on stream ciphers can be found in Exercises 4.8 and 4.9.

Example 4.21 (Stream Cipher).   Let $\Sigma = \{0, 1\}$ be the alphabet used. Σ^* is both the plaintext space and the ciphertext space. For fixed $n \in \mathbb{N}$, the key space is Σ^n. Any message $\mathbf{m} = m_1 m_2 \cdots m_z$ in Σ^* is encrypted symbol by symbol as follows. Suppose that $z \geq n$. Given a key $\mathbf{k} = (k_1, k_2, \ldots, k_n)$ in Σ^n, generate a key stream $\mathbf{s} = (s_1, s_2, \ldots, s_z, \ldots)$ that is initialized by $\mathbf{k}$ for the first n bits:

$$s_i = k_i \qquad \text{for } 1 \leq i \leq n,$$

and then continues according to the following linear recursion of order n:

$$s_i = \sum_{j=1}^{n} a_j s_{i-j} \bmod 2 \qquad \text{for } i > n, \tag{4.7}$$

where $a_1, a_2, \ldots, a_n \in \{0, 1\}$ are fixed coefficients. Denoting the first z bits of the key stream $\mathbf{s}$ by $\mathbf{s}(z)$, the encryption function $E_{\mathbf{k}}$ and the decryption function $D_{\mathbf{k}}$, both mapping from Σ^* to Σ^*, are defined by:

$$E_{\mathbf{k}}(\mathbf{m}) = \mathbf{m} \oplus \mathbf{s}(|\mathbf{m}|);$$
$$D_{\mathbf{k}}(\mathbf{c}) = \mathbf{c} \oplus \mathbf{s}(|\mathbf{c}|),$$

where $\oplus$ denotes the addition of bit vectors modulo 2. That is, the ith bit of $\mathbf{m} \oplus \mathbf{s}$ is $m_i \oplus s_i$, the exclusive-or of m_i and s_i; see Table 4.14.

For a concrete example, let $n = 5$, and fix the coefficients $a_1 = a_3 = a_4 = 0$ and $a_2 = a_5 = 1$. Then, the key stream $\mathbf{s}$ is generated by the recursion

$$s_{i+5} = s_{i+3} + s_i \bmod 2. \tag{4.8}$$

Choosing the key $\mathbf{k} = (1, 0, 0, 1, 1)$, one obtains

$$\mathbf{s} = (1, 0, 0, 1, 1, 0, 1, 0, 0, 1, 0, 0, 0, 0, 1, 0, 1, 0, 1, 1, 1, \ldots).$$

The linear recursion from (4.8) can be efficiently realized by a building block of hardware, namely a linear feedback shift register as shown in Figure 4.1. The registers store the last four bits of the key stream $\mathbf{s}$ generated. In each recursion step, the bit from the leftmost register is used as the current key. Then, the bits from the other registers are shifted by one position to the left. The rightmost register is now fed the bit that results from adding modulo 2 the bits from those registers with coefficient $a_i = 1$.

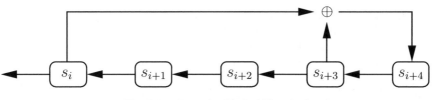

Fig. 4.1. A linear feedback shift register

4.3 Perfect Secrecy

As mentioned in the last section, the Vigenère cipher was considered unbreakable until the clever ideas of Kasiski and Babbage proved it insecure. In light of their achievement, it is natural to ask whether there exist any cryptosystems that provably guarantee *perfect secrecy*.

We turn to this question in Section 4.3.1 that describes some of the pioneering work of Claude Shannon [Sha49], who laid the foundations of modern coding and information theory. Central to Shannon's work is the notion of entropy, which is useful in physics, mathematics, computer science, and other areas. In Section 4.3.2, the notions of entropy and key equivocation are introduced and investigated. Foundations of probability theory that are crucial here are described in Section 2.5.

4.3.1 Shannon's Theorem and Vernam's One-Time Pad

Consider again the scenario given in Figure 1.1 in Chapter 1: Alice and Bob are communicating over an insecure channel, in the presence of eavesdropper Erich. Therefore, they use a cryptosystem $S = (M, C, K, \mathcal{E}, \mathcal{D})$, where M, C, and K are finite sets, and $\mathcal{E}$ and $\mathcal{D}$ are families of functions used, respectively, for encryption and decryption; see Definition 4.1.

Consider the following preliminaries and assumptions. The messages are distributed on M according to a probability distribution $\Pr_M$ that may depend on the natural language used. For each new message, Alice chooses a new key from K that is independent of the message to be encrypted. This assumption makes sense, since Alice is choosing her key before she knows what the plaintext will be.

The keys are distributed according to a probability distribution $\Pr_K$ on K. The distributions $\Pr_M$ and $\Pr_K$ induce a probability distribution $\Pr_{M \times K}$ on $M \times K$. That is, dropping the subscript, for each message $m \in M$ and for each key $k \in K$,

$$\Pr(m, k) = \Pr_M(m) \Pr_K(k)$$

is the probability that the message m is encrypted with the key k, where m and k are independent. Some more facts are in order:

- For $m \in M$, let m denote the event $\{(m, k) \mid k \in K\}$. Then, $\Pr(m) = \Pr_M(m)$ is the probability that the message m will be encrypted.

- For $k \in K$, let k denote the event $\{(m, k) \mid m \in M\}$. Then, $\Pr(k) = \Pr_K(k)$ is the probability that the key k will be used.
- For $c \in C$, let c denote the event $\{(m, k) \mid E_k(m) = c\}$. Then, $\Pr(m \mid c)$ is the probability that m is encrypted under the condition that c is received.

Suppose that eavesdropper Erich intercepts a ciphertext c that Alice sent to Bob. Erich tries to get some information about the corresponding message m encrypted by c. Since he knows the language used by Alice and Bob, he knows the probability distribution $\Pr_M$.

We now define the notion of perfect secrecy.

Definition 4.22 (Perfect Secrecy).   *A cryptosystem $S = (M, C, K, \mathcal{E}, \mathcal{D})$ is said to guarantee* perfect secrecy *if and only if*

$$(\forall m \in M)\,(\forall c \in C)\,[\Pr(m \mid c) = \Pr(m)].$$

That is, a cryptosystem guarantees perfect secrecy if and only if the event that some message m is encrypted and the event that some ciphertext c is received are independent: Erich learns nothing about m from knowing c.

We now give an example of a cryptosystem that does not guarantee perfect secrecy. Exercise 4.10 asks you to alter this cryptosystem so that it does achieve perfect secrecy. Example 4.23 will be continued in Examples 4.28 and 4.36.

Example 4.23 (Perfect Secrecy).   Consider a cryptosystem $S = (M, C, K, \mathcal{E}, \mathcal{D})$ such that the plaintext space M, the ciphertext space C, and the key space K are given by:

- $M = \{a, b\}$, where $\Pr(a) = 1/3$ and $\Pr(b) = 2/3$;
- $K = \{\$, \#\}$, where $\Pr(\$) = 1/4$ and $\Pr(\#) = 3/4$;
- $C = \{x, y\}$.

The probability that a plaintext letter $m \in M$ is encrypted with a key $k \in K$ is:

$$\Pr(a, \$) = \Pr(a) \cdot \Pr(\$) = \tfrac{1}{3} \cdot \tfrac{1}{4} = \tfrac{1}{12};$$
$$\Pr(a, \#) = \Pr(a) \cdot \Pr(\#) = \tfrac{1}{3} \cdot \tfrac{3}{4} = \tfrac{1}{4};$$
$$\Pr(b, \$) = \Pr(b) \cdot \Pr(\$) = \tfrac{2}{3} \cdot \tfrac{1}{4} = \tfrac{1}{6};$$
$$\Pr(b, \#) = \Pr(b) \cdot \Pr(\#) = \tfrac{2}{3} \cdot \tfrac{3}{4} = \tfrac{1}{2}.$$

Let the encryption functions be given by:

$$E_\$(a) = y; \quad E_\$(b) = x; \quad E_\#(a) = x; \quad E_\#(b) = y.$$

Hence, the probability that a ciphertext symbol $c \in C$ occurs is:

$$\Pr(x) = \Pr(b, \$) + \Pr(a, \#) = \tfrac{1}{6} + \tfrac{1}{4} = \tfrac{5}{12};$$
$$\Pr(y) = \Pr(a, \$) + \Pr(b, \#) = \tfrac{1}{12} + \tfrac{1}{2} = \tfrac{7}{12}.$$

Then, for each pair $(m, c) \in M \times C$, the conditional probability $\Pr(m \mid c)$ is different from the probability $\Pr(m)$:

$$\Pr(a \mid x) = \tfrac{\Pr(a,\#)}{\Pr(x)} = \tfrac{\frac{3}{12}}{\frac{5}{12}} = \tfrac{3}{5} \neq \tfrac{1}{3} = \Pr(a);$$

$$\Pr(a \mid y) = \tfrac{\Pr(a,\$)}{\Pr(y)} = \tfrac{\frac{1}{12}}{\frac{7}{12}} = \tfrac{1}{7} \neq \tfrac{1}{3} = \Pr(a);$$

$$\Pr(b \mid x) = \tfrac{\Pr(b,\$)}{\Pr(x)} = \tfrac{\frac{2}{12}}{\frac{5}{12}} = \tfrac{2}{5} \neq \tfrac{2}{3} = \Pr(b);$$

$$\Pr(b \mid y) = \tfrac{\Pr(b,\#)}{\Pr(y)} = \tfrac{\frac{6}{12}}{\frac{7}{12}} = \tfrac{6}{7} \neq \tfrac{2}{3} = \Pr(b).$$

It follows that the given cryptosystem does not achieve perfect secrecy. In particular, if Erich sees the ciphertext letter y, the odds are good that the encrypted plaintext letter was a b.

Shannon's Theorem gives conditions necessary and sufficient for a cryptosystem to achieve perfect secrecy.

Theorem 4.24 (Shannon).   *Let $S = (M, C, K, \mathcal{E}, \mathcal{D})$ be a cryptosystem with $\|C\| = \|K\|$ and $\Pr(m) > 0$ for each $m \in M$. Then, S guarantees perfect secrecy if and only if*

1. for each $m \in M$ and for each $c \in C$, there exists a unique key $k \in K$ with $E_k(m) = c$, and
2. the keys in K are uniformly distributed.

Proof.   Assume that S achieves perfect secrecy. We show that both conditions are valid.

To prove the first condition, fix an arbitrary message $m \in M$. Suppose that there is a ciphertext $c \in C$ such that no key encrypts m into c. That is, for all $k \in K$, we have $E_k(m) \neq c$. Thus,

$$\Pr(m) \neq 0 = \Pr(m \mid c).$$

Hence, S does not guarantee perfect secrecy, a contradiction. It follows that

$$(\forall c \in C)\,(\exists k \in K)\,[E_k(m) = c].$$

Now, the assumption $\|C\| = \|K\|$ implies that each ciphertext $c \in C$ has a *unique* key k with $E_k(m) = c$.

To prove the second condition, fix an arbitrary ciphertext $c \in C$. For any $m \in M$, let $k(m)$ be the unique key k with $E_k(m) = c$. By the Theorem of Bayes (see Theorem 2.55), it follows that for each $m \in M$:

$$\Pr(m \mid c) = \frac{\Pr(c \mid m)\,\Pr(m)}{\Pr(c)} = \frac{\Pr(k(m))\,\Pr(m)}{\Pr(c)}. \qquad (4.9)$$

Since S guarantees perfect secrecy, we have $\Pr(m \mid c) = \Pr(m)$. By (4.9), this implies $\Pr(k(m)) = \Pr(c)$, and the latter equality holds independently of m.

Hence, the probabilities $\Pr(k)$ are equal for all $k \in K$, which implies that $\Pr(k) = 1/\|K\|$. Thus, the keys in K are uniformly distributed.

Conversely, suppose that both conditions are true. We show that S achieves perfect secrecy. Let $k = k(m, c)$ be the unique key k with $E_k(m) = c$. By the Theorem of Bayes, it follows that

$$\Pr(m \,|\, c) = \frac{\Pr(m)\,\Pr(c \,|\, m)}{\Pr(c)}$$

$$= \frac{\Pr(m)\,\Pr(k(m, c))}{\sum_{q \in M}\Pr(q)\,\Pr(k(q, c))}. \tag{4.10}$$

Since all keys are uniformly distributed by the second condition, it follows that

$$\Pr(k(m, c)) = \frac{1}{\|K\|}.$$

Moreover, we have that

$$\sum_{q \in M}\Pr(q)\,\Pr(k(q, c)) = \frac{\sum_{q \in M}\Pr(q)}{\|K\|} = \frac{1}{\|K\|}.$$

Substituting this equality in (4.10) gives

$$\Pr(m \,|\, c) = \Pr(m).$$

Hence, S guarantees perfect secrecy.   ∎

Cryptosystems with perfect secrecy can be designed by satisfying the conditions in Theorem 4.24. One famous such cryptosystem was invented by Gilbert Vernam in 1917. His symmetric cryptosystem, a block cipher, is known as the one-time pad.

Example 4.25 (Vernam's One-Time Pad).   Fix the alphabet $\Sigma = \{0, 1\}$, and define the plaintext space, the ciphertext space, and the key space by

$$M = C = K = \{0, 1\}^n$$

for some block length $n \in \mathbb{N}$. The keys are uniformly distributed on $\{0, 1\}^n$.

For each key $\mathbf{k} \in \{0, 1\}^n$, define the encryption function $E_{\mathbf{k}}$ and the decryption function $D_{\mathbf{k}}$, both mapping from $\{0, 1\}^n$ to $\{0, 1\}^n$, by:

$$E_{\mathbf{k}}(\mathbf{x}) = \mathbf{x} \oplus \mathbf{k};$$
$$D_{\mathbf{k}}(\mathbf{y}) = \mathbf{y} \oplus \mathbf{k},$$

where $\oplus$ denotes bit-wise addition modulo 2.

By Shannon's Theorem, the one-time pad achieves perfect secrecy, since for each plaintext $\mathbf{x} \in \{0, 1\}^n$ and for each ciphertext $\mathbf{y} \in \{0, 1\}^n$, there exists a unique key $\mathbf{k} \in \{0, 1\}^n$ with $\mathbf{y} = \mathbf{x} \oplus \mathbf{k}$, namely the vector $\mathbf{k} = \mathbf{x} \oplus \mathbf{y}$.

The one-time pad has some severe disadvantages that make its usage impractical in most concrete scenarios. To guarantee perfect secrecy, every key can be used only once, and it must be as long as the block of the message encrypted by it. If Alice and Bob were using the same key twice and were to encrypt two (or more) blocks with it, the one-time pad would not achieve perfect secrecy anymore. Sure enough, since for every block of the message a new secret key must be exchanged, the one-time pad lacks efficient key management. This is one reason why it has only limited use in commercial applications.

Even worse, the one-time pad is not secure against known-plaintext attacks if the same key is used twice. Knowing a message x and a corresponding ciphertext y, Erich can determine the key used simply by computing

$$x \oplus y = x \oplus x \oplus k = k.$$

Due to its perfect secrecy and despite its drawbacks, the one-time pad has been employed in real-world applications in a diplomatic and military context. Allegedly, it has been used for the hotline between Moscow and Washington, see p. 316 in [Sim79]. Evidently, in situations where unconditional security does matter, cryptosystems that provably guarantee perfect secrecy—such as the one-time pad—are of great importance.

4.3.2 Entropy and Key Equivocation

When discussing the notion of perfect secrecy in Section 4.3.1, we assumed that a new key is used whenever a new plaintext is to be encrypted, and that the key and the plaintext are independent random variables. In contrast, we now ask what happens if more than one plaintext is encrypted with the same key. How much information can a cryptanalyst gain from the fact that keys are reused repeatedly? How likely is it that this information can be employed for a successful ciphertext-only attack? Actually, what *is* "information," and how can one measure it? The answer to the latter question is: "Entropy."

Entropy

The notion of entropy originates from physics, where it is used to describe the degree of chaos (or disorder, the opposite of ordered structure) in the universe or in any closed system. In the world of physics, entropy refers to *manifest* order or structure, as opposed to the regular, precise movement of microscopic particles, which is not considered as manifest order. The second principle of thermodynamics says that the entropy of any closed system increases with the passing of time, unless it is a "reversible" system in which case the entropy remains constant.

What does this have to do with cryptography? Entropy is so fundamental a notion that it occurs not only in physics but also in mathematics, computer science, and other fields. For example, it is a central notion in Shannon's information and coding theory and in the related theory of data compression. In algorithmics, it can be used to analyze the running time of randomized algorithms, to estimate the average search time in the data structure of optimal search trees, to estimate the average length of the linked lists for hash tables that resolve collisions by chaining, and so on. Whenever a random experiment such as tossing a coin is conducted, entropy measures the *information gained* by knowing the result of this experiment. The other way round, entropy is a measure of the *uncertainty* removed by conducting this experiment. Roughly speaking, uncertainty corresponds to chaos, whereas information corresponds to order. Not surprisingly, entropy is also useful in cryptography.

We now define the notion of entropy and state some useful properties for future reference. Consider a random experiment with finitely many results. We call such a result an *event*. If these events occur with one of the probabilities $p_1, p_2, \ldots, p_n$, then we can assign a certain number to this random experiment, namely its entropy.

Definition 4.26 (Entropy).   *Let $\mathbf{X}$ be a random variable that can take on n possible values from the set $X = \{x_1, x_2, \ldots, x_n\}$. For each i with $1 \leq i \leq n$, let $p_i = \Pr(\mathbf{X} = x_i)$ be the probability that $\mathbf{X}$ takes on the value x_i. Define the entropy of $\mathbf{X}$ by*

$$\mathcal{H}(\mathbf{X}) = -\sum_{i=1}^{n} p_i \log p_i. \tag{4.11}$$

By convention, we set $0 \log 0 = 0$.

Formally, the weighted sum in (4.11) has the form of an expectation value, see Section 2.5. The entropy expresses the degree of uncertainty associated with the result of the given experiment *before* it has been conducted. Conversely, it can be viewed as a measure for the average amount of information gained by conducting the experiment, i.e., *after* knowing its result. In other words, if the ith event occurs in this experiment, the information gained amounts to

$$-\log p_i = \log \frac{1}{p_i}.$$

If events are independent, then their probabilities are multiplied. Hence, by the logarithm laws, the corresponding amounts of information gained can be added up. Note that all logarithms are base 2; as usual, this choice is arbitrary because changing the base would change the amount of the entropy only by a constant factor, cf. Exercise 2.4.

Example 4.27 (Entropy).   Tossing a coin is a random experiment with two possible outcomes: heads or tails. Let $\mathbf{X}$ be a random variable that gives the result of this experiment: $\mathbf{X} = 1$ if the coin came down heads after being tossed, and $\mathbf{X} = 0$ if it came down tails. If it is a fair coin, both these events occur with probability $p_1 = p_2 = 1/2$. Since

$$\mathcal{H}(\mathbf{X}) = -\left(\frac{1}{2} \log \frac{1}{2} + \frac{1}{2} \log \frac{1}{2} \right) = \frac{1}{2} \log 2 + \frac{1}{2} \log 2 = 1,$$

the random experiment of tossing a coin has an information content of precisely one bit, which is either 1 for heads or 0 for tails.

However, if the coin is biased, say with the probabilities $p_1 = 1/4$ for heads and $p_2 = 3/4$ for tails, the entropy of this experiment decreases to about 0.8113 bit.

The following example illustrates how one can describe the various components of a cryptosystem by their entropies.

Example 4.28 (Entropy of a Cryptosystem: Example 4.23 continued).
Consider the cryptosystem $S = (M, C, K, \mathcal{E}, \mathcal{D})$ defined in Example 4.23. One can think of a key as a random variable $\mathbf{K}$ that takes on values in $K = \{\$, \#\}$, and thus one can compute its entropy. Similarly, let $\mathbf{M}$ and $\mathbf{C}$ be random variables that describe the plaintext and ciphertext, respectively, and take on values in M and in C.
The entropies of $\mathbf{K}$, $\mathbf{M}$, and $\mathbf{C}$ can be computed as follows:

$$\mathcal{H}(\mathbf{K}) = - \left(\frac{1}{4} \log \frac{1}{4} + \frac{3}{4} \log \frac{3}{4} \right) = \frac{1}{4} \log 4 + \frac{3}{4} \log \frac{4}{3} = 2 - \frac{3}{4} \log 3 \approx 0.8113;$$

$$\mathcal{H}(\mathbf{M}) = - \left(\frac{1}{3} \log \frac{1}{3} + \frac{2}{3} \log \frac{2}{3} \right) = \frac{1}{3} \log 3 + \frac{2}{3} \log \frac{3}{2} \approx 0.9183;$$

$$\mathcal{H}(\mathbf{C}) = - \left(\frac{5}{12} \log \frac{5}{12} + \frac{7}{12} \log \frac{7}{12} \right) = \frac{5}{12} \log \frac{12}{5} + \frac{7}{12} \log \frac{12}{7} \approx 0.9799.$$

Theorem 4.31 below collects a number of useful properties of entropy. Its proof is omitted except for the first statement. The remaining statements are left to the reader as Exercise 4.12. To prove the first statement of Theorem 4.31, we need Jensen's inequality that is stated without proof as Lemma 4.30 below.

Definition 4.29. *A real-valued function f is said to be* concave *on the interval $I \subseteq \mathbb{R}$ if and only if for all $x, y \in I$,*

$$f \left(\frac{x+y}{2} \right) \geq \frac{f(x) + f(y)}{2}.$$

The function f is said to be strictly concave *on the interval $I \subseteq \mathbb{R}$ if and only if for all $x, y \in I$ with $x \neq y$,*

$$f \left(\frac{x+y}{2} \right) > \frac{f(x) + f(y)}{2}.$$

Lemma 4.30 (Jensen's Inequality). *If f is a continuous function that is strictly concave on the real interval I, and if the positive real numbers $p_1, p_2, \ldots, p_n$ satisfy*

$$\sum_{i=1}^{n} p_i = 1,$$

then

$$\sum_{i=1}^{n} p_i f(x_i) \leq f \left(\sum_{i=1}^{n} p_i x_i \right).$$

Theorem 4.31 (Properties of Entropy).   *Let* $\mathbf{X}$ *be a random variable that can take on n possible values from the set* $X = \{x_1, x_2, \ldots, x_n\}$. *For each i with $1 \leq i \leq n$, let $p_i = \mathrm{Pr}(\mathbf{X} = x_i)$ be the probability that* $\mathbf{X}$ *takes on the value x_i.*

1. $\mathcal{H}(\mathbf{X}) \leq \log n$, *with equality if and only if* $(p_1, p_2, \ldots, p_n) = \left(\frac{1}{n}, \frac{1}{n}, \ldots, \frac{1}{n}\right)$.
2. $\mathcal{H}(\mathbf{X}) \geq 0$, *with equality if and only if $p_i = 1$ for some i, and $p_j = 0$ for $j \neq i$. Here, $\mathcal{H}(\mathbf{X}) = 0$ means that the experiment's result is completely determined, i.e., there is no uncertainty about it and it does not provide any information.*
3. *If* $\mathbf{Y}$ *is a random variable that can take on $n + 1$ possible values from the set* $Y = \{y_1, y_2, \ldots, y_{n+1}\}$ *such that* $\mathrm{Pr}(\mathbf{Y} = y_i) = p_i$ *for $1 \leq i \leq n$ and* $\mathrm{Pr}(\mathbf{Y} = y_{n+1}) = 0$, *then* $\mathcal{H}(\mathbf{Y}) = \mathcal{H}(\mathbf{X})$.
4. *If* $\pi \in \mathfrak{S}_n$ *is an arbitrary permutation of the set $\{1, 2, \ldots, n\}$ and if* $\mathbf{Y}$ *is a random variable with* $\mathrm{Pr}(\mathbf{Y} = x_i) = p_{\pi(i)}$, $1 \leq i \leq n$, *then* $\mathcal{H}(\mathbf{Y}) = \mathcal{H}(\mathbf{X})$.
5. *Grouping Property: If* $\mathbf{Y}$ *and* $\mathbf{Z}$ *are random variables such that* $\mathbf{Y}$ *can take on $n - 1$ possible values with the probabilities $p_1 + p_2, p_3, \ldots, p_n$ and* $\mathbf{Z}$ *can take on two possible values with the probabilities $p_1/(p_1 + p_2)$ and $p_2/(p_1 + p_2)$, then* $\mathcal{H}(\mathbf{X}) = \mathcal{H}(\mathbf{Y}) + (p_1 + p_2)\mathcal{H}(\mathbf{Z})$.
6. *Gibb's Lemma: Let* $\mathbf{Y}$ *be a random variable that can take on n possible values with the probabilities $q_1, q_2, \ldots, q_n$ (i.e., $0 \leq q_i \leq 1$ and $\sum_{i=1}^{n} q_i = 1$), then*

$$\mathcal{H}(\mathbf{X}) \leq -\sum_{i=1}^{n} p_i \log q_i,$$

with equality if and only if $(p_1, p_2, \ldots, p_n) = (q_1, q_2, \ldots, q_n)$.
7. *Subadditivity: Let* $\mathbf{Z} = (\mathbf{X}_1, \mathbf{X}_2, \ldots, \mathbf{X}_n)$ *be a random variable whose possible values are n-tuples of the form $(x_1, x_2, \ldots, x_n)$, i.e., x_i is the value of the random variable* $\mathbf{X}_i$. *Then,*

$$\mathcal{H}(\mathbf{Z}) \leq \mathcal{H}(\mathbf{X}_1) + \mathcal{H}(\mathbf{X}_2) + \cdots + \mathcal{H}(\mathbf{X}_n),$$

with equality if and only if the random variables $\mathbf{X}_i$ *are independent, i.e.,*

$$\mathrm{Pr}(\mathbf{X}_1 = x_1, \mathbf{X}_2 = x_2, \ldots, \mathbf{X}_n = x_n) = \prod_{i=1}^{n} \mathrm{Pr}(\mathbf{X}_i = x_i).$$

Proof.   We restrict ourselves to proving the first statement, leaving the remaining statements to the reader, see Exercise 4.12. Observe that the function $\log x$ is strictly concave on the interval $(0, \infty)$. By Jensen's inequality (Lemma 4.30), it follows that

$$\mathcal{H}(\mathbf{X}) = -\sum_{i=1}^{n} p_i \log p_i = \sum_{i=1}^{n} p_i \log \frac{1}{p_i}$$

$$\leq \log \sum_{i=1}^{n} \left(p_i \frac{1}{p_i}\right) = \log n.$$

Furthermore, we have equality if and only if $p_i = 1/n$ for each i with $1 \leq i \leq n$. ∎

Based on the notion of conditional probability from Definition 2.54, we now define conditional entropy. Intuitively, conditional entropy measures the amount of information about a random variable $\mathbf{X}$ revealed by a random variable $\mathbf{Y}$. This notion will be useful to quantify the information that cryptanalyst Erich can learn about the key used from knowing a certain ciphertext.

Definition 4.32 (Conditional Entropy).   *Let* $\mathbf{X}$ *and* $\mathbf{Y}$ *be two random variables such that* $\mathbf{X}$ *can take on* n *possible values from the set* $X = \{x_1, x_2, \ldots, x_n\}$ *and* $\mathbf{Y}$ *can take on* m *possible values from the set* $Y = \{y_1, y_2, \ldots, y_m\}$.

For each i *and* j *with* $1 \leq i \leq n$ *and* $1 \leq j \leq m$, *define the conditional probabilities* p_{ij} *and the probabilities* q_j *by:*

$$p_{ij} = \Pr(\mathbf{X} = x_i \mid \mathbf{Y} = y_j);$$
$$q_j = \Pr(\mathbf{Y} = y_j).$$

For fixed j, $1 \leq j \leq m$, *let* $\mathbf{X}_j$ *denote the random variable on* X *that is distributed according to* $p_{1j}, p_{2j}, \ldots, p_{nj}$. *Clearly,*

$$\mathcal{H}(\mathbf{X}_j) = -\sum_{i=1}^{n} p_{ij} \log p_{ij}.$$

Define the conditional entropy *by*

$$\mathcal{H}(\mathbf{X} \mid \mathbf{Y}) = \sum_{j=1}^{m} q_j \mathcal{H}(\mathbf{X}_j) = -\sum_{j=1}^{m} \sum_{i=1}^{n} q_j p_{ij} \log p_{ij}.$$

Intuitively, the conditional entropy $\mathcal{H}(\mathbf{X} \mid \mathbf{Y})$ is the weighted average (with respect to the probability distribution on Y) of the entropies $\mathcal{H}(\mathbf{X}_j)$ for all j with $1 \leq j \leq m$. This notion will be applied to cryptosystems in Example 4.36 below.

The proof of the following two statements is straightforward and thus omitted; see Exercise 4.13.

Theorem 4.33. $\mathcal{H}(\mathbf{X}, \mathbf{Y}) = \mathcal{H}(\mathbf{Y}) + \mathcal{H}(\mathbf{X} \mid \mathbf{Y})$.

Corollary 4.34. $\mathcal{H}(\mathbf{X}, \mathbf{Y}) \leq \mathcal{H}(\mathbf{X})$, *with equality if and only if* $\mathbf{X}$ *and* $\mathbf{Y}$ *are independent.*

Key Equivocation

The properties of entropy and conditional entropy are now applied to cryptosystems. It was noted in Example 4.28 that, given a cryptosystem $S = (M, C, K, \mathcal{E}, \mathcal{D})$, one can think of a key, a plaintext, and a ciphertext as a random variable $\mathbf{K}$, $\mathbf{M}$, and $\mathbf{C}$, respectively. Hence, one can compute their entropies.

We are now interested in determining the conditional entropy $\mathcal{H}(\mathbf{K} \mid \mathbf{C})$, which is called the *key equivocation of S*, and is interpreted as the amount of information about the key used that is revealed by the ciphertext observed. The following result tells us how to compute the key equivocation of a given cryptosystem.

Theorem 4.35. *Let* $S = (M, C, K, \mathcal{E}, \mathcal{D})$ *be a cryptosystem, and let* $\mathbf{K}$, $\mathbf{M}$, *and* $\mathbf{C}$ *be random variables corresponding to* K, M, *and* C. *Then,*

$$\mathcal{H}(\mathbf{K} \mid \mathbf{C}) = \mathcal{H}(\mathbf{K}) + \mathcal{H}(\mathbf{M}) - \mathcal{H}(\mathbf{C}).$$

Proof.   By applying Theorem 4.33 with $\mathbf{X} = \mathbf{C}$ and $\mathbf{Y} = (\mathbf{K}, \mathbf{M})$, we obtain

$$\mathcal{H}(\mathbf{C}, \mathbf{K}, \mathbf{M}) = \mathcal{H}(\mathbf{K}, \mathbf{M}) + \mathcal{H}(\mathbf{C} \mid \mathbf{K}, \mathbf{M}).$$

Since S is a cryptosystem, a given key $k \in K$ and a given plaintext $m \in M$ uniquely determine the ciphertext $c = E_k(m)$. Hence, $\mathcal{H}(\mathbf{C} \mid \mathbf{K}, \mathbf{M}) = 0$. It follows that

$$\mathcal{H}(\mathbf{C}, \mathbf{K}, \mathbf{M}) = \mathcal{H}(\mathbf{K}, \mathbf{M}).$$

However, since the random variables $\mathbf{K}$ and $\mathbf{M}$ are independent, the subadditivity of entropy (Property (7) in Theorem 4.31) implies that $\mathcal{H}(\mathbf{K}, \mathbf{M}) = \mathcal{H}(\mathbf{K}) + \mathcal{H}(\mathbf{M})$. Thus,

$$\mathcal{H}(\mathbf{C}, \mathbf{K}, \mathbf{M}) = \mathcal{H}(\mathbf{K}, \mathbf{M}) = \mathcal{H}(\mathbf{K}) + \mathcal{H}(\mathbf{M}). \tag{4.12}$$

Similarly, a given key $k \in K$ and a given ciphertext $c \in C$ uniquely determine the plaintext $m = D_k(c)$. Hence, $\mathcal{H}(\mathbf{M} \mid \mathbf{K}, \mathbf{C}) = 0$. It follows that

$$\mathcal{H}(\mathbf{C}, \mathbf{K}, \mathbf{M}) = \mathcal{H}(\mathbf{K}, \mathbf{C}). \tag{4.13}$$

By Theorem 4.33, the equalities (4.12) and (4.13) imply that

$$\begin{aligned}
\mathcal{H}(\mathbf{K} \mid \mathbf{C}) &= \mathcal{H}(\mathbf{K}, \mathbf{C}) - \mathcal{H}(\mathbf{C}) \\
&= \mathcal{H}(\mathbf{C}, \mathbf{K}, \mathbf{M}) - \mathcal{H}(\mathbf{C}) \\
&= \mathcal{H}(\mathbf{K}) + \mathcal{H}(\mathbf{M}) - \mathcal{H}(\mathbf{C}),
\end{aligned}$$

which proves the theorem.   ∎

To illustrate Theorem 4.35, we compute the key equivocation of the cryptosystem defined in Example 4.23.

Example 4.36 (Key Equivocation: Examples 4.23 and 4.28 continued).
Consider the cryptosystem from Example 4.23. In Example 4.28, we estimated the entropies associated with the random variables $\mathbf{K}$, $\mathbf{M}$, and $\mathbf{C}$ corresponding to the key space, plaintext space, and ciphertext space as follows: $\mathcal{H}(\mathbf{K}) \approx 0.8113$, $\mathcal{H}(\mathbf{M}) \approx 0.9183$, $\mathcal{H}(\mathbf{C}) \approx 0.9799$. By Theorem 4.35, we obtain

$$\begin{aligned}
\mathcal{H}(\mathbf{K} \mid \mathbf{C}) &= \mathcal{H}(\mathbf{K}) + \mathcal{H}(\mathbf{M}) - \mathcal{H}(\mathbf{C}) \\
&\approx 0.8113 + 0.9183 - 0.9799 \tag{4.14} \\
&= 0.7497.
\end{aligned}$$

The key equivocation of this cryptosystem can also be determined directly by applying the conditional entropy from Definition 4.32. Using the Theorem of Bayes

(Theorem 2.55), we first determine the conditional probabilities $\Pr(\mathbf{K} = k \mid \mathbf{C} = c)$ for each $k \in K = \{\$, \#\}$ and $c \in C = \{x, y\}$:

$$\Pr(\$ \mid x) = \frac{\Pr(b, \$)}{\Pr(x)} = \frac{2}{5}; \qquad \Pr(\# \mid x) = \frac{\Pr(a, \#)}{\Pr(x)} = \frac{3}{5};$$

$$\Pr(\$ \mid y) = \frac{\Pr(a, \$)}{\Pr(y)} = \frac{1}{7}; \qquad \Pr(\# \mid y) = \frac{\Pr(b, \#)}{\Pr(y)} = \frac{6}{7}.$$

Note that it is a pure coincidence that our cryptosystem satisfies:

- $\Pr(\$ \mid x) = 2/5 = \Pr(b \mid x)$,
- $\Pr(\# \mid x) = 3/5 = \Pr(a \mid x)$,
- $\Pr(\$ \mid y) = 1/7 = \Pr(a \mid y)$, and
- $\Pr(\# \mid y) = 6/7 = \Pr(b \mid y)$.

In general, this is not the case. For example, it is not necessarily the case that the key space and the plaintext space are of the same size.

Now, we can compute the key equivocation according to Definition 4.32:

$$\mathcal{H}(\mathbf{K} \mid \mathbf{C}) = \frac{5}{12}\left(\frac{2}{5}\log\frac{5}{2} + \frac{3}{5}\log\frac{5}{3}\right) + \frac{7}{12}\left(\frac{1}{7}\log 7 + \frac{6}{7}\log\frac{7}{6}\right)$$
$$\approx 0.7497,$$

confirming the result in (4.14) that was yielded by Theorem 4.35.

4.4 Exercises and Problems

Exercise 4.1 (a) Decrypt the following ciphertext that was encrypted by the permutation cipher:

O□HWEARCD□ETE□HT A R HCTECA "T□R□BEHDE I R IN□"KI"□
□BL LL"LI□U□?□TAMRMUH□ONAQU□RT INETA□NNTARO?N I

Hint: First determine the key used. The answer to the encrypted message is encrypted as "HTOB" by the permutation cipher using a *different* key.

(b) Let π_1 be the key from Exercise 4.1(a). Choose two more keys:

$$\pi_2 = \begin{pmatrix} 1\,2\,3\,4\,5\,6\,7\,8 \\ 2\,1\,8\,6\,4\,5\,3\,7 \end{pmatrix} \quad \text{and} \quad \pi_3 = \begin{pmatrix} 1\ 2\ 3\,4\ 5\ 6\,7\,8\,9\,10\,11 \\ 8\ 11\ 2\,1\ 10\ 5\,3\,7\,4\ 6\ 9 \end{pmatrix}.$$

Encrypt the plaintext from Exercise 4.1(a) by triple encryption using the keys π_1, π_2, and π_3; see Section 4.2.3. What is the size of the key space?

Exercise 4.2 Table 4.17 gives a ciphertext obtained by the affine cipher.

(a) Determine the key and the plaintext by the frequency counts method.

Hint: The plaintext is a German poem by Christian Morgenstern, taken from "Ausgewählte Werke I," Gustav Kiepenheuer Verlag, 1985. The frequencies of letters in typical German texts can be found, e.g., in [Beu02].

PWMU DZUIFDMZ WERXMNR XSZIF XUM REIFD
XSZIF UFZMO ZSCVBO HMZMRQDMR OIFEIFD
BNUMOOD WMUOOMO CGRXNUIFD
ODUNN SRX FMUDMZ
ESB UFZMR
WENXWMQ
SO
W

Table 4.17. A ciphertext obtained by the affine cipher for Exercise 4.2(a)

(b) The title of the poem in Table 4.17 has been encrypted by the affine cipher (using a different key) into the following ciphertext:

JMU DHMYBDUH

Determine the key and decrypt the ciphertext according to the known-plaintext attack in Example 4.8. The first two letters of the plaintext are "DI."

Exercise 4.3 Table 4.18 shows two ciphertexts you have intercepted, c_1 and c_2. You know that both encrypt the same plaintext and that one is encrypted by the shift cipher, the other one by the Vigenère cipher. Determine the keys and decipher both ciphertexts.

| c_1 | W K L V V H Q W H Q F H L V H Q F U B S W H G E B F D H V D U V N H B |
| c_2 | N U O S J Y A Z E E W R O S V H P X Y G N R J B P W N K S R L F Q E P |

Table 4.18. Two ciphertexts encrypting the same plaintext for Exercise 4.3

Hint: After deciphering the texts you will see that one of the ciphers used yields a true, the other one a false statement. Is the method of frequency counts useful perhaps?

Exercise 4.4 Consider the encryption of the plaintext "THE FOOL ON THE HILL" by the Hill cipher given in Ecample 4.13, see Table 4.8.

(a) Prove that $A^{-1} = \begin{pmatrix} 21 & 16 \\ 28 & 17 \end{pmatrix}$ indeed is the inverse matrix of $A = \begin{pmatrix} 3 & 4 \\ 7 & 2 \end{pmatrix}$ modulo 29, i.e., prove that $AA^{-1} = A^{-1}A = U_2 \bmod 29$.

(b) Check that the ciphertext given in Table 4.8 properly decrypts into this plaintext using the decryption key A^{-1}.

(c) Encrypt the entire text of the Beatles song "THE FOOL ON THE HILL" with block length 3 and a matrix of your choice. Determine the inverse matrix and check that your ciphertext properly decrypts into the plaintext.

(d) Table 4.19 gives a ciphertext obtained by the Hill cipher with block length two and using the alphabet $\Sigma = \{A, B, C, \ldots, Z, \Box, \&, \text{-}\}$. The corresponding plaintext starts with the following four letters: "THER." Determine the key and decrypt the ciphertext according to the known-plaintext attack in Example 4.16.

```
S B Q B Q - B K P □ R A & G Q - AU S E T H R C - □ X R Q N Q B J W & I J K B H & T DM
R & & J QM J K B K P □ R □ Q - UD QU R W & T O C X P R R R D A K I Q R R R & & E Q -
S B Q B Q - B K P □ R A & G Q - AU S E T H R C - □ X R Q N Q B J K Q N D U R W - O S A
B & R Y X K B G B K P □ R □ Q - A K R G □ I P N S B A F R C Q - I E X R K A O T R X E P
□ Z R C - & R A AW Q E R S U B - O D J R S O & P G X P R H K Z O - & V S A & V R T C X
A O Q U R H K Z C B K E P H R M K W J C M □ B & R Y X K B G S B A - R P A Y K Z A Y X Z
R C - □ K R R S S R R X S A S B Q B Q - B K P □ R A & G Q - AU S E T H R C - □ X R J D
W C B - X Z R G □ Z X R E Q R X O - A H Q U R S U B J D W C AW Q - U K S A B H & T I E
K R O & D C R I & B K R R T & T C O & V R I & B R A A K S A A P U X K O R W & T E E J K
AU C B D J R H U B T I M □ AU Y Z Z Q & T O G K R S P - L Q M A Z S E I Y C B X Z O &
S B Q B Q - B K P □ R A & G Q - AU S E T H R C - □ X R J D W C I E X R Q N Q S R W A B
Q - J D W E R A P G S B Q E R H U Z R C - □ X R J D W C M G X D Q -
```

Table 4.19. A ciphertext obtained by the Hill cipher for Exercise 4.4(d)

Hint: The plaintext was taken from the album "We're only in it for the Money" by Frank Zappa and the Mothers of Invention, Frank Zappa Music Co., Inc., 1967.

Exercise 4.5 Table 4.20 shows a ciphertext obtained by the Vigenère cipher, where spaces between words and punctuation have been dropped. Apply Kasiski's method from Example 4.15 to determine the period, the key used, and the original message.

```
P O U L Q K Z H C T M Z O J G U A Z V Y F P V Y B O P A L O
W Z O J G L V Z Q T N T Z W C S E G O U K Z A J V X M V Q N
W D D B R M V Q Z D E L D I B C G U J S M T I N W K O J G E
S S H M F G J D F L F D W X K I Y L V W Q B U G P W G U X Q
Z N R E C C A S W T N Y L I A H W E W N T Z M W Z I X N G U
K K Y C M X T N O J T F L W A C G N K F D Y E Z K R O S A Q
A L Q V J U N K G U K A V J N W T G M I X B J G O A K H N A
Z N S A R G J E Z V B B A L Z B X F P R V N I L A A M A G U
K S K H P Y I A J E C M B P P V G M A T R O V A C T N E T G
U X T M N L P E P U S A V F M A R R Y Y P M F Z A I L H R P
Q H Y A D R V K A I A Z E Q S L L G V G O J G G U X T M Y U
Y A J Z L A X F G J D G Y I Y M Z H A R M U G Q I F Q E N E
O I D Q S Y D E R O S G O U Z E S F V Y X L O K Y O K L E I
Z V Z A R G U L Q Z G E L I A H P X G P X U P R P G I I L C
A W C Y I M T Y Y K E L J L M V G K Z W G A L E P R Y W I B
U S U B B U G T F H X F W Z K W N W L W
```

Table 4.20. A ciphertext obtained by the Vigenère cipher for Exercise 4.5

Hint: The plaintext was taken from the short story "A Twenties Memory" by Woody Allen, Random House, Inc., 1971.

Exercise 4.6 There are a number of other squares similar to the Vigenère square that can be used for a polyalphabetic block cipher similar to the Vigenère cipher from Example 4.10. One famous such cryptosystem is the Beaufort cipher, which was invented by Admiral Sir Francis Beaufort (1774 until 1857), who also invented the twelve-level Beaufort scale for measuring wind speed.

Z	Y	X	W	V	U	T	S	R	Q	P	O	N	M	L	K	J	I	H	G	F	E	D	C	B	A
A	Z	Y	X	W	V	U	T	S	R	Q	P	O	N	M	L	K	J	I	H	G	F	E	D	C	B
B	A	Z	Y	X	W	V	U	T	S	R	Q	P	O	N	M	L	K	J	I	H	G	F	E	D	C
C	B	A	Z	Y	X	W	V	U	T	S	R	Q	P	O	N	M	L	K	J	I	H	G	F	E	D
D	C	B	A	Z	Y	X	W	V	U	T	S	R	Q	P	O	N	M	L	K	J	I	H	G	F	E
E	D	C	B	A	Z	Y	X	W	V	U	T	S	R	Q	P	O	N	M	L	K	J	I	H	G	F
F	E	D	C	B	A	Z	Y	X	W	V	U	T	S	R	Q	P	O	N	M	L	K	J	I	H	G
G	F	E	D	C	B	A	Z	Y	X	W	V	U	T	S	R	Q	P	O	N	M	L	K	J	I	H
H	G	F	E	D	C	B	A	Z	Y	X	W	V	U	T	S	R	Q	P	O	N	M	L	K	J	I
I	H	G	F	E	D	C	B	A	Z	Y	X	W	V	U	T	S	R	Q	P	O	N	M	L	K	J
J	I	H	G	F	E	D	C	B	A	Z	Y	X	W	V	U	T	S	R	Q	P	O	N	M	L	K
K	J	I	H	G	F	E	D	C	B	A	Z	Y	X	W	V	U	T	S	R	Q	P	O	N	M	L
L	K	J	I	H	G	F	E	D	C	B	A	Z	Y	X	W	V	U	T	S	R	Q	P	O	N	M
M	L	K	J	I	H	G	F	E	D	C	B	A	Z	Y	X	W	V	U	T	S	R	Q	P	O	N
N	M	L	K	J	I	H	G	F	E	D	C	B	A	Z	Y	X	W	V	U	T	S	R	Q	P	O
O	N	M	L	K	J	I	H	G	F	E	D	C	B	A	Z	Y	X	W	V	U	T	S	R	Q	P
P	O	N	M	L	K	J	I	H	G	F	E	D	C	B	A	Z	Y	X	W	V	U	T	S	R	Q
Q	P	O	N	M	L	K	J	I	H	G	F	E	D	C	B	A	Z	Y	X	W	V	U	T	S	R
R	Q	P	O	N	M	L	K	J	I	H	G	F	E	D	C	B	A	Z	Y	X	W	V	U	T	S
S	R	Q	P	O	N	M	L	K	J	I	H	G	F	E	D	C	B	A	Z	Y	X	W	V	U	T
T	S	R	Q	P	O	N	M	L	K	J	I	H	G	F	E	D	C	B	A	Z	Y	X	W	V	U
U	T	S	R	Q	P	O	N	M	L	K	J	I	H	G	F	E	D	C	B	A	Z	Y	X	W	V
V	U	T	S	R	Q	P	O	N	M	L	K	J	I	H	G	F	E	D	C	B	A	Z	Y	X	W
W	V	U	T	S	R	Q	P	O	N	M	L	K	J	I	H	G	F	E	D	C	B	A	Z	Y	X
X	W	V	U	T	S	R	Q	P	O	N	M	L	K	J	I	H	G	F	E	D	C	B	A	Z	Y
Y	X	W	V	U	T	S	R	Q	P	O	N	M	L	K	J	I	H	G	F	E	D	C	B	A	Z

Table 4.21. Beaufort square: plaintext "S" is encrypted with key "H" as "A"

The Beaufort cipher is based on the Beaufort square shown in Table 4.21. It looks just like the Vigenère square in Table 4.6, except that one starts with the letter "Z" in the first row and then goes backwards through the English alphabet. From row to row, this order is shifted by one position to the right. The encryption and decryption works just like the Vigenère cipher, except that one uses the Beaufort square in place of the Vigenère square.

(a) Suppose you have encrypted a plaintext by the Vigenère cipher with some key. How would you modify this key to obtain the same ciphertext from the plaintext using the Beaufort cipher?

(b) Verify your guess for Exercise 4.6(a). To this end, compare the two ciphertexts obtained from the same plaintext by the Vigenère cipher with some key and by the Beaufort cipher with the accordingly modified key. Use the plaintext from Exercise 4.5 if you were able to decipher the ciphertext in Table 4.20.

Exercise 4.7 **(a)** Apply the CBC mode to the following block encryptions:

- The Vigenère cipher with key ELLA and the plaintext given in Table 4.7 from Example 4.10. The initial vector in $\mathbb{Z}_{26}^4$ is $c_0 = $ ALLE.
- The Vigenère cipher with key PAULA and the plaintext given in Table 4.12. The initial vector in $\mathbb{Z}_{26}^5$ is $c_0 = $ ALUAP.
- The Hill cipher with key $A = \begin{pmatrix} 3 & 4 \\ 7 & 2 \end{pmatrix}$ and the plaintext given in Table 4.8 from Example 4.13. The initial vector is $c_0 = \square$B.
- The Hill cipher with key $A = \begin{pmatrix} 4 & 3 \\ 2 & 7 \end{pmatrix}$ and the plaintext corresponding to the ciphertext in Table 4.19 from Exercise 4.4(d). The initial vector is $c_0 = $ FZ.

Hint: For the Vigenère encryptions, the exclusive-or operation $\oplus$ used in the CBC mode is to be replaced by character-wise addition modulo 26. Similarly, for the Hill encryptions, replace $\oplus$ by character-wise addition modulo 29.

(b) Apply both the CFB mode and the OFB mode to the permutation cipher with the alphabet $\Sigma = \{0, 1\}$, block length 6, key $\pi = \begin{pmatrix} 1 & 2 & 3 & 4 & 5 & 6 \\ 6 & 1 & 2 & 5 & 3 & 4 \end{pmatrix}$, and initial vector $z_0 = 101001$. The plaintext is

$$m = 100110\ 111100\ 001100\ 010100.$$

Choose the shorter block length $k = 3$.

(c) Repeat Exercise 4.7(b) with the shorter block length $k = 2$.

(d) Using the permutation cipher with the alphabet $\Sigma = \{0, 1\}$, block length 3, and key

$$\pi = \begin{pmatrix} 1 & 2 & 3 \\ 3 & 2 & 1 \end{pmatrix},$$

encrypt the plaintext

$$m = 001\ 100\ 111\ 010$$

in the ECB, CBC, CFB, and OFB mode. The initial vector is 111. In the CFB and OFB mode, use the shorter block length $k = 2$.

Exercise 4.8 Consider the stream cipher that is based on a linear feedback shift register as shown in Example 4.21.

(a) Let $n = 6$, and fix the coefficients $a_2 = a_3 = a_6 = 0$ and $a_1 = a_4 = a_5 = 1$ in (4.7). Choose the key $\mathbf{k} = (1, 1, 0, 0, 1, 1)$. Encrypt the message

$$m = 1011100011011010100110101111001.$$

(b) Design a known-plaintext attack for breaking this stream cipher.

Hint: This attack is similar to the cryptanalysis of affine linear block ciphers such as the Hill cipher from Example 4.16. Note that all operations used in this stream cipher are linear. Thus, knowing a string of plaintext and a corresponding string of ciphertext, you can solve a system of linear equations to determine the values of the n unknown coefficients in the linear recursion (4.7).

Exercise 4.9 Consider the following stream cipher, which realizes one of the ideas from the infamous encryption machine *Enigma* that the Deutsche Wehrmacht used during World War II. The key space is $\mathbb{Z}_{26}$. For some fixed key $k \in \mathbb{Z}_{26}$ and for each $i \geq 1$, generate the key stream s by defining its ith element by the rule

$$s_i = (k + i - 1) \bmod 26.$$

Let π be some fixed permutation of $\mathbb{Z}_{26}$. If $s \in \mathbb{Z}_{26}$ is the current element of the key stream and x is the current plaintext letter, the encryption function E_s, which maps from $\mathbb{Z}_{26}$ to $\mathbb{Z}_{26}$, uses both π and s as follows:

$$E_s(x) = \pi((x + s) \bmod 26).$$

Similarly, the decryption function D_s, which also maps from $\mathbb{Z}_{26}$ to $\mathbb{Z}_{26}$, uses both s and the inverse permutation π^{-1} to decrypt the current ciphertext symbol y:

$$D_s(y) = (\pi^{-1}(y) - s) \bmod 26.$$

(a) Prove that this is a cryptosystem, i.e., prove that (4.1) is satisfied.

(b) Suppose that the permutation π of $\mathbb{Z}_{26}$ is given by

$$\begin{pmatrix} 0 \ 1 \ 2 \ 3 \ 4 \ 5 \ 6 \ 7 \ 8 \ 9 \ 10 \ 11 \ 12 \ 13 \ 14 \ 15 \ 16 \ 17 \ 18 \ 19 \ 20 \ 21 \ 22 \ 23 \ 24 \ 25 \\ 11 \ 8 \ 6 \ 1 \ 3 \ 4 \ 5 \ 9 \ 10 \ 2 \ 7 \ 0 \ 14 \ 12 \ 20 \ 13 \ 25 \ 21 \ 15 \ 17 \ 24 \ 18 \ 16 \ 22 \ 19 \ 23 \end{pmatrix}.$$

The following ciphertext was produced by the above stream cipher with π:

FRRMXCBEWMJWDDH TKO UACYKUK QAMT ASVZWO

Find the key used by exhaustive search of the key space, determine the complete key stream, and decrypt the ciphertext.

Exercise 4.10 Alter the given probabilities in Example 4.23 so as to obtain a cryptosystem that guarantees perfect secrecy.

Exercise 4.11 Prove that the shift cipher guarantees perfect secrecy, provided that the keys are distributed uniformly, and that a new random key is chosen to encrypt every new plaintext letter.

Exercise 4.12 Complete the proof of Theorem 4.31.

Exercise 4.13 Prove Theorem 4.33 and Corollary 4.34.

Exercise 4.14 Determine the inverse of the matrix

$$A = \begin{pmatrix} 0 \ 0 \ 1 \\ 0 \ 1 \ 1 \\ 1 \ 1 \ 1 \end{pmatrix}$$

modulo 2.

Exercise 4.15 Determine the determinant $\det B$ of the matrix

$$B = \begin{pmatrix} 3 & 1 & 2 \\ 2 & 3 & 1 \\ 1 & 2 & 3 \end{pmatrix}.$$

Problem 4.1 (Computing the Determinant)

(a) Design an algorithm in pseudocode for computing the determinant of a given matrix over $\mathbb{Z}_m$. Implement your algorithm in a programming language of your choice.

(b) Can you determine the inverse of a given matrix efficiently?

Problem 4.2 (Redundancy of a Language and Unicity Distance)

Let L be a natural language, such as Dutch or English, with the alphabet Σ. Intuitively, the *entropy of* L, denoted $\mathcal{H}_L$, measures the entropy per letter of L. If L were a random language in which each letter occurs with the same probability and independent of its context, then L would have the entropy $\log \|\Sigma\|$. However, natural languages are not random. The fraction of "additional" or "superfluous" letters is called the *redundancy of* L and is denoted by $\mathcal{R}_L$. Define these notions formally by

$$\mathcal{H}_L = \lim_{n \to \infty} \frac{\mathcal{H}(\mathbf{M}^n)}{n} \quad \text{and} \quad \mathcal{R}_L = 1 - \frac{\mathcal{H}_L}{\log \|\Sigma\|},$$

where $\mathbf{M}^n$ is some random variable that is distributed according to the probabilities with which the length n strings (i.e., all n-grams) in the language L occur.

(a) Let $S = (M, C, K, \mathcal{E}, \mathcal{D})$ be some cryptosystem, where $\|M\| = \|C\|$ and the keys are distributed uniformly. Let L be the language in which plaintexts are written. Given a ciphertext of length n, a cryptanalyst performing a ciphertext-only attack may be able to rule out certain keys, but many possible keys remain, only one of which is correct. Possible yet incorrect keys are called *spurious* keys. Let $\tilde{s}_n$ be the expected number of spurious keys, given a ciphertext of length n. Find a lower bound for $\tilde{s}_n$ in terms of the redundancy of L.

Hint: Use the ideas of entropy and conditional entropy.

(b) Define the *unicity distance of* S to be the value $n_0 \in \mathbb{N}$ for which $\tilde{s}_{n_0}$ becomes zero, i.e., the average size of ciphertext required for uniquely determining the correct key, provided one has sufficient computation time.

Give an approximation for the unicity distance n_0 based on your formula for $\tilde{s}_n$.

Problem 4.3 (Deciphering Edgar Allan Poe's Ciphertext)

Using a monoalphabetic cipher, Edgar Allan Poe created the following ciphertext in his short story "The Gold-Bug" (Random House, Inc., 1965):

```
53‡‡†305))6*;4826)4‡.)4‡);806*;48†8¶60))85;1‡(;:‡*8
†83(88)5*†;46(;88*96*?;8)*‡(;485);5*†2:*‡(;4956*2(5
*-4)8¶8*;4069285);)6†8)4‡‡ ;1(‡9;48081;8:8‡1;48†85;
4)485†528806*81(‡9;48;(88;4(‡?34;48)4‡;161;:188;‡?;
```

Determine the key and decrypt the ciphertext. Upon your solution of this enigma, go and find the hidden treasure and all the jewels of Golconda.

4.5 Summary and Bibliographic Remarks

General Remarks: Among the classics in cryptology are the books by Goldreich [Gol99, Gol01], Salomaa [Sal96], Stinson [Sti02], and Welsh [Wel98]. The book by Schneier [Sch96] provides a very comprehensive collection of literally all notions and concepts known in cryptology.

Singh [Sin99] has written a very charming, easy-to-read, fascinating book about the history of cryptography. An older but still valuable source is Kahn's book [Kah67]. Without claiming this list to be complete, we mention the texts by Bauer [Bau00a, Bau00b], Beutelspacher et al. [Beu94, BSW01, Beu02], Buchmann [Buc01], and Luby [Lub96]. More about the design and analysis of stream ciphers can be found in Rueppel's book [Rue86]. Micciancio and Goldwasser [MG02] survey the complexity of lattice problems from a cryptographic perspective.

Survey papers falling into the scope of this book are (in alphabetic order) those by Beygelzimer et al. [BHHR99], Cai [Cai99], Feigenbaum [Fei92], Goldreich [Gol88], Goldwasser [Gol89], Kumar and Sivakumar [KS01], Nguyen and Stern [NS01], Rothe [Rot04c, Rot02], and Selman [Sel92].

Specific Remarks: The beginnings of cryptography date back roughly to the ancient roots of human civilization. For example, Gaius Julius Caesar reports in his book "De Bello Gallico" that he transmitted an encrypted message to Q. Tullius Cicero (the brother of the famous speaker), who was besieged with his legion during the Gallic Wars (58 until 50 B.C.). The system used was monoalphabetic and replaced Latin letters by Greek letters. However, it is not clear from Caesar's report whether he used the shift cipher with key $k = 3$ indeed. This information was given later by Suetonius.

Vigenère's cipher rests on previous work by the Italian mathematician Leon Battista Alberti (born in 1404), the German abbot Johannes Trithemius (born in 1492), and the Italian scientist Giovanni Porta (born in 1535), see Singh [Sin99]. Kasiski's achievement of breaking the Vigenère cipher is also attributed to an unpublished work, done probably around 1854, by the British genius and eccentric Charles Babbage. More about Babbage's life, work, and ingenious inventions, including an early prototype of a computer, can be found in [Sin99].

From the example in Table 4.7, we not only learn how the Vigenère cipher works, but also that using a language that is not widely used, such as Hungarian or Finnish, often makes illegal decryption harder, and thus results in a higher level of security. This is not a purely theoretical observation. During World War II, the US Navy transmitted important messages using the language of the Navajos, a Native American tribe. The "Navajo Code" was never broken by the Japanese codebreakers, see [Sin99].

Likewise, Singh's book [Sin99] is a wonderful source for other exciting stories from the history of cryptology. For example, it reports on the thrilling struggle between the German cryptographers and the allied cryptanalysts during World War II. Eventually, the codebreakers of Bletchley Park, and most notably among them Alan Turing, succeeded in breaking the German *Enigma* code, see also Bauer [Bau00a, Bau00b]. The *Enigma*-based stream cipher given in Exercise 4.9 modifies a similar stream cipher due to Stinson [Sti02].

For the solution to Problem 4.2, which deals with the entropy and the redundancy of natural languages and with the unicity distance of cryptosystems, see Stinson [Sti02]. Denoting the English language by E, Stinson [Sti02] gives an estimate of $\mathcal{H}_E \approx 1.25$. That is, the average information content of English texts—including the book you are currently reading—is about 1.25 bits per letter. Thus, English has a redundancy of $\mathcal{R}_E \approx 0.75$. That is not to say that you could still read this book if three out of four letters had been removed.[1] Rather, it means that you can apply an encoding algorithm to compress the text to about one fourth of its original length without losing any information.

One may wonder why we speak so redundantly if we were able to convey the same information in another, compressed, language more tersely. It is worth mentioning that the redundancy of natural languages is not superfluous, it does have a purpose. Namely, it allows us to be still able to understand when transmission errors occur, for example those caused by a loud background noise in a bar. Speaking of that, the phrase "It is worth mentioning that" in a preceding sentence of this paragraph could have easily been dropped without losing much information. And likewise the phrase "Speaking of that."

The seminal idea of using the notion of entropy as a measure of information is due to Shannon [Sha49], who also proved Theorem 4.24 that characterizes the perfect secrecy of cryptosystems by necessary and sufficient conditions.

In Chapters 7 and 8, we will turn to cryptography again, focusing mainly on public-key cryptography and its relation to complexity theory, and thus omitting the presentation of more recent symmetric cryptosystems and block ciphers, notwithstanding their importance in practice. Many of those systems use very clever ideas. For example, one of the most popular symmetric, monoalphabetic block ciphers is the *Data Encryption Standard* (DES, for short), which is based on certain sophisticated transformations and is described in many textbooks on cryptography. The DES was developed by IBM and was adopted as a standard in 1977. One problem with this system is its key length, which is only 56 bits and thus too short by current standards. The DES was broken in 1999 by exhaustive key search. For more information on the mathematical properties of the DES obtained from empirical studies, see Kaliski, Rivest, and Sherman [KRS88].

---

[1] M□□□ li□□□y□ □□□□ w□□□□n□t w□□k□

A successor of this block cipher, Triple-DES, has a key length of 112 bits and is thus more secure. For more information on the *Advanced Encryption Standard* (AES, for short), which has been adopted by the National Institute of Standards and Technology (NIST) as the current encryption standard, see Daemen and Rijmen [DR01].

5

Hierarchies Based on NP

Wer reitet so spät durch Nacht und Schnee?
Es ist Gerd Wechsung mit seinem MEE;
Er hat die Formel wohl in dem Arm,
Er faßt sie sicher, er hält sie warm. –

Mein Phi, was birgst du so bang dein Gesicht? –
Siehst, Gerd, denn du den Erlkönig nicht?
Den Erlenkönig mit Kron und so? –
Mein Phi, das ist nur Theta-pe-zwo. –

"Du liebes Phi, komm, geh mit mir!
Gar schöne Spiele spiel ich mit dir;
Und bist du die kleinste Formel am End,
So macht meine Mutter dich äquivalent."

Mein Gerd, mein Gerd, und hörest du nicht,
Was Erlenkönig mir leise verspricht? –
Sei ruhig, bleibe ruhig, mein Phi!
Orakelmaschinen säuseln doch nie. –

"Gehst, feines Phi, du mit mir schnell?
Meine Töchter erfragen dich parallel;
Meine Töchter sind schön und ganz ohne Makel
Und fragen nach dir ihr NP-Orakel."

Mein Gerd, mein Gerd, und siehst du nicht dort
Erlkönigs Töchter am düstern Ort? –
Mein Phi, mein Phi, was ich da seh,
Das ist doch wieder bloß Theta-zwo-pe. –

"Ich liebe dich, mich reizt deine schöne Gestalt;
Und bist du nicht willig, so brauch ich Gewalt." –
Mein Gerd, mein Gerd, jetzt faßt er mich an!
Erlkönig hat mir ein Leids getan! –

Gerd Wechsung grauset's, er reitet wie nie,
Er hält in Armen das ächzende Phi,
Erreicht den Hof mit Phi, so zart;
In seinen Armen das MEE war hart.

(Based on the poem "Erlkönig"
by Johann W. von Goethe, see also [HW02, Rot04b])

Turning again to complexity theory, this chapter introduces some important complexity hierarchies built upon NP, such as the boolean hierarchy over NP and the polynomial hierarchy. Complete problems in the levels of these hierarchies are identified, and the properties of and the relationships between these two hierarchies are explored. Examples of problems complete for the levels of the boolean hierarchy over NP include the "exact" variants of NP-complete optimization problems and critical graph problems. Examples of problems complete for the levels of the polynomial hierarchy include variants of NP-complete problems involving quantification with a bounded number of alternating length-bounded quantifiers. Relatedly, the notion of alternating Turing machines is introduced.

Moreover, this chapter introduces the low hierarchy within NP, which provides a yardstick for measuring the complexity of NP problems that seemingly are neither in P nor NP-complete. As an example of such problems, the graph isomorphism problem will be shown to be low in Chapter 6.

5.1 Boolean Hierarchy over NP

Many important problems were shown to be NP-complete in Section 3.5.3, among them the 3-Colorability problem and the domatic number problem, DNP. The goal now is to study the "exact" variants of these two problems and to determine their exact complexity.

We start with the exact domatic number problem. Recall from Section 3.5.3 that DNP is (the decision version of) the problem of partitioning the vertex set of a given graph G into a maximum number of disjoint dominating sets, where a dominating set is a subset D of G's vertex set such that every vertex of $V(G)$ either belongs to D or is adjacent to some vertex in D.

First, what are the "exact" variants of NP-complete optimization problems such as the DNP, and why would one want to study them? As a motivation, consider the following two scenarios in which the domatic number problem arises: it is related both to the task of distributing resources in a computer network and to the task of locating facilities in a communication network. In the latter scenario, n cities are linked via communication channels. A *transmitting group* is any subset T of the cities such that each city in T can transmit messages to every city in the network. A transmitting group is nothing else than a dominating set in the network graph, and the domatic number of this graph is the maximum number of disjoint transmitting groups in the network.

In the other scenario, consider a network of n computers. Suppose that resources are to be allocated in the network such that expensive services are quickly accessible in the immediate neighborhood of each vertex. If every vertex has only a limited capacity, then there is a bound on the number of resources that can be supported. In particular, if every vertex can serve a single resource only, then the maximum number of resources that can be supported equals the domatic number of the network graph.

Expensive resources should not be wasted. Given a graph G and a positive integer i, how hard is it to determine whether or not $\delta(G)$, the domatic number of G, equals i *exactly*? That is, what is the exact complexity of the exact domatic number problem?

Definition 5.1 (Exact Domatic Number Problem).
For each fixed positive integer i, define the exact domatic number problem *by:*

$$\text{Exact-}i\text{-DNP} = \{G \mid G \text{ is a graph and } \delta(G) = i\}.$$

Fact 5.2 *For each fixed $i \geq 3$,* Exact-i-DNP *is NP-hard.*

Proof.   The proof is given for the case of $i = 3$ only; see Exercise 5.1 for the case of $i > 3$.

For $i = 3$, consider the reduction f constructed in the proof of Theorem 3.58, which witnesses that 3-Colorability $\leq_m^p$ DNP. This reduction maps any given graph G to the pair $\langle H, 3 \rangle = f(G)$, where H is a graph satisfying the implications (3.16) and (3.17) as is shown in that proof:

$$G \in \text{3-Colorability} \Longrightarrow \delta(H) = 3;$$
$$G \notin \text{3-Colorability} \Longrightarrow \delta(H) = 2.$$

Modify this reduction slightly by defining $\hat{f}(G) = H$, which yields a reduction for 3-Colorability $\leq_m^P$ Exact-3-DNP. Hence, Exact-3-DNP is NP-hard.   ∎

Is Exact-i-DNP NP-complete? That is, is it in NP? The following naive approach to show membership in NP fails: Given a positive integer i and a graph G, nondeterministically guess a partition of G's vertex set into i pairwise disjoint sets, and for each partition guessed, verify deterministically that each set in the partition is a dominating set of G. This approach works fine if $\delta(G) \leq i$, since the NP algorithm checks the other condition required for equality: $\delta(G) \geq i$. However, if $\delta(G) > i$, then G is not in Exact-i-DNP, yet the NP algorithm above incorrectly accepts G on some erroneous computation path. Thus, what is needed to accept Exact-i-DNP is an additional test that $\delta(G) > i$ does *not* hold. This, however, is a coNP predicate.

So, proving an NP upper bound for Exact-i-DNP seems hard, if not impossible. But then, what *is* the best upper bound known for this problem? Note that Exact-i-DNP can be written as the intersection of two sets:

$$\text{Exact-}i\text{-DNP} = \{G \mid \delta(G) \geq i\} \cap \{G \mid \delta(G) \leq i\}.$$

The first set, $\{G \mid \delta(G) \geq i\}$, is in NP, whereas the second set, $\{G \mid \delta(G) \leq i\}$, is in coNP. That is, Exact-i-DNP can be written as the intersection of an NP set and a coNP set. Motivated by such "exact" variants of NP-complete optimization problems, Papadimitriou and Yannakakis introduced the complexity class DP, which contains precisely the differences of any two NP sets:

$$\text{DP} = \{A - B \mid A \text{ and } B \text{ are in NP}\}.$$

In particular, Exact-i-DNP is in DP, since $A - B = A \cap \overline{B}$. Again, is it DP-complete? That is, is it DP-hard? We will see later on that the answer is yes. However, before showing DP-completeness of the exact domatic number problem, we introduce generalized versions of this problem and, relatedly, a generalization of DP. Given a graph G and a set $M_k = \{i_1, i_2, \ldots, i_k\}$ of k positive integers, how hard is it to determine whether or not $\delta(G)$ equals some i_j *exactly*?

Definition 5.3 (Exact Domatic Number Problem (Generalized Version)).
Let $M_k \subseteq \mathbb{N}$ be any set of k integers. Define the generalized version of the exact domatic number problem *by:*

$$\text{Exact-}M_k\text{-DNP} = \{G \mid G \text{ is a graph and } \delta(G) \in M_k\}.$$

In particular, for each singleton $M_1 = \{i\}$, we write Exact-i-DNP $= \{G \mid \delta(G) = i\}$.

Analogously to the above arguments that Exact-i-DNP is in DP, one can show that Exact-M_k-DNP can be written as the union of k sets in DP. This observation motivates a generalization of DP: the boolean hierarchy over NP. To define this hierarchy, we use the symbols $\wedge$ and $\vee$, respectively, to denote the *complex intersection* and the *complex union* of set classes. That is, for classes $\mathcal{C}$ and $\mathcal{D}$ of sets, define:

$$\mathcal{C} \wedge \mathcal{D} = \{A \cap B \mid A \in \mathcal{C} \text{ and } B \in \mathcal{D}\};$$
$$\mathcal{C} \vee \mathcal{D} = \{A \cup B \mid A \in \mathcal{C} \text{ and } B \in \mathcal{D}\}.$$

Definition 5.4 (Boolean Hierarchy over NP).
The boolean hierarchy over NP *is inductively defined by:*

$$\mathrm{BH}_0(\mathrm{NP}) = \mathrm{P},$$
$$\mathrm{BH}_1(\mathrm{NP}) = \mathrm{NP},$$
$$\mathrm{BH}_2(\mathrm{NP}) = \mathrm{NP} \wedge \mathrm{coNP},$$
$$\mathrm{BH}_k(\mathrm{NP}) = \mathrm{BH}_{k-2}(\mathrm{NP}) \vee \mathrm{BH}_2(\mathrm{NP}) \quad \textit{for each } k \geq 3, \textit{ and}$$
$$\mathrm{BH}(\mathrm{NP}) = \bigcup_{k \geq 0} \mathrm{BH}_k(\mathrm{NP}).$$

Note that $\mathrm{DP} = \mathrm{BH}_2(\mathrm{NP}) = \mathrm{NP} \wedge \mathrm{coNP}$. A warning is in order here: $\mathrm{NP} \wedge \mathrm{coNP}$ and $\mathrm{NP} \cap \mathrm{coNP}$ are (most likely to be) *distinct* complexity classes! Set-theoretically, the *intersection* $\mathrm{NP} \cap \mathrm{coNP}$ is performed on a different level than the *complex intersection* $\mathrm{NP} \wedge \mathrm{coNP}$ of the set classes NP and coNP. That is, $\mathrm{NP} \wedge \mathrm{coNP}$ is the set of intersections of NP sets with coNP sets, whereas $\mathrm{NP} \cap \mathrm{coNP}$ is the set of sets that are both in NP and in coNP. Certainly, if NP equals P, then so do coNP, $\mathrm{NP} \wedge \mathrm{coNP}$, $\mathrm{NP} \cap \mathrm{coNP}$, and many other classes; see Exercise 5.3. However, $\mathrm{NP} = \mathrm{P}$ is considered to be most unlikely.

The above comment about the complex intersection and union of set classes applies as well to the co operator, which applied to any class $\mathcal{C}$ of sets yields the class $\mathrm{co}\mathcal{C} = \{\overline{L} \mid L \in \mathcal{C}\}$, the class of complements of the sets in $\mathcal{C}$. For instance, coNP, the class of complements of NP sets, is quite different an animal than $\overline{\mathrm{NP}} = \{L \mid L \notin \mathrm{NP}\}$, the complement of NP, which contains every set that is not an NP set.

Definition 5.5 (Boolean Closure).   *Let $\mathcal{C}$ be any class of sets, and let A and B be any sets. Define the* boolean closure of $\mathcal{C}$, *denoted by* $\mathrm{BC}(\mathcal{C})$, *to be the smallest class $\mathcal{D}$ of languages containing $\mathcal{C}$ and closed under the following boolean operations:*

- *$\mathcal{D}$ is closed under union, i.e., if both A and B are in $\mathcal{D}$, then so is $A \cup B$;*
- *$\mathcal{D}$ is closed under intersection, i.e., if both A and B are in $\mathcal{D}$, then so is $A \cap B$;*
- *$\mathcal{D}$ is closed under complement, i.e., if A is in $\mathcal{D}$, then so is $\overline{A}$.*

In particular, consider $\mathrm{BC}(\mathrm{NP})$, the boolean closure of NP. The first two closure properties (under union and intersection) can also be expressed by $\mathrm{NP} \vee \mathrm{NP} = \mathrm{NP}$ and $\mathrm{NP} \wedge \mathrm{NP} = \mathrm{NP}$, respectively, and they are outright true for NP; see Exercise 5.4. However, the third closure property (under complement) is a major open question for NP, almost as intractable and as infamous as the P versus NP question. It is widely believed that $\mathrm{NP} \neq \mathrm{coNP}$, i.e., that NP is not closed under complement.

Hence, it is widely believed that NP $\neq$ BC(NP); see Exercise 5.5. However, any proof of NP $\neq$ BC(NP) immediately gives a proof of NP $\neq$ coNP, which in turn proves P $\neq$ NP.

Classes of sets that are closed under union and intersection and contain $\emptyset$ and Σ^*, such as NP, are called *set rings*, with the ring operations union and intersection. Set rings that in addition are closed under complement are called *boolean algebras*. For each boolean algebra $\mathcal{A}$, BC($\mathcal{A}$) $= \mathcal{A}$. Hausdorff [Hau14] introduced the boolean hierarchy over arbitrary set rings as the "union-of-differences hierarchy," which is given for the set ring NP in Definition 5.4.[1] Therefore, this boolean hierarchy normal form is sometimes called the *Hausdorff hierarchy*; see Section 5.9 for other boolean hierarchy normal forms and for boolean hierarchies over complexity classes other than NP.

One of the other boolean hierarchy normal forms hinted at above is the "nested difference hierarchy," which coincides, level by level, with the "union-of-differences hierarchy" from Definition 5.4. Theorem 5.6 below shows that these two boolean hierarchy normal forms are equivalent for set rings, level by level, and also that both capture the boolean closure of the underlying set ring. If the underlying set class is not a set ring, the corresponding equivalences are not so clear. For certain boolean hierarchy normal forms other than the two discussed here, L. Hemaspaandra and Rothe prove that closure of the underlying set class under intersection already suffices to capture the boolean closure of the class; see the discussion in Section 5.9. An example of a class closed under intersection, yet presumably not closed under union, is the class UP; see Exercise 5.6.

When writing nested differences of k sets, we agree by convention that we may omit the parentheses to enhance readability:

$$A_1 - A_2 - \cdots - A_{k-1} - A_k = A_1 - (A_2 - (\cdots - (A_{k-1} - A_k) \cdots)),$$

although set difference is not an associative operation.

Theorem 5.6. *For each set ring $\mathcal{C}$, the following two statements hold:*

1. *The nested difference hierarchy over $\mathcal{C}$ coincides, level by level, with the union-of-differences hierarchy over $\mathcal{C}$:*

$$\mathrm{BH}_k(\mathcal{C}) = \left\{ L \,\middle|\, \begin{array}{l} L = A_1 - A_2 - \cdots - A_k \text{ for sets } A_i \text{ in } \mathcal{C}, \\ 1 \leq i \leq k, \text{ satisfying } A_k \subseteq A_{k-1} \subseteq \cdots \subseteq A_1 \end{array} \right\}.$$

2. $\mathrm{BH}(\mathcal{C}) = \mathrm{BC}(\mathcal{C})$.

Proof. Both statements can be proven by elementary set transformations; see Exercise 5.7. ∎

---

[1] Substituting any set class $\mathcal{C}$ for NP in Definition 5.4 defines the levels $\mathrm{BH}_k(\mathcal{C})$ of the boolean hierarchy over $\mathcal{C}$, whose union is $\mathrm{BH}(\mathcal{C}) = \bigcup_{k \geq 0} \mathrm{BH}_k(\mathcal{C})$.

Corollary 5.7.   *1. The nested difference hierarchy over* NP *coincides, level by level, with the union-of-differences hierarchy over* NP:

$$\mathrm{BH}_k(\mathrm{NP}) = \left\{ L \left| \begin{array}{l} L = A_1 - A_2 - \cdots - A_k \text{ for sets } A_i \text{ in NP,} \\ 1 \leq i \leq k, \text{ satisfying } A_k \subseteq A_{k-1} \subseteq \cdots \subseteq A_1 \end{array} \right. \right\}.$$

2. $\mathrm{BH}(\mathrm{NP}) = \mathrm{BC}(\mathrm{NP})$.

Theorem 5.8 states the inclusion relations between the levels of the boolean hierarchy over NP, which follow immediately from Definition 5.4. Figure 5.1 shows this inclusion structure as a Hasse diagram. That is, containment of a class $\mathcal{C}$ in a class $\mathcal{D}$ is indicated by a line going from $\mathcal{C}$ upward to $\mathcal{D}$. Incomparable classes—which means that neither $\mathcal{C} \subseteq \mathcal{D}$ nor $\mathcal{D} \subseteq \mathcal{C}$ is known to hold—are not connected by a line. Figure 5.2 shows this inclusion structure as a Venn diagram, where we write BH_1 in place of $\mathrm{BH}_1(\mathrm{NP})$, etc. to enhance readability. Here, darker classes are contained in lighter classes, and incomparable classes have the same gray level. None of the inclusions is known to be strict.

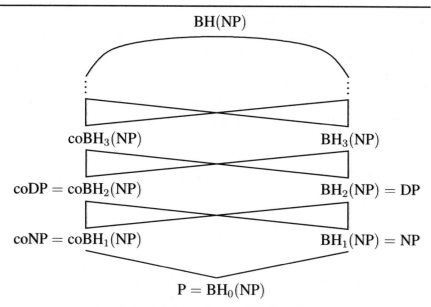

Fig. 5.1. Boolean hierarchy over NP (Hasse diagram)

Theorem 5.8.   *For each $k \geq 0$,*

$$\mathrm{BH}_k(\mathrm{NP}) \subseteq \mathrm{BH}_{k+1}(\mathrm{NP}) \ \text{and} \ \mathrm{coBH}_k(\mathrm{NP}) \subseteq \mathrm{coBH}_{k+1}(\mathrm{NP}) \qquad (5.1)$$

and, hence, $\mathrm{BH}_k(\mathrm{NP}) \cup \mathrm{coBH}_k(\mathrm{NP}) \subseteq \mathrm{BH}_{k+1}(\mathrm{NP})$.

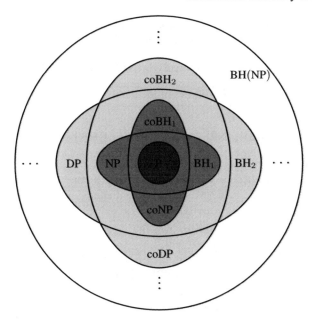

Fig. 5.2. Boolean hierarchy over NP (Venn diagram)

Story 5.9 *Think of the boolean hierarchy as a building; a huge, magnificent, splendid pair of twin towers whose floors are the* $\mathrm{BH}_k(\mathrm{NP})$ *and* $\mathrm{coBH}_k(\mathrm{NP})$ *levels, respectively. How many floors are there? Is* $\mathrm{BH}_k(\mathrm{NP})$ *a proper hierarchy consisting of an infinite number of strictly distinct levels? Or is it finite? No one knows. As so often in complexity theory, this is an open research question closely tied to the* P *versus* NP *question.*

Now imagine some evil terrorist vandalizing through the Boolean Hierarchy Tower and, with hand grenades and other explosives, damaging the 71st floor so badly that it is completely destroyed. It is clear what will happen to the building: It collapses. Theorem 5.10 shows that this is exactly what happens to the boolean hierarchy: If any one of its levels collapses down to the level preceding it, then the entire hierarchy collapses down to this specific, finite level. Even if any one of the $\mathrm{BH}_k(\mathrm{NP})$ *classes were to coincide with its complementary class,* $\mathrm{coBH}_k(\mathrm{NP})$, *the same consequence occurs. This property of a hierarchy of complexity classes is dubbed "upward collapse" or, synonymously, "downward separation."*

Theorem 5.10.

1. *For each* $k \geq 0$, *if* $\mathrm{BH}_k(\mathrm{NP}) = \mathrm{BH}_{k+1}(\mathrm{NP})$, *then*

   $$\mathrm{BH}_k(\mathrm{NP}) = \mathrm{coBH}_k(\mathrm{NP}) = \mathrm{BH}_{k+1}(\mathrm{NP}) = \mathrm{coBH}_{k+1}(\mathrm{NP}) = \cdots = \mathrm{BH}(\mathrm{NP}).$$

2. *For each* $k \geq 1$, *if* $\mathrm{BH}_k(\mathrm{NP}) = \mathrm{coBH}_k(\mathrm{NP})$, *then*

   $$\mathrm{BH}_k(\mathrm{NP}) = \mathrm{coBH}_k(\mathrm{NP}) = \mathrm{BH}_{k+1}(\mathrm{NP}) = \mathrm{coBH}_{k+1}(\mathrm{NP}) = \cdots = \mathrm{BH}(\mathrm{NP}).$$

Proof.   To prove the first statement, suppose that $\mathrm{BH}_k(\mathrm{NP}) = \mathrm{BH}_{k+1}(\mathrm{NP})$ is true for some fixed $k \geq 0$. We prove by induction on n:

$$(\forall n \geq k)\, [\mathrm{BH}_n(\mathrm{NP}) = \mathrm{coBH}_n(\mathrm{NP}) = \mathrm{BH}_{n+1}(\mathrm{NP})]. \tag{5.2}$$

The induction base, $n = k$, follows immediately from (5.1) in Theorem 5.8 and the hypothesis $\mathrm{BH}_k(\mathrm{NP}) = \mathrm{BH}_{k+1}(\mathrm{NP})$:

$$\mathrm{coBH}_k(\mathrm{NP}) \subseteq \mathrm{BH}_{k+1}(\mathrm{NP}) = \mathrm{BH}_k(\mathrm{NP}),$$

which immediately implies $\mathrm{coBH}_k(\mathrm{NP}) = \mathrm{BH}_k(\mathrm{NP})$.

The induction hypothesis says that (5.2) is true for some $n \geq k$. We have to show that $\mathrm{BH}_{n+1}(\mathrm{NP}) = \mathrm{BH}_{n+2}(\mathrm{NP})$. By an argument analogous to the induction base, this also implies $\mathrm{BH}_{n+1}(\mathrm{NP}) = \mathrm{coBH}_{n+1}(\mathrm{NP})$.

Let X be any set in $\mathrm{BH}_{n+2}(\mathrm{NP})$. Thus, there exist sets $A_1, A_2, \ldots, A_{n+2}$ in NP such that $A_{n+2} \subseteq A_{n+1} \subseteq \cdots \subseteq A_1$ and $X = A_1 - A_2 - \cdots - A_{n+2}$.

Let $Y = A_2 - A_3 - \cdots - A_{n+2}$. Thus, $Y \in \mathrm{BH}_{n+1}(\mathrm{NP})$. By induction hypothesis, Y is contained in $\mathrm{BH}_n(\mathrm{NP}) = \mathrm{BH}_{n+1}(\mathrm{NP})$. Hence, $Y = B_1 - B_2 - \cdots - B_n$, for suitable NP sets $B_1, B_2, \ldots, B_n$ satisfying $B_n \subseteq B_{n-1} \subseteq \cdots \subseteq B_1$. By our choice of the sets A_i, we have $Y \subseteq A_1$, which implies $Y \cap A_1 = Y$. It follows that

$$Y = (B_1 \cap A_1) - (B_2 \cap A_1) - \cdots - (B_n \cap A_1).$$

Each of the sets $B_i \cap A_1$ is in NP, since NP is closed under intersection; see Exercise 5.4(a). Consequently,

$$X = A_1 - Y = A_1 - (B_1 \cap A_1) - (B_2 \cap A_1) - \cdots - (B_n \cap A_1),$$

is a set in $\mathrm{BH}_{n+1}(\mathrm{NP})$, where

$$(B_n \cap A_1) \subseteq (B_{n-1} \cap A_1) \subseteq \cdots \subseteq (B_1 \cap A_1) \subseteq A_1,$$

which concludes the induction and proves (5.2).

To prove the second statement, suppose that $\mathrm{BH}_k(\mathrm{NP}) = \mathrm{coBH}_k(\mathrm{NP})$ is true for some fixed $k \geq 1$. We show that this supposition implies $\mathrm{BH}_{k+1}(\mathrm{NP}) = \mathrm{BH}_k(\mathrm{NP})$, thus reducing the second statement to the first statement of the theorem.

Let $X = A_1 - A_2 - \cdots - A_{k+1}$ be a set in $\mathrm{BH}_{k+1}(\mathrm{NP})$, where $A_1, A_2, \ldots, A_{k+1}$ are sets in NP satisfying that $A_{k+1} \subseteq A_k \subseteq \cdots \subseteq A_1$.

Hence, $Y = A_2 - A_3 - \cdots - A_{k+1}$ is a set in $\mathrm{BH}_k(\mathrm{NP})$. By our supposition, Y is in $\mathrm{coBH}_k(\mathrm{NP}) = \mathrm{BH}_k(\mathrm{NP})$. Thus, $\overline{Y}$ is a set in $\mathrm{BH}_k(\mathrm{NP})$. Let $B_1, B_2, \ldots, B_k$ be sets in NP such that $\overline{Y} = B_1 - B_2 - \cdots - B_k$ and $B_k \subseteq B_{k-1} \subseteq \cdots \subseteq B_1$. Again, since NP is closed under intersection, each of the sets $A_1 \cap B_i$, $1 \leq i \leq k$, is in NP. Furthermore, $A_1 \cap B_k \subseteq A_1 \cap B_{k-1} \subseteq \cdots \subseteq A_1 \cap B_1$. Hence,

$$X = A_1 - Y = A_1 \cap \overline{Y} = (A_1 \cap B_1) - (A_1 \cap B_2) - \cdots - (A_1 \cap B_k)$$

is a set in $\mathrm{BH}_k(\mathrm{NP})$, which proves that $\mathrm{BH}_{k+1}(\mathrm{NP}) = \mathrm{BH}_k(\mathrm{NP})$, and the argument given in the proof of the first statement of the theorem applies to prove the collapse $\mathrm{BH}_k(\mathrm{NP}) = \mathrm{BH}(\mathrm{NP})$.   ∎

Turning back to the exact domatic number problem, recall that Exact-i-DNP is in DP for each fixed i. Hence, for each $k \geq 1$ and for each set M_k of k positive integers, Exact-M_k-DNP is contained in $\mathrm{BH}_{2k}(\mathrm{NP})$. Do there exist *lower bounds* for Exact-M_k-DNP matching these $\mathrm{BH}_{2k}(\mathrm{NP})$ upper bounds? That is, is Exact-M_k-DNP complete for $\mathrm{BH}_{2k}(\mathrm{NP})$? As mentioned earlier, the answer is yes.

In his seminal paper [Wag87a], Wagner provided a set of conditions sufficient to prove $\mathrm{BH}_i(\mathrm{NP})$-hardness results for each $i \geq 1$. Replacing "odd" by "even" in (5.3) of Lemma 5.11 below, one obtains analogous sufficient conditions for $\mathrm{coBH}_i(\mathrm{NP})$-hardness.

Crucially, the Wagner technique shows how to raise NP lower bounds to lower bounds for classes above NP. Section 5.3 will provide another condition of Wagner, which is closely akin to that presented in Lemma 5.11 and which is sufficient to prove hardness for some complexity class even larger than the boolean hierarchy. Applications of Wagner's sufficient conditions will be mentioned in Section 5.9.

Lemma 5.11 (Wagner).   *Let A be some NP-complete problem, let B be an arbitrary problem, and let $k \geq 1$ be fixed. If there exists a polynomial-time computable function f such that, for all strings $x_1, x_2, \ldots, x_k \in \Sigma^*$ satisfying that $x_{j+1} \in A$ implies $x_j \in A$ for each j with $1 \leq j < k$, the equivalence*

$$||\{i \mid x_i \in A\}|| \text{ is odd} \iff f(\langle x_1, x_2, \ldots, x_k \rangle) \in B \tag{5.3}$$

is true, then B is $\mathrm{BH}_k(\mathrm{NP})$-hard.

Proof.   Fix some NP-complete problem A and some $k \geq 1$, and let B be an arbitrary problem. It is enough to prove the theorem for even k only; the case of k being odd can be proven analogously. Let $k = 2m$ for some $m \geq 1$. Suppose there exists some function $f \in \mathrm{FP}$ satisfying (5.3) for all strings $x_1, x_2, \ldots, x_k \in \Sigma^*$ for which $x_{j+1} \in A$ implies $x_j \in A$ for each j with $1 \leq j < k$.

Let X be an arbitrary set in $\mathrm{BH}_k(\mathrm{NP})$. By Theorem 5.6, there exist NP sets $Y_1, Y_2, \ldots, Y_k$ such that $Y_k \subseteq Y_{k-1} \subseteq \cdots \subseteq Y_1$ and

$$X = Y_1 - Y_2 - \cdots - Y_k = \bigcup_{i=1}^{m} (Y_{2i-1} \cap \overline{Y_{2i}}). \tag{5.4}$$

Since A is NP-complete, there exist k reductions $r_1, r_2, \ldots, r_k$ in FP such that, for each $x \in \Sigma^*$, $x \in Y_j$ if and only if $r_j(x) \in A$, for each j with $1 \leq j \leq k$.

Hence, since $Y_k \subseteq Y_{k-1} \subseteq \cdots \subseteq Y_1$, $r_{j+1}(x) \in A$ implies $r_j(x) \in A$ for each j with $1 \leq j \leq k$. By (5.4) and (5.3), for each $x \in \Sigma^*$,

$$x \in X \overset{(5.4)}{\iff} ||\{i \mid r_i(x) \in A\}|| \text{ is odd}$$

$$\overset{(5.3)}{\iff} f(\langle r_1(x), r_2(x), \ldots, r_k(x) \rangle) \in B.$$

Thus, $X \leq_{\mathrm{m}}^{\mathrm{p}} B$ via $f \in \mathrm{FP}$. Since X is an arbitrary set in $\mathrm{BH}_k(\mathrm{NP})$, it follows that B is $\mathrm{BH}_k(\mathrm{NP})$-hard.   ∎

Theorem 5.12 applies Wagner's sufficient condition from Lemma 5.11 to the exact domatic number problem: For each fixed set M_k containing k noncontiguous integers not smaller than $4k + 1$, Exact-M_k-DNP is complete for $\mathrm{BH}_{2k}(\mathrm{NP})$. In particular, for $k = 1$, Corollary 5.13 states that Exact-5-DNP is DP-complete.

Theorem 5.12. *For fixed $k \geq 1$, let $M_k = \{4k + 1, 4k + 3, \ldots, 6k - 1\}$. Then,* Exact-$M_k$-DNP *is* $\mathrm{BH}_{2k}(\mathrm{NP})$-*complete.*

Corollary 5.13. Exact-5-DNP *is DP-complete.*

Proof of Theorem 5.12.   We have already seen that Exact-M_k-DNP is contained in $\mathrm{BH}_{2k}(\mathrm{NP})$. It remains to prove $\mathrm{BH}_{2k}(\mathrm{NP})$-hardness of Exact-$M_k$-DNP. To this end, apply Lemma 5.11 with 3-Colorability being the NP-complete set A and with Exact-M_k-DNP being the set B from this lemma.

Fix any $2k$ graphs $G_1, G_2, \ldots, G_{2k}$ satisfying that for each j with $1 \leq j < 2k$, if G_{j+1} is in 3-Colorability, then so is G_j. By the proof of Theorem 3.56, which provides a reduction from 3-SAT to 3-Colorability, we may assume that:

- for each graph G_j, we have $3 \leq \chi(G_j) \leq 4$, where $\chi(G_j)$ denotes the chromatic number of G_j;
- none of the graphs G_j contains isolated vertices.

Solve Exercise 5.10 to comprehend why these assumptions can be made without loss of generality.

Let $g \in \mathrm{FP}$ be the reduction constructed in the proof of Theorem 3.58, which reduces 3-Colorability to DNP by mapping any given graph G to the pair $\langle H, 3 \rangle = g(G)$, where H is a graph satisfying the implications (3.16) and (3.17):

$$G \in \text{3-Colorability} \Longrightarrow \delta(H) = 3;$$
$$G \notin \text{3-Colorability} \Longrightarrow \delta(H) = 2.$$

Applying g to each of the graphs G_j, where $1 \leq j \leq 2k$, we obtain $2k$ graphs $H_j = g(G_j)$, each satisfying the implications (3.16) and (3.17). Hence, for each j, $\delta(H_j) \in \{2, 3\}$, and $\delta(H_{j+1}) = 3$ implies $\delta(H_j) = 3$.

Define a polynomial-time computable function f mapping the given graphs $G_1, G_2, \ldots, G_{2k}$ to a graph H such that the equivalence (5.3) from Lemma 5.11 is satisfied. The graph H is constructed from the graphs $H_1, H_2, \ldots, H_{2k}$ such that $\delta(H) = \sum_{j=1}^{2k} \delta(H_j)$.

Before the construction is given in general, consider the special case $k = 1$ first. For $k = 1$, two graphs are given, $H_1 = g(G_1)$ and $H_2 = g(G_2)$. Construct a gadget connecting H_1 and H_2 as follows. Recalling the construction from Theorem 3.58, let T_1 with $V(T_1) = \{v_q^{T_1}, u_{q,r}^{T_1}, v_r^{T_1}\}$ be any fixed triangle in H_1, and let T_2 with $V(T_2) = \{v_s^{T_2}, u_{s,t}^{T_2}, v_t^{T_2}\}$ be any fixed triangle in H_2. Connect T_1 and T_2 using the gadget that is shown in Figure 5.3. That is, add the six new vertices $a_1^{T_1,T_2}, a_2^{T_1,T_2}, \ldots, a_6^{T_1,T_2}$, and add the new edges shown in that figure by thin lines.

Using pairwise disjoint copies of the gadget from Figure 5.3, connect each pair of triangles from H_1 and H_2. Call the resulting graph H. Recall that, for any graph G,

$\delta(G) \leq$ *min-deg*$(G) + 1$, where *min-deg*(G) denotes the minimum degree of the vertices of G. (The *degree of a vertex* v in a graph G is the number of edges incident to v.) Since the degree of each gadget vertex a_i is 5, $\delta(H) \leq 6$, regardless of the domatic numbers of H_1 and H_2. We now show that $\delta(H) = \delta(H_1) + \delta(H_2)$.

Let $D_1, D_2, \ldots, D_{\delta(H_1)}$ be $\delta(H_1)$ pairwise disjoint sets dominating H_1, and let $D_{\delta(H_1)+1}, D_{\delta(H_1)+2}, \ldots, D_{\delta(H_1)+\delta(H_2)}$ be $\delta(H_2)$ pairwise disjoint sets dominating H_2. Distinguish the following three cases.

Case 1: $\delta(H_1) = \delta(H_2) = 3$.   Consider any fixed D_j, where $1 \leq j \leq 3$. Since D_j dominates H_1, every triangle T_1 of H_1 has exactly one vertex in D_j. Fix T_1, and suppose $V(T_1) = \{v_q^{T_1}, u_{q,r}^{T_1}, v_r^{T_1}\}$ and, say, $V(T_1) \cap D_j = \{v_q^{T_1}\}$; the other cases are analogous.

For each triangle T_2 of H_2, say T_2 with $V(T_2) = \{v_s^{T_2}, u_{s,t}^{T_2}, v_t^{T_2}\}$, consider the six gadget vertices $a_1^{T_1,T_2}, a_2^{T_1,T_2}, \ldots, a_6^{T_1,T_2}$ connecting T_1 and T_2 as in Figure 5.3. Note that exactly one of these gadget vertices, $a_3^{T_1,T_2}$, is not adjacent to $v_q^{T_1}$. For each triangle T_2, add the missing gadget vertex to D_j, and define

$$\hat{D}_j = D_j \cup \{a_3^{T_1,T_2} \mid T_2 \text{ is a triangle of } H_2\}.$$

Since every vertex of H_2 is contained in some triangle T_2 of H_2 and since $a_3^{T_1,T_2}$ is adjacent to each vertex in T_2, $\hat{D}_j$ dominates H_2. Also, $\hat{D}_j$, which contains D_j, dominates H_1, and since $v_q^{T_1}$ is adjacent to each $a_i^{T_1,T_2}$ except $a_3^{T_1,T_2}$ for each

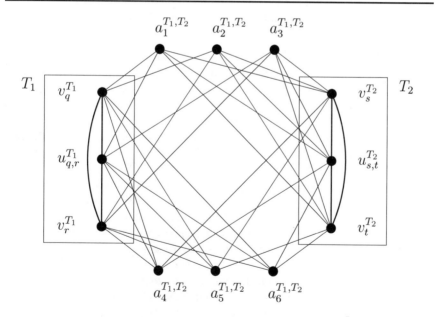

Fig. 5.3. Exact-5-DNP is DP-complete: gadget connecting two triangles T_1 and T_2

triangle T_2 of H_2, $\hat{D}_j$ dominates every gadget vertex of H. Hence, $\hat{D}_j$ dominates H.

By a symmetric argument, every set D_j, where $4 \leq j \leq 6$, dominating H_2 can be extended to a set $\hat{D}_j$ dominating the entire graph H. By construction, the sets $\hat{D}_j$ with $1 \leq j \leq 6$ are pairwise disjoint. Hence, $\delta(H) = 6 = \delta(H_1) + \delta(H_2)$.

Case 2: $\delta(H_1) = 3$ and $\delta(H_2) = 2$. As in Case 1, we can add appropriate gadget vertices to the five given sets $D_1, D_2, \ldots, D_5$ to obtain five pairwise disjoint sets $\hat{D}_1, \hat{D}_2, \ldots, \hat{D}_5$ such that each $\hat{D}_i$ dominates the entire graph H. It follows that $5 \leq \delta(H) \leq 6$. It remains to show that $\delta(H) \neq 6$.
For a contradiction, suppose that $\delta(H) = 6$. Look at Figure 5.3 showing the gadget between any two triangles T_1 and T_2 belonging to H_1 and H_2, respectively. Fix T_1 with $V(T_1) = \{v_q^{T_1}, u_{q,r}^{T_1}, v_r^{T_1}\}$. The only way (except for renaming the dominating sets) to partition the graph H into six dominating sets, say $E_1, E_2, \ldots, E_6$, is to assign to the sets E_i the vertices of T_1, of H_2, and of the gadgets connected with T_1 as follows:

- assign $\{v_q^{T_1}\} \cup \{a_3^{T_1,T_2} \mid T_2 \text{ is a triangle in } H_2\}$ to E_1;
- assign $\{u_{q,r}^{T_1}\} \cup \{a_2^{T_1,T_2} \mid T_2 \text{ is a triangle in } H_2\}$ to E_2;
- assign $\{v_r^{T_1}\} \cup \{a_1^{T_1,T_2} \mid T_2 \text{ is a triangle in } H_2\}$ to E_3;
- assign $\{v_s^{T_2}, a_6^{T_1,T_2} \mid T_2 \text{ is a triangle in } H_2\}$ to E_4;
- assign $\{u_{s,t}^{T_2}, a_5^{T_1,T_2} \mid T_2 \text{ is a triangle in } H_2\}$ to E_5;
- assign $\{v_t^{T_2}, a_4^{T_1,T_2} \mid T_2 \text{ is a triangle in } H_2\}$ to E_6.

Hence, all vertices from H_2 must be assigned to the three dominating sets E_4, E_5, and E_6, which induces a partition of H_2 into three dominating sets. This contradicts the case assumption that $\delta(H_2) = 2$. It follows that $\delta(H) = 5 = \delta(H_1) + \delta(H_2)$.

Case 3: $\delta(H_1) = \delta(H_2) = 2$. As in the previous two cases, we can add appropriate gadget vertices to the four given sets D_1, D_2, D_3, and D_4 to obtain a partition of $V(H)$ into four sets $\hat{D}_1$, $\hat{D}_2$, $\hat{D}_3$, and $\hat{D}_4$ such that each $\hat{D}_i$ dominates the entire graph H. It follows that $4 \leq \delta(H) \leq 6$. By the same arguments as in Case 2, $\delta(H) \neq 6$. It remains to show that $\delta(H) \neq 5$.
For a contradiction, suppose that $\delta(H) = 5$. Look at Figure 5.3 showing the gadget between any two triangles T_1 and T_2 belonging to H_1 and H_2, respectively. Suppose H is partitioned into five dominant sets $E_1, E_2, \ldots, E_5$.
First, we show that neither T_1 nor T_2 can have two vertices belonging to the same dominating set. Suppose otherwise, and let, say, $v_q^{T_1}$ and $u_{q,r}^{T_1}$ be both in E_1, and let $v_r^{T_1}$ be in E_2; all other cases are treated analogously. This implies that the vertices $v_s^{T_2}$, $u_{s,t}^{T_2}$, and $v_t^{T_2}$ in T_2 must be assigned to the other three dominating sets, E_3, E_4, and E_5, since otherwise one of the sets E_i would not dominate all gadget vertices $a_j^{T_1,T_2}$, $1 \leq j \leq 6$. Since T_1 is connected with each triangle of H_2 via some gadget, the same argument shows that $V(H_2)$ can be partitioned into three dominating sets, which contradicts the assumption that $\delta(H_2) = 2$.
Hence, the vertices of T_1 are assigned to three different dominating sets, say E_1, E_2, and E_3. Then, every triangle T_2 of H_2 must have one of its vertices in

E_4, one in E_5, and one in either one of E_1, E_2, and E_3. Again, this induces a partition of H_2 into three dominating sets, which contradicts the assumption that $\delta(H_2) = 2$. It follows that $\delta(H) \neq 5$, so $\delta(H) = 4 = \delta(H_1) + \delta(H_2)$.

By construction, $\delta(H_2) = 3$ implies $\delta(H_1) = 3$. Thus, the case "$\delta(H_1) = 2$ and $\delta(H_2) = 3$" cannot occur. The case distinction is complete.

Define $f(\langle G_1, G_2 \rangle) = H$. Note that f is polynomial-time computable and, by the case distinction above, f satisfies (5.3):

$$G_1 \in \text{3-Colorability and } G_2 \notin \text{3-Colorability}$$
$$\Longleftrightarrow \delta(H_1) = 3 \text{ and } \delta(H_2) = 2$$
$$\Longleftrightarrow \delta(H) = \delta(H_1) + \delta(H_2) = 5$$
$$\Longleftrightarrow f(\langle G_1, G_2 \rangle) = H \in \text{Exact-5-DNP}.$$

Applying Lemma 5.11 with $k = 1$, it follows that Exact-5-DNP is DP-complete, which directly proves Corollary 5.13.

To prove the general case, fix any $k \geq 1$. Recall that we are given the graphs $H_1, H_2, \ldots, H_{2k}$ that are constructed from $G_1, G_2, \ldots, G_{2k}$. Generalize the above construction of graph H as follows.

For any fixed sequence $T_1, T_2, \ldots, T_{2k}$ of triangles, where T_i belongs to H_i, add $6k$ new gadget vertices $a_1, a_2, \ldots, a_{6k}$ and, for each i with $1 \leq i \leq 2k$, associate the three gadget vertices $a_{1+3(i-1)}$, $a_{2+3(i-1)}$, and a_{3i} with the triangle T_i. For each i with $1 \leq i \leq 2k$, connect T_i with every T_j, where $1 \leq j \leq 2k$ and $i \neq j$, via the same three gadget vertices $a_{1+3(i-1)}$, $a_{2+3(i-1)}$, and a_{3i} associated with T_i the same way T_1 and T_2 are connected in Figure 5.3 via the vertices a_1, a_2, and a_3. It follows that the degree of a_i is $6k - 1$ for each i, so $\delta(H) \leq 6k$. An argument analogous to the above case distinction shows that $\delta(H) = \sum_{j=1}^{2k} \delta(H_j)$. Hence,

$$\|\{i \mid G_i \in \text{3-Colorability}\}\| \text{ is odd}$$
$$\Longleftrightarrow (\exists i : 1 \leq i \leq k) \left[\begin{array}{ll} \chi(G_1) & = \cdots = \chi(G_{2i-1}) = 3 \text{ and} \\ \chi(G_{2i}) & = \cdots = \chi(G_{2k}) \quad = 4 \end{array} \right]$$
$$\Longleftrightarrow (\exists i : 1 \leq i \leq k) \left[\begin{array}{ll} \delta(H_1) & = \cdots = \delta(H_{2i-1}) = 3 \text{ and} \\ \delta(H_{2i}) & = \cdots = \delta(H_{2k}) \quad = 2 \end{array} \right]$$
$$\Longleftrightarrow (\exists i : 1 \leq i \leq k) \left[\delta(H) = \sum_{j=1}^{2k} \delta(H_j) = 3(2i - 1) + 2(2k - 2i + 1) \right]$$
$$\Longleftrightarrow (\exists i : 1 \leq i \leq k) \left[\delta(H) = 4k + 2i - 1 \right]$$
$$\Longleftrightarrow \delta(H) \in \{4k + 1, 4k + 3, \ldots, 6k - 1\}$$
$$\Longleftrightarrow f(\langle G_1, G_2, \ldots, G_{2k} \rangle) = H \in \text{Exact-}M_k\text{-DNP}.$$

It follows that f satisfies (5.3). By Lemma 5.11, Exact-M_k-DNP is $\text{BH}_{2k}(\text{NP})$-complete. ∎

In contrast with Corollary 5.13, which says that Exact-5-DNP is DP-complete, Exact-2-DNP is in coNP; see Exercise 5.8(a). By Theorem 5.10, Exact-2-DNP cannot be DP-complete unless the boolean hierarchy over NP collapses; see Exercise 5.8(c). The precise complexity of the problems Exact-3-DNP and Exact-4-DNP is currently not known: they are both coNP-hard and contained in DP, yet it is not known currently whether they are complete for either one of these two classes.

The second application of Lemma 5.11 concerns the exact colorability problem. Recall that $\chi(G)$ denotes the chromatic number of graph G, i.e., the smallest number of colors needed to color the vertices of G such that no two adjacent vertices receive the same color. By Theorem 3.56 from Section 3.5.3, it is NP-complete to determine whether or not $\chi(G) \leq 3$ for a given graph G.

Definition 5.14 (Exact Colorability Problem).
For each fixed positive integer i, define the exact colorability problem *by:*

$$\text{Exact-}i\text{-Colorability} = \{G \mid G \text{ is a graph and } \chi(G) = i\}.$$

Definition 5.15 (Exact Colorability Problem (Generalized Version)).
Let $M_k \subseteq \mathbb{N}$ be any set of k integers. Define the generalized version of the exact colorability problem *by:*

$$\text{Exact-}M_k\text{-Colorability} = \{G \mid G \text{ is a graph and } \chi(G) \in M_k\}.$$

In particular, we write $\text{Exact-}i\text{-Colorability} = \{G \mid \chi(G) = i\}$ *for each singleton* $M_1 = \{i\}$.

Let $M_k = \{6k + 1, 6k + 3, \ldots, 8k - 1\}$. A straightforward application of Wagner's technique shows that, for each $k \geq 1$, Exact-M_k-Colorability is $\text{BH}_{2k}(\text{NP})$-complete. Hence, for the special case of $k = 1$, Exact-7-Colorability is DP-complete; see Exercise 5.11. In contrast, the following proposition shows that, for the special case of $k = 1$, Exact-3-Colorability is in NP. By Theorem 5.10, Exact-3-Colorability cannot be DP-complete unless the boolean hierarchy over NP collapses to its first level.

Proposition 5.16. *Fix any $k \geq 1$, and let M_k be any set of k positive integers including 3. Then,* Exact-M_k-Colorability *is in* $\text{BH}_{2k-1}(\text{NP})$ *and thus is not* $\text{BH}_{2k}(\text{NP})$-complete *unless the boolean hierarchy over NP collapses.*

Proof.   See Exercise 5.12.   ∎

Again, there is a gap in determining the precise threshold $i \in \{4, 5, 6, 7\}$ for which the problem Exact-i-Colorability jumps from NP to DP-completeness. Closing this gap, we will show in Corollary 5.21 below that the minimum number of colors needed to prove DP-completeness is in fact four: Exact-4-Colorability is DP-complete. This result follows from the more general statement about the hardness of the generalized exact colorability problem for higher levels of the boolean hierarchy given in Theorem 5.20 below.

To this end, we again apply Lemma 5.11, and we apply two known reductions from 3-SAT to 3-Colorability, which have certain useful properties that are stated in the following two lemmas. The first reduction is the standard reduction from 3-SAT to 3-Colorability given in the proof of Theorem 3.56. The second reduction is due to Guruswami and Khanna [GK00] and, originally, was not motivated by issues concerning the hardness of exact colorability, but by issues related to the hardness of approximating the chromatic number of 3-colorable graphs. Intuitively, their result says that it is NP-hard to 4-color a 3-colorable graph.

Lemma 5.17. *There exists a polynomial-time computable function σ that $\leq^{p}_{m}$-reduces 3-SAT to 3-Colorability and satisfies the following two properties:*

$$\varphi \in \text{3-SAT} \implies \chi(\sigma(\varphi)) = 3; \tag{5.5}$$
$$\varphi \notin \text{3-SAT} \implies \chi(\sigma(\varphi)) = 4. \tag{5.6}$$

Lemma 5.18 (Guruswami and Khanna; cf. proof of Theorem 1 of [GK00]).
There exists a polynomial-time computable function ρ that $\leq^{p}_{m}$-reduces 3-SAT to 3-Colorability and satisfies the following two properties:

$$\varphi \in \text{3-SAT} \implies \chi(\rho(\varphi)) = 3; \tag{5.7}$$
$$\varphi \notin \text{3-SAT} \implies \chi(\rho(\varphi)) = 5. \tag{5.8}$$

Proof Sketch. The Guruswami–Khanna reduction, call it ρ, is the composition of two subsequent reductions: first a reduction from 3-SAT to the independent set problem, and then from the independent set problem to 3-Colorability. Recall that the independent set problem asks, given a graph G and an integer m, whether or not the size of a maximum independent set of G (i.e., of a maximum subset of G's vertex set in which no two vertices are adjacent) is at least m.

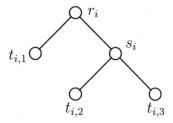

Fig. 5.4. Tree-like structure S_i in the Guruswami–Khanna reduction

We give only a rough outline of Guruswami and Khanna's very sophisticated construction, which involves tree-like structures and various types of gadgets connecting them. Using the standard reduction from 3-SAT to the independent set problem given in the proof of Theorem 3.54 (see Figure 3.3), construct from the given boolean formula φ a graph G consisting of m triangles (i.e., of m cliques of size 3 each) such that each triangle corresponds to some clause of φ and the vertices of any two distinct triangles are connected by an edge if and only if they represent some literal and its negation, respectively, in the corresponding clauses.

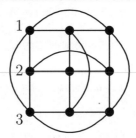

Fig. 5.5. Basic template in the Guruswami–Khanna reduction

Denote the m triangles by $T_1, T_2, \ldots, T_m$. To each T_i in G, there corresponds a tree-like structure S_i that is shown in Figure 5.4, where the three "leaves" $t_{i,1}$, $t_{i,2}$, and $t_{i,3}$ correspond to the three corners of the triangle T_i. Every individual "vertex" of the tree-like structures has the form of the basic template shown in Figure 5.5. Such a template consists of a 3×3 grid such that the vertices in each row and in each column of the grid induce a 3-clique. The three vertices in the first column of any such basic template, which are called the "ground vertices," in fact are shared among all the basic templates in each of the tree-like structures. Since the ground vertices form a 3-clique, every legal coloring assigns three distinct colors to them, say 1, 2, and 3.

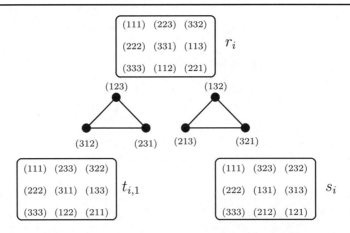

Fig. 5.6. Connection pattern between the templates of a tree-like structure

The connection pattern between the five basic templates of a tree-like structure can be seen in Figure 5.6, which shows a parent "vertex" and its two "children," each consisting of the nine vertices in the basic template. In addition, there are two more triangles. Every vertex of the templates and the triangles is labeled by a triple of colors. The simple rule is that two vertices are connected by an edge if and only if their labels differ in each coordinate. Figure 5.6 shows this pattern for the "vertices" r_i, $t_{i,1}$, and s_i; an analogous pattern applies to s_i, $t_{i,2}$, and $t_{i,3}$.

Before describing how the tree-like structures S_i are connected with each other, we explain the intuitive idea of this construction. Any coloring of S_i selects certain "vertices" of S_i. A "vertex" in some S_i is said to be *selected* if and only if at least one of the three rows in its basic template receives colors that form an even permutation of $\{1, 2, 3\}$, i.e., the first row has colors $1, 2, 3$ from left to right, or the second row has colors $2, 3, 1$, or the third row has colors $3, 1, 2$. Clearly, for each legal 4-coloring of S_i, every "vertex" is either selected or not selected.

Our goal is to guarantee that any legal 4-coloring of S_i selects at least one of the three "leaves," $t_{i,1}$, $t_{i,2}$, or $t_{i,3}$. The idea is to enforce that the root r_i must be selected, and that if some internal "vertex," r_i or s_i, is selected, at least one of its "children" must be selected. This property is summarized in the following key lemma. The proof of Lemma 5.19 is left to the reader, see Problem 5.2.

Lemma 5.19. *Every legal 4-coloring of S_i selects at least one of $t_{i,1}$, $t_{i,2}$, or $t_{i,3}$.*

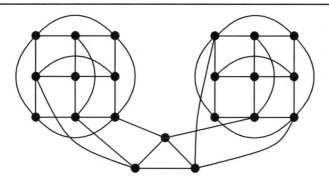

Fig. 5.7. Gadget connecting two "leaves" of the "same row" kind

Finally, we specify how to connect the "leaves" of distinct tree-like structures S_i and S_j, $i \neq j$. For each pair of "vertices," $t_{i,k}$ and $t_{j,\ell}$, that correspond to adjacent vertices in graph G, appropriate gadgets are inserted to prevent both these "leaves" being selected simultaneously. (This is necessary, since otherwise any 4-coloring of the graph we construct would imply that G has an independent set of size m.)

Two kinds of gadgets are used. The first kind of gadget is called the "same row" kind and can be seen in Figure 5.7. Its purpose is to prevent the two "leaves" being simultaneously selected because of the same row; for example, because both have a third row colored $3, 1, 2$. The second kind of gadget is called the "different rows" kind and can be seen in Figure 5.8. Its purpose is to prevent the two "leaves" being simultaneously selected because of different rows; for example, because $t_{i,k}$ has a third row colored $3, 1, 2$ and $t_{j,\ell}$ has a first row colored $1, 2, 3$, in some 4-coloring. Note, however, that there is some legal 3-coloring whenever the third row of $t_{i,k}$ is colored $3, 2, 1$ and the first row of $t_{j,\ell}$ is colored $1, 3, 2$, i.e., whenever $t_{i,k}$ and $t_{j,\ell}$ are *not* selected due to these two different rows.

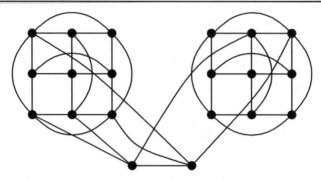

Fig. 5.8. Gadget connecting two "leaves" of the "different rows" kind

This completes our description of the reduction ρ that transforms the formula φ via the graph G to a graph $H = \rho(\varphi)$. We omit presenting the details of Guruswami and Khanna's clever proof of correctness. A rough outline of the idea should be clear from the above explanations. The details are left to the reader as Problem 5.2.

The above construction guarantees that

- $\varphi \in$ 3-SAT implies $\chi(\rho(\varphi)) = 3$, and
- $\varphi \notin$ 3-SAT implies $\chi(\rho(\varphi)) = 5$.

In other words, the graph H never has a chromatic number of exactly four, no matter whether or not φ is satisfiable. Thus, (5.7) and (5.8) are proven.   ∎

Theorem 5.20. *For each fixed $k \geq 1$, let $M_k = \{3k + 1, 3k + 3, \ldots, 5k - 1\}$. Then,* Exact-$M_k$-Colorability *is* $\text{BH}_{2k}(\text{NP})$-*complete.*

In particular, for $k = 1$, Theorem 5.20 has the following corollary. Both the theorem and its corollary can be proven by Wagner's technique, using Lemma 5.18.

Corollary 5.21. Exact-4-Colorability *is* DP-*complete.*

Proof of Theorem 5.20.   Fix $k \geq 1$. Apply Lemma 5.11 with A being the NP-complete problem 3-SAT and B being the problem Exact-M_k-Colorability, where $M_k = \{3k + 1, 3k + 3, \ldots, 5k - 1\}$.

Let σ be the standard reduction from 3-SAT to 3-Colorability according to Lemma 5.17, and let ρ be the Guruswami–Khanna reduction from 3-SAT to 3-Colorability according to Lemma 5.18.

The *join operation on graphs*, denoted by $\bowtie$, is defined as follows: Given two disjoint graphs A and B, their join $A \bowtie B$ is the graph whose vertex and edge set, respectively, are:

$$V(A \bowtie B) = V(A) \cup V(B);$$
$$E(A \bowtie B) = E(A) \cup E(B) \cup \{\{a,b\} \mid a \in V(A) \text{ and } b \in V(B)\}.$$

Note that $\chi(A \bowtie B) = \chi(A) + \chi(B)$ and $\bowtie$ is an associative operation on graphs; see Exercise 5.13.

Let $\varphi_1, \varphi_2, \ldots, \varphi_{2k}$ be $2k$ given boolean formulas satisfying that $\varphi_{j+1} \in$ 3-SAT implies $\varphi_j \in$ 3-SAT for each j with $1 \leq j < 2k$. Define $2k$ graphs $H_1, H_2, \ldots, H_{2k}$ as follows. For each i with $1 \leq i \leq k$, define $H_{2i-1} = \rho(\varphi_{2i-1})$ and $H_{2i} = \sigma(\varphi_{2i})$. By (5.5), (5.6), (5.7), and (5.8) from Lemmas 5.17 and 5.18, it follows that

$$\chi(H_j) = \begin{cases} 3 \text{ if } 1 \leq j \leq 2k \text{ and } \varphi_j \in \text{3-SAT} \\ 4 \text{ if } j = 2i \text{ for some } i \in \{1, 2, \ldots, k\} \text{ and } \varphi_j \notin \text{3-SAT} \\ 5 \text{ if } j = 2i-1 \text{ for some } i \in \{1, 2, \ldots, k\} \text{ and } \varphi_j \notin \text{3-SAT}. \end{cases} \quad (5.9)$$

For each i with $1 \leq i \leq k$, define the graph G_i to be the disjoint union of the graphs H_{2i-1} and H_{2i}. Thus, $\chi(G_i) = \max\{\chi(H_{2i-1}), \chi(H_{2i})\}$, for each i, $1 \leq i \leq k$. The construction of our reduction f is completed by defining

$$f(\langle \varphi_1, \varphi_2, \ldots, \varphi_{2k} \rangle) = G,$$

where the graph G is the join of the graphs $G_1, G_2, \ldots, G_k$. Thus,

$$\chi(G) = \sum_{i=1}^{k} \chi(G_i) = \sum_{i=1}^{k} \max\{\chi(H_{2i-1}), \chi(H_{2i})\}. \quad (5.10)$$

It follows from our construction that:

$\|\{i \mid \varphi_i \in \text{3-SAT}\}\|$ is odd

$\Longleftrightarrow \quad (\exists i : 1 \leq i \leq k) [\varphi_1, \ldots, \varphi_{2i-1} \in \text{3-SAT and } \varphi_{2i}, \ldots, \varphi_{2k} \notin \text{3-SAT}]$

$\overset{(5.9),\,(5.10)}{\Longleftrightarrow} \quad (\exists i : 1 \leq i \leq k) \left[\begin{array}{l} \sum_{j=1}^{k} \chi(G_j) = 3(i-1) + 4 + 5(k-i) \\ \qquad\qquad = 5k - 2i + 1 \end{array} \right]$

$\overset{(5.10)}{\Longleftrightarrow} \quad \chi(G) \in M_k = \{3k+1, 3k+3, \ldots, 5k-1\}$

$\Longleftrightarrow \quad f(\langle \varphi_1, \varphi_2, \ldots, \varphi_{2k} \rangle) = G \in \text{Exact-}M_k\text{-Colorability}.$

Hence, (5.3) is satisfied. By Lemma 5.11, Exact-M_k-Colorability is BH$_{2k}$(NP)-complete. ∎

Section 5.9 mentions further applications of Wagner's technique for proving BH$_k$(NP) lower bounds.

5.2 Polynomial Hierarchy

Just like the boolean hierarchy, the polynomial hierarchy is an NP-based hierarchy of complexity classes. The levels of this hierarchy can be characterized in two equivalent ways: first, by alternating length-bounded $\exists$ and $\forall$ quantifiers; second, by a stack of NP oracle machines accessing NP oracles.

We start with the quantifier representation for the hierarchy's first level, i.e., for NP itself. NP algorithms typically consist of two phases: a nondeterministic guessing phase in which potential problem solutions are guessed, followed by a deterministic checking phase in which the correctness of the solution guessed is verified. Both phases are polynomial-time bounded.

Problem solutions $\mathbf{w}$ that can be verified in deterministic polynomial time are also referred to as "witnesses" or as "certificates," for they witness (or certify) membership of the given instance in the given NP problem. For illustration, consider the following examples of NP problems.

Example 5.22 (Witnesses for Problems in NP).

- Consider the NP-complete problem SOS. The standard NP machine for SOS proceeds as follows: Given an instance $\langle s_1, s_2, \ldots, s_n, T \rangle$, nondeterministically guess a solution $\mathbf{w} \in \{0,1\}^n$, $\mathbf{w} = (w_1, w_2, \ldots, w_n)$, and for each solution $\mathbf{w}$ guessed, compute deterministically the sum $\sum_{i=1}^{n} w_i s_i$, and accept the input if and only if $\sum_{i=1}^{n} w_i s_i = T$.
- Consider the NP problem GI. The standard NP machine for GI proceeds as follows: Given an instance $\langle G, H \rangle$, where G and H are undirected graphs with n vertices each, nondeterministically guess a solution $\pi \in \mathfrak{S}_n$ (i.e., a permutation of the vertices of G), and for each solution π guessed, check deterministically whether or not it is an isomorphism (i.e., an edge-preserving bijection) between the vertices of G and H.

We briefly mention some further examples: solutions of the clique problem, given an instance $\langle G, k \rangle$, are (suitably encoded) size k cliques of the graph G; solutions of the satisfiability problem are satisfying truth assignments of the given formula; solutions of the 3-DM problem are tripartite matchings of the given 3-DM instance; and so on.

Polynomially time-bounded nondeterministic guessing thus corresponds to polynomially length-bounded existential quantification. All NP problems are of this form: A is in NP (via some NP machine M) if and only if A comprises precisely those input strings x for which there *exists* a polynomially length-bounded, polynomial-time checkable witness w (with respect to M). In other words, witnesses are nothing else than accepting computation paths of $M(x)$, suitably encoded as binary strings of length $p(|x|)$ for some $p \in \text{Pol}$. The ith bit of a witness w corresponds to the ith nondeterministic branching of $M(x)$ along the computation path w.

Definition 5.23 (Witness Set).   *Let $A \in$ NP, and let M be some NP machine accepting A in time $p \in \text{Pol}$. For each x of length n, define the set of witnesses for "$x \in A$" with respect to M by*

$\text{Wit}_M(x) = \{w \in \{0,1\}^{p(n)} \mid w \text{ is an accepting computation path of } M(x)\}.$

Note that $x \in A$ if and only if $\text{Wit}_M(x)$ is nonempty.

Theorem 5.24 is the complexity-theoretic analog of the projection theorem from recursive function theory, which says that any given set is recursively enumerable if and only if it is the projection of some decidable set; see the second item of Theorem 2.20 in Section 2.2. This theorem can easily be proven by turning the above comments into formal arguments. The proof is left to the reader as Exercise 5.16.

Theorem 5.24. $A \in \text{NP}$ *if and only if there exist a set* $B \in \text{P}$ *and a polynomial p such that for each $x \in \Sigma^*$,*

$$x \in A \iff (\exists w)\,[|w| \leq p(|x|) \text{ and } \langle x, w \rangle \in B]. \tag{5.11}$$

For polynomially length-bounded quantifiers, we use the following notation.

Definition 5.25 (Polynomially Length-Bounded Quantifier).
For each predicate B, for each polynomial p, and for each string x, define:

$$(\exists^p y)\,[B(x,y)] \iff (\exists y)\,[|y| \leq p(|x|) \text{ and } B(x,y)];$$
$$(\forall^p y)\,[B(x,y)] \iff (\forall y)\,[|y| \leq p(|x|) \text{ implies } B(x,y)].$$

Now, we turn to the NP oracle machine approach. Oracle Turing machines are formally defined in Definition 2.22 of Section 2.2. In particular, they are useful for certain search techniques such as *binary search* or *prefix search*, as illustrated by the following example.

Example 5.26 (Prefix Search by an Oracle Turing Machine).   The graph isorphism problem GI was defined in Definition 2.49 of Section 2.4. Let G and H be two given graphs with $n \geq 1$ vertices each. The set $\text{ISO}(G, H)$ of isomorphisms between G and H contains all solutions (or witnesses) of "$\langle G, H \rangle \in$ GI," with respect to the standard NPTM for solving GI. Note that

$$\text{ISO}(G, H) \neq \emptyset \iff \langle G, H \rangle \in \text{GI}. \tag{5.12}$$

We want to find the lexicographically smallest graph isomorphism in $\text{ISO}(G, H)$ if $\langle G, H \rangle \in$ GI; otherwise, "$\langle G, H \rangle \notin$ GI" is to be indicated by returning the empty string ε. That is, we want to compute the function f that is defined by

$$f(G, H) = \begin{cases} \min\{\pi \mid \pi \in \text{ISO}(G, H)\} & \text{if } \langle G, H \rangle \in \text{GI} \\ \varepsilon & \text{if } \langle G, H \rangle \notin \text{GI}. \end{cases}$$

Here, the minimum is taken with respect to the lexicographical order on $\mathfrak{S}_n$, which is defined as follows. We view a permutation $\pi \in \mathfrak{S}_n$ as the length n string $\pi(1)\pi(2)\cdots\pi(n)$ over the alphabet $[n] = \{1, 2, \ldots, n\}$, and for $\sigma, \tau \in \mathfrak{S}_n$, we write $\sigma < \tau$ if and only if there exists a $j \in [n]$ such that $\sigma(i) = \tau(i)$ for all $i < j$, and $\sigma(j) < \tau(j)$. For example, if $\sigma = \left(\begin{smallmatrix} 1 & 2 & 3 & 4 & 5 \\ 3 & 4 & 1 & 5 & 2 \end{smallmatrix}\right)$ and $\tau = \left(\begin{smallmatrix} 1 & 2 & 3 & 4 & 5 \\ 3 & 4 & 2 & 1 & 5 \end{smallmatrix}\right)$, then

```
N^Pre-Iso(G, H) {
   if (⟨G, H, ε⟩ ∉ Pre-Iso) return ε;
   else {
      π := ε;   j := 0;
      while (j < n) {                              // G and H both have n vertices
         i := 1;
         while (⟨G, H, πi⟩ ∉ Pre-Iso) {i := i + 1; }
         π := πi;   j := j + 1;
      }
   }
   return π;
}
```

Fig. 5.9. Prefix search to find the smallest graph isomorphism in ISO(G, H)

$\sigma = 3\,4\,1\,5\,2 < 3\,4\,2\,1\,5 = \tau$, since they coincide in the first two positions and differ in the third, where $\sigma(3) = 1 < 2 = \tau(3)$.

Canceling some pairs $(i, \sigma(i))$ out of a permutation $\sigma \in \mathfrak{S}_n$, one obtains a *partial permutation*, which can also be viewed as a string over $[n] \cup \{*\}$, where $*$ indicates an undefined position. A *prefix of length k of $\sigma \in \mathfrak{S}_n$*, where $k \leq n$, is a partial permutation of σ that contains every pair $(i, \sigma(i))$ with $i \leq k$, but none of the pairs $(i, \sigma(i))$ with $i > k$. In particular, if $k = 0$ then the empty string ε is the (unique) length 0 prefix of σ, and if $k = n$ then the total permutation σ is the (unique) length n prefix of itself. For example, if $\sigma = \left(\begin{smallmatrix} 1 & 2 & 3 & 4 & 5 \\ 3 & 4 & 1 & 5 & 2 \end{smallmatrix}\right)$, then $\tau = \left(\begin{smallmatrix} 1 & 3 & 5 \\ 3 & 1 & 2 \end{smallmatrix}\right)$ is a partial permutation of σ, and $\pi = \left(\begin{smallmatrix} 1 & 2 & 3 \\ 3 & 4 & 1 \end{smallmatrix}\right)$ is a prefix of length 3 of σ. As a string over $[n] \cup \{*\}$, the partial permutation τ is written $\tau = 3 * 1 * 2$. For prefixes like $\pi = 3\,4\,1 * * = 3\,4\,1$, the placeholders $*$ may be dropped.

If π is a prefix of length $k < n$ of $\sigma \in \mathfrak{S}_n$ and if $w = i_1 i_2 \cdots i_{|w|}$ is a string over $[n]$ of length $|w| \leq n - k$ with none of the i_j occurring in π, then πw denotes the partial permutation that extends π by the pairs

$$(k + 1, i_1), (k + 2, i_2), \ldots, (k + |w|, i_{|w|}).$$

If in addition $\sigma(k + j) = i_j$ for $1 \leq j \leq |w|$, then πw is also a prefix of σ. For example, if $\pi = \left(\begin{smallmatrix} 1 & 2 & 3 \\ 3 & 4 & 1 \end{smallmatrix}\right)$ is a prefix of $\sigma = \left(\begin{smallmatrix} 1 & 2 & 3 & 4 & 5 \\ 3 & 4 & 1 & 5 & 2 \end{smallmatrix}\right)$, then π is extended by each of the strings $w_1 = 2$, $w_2 = 5$, $w_3 = 2\,5$, and $w_4 = 5\,2$, but only $\pi w_2 = 3\,4\,1\,5$ and $\pi w_4 = 3\,4\,1\,5\,2$ are prefixes of σ.

For any two graphs G and H, define the set of prefixes of isomorphisms in ISO(G, H) by

$$\text{Pre-Iso} = \{\langle G, H, \pi \rangle \mid (\exists w \in [n]^*)\,[w = i_1 i_2 \cdots i_{n-|\pi|} \text{ and } \pi w \in \text{ISO}(G, H)]\}.$$

Note that for $n \geq 1$, the empty string ε does not encode a permutation in $\mathfrak{S}_n$, and that ISO(G, H) = ∅ if and only if $\langle G, H, \varepsilon \rangle \notin$ Pre-Iso, which by (5.12) is the case exactly if $\langle G, H \rangle \notin$ GI. Using Pre-Iso as an oracle set, the DPOTM N in Figure 5.9

computes the function f by prefix search. Thus, $f \in \text{FP}^{\text{Pre-Iso}}$. It is not difficult to prove that Pre-Iso is a set in NP; see Exercise 5.17(a). Since Pre-Iso is in NP, we have $f \in \text{FP}^{\text{NP}}$. See also Exercise 5.17(b) and Problem 5.3.

The algorithm given in Figure 5.9 describes a Turing reduction to the oracle set Pre-Iso. Note that polynomial-time Turing reductions can ask polynomially many queries, whereas polynomial-time many-one reductions ask only one query. Moreover, $\leq_m^P$-reductions accept the given input if and only if this query is answered in the affirmative, a severe restriction not required for $\leq_T^P$-reductions. Hence, the Turing reducibility is much more flexible than the many-one reducibility.

Definition 5.27 (Polynomial-Time Turing Reducibility and Completeness).
Let $\Sigma = \{0, 1\}$ be a fixed alphabet, and let A and B be sets of strings over Σ. Let C be any complexity class.

1. *Define the polynomial-time Turing reducibility, denoted by $\leq_T^P$, as follows: $A \leq_T^P B$ if and only if there is a deterministic polynomial-time oracle Turing machine (DPOTM, for short) M such that $A = L(M^B)$.*
2. *Define the nondeterministic polynomial-time Turing reducibility, denoted $\leq_T^{\text{NP}}$, as follows: $A \leq_T^{\text{NP}} B$ if and only if there is a nondeterministic polynomial-time oracle Turing machine (NPOTM, for short) M such that $A = L(M^B)$.*
3. *A set B is $\leq_T^P$-hard for C if and only if $A \leq_T^P B$ for each $A \in C$.*
4. *A set B is $\leq_T^P$-complete for C if and only if B is $\leq_T^P$-hard for C and $B \in C$.*
5. *C is said to be closed under the $\leq_T^P$-reducibility ($\leq_T^P$-closed, for short) if and only if for any two sets A and B, if $A \leq_T^P B$ and $B \in C$, then $A \in C$. The notion of C being $\leq_T^{\text{NP}}$-closed is defined analogously. The Turing closure of C and the $\leq_T^{\text{NP}}$-closure of C, respectively, are defined by:*

$$\mathbf{P}^C = \{A \mid (\exists B \in C)\,[A \leq_T^P B]\};$$
$$\mathbf{NP}^C = \{A \mid (\exists B \in C)\,[A \leq_T^{\text{NP}} B]\}.$$

The following proposition summarizes some basic properties of the reducibilities defined above. The proof of Proposition 5.28 is left to the reader as Exercise 5.18. For the first item of Proposition 5.28, recall that we may view the relations $\leq_T^P$ and $\leq_T^{\text{NP}}$ as sets of pairs, i.e., $\leq_T^P \;=\; \{(A, B) \mid A \leq_T^P B\}$ and $\leq_T^{\text{NP}} \;=\; \{(A, B) \mid A \leq_T^{\text{NP}} B\}$. The last item of Proposition 5.28 is analogous to Theorem 3.41. This item says that if $\leq_T^{\text{NP}}$ and $\leq_m^{\log}$ coincide on NP, then NP collapses down to L. In contrast with $\leq_m^{\log}$, $\leq_m^P$, and $\leq_T^P$, it is known that $\leq_T^{\text{NP}}$ is not a transitive relation.

Proposition 5.28.   *1. $\leq_m^{\log} \subseteq \leq_m^P \subseteq \leq_T^P \subseteq \leq_T^{\text{NP}}$.*
    2. The relation $\leq_T^P$ is both reflexive and transitive, yet not antisymmetric.
    3. P and PSPACE are $\leq_T^P$-closed, i.e., $\mathbf{P}^P = \text{P}$ and $\mathbf{P}^{\text{PSPACE}} = \text{PSPACE}$.
    4. $\text{NP}^P = \text{NP}$ and $\text{NP}^{\text{PSPACE}} = \text{PSPACE}$.
    5. If $A \leq_T^P B$ and A is $\leq_T^P$-hard for a complexity class C, then B is $\leq_T^P$-hard for C.
    6. If $\text{L} \neq \text{NP}$, then there exist sets A and B in NP such that $A \leq_T^{\text{NP}} B$, yet $A \not\leq_m^{\log} B$.

By Proposition 5.28, $P^P = P$ and $NP^P = NP$. Thus, neither for P nor for NP do P oracle sets provide any additional computational power. What about an NP oracle set? Does NP equal P^{NP} or even NP^{NP}? Both equalities are considered most unlikely. That is, NP is most likely neither $\leq^P_T$-closed nor $\leq^{NP}_T$-closed. In contrast, NP is closed under polynomial-time *positive* Turing reductions; see Exercise 5.19.

The naive approach to prove $P^{NP} = NP$ seeks to simulate oracle queries to the NP oracle B directly. Suppose that the input x is rejected in the P^B computation and that some oracle query, say q_i, belongs to B. Thus, the correct oracle answer for q_i is "yes." Simulating the NP machine M for B on input q_i may yield both accepting computation paths (which are correct, since q_i is in B) and (incorrect) rejecting computation paths. However, the rejecting paths do not "know" that $q_i \in B$. Neither do they "know" that they in fact are incorrect, since they cannot "see" what is happening on the other paths of $M(q_i)$. Hence, it might happen that such an incorrect rejecting path of $M(q_i)$ causes an incorrect acceptance of the input x, which demonstrates that the naive approach to show that $P^{NP} = NP$ fails. In fact, NP is most likely to be distinct from both P^{NP} and NP^{NP}. This observation motivates the following definition introducing the polynomial hierarchy.

Definition 5.29 (Polynomial Hierarchy).
The polynomial hierarchy *is inductively defined by:*

$$\Delta^p_0 = \Sigma^p_0 = \Pi^p_0 = P;$$
$$\Delta^p_{i+1} = P^{\Sigma^p_i}, \quad \Sigma^p_{i+1} = NP^{\Sigma^p_i}, \ and \quad \Pi^p_{i+1} = co\Sigma^p_{i+1} \quad for\ i \geq 0;$$
$$PH = \bigcup_{k \geq 0} \Sigma^p_k.$$

Note that, in particular, $\Delta^p_1 = P^{\Sigma^p_0} = P^P = P$ and $\Sigma^p_1 = NP^{\Sigma^p_0} = NP^P = NP$ and $\Pi^p_1 = co\Sigma^p_1 = coNP$.

Theorem 5.30.   *1. For each $i \geq 0$, $\Sigma^p_i \cup \Pi^p_i \subseteq \Delta^p_{i+1} \subseteq \Sigma^p_{i+1} \cap \Pi^p_{i+1}$.*
2. PH $\subseteq$ PSPACE.
3. Each of the classes Δ^p_i, Σ^p_i, Π^p_i, and PH is $\leq^P_m$-closed. The Δ^p_i levels of the polynomial hierarchy are even closed under $\leq^P_T$-reductions.

Proof.   1. For each class $\mathcal{C}$, we have $\mathcal{C} \subseteq P^{\mathcal{C}}$, since $\leq^P_T$ is reflexive by Proposition 5.28: If A is in $\mathcal{C}$, then $A = L(M^A)$ for some DPOTM M, so A is in $P^{\mathcal{C}}$. Hence, $\Sigma^p_i \subseteq P^{\Sigma^p_i} = \Delta^p_{i+1}$. Since $\Delta^p_{i+1} = co\Delta^p_{i+1}$, we have $\Pi^p_i = co\Sigma^p_i \subseteq \Delta^p_{i+1}$. Moreover, $\Delta^p_{i+1} = P^{\Sigma^p_i} \subseteq NP^{\Sigma^p_i} = \Sigma^p_{i+1}$ and $\Delta^p_{i+1} = co\Delta^p_{i+1} \subseteq co\Sigma^p_{i+1} = \Pi^p_{i+1}$.
2. We prove by induction on i:

$$(\forall i \geq 0)\, [\Sigma^p_i \subseteq PSPACE]. \tag{5.13}$$

The induction base, $i = 0$, is trivial: $\Sigma^p_0 = P \subseteq PSPACE$. The induction hypothesis says that (5.13) is true for some $i \geq 0$: $\Sigma^p_i \subseteq PSPACE$. Then,

$$\Sigma^p_{i+1} = NP^{\Sigma^p_i} \subseteq NP^{PSPACE} \subseteq PSPACE,$$

where the last inclusion, which is also stated in the fourth item of Proposition 5.28, can be proven analogously to the inclusion NP $\subseteq$ PSPACE proven in Theorem 3.27 plus a direct PSPACE simulation of the oracle queries.

3. The proof of this claim is left to the reader as Exercise 5.20.   ∎

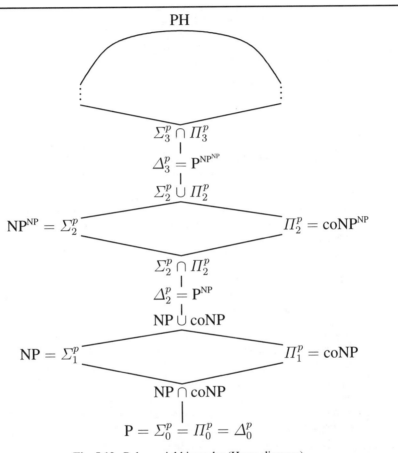

Fig. 5.10. Polynomial hierarchy (Hasse diagram)

Theorem 5.30 states the inclusion relations between the classes of the polynomial hierarchy. Figure 5.10 shows this inclusion structure as a Hasse diagram. Again, in this figure, containment of a class C in a class D is indicated by a line going from C upward to D, and incomparable classes are not connected. Figure 5.11 shows this inclusion structure as a Venn diagram. Here, darker classes are contained in lighter classes, and incomparable classes have the same gray level. None of the inclusions is known to be strict.

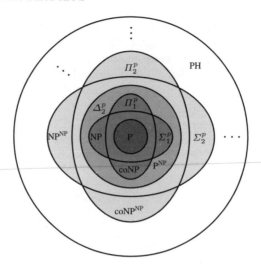

Fig. 5.11. Polynomial hierarchy (Venn diagram)

The following theorem generalizes the existential quantifier representation of NP from Theorem 5.24 to an alternating quantifier representation of all levels of the polynomial hierarchy.

Theorem 5.31. *For each $i \geq 0$, $A \in \Sigma_i^p$ if and only if there exist a set $B \in$ P and a polynomial p such that for each $x \in \Sigma^*$,*

$$x \in A \iff (\exists^p w_1)(\forall^p w_2) \cdots (\mathfrak{Q}^p w_i)[\langle x, w_1, w_2, \ldots, w_i \rangle \in B], \quad (5.14)$$

where $\mathfrak{Q}^p = \exists^p$ if i is odd, and $\mathfrak{Q}^p = \forall^p$ if i is even.

Proof.   The theorem is proven by induction on i. The induction base $i = 0$ is trivial (and the case $i = 1$ is stated as Theorem 5.24). The induction hypothesis says that the assertion of Theorem 5.31 is true for some $i \geq 0$. We have to show that this assertion also holds for $i + 1$.

For the direction from left to right, suppose that A is a set in $\Sigma_{i+1}^p = \mathrm{NP}^{\Sigma_i^p}$. Let M be some NPOTM accepting A in time $q \in \mathbb{P}$ol, and let $C \in \Sigma_i^p$ be M's oracle set, i.e., $A = L(M^C)$. Define a set D as follows:

$$D = \left\{ \langle x, u, v, w \rangle \;\middle|\; \begin{array}{l} w \in \mathrm{Wit}_{M(\cdot)}(x),\ u = \langle u_1, u_2, \ldots, u_k \rangle,\ v = \langle v_1, v_2, \ldots, v_\ell \rangle, \\ \text{where } u \text{ comprises the queries on path } w \text{ with answer "yes"} \\ \text{and } v \text{ comprises the queries on path } w \text{ with answer "no"} \end{array} \right\}.$$

Note that $D \in$ P. It follows from the definition of D that:

$$\begin{aligned}
x \in A &\iff M^C \text{ accepts } x \qquad\qquad\qquad\qquad\qquad\qquad\quad (5.15) \\
&\iff (\exists^q w)[w \in \mathrm{Wit}_{M^C}(x)] \\
&\iff (\exists^q w)(\exists^q u)(\exists^q v)[u = \langle u_1, u_2, \ldots, u_k \rangle \wedge v = \langle v_1, v_2, \ldots, v_\ell \rangle \\
&\qquad\qquad \wedge \langle x, u, v, w \rangle \in D \wedge u_1, u_2, \ldots, u_k \in C \wedge v_1, v_2, \ldots, v_\ell \notin C].
\end{aligned}$$

Define the sets

$$C_{\text{yes}} = \{u \mid u = \langle u_1, u_2, \ldots, u_k \rangle \text{ and } u_1, u_2, \ldots, u_k \in C\};$$
$$C_{\text{no}} = \{v \mid v = \langle v_1, v_2, \ldots, v_\ell \rangle \text{ and } v_1, v_2, \ldots, v_\ell \notin C\}.$$

Since $C \in \Sigma_i^p$, $k \leq q(|x|)$, and Σ_i^p is closed under pairing, we have $C_{\text{yes}} \in \Sigma_i^p$. Similarly, since $\overline{C} \in \Pi_i^p$, $\ell \leq q(|x|)$, and Π_i^p is closed under pairing, we have $C_{\text{no}} \in \Pi_i^p$; see Exercise 5.21.

By the induction hypothesis, for $C_{\text{yes}} \in \Sigma_i^p$ and $C_{\text{no}} \in \Pi_i^p$, there exist sets E and F in P and polynomials r and s such that:

$$u \in C_{\text{yes}} \iff (\exists^r y_1)(\forall^r y_2) \cdots (\mathfrak{Q}^r y_i)[\langle u, y_1, y_2, \ldots, y_i \rangle \in E]; \quad (5.16)$$

$$v \in C_{\text{no}} \iff (\forall^s z_1)(\exists^s z_2) \cdots (\overline{\mathfrak{Q}}^s z_i)[\langle v, z_1, z_2, \ldots, z_i \rangle \in F], \quad (5.17)$$

where $\mathfrak{Q}^r = \exists^r$ and $\overline{\mathfrak{Q}}^s = \forall^s$ if i is odd, and $\mathfrak{Q}^r = \forall^r$ and $\overline{\mathfrak{Q}}^s = \exists^s$ if i is even. Substituting the equivalences (5.16) and (5.17) in (5.15) above gives:

$$
\begin{aligned}
x \in A \iff & (\exists^q w)(\exists^q u)(\exists^q v)[\langle x, u, v, w \rangle \in D \,\wedge \qquad\qquad (5.18)\\
& (\exists^r y_1)(\forall^r y_2) \cdots (\mathfrak{Q}^r y_i)[\langle u, y_1, y_2, \ldots, y_i \rangle \in E] \,\wedge\\
& (\forall^s z_1)(\exists^s z_2) \cdots (\overline{\mathfrak{Q}}^s z_i)[\langle v, z_1, z_2, \ldots, z_i \rangle \in F]].
\end{aligned}
$$

Alternatingly extracting the quantifiers from the last two lines of equivalence (5.18) and combining contiguous equal quantifiers to one quantifier of the same type, we obtain:

$$
\begin{aligned}
x \in A \iff & \underbrace{(\exists^q w)(\exists^q u)(\exists^q v)(\exists^r y_1)}_{\text{combine to }(\exists^P w_1)} \ \underbrace{(\forall^r y_2)(\forall^s z_1)}_{\text{combine to }(\forall^P w_2)} \cdots \underbrace{(\mathfrak{Q}^r y_i)(\mathfrak{Q}^s z_{i-1})}_{\text{combine to }(\mathfrak{Q}^P w_i)}(\overline{\mathfrak{Q}}^s z_i)\\
& [\langle x, u, v, w \rangle \in D \,\wedge\, \langle u, y_1, y_2, \ldots, y_i \rangle \in E \,\wedge\, \langle v, z_1, z_2, \ldots, z_i \rangle \in F]\\
\iff & (\exists^P w_1)(\forall^P w_2) \cdots (\overline{\mathfrak{Q}}^P w_{i+1})[\langle x, w_1, w_2, \ldots, w_{i+1} \rangle \in B], \quad (5.19)
\end{aligned}
$$

where $p = \max\{3q + r, r + s\} + c$ is a polynomial depending on the polynomials q, r, and s, and on a constant c, which is due to the pairing of strings when combining quantifiers. According to the quantifier combination, the set B is suitably defined so as to satisfy:

$$
\begin{aligned}
& \langle x, w_1, w_2, \ldots, w_{i+1} \rangle \in B\\
\iff & \langle x, u, v, w \rangle \in D \,\wedge\, \langle u, y_1, y_2, \ldots, y_i \rangle \in E \,\wedge\, \langle v, z_1, z_2, \ldots, z_i \rangle \in F.
\end{aligned}
$$

Since the sets D, E, and F each are in P, so is B. By equivalence (5.19), A satisfies the representation (5.14) for $i + 1$. The induction proof is complete for the direction from left to right.

Conversely, for the direction from right to left, suppose that there exist a set $B \in P$ and a polynomial p such that A can be represented as follows:

$$A = \{x \mid (\exists^P w_1)(\forall^P w_2) \cdots (\mathfrak{Q}^P w_{i+1})[\langle x, w_1, w_2, \ldots, w_{i+1} \rangle \in B],$$

where $\mathfrak{Q}^p = \exists^p$ if i is even, and $\mathfrak{Q}^p = \forall^p$ if i is odd. Define a set C by:

$$C = \{\langle x, w_1 \rangle \mid |w_1| \le p(|x|) \wedge (\forall^p w_2) \cdots (\mathfrak{Q}^p w_{i+1}) [\langle x, w_1, w_2, \ldots, w_{i+1} \rangle \in B].$$

Hence,

$$x \in A \iff (\exists^p w_1) [\langle x, w_1 \rangle \in C].$$

By induction hypothesis, C is in Π_i^p; so its complement, $\overline{C}$, is in Σ_i^p. Let M be an NPOTM that, using $\overline{C}$ as an oracle, accepts A as follows: On input x,

- nondeterministically guess a string w_1 with $|w_1| \le p(|x|)$,
- for each w_1 guessed, query the oracle about the pair $\langle x, w_1 \rangle$, and
- accept the input x if and only if the answer is "no."

It follows that $A = L(M^{\overline{C}})$. Thus, $A \in \mathrm{NP}^{\Sigma_i^p} = \Sigma_{i+1}^p$, which completes the induction proof. ∎

Corollary 5.32. *For each $i \ge 0$, $A \in \Pi_i^p$ if and only if there exist a set $B \in \mathrm{P}$ and a polynomial p such that for each $x \in \Sigma^*$,*

$$x \in A \iff (\forall^p w_1)(\exists^p w_2) \cdots (\mathfrak{Q}^p w_i) [\langle x, w_1, w_2, \ldots, w_i \rangle \in B],$$

where $\mathfrak{Q}^p = \forall^p$ if i is odd, and $\mathfrak{Q}^p = \exists^p$ if i is even.

The following theorem shows that the polynomial hierarchy shares with the boolean hierarchy (cf. Theorem 5.10) the "upward collapse" property: If any one of its levels collapses down to the level preceding it, then the entire hierarchy collapses down to this specific, finite level. Even if any one of the Σ_i^p classes were to coincide with its complementary class, Π_i^p, the same consequence occurs.

Theorem 5.33.   *1. For each $i \ge 0$, if $\Sigma_i^p = \Sigma_{i+1}^p$, then*

$$\Sigma_i^p = \Pi_i^p = \Delta_{i+1}^p = \Sigma_{i+1}^p = \Pi_{i+1}^p = \cdots = \mathrm{PH}.$$

2. For each $i \ge 1$, if $\Sigma_i^p = \Pi_i^p$, then

$$\Sigma_i^p = \Pi_i^p = \Delta_{i+1}^p = \Sigma_{i+1}^p = \Pi_{i+1}^p = \cdots = \mathrm{PH}.$$

Proof.   First, we show that the hypothesis of the first statement implies that of the second statement. Supposing $\Sigma_i^p = \Sigma_{i+1}^p$ for $i \ge 0$, it follows that:

$$\Pi_i^p \subseteq \Sigma_{i+1}^p = \Sigma_i^p,$$

which implies $\Sigma_i^p = \Pi_i^p$; see Exercise 5.22.

Now suppose that $\Sigma_i^p = \Pi_i^p$ for $i \ge 1$.[2] We show that this implies $\Sigma_i^p = \Sigma_{i+1}^p$. Let A be any set in Σ_{i+1}^p. By Theorem 5.31, there exist a set $B \in \mathrm{P}$ and a polynomial p such that for each $x \in \Sigma^*$,

---

[2] By definition, $\Sigma_0^p = \mathrm{P} = \Pi_0^p$ is outright true, yet $\mathrm{P} = \Sigma_0^p = \Sigma_1^p = \mathrm{NP}$ is very doubtful. Where does the argument in this proof fail to prove $\Sigma_0^p = \Pi_0^p \implies \Sigma_0^p = \Sigma_1^p$? See Exercise 5.23.

$$x \in A \iff (\exists^p w_1)(\forall^p w_2) \cdots (\mathfrak{Q}^p w_{i+1})[\langle x, w_1, w_2, \ldots, w_{i+1}\rangle \in B],$$

where $\mathfrak{Q}^p = \exists^p$ if i is even, and $\mathfrak{Q}^p = \forall^p$ if i is odd. Define a set C by:

$$C = \left\{\langle x, w_1\rangle \;\middle|\; \begin{array}{l} |w_1| \leq p(|x|) \wedge (\forall^p w_2)(\exists^p w_3) \cdots \\ (\mathfrak{Q}^p w_{i+1})[\langle x, w_1, w_2, \ldots, w_{i+1}\rangle \in B] \end{array}\right\}.$$

By Theorem 5.31, $C \in \Pi_i^p = \Sigma_i^p$. Again by Theorem 5.31, for $C \in \Sigma_i^p$, there exist a set $D \in P$ and a polynomial q such that for each $x \in \Sigma^*$,

$$C = \left\{\langle x, w_1\rangle \;\middle|\; \begin{array}{l} |w_1| \leq q(|x|) \wedge (\exists^q w_2)(\forall^q w_3) \cdots \\ (\overline{\mathfrak{Q}}^q w_{i+1})[\langle x, w_1, w_2, \ldots, w_{i+1}\rangle \in D] \end{array}\right\},$$

where $\overline{\mathfrak{Q}}^q = \forall^q$ if i is even, and $\overline{\mathfrak{Q}}^q = \exists^q$ if i is odd. Hence,

$$x \in A \iff \underbrace{(\exists^p w_1)(\exists^q w_2)}_{\text{combine to } (\exists^r w)}(\forall^q w_3) \cdots (\overline{\mathfrak{Q}}^q w_{i+1})[\langle x, w_1, w_2, \ldots, w_{i+1}\rangle \in D].$$

Combining the first two existential quantifiers to one existential quantifier whose length is bounded by the polynomial $r = p + q$ (neglecting the constant overhead for the pairing) and once more applying Theorem 5.31, we obtain $A \in \Sigma_i^p$. Since A was arbitrarily chosen from Σ_{i+1}^p, we have $\Sigma_i^p = \Sigma_{i+1}^p$.

An easy induction now shows that every level Σ_k^p with $k \geq i$ collapses down to Σ_i^p:

$$\Sigma_{i+2}^p = NP^{\Sigma_{i+1}^p} = NP^{\Sigma_i^p} = \Sigma_{i+1}^p = \Sigma_i^p,$$

and so on. ∎

Do there exist complete sets in the polynomial hierarchy? Which problems are complete for the Σ_i^p levels, and which for the Π_i^p levels? The quantifier characterization of Σ_i^p and Π_i^p stated in Theorem 5.31 and Corollary 5.32 suggests that generalizing the satisfiability problem so as to also allow *quantified* boolean formulas yields good candidates for complete problems.

Definition 5.34 (Quantified Boolean Formula Problem).
Define the quantified boolean formula problem *by:*

$$QBF = \{F \mid F \text{ is a closed QBF that evaluates to true}\}.$$

We now define restrictions of QBF with a bounded number of alternating quantifiers. Recall from Section 2.3 that every QBF can be transformed into an equivalent QBF in prenex form, see Definition 2.28. Recall also that one can combine contiguous equal quantifiers to one quantifier of the same type, which thus may quantify a set of variables. By renaming the quantified variables, the variable sets after each quantifier can be made pairwise disjoint.

We now restrict the general QBF problem by bounding the number of alternating quantifiers, thus obtaining the problems Σ_iSAT and Π_iSAT for each i. Σ_iSAT contains those formulas from QBF that are in prenex form and have a prefix of i alternating quantifiers starting with $\exists$. Π_iSAT contains those formulas from QBF that are in prenex form and have a prefix of i alternating quantifiers starting with $\forall$.

Definition 5.35 (QBF Problem with a Bounded Number of Alternations).

1. For each $i \geq 1$, a QBF F is said to be a Σ_iSAT formula if and only if F is closed and of the form:

$$F = (\exists X_1)(\forall X_2) \cdots (\mathfrak{Q} X_i) H(X_1, X_2, \ldots, X_i),$$

where the X_j are pairwise disjoint variable sets, $\mathfrak{Q} \in \{\exists, \forall\}$, the i quantifiers alternate between $\exists$ and $\forall$, and H is a boolean formula without quantifiers. For each $i \geq 1$, define the problem

$$\Sigma_i \text{SAT} = \{F \mid F \text{ is a true } \Sigma_i \text{SAT formula}\}.$$

2. For each $i \geq 1$, a QBF F is said to be a Π_iSAT formula if and only if F is closed and of the form:

$$F = (\forall X_1)(\exists X_2) \cdots (\mathfrak{Q} X_i) H(X_1, X_2, \ldots, X_i),$$

where the X_j are pairwise disjoint variable sets, $\mathfrak{Q} \in \{\exists, \forall\}$, the i quantifiers alternate between $\forall$ and $\exists$, and H is a boolean formula without quantifiers. For each $i \geq 1$, define the problem

$$\Pi_i \text{SAT} = \{F \mid F \text{ is a true } \Pi_i \text{SAT formula}\}.$$

Theorem 5.36. *1. QBF is PSPACE-complete.*
2. For each $i \geq 1$, Σ_iSAT is Σ_i^p-complete and Π_iSAT is Π_i^p-complete.
3. If there exists a complete set for PH, then PH collapses down to some finite level: PH $= \Sigma_i^p = \Pi_i^p$ for some i.

Proof.   1. The theorem's first statement can be proven using the method applied in the proof of Savitch's Theorem (see Theorem 3.29); see Exercise 5.24. Alternatively, the theorem's first statement can be proven analogously to the proof of the theorem's second statement.

2. For the second statement, membership of Σ_iSAT in Σ_i^p and of Π_iSAT in Π_i^p immediately follows from Theorem 5.31 and Corollary 5.32, respectively.

Suppose that i is odd. The case of even i can be proven in a similar fashion. To prove that Σ_iSAT is Σ_i^p-hard, let A be any set in Σ_i^p. Again by Theorem 5.31, there exist a set $B \in$ P and a polynomial p such that for each $x \in \Sigma^*$,

$$x \in A \iff (\exists^p y_1)(\forall^p y_2) \cdots (\exists^p y_i)[\langle x, y_1, y_2, \ldots, y_i \rangle \in B]. \quad (5.20)$$

Let M be some deterministic polynomial-time Turing machine deciding B, i.e., $L(M) = B$. By Cook's Theorem (see Theorem 3.49), the computation of M on any input of the form $\langle x, y_1, y_2, \ldots, y_i \rangle$ can be encoded by a boolean formula $\varphi_M(X, Y_1, Y_2, \ldots, Y_i, Z)$, where $X \cup \bigcup_{j=1}^{i} Y_j$ is the set of input variables and Z is the set of all the remaining variables in the Cook reduction. Note that each variable in $X \cup \bigcup_{j=1}^{i} Y_j$ corresponds to one bit in the input strings $x, y_1, y_2, \ldots, y_i$, and setting these bits to 1 or 0 sets the corresponding variables to true or false. In particular, fixing all bits in the string x creates a boolean formula $\varphi_{\langle M,x\rangle}$ depending only on the variables from $Z \cup \bigcup_{j=1}^{i} Y_j$.

By Cook's Theorem, for each input $\langle x, y_1, y_2, \ldots, y_i \rangle$,

$$\langle x, y_1, y_2, \ldots, y_i \rangle \in B \iff \varphi_{\langle M,x,y_1,y_2,\ldots,y_i \rangle}(Z) \in \mathsf{SAT} \tag{5.21}$$
$$\iff (\exists^q z)\, [\varphi_{\langle M,x,y_1,y_2,\ldots,y_i,z \rangle} \text{ evaluates to true}],$$

where q is a polynomial in $|x|$ bounding the number of variables in Z; see the proof of Theorem 3.49. Equivalences (5.20) and (5.21) now imply that for each $x \in \Sigma^*$,

$$x \in A \iff (\exists^p y_1)\,(\forall^p y_2) \cdots (\exists^p y_i)\, [\langle x, y_1, y_2, \ldots, y_i \rangle \in B] \tag{5.22}$$
$$\iff (\exists^p y_1)\,(\forall^p y_2) \cdots \underbrace{(\exists^p y_i)\,(\exists^q z)}_{\text{combine to } (\exists^r z_1)}\, [\varphi_{\langle M,x,y_1,y_2,\ldots,y_i,z \rangle} \text{ evaluates to true}],$$

where $r = p + q$ is a polynomial. Let $V = Y_i \cup Z$ be the variable set containing all variables from Y_i and Z. Mapping any given x to the $\Sigma_i\mathsf{SAT}$ formula

$$F_x = (\exists Y_1)\,(\forall Y_2) \cdots (\forall Y_{i-1})\,(\exists V)\, \varphi_{\langle M,x\rangle}(Y_1, Y_2, \ldots, Y_{i-1}, V)$$

defines the $\leq_m^P$-reduction from A to $\Sigma_i\mathsf{SAT}$. Since the Cook reduction is polynomial-time computable, F_x can be computed from x in time polynomially in $|x|$. By Equivalence (5.22), x is in A if and only if $F_x \in \Sigma_i\mathsf{SAT}$, which shows that $\Sigma_i\mathsf{SAT}$ is Σ_i^p-complete. Π_i^p-completeness of $\Pi_i\mathsf{SAT}$ is proven analogously.

3. To prove the theorem's third statement, suppose L is a set complete for PH. Since L is in PH, there exists a smallest i such that $L \in \Sigma_i^p$. Since L is hard for PH, $X \leq_m^P L$ for each X in PH. Since Σ_i^p is $\leq_m^P$-closed, it follows that $X \in \Sigma_i^p$ for each $X \in$ PH. Thus, PH $= \Sigma_i^p = \Pi_i^p$. ∎

Corollary 5.37. PSPACE $= \Sigma_i^p$ *if and only if* QBF $\in \Sigma_i^p$.

5.3 Parallel Access to NP

As an example of a polynomial-time Turing reduction, Figure 5.9 shows a prefix search algorithm for finding the lexicographically smallest solution of a given GI instance. Since the number of all solutions is exponential in the size n of the given input, say 2^{n^c} for some constant c, this algorithm makes at most $\mathcal{O}(\log 2^{n^c}) = \mathcal{O}(n^c)$ oracle queries and thus terminates in polynomial time. If the solution space itself is bounded by a polynomial in the input size, say n^k for some constant k, a binary (or prefix) search succeeds in time $\mathcal{O}(\log n^k) = \mathcal{O}(\log n)$.

For illustration, consider the problem of determining whether or not the independence number of a given graph is odd, or the problem of comparing the independence numbers of two given graphs. Recall that an independent set of a graph is a subset I of its vertices such that no two vertices in I are adjacent. The size of I is the number of vertices in I.

Definition 5.38 (Independence Number Problems).
For any graph G, the independence number *of G, denoted by $\alpha(G)$, is the size of a maximum independent set of G. Define the problems:*

$$\text{IN-Odd} = \{G \mid G \text{ is a graph such that } \alpha(G) \text{ is odd}\};$$
$$\text{IN-Equ} = \{\langle G, H \rangle \mid G \text{ and } H \text{ are graphs such that } \alpha(G) = \alpha(H)\};$$
$$\text{IN-Geq} = \{\langle G, H \rangle \mid G \text{ and } H \text{ are graphs such that } \alpha(G) \geq \alpha(H)\}.$$

Note that $\alpha(G) \leq n$ for each graph G with n vertices. Thus, for example, deciding whether or not G is in IN-Odd takes no more than $\mathcal{O}(\log n)$ sequential Turing queries. Papadimitriou and Zachos introduced the corresponding complexity class, $P^{NP[\mathcal{O}(\log)]}$, which has become later a "named" level of the polynomial hierarchy, Θ_2^p.

Definition 5.39. *1. Define $P^{NP[\mathcal{O}(\log)]}$ to be the class of problems A solvable by some DPOTM M with oracle $B \in NP$, i.e., $A = L(M^B)$, such that M on each input of length n makes at most $\mathcal{O}(\log n)$ sequential Turing queries to B.*
2. Define $\Theta_2^p = P^{NP[\mathcal{O}(\log)]}$.
3. Analogously, define $\Theta_i^p = P^{\Sigma_{i-1}^p[\mathcal{O}(\log)]}$ for each $i \geq 1$.

By definition, $\Sigma_{i-1}^p \cup \Pi_{i-1}^p \subseteq \Theta_i^p \subseteq \Delta_i^p$ for each $i \geq 1$. The comments above immediately provide a Θ_2^p upper bound on the independence number problems from Definition 5.38. The details of the formal proof are left to the reader as Exercise 5.25(a). We will see later on (in Theorem 5.44) that Θ_2^p also provides a lower bound for these problems.

Proposition 5.40. IN-Odd, IN-Equ, *and* IN-Geq *each are in* Θ_2^p.

There are about a dozen of characterizations of the complexity class $\Theta_2^p = P^{NP[\mathcal{O}(\log)]}$; see [Wag90]. Most central among them is the characterization of Θ_2^p as the closure of NP under the polynomial-time truth-table reducibility.

Definition 5.41 (Polynomial-Time Truth-Table Reducibility and Completeness).
Let $\Sigma = \{0, 1\}$ be a fixed alphabet, let A and B be any sets of strings over Σ, and let $\mathcal{C}$ be any complexity class. The characteristic function *of B, denoted by χ_B, is defined by $\chi_B(q) = 1$ if $q \in B$, and $\chi_B(q) = 0$ if $q \notin B$.*

1. Define the polynomial-time truth-table reducibility, *denoted by $\leq_{tt}^P$, as follows: $A \leq_{tt}^P B$ if and only if there is a function $f \in FP$ such that, for each input x, $f(x) = \langle \tau, q_1, q_2, \ldots, q_k \rangle$, where $q_1, q_2, \ldots, q_k$ are the truth-table queries generated and τ is a k-ary boolean function encoded as a boolean circuit, and:*

$$x \in A \iff \tau(\chi_B(q_1), \chi_B(q_2), \ldots, \chi_B(q_k)) = 1.$$

Note that the number k of queries is polynomial in $|x|$, since f is in FP.
2. A set B is $\leq_{tt}^P$-hard for $\mathcal{C}$ if and only if $A \leq_{tt}^P B$ for each $A \in \mathcal{C}$.
3. A set B is $\leq_{tt}^P$-complete for $\mathcal{C}$ if and only if B is $\leq_{tt}^P$-hard for $\mathcal{C}$ and $B \in \mathcal{C}$.

4. *The $\leq_{tt}^P$-closure of $\mathcal{C}$ is defined by:*

$$P_{tt}^{\mathcal{C}} = \{A \mid (\exists B \in \mathcal{C})\,[A \leq_{tt}^P B]\}.$$

A class $\mathcal{C}$ is said to be closed under the $\leq_{tt}^P$-reducibility *($\leq_{tt}^P$-closed, for short) if and only if $\mathcal{C} = P_{tt}^{\mathcal{C}}$.*

The truth-table reducibility is more flexible than the many-one reducibility, yet less flexible than the Turing reducibility. Crucially, the oracle queries in Turing reductions may depend on the answers to previously asked queries. In this sense, Turing reductions are *adaptive*. In contrast, truth-table queries are *nonadaptive*, since they are all precomputed in advance—before any of them is asked—and then they all are asked in parallel. That is why the truth-table oracle access is also called *parallel oracle access*. In particular, the complexity class P_{tt}^{NP} is often referred to as capturing "parallel access to NP." Corollary 5.55 will establish the equality $P_{tt}^{NP} = \Theta_2^p$.

Example 5.42 (Polynomial-Time Truth-Table Reducibility). For illustration, we construct a $\leq_{tt}^P$-reduction f from IN-Odd to IS. Recall that IS $= \{\langle G, k\rangle \mid \alpha(G) \geq k\}$ is an NP-complete set. Thus, since IS is in NP and IN-Odd $\leq_{tt}^P$ IS, the upcoming Corollary 5.55 implies that IN-Odd is in Θ_2^p.

Given a graph G with n vertices, define $f(G) = \langle \tau, q_1, q_2, \ldots, q_n\rangle$, where for each i, $1 \leq i \leq n$, the ith query is $q_i = \langle G, i\rangle$, and τ is the truth table defined by:

$$\tau(b_1, b_2, \ldots, b_n) = \begin{cases} 1 & b_1 = \cdots = b_i = 1 \wedge b_{i+1} = \cdots = b_n = 0 \text{ for some odd } i \\ 0 & \text{otherwise,} \end{cases}$$

where $b_i = \chi_{IS}(q_i)$ for $1 \leq i \leq n$. That is, $b_i = 1$ if and only if $\alpha(G) \geq i$.

Table 5.1 illustrates this $\leq_{tt}^P$-reduction for the case of four queries, i.e., for a graph with four vertices. Note that only the boldfaced columns are relevant for the definition of τ, since the cases corresponding to the other columns cannot occur. That is, the value of τ can be chosen arbitrarily for the non-boldfaced columns.

b_1: "$q_1 = \langle G, 1\rangle \in$ IS?"	0 0 0 0	0 0 0 0	1 1 1 1	1 1 1 1
b_2: "$q_2 = \langle G, 2\rangle \in$ IS?"	0 0 0 0	1 1 1 1	0 0 0 0	1 1 1 1
b_3: "$q_3 = \langle G, 3\rangle \in$ IS?"	0 0 1 1	0 0 1 1	0 0 1 1	0 0 1 1
b_4: "$q_4 = \langle G, 4\rangle \in$ IS?"	0 1 0 1	0 1 0 1	0 1 0 1	0 1 0 1
$\tau(b_1, b_2, b_3, b_4)$	0 0 0 0	0 0 0 0	1 0 0 0	0 0 1 0

Table 5.1. Example of a $\leq_{tt}^P$-reduction from IN-Odd to IS with four queries

The following lemma provides a sufficient condition for proving Θ_2^p-hardness. It is another example of Wagner's technique of raising NP lower bounds to lower bounds for classes above NP. The difference with Lemma 5.11, which provides an analogous condition sufficient to prove BH$_k$(NP)-hardness for each given k, is that the value of k is not fixed in Lemma 5.43.

Lemma 5.43 (Wagner).   *Let A be some NP-complete set, and let B be any set. If there exists a polynomial-time computable function f such that, for all $k \geq 1$ and all strings $x_1, \ldots, x_{2k} \in \Sigma^*$ satisfying $\chi_A(x_1) \geq \chi_A(x_2) \geq \cdots \geq \chi_A(x_{2k})$, we have*

$$||\{i \mid x_i \in A\}|| \text{ is odd } \iff f((x_1, x_2, \ldots, x_{2k})) \in B, \qquad (5.23)$$

then B is Θ_2^p-hard.

We illustrate the application of Lemma 5.43 by proving Θ_2^p-completeness of the three independence number problems defined above.

Theorem 5.44. IN-Odd, IN-Equ, *and* IN-Geq *each are* Θ_2^p-complete.

Proof.   Membership in Θ_2^p has already been stated in Proposition 5.40 for each of these problems. Using Lemma 5.43, we now prove that IN-Equ is Θ_2^p-hard. The proof of the Θ_2^p-hardness of both IN-Odd and IN-Geq is similar; see Exercise 5.25(b).

We apply Lemma 5.43 with 3-SAT being the NP-complete set A and with $B =$ IN-Equ. Since Θ_2^p is closed under complementation, it suffices to define a polynomial-time computable function f such that the equivalence

$$||\{i \mid \varphi_i \in \text{3-SAT}\}|| \text{ is even } \iff f((\varphi_1, \ldots, \varphi_{2k})) \in \text{IN-Equ} \qquad (5.24)$$

is true for all $k \geq 1$ and all boolean formulas $\varphi_1, \varphi_2, \ldots, \varphi_{2k}$ (suitably encoded as strings in Σ^*) satisfying that $\varphi_{i+1} \in$ 3-SAT implies $\varphi_i \in$ 3-SAT for each i with $1 \leq i < 2k$. Let g be a reduction that $\leq_m^p$-reduces 3-SAT to IS such that the following property is satisfied: For each boolean formula φ, $g(\varphi) = \langle G, \ell \rangle$, where G is a graph and ℓ is a positive integer (namely the number of clauses of φ), and it holds that:

$$\varphi \in \text{3-SAT} \implies \alpha(G) = \ell; \qquad (5.25)$$
$$\varphi \notin \text{3-SAT} \implies \alpha(G) = \ell - 1. \qquad (5.26)$$

The construction of g such that (5.25) and (5.25) are satisfied is left to the reader as Exercise 5.25(b). (Note that the reduction for 3-SAT $\leq_m^p$ IS constructed in the proof of Theorem 3.54 does not have the desired properties.)

Let $k \geq 1$, and let $\varphi_1, \varphi_2, \ldots, \varphi_{2k}$ be boolean formulas such that $\varphi_{i+1} \in$ 3-SAT implies $\varphi_i \in$ 3-SAT for each $i < 2k$. For each i with $1 \leq i \leq 2k$, let $g(\varphi_i) = \langle G_i, \ell_i \rangle$. Note that $||\{i \mid \varphi_i \in \text{3-SAT}\}|| = m$ if and only if $\varphi_1, \varphi_2, \ldots, \varphi_m \in$ 3-SAT and $\varphi_{m+1}, \varphi_{m+2}, \ldots, \varphi_{2k} \notin$ 3-SAT. It follows that:

- If $||\{i \mid \varphi_i \in \text{3-SAT}\}||$ is even, then for each $i \in \{1, 2, \ldots, k\}$:

$$\varphi_{2i-1} \in \text{3-SAT} \iff \varphi_{2i} \in \text{3-SAT}.$$

This implies that for each $i \in \{1, 2, \ldots, k\}$:

$$\alpha(G_{2i-1}) + \ell_{2i} = \alpha(G_{2i}) + \ell_{2i-1}.$$

- If $||\{i \mid \varphi_i \in 3\text{-SAT}\}||$ is odd, then there exists some $i \in \{1, 2, \ldots, k\}$ such that:

$$\varphi_{2i-1} \in 3\text{-SAT} \quad \text{and} \quad \varphi_{2i} \notin 3\text{-SAT} \quad \text{and}$$
$$(\forall j \in \{1, 2, \ldots, k\}, j \neq i)\,[\varphi_{2j-1} \in 3\text{-SAT} \iff \varphi_{2j} \in 3\text{-SAT}].$$

This implies that for this integer i:

$$\alpha(G_{2i-1}) + \ell_{2i} - 1 = \alpha(G_{2i}) + \ell_{2i-1};$$
$$(\forall j \in \{1, 2, \ldots, k\}, j \neq i)\,[\alpha(G_{2j-1}) + \ell_{2j} = \alpha(G_{2j}) + \ell_{2j-1}].$$

For any two disjoint graphs G and H, their *disjoint union* is the graph $G \cup H$ with vertex set $V(G \cup H) = V(G) \cup V(H)$ and edge set $E(G \cup H) = E(G) \cup E(H)$. It is important to note that $\alpha(G \cup H) = \alpha(G) + \alpha(H)$. Without loss of generality, we assume that the graphs $G_1, G_2, \ldots, G_{2k}$ are pairwise disjoint. Define the sum of the ℓ_j's and the disjoint union of the G_j's with odd (respectively, with even) subscript j by:

$$\ell_{\text{odd}} = \sum_{1 \leq i \leq k} \ell_{2i-1} \quad \text{and} \quad \ell_{\text{even}} = \sum_{1 \leq i \leq k} \ell_{2i};$$
$$G_{\text{odd}} = \bigcup_{1 \leq i \leq k} G_{2i-1} \quad \text{and} \quad G_{\text{even}} = \bigcup_{1 \leq i \leq k} G_{2i}.$$

For $m > 0$, let H_m be the graph consisting of m isolated points, and assume that H_m is disjoint from G_{odd} and G_{even}. Note that $\alpha(H_m) = m$. Define the reduction:

$$f(\langle \varphi_1, \varphi_2, \ldots, \varphi_{2k} \rangle) = \langle G_{\text{odd}} \cup H_{\ell_{\text{even}}}, G_{\text{even}} \cup H_{\ell_{\text{odd}}} \rangle.$$

Clearly, f is computable in polynomial time. To satisfy (5.24), it remains to show that:

$$||\{i \mid \varphi_i \in 3\text{-SAT}\}|| \text{ is even} \iff \alpha(G_{\text{odd}} \cup H_{\ell_{\text{even}}}) = \alpha(G_{\text{even}} \cup H_{\ell_{\text{odd}}}).$$

From left to right:

$$||\{i \mid \varphi_i \in 3\text{-SAT}\}|| \text{ is even}$$
$$\implies (\forall i \in \{1, 2, \ldots, k\})\,[\alpha(G_{2i-1}) + \ell_{2i} = \alpha(G_{2i}) + \ell_{2i-1}]$$
$$\implies \sum_{1 \leq i \leq k} (\alpha(G_{2i-1}) + \ell_{2i}) = \sum_{1 \leq i \leq k} (\alpha(G_{2i}) + \ell_{2i-1})$$
$$\implies \alpha(G_{\text{odd}}) + \ell_{\text{even}} = \alpha(G_{\text{even}}) + \ell_{\text{odd}}$$
$$\implies \alpha(G_{\text{odd}} \cup H_{\ell_{\text{even}}}) = \alpha(G_{\text{even}} \cup H_{\ell_{\text{odd}}}).$$

From right to left:

$$||\{i \mid \varphi_i \in 3\text{-SAT}\}|| \text{ is odd}$$
$$\implies (\exists i \in \{1, 2, \ldots, k\})\,[\alpha(G_{2i-1}) + \ell_{2i} - 1 = \alpha(G_{2i}) + \ell_{2i-1} \text{ and}$$
$$(\forall j \in \{1, 2, \ldots, k\}, j \neq i)\,[\alpha(G_{2j-1}) + \ell_{2j} = \alpha(G_{2j}) + \ell_{2j-1}]]$$
$$\implies -1 + \sum_{1 \leq j \leq k} (\alpha(G_{2j-1}) + \ell_{2j}) = \sum_{1 \leq j \leq k} (\alpha(G_{2j}) + \ell_{2j-1})$$
$$\implies \alpha(G_{\text{odd}}) + \ell_{\text{even}} - 1 = \alpha(G_{\text{even}}) + \ell_{\text{odd}}$$
$$\implies \alpha(G_{\text{odd}} \cup H_{\ell_{\text{even}}}) - 1 = \alpha(G_{\text{even}} \cup H_{\ell_{\text{odd}}})$$
$$\implies \alpha(G_{\text{odd}} \cup H_{\ell_{\text{even}}}) \neq \alpha(G_{\text{even}} \cup H_{\ell_{\text{odd}}}).$$

Thus, (5.24) is satisfied. By Lemma 5.43, IN-Equ is Θ_2^p-hard, which completes the proof.   ∎

Lemma 5.43 has yielded a host of Θ_2^p-completeness results. Take Favorite, your favorite NP-complete problem. Analogously to IN-Odd, IN-Equ, and IN-Geq defined in Definition 5.38, define the variants Favorite-Odd, Favorite-Equ, and Favorite-Geq corresponding to Favorite, and apply the Wagner technique of Lemma 5.43 to prove them Θ_2^p-complete. Section 5.9 provides further applications.

One might argue that problems such as Favorite-Odd, Favorite-Equ, and Favorite-Geq are not overly natural. However, there are some quite natural problems for which this technique has also yielded Θ_2^p-completeness results. Some of them are related to social choice theory and computational politics. In particular, Lemma 5.43 was applied successfully to prove that the winner problem for certain election systems is Θ_2^p-complete. The remaining part of this section introduces one such result by giving a careful analysis of the winner problem for Young elections and pinpointing its precise computational complexity: Determining Young winners is complete for parallel access to NP. The proof of this result, which is due to Rothe, Spakowski, and Vogel [RSV02, RSV03], does not explicitly apply Lemma 5.43. However, it does use Lemma 5.43 implicitly, as it applies a reduction from the problem IN-Geq, which is Θ_2^p-complete by Theorem 5.44.

Before turning to the actual complexity analysis, let us briefly digress to give some background from social choice theory. More information on the issues and results in computational politics can be found in the survey by E. and L. Hemaspaandra [HH00].

5.3.1 A Brief Digression to Social Choice Theory

The following quote is from the blurb of Saari's book "Chaotic Elections! A Mathematician Looks at Voting" [Saa01]:

> "What does the 2000 U.S. Presidential Election have in common with selecting a textbook for a calculus course in your department? Was Ralph Nader's influence on the election of George W. Bush greater than the now-famous chads? In Chaotic Elections!, Don Saari analyzes these questions, placing them in the larger context of voting systems in general. His analysis shows that the fundamental problems with the 2000 presidential election are not with the courts, recounts or defective ballots, but are caused by the very way Americans vote for president."

> (From "Chaotic Elections!" by Don Saari, American Mathematical Society, 2001)

In other words, before blaming anything or anybody else for the perhaps undesired outcome of an election, you should take a close look at the mathematics that underpins the electoral system used. Is it a "fair" system? Can there exist "fair" election systems at all? And what are the fundamental properties of election systems? Questions like these have been studied by social choice theorists and mathematicians for centuries now. Among the properties that any "reasonable" election procedure arguably should satisfy are nondictatorship, monotonicity, the Pareto Principle, and independence of irrelevant alternatives. One of the most notable results in social choice theory is Arrow's famous impossibility theorem [Arr63], which says that the just-mentioned four properties are logically inconsistent whenever there are at least three candidates, and thus no "fair" voting scheme can exist.

To describe voting systems, we need candidates (or alternatives) and voters and some rule that tells us who has won the election according to the voters' preferences over the candidates. An election is given by a *preference profile*, a pair $\langle C, V \rangle$ such that C is a set of candidates and V is the multiset[3] of the voters' preference orders on C. Assume that each voter has strict preferences over the candidates. Formally, the preference order of each voter is a strict (i.e., irreflexive and antisymmetric), transitive, and complete (i.e., all candidates are ranked by each voter) relation on C.

A *voting scheme* (or *social choice function*, SCF for short) is a rule for how to determine the winner(s) of an election. That is, an SCF maps any given preference profile to society's aggregate *choice set*, i.e., to those candidates who have won the election. That is, the choice set $f(\langle C, V \rangle)$ gives the set of winning candidates for any SCF f and any preference profile $\langle C, V \rangle$. For example, the *majority rule* says that a candidate A *defeats* a candidate B if and only if A is preferred to B by a strict majority of the voters. To *win an election according to the majority rule*, a candidate must defeat every other candidate in a pairwise contest. Such a candidate is called the *Condorcet winner* of the election.

Example 5.45 (Condorcet Paradox). In 1785, Marie-Jean-Antoine-Nicolas de Caritat, the Marquis de Condorcet, observed in his seminal essay [Con85] that whenever there are at least three candidates, say a, b, and c, the majority rule can yield cycles. His example consists of the following three voters:

$$\text{Voter 1:} \quad a > b > c;$$
$$\text{Voter 2:} \quad b > c > a;$$
$$\text{Voter 3:} \quad c > a > b.$$

In this example, a defeats b and b defeats c, and yet c defeats a. Consequently, even though each individual voter has a rational (i.e., transitive or noncyclic) preference order, society can behave irrationally, and Condorcet winners do not always exist. This observation is known as the Condorcet Paradox.

The *Condorcet Principle* says that the majority rule determines the winner of the election for each given preference profile. An SCF is said to be a *Condorcet SCF* if and only if it respects the Condorcet Principle in the sense that the Condorcet winner is elected whenever one exists. Condorcet winners are uniquely determined if they exist. Many Condorcet SCFs have been proposed in the social choice literature; see Fishburn's work [Fis77] for an overview of the most central ones. Condorcet SCFs extend the Condorcet Principle in a way that avoids the troubling feature of the majority rule. In what follows, we will focus on the Young voting scheme [You77], which is one of the Condorcet SCFs listed in [Fis77].

---

[3] A *multiset* is a list of elements in which the same element may occur more than once. Multisets are used for the voters' preference orders, since distinct voters may have the same preferences over the candidates.

5.3.2 Determining Young Winners Is Complete for Parallel Access to NP

H. Young's [You77] approach to extending the Condorcet Principle is based on altered preference profiles. He suggests that we remain most faithful to the Condorcet
Principle if we require that an election is won by any candidate who can be made
a Condorcet winner by removing the fewest possible number of voters. To study
computational complexity issues related to the Young voting scheme, define the following two decision problems.

Definition 5.46 (Young Winner and Young Ranking Problems).
For each candidate c in a given preference profile $\langle C, V \rangle$, define the Young score,
denoted by $\mathrm{YScore}(C, c, V)$, *to be the size of a largest submultiset of V for which
c is a Condorcet winner. A* Young winner *is any candidate with a maximum Young
score. Define the problems:*

$$\texttt{YoungWinner} = \left\{ \langle C, c, V \rangle \,\middle|\, \begin{array}{l} \langle C, V \rangle \text{ is a preference profile, } c \in C \text{ is a} \\ \text{designated candidate, and for each } d \in C, \\ \mathrm{YScore}(C, c, V) \geq \mathrm{YScore}(C, d, V) \end{array} \right\};$$

$$\texttt{YoungRanking} = \left\{ \langle C, c, d, V \rangle \,\middle|\, \begin{array}{l} \langle C, V \rangle \text{ is a preference profile and } c \text{ and } d \\ \text{are designated candidates in } C \text{ such that} \\ \mathrm{YScore}(C, c, V) \geq \mathrm{YScore}(C, d, V) \end{array} \right\}.$$

Theorems 5.49 and 5.51 below prove the two problems defined above Θ_2^p-
hard using reductions from the problem Max-SetPacking-Geq. Recall the definition
of the related NP-complete problem SetPacking; see Definition 3.64 and Theorem 3.65.

Definition 5.47 (Maximum Set Packing Compare Problem).
*For any collection S of sets, $\kappa(S)$ denotes the maximum number of pairwise disjoint
sets in S. Define the problem:*

Max-SetPacking-Geq
$$= \left\{ \langle U_1, U_2, S_1, S_2 \rangle \,\middle|\, \begin{array}{l} U_i \text{ is a finite set and } S_i \subseteq \mathfrak{P}(U_i), \, i \in \{1, 2\}, \text{ is a} \\ \text{collection of nonempty sets such that } \kappa(S_1) \geq \kappa(S_2) \end{array} \right\}.$$

Lemma 5.48. Max-SetPacking-Geq *is Θ_2^p-complete.*

Proof.   It is not difficult to construct a reduction from the problem IN-Geq, which
is Θ_2^p-complete by Theorem 5.44, to Max-SetPacking-Geq. The details of the construction are left to the reader as Exercise 5.25(c).   ∎

Theorem 5.49. YoungRanking *is Θ_2^p-complete.*

Proof of Theorem 5.49.   It is easy to see that YoungRanking and YoungWinner
are both in Θ_2^p. The details of the construction are left to the reader as Exercise 5.26.

To prove the Θ_2^p lower bound, we give a polynomial-time many-one reduction from the problem Max-SetPacking-Geq. Let $U_1 = \{x_1, x_2, \ldots, x_m\}$ and $U_2 = \{y_1, y_2, \ldots, y_n\}$ be two given sets, and let $\mathcal{S}_1$ and $\mathcal{S}_2$ be given collections of subsets of U_1 and U_2, respectively. Recall that $\kappa(\mathcal{S}_i)$, for $i \in \{1, 2\}$, is the maximum number of pairwise disjoint sets in $\mathcal{S}_i$. Without loss of generality, we may assume that $\kappa(\mathcal{S}_i) > 2$.

The goal is to construct a preference profile $\langle C, V \rangle$ with the designated candidates c and d in C such that:

$$\text{YScore}(C, c, V) = 2 \cdot \kappa(\mathcal{S}_1) + 1; \tag{5.27}$$
$$\text{YScore}(C, d, V) = 2 \cdot \kappa(\mathcal{S}_2) + 1. \tag{5.28}$$

Define the set C of candidates by creating:

- the two designated candidates c and d,
- a candidate x_i for each element x_i of U_1,
- a candidate y_i for each element y_i of U_2, and
- two auxiliary candidates, a and b.

Define the set V of voters as follows:

- **Voters representing $\mathcal{S}_1$:** For each set $E \in \mathcal{S}_1$, create a single voter v_E as follows:
    - Enumerate E as $\{e_1, e_2, \ldots, e_{\|E\|}\}$ (renaming the candidates e_i chosen from $\{x_1, x_2, \ldots, x_m\}$ for notational convenience), and enumerate its complement $\overline{E} = U_1 - E$ as $\{\overline{e}_1, \overline{e}_2, \ldots, \overline{e}_{m - \|E\|}\}$.
    - To make the preference orders easier to parse, we use the notation:

"**E**"	to represent the text string "$e_1 > e_2 > \cdots > e_{\|E\|}$";
"**$\overline{E}$**"	to represent the text string "$\overline{e}_1 > \overline{e}_2 > \cdots > \overline{e}_{m - \|E\|}$";
"**U$_1$**"	to represent the text string "$x_1 > x_2 > \cdots > x_m$";
"**U$_2$**"	to represent the text string "$y_1 > y_2 > \cdots > y_n$".

    - Create one voter v_E with preference order:

    $$\mathbf{E} > a > c > \overline{\mathbf{E}} > \mathbf{U_2} > b > d. \tag{5.29}$$

- Additionally, create two voters with preference order:

$$c > \mathbf{U_1} > a > \mathbf{U_2} > b > d. \tag{5.30}$$

- Finally, create $\|\mathcal{S}_1\| - 1$ voters with preference order:

$$\mathbf{U_1} > c > a > \mathbf{U_2} > b > d. \tag{5.31}$$

- **Voters representing $\mathcal{S}_2$:** The case of $\mathcal{S}_2$ is treated analogously with the roles of respectively $\mathcal{S}_1$, U_1, x_i, c, a, E, e_j, and $\overline{e}_k$ interchanged with $\mathcal{S}_2$, U_2, y_i, d, b, F, f_j, and $\overline{f}_k$. More precisely, for each set $F \in \mathcal{S}_2$, create a single voter v_F as follows:

- Enumerate F as $\{f_1, f_2, \ldots, f_{\|F\|}\}$ (renaming the candidates f_j chosen from $\{y_1, y_2, \ldots, y_n\}$ for notational convenience), and enumerate its complement $\overline{F} = U_1 - F$ as $\{\overline{f}_1, \overline{f}_2, \ldots, \overline{f}_{n-\|F\|}\}$.
- To make the preference orders easier to parse, we use the notation:

   "$\mathbf{F}$" to represent the text string "$f_1 > f_2 > \cdots > f_{\|F\|}$";
   "$\overline{\mathbf{F}}$" to represent the text string "$\overline{f}_1 > \overline{f}_2 > \cdots > \overline{f}_{n-\|F\|}$".

- Create one voter v_F with preference order:

$$\mathbf{F} > b > d > \overline{\mathbf{F}} > \mathbf{U_1} > a > c. \tag{5.32}$$

• Additionally, create two voters with preference order:

$$d > \mathbf{U_2} > b > \mathbf{U_1} > a > c. \tag{5.33}$$

• Finally, create $\|S_2\| - 1$ voters with preference order:

$$\mathbf{U_2} > d > b > \mathbf{U_1} > a > c. \tag{5.34}$$

We now prove (5.27): $\text{YScore}(C, c, V) = 2 \cdot \kappa(S_1) + 1$.

Let $E_1, E_2, \ldots, E_{\kappa(S_1)} \in S_1$ be $\kappa(S_1)$ pairwise disjoint subsets of U_1. Consider the submultiset $\widehat{V}$ of V that consists of:

• every voter v_{E_i} corresponding to the set E_i, where $1 \leq i \leq \kappa(S_1)$;
• the two voters given in (5.30);
• $\kappa(S_1) - 1$ voters of the form given in (5.31).

Clearly, $\|\widehat{V}\| = 2 \cdot \kappa(S_1) + 1$. Note that a strict majority of the voters in $\widehat{V}$ prefer c over any other candidate, and thus c is a Condorcet winner in $\langle C, \widehat{V} \rangle$. Hence,

$$\text{YScore}(C, c, V) \geq 2 \cdot \kappa(S_1) + 1.$$

Conversely, to prove that $\text{YScore}(C, c, V) \leq 2 \cdot \kappa(S_1) + 1$, we need the following lemma.

Lemma 5.50. *For any λ with $3 < \lambda \leq \|S_1\| + 1$, let V_λ be any submultiset of V such that V_λ contains exactly λ voters of the form (5.30) or (5.31) and c is a Condorcet winner in $\langle C, V_\lambda \rangle$. Then, V_λ contains exactly $\lambda - 1$ voters of the form (5.29) and no voters of the form (5.32), (5.33), or (5.34). Moreover, the $\lambda - 1$ voters of the form (5.29) in V_λ represent pairwise disjoint sets from S_1.*

Proof of Lemma 5.50.   For fixed λ, let V_λ be given as above. Consider the submultiset of V_λ that consists of the λ voters of the form (5.30) or (5.31). Every candidate x_i, $1 \leq i \leq m$, is preferred to c by the at least $\lambda - 2$ voters of the form (5.31). Since c is a Condorcet winner in $\langle C, V_\lambda \rangle$, there exist, for every x_i, at least $\lambda - 1 > 2$ voters in V_λ who prefer c to x_i. By construction, these voters must be of the form (5.29) or (5.30). Since there are at most two voters of the form (5.30), there exists at least one voter of the form (5.29), say $\tilde{v}$. Since the voters of the form (5.29) represent $\mathcal{S}_1$, which contains only nonempty sets, there exists some candidate x_j who is preferred to c by $\tilde{v}$. In particular, c must outpoll x_j in $\langle C, V_\lambda \rangle$ and thus needs more than $(\lambda - 2) + 1$ votes of the form (5.29) or (5.30). There are at most two voters of the form (5.30). Hence, c must be preferred by at least $\lambda - 2$ voters of the form (5.29) that are distinct from $\tilde{v}$. Summing up, V_λ contains at least $\lambda - 1$ voters of the form (5.29).

On the other hand, since c is a Condorcet winner in $\langle C, V_\lambda \rangle$, c must in particular outpoll a, who is not preferred to c by the λ voters of the form (5.30) or (5.31) and who is preferred to c by all other voters. Hence, V_λ may contain at most $\lambda - 1$ voters of the form (5.29), (5.32), (5.33), or (5.34). It follows that V_λ contains exactly $\lambda - 1$ voters of the form (5.29) and no voters of the form (5.32), (5.33), or (5.34).

For a contradiction, suppose that there is a candidate x_j who is preferred to c by more than one voter of the form (5.29) in V_λ. Then,

- c is preferred to x_j by at most two voters of the form (5.30) and by at most $(\lambda - 1) - 2 = \lambda - 3$ voters of the form (5.29);
- x_j is preferred to c by at least $\lambda - 2$ voters of the form (5.31) and by at least two voters of the form (5.29).

Since c thus has at most $\lambda - 1$ votes and x_j has at least λ votes in V_λ, c is not a Condorcet winner in $\langle C, V_\lambda \rangle$, a contradiction. Thus, every candidate x_i, $1 \leq i \leq m$, is preferred to c by at most one voter of the form (5.29) in V_λ, which means that the $\lambda - 1$ voters of the form (5.29) in V_λ represent pairwise disjoint sets from $\mathcal{S}_1$. The lemma is proven.   ∎ Lemma 5.50

To continue the proof of Theorem 5.49, let $k = \text{YScore}(C, c, V)$. Let $\widehat{V} \subseteq V$ be a submultiset of size k such that c is a Condorcet winner in $\langle C, \widehat{V} \rangle$. Suppose that there are exactly $\lambda \leq \|\mathcal{S}_1\| + 1$ voters of the form (5.30) or (5.31) in $\widehat{V}$. Since c, the Condorcet winner of $\langle C, \widehat{V} \rangle$, must in particular outpoll a, we have $\lambda \geq \left\lceil \frac{k+1}{2} \right\rceil$, where for each real number r, $\lceil r \rceil$ denotes the smallest integer s with $s \geq r$. By our assumption that $\kappa(\mathcal{S}_1) > 2$, it follows from $k \geq 2 \cdot \kappa(\mathcal{S}_1) + 1$ that $\lambda > 3$.

Lemma 5.50 then implies that there are exactly $\lambda - 1$ voters of the form (5.29) in $\widehat{V}$, which represent pairwise disjoint sets from $\mathcal{S}_1$, and $\widehat{V}$ contains no voters of the form (5.32), (5.33), or (5.34). Hence, $k = 2 \cdot \lambda - 1$ is odd, and

$$\frac{k-1}{2} = \lambda - 1 \leq \kappa(\mathcal{S}_1),$$

which proves (5.27).

Equation (5.28) can be proven analogously. It follows that:

$$\kappa(\mathcal{S}_1) \geq \kappa(\mathcal{S}_2) \iff \text{YScore}(C, c, V) \geq \text{YScore}(C, d, V).$$

The proof of Theorem 5.49 is complete.   ∎ Theorem 5.49

Theorem 5.51. YoungWinner *is* Θ_2^p-*complete.*

Proof.   Membership of YoungWinner in Θ_2^p has already been stated in the proof of Theorem 5.49. To prove Θ_2^p-hardness, we modify the reduction from Theorem 5.49 to a reduction from the problem Max-SetPacking-Geq to the problem YoungWinner as follows. Let $\langle C, V \rangle$ be the preference profile constructed in the proof of Theorem 5.49 with the designated candidates c and d. We alter this profile such that all other candidates do worse than c and d. That is, from $\langle C, V \rangle$, we construct a new preference profile $\langle D, W \rangle$. To define the new set D of candidates, replace every candidate $g \in C$ except c and d by $\|V\|$ candidates $g^1, g^2, \ldots, g^{\|V\|}$.

To define the new voter set W, replace each occurrence of candidate g in the ith voter of V by the text string:

$$g^{i \mod \|V\|} > g^{i+1 \mod \|V\|} > g^{i+2 \mod \|V\|} > \cdots > g^{i+\|V\|-1 \mod \|V\|}.$$

Let $\tilde{V}$ be any submultiset of V, and let $\tilde{W}$ be the submultiset of W corresponding to $\tilde{V}$. It is easy to see that c is a Condorcet winner in $\tilde{V}$ if and only if c is a Condorcet winner in $\tilde{W}$. Thus, changing $\langle C, V \rangle$ to $\langle D, W \rangle$ does not alter the Young score of c and d. On the other hand, the Young score of any other candidate now is at most 1. Thus, there is no candidate b with $\text{YScore}(D, b, W) > \text{YScore}(D, c, W)$ or $\text{YScore}(D, b, W) > \text{YScore}(D, d, W)$. Hence, $\kappa(\mathcal{S}_1) \geq \kappa(\mathcal{S}_2)$ if and only if c is a Young winner of the election $\langle D, W \rangle$.   ∎

5.4 Query Hierarchies over NP

Both the polynomial hierarchy and the boolean hierarchy over NP share NP and coNP, respectively, as their first level. This section shows that the boolean hierarchy over NP is completely contained in the second level of the polynomial hierarchy, and even in its Θ_2^p level. By definition, Θ_2^p equals $\text{P}^{\text{NP}[\mathcal{O}(\log)]}$, the class of problems solvable by some DPOTM that makes logarithmically many Turing queries to an NP oracle. Similarly, the class $\text{P}^{\text{NP}[\mathcal{O}(1)]}$ contains precisely those problems L solvable by a DPOTM M^A that accesses its NP oracle A in the fashion of a Turing reduction and asks at most a constant number of queries. Analogously, one can define classes of sets solvable by some DPOTM that makes a bounded number of *parallel* queries to its NP oracle, i.e., the oracle access is made in the fashion of a truth-table reduction. Using these concepts, one can define the *query hierarchy* and the *parallel (a.k.a. truth-table) query hierarchy* over NP.

Definition 5.52 (Query Hierarchy and Parallel Query Hierarchy over NP).

1. The query hierarchy over NP *is defined by:*

$$\text{P}^{\text{NP}[k]} = \left\{ L \mid \begin{array}{l} L = L(M^{\text{SAT}}) \text{ for some DPOTM } M \text{ making no} \\ \text{more than } k \text{ oracle queries in a Turing fashion} \end{array} \right\},$$

$$\text{P}^{\text{NP}[\mathcal{O}(1)]} = \bigcup_{k \in \mathbb{N}} \text{P}^{\text{NP}[k]}, \quad and \quad \text{P}^{\text{NP}[\mathcal{O}(\log)]} = \bigcup_{k \in \mathcal{O}(\log)} \text{P}^{\text{NP}[k]},$$

where in the latter case $k \in \mathcal{O}(\log)$ is a function of the input size.

2. *The* parallel query hierarchy over NP *is defined by:*

$$P_{k\text{-tt}}^{NP} = \left\{ L \;\middle|\; \begin{array}{l} L = L(M^{SAT}) \text{ for some DPOTM } M \text{ making no} \\ \text{more than } k \text{ oracle queries in a truth-table fashion} \end{array} \right\},$$

$$P_{btt}^{NP} = \bigcup_{k \in \mathbb{N}} P_{k\text{-tt}}^{NP}, \quad \text{and} \quad P_{tt}^{NP} = \bigcup_{p \in \mathbb{Pol}} P_{p\text{-tt}}^{NP},$$

where in the latter case $p \in \mathbb{Pol}$ *is a function of the input size.*
3. *For any oracle set* A *and for any class* $\mathcal{C}$ *of oracle sets, the classes* $P^{A[k]}$, $P_{k\text{-tt}}^{A}$, $P^{\mathcal{C}[k]}$, $P_{k\text{-tt}}^{\mathcal{C}}$, *etc. are defined analogously.*

Note that P_{tt}^{NP} is precisely the $\leq_{tt}^{P}$-closure of NP, since a DPOTM can make at most a polynomial number of queries. The following result shows the relations between the boolean hierarchy and the query hierarchies over NP. In particular, it shows that these hierarchies are intertwined, which implies that all three hierarchies stand or fall together.

Theorem 5.53. *1.* $P_{k\text{-tt}}^{NP} = P^{A[1]}$ *for some set* A *that is* $\leq_{m}^{P}$*-complete for* $BH_k(NP)$.
2. $P^{NP[k]} = P_{(2^k-1)\text{-tt}}^{NP}$.
3. $BH_k(NP) \cup coBH_k(NP) \subseteq P_{k\text{-tt}}^{NP} \subseteq BH_{k+1}(NP) \cap coBH_{k+1}(NP)$.
4. $BH_{2^k-1}(NP) \cup coBH_{2^k-1}(NP) \subseteq P^{NP[k]} \subseteq BH_{2^k}(NP) \cap coBH_{2^k}(NP)$.

Proof. 1. For fixed $k \geq 1$, define the problem

$$\text{Odd-}k\text{-SAT} = \left\{ \langle \varphi_1, \varphi_2, \ldots, \varphi_k \rangle \;\middle|\; \begin{array}{l} \varphi_1, \varphi_2, \ldots, \varphi_k \text{ are boolean formulas} \\ \text{such that } \|\{i \mid \varphi_i \in SAT\}\| \text{ is odd} \end{array} \right\}.$$

Note that Odd-k-SAT is in $BH_k(NP)$. By Lemma 5.11, Odd-k-SAT is even $BH_k(NP)$-complete; see Exercise 5.29.

To prove that $P_{k\text{-tt}}^{NP} \subseteq P^{A[1]}$ for $A = $ Odd-k-SAT, let L be any set in $P_{k\text{-tt}}^{NP}$. By definition, there exist a set $B \in NP$ and a polynomial-time computable function f such that, for each input x, $f(x) = \langle \tau, q_1, q_2, \ldots, q_k \rangle$, where

- $q_1, q_2, \ldots, q_k$ are the k truth-table queries generated, and
- τ is a k-ary boolean function encoded as a boolean circuit whose input variables $b_1, b_2, \ldots, b_k$ are the k values of the characteristic function of B on q_i, where $1 \leq i \leq k$, and such that $\tau(b_1, b_2, \ldots, b_k)$ evaluates to true if and only if $x \in L$. That is, setting $b_i = \chi_B(q_i) = 1$ if $q_i \in B$, and $b_i = \chi_B(q_i) = 0$ if $q_i \notin B$, where $1 \leq i \leq k$, it holds that:

$$x \in L \iff \tau(b_1, b_2, \ldots, b_k) = 1. \tag{5.35}$$

Think of the right-hand side of (5.35) as the sentence in a trial with x being accused of having committed a murder, L being the state prison, and τ being the jury. The question τ has to decide is whether or not x is guilty and belongs to jail. The answer to this question depends on the (hopefully correct) answers to k other queries of the form "$q_i \in B$?" that are to be found during the trial. Unfortunately, for each query "$q_i \in B$?," contradictory answers are given by the prosecuting authorities and by x's defense lawyers. Think of any sequence of oracle answers as a k-dimensional bit vector $\mathbf{v} = (v_1, v_2, \ldots, v_k)$, where $v_i = 1$ means "yes" (i.e., $q_i \in B$), and $v_i = 0$ means "no" (i.e., $q_i \notin B$). Using a truth table to evaluate any given answer vector $\mathbf{v}$, τ's objective is to come to a decision on whether or not x belongs to L. With this interpretation in mind, (5.35) reads as follows: x belongs to jail if and only if the jury τ passes the verdict that x is guilty, based on the information on whether or not the q_i are in B. The difficulty for τ is to determine the truth value of the answers given by the prosecution and the defense.

Distinct answer vectors represent distinct opinions of the prosecutor and of x's lawyers on the membership of the query strings $q_1, q_2, \ldots, q_k$ in B. Unfortunately, the jury τ does not know whether a prosecutor's or a lawyer's claim that some q_i does or does not belong to B is reliable. However, since B is in NP, by Theorem 5.24, every claim that "$q_i \in B$" has an efficiently checkable witness. Asking the witness for "$q_i \in B$," τ can verify each positive answer.

If some witness's testimony makes τ believe that some q_i, which was previously thought to be not in B, in fact does belong to B and if this updated information causes τ to change its decision on whether x belongs to L, we say that τ *has changed its mind*. That is why this proof technique has been dubbed the "mind-change technique."

Interpreting bit vectors $\mathbf{v} = (v_1, v_2, \ldots, v_k)$ as bit strings $v_1 v_2 \cdots v_k \in \{0, 1\}^k$, the standard lexicographical ordering of $\{0, 1\}^k$ induces an ordering of answer vectors: $\mathbf{u} \leq \mathbf{v}$ if and only if $u_i \leq v_i$ for each i, and $\mathbf{u} < \mathbf{v}$ if and only if $\mathbf{u} \leq \mathbf{v}$ and $u_j < v_j$ for some j. If we consider only increasing chains of answer vectors, at most k mind changes can occur. However, there is no obvious way to efficiently detect exactly when a mind change occurs, not even nondeterministically. Fortunately, it can be tested in NP if at least m mind changes occur: Initially, τ cautiously starts with the all-zero vector $\mathbf{v}^0 = (0, 0, \ldots, 0)$ assuming all answers are negative. Then, τ guesses $\mathbf{v}^1, \mathbf{v}^2, \ldots, \mathbf{v}^m$, a lexicographically increasing sequence of m distinct answer vectors. For each j with $1 \leq j \leq m$, τ checks that:

(a) each "yes" in $\mathbf{v}^{j-1}$ is also a "yes" in $\mathbf{v}^j$, in order to keep the already verified correct answers, and

(b) $\tau(\mathbf{v}^{j-1}) \neq \tau(\mathbf{v}^j)$, i.e., a mind change has occurred.

Then, τ guesses witnesses for "$q_i \in B$" corresponding to each "yes" answer in $\mathbf{v}^m$ and checks each such witness deterministically in polynomial time. Using the notations above, define the set T by:

$$T = \left\{ \langle x, m \rangle \,\middle|\, \begin{array}{l} (\exists \mathbf{v}^1, \mathbf{v}^2, \ldots, \mathbf{v}^m) \, [(\forall i \leq k) \, [v_i^m = 1 \implies q_i \in B] \\ \wedge \, (\forall j \leq m) \, [\mathbf{v}^{j-1} < \mathbf{v}^j \wedge \tau(\mathbf{v}^{j-1}) \neq \tau(\mathbf{v}^j)]] \end{array} \right\}.$$

It follows from the considerations above that T is in NP. Let $\mathbf{b} = (b_1, b_2, \ldots, b_k)$ be the correct answer vector according to B. Let $\hat{m}(x) = \max_{\langle x, m \rangle \in T} m$ be the largest m with $\langle x, m \rangle \in T$, and let $\mathbf{v}^1, \mathbf{v}^2, \ldots, \mathbf{v}^{\hat{m}(x)}$ be vectors witnessing this fact. Note that $\hat{m}(x) \leq k$ is the maximum number of mind changes. By construction of T,

$$\tau(\mathbf{v}^{\hat{m}(x)}) = \tau(\mathbf{b}), \qquad (5.36)$$

since otherwise the sequence $\mathbf{v}^1, \mathbf{v}^2, \ldots, \mathbf{v}^{\hat{m}(x)}, \mathbf{b}$ of $\hat{m}(x)+1$ answer vectors would witness that $\langle x, \hat{m}(x) + 1 \rangle \in T$, which contradicts the choice of $\hat{m}(x)$.

Since $\tau(\mathbf{v}^j) \equiv 1 + \tau(\mathbf{v}^{j-1}) \mod 2$ for each j, it follows that:

$$\tau(\mathbf{v}^{\hat{m}(x)}) \equiv \tau(\mathbf{v}^0) + \hat{m}(x) \mod 2. \qquad (5.37)$$

Equations (5.35), (5.36), and (5.37) now imply that:

$$x \in L \iff \tau(\mathbf{v}^0) + \hat{m}(x) \equiv 1 \mod 2. \qquad (5.38)$$

By construction, $\hat{m}(x) = ||\{m \mid 1 \le m \le k \text{ and } \langle x, m \rangle \in T\}||$. Since T is in NP, $T \le_m^P \mathrm{SAT}$ via some reduction h. For each m with $1 \le m \le k$, let $\varphi_m = h(\langle x, m \rangle)$ be the corresponding boolean formula. It follows that:

$$\hat{m}(x) = ||\{m \mid 1 \le m \le k \text{ and } \varphi_m \in \mathrm{SAT}\}||. \qquad (5.39)$$

Define the DPOTM M with oracle $\mathrm{Odd}\text{-}k\text{-}\mathrm{SAT}$ as follows. On input x, M first computes deterministically $f(x) = \langle \tau, q_1, q_2, \ldots, q_k \rangle$, the value of $\tau(\mathbf{v}^0)$, and the k formulas $\varphi_1, \varphi_2, \ldots, \varphi_k$ as defined above. Then, M makes one query asking whether or not $\langle \varphi_1, \varphi_2, \ldots, \varphi_k \rangle$ belongs to its oracle $\mathrm{Odd}\text{-}k\text{-}\mathrm{SAT}$. Let $a \in \{0, 1\}$ be the oracle answer, where $a = 1$ if $\langle \varphi_1, \varphi_2, \ldots, \varphi_k \rangle \in \mathrm{Odd}\text{-}k\text{-}\mathrm{SAT}$, and $a = 0$ otherwise. By (5.39), $\hat{m}(x)$ is odd if and only if $a = 1$. Finally, M accepts x if and only if $\tau(\mathbf{v}^0) + a \equiv 1 \mod 2$. By (5.38), $L(M^A) = L$, where M makes one oracle call to $A = \mathrm{Odd}\text{-}k\text{-}\mathrm{SAT}$. Thus, M witnesses that $\mathrm{P}_{k\text{-tt}}^{\mathrm{NP}} \subseteq \mathrm{P}^{A[1]}$ for some set A that is $\le_m^P$-complete for $\mathrm{BH}_k(\mathrm{NP})$.

The converse inclusion, $\mathrm{P}^{A[1]} \subseteq \mathrm{P}_{k\text{-tt}}^{\mathrm{NP}}$, follows immediately from the fact that $\mathrm{Odd}\text{-}k\text{-}\mathrm{SAT} \in \mathrm{P}_{k\text{-tt}}^{\mathrm{NP}}$.

2. The inclusion $\mathrm{P}^{\mathrm{NP}[k]} \subseteq \mathrm{P}_{(2^k-1)\text{-tt}}^{\mathrm{NP}}$ is proven by directly simulating the $\mathrm{P}^{\mathrm{NP}[k]}$ computation without making any queries. Imposing a polynomial-time clock on each computation path ensures that the simulation terminates in polynomial time. Since no more than k queries are made in the $\mathrm{P}^{\mathrm{NP}[k]}$ computation, at most 2^{k-1} possible queries occur in the potential query tree of $\mathrm{P}^{\mathrm{NP}[k]}$. Making all these queries simultaneously in the $\mathrm{P}_{(2^k-1)\text{-tt}}^{\mathrm{NP}}$ simulation determines which is the correct path.

Conversely, for $\mathrm{P}_{(2^k-1)\text{-tt}}^{\mathrm{NP}} \subseteq \mathrm{P}^{\mathrm{NP}[k]}$, consider the set $A = \mathrm{Odd}\text{-}(2^k - 1)\text{-}\mathrm{SAT}$. A straightforward binary search with k queries to the NP oracle set SAT determines how many of the $2^k - 1$ input formulas are satisfiable. Thus, $\mathrm{Odd}\text{-}(2^k - 1)\text{-}\mathrm{SAT} \in \mathrm{P}^{\mathrm{NP}[k]}$. Hence, by the first item of this proof,

$$\mathrm{P}_{(2^k-1)\text{-tt}}^{\mathrm{NP}} = \mathrm{P}^{A[1]} \subseteq \mathrm{P}^{\mathrm{NP}[k]}.$$

3. The inclusion $\mathrm{BH}_k(\mathrm{NP}) \cup \mathrm{coBH}_k(\mathrm{NP}) \subseteq \mathrm{P}_{k\text{-tt}}^{\mathrm{NP}}$ follows from the definitions. To prove the inclusion $\mathrm{P}_{k\text{-tt}}^{\mathrm{NP}} \subseteq \mathrm{BH}_{k+1}(\mathrm{NP}) \cap \mathrm{coBH}_{k+1}(\mathrm{NP})$, it is enough to show that $\mathrm{P}_{k\text{-tt}}^{\mathrm{NP}} \subseteq \mathrm{BH}_{k+1}(\mathrm{NP})$, since $\mathrm{P}_{k\text{-tt}}^{\mathrm{NP}}$ is closed under complement. To show the inclusion $\mathrm{P}_{k\text{-tt}}^{\mathrm{NP}} \subseteq \mathrm{BH}_{k+1}(\mathrm{NP})$, Lemma 3.36 implies that it is enough to prove that

Odd-$(k+1)$-SAT is $\leq^{\mathrm{p}}_{\mathrm{m}}$-hard for $\mathrm{P}^{\mathrm{NP}}_{k\text{-tt}}$, since Odd-$(k+1)$-SAT is in $\mathrm{BH}_{k+1}(\mathrm{NP})$ and $\mathrm{BH}_{k+1}(\mathrm{NP})$ is $\leq^{\mathrm{p}}_{\mathrm{m}}$-closed.

Let L be any set in $\mathrm{P}^{\mathrm{NP}}_{k\text{-tt}}$. By the first item of this theorem, $L \in \mathrm{P}^{A[1]}$ for the oracle set $A = $ Odd-k-SAT. Hence, there exists a DPOTM M that decides L by making one oracle call to Odd-k-SAT. For a given input x, let $q_x = \langle \varphi^x_1, \varphi^x_2, \ldots, \varphi^x_k \rangle$ be this oracle query of $M^A(x)$. Let $\psi \in $ SAT be some fixed satisfiable formula, and let $\bar{\psi} \in \overline{\mathrm{SAT}}$ be some fixed unsatisfiable formula. Define the boolean formula φ^x_0 as follows:

$$\varphi^x_0 = \begin{cases} \psi & \text{if } (M^A \text{ accepts } x \iff \text{the answer to } q_x \text{ is ``no'')} \\ \bar{\psi} & \text{otherwise.} \end{cases}$$

Let f be the function that maps any given x to the $(k+1)$-tuple $\langle \varphi^x_0, \varphi^x_1, \ldots, \varphi^x_k \rangle$ of boolean formulas. Clearly, f is polynomial-time computable, and for each $x \in \Sigma^*$,

$$
\begin{aligned}
x \in L &\iff M^A \text{ accepts } x \\
&\iff (\varphi^x_0 \in \mathrm{SAT} \wedge q_x \text{ has the answer ``no''}) \vee \\
&\qquad (\varphi^x_0 \notin \mathrm{SAT} \wedge q_x \text{ has the answer ``yes''}) \\
&\iff (\varphi^x_0 \in \mathrm{SAT} \wedge q_x \notin \text{Odd-}k\text{-SAT}) \vee (\varphi^x_0 \notin \mathrm{SAT} \wedge q_x \in \text{Odd-}k\text{-SAT}) \\
&\iff f(x) = \langle \varphi^x_0, \varphi^x_1, \ldots, \varphi^x_k \rangle \in \text{Odd-}(k+1)\text{-SAT}.
\end{aligned}
$$

Hence, f is a $\leq^{\mathrm{p}}_{\mathrm{m}}$-reduction from L to Odd-$(k+1)$-SAT. Since L is an arbitrary set in $\mathrm{P}^{\mathrm{NP}}_{k\text{-tt}}$, Odd-$(k+1)$-SAT is $\leq^{\mathrm{p}}_{\mathrm{m}}$-hard for $\mathrm{P}^{\mathrm{NP}}_{k\text{-tt}}$.

4. This item follows immediately from the second and the third item.   ∎

As an immediate corollary, both $\mathrm{P}^{\mathrm{NP}[\mathcal{O}(1)]}$ and $\mathrm{P}^{\mathrm{NP}}_{\mathrm{btt}}$ capture precisely the boolean hierarchy over NP and, by Theorem 5.6, also the boolean closure of NP.

Corollary 5.54. $\mathrm{BH}(\mathrm{NP}) = \mathrm{P}^{\mathrm{NP}[\mathcal{O}(1)]} = \mathrm{P}^{\mathrm{NP}}_{\mathrm{btt}} = \mathrm{BC}(\mathrm{NP})$.

Proof.   The first two equalities follow from Theorem 5.53. The last equality follows from Corollary 5.7.   ∎

The proof of the second item of Theorem 5.53, which states the equality of $\mathrm{P}^{\mathrm{NP}[k]}$ and $\mathrm{P}^{\mathrm{NP}}_{(2^k-1)\text{-tt}}$, also works if the constant number k of queries is replaced by $c \cdot \log n$ queries for some rational constant c and for inputs of length n. Consequently, the boolean hierarchy over NP is contained in the Θ^p_2 level of the polynomial hierarchy.

Corollary 5.55. $\mathrm{BH}(\mathrm{NP}) \subseteq \mathrm{P}^{\mathrm{NP}[\mathcal{O}(\log)]} = \mathrm{P}^{\mathrm{NP}}_{\mathrm{tt}} = \Theta^p_2$.

The equality $\mathrm{P}^{\mathrm{NP}[\mathcal{O}(\log)]} = \mathrm{P}^{\mathrm{NP}}_{\mathrm{tt}}$ in the corollary above is due to L. Hemaspaandra [Hem87, Hem89] and, independently, to Buss and Hay [BH88, BH91], and to Köbler, Schöning, and Wagner [KSW87, Wag90].

5.5 The Boolean Hierarchy Collapsing the Polynomial Hierarchy

In this section, the interrelations between the polynomial hierarchy and the boolean hierarchy over NP are explored further by establishing an interesting, close connection between these two hierarchies.

The following story illustrates this quite amazing connection. Do you still remember Paula and Ella, the two little girls introduced in Section 3.3 to illustrate Book's upward separation technique? Do you still remember the Boolean Hierarchy Tower (BHT, for short), the splendid building introduced in Section 5.1 to illustrate the upward collapse property of the boolean hierarchy? You do? Alright,[4] then listen:

Story 5.56 *Paula and Ella are living in the second floor of the Polynomial Hierarchy Tower (PHT, for short), one of the tallest buildings in the skyline of their city, even higher and even more magnificent than the BHT. In fact, Corollary 5.55 above says that the entire BHT fits into the second floor of the PHT. It may not be easy to imagine a huge building with a potential infinity of floors like the BHT being entirely contained in just the first two floors of another building like the PHT. So, think of the BHT now as a toy model of a building standing in Paula and Ella's room for them to play with. To ensure that the possibly infinitely many levels of the BHT conveniently fit into their room, suppose that each floor of the BHT toy model is only half as high as the floor preceding it.*

The two little dears are in an aggressive, destructive mood today: On purpose, they damage the BHT toy model with hammers so badly that one of its lower levels, the fifth floor, is completely destroyed and collapses down to the fourth floor. Knowing Theorem 5.10, Paula and Ella now expect the entire BHT to collapse down to its fourth floor, and to their great pleasure this is exactly what happens. They fall over screaming with laughter.

Unfortunately, though, they do not know Theorem 5.57 yet. That is why they do not expect what is about to happen too in this very moment: First they hear a hollow rumbling from far above, then they see some little cracks on the walls and the ceiling of their room, the building is shaking and quaking like in an earthquake, and all of a sudden it is crashing down with a terribly loud noise. Coughing and crying, the terrified children hurry downstairs through the dust and run outside. Out of the building, they see what they have done by thoughtlessly destroying the BHT toy model: The entire PHT has collapsed down to its third level, and parts of its second level are damaged too.

Luckily, no one was hurt, since in the third and higher floors of the PHT there are only offices unoccupied at this hour of the day. Paula and Ella now see their puzzled and scared parents coming out of the PHT—or what is left of it. After having reported to the police and to the insurance company everything they have done, and after having received an adequate punishment, Paula and Ella listen very carefully to their parents' emphatic and very clear explanations about Theorem 5.57.

Theorem 5.57 (Kadin).   *If there is some $k \geq 1$ such that $\mathrm{BH}_k(\mathrm{NP}) = \mathrm{coBH}_k(\mathrm{NP})$, then the polynomial hierarchy collapses down to its third level:* $\mathrm{PH} = \Sigma_3^p \cap \Pi_3^p$.

---

[4] You don't? Alright, then go back to Stories 3.23 and 5.9 in Sections 3.3 and 5.1.

Theorem 5.57 states Kadin's original result [Kad88]. The collapse consequence of Theorem 5.57 has been strenghtened later on. In particular, Wagner [Wag87b, Wag89] proved that the hypothesis $\mathrm{BH}_k(\mathrm{NP}) = \mathrm{coBH}_k(\mathrm{NP})$ implies $\mathrm{PH} = \Delta_3^p$ and even $\mathrm{PH} = \mathrm{BH}(\Sigma_2^p)$. Under the same hypothesis, Chang and Kadin [Cha91, CK96] strengthened the collapse consequence of PH down to $\mathrm{BH}_k(\Sigma_2^p)$, which is contained in $\mathrm{BH}(\Sigma_2^p) \subseteq \Theta_3^p$. Further improvements were obtained by Beigel, Chang, and Ogihara [BCO93] and by E. and L. Hemaspaandra and Hempel [HHH98b], see also [Hem98]. Section 5.9 provides more details.

The proof of Theorem 5.57 applies a method called the "easy-hard technique." Crucial to this technique is the notion of sparse sets and a result of Yap [Yap83] saying that if there exists a sparse set that is $\leq_T^{\mathrm{NP}}$-hard for coNP, then the collapse consequence of Theorem 5.57 occurs. Intuitively, sparse sets are sets of low information content: up to each given length, they contain no more than polynomially many strings. Yap's result is stated as Lemma 5.59 below without proof. For improvements of Yap's result and for related results, see Section 5.9.

Definition 5.58 (Sparse Language).   *For any language S and any $n \in \mathbb{N}$, define the* set of strings of length up to n *by $S^{\leq n} = \{x \mid x \in S$ and $|x| \leq n\}$. A language S is said to be* sparse *if and only if*

$$(\exists p \in \mathbb{P}\mathrm{ol}) \, (\forall n \in \mathbb{N}) \, \left[||S^{\leq n}|| \leq p(n) \right].$$

Lemma 5.59 (Yap).
If there exists a sparse set S such that $\mathrm{coNP} \subseteq \mathrm{NP}^S$, then $\mathrm{PH} = \Sigma_3^p \cap \Pi_3^p$.

Proof of Theorem 5.57.   For $k = 1$, Theorem 5.33 immediately implies an even stronger collapse: $\mathrm{PH} = \mathrm{NP} \cap \mathrm{coNP}$. We give a proof for the case of $k = 2$; the general case of $k \geq 2$ can be proven analogously.

Suppose that $\mathrm{BH}_2(\mathrm{NP}) = \mathrm{coBH}_2(\mathrm{NP})$, i.e., $\mathrm{DP} = \mathrm{coDP}$. Note that the set

$$\overline{\mathrm{SAT}} = \{\varphi \mid \varphi \text{ is an unsatisfiable boolean formula}\}$$

is coNP-complete. Thus, it is enough to prove that $\overline{\mathrm{SAT}}$ is in NP^S for some sparse set S, which implies the hypothesis $\mathrm{coNP} \subseteq \mathrm{NP}^S$ of Lemma 5.59. By Lemma 5.59, the collapse $\mathrm{PH} = \Sigma_3^p \cap \Pi_3^p$ then follows.

Define the set SAT-UNSAT by:

$$\mathrm{SAT\text{-}UNSAT} = \left\{ \langle \varphi, \psi \rangle \; \middle| \; \begin{array}{l} \varphi \text{ and } \psi \text{ are boolean formulas in CNF such} \\ \text{that } \varphi \text{ is satisfiable and } \psi \text{ is not satisfiable} \end{array} \right\}.$$

Note that SAT-UNSAT is DP-complete; see Exercise 5.2. By our supposition that $\mathrm{DP} = \mathrm{coDP}$, SAT-UNSAT is also $\leq_m^p$-complete for coDP. In particular, it follows that $\mathrm{SAT\text{-}UNSAT} \leq_m^p \overline{\mathrm{SAT\text{-}UNSAT}}$. Let $f \in \mathrm{FP}$ be the $\leq_m^p$-reduction from SAT-UNSAT to $\overline{\mathrm{SAT\text{-}UNSAT}}$. Encoding boolean formulas suitably by strings over the alphabet $\{0, 1\}$, for each pair $\langle \varphi, \psi \rangle$ of strings, we have:

$$\langle \varphi, \psi \rangle \in \mathrm{SAT\text{-}UNSAT} \iff f(\langle \varphi, \psi \rangle) \in \overline{\mathrm{SAT\text{-}UNSAT}}. \tag{5.40}$$

Note that f maps pairs of strings encoding boolean formulas to pairs of strings encoding boolean formulas. Let g and h be functions in FP satisfying that, for each pair $\langle \varphi, \psi \rangle$,

$$f(\langle \varphi, \psi \rangle) = \langle g(\langle \varphi, \psi \rangle), h(\langle \varphi, \psi \rangle) \rangle.$$

Equivalence (5.40) then implies:

$$\varphi \in \mathrm{SAT} \wedge \psi \in \overline{\mathrm{SAT}}$$
$$\iff g(\langle \varphi, \psi \rangle) \in \overline{\mathrm{SAT}} \vee h(\langle \varphi, \psi \rangle) \in \mathrm{SAT}. \tag{5.41}$$

The following notation explains why this proof technique is called the "easy-hard technique":

• A string $\psi \in \{0, 1\}^*$ is said to be *easy* if and only if

$$(\exists \varphi \in \{0, 1\}^*) \, [|\varphi| = |\psi| \wedge h(\langle \varphi, \psi \rangle) \in \mathrm{SAT}]. \tag{5.42}$$

• A string $\psi \in \{0, 1\}^*$ is said to be *hard* if and only if

$$\psi \text{ is not easy and } \psi \in \overline{\mathrm{SAT}}. \tag{5.43}$$

Proposition 5.60. *1. The set $E = \{\psi \in \{0, 1\}^* \mid \psi \text{ is easy}\}$ is in NP.*
2. If ψ is in E, then ψ is in $\overline{\mathrm{SAT}}$.
3. If ψ is hard, then for each φ with $|\varphi| = |\psi|$,

$$\varphi \in \mathrm{SAT} \iff g(\langle \varphi, \psi \rangle) \in \overline{\mathrm{SAT}}. \tag{5.44}$$

Proof of Proposition 5.60.   1. The first statement is easy to prove using Theorem 5.24; the details are left to the reader as Exercise 5.28.
    2. Let $\psi \in E$. Since ψ is easy, there exists a string φ, $|\varphi| = |\psi|$, such that $h(\langle \varphi, \psi \rangle) \in \mathrm{SAT}$. Hence, the right-hand side of equivalence (5.41) is true, regardless of whether or not $g(\langle \varphi, \psi \rangle)$ is in $\overline{\mathrm{SAT}}$. Thus, the left-hand side of (5.41) is also true, which implies that $\psi \in \overline{\mathrm{SAT}}$.
    3. If ψ is hard, it cannot be easy. Hence, by (5.42), there exists no φ of length $|\psi|$ such that $h(\langle \varphi, \psi \rangle) \in \mathrm{SAT}$. Moreover, since ψ is hard, $\psi \in \overline{\mathrm{SAT}}$. It follows that the equivalence (5.41) reduces to the equivalence (5.44).   ■ Proposition 5.60

To continue the proof of Theorem 5.57, let 2 be a new letter. Define the set S over the alphabet $\{0, 1, 2\}$ as follows. For each $n \in \mathbb{N}$, define the census set S_n at length n by:

$$S_n = \left\{ \psi 2^{n-|\psi|} \;\middle|\; \begin{array}{l} (\exists \alpha \in \{0, 1\}^*) \, [|\alpha| = n \text{ and } \alpha \text{ is hard}] \text{ and} \\ \psi \in \{0, 1\}^* \text{ is a prefix of the lexicographically} \\ \text{smallest hard string of length } n \end{array} \right\}.$$

Define $S = \bigcup_{n \in \mathbb{N}} S_n$. Note that, for each $n \in \mathbb{N}$, either S_n does not contain any hard string and thus $||S_n|| = 0$, or $||S_n|| = n + 1$ otherwise. Hence, for each $n \in \mathbb{N}$, $||S^{\leq n}|| \leq (n + 1)^2$. Thus, S is a sparse set.
    To prove that $\overline{\mathrm{SAT}}$ is in NP^S, consider the NPOTM M^S that works as follows on input φ of length n:

Step 1: M^S determines whether or not S_n is empty by asking one query: "$2^n \in S$?"

Step 2: There are two cases to distinguish, a positive and a negative oracle answer.

> **Case 1: Oracle answer is "yes," i.e., $2^n \in S$ and $S_n \neq \emptyset$.** In this case, M^S on input φ works as follows. First, by prefix search with n queries to the oracle S, M^S determines $\psi \in S_n$, the lexicographically smallest hard string of length n. The prefix search algorithm is given in Figure 5.12.

```
M^S(φ) {
    // input string φ ∈ {0, 1}*, |φ| = n, encodes a boolean formula
    ψ := ε;
    for (i = n, n − 1, . . . , 1) {
        if (ψ02^{i−1} ∈ S) ψ := ψ0;
        else ψ := ψ1;
    }
    return ψ
}
```

Fig. 5.12. Easy-hard technique: finding the smallest hard length n string by prefix search

---

Since ψ is hard, equivalence (5.44) of Proposition 5.60.3 implies that for each φ with $|\varphi| = |\psi|$:

$$\varphi \in \overline{\text{SAT}} \iff g(\langle \varphi, \psi \rangle) \in \text{SAT}.$$

To accept $\overline{\text{SAT}}$, $M^S(\varphi)$ now computes the formula $g(\langle \varphi, \psi \rangle)$ deterministically in polynomial time, simulates the standard NP machine for SAT on input $g(\langle \varphi, \psi \rangle)$, and accepts φ if and only if $g(\langle \varphi, \psi \rangle) \in \text{SAT}$. It follows that $L(M^S) = \overline{\text{SAT}}$.

> **Case 2: Oracle answer is "no," i.e., $2^n \notin S$ and $S_n = \emptyset$.** In this case, there is no hard string of length n in S. In particular, φ is not hard. By the definition of "hard," negating (5.43), φ is easy or $\varphi \notin \overline{\text{SAT}}$. Equivalently, $\varphi \in \overline{\text{SAT}}$ implies that φ is easy. By Proposition 5.60.2, it follows that $\varphi \in \overline{\text{SAT}}$ if and only if φ is easy. By Proposition 5.60.1, there exists an NP machine N that accepts exactly the easy input strings. So, in the current case, $M^S(\varphi)$ simply simulates N on input φ. It follows that $L(M^S) = L(N) = \overline{\text{SAT}}$.

Since $L(M^S) = \overline{\text{SAT}}$ is true in both cases, $\overline{\text{SAT}}$ is in NP^S for the sparse set S, which satisfies the hypothesis $\text{coNP} \subseteq \text{NP}^S$ of Lemma 5.59. This lemma in turn implies the collapse $\text{PH} = \Sigma_3^p \cap \Pi_3^p$. The proof is complete.   ■   Theorem 5.57

5.6 Alternating Turing Machines

The classes of the polynomial hierarchy, which can be characterized by alternating existential and universal quantifiers according to Theorem 5.31, generalize the classes P and NP. Therefore, this characterization suggests that *alternation* is a natural generalization of both determinism and nondeterminism, which were introduced as the basic computational paradigms in Chapter 3.

In this section, this idea is formalized by introducing yet another type of Turing machine, the *alternating Turing machine*. Syntactically, alternating Turing machines (ATMs, for short) are nothing else than nondeterministic Turing machines (NTMs; see Definitions 2.15 and 2.16 in Section 2.2 for the formal definition) whose non-halting states are labeled to be either "existential" or "universal" states. Semantically, ATMs have an acceptance mode different from that of NTMs in that they accept an input via the concept of "accepting alternating subtrees."

Definition 5.61 (Alternating Turing Machines).

1. **Syntax:**   *An NTM M is said to be an* alternating Turing machine (ATM, *for short) if and only if the set S of M's states is partitioned into four disjoint subsets $S = E \cup U \cup A \cup R$, where:*
   - *the elements of E are the* existential states *of M,*
   - *the elements of U are the* universal states *of M,*
   - *the elements of A are the* accepting states *of M, and*
   - *the elements of R are the* rejecting states *of M.*
2. **Semantics:**   *Let M be any ATM, let x be any input string, and let $M(x)$ be the computation tree of M on input x. For any configuration C in $M(x)$, if $s \in S$ is the state in C, then C is said to be:*
   - *an* existential configuration *of $M(x)$ (marked by $\vee$) if and only if $s \in E$,*
   - *a* universal configuration *of $M(x)$ (marked by $\wedge$) if and only if $s \in U$,*
   - *an* accepting configuration *of $M(x)$ (marked by 1) if and only if $s \in A$, and*
   - *a* rejecting configuration *of $M(x)$ (marked by 0) if and only if $s \in R$.*

   Accepting and rejecting configurations are the only halting configurations—and, as such, the leaves—of $M(x)$. Existential and universal configurations are the internal vertices of $M(x)$. Since we may assume, without loss of generality, that the nondeterministic branching degree of M is 2 for any input, every existential or universal configuration has exactly two immediate successor configurations. Let $\mathfrak{K}_M$ be the set of all configurations of M, and define the evaluation function $\texttt{eval} : \mathfrak{K}_M \to \{0,1\}$ *as follows:*

$$\texttt{eval}(C) = \begin{cases} 0 & \text{if } C \text{ is rejecting} \\ 1 & \text{if } C \text{ is accepting} \\ \texttt{eval}(C_1) \vee \texttt{eval}(C_2) & \text{if } C \text{ is existential} \\ \texttt{eval}(C_1) \wedge \texttt{eval}(C_2) & \text{if } C \text{ is universal,} \end{cases}$$

where C_1 and C_2 are the two immediate successor configurations of C.

Let START$_M(x)$ *be the unique start configuration of M on input x. M is said to accept the input x if and only if* eval$($START$_M(x)) = 1$. *The* language accepted by M *is defined by:*

$$L(M) = \{x \in \Sigma^* \mid \text{eval}(\text{START}_M(x)) = 1\}.$$

In other words, the function eval evaluates the tree $M(x)$ bottom-up, viewing it as a boolean circuit with the leaves of the tree being the input gates of the circuit and the root of the tree being the output gate of the circuit.

To define alternating complexity measures and classes associated with ATMs, the concept of "accepting alternating subtrees" is introduced below.

Definition 5.62 (Accepting Alternating Subtree of $M(x)$).   *Let M be any ATM, let x be any input string, and let $M(x)$ be the computation tree of M on input x. For any subtree T of $M(x)$, let* eval$_T$ *denote the evaluation function* eval *from Definition 5.61 restricted to T.*

T is said to be an accepting alternating subtree of $M(x)$ *if and only if*

1. *T contains* START$_M(x)$*, the root of $M(x)$, and*
2. eval$_T($START$_M(x)) = 1$.

Figure 5.13 gives an example of an accepting alternating subtree of the computation tree of an ATM M on some input x. The internal vertices of the tree $M(x)$ are labeled by $\vee$ or $\wedge$ to represent existential or universal configurations. The leaves of $M(x)$ are labeled by 1 or 0 to represent accepting or rejecting configurations. The shadowed vertices of $M(x)$ represent some accepting alternating subtree, since the root of this tree evaluates to 1 according to the function eval.

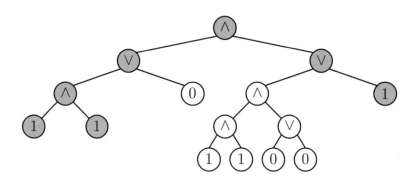

Fig. 5.13. An accepting alternating subtree of an ATM

Definition 5.63 (Alternating Time and Space Complexity Measures and Classes).
Let M be any ATM, and let x be any input string, and let t and s be functions in $\mathbb{R}$ mapping from $\mathbb{N}$ to $\mathbb{N}$.

1. M accepts x in time k *if and only if $M(x)$ has an accepting alternating subtree of depth at most k.*
2. M accepts a language L in time t *if and only if $L(M) = L$ and, for each $x \in L$, M accepts x in time $t(|x|)$.*
3. M accepts x in space k *if and only if $M(x)$ has an accepting alternating subtree each configuration of which has size at most k.*
4. M accepts a language L in space s *if and only if $L(M) = L$ and, for each $x \in L$, M accepts x in space $s(|x|)$.*

Define the following alternating complexity classes with resource function t and s, *respectively:*

$$\text{ATIME}(t) = \{A \mid \text{there is some ATM } M \text{ accepting } A \text{ in time } t\} \, ;$$
$$\text{ASPACE}(s) = \{A \mid \text{there is some ATM } M \text{ accepting } A \text{ in space } s\} \, .$$

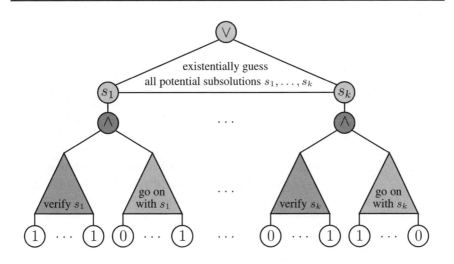

Fig. 5.14. ATMs as a model of parallel computation

Alternating Turing machines are a "parallel" model of computation. Parallelism means that a given task is subdivided into smaller subtasks that are processed *in parallel*, i.e., simultaneously. Continue this process recursively by dividing subtasks into smaller subsubtasks, which again are processed in parallel, and so on until you end up with tasks so small that they can be solved immediately. The result is a large number of solutions to very small tasks at the leaf level of the computation tree, where the leaves represent either accepting or rejecting configurations. These small subsolutions must be combined now to obtain a solution to the original task of accepting or rejecting the input string at the root of the tree, which represents the start configuration. Parallelism thus requires a means to convey the information contained in the final subsolutions backwards. In the case of ATMs, this can be achieved by the evaluation function `eval` from Definition 5.61 and the acceptance mode of accepting alternating subtrees from Definition 5.62. By conveying the information at the leaves of the tree backwards to evaluate the start configuration at its root, the combination of small subsolutions to a solution of the original task can be accomplished as desired.

Figure 5.14 shows the computation of an ATM as a parallel model of computation. First, in an existential phase, all potential subsolutions $s_1, s_2, \ldots, s_k$ are guessed. Then, the ATM branches universally: On its left branch, it checks the correctness of s_i, the subsolution guessed; on its right branch, it keeps computing with s_i assuming it was a correct guess. Only if both these subtrees are accepting, does the corresponding universal configuration convey the value 1 upwards. On this right subtree below s_i, the ATM is again in an existential phase, guessing an extension $s_{i,j}$ of s_i, where $1 \leq j \leq \ell$. Then, it again branches universally, in parallel verifying this extension $s_{i,j}$ and continuing the computation with $s_{i,j}$. Recursively proceeding in this way, the computation eventually reaches the leaf level, where it either accepts or rejects.

Intuitively, alternation is quite a powerful computational paradigm, much more powerful than nondeterminism. Tradeoffs between alternating space and time and deterministic space and time will be proven later in this section.

In the following example, an interesting observation is made: The parallelism inherent in the computation of ATMs allows us to speak about *alternating logarithmic time*. This observation is in contrast with the case of DTMs and NTMs for which it does not make sense to consider logarithmic time, since in only a logarithmic number of steps those machines could not even scan all inputs bits. However, all bits of some input string x of length n can be scanned in parallel in $\log n$ steps. To this end, the ATM model from Definition 5.61 is equipped with an additional read-only tape called the *index tape* or the *address register* by which the ATM has direct access to the input tape. If some number i is written in binary on the index tape, then the ATM scans the ith input bit within one step.

Example 5.64 (Alternating Logarithmic Time). Define ALOGTIME = ATIME(log). The set $L = \{0^n 1^n \mid n \geq 1\}$ is in ALOGTIME.

An ATM M accepting L in time $\mathcal{O}(\log n)$ works as follows on a given input $x = x_1 x_2 \cdots x_n$, where each $x_i \in \{0, 1\}$:

Step 1: First, determine the length n of the input as follows:
- Successively, write the strings 1, 10, 100, ..., which represent the numbers $2^0, 2^1, 2^2, \ldots$ in binary, onto the index tape and scan the corresponding input bit until the first blank symbol is scanned.
- If k input bits were scanned and the 2^{k+1}st input tape cell contains a blank, we know that $2^k \leq n < 2^{k+1}$. A binary search on the interval $[2^k, 2^{k+1})$ now determines the exact value of n.

Step 2: Distinguish two cases:
- If n is odd, M rejects x.

- If n is even, M branches universally and checks whether or not, for each $i \leq \frac{n}{2}$, $x_i = 0$ and $x_{n-i+1} = 1$ by writing the binary representation of i and $n - i + 1$, respectively, onto the index tape.

Since by definition NTIME(t) is contained in ATIME(t), the following result improves upon Corollary 3.28, which says that NTIME(t) is contained in DSPACE(t).

Theorem 5.65. *For each space-constructible function $t \geq \log$,*

$$\text{ATIME}(t) \subseteq \text{DSPACE}(t).$$

Proof.   Let A be any set in ATIME(t), and let M be some ATM with k tapes accepting A in time t. Construct a DTM N with $k+1$ tapes that decides A in space t. The first k tapes of N are used to simulate M, and the $(k + 1)^{\text{st}}$ tape of N is used to decide by depth-first search whether or not, for a given input x, $M(x)$ has an accepting alternating subtree. On input x of length n, N works as follows:

Phase 1: Initialization. N marks exactly $t(n) + 1$ tape cells on its $(k+1)^{\text{st}}$ tape, which is subdivided into two tracks. Then, N writes the lexicographically first path name, $0^{t(n)}$, onto the tape cells $1, 2, \ldots, t(n)$ of the first track and leaves the zeroth tape cell of this track blank; see Figure 5.15.

Track 1:	□	0	0	0	$\cdots$	0	0	0	$\cdots$
Track 2:	#				$\cdots$		$		$\cdots$

| Tape cell number: | 0 | 1 | 2 | 3 | $\cdots$ | $t(n)$ | $\cdots$ |

Fig. 5.15. Initializing the $(k+1)^{\text{st}}$ tape of DTM N in the proof of ATIME(t) $\subseteq$ DSPACE(t)

Phase 2: Simulation.   Using the first k of its tapes, N simulates the computation of $M(x)$ along the path whose name is written onto the first track of its $(k+1)^{\text{st}}$ tape. For each $i \geq 0$, after the ith step has been executed in this simulation and after the ith configuration, C_i, has been reached along the current path, N writes onto the ith tape cell of the second track of its $(k + 1)^{\text{st}}$ tape the symbol:

$$0 \text{ if } C_i \text{ is rejecting;} \quad 1 \text{ if } C_i \text{ is accepting;}$$
$$\vee \text{ if } C_i \text{ is existential;} \quad \wedge \text{ if } C_i \text{ is universal.}$$

In particular, the zeroth tape cell on the second track of N's $(k + 1)^{\text{st}}$ tape contains the information of whether the start configuration $C_0 = \text{START}_M(x)$ is existential or universal, etc.

Figure 5.16 gives an example in which the start configuration is universal and an accepting final configuration is reached after $t(n) - 1$ steps. If no final configuration is reached up to the $t(n)^{\text{th}}$ step of the simulation, N aborts the simulation of $M(x)$ along the current path and writes a "0" onto the $t(n)^{\text{th}}$ tape cell on the second track of its $(k + 1)^{\text{st}}$ tape.

| Track 1: | □ | 0 | 0 | 0 | · · · | 0 | 0 | 0 | · · · |
| Track 2: | ∧ | ∨ | ∨ | ∧ | · · · | ∧ | 1 | $ | · · · |

| Tape cell number: | 0 | 1 | 2 | 3 | · · · | $t(n)$ | · · · |

Fig. 5.16. Simulating ATM M on input x in the proof of $\text{ATIME}(t) \subseteq \text{DSPACE}(t)$

Phase 3: Evaluation.   If N has written a "0" or a "1" onto the second track of its $(k+1)^{\text{st}}$ tape, say in the ith tape cell, N alters the content of the $(i-1)^{\text{st}}$ and the ith tape cell on this track according to the function e_i that is defined by (5.45) through (5.50) below. Let $\Gamma = \{\Box, 0, 1, \wedge, \vee, \wedge_1, \vee_0\}$ be an alphabet. To describe the evaluation function eval from Definition 5.61, the function

$$e_i : \Gamma \times \Gamma \to \Gamma \times \Gamma$$

maps pairs of symbols from Γ to pairs of symbols from Γ as follows:

$$e_i(\wedge, 0) = (0, \Box) \tag{5.45}$$
$$e_i(\vee, 1) = (1, \Box) \tag{5.46}$$
$$e_i(\wedge, 1) = (\wedge_1, \Box) \tag{5.47}$$
$$e_i(\vee, 0) = (\vee_0, \Box). \tag{5.48}$$

The first component of such a pair corresponds to the content of the $(i-1)^{\text{st}}$ tape cell on the second track of N's $(k+1)^{\text{st}}$ tape, and the second component corresponds to the content of the ith tape cell. Equations (5.45) and (5.46) imply that the evaluation can be continued recursively with e_{i-1} in order to evaluate the simulation for the $(i-1)^{\text{st}}$ tape cell, and so on.

However, if either one of (5.47) or (5.48) applies, more information is needed to evaluate C_{i-1}, the $(i-1)^{\text{st}}$ configuration of the path currently written onto the first track of N's $(k+1)^{\text{st}}$ tape. Continuing the example from Figure 5.16, Figure 5.17 shows an application of (5.47): $e_{t(n)-1}(\wedge, 1) = (\wedge_1, \Box)$.

| Track 1: | □ | 0 | 0 | 0 | · · · | 0 | 0 | 0 | · · · |
| Track 2: | ∧ | ∨ | ∨ | ∧ | · · · | $\wedge_1$ | □ | $ | · · · |

| Tape cell number: | 0 | 1 | 2 | 3 | · · · | $t(n)$ | · · · |

Fig. 5.17. Evaluating the simulation of $M(x)$ in the proof of $\text{ATIME}(t) \subseteq \text{DSPACE}(t)$

C_{i-1} has two immediate successor configurations, C_i and C_j, in the computation tree $M(x)$. Knowing $\text{eval}(C_i)$ is not enough to determine $\text{eval}(C_{i-1})$; N must also know $\text{eval}(C_j)$. Thus, N continues the depth-first search by updating the path name currently written onto the first track of its $(k+1)^{\text{st}}$ tape:

- the tape cells $0, 1, \ldots, i - 1$ remain unchanged,
- the ith tape cell is updated from "0" to "1," and
- the tape cells $i + 1, i + 2, \ldots, t(n)$ contain a "0."

Since C_{i-1} has not been stored, $M(x)$ is simulated from the beginning (see Phase 2) along the updated path in order to determine the value of $\texttt{eval}(C_j)$. Observe that the simulation of $M(x)$ and its evaluation is a recursive process. However, since space is re-usable, this recursion can be done by N within the space marked. As soon as it has determined the value of $\texttt{eval}(C_j) \in \{0, 1\}$ recursively, N updates the $(i-1)^{\text{st}}$ and the ith tape cell on the second track of its $(k+1)^{\text{st}}$ tape according to:

$$e_i(\wedge_1, \texttt{eval}(C_j)) = (\texttt{eval}(C_j), \square) \tag{5.49}$$

$$e_i(\vee_0, \texttt{eval}(C_j)) = (\texttt{eval}(C_j), \square), \tag{5.50}$$

and proceeds recursively with e_{i-1} in order to evaluate the simulation for the $(i-1)^{\text{st}}$ tape cell, and so on.

Phase 4: Acceptance.   As soon as the zeroth tape cell on N's second track of its $(k+1)^{\text{st}}$ tape has been evaluated this way, N accepts x if and only if this tape cell contains a "1," which by construction is the case if and only if $M(x)$ has an accepting alternating subtree.

This completes the description of N. Clearly, N works in space $\mathcal{O}(t(n))$ and $L(N) = L(M) = A$. Thus, A is in $\text{DSPACE}(t)$.   ∎

The converse containment of that stated in Theorem 5.65 can almost be accomplished. Trading deterministic space for alternating time exacts a small price: only a quadratic increase in the resource used.

Theorem 5.66. *For each time-constructible function $s \geq \log$,*

$$\text{DSPACE}(s) \subseteq \text{ATIME}(s^2).$$

Proof Sketch.   The proof idea is based on the proof technique of Savitch's Theorem; see Theorem 3.29. The details of the proof are left to the reader as Exercise 5.30.

Let A be any set in $\text{DSPACE}(s)$, and let M be some DTM deciding A in space s. By Theorem 3.6, $\text{DSPACE}(s) \subseteq \text{DTIME}(2^{\mathbf{Lin}(s)})$ for $s \geq \log$. Thus, there is some constant c such that M works in time $2^{c \cdot s(n)}$. Let k be the smallest integer such that $2^{c \cdot s(n)} \leq 2^k$. Let ACCEPT_M be the unique accepting configuration of M on any input, and let $\text{START}_M(x)$ be the unique start configuration of M on input x. Then,

$$x \in A \iff \text{START}_M(x) \vdash_M^{2^k} \text{ACCEPT}_M$$
$$\iff (\exists i) [\text{START}_M(x) \vdash_M^{2^{k-1}} C_i \text{ and } C_i \vdash_M^{2^{k-1}} \text{ACCEPT}_M]. \tag{5.51}$$

Construct an ATM N that accepts A in time $\mathcal{O}((s(n))^2)$ as follows. On input x of length n, N does the following:

1. Existential Guessing Phase: According to Equation (5.51), existentially guess a configuration C_i of size at most $s(n)$ in $\mathcal{O}(s(n))$ steps.

2. Universal Checking Phase: For each configuration C_i guessed, universally verify the statement of (5.51):

$$\text{START}_M(x) \vdash_M^{2^{k-1}} C_i \ \text{ and } \ C_i \vdash_M^{2^{k-1}} \text{ACCEPT}_M.$$

To this end, recursively do existential guesses and universal verifications as above in parallel until after at most k recursive calls of this procedure only $C_j \vdash_M C_\ell$ must be verified for pairs of configurations C_j and C_ℓ.

Since there are at most $k \in \mathcal{O}(s(n))$ guessing and checking phases of at most $\mathcal{O}(s(n))$ steps each, N needs no more than $\mathcal{O}((s(n))^2)$ steps. ∎

Theorems 5.65 and 5.66 have the following corollary that in particular says that alternating polynomial time, which is defined by AP = ATIME($\mathbb{P}$ol), equals deterministic polynomial space. This result sharply contrasts with the case of nondeterministic time for which the inclusion DSPACE($\mathbb{P}$ol(t)) $\subseteq$ NTIME($\mathbb{P}$ol(t)) is not known. The most famous incarnation of this major open question is whether or not PSPACE is contained in NP.

Corollary 5.67. ATIME($\mathbb{P}$ol(t)) = DSPACE($\mathbb{P}$ol(t)) *for each space-constructible function* $t \geq \log$. *In particular,* AP = PSPACE.

Corollary 5.67 can be used to identify PSPACE-complete problems by defining "alternating" variants of NP-complete problems. One such example is already known from Theorem 5.36: QBF is PSPACE-complete. Note that QBF can be viewed as an "alternating" generalization of the NP-complete satisfiability problem.

Corollary 5.67 says that the alternating Turing machine is a sensible model of parallel computation, since it satisfies Cook's criterion:

Parallel time corresponds to sequential (i.e., deterministic) space.

"Correspondence" here means that there is a polynomial tradeoff between the two complexity measures.

We now turn to the tradeoff between the complexity measures alternating space and deterministic time. Since by definition NSPACE(s) is contained in ASPACE(s), Theorem 5.68 below strengthens the containment NSPACE(s) $\subseteq$ DTIME($2^{\mathbb{L}\text{in}(s)}$) from Corollary 3.28.

Theorem 5.68. *If* $s \geq \log$ *is constructible in time* $2^{\mathbb{L}\text{in}(s)}$, *then*

$$\text{ASPACE}(s) \subseteq \text{DTIME}(2^{\mathbb{L}\text{in}(s)}).$$

Proof Sketch.   The proof follows the lines of the proof of "NL $\subseteq$ P" stated in Theorem 3.27. The difference is that now we are given not only an NTM but an ATM M, and the computation of M on input x is to be simulated deterministically in time $2^{\mathbb{L}\text{in}(s)}$. Thus, not only one accepting path must be found in the computation tree of $M(x)$, if one exists, but the deterministic simulation must decide whether or not $M(x)$ has an accepting alternating subtree.

It is not difficult to design a DTM N that accepts a given input x if and only if $\mathtt{eval}(\mathrm{START}_M(x)) = 1$, where $\mathtt{eval}$ is the evaluation function from Definition 5.61 and $\mathrm{START}_M(x)$ is the unique start configuration of M on input x. The details of how to construct N are left to the reader as Exercise 5.31. ∎

For the alternating space measure, the converse containment of that stated in Theorem 5.68 can be shown. The proof of Theorem 5.69 makes the most radical use of parallelism.

Theorem 5.69. *For each function $s \geq \log$, $\mathrm{DTIME}(2^{\mathbf{Lin}(s)}) \subseteq \mathrm{ASPACE}(s)$.*

Proof.   Let A be any set in $\mathrm{DTIME}(2^{\mathbf{Lin}(s)})$, and let M be some one-tape DTM accepting A in time $2^{\mathbf{Lin}(s)}$. This assumption of M having only one tape can be made without loss of generality, since the quadratic blow-up of the time resource that is caused by simulating a multi-tape DTM by a one-tape DTM (see Exercise 3.8(c)) is negligible for resource functions in $2^{\mathbf{Lin}(s)}$.

The goal is to construct an ATM N that accepts A in space $s(n)$ by simulating the computation of M running on any input x of length n. Figure 5.18 shows the movement of M's head as a function of the time.

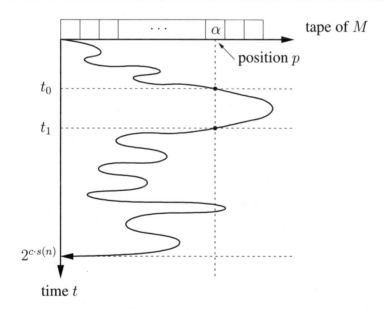

Fig. 5.18. Head movement of DTM M in the proof of $\mathrm{DTIME}(2^{\mathbf{Lin}(s)}) \subseteq \mathrm{ASPACE}(s)$

Every step of $M(x)$ is determined by a triple (z, t, p), where z is the current state of M, t is the current step of M, and p is the number of the tape cell currently scanned by M's head. In order to simulate the computation of M, ATM N cannot store the entire inscription of M's tape, which is way too long: M's head can move by up to $2^{c \cdot s(n)}$ tape cells in $2^{c \cdot s(n)}$ steps. However, N can make massive use of its parallelism: N *existentially guesses* the content of some tape cell of M and keeps computing with this guess assuming it is correct, while it *universally checks* the guess in parallel. For example, suppose $N(x)$ has simulated the computation of $M(x)$ until step t_1, and N has guessed that M's head currently scans the symbol α at position p; see Figure 5.18. In parallel with the further simulation that uses this guess, N checks the correctness of its guess. To this end, N restarts the computation of $M(x)$ from the beginning to see whether or not: (a) there exists some step $t_0 < t_1$ in which the symbol α was indeed written onto the tape cell with number p, and (b) t_0 was the last time M's head was at position p prior to step t_1.

In some more detail, suppose that Z is the set of M's states and Γ is M's working alphabet. Then, for each $z \in Z$ and each $\alpha \in \Gamma$, N has states of the form z, z_α, and α. Moreover, N is equipped with extra working tapes to keep track of the current step t and the current head position p in the simulation of $M(x)$. Storing these numbers in binary requires no more than $\mathcal{O}(s(n))$ space, since both the number of steps of $M(x)$ and the number of M's head positions during the computation are bounded above by $2^{c \cdot s(n)}$ for some constant c.

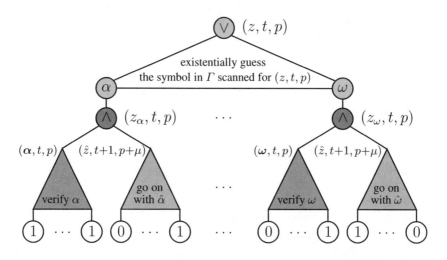

Fig. 5.19. Computation tree of ATM N in the proof of $\mathrm{DTIME}(2^{\mathbf{Lin}(s)}) \subseteq \mathrm{ASPACE}(s)$

Suppose that some triple (z, t, p) is given, and let $z\alpha \to \hat{z}\hat{\alpha}\mu$ be some Turing transition of M, where $z, \hat{z} \in Z$ are states, $\alpha, \hat{\alpha} \in \Gamma$ are symbols, and $\mu \in \{-1, 0, 1\}$ is the head movement of M. Look at Figure 5.19 that is based on the general pattern of Figure 5.14. First, N guesses the symbol M's head currently scans for the triple (z, t, p), i.e., in state z and step t and at position p.

Suppose that N's guess is the symbol α. Then, N uses the universal state z_α to branch universally as shown in Figure 5.19. The right subtree below (z_α, t, p), which is marked by $(\hat{z}, t + 1, p + \mu)$, continues the simulation of $M(x)$ assuming the guess was correct and applying the transition $z\alpha \rightarrow \hat{z}\hat{\alpha}\mu$. The left subtree below (z_α, t, p), which is marked by (α, t, p), verifies in parallel that the guess α was correct. To this end, N switches to the state α, stores the current value of step t and position p on an extra working tape, and initiates a recomputation of $M(x)$ from the beginning up to step t during which the symbol at position p is stored. The recomputation initiated by α accepts if and only if this symbol equals α in the end.

Observe that each such recomputation permanently initiates new verification processes that trigger new recomputations, and so on. However, since each recomputation stores only its "own" triple (α, t, p) and not those of the previous recomputations, the overall procedure terminates in space $\mathcal{O}(s(n))$. Hence, $A \in \mathrm{ASPACE}(s)$, which proves the theorem.   ∎

Theorems 5.68 and 5.69 have the following corollary that in particular says that alternating logarithmic space, which is defined by $\mathrm{AL} = \mathrm{ASPACE}(\log)$, equals deterministic polynomial time. Again, this result sharply contrasts with the case of nondeterministic space for which the inclusion $\mathrm{DTIME}(2^{\mathbf{Lin}(s)}) \subseteq \mathrm{NSPACE}(s)$ is not known. The most famous incarnation of this major open question is whether or not P is contained in NL.

Corollary 5.70. $\mathrm{ASPACE}(s) = \mathrm{DTIME}(2^{\mathbf{Lin}(s)})$ *for each function* $s \geq \log$ *constructible in time* $2^{\mathbf{Lin}(s)}$. *In particular,* $\mathrm{AL} = \mathrm{P}$.

Using Corollary 5.70, it is possible to identify problems $\leq_{\mathrm{m}}^{\log}$-complete for P by defining "alternating" variants of NL-complete problems. One such example is presented below: the "alternating" graph accessibility problem. Recall that the graph accessibility problem, GAP, has been shown $\leq_{\mathrm{m}}^{\log}$-complete for NL in Theorem 3.43.

Definition 5.71 (Alternating Graph Accessibility Problem).

An alternating graph is a directed, acyclic graph whose internal vertices (i.e., those vertices with outgoing edges) are either existential *(i.e., labeled by $\vee$) or* universal *(i.e., labeled by $\wedge$). Define the notion of* reachability *in an alternating graph G inductively as follows. For each vertex $x \in V(G)$:*

- *x is reachable from x;*
- *if x is existential, i.e., labeled by $\vee$, then any vertex $z \in V(G)$ is reachable from x if and only if there exists a vertex $y \in V(G)$ such that $(x, y) \in E(G)$ is an edge in G and z is reachable from y;*
- *if x is universal, i.e., labeled by $\wedge$, then any vertex $z \in V(G)$ is reachable from x if and only if for each vertex $y \in V(G)$ with $(x, y) \in E(G)$, z is reachable from y.*

Define the alternating graph accessibility problem *by:*

$$\text{AGAP} = \left\{ \langle G, s, t \rangle \,\middle|\, \begin{array}{l} G \text{ is an alternating graph with } s, t \in V(G), \\ \text{and } t \text{ is reachable from } s \text{ in } G \end{array} \right\}.$$

Theorem 5.72. AGAP *is* $\leq_{\mathrm{m}}^{\log}$-*complete for* P.

Proof.   An argument analogous to that of Theorem 3.43, which shows that GAP is $\leq_{\mathrm{m}}^{\log}$-complete for NL, shows that AGAP is $\leq_{\mathrm{m}}^{\log}$-complete for AL. Corollary 5.70 then completes the proof.   ∎

5.7 The Low and the High Hierarchy within NP

Let H be any NP-complete set, and let M and N be some DPOTM and some NPOTM, respectively, using H as an oracle set. How much additional computing power does H provide for M and N? Since H is NP-complete, NP $\subseteq$ P^H and NP$^{\text{NP}} \subseteq$ NP^H. Thus, using H, both M and N "jump" one level higher in the polynomial hierarchy: M^H can solve every NP problem, and N^H can solve every Σ_2^p problem. In this sense, the NP-complete sets such as H are the most powerful (or "highest") sets in NP.

Now consider any set L in P as an oracle for M and N. By Proposition 5.28, P^P = P and NP^P = NP. Thus, L does not add any more power to M or N than the empty set: L is completely useless as an oracle set for both M and N. In this sense, the P sets such as L are the weakest (or "lowest") sets in NP. In particular, assuming P $\neq$ NP, no NP-complete set can be in P: the classes of "low" and of "high" sets in NP are disjoint.

What if your oracle machine is not a DPOTM or an NPOTM but a Σ_k^p oracle machine for some $k > 1$? That is, which sets are "low" and which sets are "high" for Σ_k^p, the kth level of the polynomial hierarchy? Schöning [Sch83] introduced the low and the high hierarchy within NP, which provide a refined structure of this central complexity class. Lowness and highness both provide a means to measure the usefulness of an NP set as an oracle for the levels of the polynomial hierarchy.

Definition 5.73 (Low Hierarchy and High Hierarchy within NP).

1. The low hierarchy within NP *is defined by:*

$$\text{Low}_k = \{ L \mid L \in \text{NP and } \Sigma_k^{p,L} \subseteq \Sigma_k^p \} \quad \textit{for each } k \geq 0, \textit{ and}$$

$$\text{LH} = \bigcup_{k \geq 0} \text{Low}_k.$$

2. The high hierarchy within NP *is defined by:*

$$\text{High}_k = \{ H \mid H \in \text{NP and } \Sigma_{k+1}^p \subseteq \Sigma_k^{p,H} \} \quad \textit{for each } k \geq 0, \textit{ and}$$

$$\text{HH} = \bigcup_{k \geq 0} \text{High}_k.$$

The low levels of the low and the high hierarchies can be characterized by well-known complexity classes and by classes of complete sets with respect to certain reducibilities, respectively. One such reducibility notion is introduced below.

Definition 5.74 (Strong Nondeterministic Turing Reducibility).
Let $\Sigma = \{0, 1\}$ be a fixed alphabet, and let A and B be sets of strings over Σ. Let $\mathcal{C}$ be any complexity class.

1. *Define the* strong nondeterministic polynomial-time Turing reducibility, *denoted by $\leq_{sT}^{NP}$, as follows: $A \leq_{sT}^{NP} B$ if and only if there exists some NPOTM M with three types of final states (an accepting state s_a, a rejecting state s_r, and a "don't know" state $s_?$) such that:*

$$x \in A \implies M^B(x) \text{ has an accepting path and no rejecting path;}$$
$$x \notin A \implies M^B(x) \text{ has a rejecting path and no accepting path.}$$

   In both cases, $M^B(x)$ may have paths that halt in the state $s_?$.
2. *A set B is $\leq_{sT}^{NP}$-hard for $\mathcal{C}$ if and only if $A \leq_{sT}^{NP} B$ for each $A \in \mathcal{C}$.*
3. *A set B is $\leq_{sT}^{NP}$-complete for $\mathcal{C}$ if and only if B is $\leq_{sT}^{NP}$-hard for $\mathcal{C}$ and $B \in \mathcal{C}$.*

The following lemma is due to Selman [Sel78]. It provides equivalent conditions for the $\leq_{sT}^{NP}$-reducibility, analogously with the corresponding characterizations of the $\leq_{T}^{P}$-reducibility: $A \leq_{T}^{P} B$ is equivalent to $A \in P^B$, which in turn is equivalent to $P^A \subseteq P^B$. The proof of Lemma 5.75 is left to the reader as Exercise 5.32(a).

Lemma 5.75. *The following three statements are pairwise equivalent:*

1. *$A \leq_{sT}^{NP} B$.*
2. *$A \in NP^B \cap coNP^B$.*
3. *$NP^A \subseteq NP^B$.*

Theorem 5.76.   *1. $Low_0 = P$.*
   2. $Low_1 = NP \cap coNP$.
   3. $High_0 = \{H \mid H \text{ is } \leq_{T}^{P}\text{-complete for } NP\}$.
   4. $High_1 = \{H \mid H \text{ is } \leq_{sT}^{NP}\text{-complete for } NP\}$.

Proof.   1. By definition, any NP set L is in Low_0 if and only if $P^L \subseteq P$, which in turn is equivalent to L being in P. Hence, $Low_0 = P$.

2. By definition, any NP set L is in Low_1 if and only if $NP^L \subseteq NP = NP^\emptyset$, which by Lemma 5.75 is the case exactly if $L \in NP^\emptyset \cap coNP^\emptyset = NP \cap coNP$. Hence, $Low_1 = NP \cap coNP$.

3. By definition, any NP set H is in $High_0$ if and only if $NP \subseteq P^H$, which in turn is equivalent to H being $\leq_{T}^{P}$-complete for NP. Hence,

$$High_0 = \{H \mid H \text{ is } \leq_{T}^{P}\text{-complete for } NP\}.$$

4. By definition, any NP set H is in $High_1$ if and only if $NP^{NP} \subseteq NP^H$, which in turn is true exactly if $NP^{SAT} \subseteq NP^H$. By Lemma 5.75, this is the case if and only if

$\mathtt{SAT} \leq^{\mathrm{NP}}_{\mathrm{sT}} H$. Since $\mathtt{SAT}$ is $\leq^{\mathrm{P}}_{\mathrm{m}}$-complete for NP and since $A \leq^{\mathrm{P}}_{\mathrm{m}} B$ implies $A \leq^{\mathrm{NP}}_{\mathrm{sT}} B$ for any sets A and B, it follows that H is $\leq^{\mathrm{NP}}_{\mathrm{sT}}$-complete for NP. Hence,

$$\mathrm{High}_1 = \{H \mid H \text{ is } \leq^{\mathrm{NP}}_{\mathrm{sT}}\text{-complete for NP}\}.$$

The proof is complete.   ∎

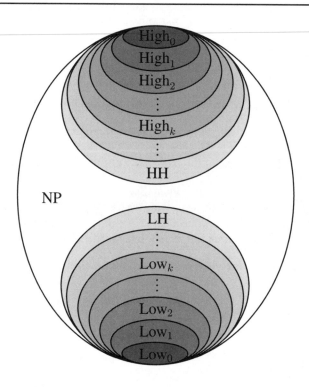

Fig. 5.20. The low and the high hierarchy within NP

Some basic properties of the low and the high hierarchy are summarized below. Figure 5.20 shows the inclusion structure of the levels of these two hierarchies that refine NP. The degree of darkness of the shadowed classes in Figure 5.20 indicates containment: Darker classes are contained in lighter classes.

Theorem 5.77.   *1.* $\mathrm{Low}_0 \subseteq \mathrm{Low}_1 \subseteq \cdots \subseteq \mathrm{Low}_k \subseteq \cdots \subseteq \mathrm{LH} \subseteq \mathrm{NP}$.
    2. $\mathrm{High}_0 \subseteq \mathrm{High}_1 \subseteq \cdots \subseteq \mathrm{High}_k \subseteq \cdots \subseteq \mathrm{HH} \subseteq \mathrm{NP}$.
    3. For each $k \geq 0$, $\mathrm{Low}_k \cap \mathrm{High}_k \neq \emptyset$ *if and only if* $\Sigma^p_k = \Sigma^p_{k+1} = \cdots = \mathrm{PH}$.

Proof.   1. Fix any k, and let L be any set in Low_k. By definition, $\Sigma^{p,L}_k \subseteq \Sigma^p_k$. Hence,

$$\Sigma_{k+1}^{p,L} = \mathrm{NP}^{\Sigma_k^{p,L}} \subseteq \mathrm{NP}^{\Sigma_k^p} = \Sigma_{k+1}^p,$$

which implies that L is in Low_{k+1}.

2. Fix any k, and let H be any set in High_k. By definition, $\Sigma_{k+1}^p \subseteq \Sigma_k^{p,H}$. Hence,

$$\Sigma_{k+2}^p = \mathrm{NP}^{\Sigma_{k+1}^p} \subseteq \mathrm{NP}^{\Sigma_k^{p,H}} = \Sigma_{k+1}^{p,H},$$

which implies that H is in High_{k+1}.

3. For the implication from left to right, suppose that $\mathrm{Low}_k \cap \mathrm{High}_k$ is nonempty, and let A be a set in $\mathrm{Low}_k \cap \mathrm{High}_k$. Then, $\Sigma_{k+1}^p \subseteq \Sigma_k^{p,A} \subseteq \Sigma_k^p$, and the collapse follows from Theorem 5.33.

For the implication from right to left, suppose that $\Sigma_{k+1}^p = \Sigma_k^p$. Then, for each set A in NP,

$$\Sigma_{k+1}^p = \Sigma_k^p \subseteq \Sigma_k^{p,A} \subseteq \Sigma_{k+1}^p.$$

Hence, every NP set is simultaneously in Low_k and in High_k. Thus, we even have that $\mathrm{NP} = \mathrm{Low}_k = \mathrm{High}_k$. In particular, $\mathrm{Low}_k \cap \mathrm{High}_k$ is nonempty. ∎

Corollary 5.78.

1. For each $k \geq 0$, either $\mathrm{Low}_k \cap \mathrm{High}_k = \emptyset$ or $\mathrm{NP} = \mathrm{Low}_k = \mathrm{High}_k$.
2. The polynomial hierarchy is strictly infinite if and only if $\mathrm{LH} \cap \mathrm{HH} = \emptyset$.

If the polynomial hierarchy is proper up to its $(k+1)^{\mathrm{st}}$ level, i.e., if $\Sigma_k^p \neq \Sigma_{k+1}^p$, Theorem 5.77 and the first part of Corollary 5.78 above say that Low_k and High_k are disjoint subclasses of NP. Do there exist sets in NP that are neither in Low_k nor in High_k? Similarly, the second part of Corollary 5.78 says that if the polynomial hierarchy is properly infinite, then the hierarchies LH and HH are disjoint subclasses of NP. Again, do there exist sets in NP that are neither in LH nor in HH?

These questions will be answered later on in terms of collapses and separations of the levels of the polynomial hierarchy. To prove these results, we need some useful characterizations of the levels of the low and high hierarchies in terms of $\leq_m^p$-reducibilities and the iterated K-operator that is defined below.

Schöning's [Sch83] original definition of the low and high hierarchies slightly differs from Definition 5.73. He defines a complexity-theoretic version of the *jump operator* from recursive function theory: The *jump of any set A*, denoted by A', is defined to be the halting problem relativized to A; see H. Rogers's book [Rog67] for more background. The crucial property of the halting problem here is that it is many-one complete (in the recursion-theoretic sense, i.e., the reduction must be computable, but not necessarily in polynomial time) for the class RE of recursively enumerable sets. The complexity-theoretic analog of RE is NP; see Theorems 5.24 and 2.20. Hence, to define a complexity-theoretic analog of the jump operator, it suffices to pick some $\leq_m^p$-complete set for NP and relativize it. This is done in Definition 5.79 below that introduces the K-operator, which is based on the generic $\leq_m^p$-complete set K for NP defined by:

$$\mathrm{K} = \left\{ \langle M, x, 1^t \rangle \, \middle| \, \begin{array}{l} M \text{ is a representation of an NTM that} \\ \text{accepts the input } x \text{ in } t \text{ or fewer steps} \end{array} \right\}.$$

Definition 5.79 (K-Operator and Iterated K-Operator).

1. For any set A, define the set $K(A)$, the K-operator applied to A, as follows:

$$K(A) = \left\{ \langle M, x, 1^t \rangle \,\middle|\, \begin{array}{l} M \text{ is a representation of an NOTM that uses the} \\ \text{oracle } A \text{ to accept the input } x \text{ in } t \text{ or fewer steps} \end{array} \right\}.$$

2. For any set A, the iterated K-operator *applied to A is inductively defined by:*

$$K^0(A) = A;$$
$$K^n(A) = K(K^{n-1}(A)) \quad \text{for } n \geq 1.$$

If $A = \emptyset$, we write $K^n = K^n(\emptyset)$.

An alternative approach would be to choose some natural $\leq_m^P$-complete set for NP and to define a suitably relativized version thereof. This has been done by Schöning [Sch81] for the satisfiability problem. However, this approach is somewhat more complicated and yields some technical subtleties that must be coped with.

Lemma 5.80 collects some useful properties of the K-operator. In particular, the third part of Lemma 5.80 adds another equivalent condition to the characterizations of the $\leq_{sT}^{NP}$-reducibility given in Lemma 5.75.

Lemma 5.80.   *1. For each set A, the set $K(A)$ is $\leq_m^P$-complete for NP^A. In particular, for $A = \emptyset$, K is $\leq_m^P$-complete for NP.*
2. For each set A, $A \leq_m^P K(A)$.
3. For any two sets A and B, $A \leq_{sT}^{NP} B$ if and only if $K(A) \leq_m^P K(B)$.

Proof.   1. The proof of the lemma's first part is left to the reader as Exercise 5.33(a).

2. Define the following NOTM M: On input x, M queries its oracle about x. If the answer is "yes," M accepts; otherwise, M rejects. It follows that $A = L(M^A)$ for each set A. Moreover, M runs in time p for some polynomial p. Hence, the function f defined by $f(x) = \langle M, x, 1^{p(|x|)} \rangle$ is a $\leq_m^P$-reduction from A to $K(A)$.

3. For the direction from right to left, suppose that $K(A) \leq_m^P K(B)$ is witnessed by some reduction f in FP. Let $\langle \cdot, \cdot, \cdot \rangle : \Sigma^* \times \Sigma^* \times \Sigma^* \to \Sigma^*$ be a standard pairing function that is polynomial-time computable and has polynomial-time computable projections π_1, π_2, and π_3. Let M and $\bar{M}$ be the trivial NPOTMs with $A = L(M^A)$ and $\bar{A} = L(\bar{M}^A)$, respectively. Let $p \in \text{Pol}$ be the time bound for both M and $\bar{M}$. To show that $A \leq_{sT}^{NP} B$, define an NPOTM N that works as follows on input x:

Step 1: N computes the string $y = f(\langle M, x, 1^{p(|x|)} \rangle)$ in Σ^*. Then, N checks whether y has the form $y = \langle \pi_1(y), \pi_2(y), \pi_3(y) \rangle$, where $M_1 = \pi_1(y)$ encodes the syntactically correct representation of an NOTM, $x_1 = \pi_2(y)$ is a string, and $t_1 = |\pi_3(y)|$ is a number in $\mathbb{N}$. If y is not of the desired form, N rejects. Otherwise, N nondeterministically simulates M_1 with oracle B on input x_1 for t_1 steps. On those paths in the simulation of $M_1^B(x_1)$ that accept after t_1 or fewer steps, N accepts. On those paths that do not accept after t_1 or fewer steps, N proceeds to Step 2.

Step 2: As in Step 1, N computes $z = f(\langle \bar{M}, x, 1^{p(|x|)} \rangle)$ and checks that the string $z = \langle \pi_1(z), \pi_2(z), \pi_3(z) \rangle$ has the syntactically correct form. Let $M_2 = \pi_1(z)$, $x_2 = \pi_2(z)$, and $t_2 = |\pi_3(z)|$. As in Step 1, N nondeterministically simulates M_2 on input x_2 for t_2 steps, using B as an oracle. For each accepting path in this simulation, N rejects. For all other paths, N halts in the "don't know" state $s_?$.

If $x \in A = L(M^A)$, then $\langle M, x, 1^{p(|x|)} \rangle$ is in $K(A)$, which implies that the triple $f(\langle M, x, 1^{p(|x|)} \rangle) = \langle M_1, x_1, 1^{t_1} \rangle$ is in $K(B)$. Thus, $M_1^B(x_1)$ accepts in time t_1 on some path. By construction, $N^B(x)$ accepts on some path in Step 1. On the other hand, since $x \notin \bar{A} = L(\bar{M}^A)$, we have $\langle \bar{M}, x, 1^{p(|x|)} \rangle \notin K(A)$. It follows that $f(\langle \bar{M}, x, 1^{p(|x|)} \rangle) = \langle M_2, x_2, 1^{t_2} \rangle$ is not in $K(B)$. By construction, $N^B(x)$ has no rejecting paths in Step 2.

An analogous argument shows that $x \notin A$ implies that $N^B(x)$ has some rejecting path in Step 2, yet no accepting path in Step 1. Hence, N witnesses that $A \leq_{sT}^{NP} B$.

For the direction from left to right, suppose that $A \leq_{sT}^{NP} B$. By Lemma 5.75, A is in $NP^B \cap coNP^B$. Let M and $\bar{M}$ be NPOTMs such that $A = L(M^B)$ and $\bar{A} = L(\bar{M}^B)$. The goal is to construct a reduction $f \in FP$ that $\leq_m^p$-reduces $K(A)$ to $K(B)$. That is, f maps triples of the form $\langle N_1, x_1, 1^{t_1} \rangle$ to triples of the form $\langle N_2, x_2, 1^{t_2} \rangle$ such that:

$$N_1^A \text{ accepts } x_1 \text{ in at most } t_1 \text{ steps}$$
$$\Longleftrightarrow N_2^B \text{ accepts } x_2 \text{ in at most } t_2 \text{ steps.} \tag{5.52}$$

Given N_1, M, and $\bar{M}$, the NPOTM N_2 is constructed as follows. N_2 behaves exactly as N_1 except that it handles its oracle queries differently. Whenever N_1 queries its oracle for a string, say q, N_2 nondeterministically guesses whether the answer is "yes" or "no," and verifies its guess by simulating $M^B(q)$ if the guess is "yes" and simulating $\bar{M}^B(q)$ if the guess is "no," respectively. In both cases, the correct guess is witnessed by some accepting computation path, and the incorrect guess yields only rejecting computation paths. On the accepting paths certifying the correct guess, N_2 proceeds with the simulation of N_1 using the correct answer, and it rejects on all other paths.

For suitable representations of NPOTMs, the string encoding N_2 can be computed in polynomial time from the string encoding N_1. Let p be some monotonic increasing polynomial bounding the running time of both M and $\bar{M}$. In at most t_1 steps, N_1 can query only strings of length at most t_1. Hence, N_1^A accepts some input x_1 in at most t_1 steps if and only if N_2^B accepts x_1 in at most $t_1 p(t_1)$ steps. Setting $x_2 = x_1$ and $t_2 = t_1 p(t_1)$ completes the construction of f and proves (5.52). Hence, $K(A) \leq_m^p K(B)$ via f. ∎

An immediate consequence of the first part of Lemma 5.80 is the following corollary that can be proven by an easy induction; see Exercise 5.33(b).

Corollary 5.81. *1. For each set A, the set $K^n(A)$ is $\leq_m^p$-complete for $\Sigma_n^{p,A}$. In particular, for $A = \emptyset$, K^n is $\leq_m^p$-complete for Σ_n^p.*
2. For each $k, n \in \mathbb{N}$, if A is $\leq_m^p$-complete for Σ_k^p, then $K^n(A)$ is $\leq_m^p$-complete for Σ_{k+n}^p.

Since $A \leq_T^P B$ implies $A \leq_{sT}^{NP} B$ for any two sets A and B, the third part of Lemma 5.80 has the following corollary. Schöning [Sch83] has shown that the converse of the implications in Corollary 5.82 does not hold.

Corollary 5.82. *1. If $A \leq_T^P B$, then $K(A) \leq_m^P K(B)$.*
2. If $A \leq_m^P B$, then $K(A) \leq_m^P K(B)$.

Next, we show that the definition of lowness and highness according to Definition 5.73 is equivalent to Schöning's [Sch83] original definition that uses Corollary 5.84 below. Interestingly, Theorem 5.83 and Corollary 5.84 do not apply to the case of $n = 0$. For Low_0, the reason is that $K^0(L)$ and K^0 are defined as L and the empty set, respectively, which implies a trivial problem with the $\leq_m^P$-reduction from $K^0(L) = L$ to $K^0 = \emptyset$.

Defining K^0 as any fixed nontrivial set B in P (i.e., $B \neq \emptyset$ and $B \neq \Sigma^*$), Equation (5.53) in Theorem 5.83 and the characterization of Low_n in Corollary 5.84 also apply to the case of $n = 0$: Any NP set L is in Low_0 if and only if $K^0(L) = L$ is $\leq_m^P$-reducible to $B = K^0$, which in turn is equivalent to $K^0(L)$ being $\leq_m^P$-complete for P.

In contrast, for $High_0$, it is not known whether or not (5.54) is true for $n = 0$. By Theorem 5.76, $High_0$ equals the class of sets $\leq_T^P$-complete for NP, whereas the characterization of Theorem 5.83 would require, for $n = 0$, equality of $High_0$ with the class of sets $\leq_m^P$-complete for NP.

Theorem 5.83. *For each $n > 0$ and for all sets L and H in NP:*

$$L \in Low_n \iff K^n(L) \leq_m^P K^n; \tag{5.53}$$

$$H \in High_n \iff K^{n+1} \leq_m^P K^n(H). \tag{5.54}$$

Proof.   To prove (5.53), let L be any set in Low_n. Thus, $\Sigma_n^{p,L} \subseteq \Sigma_n^p$. Since $K^n(L)$ is in $\Sigma_n^{p,L} \subseteq \Sigma_n^p$ and since K^n is $\leq_m^P$-complete for Σ_n^p by Corollary 5.81, it follows that $K^n(L) \leq_m^P K^n$.

Conversely, suppose $K^n(L) \leq_m^P K^n$. Since $K^n(L)$ is $\leq_m^P$-complete for $\Sigma_n^{p,L}$ by Corollary 5.81, every set from $\Sigma_n^{p,L}$ is $\leq_m^P$-reducible to $K^n \in \Sigma_n^p$. Since Σ_n^p is closed under $\leq_m^P$-reductions, $\Sigma_n^{p,L} \subseteq \Sigma_n^p$. Hence, L is in Low_n.

Equation (5.54) can be proven analogously; see Exercise 5.34.   ■

Corollary 5.84. *For each $n > 0$,*

$$Low_n = \{L \in NP \mid K^n(L) \text{ is } \leq_m^P\text{-complete for } \Sigma_n^p\};$$
$$High_n = \{H \in NP \mid K^n(H) \text{ is } \leq_m^P\text{-complete for } \Sigma_{n+1}^p\}.$$

We now turn to the questions raised after Corollary 5.78: Do there exist sets in NP that are neither in Low_k nor in $High_k$ for some k, and do there exist sets in NP that are neither in LH nor in HH? The answer to these questions requires two somewhat technical prerequisites that the classes Low_n, $High_n$, LH, and HH must satisfy: recursive presentability and closure under finite variations.

Definition 5.85 (Recursive Presentability and Closure under Finite Variations).
Let C be any class of decidable sets.

1. *C is said to be* recursively presentable *if and only if there is a recursively enumerable sequence $M_0, M_1, M_2, \ldots$ of Turing machines such that:*
   a) *$C = \{L(M_i) \mid i \geq 0\}$, and*
   b) *each of the Turing machines M_i halts for each input.*
2. *C is said to be* closed under finite variations *if and only if for any two sets A and B, if $A \in C$ and $A \Delta B = (A - B) \cup (B - A)$, the symmetric difference of A and B, is a finite set, then $B \in C$.*

Lemma 5.86. *For each $n \geq 0$, the classes Low_n, High_n, LH, and HH are recursively presentable and closed under finite variations.*

Proof.   The proof of these classes being closed under finite variations is left to the reader as Exercise 5.35(a). To prove that Low_n is recursively presentable, let $N_0, N_1, N_2, \ldots$ be a fixed Gödelization (i.e., an effective enumeration) of all NPTMs. Let $T_0, T_1, T_2, \ldots$ be a fixed Gödelization of all deterministic, polynomial-time Turing transducers.[5] That is,

$$\mathrm{NP} = \{L(N_i) \mid i \geq 0\};$$
$$\mathrm{FP} = \{f_i \mid i \geq 0 \text{ and } f_i \text{ is the function computed by } T_i\}.$$

Since every N_i halts on each input, the set $\{\langle x, i, n \rangle \mid x \in \mathrm{K}^n(L(N_i))\}$ is decidable. Construct a recursively enumerable sequence of Turing machines $M_0, M_1, M_2, \ldots$ satisfying that $\mathrm{Low}_n = \{L(M_i) \mid i \geq 0\}$ as follows. By (5.53) in Theorem 5.83, any set L is in Low_n if and only if $\mathrm{K}^n(L) \leq_{\mathrm{m}}^{\mathrm{P}} \mathrm{K}^n$. Note that the Σ_n^p-complete set K^n in this reduction can be replaced by $\mathrm{K}^n(A)$ for any nontrivial set A in P, i.e., for any set A in P such that $A \neq \emptyset$ and $A \neq \Sigma^*$. This follows from Lemma 3.37, which says that every nontrivial set in P is $\leq_{\mathrm{m}}^{\mathrm{P}}$-complete for P, and from the second part of Corollary 5.81. Thus, fixing any nontrivial set A in P, we have

$$L \in \mathrm{Low}_n \iff \mathrm{K}^n(L) \leq_{\mathrm{m}}^{\mathrm{P}} \mathrm{K}^n(A). \tag{5.55}$$

For $i = \langle j, k \rangle$, define the ith Turing machine M_i as follows:

Step 1: On input x, M_i tests for each string y with $|y| < |x|$ whether or not

$$y \in \mathrm{K}^n(L(N_j)) \iff T_k(y) \in \mathrm{K}^n(A). \tag{5.56}$$

Step 2: If (5.56) is true for all such strings y, then M_i accepts x if and only if $x \in L(N_j)$. Otherwise, M_i accepts x if and only if i is even.

Clearly, M_i halts on each input. It remains to show that $\mathrm{Low}_n = \{L(M_i) \mid i \geq 0\}$. Let $L = L(M_i)$ for some $i \geq 0$ with $i = \langle j, k \rangle$. By construction of M_i, either (a) L is a finite or a cofinite set (i.e., a set with a finite complement), or (b) $L =$

---

[5] A transducer is a Turing machine that computes a function.

$L(M_i) = L(N_j)$. In case (a), L is trivially in Low_n, since already $Low_0 = P$ contains all finite and cofinite sets. In case (b), T_k witnesses that $K^n(L) \leq^P_m K^n(A)$. By (5.55), L is in Low_n.

Conversely, suppose that L is in Low_n. Then, in particular, L is in NP. Let N_j be some NPTM accepting L, i.e., $L(N_j) = L$. Moreover, by (5.55), there exists a k such that $K^n(L) \leq^P_m K^n(A)$ via T_k. It follows that $L = L(M_{\langle j,k \rangle})$. Thus, Low_n is recursively presentable.

The proof that LH is recursively presentable is analogous except that now we consider triples $i = \langle j, k, n \rangle$ instead of pairs $i = \langle j, k \rangle$ in the construction of M_i.

The proof that $High_n$ and HH are recursively presentable is similar to the above proof and is left to the reader as Exercise 5.35(b). ∎

Lemma 5.86 shows that the low and the high classes satisfy the hypothesis of the uniform diagonalization theorem that is presented here as Lemma 5.87 below without proof. The uniform diagonalization theorem is due to Schöning [Sch82] and will be applied in proving Theorem 5.88 below.

Lemma 5.87 (Uniform Diagonalization Theorem).

Let A and B be decidable sets and let C and D be classes of decidable sets satisfying the following properties:

(a) $A \notin C$ and $B \notin D$,
(b) C and D are recursively presentable, and
(c) C and D are closed under finite variations.

Then there exists a decidable set X such that:

1. $X \notin C$ and $X \notin D$.
2. *If $A \in P$ and B is nontrivial, then $X \leq^P_m B$.*

Using the lemmas above, the questions as to whether or not there exist sets in NP that are neither low nor high can be characterized in terms of collapses and separations of the levels of the polynomial hierarchy.

Theorem 5.88 (Schöning).

1. *For each $n \geq 0$, there are sets in NP that are neither in Low_n nor in $High_n$ if and only if $\Sigma^p_n \neq \Sigma^p_{n+1}$.*
2. *There are sets in NP that are neither in LH nor in HH if and only if the polynomial hierarchy is strictly infinite.*

Proof.   1. Fix $n \geq 0$. For the direction from right to left, suppose that $\Sigma^p_n \neq \Sigma^p_{n+1}$. To apply Lemma 5.87, choose $A = \emptyset$, $B = SAT$, $C = High_n$, and $D = Low_n$.

Note that $A = \emptyset$ is in $P = Low_0 \subseteq Low_n$ and the NP-complete set $B = SAT$ is in $High_0 \subseteq High_n$ by Theorems 5.76 and 5.77. Hence, by the third part of Theorem 5.77, our supposition $\Sigma^p_n \neq \Sigma^p_{n+1}$ implies that $A = \emptyset$ is not in $C = High_n$ and $B = SAT$ is not in $D = Low_n$, which satisfies hypothesis (a) of Lemma 5.87. Hypotheses (b) and (c) of Lemma 5.87 are satisfied by Lemma 5.86.

Now, applying Lemma 5.87, there is a decidable set X such that X is neither in $\mathcal{C} = \text{High}_n$ nor in $\mathcal{D} = \text{Low}_n$. Moreover, since $A = \emptyset$ is in P and $B = \text{SAT}$ is nontrivial, $X \leq^p_m \text{SAT}$. Hence, X is in NP.

The direction from left to right is proven by contraposition. The third part of Theorem 5.77 says that $\Sigma^p_n = \Sigma^p_{n+1}$ implies $\text{Low}_n \cap \text{High}_n \neq \emptyset$. By Corollary 5.78, $\text{NP} = \text{Low}_n = \text{High}_n$.

2. This part follows analogously to the first part of the theorem by applying Corollary 5.78 and the uniform diagonalization theorem stated in Lemma 5.87. ■

Note that the special case of $n = 0$ in the first part of Theorem 5.88 is nothing else than Ladner's result [Lad75], which says that P $\neq$ NP if and only if there exist sets in NP that are neither in P nor NP-complete; see Theorem 3.68.

In Chapter 6, concrete examples of natural problems and classes of problems that are low will be presented, including the graph isomorphism problem and certain classes involving randomized algorithms.

5.8 Exercises and Problems

Exercise 5.1 Complete the proof of Fact 5.2: Exact-i-DNP is NP-hard for $i > 3$.

Exercise 5.2 Consider the problem SAT-UNSAT, which in the proof of Theorem 5.57 is defined by

$$\text{SAT-UNSAT} = \left\{ \langle \varphi, \psi \rangle \;\middle|\; \begin{array}{l} \varphi \text{ and } \psi \text{ are boolean formulas in CNF such} \\ \text{that } \varphi \text{ is satisfiable and } \psi \text{ is not satisfiable} \end{array} \right\}.$$

Prove that SAT-UNSAT is DP-complete.

Hint: Any given language L in DP can be represented by $L = A \cap \overline{B}$ for sets A and B in NP, and use the reductions from A and B, respectively, to the NP-complete set SAT.

Exercise 5.3 Prove that:

(a) $\text{NP} \cap \text{coNP} \subseteq \text{NP} \subseteq \text{NP} \cup \text{coNP} \subseteq (\text{NP} \wedge \text{coNP}) \cup (\text{NP} \vee \text{coNP})$.

   (Can you prove equality for any of these inclusions?

   Hint: If so, congratulations! You have just collapsed both the boolean and the polynomial hierarchy. You should publish your result in one of the top computer science journals ... after you have carefully checked your proof.)

(b) $\text{NP} \wedge \text{coNP} = \text{co}(\text{NP} \vee \text{coNP})$.

(c) If P $=$ NP then P $=$ coNP $=$ NP $\cap$ coNP $=$ NP$\wedge$coNP $=$ NP$\vee$coNP.

Exercise 5.4 Prove that:

(a) NP is a set ring, i.e., NP is closed under union and intersection.

(b) P and PSPACE both are boolean algebras, i.e., closed under intersection, union, and complement. What is BC(P), and what is BC(PSPACE)?

Exercise 5.5 **(a)** Prove that NP = coNP if and only if NP = BC(NP).

(b) Prove that P = NP if and only if P = BC(NP).

(c) Why does NP $\neq$ BC(NP) imply P $\neq$ NP?

Exercise 5.6 **(a)** Prove that UP is closed under intersection.

(b) Is UP closed under union? Is it closed under complement?

(c) Which complexity classes are known to be closed under intersection yet not known to be closed under union?

Exercise 5.7 Prove Theorem 5.6: For each set ring $\mathcal{C}$, the following statements hold:

1. The nested difference hierarchy over $\mathcal{C}$ coincides, level by level, with the union-of-differences hierarchy over $\mathcal{C}$:

$$\mathrm{BH}_k(\mathcal{C}) = \left\{ L \,\middle|\, \begin{array}{l} L = A_1 - A_2 - \cdots - A_k \text{ for sets } A_i \text{ in } \mathcal{C}, \\ 1 \leq i \leq k, \text{ satisfying } A_k \subseteq A_{k-1} \subseteq \cdots \subseteq A_1 \end{array} \right\}.$$

2. $\mathrm{BH}(\mathcal{C}) = \mathrm{BC}(\mathcal{C})$.

Exercise 5.8 Corollary 5.13 says that Exact-5-DNP is DP-complete. Prove that, in contrast, Exact-2-DNP is very unlikely to be DP-complete. In particular:

(a) Prove that Exact-2-DNP is in coNP.

Hint: Prove that every graph without isolated vertices has a domatic number of at least 2, and determine the complexity of the set $\{G \mid \delta(G) \geq 2\}$.

(b) Prove that Exact-2-DNP is even coNP-complete.

(c) Suppose that Exact-2-DNP were DP-complete. Which consequences follow from this hypothesis for the boolean hierarchy over NP and which for the polynomial hierarchy?

Exercise 5.9 Does the class $\mathrm{BH}(\mathrm{NP}) = \bigcup_{k \geq 0} \mathrm{BH}_k(\mathrm{NP})$ have $\leq_m^{\mathrm{P}}$-complete sets?

Exercise 5.10 Look at the proof of Theorem 5.12. Argue why the assumptions made in this proof can be made without loss of generality. In particular, argue why:

(a) for each graph G_j, we have $3 \leq \chi(G_j) \leq 4$, where $\chi(G_j)$ denotes the chromatic number of G_j;

(b) none of the graphs G_j contains isolated vertices.

Exercise 5.11 Without using Lemma 5.18 and without using Theorem 5.20, apply Lemmas 5.11 and 5.17 directly to prove that:

(a) Exact-7-Colorability is DP-complete;

(b) Exact-M_k-Colorability is $\mathrm{BH}_{2k}(\mathrm{NP})$-complete for the k-element set

$$M_k = \{6k + 1, 6k + 3, \ldots, 8k - 1\}.$$

Exercise 5.12 Prove Proposition 5.16: Fix any $k \geq 1$, and let M_k be any set of k positive integers including 3. Then, Exact-M_k-Colorability is in $\mathrm{BH}_{2k-1}(\mathrm{NP})$ and cannot be $\mathrm{BH}_{2k}(\mathrm{NP})$-complete unless the boolean hierarchy over NP collapses.

Exercise 5.13 Prove that the join operation $\bowtie$ on graphs, which is defined in the proof of Theorem 5.20, is an associative operation, and that for any two graphs A and B, $\chi(A \bowtie B) = \chi(A) + \chi(B)$, where $\chi(G)$ denotes the chromatic number of any graph G.

Exercise 5.14 **(a)** Analogously with the exact domatic number problem and with the exact colorability problem, define the following exact variants of other NP-complete optimization problems. For each $i \geq 1$ and for any k-element set M_k of positive integers, define the exact variants of the clique problem, the independent set problem, and a third NP-complete problem of your choice:

- Exact-i-Clique and Exact-M_k-Clique;
- Exact-i-IS and Exact-M_k-IS;
- Exact-i-Favorite and Exact-M_k-Favorite, where Favorite is your favorite NP-complete problem.

(b) Prove the problems defined in (a) complete for the levels of the boolean hierarchy over NP. What can be said about the optimality of the problem parameters i and the integers in M_k?

(c) Prove that the problem Clique-Facet, which is defined in Section 5.9, is DP-complete.

Hint: Do not look into the paper [PY84] before you have tried to find a reduction from Exact-i-Clique to Clique-Facet by yourself.

Exercise 5.15 **(a)** Show that Unique-SAT is coNP-hard and contained in DP.

(b) Prove that if Unique-SAT is in NP then NP $=$ coNP.

Exercise 5.16 **(a)** Prove Theorem 5.24: $A \in$ NP if and only if there exist a set $B \in$ P and a polynomial p such that for each $x \in \Sigma^*$,

$$x \in A \iff (\exists w) \left[|w| \leq p(|x|) \text{ and } \langle x, w \rangle \in B \right].$$

(b) Prove the analogous quantifier characterization of coNP.

Hint: Do not use Theorem 5.31 nor Corollary 5.32.

Exercise 5.17 **(a)** Prove that the set Pre-Iso defined in Example 5.26 is contained in NP, and that the machine N given in Figure 5.9 indeed is a DPOTM; i.e., show that N runs in polynomial time.

(b) Let M be the standard NP machine for the SOS problem. Define the function

$$g(x) = \begin{cases} \min\{w \mid w \in \text{Wit}_M(x)\} & \text{if } x \in \text{SOS} \\ \varepsilon & \text{otherwise,} \end{cases}$$

where the minimum is taken with respect to the lexicographic ordering of strings. Without loss of generality, assume that ε, the empty string, does not encode an accepting path of $M(x)$. Prove that $g \in \text{FP}^{\text{NP}}$.

Hint: Perform a prefix search similar to the one given in Figure 5.9 of Example 5.26.

Exercise 5.18 Prove Proposition 5.28:

1. $\leq_m^{\log} \subseteq \leq_m^P \subseteq \leq_T^P \subseteq \leq_T^{NP}$.
2. The relation $\leq_T^P$ is both reflexive and transitive, yet not antisymmetric.
3. P and PSPACE are $\leq_T^P$-closed, i.e., $P^P = P$ and $P^{PSPACE} = PSPACE$.
4. $NP^P = NP$ and $NP^{PSPACE} = PSPACE$.
5. If $A \leq_T^P B$ and A is $\leq_T^P$-hard for some complexity class $\mathcal{C}$, then B is $\leq_T^P$-hard for $\mathcal{C}$.
6. If $L \neq NP$, then there exist sets A and B in NP such that $A \leq_T^{NP} B$, yet $A \not\leq_m^{\log} B$.

Exercise 5.19 A DPOTM M is said to be *positive* if and only if $A \subseteq B$ implies $L(M^A) \subseteq L(M^B)$. Define the *polynomial-time positive Turing reducibility*, denoted by $\leq_{pos\text{-}T}^P$, as follows: $A \leq_{pos\text{-}T}^P B$ if and only if there exists a positive DPOTM M such that $A = L(M^B)$.

(a) Show that NP is closed under $\leq_{pos\text{-}T}^P$-reductions.

(b) Which other complexity classes are closed under $\leq_{pos\text{-}T}^P$-reductions?

Exercise 5.20 Prove the third item of Theorem 5.30:

(a) Each of the classes Δ_i^p, Σ_i^p, Π_i^p, and PH is $\leq_m^P$-closed.

(b) The Δ_i^p levels of the polynomial hierarchy are even closed under $\leq_T^P$-reductions.

Exercise 5.21 Consider the sets C_{yes} and C_{no} defined in the proof of Theorem 5.31. It is claimed in this proof that $C_{yes} \in \Sigma_i^p$ and $C_{no} \in \Pi_i^p$. Prove these claims.

Exercise 5.22 Show that for each class $\mathcal{C}$, $co\mathcal{C} \subseteq \mathcal{C}$ implies $\mathcal{C} = co\mathcal{C}$.

Exercise 5.23 Look at the proof of Theorem 5.33, which establishes the equivalence $\Sigma_i^p = \Pi_i^p \iff \Sigma_i^p = \Sigma_{i+1}^p$ for each $i \geq 1$, yet only the implication from right to left for $i = 0$. Where does the argument in this proof fail to prove the converse implication: $\Sigma_0^p = \Pi_0^p \implies \Sigma_0^p = \Sigma_1^p$?

Exercise 5.24 **(a)** Show that $\Sigma_1 SAT = SAT$. Compare $\Pi_1 SAT$ with the tautology problem defined in Exercise 5.27. What can you say about these two problems?

(b) Prove the first claim of Theorem 5.36: QBF is PSPACE-complete.

  Hint: Use the method applied in the proof of Savitch's Theorem; see Theorem 3.29. Alternatively, you may apply the method used in the proof of the second statement of Theorem 5.36.

(c) A QBF F is said to be *simple* if and only if for each occurrence of every variable x_i in F, there is at most one $\forall$ quantifier between x_i and the point of x_i's quantification. Simple QBFs are important for A. Shamir's proof [Sha92] that PSPACE equals IP, which is mentioned in Sections 6.7 and 8.8.

  Prove that the following restriction of QBF is PSPACE-complete:

$$QBF_{simple} = \{F \mid F \text{ is a valid simple QBF}\}.$$

(d) Prove Corollary 5.37: PSPACE $= \Sigma_i^p$ if and only if QBF $\in \Sigma_i^p$.

Exercise 5.25 (a) Prove Proposition 5.40: IN-Odd, IN-Equ, and IN-Geq are in Θ_2^p.

(b) Complete the proof of Theorem 5.44: Show that there is a reduction g for 3-SAT $\leq_m^p$ IS satisfying (5.25) and (5.26), and show that both IN-Odd and IN-Geq are Θ_2^p-hard.

Hint: Explicit proofs that the problems IN-Odd and IN-Geq are Θ_2^p-complete can be found in [Wag87a, Cor. 6.4] and in [SV00, Thm. 12], respectively.

(c) Prove Lemma 5.48: Max-SetPacking-Geq is Θ_2^p-complete.

Hint: Construct a reduction from IN-Geq: Given two graphs G_1 and G_2, define $U_i = E(G_i)$ for $i \in \{1, 2\}$, and for each vertex v of G_i, add to S_i the set of edges incident to v. Argue that $\alpha(G_i) = \kappa(S_i)$. See [RSV03] for more details.

Exercise 5.26 Prove that YoungRanking and YoungWinner both are in Θ_2^p.

Exercise 5.27 (a) Prove that the problem MEE-DNF, which is defined in Section 5.9, is contained in Σ_2^p.

(b) Prove that MEE-DNF is coNP-hard.   **Hint:** Find a reduction from the coNP-complete tautology problem: Given a boolean formula φ, is φ a tautology? That is, is φ true under every possible truth assignment?

Exercise 5.28 Prove Proposition 5.60.1: The set $E = \{\psi \in \{0, 1\}^* \mid \psi \text{ is easy}\}$ is in NP.   **Hint:** Apply Theorem 5.24.

Exercise 5.29 (a) Prove that the problem Odd-k-SAT, which is defined in the proof of Theorem 5.53, is $\mathrm{BH}_k(\mathrm{NP})$-complete.   **Hint:** Apply Lemma 5.11.

(b) Define the problem

$$\text{Odd-SAT} = \left\{ \langle \varphi_1, \varphi_2, \dots, \varphi_k \rangle \,\middle|\, \begin{array}{l} k \in \mathbb{N} \text{ and } \varphi_1, \varphi_2, \dots, \varphi_k \text{ are boolean} \\ \text{formulas and } ||\{i \mid \varphi_i \in \text{SAT}\}|| \text{ is odd} \end{array} \right\}.$$

For which complexity class is Odd-SAT complete? Prove your conjecture.

Exercise 5.30 Give a detailed proof of Theorem 5.66: For each time-constructible function $s \geq \log$, $\mathrm{DSPACE}(s) \subseteq \mathrm{ATIME}(s^2)$.

Exercise 5.31 Give a detailed proof of Theorem 5.68: If $s \geq \log$ is constructible in time $2^{\mathbf{Lin}(s)}$, then $\mathrm{ASPACE}(s) \subseteq \mathrm{DTIME}(2^{\mathbf{Lin}(s)})$.

Exercise 5.32 (a) Prove Lemma 5.75, which states that the following three statements are pairwise equivalent:

- $A \leq_{\mathrm{sT}}^{\mathrm{NP}} B$.
- $A \in \mathrm{NP}^B \cap \mathrm{coNP}^B$.
- $\mathrm{NP}^A \subseteq \mathrm{NP}^B$.

(b) Prove the analogous assertion for the $\leq_{\mathrm{T}}^{\mathrm{p}}$-reducibility, i.e., show that the following three statements are pairwise equivalent:

- $A \leq_{\mathrm{T}}^{\mathrm{p}} B$.
- $A \in \mathrm{P}^B$.
- $\mathrm{P}^A \subseteq \mathrm{P}^B$.

Exercise 5.33 (a) Prove Lemma 5.80.1: For each set A, the set $K(A)$ is $\leq^P_m$-complete for NP^A. In particular, for $A = \emptyset$, K is $\leq^P_m$-complete for NP.

(b) Prove Corollary 5.81:

    a) For each set A, the set $K^n(A)$ is $\leq^P_m$-complete for $\Sigma^{p,A}_n$.

    b) For each $k, n \in \mathbb{N}$, if A is $\leq^P_m$-complete for Σ^p_k, then $K^n(A)$ is $\leq^P_m$-complete for Σ^p_{k+n}.

Exercise 5.34 Prove (5.54) from Theorem 5.83: For each $n > 0$, H is in High_n if and only if $K^{n+1} \leq^P_m K^n(H)$.

Exercise 5.35 Complete the proof of Lemma 5.86:

(a) For each $n \geq 0$, the classes Low_n, High_n, LH, and HH are closed under finite variations.

(b) Prove that High_n and HH are recursively presentable.

Exercise 5.36 Do there exist complete sets in the levels Low_k of the low hierarchy?

Problem 5.1 (Critical Graph Problems)   A *hamiltonian circuit* in an undirected graph G with n vertices is a sequence $(v_1, v_2, \ldots, v_n)$ of vertices from $V(G)$ such that $\{v_n, v_1\} \in E(G)$ and $\{v_i, v_{i+1}\} \in E(G)$ for each i, $1 \leq i < n$. Hamiltonian circuits in directed graphs are defined analogously. The *hamiltonian circuit problem*, which asks whether or not a given graph has a hamiltonian circuit, is known to be NP-complete both for directed and for undirected graphs.

(a) Prove the above claim.

    Hint: First, reduce the vertex cover problem to the hamiltonian circuit problem for undirected graphs. Then, reduce the hamiltonian circuit problem for undirected graphs to that for directed graphs. Both reductions can be found in [GJ79].

(b) Define the *maximal non-hamiltonian circuit problem* (MNHC, for short) as follows: Given an undirected graph G, is it true that G has no hamiltonian circuit, yet adding any one edge to G creates one? Call the analogous problem for directed graphs MDNHC, and prove that both MNHC and MDNHC are contained in DP.

(c) Show that MNHC $\leq^P_m$ MDNHC.

    Hint: Use the reduction from the hamiltonian circuit problem for undirected graphs to that for directed graphs from (a). This reduction happens to preserve criticality. (However, this is quite a lucky strike. In general, it cannot be taken for granted that reductions preserve criticality. In fact, in most of the cases they fail to do so. The MNHC $\leq^P_m$ MDNHC case is one of the rare occasions at which the standard NP-completeness reduction happens to also work for the critical problem variant.)

(d) Can you prove that MNHC is DP-complete? What about the critical problem TSP-Facet mentioned in Section 5.9 and defined in [PY84]?

> **Hint:** If not, don't be discouraged. Rather, look into [PW88], which gives a very sophisticated reduction from Minimal-3-UNSAT to MNHC. Then, look into [PY84] for the reduction from MNHC to TSP-Facet.

Problem 5.2 (Correctness of the Guruswami–Khanna Reduction)

Look at the proof of Lemma 5.18 that gives the Guruswami–Khanna reduction from 3-SAT to 3-Colorability. Intuitively, it is argued that every 4-coloring of the graph $H = \rho(G)$ selects the "root" r_i of each tree-like structure S_i, and that this selection is inherited downwards to the "leaves" of S_i. Give a formal proof that the reduction is correct. In particular, prove the following claims:

(a) For each i with $1 \leq i \leq m$, there exists a 3-coloring of the vertices in S_i such that exactly one of the three "leaves" $t_{i,1}$, $t_{i,2}$, and $t_{i,3}$ is selected.

(b) Prove Lemma 5.19: Every legal 4-coloring of S_i selects one of $t_{i,1}$, $t_{i,2}$, or $t_{i,3}$.

> **Hint:** Construct a basic template for r_i that slightly modifies the one given in Figure 5.5 such that the modified template enforces selection of the "root." Then, looking at the connection pattern between the templates of a tree-like structure S_i in Figure 5.6, prove that if an internal "vertex" of S_i is selected, so is one of its "children."

(c) Prove that the gadgets shown in Figures 5.7 and 5.8 that connect two "leaves" of S_i and S_j, $i \neq j$, prevent both these "leaves" being selected by the same 4-coloring. Why is it necessary to guarantee that "vertices," say $t_{i,k}$ in S_i and $t_{j,\ell}$ in S_j, which correspond to adjacent vertices in G, cannot be selected by the same 4-coloring?

Problem 5.3 (Computing Complete Graph Isomorphisms from Partial Ones)

(a) Let g be some function oracle that, given any two isomorphic graphs with n vertices each, outputs a partial isomorphism between the graphs consisting of at least $(3 + \epsilon) \log n$ vertices for some constant $\epsilon > 0$. Prove that there exists a DPOTM M that uses the oracle g to compute a complete isomorphism between any two isomorphic graphs.

> **Hint:** This problem and its solution are due to Gál, Halevi, Lipton, and Petrank [GHLP99].

(b) Improve the above result by showing the same consequence under the following assumption: Suppose you are given a function oracle f that provides *only one vertex pair* belonging to an isomorphism between two given isomorphic graphs; that is, $f(G, H)$ computes a partial isomorphism consisting of the pair (x, y) only, where $x \in V(G)$ and $y \in V(H)$ with $\sigma(x) = y$ for some $\sigma \in \mathrm{ISO}(G, H)$. Prove that there exists a DPOTM M that uses the oracle f to compute a total isomorphism $\varphi \in \mathrm{ISO}(G, H)$, where φ possibly may be distinct from σ.

> **Hint:** The solution is due to Große, Rothe, and Wechsung [GRW02], whose result is based on the techniques to prove that GI is self-reducible; see also the comments in Section 3.8.

5.9 Summary and Bibliographic Remarks

The class DP, which constitutes the second level of the boolean hierarchy over NP, was introduced by Papadimitriou and Yannakakis in their seminal paper [PY84]. In addition to the exact variants of NP-complete optimization problems, they also studied various other important classes of problems belonging to DP, including *critical problems*, *facet problems*, and *unique solution problems*, and they proved many of them complete for DP.

Critical Problems: A graph is said to be *critical* if it does not have a certain property, but deleting any one of its vertices or edges (or inserting a single new vertex or edge anywhere in the graph) creates a graph with this property. Critical graph problems ask whether or not a given graph is critical with respect to some given property. For instance, Minimal-3-Uncolorability is a critical graph problem that asks whether a given graph is not 3-colorable, but deleting any one of its vertices makes it 3-colorable. Papadimitriou and Yannakakis [PY84] noted that critical problems tend to be extremely elusive and very hard to tackle:

> "This difficulty seems to reflect the extremely delicate and deep structure of critical problems—too delicate to sustain any of the known reduction methods. One way to understand this is that critical graphs is usually the object of hard theorems."

The first critical problem proven to be DP-complete was Minimal-3-UNSAT: Given a boolean formula φ in 3-CNF (and with at most three occurrences of each variable), is it true that φ is unsatisfiable, yet removing any one of its clauses makes it satisfiable? This result is due to Papadimitriou and Wolfe [PW88] who gave a reduction from SAT-UNSAT, which is defined in Exercise 5.2.

By a very sophisticated construction, Cai and G. Meyer [CM87] proved that the problem Minimal-3-Uncolorability is DP-complete, even when the problem is restricted to planar graphs. Their reduction is from Minimal-3-UNSAT.

V. Vazirani, as attributed in [PW88], proved DP-completeness of the problem Critical-Clique: Given a graph G and an integer k, is it true that G has no clique of size k, yet adding any one edge creates a k-clique?

Facet Problems: Many combinatorial optimization problems, including the NP-complete traveling salesperson problem[6] and the clique problem, require the optimization of a linear functional over some discrete set of vectors. For example,

---

[6] For any set $C = \{c_1, c_2, \ldots, c_n\}$ of n cities, a *distance map on* C is an $n \times n$ matrix D whose entries are $d(c_i, c_i) = 0$ on the diagonal, where $1 \leq i \leq n$, and $d(c_i, c_j) \in \mathbb{Z}^+$ for each pair of distinct cities c_i and c_j in C, where $\mathbb{Z}^+$ denotes the set of positive integers. A *traveling salesperson tour on* C is a tour that visits each city exactly once and returns to the point of origin. Formally, it is given by a permutation π on $\{1, 2, \ldots, n\}$, where the cities $c_{\pi(1)}, c_{\pi(2)}, \ldots, c_{\pi(n)}, c_{\pi(1)}$ are visited in this order, and its length is $d(c_{\pi(n)}, c_{\pi(1)}) + \sum_{i=1}^{n-1} d(c_{\pi(i)}, c_{\pi(i+1)})$. The *traveling salesperson problem* asks for a minimum length traveling salesperson tour on C. The decision version TSP is defined as follows: Given a set C of n cities, a distance map D on C, and a positive integer $k \in \mathbb{Z}^+$, does there exist a traveling salesperson tour on C of length at most k?

the clique problem calls for the maximization of $c'x$ subject to $x \in C$, where x is an n-dimensional variable vector, c is the vector of n ones, and C is the set of characteristic vectors of the cliques of the given graph. Equivalently, the clique problem calls for the maximization of $c'x$ subject to $x \in \text{Polytope}(C)$, where $\text{Polytope}(C)$ is the *clique polytope of C*, i.e., the convex hull of C. Optimizing a linear functional over a convex polytope by linear programming requires a characterization of the *facets* of this polytope, i.e., it requires the nonredundant system of linear inequalities defining this polytope.

Define Clique-Facet to be the following problem: Given a graph G and a linear inequality $\sum_{i=1}^{n} x_i \leq k$, is the inequality a facet of the clique polytope of G? Papadimitriou and Yannakakis [PY84] proved that Clique-Facet is DP-complete; see Exercise 5.14(c). An alternative proof, which reduces Critical-Clique to Clique-Facet, is attributed to Lovász in [PW88]. TSP-Facet, the traveling salesperson facet problem, was proven DP-complete by Papadimitriou and Wolfe [PW88]. Their reduction to TSP-Facet is from the maximal non-hamiltonian circuit problem (MNHC), a critical graph problem defined in Problem 5.1. Exercises 5.2, 5.14(c), and 5.15 and Problem 5.1 are from [PY84].

Unique Solution Problems: For example, define Unique-SAT to be the set of all boolean formulas having exactly one satisfying assignment. It is not difficult to show that Unique-SAT is coNP-hard and contained in DP; see Exercise 5.15. The precise complexity of Unique-SAT is still unknown.

The natural question of whether or not Unique-SAT is DP-complete was studied intensely. Here are some of the partial answers obtained: Blass and Gurevich [BG82] showed that the question of whether or not Unique-SAT is DP-complete is tied to the question of whether or not Unique-SAT is NP-hard:

$$\text{Unique-SAT is DP-complete} \iff \text{SAT-UNSAT} \leq_m^P \text{Unique-SAT}$$
$$\iff \text{SAT} \leq_m^P \text{Unique-SAT}.$$

They constructed an oracle relative to which no $\leq_m^P$-reduction from SAT to Unique-SAT can exist. In contrast, Valiant and V. Vazirani established in their pathbreaking paper [VV86] a polynomial-time *randomized* reduction from SAT to Unique-SAT; see Chapter 6. Thus, Unique-SAT is DP-complete under polynomial-time randomized reductions. Chang, Kadin, and Rohatgi [CKR95] took things a step further by analyzing the threshold behavior of randomized reductions and proving that if Unique-SAT is $\leq_m^P$-equivalent with its complement, then DP = coDP and the boolean hierarchy over NP and the polynomial hierarchy collapse. Similarly, if Unique-SAT is in coDP, then the PH collapses.

Cai et al. [CGH+88, CGH+89] generalized DP by introducing the boolean hierarchy over NP. Merging, unifying, and expanding the results that originally were obtained independently by Cai and L. Hemaspaandra [CH86] and by Gundermann, Wagner, and Wechsung [Wec85, GW87], the papers [CGH+88, CGH+89] thoroughly study the basic structural properties of the boolean hierarchy and their complexity-theoretic applications. Based on the early work by Hausdorff [Hau14], which studies the boolean hierarchy over arbitrary set rings, the level-by-level equivalence of the various boolean hierarchy normal forms over the set ring NP is shown in [CGH+88, Wag87a, KSW87]. Theorems 5.6, 5.8, and 5.10 and Corollary 5.7 can be found in these papers.

Their work inspired many further papers studying the boolean hierarchy over NP and over other classes. Wagner [Wag87a, Wag90], Köbler, and Schöning [KSW87] studied the nested difference hierarchy, the symmetric difference hierarchy, and the extended boolean hierarchy, and they identified many natural problems complete for the levels of the boolean hierarchy over NP. In particular, the sufficient condition for proving $BH_k(NP)$-hardness stated in Lemma 5.11 is from [Wag87a], and so are Exercises 5.11, 5.13, 5.14(a), and 5.14(b). Exercise 5.12 is from [Rot03].

Gundermann, Nasser, and Wechsung [GNW90] and Beigel, Chang, and Ogihara [BCO93] investigated boolean hierarchies over counting classes. Bertoni et al. [BBJ+89] studied boolean hierarchies over the class RP, "random polynomial time" (see Chapter 6), and over other classes. L. Hemaspaandra and Rothe [HR95, HR97b] thoroughly investigated the boolean hierarchy normal forms over UP, "unambiguous polynomial time," which is defined in Section 3.6.2. Although UP is closed under intersection, it is very unlikely to be closed under union, and thus it is not a set ring; see Exercise 5.6. In [HR95, HR97b], it is shown that, for certain boolean hierarchy normal forms, closure under intersection suffices to capture the boolean closure of the underlying class: Both the alternating sums and the symmetric difference hierarchy over any class closed under intersection (yet possibly not closed under union) capture the boolean closure of the class. In particular, this result applies to UP. In contrast to the NP case, the Hausdorff hierarchy and the nested difference hierarchy over UP both fail to capture the boolean closure of UP in some relativized worlds [HR97b].

Theorem 5.12 is due to Riege and Rothe [RR04]. In this paper, it is also shown that the exact versions of certain generalized dominating set problems are complete for the levels of the boolean hierarchy over NP. Generalized dominating set problems were introduced by Heggernes and Telle [HT98]; their framework provides a uniform approach to define a great variety of graph problems by partitioning the vertex set of a graph such that the number of neighbors for each vertex in the partition is constrained. In addition, it is proven in [RR04] that the exact conveyor flow shop problem is complete for the levels of the boolean hierarchy over NP. The conveyor flow shop problem arises in real-world applications in the wholesale business, where warehouses are supplied with goods from a central storehouse. This problem was introduced and extensively studied by Espelage and Wanke [EW00, Esp01, EW01, EW03].

Lemma 5.17, which is proven in Chapter 3 and which gives the standard reduction from 3-SAT to 3-Colorability, is due to Stockmeyer [Sto73], Garey, and Johnson [GJS76]. Lemma 5.18 gives an even stronger reduction from 3-SAT to 3-Colorability, which is due to Guruswami and Khanna [GK00]. Originally, their work was not motivated by issues concerning the hardness of exact colorability, but by issues related to the hardness of approximating the chromatic number of 3-colorable graphs.

A very powerful tool for proving the nonapproximability of hard combinatorial problems is the PCP theorem, which is related to the notion of interactive proof systems; see Sections 6.3 and 8.4 for the related notion of Arthur-Merlin games. For example, Arora, Lund, Motwani, Sudan, and Szegedy [ALM+98] employ proof verification for proving the hardness of approximation problems. More about approximation and nonapproximability can be found, e.g., in Ausiello et al.[ACG+03], Vazirani [Vaz03], and the comprehensive, up-to-date compendium of NP optimization problems edited by Crescenzi, Kann, Halldórsson, Karpinski, and Woeginger: http://www.nada.kth.se/~viggo/problemlist/compendium.html.

PCP is an acronym for "probabilistically checkable proof system." The PCP theorem, which is due to Arora et al. [AS98, ALM+98], says that NP can be characterized by such proof systems with only logarithmically many random bits of the verifier and with a constant number of verifier queries. For precise definitions and more details and pointers to the literature, we refer to Goldreich's survey [Gol97] and to the theses of Arora [Aro94] and Sudan [Sud95]; see also Zimand [Zim04].

Using the PCP theorem, Khanna, Linial, and Safra [KLS00] showed that it is NP-hard to color a 3-colorable graph with only four colors. Guruswami and Khanna [GK00] gave a novel proof of the same result by providing the clever construction presented in the proof of Lemma 5.18. This direct transformation, which does not rely on the PCP theorem, is here employed to settle the question of the exact complexity of the exact colorability problem, which was explicitly raised by Wagner [Wag87a, p. 70] in 1987. Drawing on Lemmas 5.17 and 5.18, Theorem 5.20 says that Exact-4-Colorability is DP-complete. This result is due to Rothe [Rot03]; see also his joint work with Spakowski and Vogel [RSV02]. In contrast to this completeness result, Exact-3-Colorability is in NP by Proposition 5.16.

The polynomial hierarchy was introduced by A. Meyer and Stockmeyer [MS72, Sto77]. Theorems 5.24, 5.30, 5.31, and 5.33 and Corollary 5.32 are due to them and to Wrathall [Wra77]. Historically, one of the motivations for introducing the polynomial hierarchy was the desire to pinpoint the precise complexity of the minimum equivalent expression problem and its variations. For example, define MEE-DNF to be the following decision problem: Given a pair $\langle \varphi, k \rangle$, where φ is a boolean formula in DNF and k is a positive integer, does there exist a boolean formula ψ equivalent to φ such that at most k variables occur in ψ? It is easy to see that MEE-DNF is coNP-hard; see Exercise 5.27(b). However, every attempt to prove coNP-completeness failed. Using the Wagner technique, E. Hemaspaandra and Wechsung [HW97, HW02] raised the coNP-hardness of MEE-DNF to a Θ_2^p lower bound. On the other hand, MEE-DNF is immediately seen to be contained in Σ_2^p; see Exercise 5.27(a). Umans [Uma98] ultimately resolved the question of the precise complexity of MEE-DNF by proving it Σ_2^p-complete. Dropping the restriction to DNF formulas in the definiton of MEE-DNF, we obtain the problem MEE, which trivially is in Σ_2^p and which is known to be Θ_2^p-hard by E. Hemaspaandra and Wechsung's result [HW97]. The precise complexity of MEE is still unknown.

Eiter and Gottlob [EG93] studied problems related to logic and artificial intelligence. They proved Π_2^p-completeness of the deduction problem for arbitrary propositional theories under the extended closed-world assumption or under circumscription. These are techniques arising in nonmonotonic logic, which is concerned with reasoning with incomplete knowledge.

Schaefer and Umans [SU02a, SU02b] provide a very comprehensive, two-part compendium surveying a host of natural problems complete for the second or higher levels of the polynomial hierarchy. They also state a number of interesting open problems, including the above-mentioned issue of the precise complexity of MEE.

Agrawal and Thierauf [AT01] studied FI, the formula isomorphism problem: Given two boolean formulas φ and ψ, decide whether or not there exists a permutation of the variables of φ such that φ and ψ become equivalent. Clearly, FI is contained in Σ_2^p. Using techniques related to interactive proof systems and using a result from learning theory due to Bshouty et al. [BCKT94], they proved that FI cannot be Σ_2^p-complete unless the polynomial hierarchy collapses. Thus, the complexity of the formula isomorphism problem seems to be intermediate between the first and second levels of the PH, just like the complexity of the graph isomorphism problem seems to be intermediate between the zeroth and first levels of the PH. More information on boolean isomorphism and equivalence problems can be found in [Thi00]; see also the related work of Borchert, Ranjan, and Stephan [BRS98, BR93] and of Borchert, L. Hemaspaandra, and Rothe [BHR00].

The FP^{NP} prefix search algorithm from Figure 5.9 is the standard method for finding the lexicographically smallest solutions of NP problems. Note that FP^{NP} is the function analog of $\Delta_2^p = \text{P}^{\text{NP}}$. Krentel [Kre88] and Wagner [Wag87a] established many Δ_2^p-completeness results for optimization problems related to NP, including the problem Odd-Max-SAT that asks whether or not the maximum satisfying assignment of a given boolean formula is odd. Papadimitriou [Pap84] proved Δ_2^p-completeness for the problem of deciding whether or not there exists a *unique* optimal traveling salesperson tour for a given distance map on a set of cities. Große, Rothe, and Wechsung [GRW01] proved that computing the lexicographically smallest four-coloring for planar graphs is Δ_2^p-hard. This result optimally improves upon a result of Khuller and V. Vazirani [KV91] who provided an NP-hardness lower bound for this problem, concluding that it is not self-reducible in the sense of Schnorr [Sch76, Sch79] unless P $=$ NP. Chen and Toda [CT95] proposed a general framework for studying the complexity of solving maximality problems and obtained completeness results for coNP, DP, and Π_2^p.

The polynomial-time Turing reducibility, $\leq_{\text{T}}^{\text{p}}$, is due to Cook [Coo71]. The polynomial-time truth-table reducibility, $\leq_{\text{tt}}^{\text{p}}$, was introduced and thoroughly investigated by Ladner, Lynch, and Selman [LLS75]. Their work provides the most profound source on polynomial-time reducibilities, while the best source on logarithmically space-bounded reducibilities is [LL76]; see the work by Buhrman, E. Hemaspaandra, and Torenvliet [BST93b, BST93a] for a comparison. Every reducibility discussed here is the complexity-bounded analog of its respective counterpart in recursive function theory. Selman [Sel82b] introduced the notion of positive Turing reducibility, $\leq_{\text{pos-T}}^{\text{P}}$; Exercise 5.19 is due to him. In addition, he extensively studied various polynomial-time reducibilities on NP, linking their behavior to other complexity-theoretic notions such as self-reducibility, p-selectivity, and tally sets; see [Sel79, Sel82a, Sel82b, Sel88a]. A wonderful source on the theory of p-selectivity is the book by L. Hemaspaandra and Torenvliet [HT03a].

Proposition 5.40, Lemma 5.43, and Theorem 5.44 are due to Wagner [Wag87a]. Explicit proofs that IN-Equ and IN-Geq are both Θ_2^p-complete are not presented in his paper [Wag87a] but can be found in [HR97a] and [SV00], respectively. Note also that, unlike the statement in Lemma 5.43, Wagner actually states a criterion for P_{bf}^{NP}-hardness in [Wag87a], where P_{bf}^{NP} is defined as the closure of NP under a restriction of the $\leq_{tt}^{p}$-reducibility in which the boolean function τ from Definition 5.41 is not encoded as a boolean circuit but as a boolean formula. However, among other characterizations of Θ_2^p, Wagner proved in [Wag90] that $P_{bf}^{NP} = P_{tt}^{NP} = \Theta_2^p$.

Bartholdi, Tovey, and Trick [BTT89b, BTT89a, BTT92] initiated the study of election systems with respect to their computational properties. They established NP-hardness lower bounds for both the winner and the ranking problem for Dodgson and for Kemeny elections [BTT89b]. Dodgson elections were proposed in 1876 by Charles L. Dodgson [Dod76] who is better known today by his pen name, Lewis Carroll. His voting scheme is similar to H. Young's voting scheme in that it also extends the Condorcet Principle by altering preference profiles. Unlike Young, however, Dodgson suggests that we remain most faithful to the Condorcet Principle if the election is won by any candidate who is "closest" to being a Condorcet winner. To define "closeness," each candidate c in a given election $\langle C, V \rangle$ is assigned the Dodgson score, the smallest number of sequential interchanges of adjacent candidates in the voters' preferences that are needed to make c a Condorcet winner. Any candidate with minimum Dodgson score is called a Dodgson winner. The problem of deciding whether or not the Dodgson score of a given preference profile exceeds a given value is NP-complete [BTT89b].

Bartholdi, Tovey, and Trick's NP-hardness results for the Dodgson winner and ranking problems [BTT89b] were optimally improved to Θ_2^p-completeness by E. and L. Hemaspaandra and Rothe [HHR97a] who directly applied Lemma 5.43. E. Hemaspaandra, Spakowski, and Vogel [HSV] obtained the analogous results for Kemeny elections. Theorems 5.49 and 5.51, which provide the corresponding results for Young elections, are due to Rothe, Spakowski, and Vogel [RSV02, RSV03]. In addition, they proved that the winner and ranking problems in Fishburn's [Fis77] homogeneous[7] variant of Dodgson elections can be solved efficiently by linear programming. Their linear program is based on an integer linear program of Bartholdi et al. [BTT89b]. Young [You77] originally defined his voting scheme in the homogenous variant and showed that the corresponding problems can be solved efficiently by linear programming, which contrasts with Theorems 5.49 and 5.51.

Bartholdi, Tovey, and Trick [BTT89a, BTT92] also studied complexity issues related to strategic voting and manipulation and control of election systems (see also,

---

[7] Homogeneity is another quite natural property of voting schemes that has been studied extensively in social choice theory. Informally stated, a voting scheme f is *homogeneous* if and only if splitting each voter $v \in V$ into n voters, each of whom has the same preference order as v, yields exactly the same choice set of winning candidates. Fishburn [Fis77] proved that neither the Dodgson nor the Young voting schemes (as defined in Section 5.3.2) are homogeneous.

e.g., [CLS03, CS02, HHR05]). Dwork, Kumar, Naor und Sivakumar [DKNS01] proved that aggregation systems inspired by the Kemeny election system can provide a useful protection against spamming, the manipulation of website rankings by search engines. They developed an efficient heuristic, called *local Kemenization*, that is based on an extension of the Condorcet Principle. L. Hemaspaandra, Rajasethupathy, Sethupathy, and Zimand [HRSZ98] did an experimental study of various apportioning algorithms, including a simulated annealing heuristic, for the Congress of the United States. For further details, the reader is referred to the excellent survey [HH00], which is a rich source of reference on the issues and results in computational politics. For a deeper background in social choice theory, the reader is referred to the books [MU95, Bla58, Arr63, Saa95, Saa01].

Further applications of Lemma 5.43 can be found in the literature; see [HHR97b]. For example, E. Hemaspaandra, Rothe [HR98], and Spakowski [HRS] proved that recognizing those graphs for which certain efficient approximation heuristics for the independent set and the vertex cover problem do well is complete for parallel access to NP.

Köbler, Schöning, Wagner, and Wechsung [Wec85, KSW87, Wag87b, Wag89, Wag90], Krentel [Kre88], Buss and Hay [BH88, BH91], and Beigel [Bei91a] investigated the boolean hierarchy and the query hierarchies over NP. Theorem 5.53 is from [Bei91a], which attributes the theorem's first item to Wagner and Wechsung (see [Wec85]) and its third item to Köbler, Schöning, and Wagner [KSW87]. The equality $\mathrm{BH}(\mathrm{NP}) = \mathrm{P}^{\mathrm{NP}}_{\mathrm{btt}}$ from Corollary 5.54 is due to Cai et al. [CGH+88]. The equality $\mathrm{P}^{\mathrm{NP}[\mathcal{O}(\log)]} = \mathrm{P}^{\mathrm{NP}}_{\mathrm{tt}}$ from Corollary 5.55 was independently discovered by L. Hemaspaandra [Hem87, Hem89], Buss and Hay [BH88, BH91], and Köbler, Schöning, and Wagner [KSW87, Wag90]. Further characterizations of $\Theta^p_2 = \mathrm{P}^{\mathrm{NP}[\mathcal{O}(\log)]}$ can be found in [Wag90].

Eiter and Gottlob [EG97] provided logical characterizations of Θ^p_2 and proved a number of problems from artificial intelligence and modal logic Θ^p_2-complete. Castro and Seara [CS92] characterized the classes $\mathrm{P}^{\mathrm{NP}[\mathcal{O}(\log^k)]}$ that are sandwiched inbetween Θ^p_2 and Δ^p_2. Rohatgi [Roh95] established tight bounds on the thresholds of polynomial-time randomized reductions for the classes in the boolean and in the query hierarchies.

Kadin [Kad88] initiated the study of the connection between the boolean and the polynomial hierarchy presented in Section 5.5. Theorem 5.57 is due to him. Yap's result, stated as Lemma 5.59 and applied in the proof of Theorem 5.57, is interesting in its own right. There is a number of results related to or even stronger than Lemma 5.59. The original motivation of Lemma 5.59 comes from the Karp–Lipton Theorem [KL80]: If NP has a $\leq^p_T$-hard sparse set S (i.e., if NP $\subseteq$ P^S or, equivalently,[8] if NP has polynomial-size circuits), then PH $= \Sigma^p_2 \cap \Pi^p_2$. Comparing the two results, note that Lemma 5.59, which says that if coNP $\subseteq$ NP^S then PH $= \Sigma^p_3 \cap \Pi^p_3$, has both a weaker hypothesis and a weaker conclusion than the Karp–Lipton Theorem. Thus, the two results are related, yet incomparable.

---

[8] This equivalence, which was first noted by A. Meyer, appears in [BH77]. The Karp–Lipton Theorem is due to Karp and Lipton [KL80] who also acknowledge a contribution by Sipser.

Mahaney [Mah82] proved that if the sparse oracle set is itself in NP (i.e., if there exists a sparse set that is $\leq_T^P$-complete for NP), then the PH collapses to $\Delta_2^p = P^{NP}$. Long [Lon82a] generalized Mahaney's result by proving that if there exists a sparse set S in Δ_2^p such that NP $\subseteq P^S$, then PH $= \Delta_2^p$. Strengthening Mahaney's result, Kadin [Kad89] proved the optimal collapse: If there exists a sparse set S in NP such that coNP $\subseteq NP^S$, then PH $= \Theta_2^p = P^{NP[\mathcal{O}(\log)]}$. Thus, if there exists a sparse $\leq_T^P$-complete set in NP, then PH $= \Theta_2^p = P^{NP[\mathcal{O}(\log)]}$. This result is optimal, since Kadin [Kad89] also proved that, for each function f in $o(\log n)$, there is a relativized world such that $P^{NP[\mathcal{O}(\log)]} \not\subseteq P^{NP[f(n)]}$ and yet NP has a sparse $\leq_T^P$-complete set.

The study of reductions to sparse sets has a long and rich history in complexity theory; see the surveys [Mah86, Mah89, HOW92, You92, AHH+93]. In particular, this study is related to the famous isomorphism conjecture of Berman and Hartmanis; see Conjecture 3.73 in Section 3.6.2. Recall from this section that Mahaney [Mah82] resolved a related conjecture of Berman and Hartmanis by proving that if there exists some sparse $\leq_m^P$-complete set in NP, then P $=$ NP; see Theorem 3.75. Comparing this result with Kadin's result above, one sees that Mahaney's implication has both a stronger hypothesis ($\leq_m^P$-completeness versus $\leq_T^P$-completeness) and a stronger collapse consequence (P $=$ NP $=$ PH versus PH $= \Theta_2^p$) than Kadin's implication. What about the reductions in between $\leq_m^P$ and $\leq_T^P$? In particular, what happens if every NP set is $\leq_{tt}^P$-reducible (with an unbounded or a bounded number of queries) to some sparse set? Watanabe studied polynomial-time 1-truth-table reductions of NP sets to sparse sets. In particular, he proved that if NP $\subseteq P_{1\text{-tt}}^S$ for some sparse set S, then P $=$ FewP and NP $=$ RP, where RP is the class "random polynomial time" to be defined in Chapter 6. Ogihara and Watanabe [OW91] strengthened Mahaney's result by proving that if NP $\subseteq P_{btt}^S$ for some sparse set S, then P $=$ NP. Homer and Longpré [HL94] simplified their proof and extended their result to $\leq_{tt}^P$- and $\leq_T^P$-reductions of NP sets to sparse sets with a logarithmic number of queries. Arvind and Torán [AT99] proved that if an NP-complete set or a coNP-complete set is polynomial-time disjunctive truth-table reducible to a sparse set, then the function analogs of P_{tt}^{NP} and $P^{NP[\mathcal{O}(\log)]}$ coincide. The disjunctive truth-table reducibility is a special $\leq_{tt}^P$-reducibility that accepts exactly if at least one query is answered positively. They also showed in [AT99] that if an NP-complete set or a coNP-complete set is polynomial-time disjunctive truth-table reducible to a sparse set of polylogarithmic density, then P $=$ NP.

Note that Kadin's collapse result has both a stronger hypothesis and a stronger conclusion than the Karp–Lipton Theorem. Köbler and Watanabe [KW98] obtained a genuine improvement of the Karp–Lipton Theorem: If NP $\subseteq P^S$ for some sparse set S, then PH $=$ ZPP^{NP}, where ZPP is the class "zero-error probabilistic polynomial time" to be defined in Section 6.2.1. Note that ZPP $\subseteq$ NP. The strongest Karp–Lipton-type theorem currently known is due to Cai, Chakaravarthy, L. Hemaspaandra, and Ogihara [CCHO03]: If NP $\subseteq P^S$ for some sparse set S, then PH $\subseteq S_2^p$. The class S_2^p was introduced independently by Canetti [Can96] and by Russell and Sundaram [RS98]. S_2^p is akin to Σ_2^p in that it is also defined via two alternating quantifiers. The difference is that S_2^p is based on the *symmetric alternation* of $\exists^p$ and $\forall^p$ quantifiers: A set A is in S_2^p if and only if there exist a set $B \in P$ and a polynomial p such that for each $x \in \Sigma^*$, $x \in A$ implies $(\exists^p y)\,(\forall^p z)\,[\langle x, y, z \rangle \in B]$, and $x \notin A$ implies $(\exists^p z)\,(\forall^p y)\,[\langle x, y, z \rangle \in B]$. Compare this definition of S_2^p with the quantifier characterization of Σ_2^p given in Theorem 5.31. S_2^p is also related to the notion of competing provers in the area of interactive proof systems. By definition, $S_2^p \subseteq \Sigma_2^p \cap \Pi_2^p$. Cai [Cai01] proved that $S_2^p \subseteq \text{ZPP}^{\text{NP}}$.

Turning back to Kadin's result that the polynomial hierarchy collapses if the boolean hierarchy does, Wagner achieved stronger collapses of the PH under the same hypothesis: first, in [Wag87b], a collapse down to Δ_3^p; then, in [Wag89], a collapse down to $\text{BH}(\Sigma_2^p)$, which is contained in $\Theta_3^p \subseteq \Delta_3^p$. Chang and Kadin [Cha91, CK96] took things a step further by proving that $\text{BH}_k(\text{NP}) = \text{coBH}_k(\text{NP})$ implies a collapse of the PH even down to $\text{BH}_k(\Sigma_2^p)$. Beigel, Chang, and Ogihara [BCO93] proved that $\text{BH}_k(\text{NP}) = \text{coBH}_k(\text{NP})$ implies $\text{PH} = (\text{P}_{(k-1)\text{-tt}}^{\text{NP}})^{\text{NP}}$; note that Theorem 5.53 implies that $(\text{P}_{(k-1)\text{-tt}}^{\text{NP}})^{\text{NP}} \subseteq \text{BH}_k(\Sigma_2^p)$. E. and L. Hemaspaandra and Hempel [HHH98b] (see also Hempel's thesis [Hem98]) and, independently, Reith and Wagner [RW01] proved that, for each $k > 0$ and each $i > 0$, $\text{BH}_k(\Sigma_i^p) = \text{coBH}_k(\Sigma_i^p)$ implies $\text{PH} = \text{BH}_k(\Sigma_i^p) \,\Delta\, \text{BH}_{k-1}(\Sigma_{i+1}^p)$, where Δ denotes the complex symmetric difference of set classes.[9] In particular, for $i = 1$, $\text{BH}_k(\text{NP}) = \text{coBH}_k(\text{NP})$ implies $\text{PH} = \text{BH}_k(\text{NP}) \,\Delta\, \text{BH}_{k-1}(\Sigma_2^p)$. Currently, this is the strongest result linking a collapse of the polynomial hierarchy to a collapse of the boolean hierarchy over NP.

E. and L. Hemaspaandra and Hempel [HHH99] initiated a related line of research that studies downward collapses within the polynomial hierarchy. An immediate consequence of Theorems 5.53 and 5.57 is that $\text{P}^{\text{NP}[1]} = \text{P}^{\text{NP}[2]}$ implies $\text{PH} = \Sigma_3^p \cap \Pi_3^p$. Can one expect to obtain a collapse down to $\text{PH} = \Sigma_1^p \cap \Pi_1^p = \text{NP} \cap \text{coNP}$ under the same hypothesis? A result in [HHH99] says that such a strong downward collapse can be shown indeed for the higher levels of the polynomial hierarchy: For each $i > 2$, $\text{P}^{\Sigma_i^p[1]} = \text{P}^{\Sigma_i^p[2]}$ implies $\Sigma_i^p = \Pi_i^p$. Shortly thereafter, Buhrman and Fortnow [BF98] established the analogous result for $i = 2$: $\text{P}^{\Sigma_2^p[1]} = \text{P}^{\Sigma_2^p[2]}$ implies $\Sigma_2^p = \Pi_2^p$. In contrast, they provided a relativized counterexample for the case of $i = 1$: There exists an oracle relative to which $\text{P}^{\text{NP}[1]} = \text{P}^{\text{NP}[2]}$, and yet $\text{NP} \neq \text{coNP}$. Unifying and strengthening the techniques of the previous papers, E. and L. Hemaspaandra and Hempel [HHH01] proved the most general and strongest result currently known: For each $k > 0$ and each $i > 1$,

$$\text{P}_{k\text{-tt}}^{\Sigma_i^p} = \text{P}_{(k+1)\text{-tt}}^{\Sigma_i^p} \implies \text{BH}_k(\Sigma_i^p) = \text{coBH}_k(\Sigma_i^p).$$

This downward translation of equality result tightly links a collapse of the parallel query hierarchy over Σ_i^p to a collapse of the boolean hierarchy over Σ_i^p.

Another related line of research was initiated by L. Hemaspaandra, Hempel, and Wechsung [HHW99], who studied the question of whether and to what extent the order matters in which various oracle sets are accessed. In particular, for DPOTMs making at most one query each to two oracle sets from distinct levels of the boolean

---

[9] For classes $\mathcal{C}$ and $\mathcal{D}$ of sets, $\mathcal{C} \,\Delta\, \mathcal{D}$ is the class of symmetric differences of any two sets A and B, where $A \in \mathcal{C}$ and $B \in \mathcal{D}$.

hierarchy over NP, they precisely characterized those cases for which query order does matter, unless the polynomial hierarchy collapses. In contrast to oracle sets from the boolean hierarchy, E. and L. Hemaspaandra and Hempel [HHH98a] showed that query order never matters if the oracle sets are in the polynomial hierarchy.

Hierarchies similar to the polynomial hierarchy but based on classes other than NP have also been introduced. For example, based on the promise class UP, various unambiguous polynomial hierarchies and various ways of oracle access in such hierarchies were studied by Lange, Niedermeier, and Rossmanith [LR94, NR98], by Cai, L. Hemaspaandra, and Vyskoč [CHV92, CHV93], and by L. Hemaspaandra and Rothe [HR97b].

The concept of alternating Turing machines was introduced by Chandra, Kozen, and Stockmeyer [CKS81]. Theorems 5.65, 5.66, 5.68, and 5.69 and Corollaries 5.67 and 5.70 are due to them. Note that the constructibility requirements for the resource functions, which are stated in all these results except in Theorem 5.69, can be removed with a little care. Note also that Theorems 5.65 and 5.66 are stated for resource functions $\geq \log$, whereas the corresponding results in [CKS81] are stated for resource functions $\geq$ id only.

The concepts of lowness and highness were introduced by Schöning [Sch83] in complexity theory, and Section 5.7 follows his presentation in large parts. Theorems 5.76, 5.77, 5.83, and 5.88, Lemmas 5.80, 5.86, and 5.87, and Corollaries 5.78, 5.81, 5.82, and 5.84 are due to him. The notions of lowness and highness are inspired by similar ideas from recursive function theory; see [Soa77] and the books by H. Rogers [Rog67] and Soare [Soa87]. The strong nondeterministic polynomial-time Turing reducibility, $\leq^{NP}_{sT}$, from Definition 5.74 is due to Long [Lon82b]. This reducibility notion is based on the γ-reducibility introduced by Adleman and Manders [AM77]. The γ-reducibility is the many-one version of $\leq^{NP}_{sT}$. The characterization of $\leq^{NP}_{sT}$ in Lemma 5.75 is due to Selman [Sel78].

Following Schöning's initial work [Sch83], the study of low sets was pursued intensely. In particular, the lowness properties of the graph isomorphism problem and of certain probabilistic complexity classes were investigated in [Sch88, Sch87]. Some of this work will be presented in Chapter 6. Ko and Schöning [KS85] proved that sets with polynomial-size circuits, including the p-selective sets, are low. They also studied a refinement of the low hierarchy with respect to the Δ^p_k levels of the polynomial hierarchy. Book, Orponen, Russo, and Watanabe [BORW88] investigated lowness in the exponential-time hierarchy. Köbler, Schöning, Toda, and Torán [KSTT92, KST92] showed that problems solvable by NPTMs with few accepting paths (in particular, the problems in FewP) and the graph isomorphism problem are low for PP, probabilistic polynomial time. Further references to lowness results for the graph isomorphism problem will be presented in Chapter 6, where some of these results will be proven.

Balcázar, Book, and Schöning studied lowness and highness with respect to sparse sets. In their paper [BBS86b], they introduced interesting generalizations of lowness and highness, including the extended low hierarchy. The kth level of the extended low hierarchy is defined by

$$\mathrm{ELow}_k = \{L \mid \Sigma_k^{p,L} = \Sigma_{k-1}^{p,L \oplus \mathrm{SAT}}\}.$$

Here, $\oplus$ denotes the *join* (a.k.a. the marked union) of any two sets A and B, which is defined by $A \oplus B = \{0a \mid a \in A\} \cup \{1b \mid b \in B\}$. Among the most notable results about extended lowness are Sheu and Long's result that the extended low hierarchy is a strictly infinite hierarchy [SL94], and Köbler's result of optimally locating in the extended low hierarchy the class of sets with polynomial-size circuits [Köb94]. Allender and Hemaspaandra [AH92b] established lower bounds for the classes Low_k and ELow_k of the low and the extended low hierarchy.

The classes ELow_k behave differently from most other complexity classes in various ways. For example, unlike most standard complexity classes, the class ELow_2 is not closed under $\leq_m^p$-reductions [AH92b]. Moreover, L. Hemaspaandra, Jiang, Rothe, and Watanabe [HJRW98] proved that (a) ELow_2 is not closed under certain boolean operations such as union or intersection, and that (b) the join operator defined above can "lower" complexity with respect to extended lowness: There exist sets that are not in ELow_2, yet their join is in ELow_2. This result appears counterintuitive at first glance, if one's intuition about complexity is based on reductions. However, extended lowness is not a reduction-based measure of complexity. Rather, it is a measure of how hard it is to extract useful information from oracles. In [HJRW97], lower bounds for certain classes generalizing Selman's p-selectivity [Sel79] are established in terms of ELow_2. For more background on lowness and extended lowness, the reader is referred to the excellent surveys by L. Hemaspaandra [Hem93] and Köbler [Köb95].

We conclude this chapter by mentioning a number of relativization results, i.e., results of the form: "There exists an oracle A such that $\mathcal{C}^A \neq \mathcal{D}^A$," or: "There exists an oracle B such that $\mathcal{C}^B = \mathcal{D}^B$," or combinations of these two statements. Here, $\mathcal{C}$ and $\mathcal{D}$ are relativizable complexity classes, i.e., they are defined via some type of oracle Turing machine. When proving such assertions, one often focuses also on the quality of the separation achieved; for example, regarding the properties of the separating set constructed or regarding the properties of the oracle set constructed. For example, a "strong separation" is witnessed by an immune set. For any class $\mathcal{C}$ of sets, a set is $\mathcal{C}$-*immune* if it is an infinite set having no infinite subset in $\mathcal{C}$. Many strong separation results are known; see, e.g., [HM83, SB84, Bal85, BR88, TvEB89, BJY90, Ko90, Bru92, EHTY92, BCS92, HRW97a, Rot99]. The notion of immunity originates from recursive function theory. Without going into details here, we mention some even more demanding variants of immunity such as "bi-immunity" or Müller's "balanced immunity" [Mül93]. Lischke [Lis86, Lis99] studied the relativized relationship between NP and exponential time.

As to properties of the oracle set, we mention Cai and Watanabe's collapses by "stringent" oracle access [CW04] and separations by "generic" oracles (see, e.g., Fortnow and Yamakami [FY96]) and by "random" oracles. Regarding the latter, Baker, Gill, and Solovay [BGS75] proved that, relative to a random oracle R, NP^R contains a P^R-bi-immune set with probability one. In particular, $\mathrm{NP} \neq \mathrm{P} = \mathrm{NP} \cap \mathrm{coNP}$ holds in this world. L. Hemaspaandra and Zimand [HZ96] showed that, relative to a random oracle R, NP^R contains even a P^R-balanced-immune set with probability one.

6

Randomized Algorithms and Complexity Classes

"Yet in vain a paynim foe
Armed with fate the mighty blow;
For when he fell, the Elfin queen,
All in secret and unseen,
O'er the fainting hero threw
Her mantle of ambrosial blue,
And bade her spirits bear him far,
In Merlin's agate-axled car,
To her green isle's enamelled steep,
Far in the navel of the deep.
O'er his wounds she sprinkled dew
From flowers that in Arabia grew.

There he reigns a mighty king,
Thence to Britain shall return,
If right prophetic rolls I learn,
Borne on victory's spreading plume,
His ancient sceptre to resume,
His knightly table to restore,
And brave the tournaments of yore."

"When Arthur bowed his haughty crest,
No princess veiled in azure vest
Snatched him, by Merlin's powerful spell,
In groves of golden bliss to dwell;
But when he fell, with winged speed,
His champions, on a milk-white steed,
From the battle's hurricane
Bore him to Joseph's towered fane,

In the fair vale of Avalon;
There, with chanted orison
And the long blaze of tapers clear,
The stoled fathers met the bier;
Through the dim aisles, in order dread
Of martial woe, the chief they led,
And deep entombed in holy ground,
Before the altar's solemn bound."

(Taken from "Wharton's Ode")

This chapter deals with randomized algorithms and the corresponding probabilistic complexity classes. Randomized algorithms are often more efficient than the best known deterministic algorithms solving the same problem, yet only so at the cost of making errors. This point is made in Section 6.1, which presents selected (exponential-time) deterministic and randomized algorithms for the satisfiability problem. Randomized algorithms with bounded-error, including Monte Carlo and Las Vegas algorithms, allow very useful probability amplification techniques by which the error probability can be made exponentially small in the input size. In Section 6.2, the related probabilistic polynomial-time complexity classes such as PP, RP, ZPP, and BPP are reviewed. Efficient Monte Carlo algorithms for testing primality will be presented later on in Chapter 7. These algorithms are very important for practical purposes, especially in cryptographic applications, which often require efficient generation of large random prime numbers.

Section 6.3 introduces the notion of Arthur-Merlin games and studies the Arthur-Merlin hierarchy. Just as the polynomial hierarchy, the Arthur-Merlin hierarchy can be described by polynomially length-bounded quantifiers, where randomization is captured by the majority quantifier that corresponds to BPP. Arthur-Merlin games are closely related to the notion of interactive proof systems. Both concepts combine randomization with nondeterminism in a powerful way and are interesting both in a complexity-theoretic and in a cryptographic context. In particular, zero-knowledge protocols are interactive proof systems with certain cryptographically useful properties. They can be used for authentication. A zero-knowledge protocol for the graph isomorphism problem will be presented later on in Section 8.4.

Section 6.4 introduces the counting classes #P and GapP, which are suitable to characterize probabilistic complexity classes based on the number of accepting and rejecting paths of nondeterministic Turing machines. In Section 6.5, certain lowness properties of the graph isomorphism problem are proven, including lowness for probabilistic classes. These proofs involve Arthur-Merlin games, universal hashing, group-theoretic algorithms, and other concepts related to randomization.

6.1 The Satisfiability Problem of Propositional Logic

The satisfiability problem SAT and its restriction 3-SAT are NP-complete by Theorems 3.49 and 3.51. Hence, if SAT were in P, we had immediately P = NP, which is considered unlikely. Thus, it is considered equally unlikely that there exist efficient deterministic algorithms for SAT or 3-SAT.

But what *is* the best known running time of a deterministic algorithm for the satisfiability problem? Obviously, it depends on the structure of the given formula. For convenience, we will focus here on 3-SAT, where every clause has exactly three literals. The results presented in this section can straightforwardly be generalized to k-SAT, where every clause has exactly k literals.

The "naive" deterministic algorithm for 3-SAT works as follows: Given a boolean formula φ with n variables, check sequentially all possible assignments, and accept if and when a satisfying assignment is found. If φ is unsatisfiable, then the algorithms rejects its input after all 2^n assignments failed to satisfy the formula. This algorithm needs at least 2^n steps; it runs in time $\tilde{\mathcal{O}}(2^n)$.[1] Is there a better upper bound?

Yes, there is. But before showing *how* to beat the $\tilde{\mathcal{O}}(2^n)$ bound, let us ask: *Why?* What is the point of improving the trivial upper time bound $t \in \tilde{\mathcal{O}}(2^n)$ for 3-SAT to a slightly better, but still exponential-time bound, say to $\hat{t} \in \tilde{\mathcal{O}}(c^n)$ for some constant c with $1 < c < 2$? For small input sizes, even exponential-time algorithms may be considered feasible, although at some point n_0 the exponential growth will hit and the absolute running time of the algorithm becomes too large to be still feasible. To illustrate this point, suppose that T is a constant giving the absolute running time we can afford to spend. Improving the bound $t \in \tilde{\mathcal{O}}(2^n)$ to the bound $\hat{t} \in \tilde{\mathcal{O}}(c^n)$, where $1 < c < 2$, then means that the maximum input size $n_{\hat{t}}$ with $\hat{t}(n_{\hat{t}}) \leq T$ may be substantially larger than the maximum input size n_t with $t(n_t) \leq T$.

For example, if you can beat the trivial $\tilde{\mathcal{O}}(2^n)$ bound of the "naive" deterministic algorithm for 3-SAT by an $\tilde{\mathcal{O}}(c^n)$ algorithm for the constant $c = \sqrt{2} \approx 1.4142$,

---

[1] In this section, we drop polynomial factors in the time bounds of exponential-time algorithms, indicating this usage by the $\tilde{\mathcal{O}}$ notation.

then you have $\tilde{\mathcal{O}}(\sqrt{2}^{2n}) = \tilde{\mathcal{O}}(2^n)$. Thus, you can deal with inputs twice as large as before. Doubling the size of inputs your algorithm can handle in reasonable time is not only of theoretical importance but also very useful in practice. For example, it does make a difference whether an engineer is able to build bridges twice as long, and it does make a difference whether an architect is able to design buildings twice as high, and likewise so for the software engineer and for the algorithm designer.

Table 6.1 gives an overview of some selected algorithms and their running times for the satisfiability problem. Here, both deterministic and randomized algorithms are considered, and the upper bounds of k-SAT are given for the values of $k \in \{3, 4, 5, 6\}$. The currently best results are boldfaced.

Algorithm / Authors	Type	3-SAT	4-SAT	5-SAT	6-SAT
Backtracking	det.	$\tilde{\mathcal{O}}(1.913^n)$	$\tilde{\mathcal{O}}(1.968^n)$	$\tilde{\mathcal{O}}(1.987^n)$	$\tilde{\mathcal{O}}(1.995^n)$
Monien and Speckenmeyer [MS85]	det.	$\tilde{\mathcal{O}}(1.618^n)$	$\tilde{\mathcal{O}}(1.839^n)$	$\tilde{\mathcal{O}}(1.928^n)$	$\tilde{\mathcal{O}}(1.966^n)$
Dantsin et al. [DGH$^+$02]	det.	$\tilde{\mathcal{O}}(\mathbf{1.481^n})$	$\tilde{\mathcal{O}}(\mathbf{1.6^n})$	$\tilde{\mathcal{O}}(\mathbf{1.667^n})$	$\tilde{\mathcal{O}}(\mathbf{1.714^n})$
Paturi et al. [PPSZ98]	rand.	$\tilde{\mathcal{O}}(1.362^n)$	$\tilde{\mathcal{O}}(1.476^n)$	$\tilde{\mathcal{O}}(\mathbf{1.569^n})$	$\tilde{\mathcal{O}}(\mathbf{1.637^n})$
Schöning [Sch99]	rand.	$\tilde{\mathcal{O}}(1.334^n)$	$\tilde{\mathcal{O}}(1.5^n)$	$\tilde{\mathcal{O}}(1.6^n)$	$\tilde{\mathcal{O}}(1.667^n)$
Iwama and Tamaki [IT03]	rand.	$\tilde{\mathcal{O}}(\mathbf{1.324^n})$	$\tilde{\mathcal{O}}(\mathbf{1.474^n})$	—	—

Table 6.1. Running times of selected algorithms for the satisfiability problem

6.1.1 Deterministic Time Complexity

In this section, a deterministic algorithm for 3-SAT is presented that works according to the algorithmic principle of "*backtracking*." This algorithm design technique is suitable for problems whose solutions are composed of n components such that there is more than one choice option for each component. For example, a solution for a 3-SAT instance φ with n variables consists of the n truth values in a satisfying assignment, and for each such truth value, there are two choices possible: *true* (represented by 1) or *false* (represented by 0).

The idea now is to start with the empty solution, which assigns no values to the variables, and then to recursively construct, step by step, larger and larger partial solutions until, eventually, a complete solution is found, if one exists. In the case of 3-SAT, partial solutions are partial assignments to some of the variables in the given formula (cf. the notion of partial permutations in Example 5.26). In each recursion step of this procedure, the partial assignment constructed as yet is extended by assigning a truth value to one new variable.

The vertices of the resulting recursion tree correspond to the (nested) recursive calls of the procedure, and they are labeled with partial assignments. In particular, the root corresponds to the first recursive call and is labeled with the empty assignment. The inner vertices of the recursion tree correspond to the further recursive calls. A vertex $\tilde{v}$ in the recursion tree is the child of a vertex v if and only if $\tilde{v}$ is called within the computation triggered by v. Eventually, the algorithm terminates at the leaves of the recursion tree with no further recursive call, and some of the leaves are labeled with complete satisfying assignments if there exist any.

Other leaves represent "dead branches," which means that the computation was aborted there unsuccessfully. If one observes during the computation that the current branch of the recursion tree is "dead," i.e., the partial solution constructed as yet can in no way be extended to a complete solution of the given 3-SAT instance, then this recursion is aborted, pruning the whole subtree below it, and the procedures tracks back to the recursion one level up and tries to find another, more promising extension of the previously constructed partial solution. The term "backtracking" is due to this principle. Note that it may save time to prune large "dead" parts of the recursion tree.

BACKTRACKING-SAT(φ, β) {
    if (β assigns all variables of φ) return $\varphi(\beta)$;
      else if (β makes one clause of φ false) return 0;   // "dead branch"
        else if (BACKTRACKING-SAT$(\varphi, \beta 0)$) return 1;
           else return BACKTRACKING-SAT$(\varphi, \beta 1)$);
}

Fig. 6.1. Backtracking algorithm for 3-SAT

Figure 6.1 shows the algorithm BACKTRACKING-SAT. Given a boolean formula φ and a partial assignment β that assigns truth values to some of φ's variables, BACKTRACKING-SAT returns a boolean value: it returns 1 if the partial assignment β can be extended to a complete assignment to all of φ's variables, and it returns 0 otherwise. Here, partial assignments are viewed as strings of length at most n over the alphabet $\{0, 1\}$.

The first call of the algorithm is BACKTRACKING-SAT(φ, ε), where ε is the empty assignment. If the algorithm determines that the partial assignment β as yet constructed makes one of the clauses of φ false, then β cannot be extended to a satisfying assignment of φ. Hence, the corresponding branch in the recursion tree is "dead," and the subtree underneath it can safely be pruned. See also Exercise 6.1.

To estimate the running time of BACKTRACKING-SAT, note that the algorithm in Figure 6.1 can be specified so as to select the variables in an "intelligent" order that minimizes the number of steps needed to evaluate the variables in any clause. Consider an arbitrary, fixed clause C_j of the given formula φ. Every satisfying assignment β of φ in particular assigns truth values to the three variables occurring in C_j. Out of the $2^3 = 8$ possibilities to assign a 0 or 1 to these variables, one can be definitely excluded: the assignment that makes C_j false. The corresponding vertex in the recursion tree of BACKTRACKING-SAT(φ, β) thus leads to a "dead" branch, and the subtree underneath it can safely be pruned. Depending on the structure of φ, there may exist further "dead" branches whose subtreees could be pruned. Since we are trying to find an upper bound in the worst case here, we do not take these further "dead" subtrees into consideration. We thus obtain

$$\tilde{\mathcal{O}}\left(\left(2^3 - 1\right)^{\frac{n}{3}}\right) = \tilde{\mathcal{O}}(\sqrt[3]{7}^{\,n}) \approx \tilde{\mathcal{O}}(1.9129^n)$$

as an upper bound for BACKTRACKING-SAT in the worst case. This bound slightly improves the $\tilde{\mathcal{O}}(2^n)$ upper bound of the "naive" algorithm for 3-SAT.

The deterministic time complexity of 3-SAT can be improved even further. For example, Monien and Speckenmeyer's divide-and-conquer algorithm [MS85] provides an upper bound of $\tilde{\mathcal{O}}(1.618^n)$. Based on a local search technique, Dantsin et al. [DGH$^+$02] provided an $\tilde{\mathcal{O}}(1.481^n)$ upper bound, which is the best known bound for deterministic 3-SAT algorithms. In this discipline, they currently hold the world record; see Table 6.1.

6.1.2 Probabilistic Time Complexity

Now we turn to a randomized algorithm for 3-SAT that is due to Schöning. His "random walk" algorithm, which is based on a "constrained local search with restart," beats all known deterministic algorithms for 3-SAT, although there are even more efficient randomized algorithms for this problem now; see Section 6.7.

A *random walk* can take place on a variety of structures; for example, in the Euclidean space, on a finite or an infinite lattice, or on a finite or an infinite graph. Here, we consider random walks on a directed, finite graph that may be viewed as the transition graph of a stochastic automaton. A stochastic automaton is a special finite automaton, see Definitions 2.11 and 2.12 in Section 2.2.

Recall that the edges in the transition graph of any finite automaton are marked by the symbols of a given alphabet. The edges of a stochastic automaton $\mathcal{S}$ are in addition marked by real numbers between 0 and 1 that represent probabilities. Marking an edge from x to y by p_{xy} with $0 \leq p_{xy} \leq 1$ indicates the transition from state x to state y in $\mathcal{S}$ is with probability p_{xy}. The probabilities of all edges going out of any vertex of $\mathcal{S}$ add up to one. In the terms of probability theory, the process of randomly moving from state to state according to the designated probabilities of $\mathcal{S}$ is called a Markov chain. Final states, from which there are no transitions to other states with a non-zero probability, are called *absorbing states*. Just like finite automata, a stochastic automaton $\mathcal{S}$ can be used to recognize strings and to accept languages, even though only with a certain probability, of course. However, we are not interested in accepting languages by stochastic automata here. Rather, we use them to illustrate the computation of the randomized algorithm RANDOM-SAT shown in Figure 6.2. Given a boolean formula φ with n variables, RANDOM-SAT tries to find a satisfying assignment of φ, if there exists one. The computation of RANDOM-SAT(φ) can be thought of as a random walk on the transition graph of a stochastic automaton $\mathcal{S}$, which is shown in Figure 6.3. Here, the edges are not marked by the symbols of an alphabet but only by the corresponding transition probabilities.

On input φ, RANDOM-SAT starts by randomly choosing an initial assignment β every bit of which is chosen independently according to the uniform distribution. That is, every bit of β takes on the value 0 or 1 with probability $1/2$.

```
RANDOM-SAT(φ) {
    for (i = 1, 2, ..., ⌈(4/3)ⁿ⌉) {                    // n is the number of variables in φ
        Randomly choose an assignment β ∈ {0, 1}ⁿ under the uniform distribution;
        for (j = 1, 2, ..., n) {
            if (φ(β) = 1) return the satisfying assignment β of φ and halt;
            else {
                Choose any clause C = (x ∨ y ∨ z) with C(β) = 0;
                Randomly choose a literal ℓ ∈ {x, y, z} under the uniform distribution;
                Determine the bit βℓ ∈ {0, 1} in β that assigns ℓ;
                Modify βℓ to 1 − βℓ in β;
            }
        }
    }
    return "φ is not satisfiable";
}
```

Fig. 6.2. Algorithm RANDOM-SAT

If φ is not satisfiable, RANDOM-SAT(φ) can never output a satisfying assignment of φ; so, it does not make any error in this case. Suppose now that φ is satisfiable. Let α be an arbitrary, fixed satisfying assignment of φ. (Note that RANDOM-SAT does not need to know α; it is used only to explain how RANDOM-SAT works.) Let $\mathbf{X}$ be a random variable that describes the *Hamming distance between α and β*, i.e., the number of bits in which α and β differ. Obviously, $\mathbf{X}$ can take on the values $j \in \{0, 1, \ldots, n\}$, and is distributed according to the binomial distribution with parameters n and $1/2$. That is, the probability of the event $\mathbf{X} = j$ is $\binom{n}{j} 2^{-n}$.

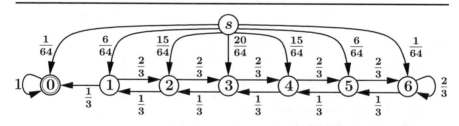

Fig. 6.3. Transition graph of a stochastic automaton for the random walk of RANDOM-SAT

The initial step of RANDOM-SAT(φ) described above can now be thought of as the initial step of the random walk on the transition graph of $\mathcal{S}$ that moves from the initial state s to one of the states $j \in \{0, 1, \ldots, n\}$ according to the distribution of $\mathbf{X}$. To be in state j means that the randomly chosen initial assignment β and the fixed satisfying assignment α have Hamming distance j. Figure 6.3 shows the transition graph of $\mathcal{S}$ for the case of $n = 6$.

Then, RANDOM-SAT(φ) checks whether or not the initial assignment β already satisfies φ, and if so, it accepts. Otherwise, since β does not satisfy φ, there must exist some clause in φ not satisfied by β. RANDOM-SAT(φ) chooses an arbitrary such clause, and in this clause, it randomly chooses some literal according to the uniform distribution. The bit in the current assignment β that assigns a truth value to the chosen literal is then flipped, in the hope that the thus modified assignment is "closer" to being a satisfying assignment. Being "closer" means that the Hamming distance to α is smaller. Flipping a bit β_ℓ to $1 - \beta_\ell$ in the current assignment as described above can be thought of as one step to the left or to the right in the random walk on the transition graph of $\mathcal{S}$, moving from state $j > 0$ either to state $j - 1$ or to state $j + 1$, where only states less than or equal to n can be reached.

There are three literals in each clause. The fixed assignment α satisfies φ; hence, it satisfies at least one literal in each clause. If we fix in each clause *exactly* one of the literals satisfied by α, say ℓ, then RANDOM-SAT(φ) makes a step to the left if and only if ℓ was chosen by RANDOM-SAT(φ). Thus, the probability of moving from state $j > 0$ to state $j - 1$ is $1/3$, and the probability of moving from state $j > 0$ to state $j + 1$ is $2/3$.

The above process is repeated as long as $j \neq 0$, and at most n times. As soon as the state $j = 0$ is reached, the current assignment β and the fixed assignment α have Hamming distance 0. Thus, RANDOM-SAT(φ) has found a satisfying assignment of φ, and accepts its input. Of course, one might also hit a satisfying assignment (distinct from α) in some state $j \neq 0$. However, this would only increase the acceptance probability, so we do not take this possibility into account here.

If the above process is repeated n times without success, then the initial assignment β was chosen so unlucky that RANDOM-SAT(φ) now drops it, and restarts the whole process from scratch by choosing a new initial assignment. The entire procedure is repeated at most t times, where $t = \lceil (4/3)^n \rceil$. If it is still unsuccessful after t trials, RANDOM-SAT(φ) rejects its input.

Here is a rough sketch of how to estimate, assuming that φ is satisfiable, the acceptance probability and running time of RANDOM-SAT(φ), omitting most of the technical details and focusing mainly on the key ideas. For convenience, suppose that 3 divides n. The probability of moving to the right is greater than the probability of moving to the left, towards the final state 0. Thus, one might be tempted to think that the acceptance probability of RANDOM-SAT(φ) is rather small. However, one should not underestimate the chance to go right away from the initial state s to a state j close to 0. The closer to state 0 one starts, the higher is the probability of eventually reaching 0 during the remaining n steps of the random walk.

Let p_i be the probability for the event that RANDOM-SAT(φ) reaches the state 0 within n steps after the initial step, under the condition that it reaches some state $i \leq n/3$ with the initial step. For example, if one reaches state $n/3$ with the initial step and does no more than $n/3$ steps to the right, then one can still reach the final state 0 by a total of at most n steps. If one does more than $n/3$ steps to the right starting from state $n/3$, then the final state cannot be reached within n steps. In general, starting from state i after the initial step, no more than $(n - i)/2$ steps to the right may be done. It was noted above that a step to the right is done with probability $2/3$, and a step to the left is done with probability $1/3$. Thus, we have

$$p_i = \binom{n}{\frac{n-i}{2}} \left(\frac{2}{3}\right)^{\frac{n-i}{2}} \left(\frac{1}{3}\right)^{n - \frac{n-i}{2}}. \tag{6.1}$$

Let q_i be the probability for the event that RANDOM-SAT(φ) reaches some state $i \leq n/3$ with the initial step. Clearly, we have that

$$q_i = \binom{n}{i} \cdot 2^{-n}. \tag{6.2}$$

Let p be the probability for the event that RANDOM-SAT(φ) reaches the final state 0 within the inner for loop. Of course, this event can occur also when starting from a state $j > n/3$. Hence, we have

$$p \geq \sum_{i=0}^{n/3} p_i \cdot q_i.$$

The above sum can be suitably approximated using the entropy function, which is defined in Definition 4.26 of Section 4.3.2. Moreover, the binomial coefficients in (6.1) and (6.2) can be suitably estimated using Stirling's formula. Thus, one obtains a lower bound of at least (up to constant factors) $(3/4)^n$ for p.

The error probability of RANDOM-SAT(φ) can be made sufficiently small by executing $t = \lceil (4/3)^n \rceil$ independent trials, each starting with a new initial assignment β. For each trial, the acceptance probability is at least $(3/4)^n$, so the error is bounded by $1 - (3/4)^n$. Since the trials are independent, these error probabilities multiply, yielding an error of $(1 - (3/4)^n)^t \leq e^{-1}$. Thus, the total acceptance probabilitiy of RANDOM-SAT(φ) is at least $1 - 1/e \approx 0.632$ if φ is satisfiable, and RANDOM-SAT(φ) does not make any error at all if φ is unsatisfiable. The hint for Exercise 6.2 explains the particular choice of this value of t, which also implies the running time $\tilde{\mathcal{O}}(1.334^n)$ of RANDOM-SAT, neglecting factors polynomially in n. As a rule of thumb, to achieve a sufficiently small error probability, the number of repetitions needed is roughly reciprocal to the success probability of one trial.

6.2 Probabilistic Polynomial-Time Classes

6.2.1 PP, RP, and ZPP: Monte Carlo and Las Vegas Algorithms

Deterministic and nondeterministic Turing machines were introduced in Chapter 3, alternating Turing machines in Chapter 5. In this chapter, we are concerned with still another type of Turing machine, the probabilistic Turing machine, which embodies still another computational paradigm: *randomization*. Probabilistic Turing machines formalize the notion of randomized algorithms, algorithms that are able to flip coins and to perform their computation based on the resulting random choices. An example of a randomized algorithm is given in Section 6.1.2. Randomization often yields more efficient algorithms for a given problem. However, there is a price to pay: randomized algorithms can make errors.

The probabilistic Turing machine model can be described by nondeterministic Turing machines (NTMs). Syntactically, a *probabilistic Turing machine* simply is an NTM N, where we agree by convention that the nondeterministic branching degree of N is at most two. Moreover, it is often useful to require that NTMs be *normalized*, i.e., to require that for each input x, all computations paths in $N(x)$ have the same number of nondeterministic branching points and can thus be described by binary strings of the same length. In other words, normalized machines always have a full binary computation tree (not allowing for the deterministic steps of the machine).

The semantics of probabilistic Turing machines is defined by specifying an acceptance behavior of NTMs suitable for randomization. To this end, for any given NTM N and any input x, we define a probability measure μ_T on the set of computation paths in the tree $T = N(x)$, whose vertices represent the configurations of N on input x. Note that there is a one-to-one correspondence between the computation paths and the leaves in the tree T.

Definition 6.1 (Semantics of Probabilistic Turing Machines).
For any NTM N and any input x, consider any subtree T of the computation tree $N(x)$ such that the root of T is the root of $N(x)$. The probability measure μ_T on the set of leaves of T is defined inductively as follows:

- *Initially, if T consists of only the root r of $N(x)$ (i.e., r is the start configuration of $N(x)$), then set $\mu_T(r) = 1$.*
- *While $T \neq N(x)$, fix some leaf ℓ of T that is not a leaf of $N(x)$, and consider the new subtree T_ℓ of $N(x)$ that is obtained from T by adding the immediate successor configuration(s) of ℓ. From the probability measure μ_T on the leaves of T, define the probability measure μ_{T_ℓ} on the leaves of T_ℓ as follows:*

$$\mu_{T_\ell}(c) = \begin{cases} \mu_T(\ell)/2 & \text{if } c \text{ is one out of two successor configurations of } \ell \\ \mu_T(\ell) & \text{if } c \text{ is the only one successor configuration of } \ell \\ \mu_T(c) & \text{if } c \text{ is not a successor configuration of } \ell. \end{cases}$$

We will be interested only in polynomial-time probabilistic Turing machines. Every computation path of a given NPTM N running on some input x is represented by a binary string α of length $p(|x|)$ for some $p \in \mathbb{P}ol$, where the ith bit of α corresponds to the ith nondeterministic branching of $N(x)$ along α. If α leads to some leaf ℓ of $T = N(x)$, we write $\mu_T(\alpha) = \mu_T(\ell)$. Note that μ_T indeed is a probability measure, since for each finite tree T:

$$\sum_{\alpha \text{ is some path of } T} \mu_T(\alpha) = 1.$$

Every subset of paths of T is an event. The probability that some event E occurs with respect to μ_T is given by:

$$\Pr(E) = \sum_{\alpha \in E} \mu_T(\alpha) = \sum_{\alpha \in E} 2^{-|\alpha|}.$$

Using the above notation, we can now define the first two probabilistic complexity classes: the class PP, "probabilistic polynomial time," and the class RP, "random polynomial time."

Definition 6.2 (Probabilistic Polynomial Time and Random Polynomial Time).

1. Probabilistic polynomial time *is defined by*

$$\mathrm{PP} = \left\{ A \,\middle|\, \begin{array}{l} \textit{there is some NPTM } M \textit{ such that for each input } x, \\ x \in A \iff \Pr(\{\alpha \mid M \textit{ accepts } x \textit{ on path } \alpha\}) \geq 1/2 \end{array} \right\}.$$

2. Random polynomial time *is defined by*

$$\mathrm{RP} = \left\{ A \,\middle|\, \begin{array}{l} \textit{there is some NPTM } M \textit{ such that for each input } x, \\ x \in A \implies \Pr(\{\alpha \mid M \textit{ accepts } x \textit{ on path } \alpha\}) \geq 1/2; \\ x \notin A \implies \Pr(\{\alpha \mid M \textit{ accepts } x \textit{ on path } \alpha\}) = 0 \end{array} \right\}.$$

Remark 6.3 (Normalized Turing Machines and Threshold Computation).

1. Every NPTM whose acceptance criterion is based on probability weights according to Definitions 6.1 and 6.2 can easily be normalized: Just extend every computation path up to a fixed polynomial length by appending a full binary subtree to it and, on each path thus obtained, accept if and only if the original path was accepting. The modified normalized machine has the same acceptance probability as the original machine.

2. The acceptance criterion of the probabilistic machines for PP and RP from Definition 6.2 is determined by the probability weight of accepting paths according to Definition 6.1. Alternatively, the acceptance criterion for PP and RP can be based on the number of accepting paths of NPTMs; see also Definitions 6.31 and 6.34. For any NPTM M, define the function $\mathrm{acc}_M : \Sigma^* \to \mathbb{N}$ by $\mathrm{acc}_M(x) = \|\{\alpha \mid M \text{ accepts } x \text{ on path } \alpha\}\|$. Then, the following characterizations of PP and RP can be shown:

   a) A is in PP if and only if there exists some normalized NPTM M and some polynomial p such that for each x:

   $$x \in A \iff \mathrm{acc}_M(x) \geq 2^{p(|x|)-1}.$$

   b) A is in RP if and only if there exists some normalized NPTM M and some polynomial p such that for each x:

   $$x \in A \implies \mathrm{acc}_M(x) \geq 2^{p(|x|)-1};$$
   $$x \notin A \implies \mathrm{acc}_M(x) = 0.$$

Observe that this equivalence of the probability weight interpretation and the acc_M interpretation uses normalized machines. In fact, for PP, the normalization requirement may be dropped; see Problem 6.1(a). However, for RP, having normalized machines appears to be a crucial requirement; see Problem 6.1(b).

Unlike PP, the class RP is a so-called "promise class." Complexity classes are usually represented by machines (e.g., NPTMs) defining the class by their acceptance and rejection criteria. In many cases, exactly one of the two criteria holds for each input. For example, PP machines accept if at least half of the total number of paths accept, and they reject otherwise. In contrast, a promise class such as RP has a rejection criterion that is *more restrictive* than the logical negation of the acceptance criterion,[2] which leaves open the possibility that for some inputs none of the two criteria applies. The burdon to avoid this obstacle is shouldered by the machines representing the promise class: Every machine "promises" that for each input exactly one of the two criteria holds. For example, according to Definition 6.2, RP machines "promise" that they never have an acceptance probability of $1/4$ (note, however, Theorem 6.6). Other examples of promise classes are UP and FewP defined in Chapter 3. Promise classes appear to have different properties than non-promise complexity classes. For example, the promise classes RP, UP, and FewP seem to lack complete sets; see also Corollary 3.83.

RP and coRP algorithms both have a one-sided error probability. Such algorithms are also called *Monte Carlo algorithms*. Let L be a set in RP, and let A be an RP algorithm for L. By definition, A may make errors for instances x in L, but A never lies for instances x not in L. Thus, the answer "yes" (i.e., an accepting path) of A on input x can occur only if x is in L and is thus always correct, whereas the answer "no" (i.e., a rejecting path) can occur both erroneously (if x is in L) and correctly (if x is not in L). Therefore, RP algorithms are sometimes called *no-biased* Monte Carlo algorithms. Similarly, coRP algorithms always give reliable "no" answers, but perhaps erroneous "yes" answers. Therefore, coRP algorithms are sometimes called *yes-biased* Monte Carlo algorithms. Unlike PP, the class RP seems to be not closed under complementation (unless, of course, it turns out that RP = P).

Theorem 6.4.   *1.* P $\subseteq$ RP $\subseteq$ NP $\subseteq$ PP $\subseteq$ PSPACE.
   2. PP *is closed under complementation.*

Proof.   1. The first two inclusions, P $\subseteq$ RP $\subseteq$ NP, follow immediately from the definitions. The inclusion PP $\subseteq$ PSPACE can be proven similar to the inclusion NP $\subseteq$ PSPACE from Theorem 3.27: Given a PP machine M running on input x, the simulating PSPACE machine performs a depth-first search through the computation tree of $M(x)$. However, rather than searching for *some* accepting path as in the proof of NP $\subseteq$ PSPACE, the PSPACE machine now counts *all* accepting paths of $M(x)$, and it accepts the input if and only if this number is at least half of the total number of paths.

For the inclusion NP $\subseteq$ PP, let A be any set in NP, and let M be a given NP machine accepting A. Suppose that M is normalized so that on each input x, the

---

[2] A bit more carefully phrased, *all known* acceptance/rejection criteria for the class share the property that the rejection criterion is more restrictive than the logical negation of the acceptance criterion. For example, although the class RP_{path} is defined in Problem 6.1 via a rejection criterion that is more restrictive than the logical negation of the acceptance criterion, RP_{path} is known to be equal to NP. Thus, RP_{path} is *not* a promise class.

computation tree $M(x)$ is a complete binary tree of depth $p(|x|)$ for some $p \in \mathbb{P}\mathrm{ol}$. Construct a new NPTM N accepting A in the sense of PP as follows. On input x, N branches nondeterministically. On the left branch, N simulates the computation of $M(x)$. On the right branch, N creates a complete binary tree of depth $p(|x|)$, accepts on $2^{p(|x|)} - 1$ of its paths, and rejects on one of its paths.

If $x \in A$, then $M(x)$ accepts on at least one of its $2^{p(|x|)}$ paths. Thus, $N(x)$ accepts on at least $2^{p(|x|)}$ of its $2^{p(|x|)+1}$ paths, i.e., N accepts x with probability at least one half. If $x \notin A$, then all $2^{p(|x|)}$ paths of $M(x)$ are rejecting. Thus, $N(x)$ accepts on at most $2^{p(|x|)} - 1$ of its $2^{p(|x|)+1}$ paths, i.e., N accepts x with probability less than one half. It follows that A is in PP.

2. The proof of PP $=$ coPP is left to the reader as Exercise 6.3. ∎

The acceptance threshold of $1/2$ in the definition of RP is chosen at will. Other thresholds would work as well and would define the same class of sets. We will now see that the acceptance threshold of an RP computation can be made very small: it is enough to require that the acceptance probability is at least a reciprocal polynomial in the input size. Thus, the error probability of RP algorithms can be made smaller than $1/q(|x|)$ for each fixed polynomial q.

Definition 6.5. *Let q be a fixed polynomial. Define the class*

$$
\mathrm{RP}_q = \left\{ A \left| \begin{array}{l} \text{there is some NPTM } M \text{ such that for each input } x, \\ x \in A \implies \Pr(\{\alpha \mid M \text{ accepts } x \text{ on path } \alpha\}) \geq 1/q(|x|); \\ x \notin A \implies \Pr(\{\alpha \mid M \text{ accepts } x \text{ on path } \alpha\}) = 0 \end{array} \right. \right\}.
$$

Theorem 6.6. *Let q be a nondecreasing polynomial such that for each n, $q(n) \geq 2$. Then, $\mathrm{RP}_q = \mathrm{RP}$.*

Proof.   Since $q(n) \geq 2$ for each n, the inclusion RP $\subseteq \mathrm{RP}_q$ holds by definition.

Conversely, to prove $\mathrm{RP}_q \subseteq \mathrm{RP}$, let A be any set in RP_q for some fixed polynomial q, and let M be some NPTM for A according to Definition 6.5. Construct an NPTM N that accepts A in the sense of RP as follows. On input x of length n, N successively simulates the computation of $M(x)$ in $q = q(n)$ independent trials. Thus, every path $\alpha = \alpha_1 \alpha_2 \cdots \alpha_q$ of $N(x)$ consists of a sequence of q paths α_i of $M(x)$, and α is defined to accept if and only if at least one of its subpaths α_i accepts.

Since q is a polynomial and M runs in polynomial time, so does N. It remains to show that N witnesses membership of A in RP. Let x be the given input string. If $x \notin A$, no path of $M(x)$ accepts. Thus, $N(x)$ has no accepting paths and the acceptance probability is zero.

We now estimate the error probability $E_N(x)$ of N for $x \in A$, which is given by

$$
E_N(x) = \Pr(\{\alpha \mid N \text{ rejects } x \text{ on path } \alpha\}).
$$

The error probability of $M(x)$ is bounded above by $1 - 1/q$. For each path α of $N(x)$, all subpaths α_i of α are independently chosen. This implies for the error probability of N that

$$E_N(x) < \left(1 - \frac{1}{q(n)}\right)^{q(n)} < \frac{1}{2}. \tag{6.3}$$

The latter inequality of (6.3) follows from the fact that $\lim_{k \to \infty} (1 + \frac{a}{k})^k = e^a$, where $e = 2.71828 \cdots$ is the base of the natural logarithm. Thus, for $a = -1$, we have that $(1 - 1/q(n))^{q(n)}$ is close to e^{-1}, which is less than one half. Hence,

$$\Pr(\{\alpha \mid N \text{ accepts } x \text{ on path } \alpha\}) \geq \frac{1}{2},$$

which completes the proof.   ∎

Theorem 6.6 has an easy corollary the proof of which is left to the reader as Exercise 6.4.

Corollary 6.7. RP *is closed under union and intersection.*

PP is also closed under union and intersection, and even under $\leq_{tt}^P$-reductions. Whereas closure under complementation is easy to see for PP, the proof of closure under intersection is not at all trivial; see Problem 6.2.

RP algorithms have a one-sided error, and Theorem 6.6 tells us that this error can be made very small. This is a clear advantage of RP over PP algorithms. As pointed out above, RP algorithms can give false "no" answers, whereas coRP algorithms always give reliable "no" answers. On the other hand, coRP algorithms can give false "yes" answers, whereas RP algorithms always give reliable "yes" answers. The class ZPP collects all problems solvable by polynomial-time randomized algorithms with zero error probability, combining the advantages of yes-biased and no-biased Monte Carlo algorithms.

Definition 6.8 (Zero-Error Probabilistic Polynomial Time).
Define the class zero-error probabilistic polynomial time *by* ZPP = RP ∩ coRP.

Just like RP, the class ZPP is a promise class. ZPP algorithms, which are also dubbed *Las Vegas algorithms*, never give a wrong answer, although it might happen that they do not give any useful answer at all. This justifies the name "zero-error" probabilistic polynomial time. Similar as in Definition 5.74, a ZPP algorithm can be viewed as an NPTM M with three types of final states: an accepting state, s_a, a rejecting state, s_r, and a "don't know" state, $s_?$. Let A be any language in ZPP, and let M and N be NPTMs witnessing that $A \in$ RP and $\overline{A} \in$ RP, respectively. Consider the machine $M \circ N$, which is defined as follows: On input x, $M \circ N$ first simulates $M(x)$ and then it simulates $N(x)$. Thus, every path of $(M \circ N)(x)$ has the form $\langle \alpha, \beta \rangle$, where α is a path of $M(x)$ and β is a path of $N(x)$. For paths α and β, denote acceptance by $+$ and rejection by $-$, respectively. Table 6.2 shows all the possibilities for the paths α and β and the way $M \circ N$ handles these cases by assigning the final states s_a, s_r, and $s_?$ to each possible pair $\langle \alpha, \beta \rangle$. Thus, we have the following corollary.

	path α of $M(x)$	path β of $N(x)$	path $\langle \alpha, \beta \rangle$ of $(M \circ N)(x)$
$x \in A$	$+$	$-$	$(+, -) = s_a$
	$-$	$-$	$(-, -) = s_?$
$x \notin A$	$-$	$+$	$(-, +) = s_r$
	$-$	$-$	$(-, -) = s_?$

Table 6.2. A ZPP computation

Corollary 6.9. *A is in* ZPP *if and only if there exists an NPTM M with three types of final states (an accepting state, s_a, a rejecting state, s_r, and a "don't know" state, $s_?$) such that for each x,*

$$x \in A \implies \Pr(\{\alpha \mid M \text{ accepts } x \text{ on path } \alpha\}) \geq 1/2 \text{ and}$$
$$\Pr(\{\alpha \mid M \text{ rejects } x \text{ on path } \alpha\}) = 0;$$
$$x \notin A \implies \Pr(\{\alpha \mid M \text{ rejects } x \text{ on path } \alpha\}) \geq 1/2 \text{ and}$$
$$\Pr(\{\alpha \mid M \text{ accepts } x \text{ on path } \alpha\}) = 0.$$

We conclude this section by presenting two problems complete for PP.

Definition 6.10 (Majority Satisfiability and Threshold Satisfiability).
Define the following two problems:

$$\texttt{Majority-SAT} = \left\{ \varphi \,\middle|\, \begin{array}{l} \varphi \text{ is a boolean formula with } n \text{ variables} \\ \text{and at least } 2^{n-1} \text{ satisfying assignments} \end{array} \right\};$$

$$\texttt{Threshold-SAT} = \left\{ \langle \varphi, i \rangle \,\middle|\, \begin{array}{l} \varphi \text{ is a boolean formula with at} \\ \text{least } i \text{ satisfying assignments} \end{array} \right\}.$$

For example, $\varphi(x, y) = x \wedge y$ is not in $\texttt{Majority-SAT}$, since only one out of four possible assignments satisfies φ. However, $\psi(x, y) = x \vee y$ is in $\texttt{Majority-SAT}$, since it has three satisfying assignments. Note also that, for these formulas φ and ψ, the instances $\langle \varphi, 0 \rangle$, $\langle \varphi, 1 \rangle$, $\langle \psi, 0 \rangle$, $\langle \psi, 1 \rangle$, $\langle \psi, 2 \rangle$, and $\langle \psi, 3 \rangle$ each belong to $\texttt{Threshold-SAT}$, wheras none of the instances $\langle \varphi, 2 \rangle$, $\langle \varphi, 3 \rangle$, $\langle \varphi, 4 \rangle$, and $\langle \psi, 4 \rangle$ belongs to $\texttt{Threshold-SAT}$.

Theorem 6.11. *Both* $\texttt{Majority-SAT}$ *and* $\texttt{Threshold-SAT}$ *are* $\leq_{\mathrm{m}}^{\mathrm{P}}$-*complete for* PP.

Proof.   It is easy to see that $\texttt{Majority-SAT}$ belongs to PP. We now prove that (1) $\texttt{Threshold-SAT}$ is $\leq_{\mathrm{m}}^{\mathrm{P}}$-hard for PP, and (2) $\texttt{Threshold-SAT} \leq_{\mathrm{m}}^{\mathrm{P}} \texttt{Majority-SAT}$. Since PP is closed under $\leq_{\mathrm{m}}^{\mathrm{P}}$-reductions (see Exercise 6.5), both statements of the theorem follow.

1. $\texttt{Threshold-SAT}$ is $\leq_{\mathrm{m}}^{\mathrm{P}}$-hard for PP: Let A be any set in PP, and let M be some NPTM accepting A in the sense of PP. By Remark 6.3, we may assume that M is a normalized machine and there is a polynomial p such that for each x of length n:

$$x \in A \iff \mathrm{acc}_M(x) \geq 2^{p(n)-1}.$$

Let f_M be the Cook reduction from Theorem 3.49, and let $\varphi_{M,x} = f_M(x)$ be the corresponding boolean formula. Since the Cook reduction is parsimonious,

$$\mathrm{acc}_M(x) = ||\{\beta \mid \beta \text{ is a satisfying assignment for } \varphi_{M,x}\}||.$$

Thus, the reduction $g(x) = \langle \varphi_{M,x}, 2^{p(|x|)-1} \rangle$ shows that $A \leq^{\mathrm{P}}_{\mathrm{m}}$ Threshold-SAT.

2. Threshold-SAT $\leq^{\mathrm{P}}_{\mathrm{m}}$ Majority-SAT: Let $\langle \varphi, i \rangle$ be any given Threshold-SAT instance, where φ is a boolean formula in the variables $x_1, x_2, \ldots, x_m$. Construct a formula $\psi = \psi(x_1, x_2, \ldots, x_m)$ such that ψ has *exactly* $j = 2^m - i$ satisfying assignments, where we assume that $i \leq 2^m$. Consider the binary representation of

$$j = 2^{m-s_1} + 2^{m-s_2} + \cdots + 2^{m-s_k},$$

where $0 \leq s_1 < s_2 < \cdots < s_k \leq m$. Define

$$
\begin{aligned}
\psi = {}& (x_1 \wedge \cdots \wedge x_{s_1-1} \wedge x_{s_1}) \vee \\
& (x_1 \wedge \cdots \wedge x_{s_1-1} \wedge \neg x_{s_1} \wedge x_{s_1+1} \wedge \cdots \wedge x_{s_2-1} \wedge x_{s_2}) \vee \\
& \qquad\qquad \vdots \\
& (x_1 \wedge \cdots \wedge x_{s_1-1} \wedge \neg x_{s_1} \wedge x_{s_1+1} \wedge \cdots \wedge x_{s_2-1} \wedge \neg x_{s_2} \wedge x_{s_2+1} \\
& \quad \wedge \cdots \wedge x_{s_{k-1}-1} \wedge \neg x_{s_{k-1}} \wedge x_{s_{k-1}+1} \wedge \cdots \wedge x_{s_k}).
\end{aligned}
$$

Observe that the ℓth clause in ψ contributes exactly 2^{m-s_ℓ} satisfying assignments, and due to the negations in ψ no assignment satisfying one clause can also satisfy another. Thus, none of the satisfying assignments is counted twice. Hence, the number of assignments satisfying ψ adds up to:

$$2^{m-s_1} + 2^{m-s_2} + \cdots + 2^{m-s_k} = j$$

as desired.

Now, fix some formula $\gamma \notin$ Majority-SAT; for example, pick $\gamma = x \wedge y$. Define the reduction Threshold-SAT $\leq^{\mathrm{P}}_{\mathrm{m}}$ Majority-SAT by

$$
f(\langle \varphi, i \rangle) = \begin{cases} \gamma & \text{if } i > 2^m \\ (x_0 \wedge \varphi(x_1, \ldots, x_m)) \vee (\neg x_0 \wedge \psi(x_1, \ldots, x_m)) & \text{if } i \leq 2^m. \end{cases}
$$

It is easy to see that if $i > 2^m$, then both $\langle \varphi, i \rangle \notin$ Threshold-SAT and $f(\langle \varphi, i \rangle) = \gamma \notin$ Majority-SAT. On the other hand, if $i \leq 2^m$, then $\langle \varphi, i \rangle$ belongs to Threshold-SAT if and only if $f(\langle \varphi, i \rangle)$ is satisfied by at least $i + 2^m - i = 2^m$ out of the 2^{m+1} possible assignments. ∎

6.2.2 BPP: Bounded-Error Probabilistic Polynomial Time

The acceptance criterion for PP machines is not very robust, since adding or deleting just one accepting path may result in a different outcome with regard to accepting or rejecting the input. In other words, as the input size grows to infinity, the error probability asymptotically can go to one half. Our goal now is to bound the error probability away from one half. To this end, we introduce the complexity class BPP.

Definition 6.12 (Bounded-Error Probabilistic Polynomial Time).
The class bounded-error probabilistic polynomial time *is defined by*

$$\text{BPP} = \left\{ A \;\middle|\; \begin{array}{l} \textit{there is some NPTM } M \textit{ and a constant } c,\, 0 < c \le 1/2, \\ \textit{such that for each input } x, \\ x \in A \implies \Pr(\{\alpha \mid M \textit{ accepts } x \textit{ on path } \alpha\}) \ge 1/2 + c; \\ x \notin A \implies \Pr(\{\alpha \mid M \textit{ accepts } x \textit{ on path } \alpha\}) \le 1/2 - c \end{array} \right\}.$$

That is, a BPP computation either accepts or rejects its input with high probability, leaving a proper gap around the value of one half that is strictly avoided by the acceptance or rejection probability. That is why BPP is a promise class as well.

Let r be a function from $\mathbb{N}$ to the real interval $[0, 1]$. We say that *an NPTM M accepts a set A in the sense of* BPP *with error probability at most r* if and only if

$$\Pr(\{\alpha \mid M(x) = \chi_A(x) \text{ on path } \alpha\}) \ge 1 - r(|x|),$$

where χ_A denotes the characteristic function of A. We now show that the error probability of BPP computations can be made exponentially small in the input size. Thus, the error in such a BPP computation is "negligibly small."

Theorem 6.13. *Let p be some fixed polynomial, and let A be any set in* BPP. *Then, there exists an NPTM N accepting A in the sense of* BPP *with error probability at most $2^{-p(n)}$.*

Proof.   Fix a polynomial p. Given any set A in BPP, let M be some NPTM and c with $0 < c \le 1/2$ be some constant such that:

$$\Pr(\{\alpha \mid M(x) = \chi_A(x) \text{ on path } \alpha\}) \ge \frac{1}{2} + c.$$

For any given input x of length n and for some polynomial q to be specified below, set $k = 2q(n) + 1$. As in the proof of Theorem 6.6, construct an NPTM N that, on input x, simulates the computation of $M(x)$ in k successive, independent trials. Thus, every path $\alpha = \alpha_1 \alpha_2 \cdots \alpha_k$ of $N(x)$ consists of a sequence of k paths α_i of $M(x)$. However, now we define α to accept if and only if a majority (i.e., at least $q(n) + 1$) of the paths α_i of $M(x)$ along α accept.

We have to show that we can find a polynomial q such that the error proability of $N(x)$, which is given by

$$E_N(x) = \Pr(\{\alpha \mid N(x) \ne \chi_A(x) \text{ on path } \alpha\})$$

is bounded above by $2^{-p(n)}$. By the way acceptance of a path $\alpha = \alpha_1 \alpha_2 \cdots \alpha_k$ is defined, for $a\alpha$ to be such an erroneous computation, there must exist some j satisfying that:

- $j \le q(n)$,
- j subpaths α_i along α are correct, i.e., $M(x) = \chi_A(x)$, and
- the remaining $k - j$ subpaths α_i along α are incorrect, i.e., $M(x) \ne \chi_A(x)$.

Denote the success probability of $M(x)$ by $\sigma = 1/2 + c$ and the error probability of $M(x)$ by $\epsilon = 1/2 - c$. Choosing among the k possible subpaths α_i of α the j correct ones and summing over all possible j, we can estimate the error probability of $N(x)$ as follows:

$$E_N(x) \leq \sum_{j=0}^{q(n)} \binom{k}{j} \sigma^j \epsilon^{k-j}. \tag{6.4}$$

Let $m > 0$ be chosen such that $j = \frac{k}{2} - m$ and $k - j = \frac{k}{2} + m$. Since $\epsilon < \sigma$, it follows that:

$$\sigma^j \epsilon^{k-j} = (\sigma \cdot \epsilon)^{\frac{k}{2}} \cdot \sigma^{-m} \cdot \epsilon^m = (\sigma \cdot \epsilon)^{\frac{k}{2}} \cdot \left(\frac{\epsilon}{\sigma}\right)^m < (\sigma \cdot \epsilon)^{\frac{k}{2}}. \tag{6.5}$$

The Binomial Theorem, which says that $(a + b)^k = \sum_{j=0}^{k} \binom{k}{j} a^j b^{k-j}$, implies for the special case of $a = b = 1$ that:

$$\sum_{j=0}^{k} \binom{k}{j} = 2^k. \tag{6.6}$$

Substituting (6.5) and (6.6) in (6.4) gives:

$$\begin{aligned}
E_N(x) &< (\sigma \cdot \epsilon)^{\frac{k}{2}} \cdot 2^k \\
&= (4\sigma\epsilon)^{\frac{k}{2}} \\
&= (1 - 4c^2)^{\frac{k}{2}}, \quad \text{since } \sigma\epsilon = (\tfrac{1}{2} + c)(\tfrac{1}{2} - c) = \tfrac{1}{4} - c^2 \\
&\leq (1 - 4c^2)^{q(n)},
\end{aligned}$$

where the latter inequality follows from

$$1 - 4c^2 < 1 \quad \text{and} \quad \frac{k}{2} = q(n) + \frac{1}{2} > q(n).$$

Since $1 - 4c^2 < 1$, we have $(1 - 4c^2)^t \leq 1/2$ for some integer t. Now, setting $q(n) = t \cdot p(n)$ gives

$$E_N(x) \leq (1 - 4c^2)^{t \cdot p(n)} \leq \left(\frac{1}{2}\right)^{p(n)} \leq 2^{-p(n)},$$

as desired.   ∎

The definitions immediately imply the following containments and the closure of BPP under complementation. Thus, Theorem 6.13 in particular applies to RP and coRP.

Fact 6.14 RP $\subseteq$ BPP $=$ coBPP $\subseteq$ PP.

What is the relationship between BPP and NP and between BPP and the polynomial hierarchy? We will see later that BPP is contained in the second level of the polynomial hierarchy. In contrast, BPP and NP are most likely to be incomparable, i.e., it is widely believed that neither BPP $\subseteq$ NP nor NP $\subseteq$ BPP. The following result gives some evidence that NP $\subseteq$ BPP is unlikely to hold. Note that the converse of Theorem 6.15 follows immediately from Fact 6.14.

Theorem 6.15. *If* NP $\subseteq$ BPP *then* NP $=$ RP.

Proof.   Suppose that NP $\subseteq$ BPP. By Theorem 6.13, there is some NPTM M accepting SAT in the sense of BPP with error probability at most 2^{-n}:

$$\Pr(\{\alpha \mid M(\varphi) = \chi_{\text{SAT}}(\varphi) \text{ on path } \alpha\}) \geq 1 - 2^{-n}, \qquad (6.7)$$

where $n = |\varphi|$ is the length of the boolean formula φ in some suitable encoding. Our goal is to show that SAT $\in$ RP by constructing an RP machine for SAT. Since SAT is $\leq_{\text{m}}^{\text{P}}$-complete in NP and since RP is $\leq_{\text{m}}^{\text{P}}$-closed, NP $=$ RP follows.

For any given boolean formula $\varphi = \varphi(x_1, x_2, \ldots, x_m)$ and for any bit string $s \in \{0, 1\}^*$, $|s| \leq m$, define the formula φ_s in $m - |s|$ variables that is obtained from φ by substituting the ith bit of s as the truth value of the ith variable in φ:

$$\varphi_0(x_2, x_3, \ldots x_m) = \varphi(0, x_2, x_3, \ldots, x_m)$$
$$\varphi_1(x_2, x_3, \ldots x_m) = \varphi(1, x_2, x_3, \ldots, x_m)$$
$$\varphi_{00}(x_3, x_4, \ldots x_m) = \varphi(0, 0, x_3, x_4, \ldots, x_m)$$
$$\vdots$$

Depending on the encoding used, simplifying φ to some formula φ_s may result in a shorter encoding string, so $|\varphi_s| \leq |\varphi|$. However, since the error probability of M depends on the input size, we want to make sure that $|\varphi_s| \geq |\varphi|$. To this end, we pad φ_s with a sufficient number of new variables $v_1, v_2, \ldots, v_{k(s)}$. For each φ_s, where $s \in \{0, 1\}^*$ and $|s| \leq m$, define the padded formula ψ_s in the variables $x_{m-|s|+1}, \ldots, x_m, v_1, \ldots, v_{k(s)}$ by

$$\psi_s = \varphi_s(x_{m-|s|+1}, \ldots, x_m) \wedge v_1 \wedge \ldots \wedge v_{k(s)},$$

where $k(s)$ is chosen large enough to ensure $|\psi_s| \geq |\varphi|$. Note that ψ_s is satisfiable if and only if φ_s is satisfiable.

To show that SAT $\in$ RP, we describe an NPTM N accepting SAT in the sense of RP. On input $\varphi(x_1, x_2, \ldots, x_m)$ of length n, N seeks to find a satisfying assignment for φ, if one exists. To this end, N first nondeterministically branches and uses M to construct, step by step, candidates of satisfying assignments for φ on each of its nondeterministic computation paths. Then, on each such path, N verifies deterministically whether or not the candidate constructed indeed satisfies φ.

In more detail, N on input $\varphi(x_1, x_2, \ldots, x_m)$ works as follows:

Step 1: Simulate $M(\psi_0)$. Since $|\psi_0| \geq |\varphi| = n$, Equation (6.7) implies that:

$$\Pr(\{\alpha \mid M(\psi_0) = \chi_{\text{SAT}}(\psi_0) \text{ on path } \alpha\}) \geq 1 - 2^{-|\psi_0|}$$
$$\geq 1 - 2^{-n}. \qquad (6.8)$$

- On the accepting paths α of $M(\psi_0)$, N stores the assignment 0 for the variable x_1 by setting the first bit of s_α to 0, and continues recursively by simulating $M(\psi_{00})$.
- On the rejecting paths α of $M(\psi_0)$, N stores the assignment 1 for the variable x_1 by setting the first bit of s_α to 0, and continues recursively by simulating $M(\psi_{10})$.

After m such steps, N has found on each path α a candidate s_α of a satisfying assignment for φ.

Step 2: On each path α, N checks deterministically whether s_α indeed satisfies φ. If so, N accepts on α; otherwise, N rejects on α.

If $\varphi \notin \text{SAT}$, $N(\varphi)$ rejects on all paths, due to the checking in Step 2. Thus,

$$\Pr(\{\alpha \mid N \text{ accepts } \varphi \text{ on path } \alpha\}) = 0.$$

Suppose now that $\varphi \in \text{SAT}$. By (6.8), the error probability of M is at most 2^{-n} in each of the m simulations in Step 1. Since each of these m trials are independent, the acceptance probability of $N(\varphi)$ can be estimated as follows:

$$\Pr(\{\alpha \mid N \text{ accepts } \varphi \text{ on path } \alpha\}) \geq \left(1 - 2^{-n}\right)^m$$
$$\geq \left(1 - m2^{-n}\right)$$
$$\geq \frac{1}{2},$$

where the latter inequality follows from the obvious fact that $m \leq n$, which implies $m2^{-n} \leq 2^{-1} = 1/2$. ∎

6.3 Quantifiers and Arthur-Merlin Games

6.3.1 Quantifiers and BPP

Recall Theorem 5.24, which characterizes the class NP by polynomially length-bounded existential quantifiers: A is in NP if and only if there is some set $B \in \text{P}$ and a polynomial p such that for each $x \in \Sigma^*$, $x \in A \iff (\exists^p w)\,[\langle x, w \rangle \in B]$. This can be rewritten as:

$$x \in A \implies (\exists^p w)\,[\langle x, w \rangle \in B];$$
$$x \notin A \implies (\forall^p w)\,[\langle x, w \rangle \notin B].$$

Thus, acceptance is expressed by the $\exists^p$ quantifier and rejection by the $\forall^p$ quantifier. Since all quantifiers considered are polynomially length-bounded, we drop their superscripts for convenience. For example, we simply write NP $= (\exists \mid \forall)$ to indicate the above characterization of NP. Similarly, coNP $= (\forall \mid \exists)$. More generally, the quantifier representations of the classes of the polynomial hierarchy given in Theorem 5.31 can be succinctly written in this notation. For example, $\Sigma_3^p = (\exists \forall \exists \mid \forall \exists \forall)$ and $\Pi_3^p = (\forall \exists \forall \mid \exists \forall \exists)$.

We will define complexity classes uniformly via their acceptance/rejection criteria using pairs of quantifier sequences as above. Of course, not all pairs of quantifier sequences are compatible with each other. It is sensible to require that they are consistent in the sense that they do not "overlap." For example, in the case of NP $= (\exists \mid \forall)$, it never happens that $(\exists w) [\langle x, w \rangle \in B] \wedge (\forall w) [\langle x, w \rangle \notin B]$, so $(\exists, \forall)$ is a sensible pair of quantifiers.

Definition 6.16. *1. Let $\mathfrak{Q}_1$ and $\mathfrak{Q}_2$ be two strings of n quantifiers each. The pair $(\mathfrak{Q}_1, \mathfrak{Q}_2)$ is sensible if and only if for each $(n + 1)$-ary predicate B, for each x, and for each $\mathbf{y} = (y_1, y_2, \ldots, y_n)$,*

$$(\mathfrak{Q}_1 \mathbf{y}) [B(x, \mathbf{y})] \wedge (\mathfrak{Q}_2 \mathbf{y}) [\neg B(x, \mathbf{y})]$$

is a contradiction. Here, y_i is the variable quantified by the ith quantifier in $\mathfrak{Q}_1$ and $\mathfrak{Q}_2$, respectively.

2. Let $(\mathfrak{Q}_1, \mathfrak{Q}_2)$ be a sensible pair of strings consisting of n (polynomially length-bounded) quantifiers each. Define the complexity class $(\mathfrak{Q}_1 \mid \mathfrak{Q}_2)$ as follows: L belongs to $(\mathfrak{Q}_1 \mid \mathfrak{Q}_2)$ if and only if there exists an $(n + 1)$-ary predicate $B \in$ P such that for each $x \in \Sigma^*$:

$$x \in L \implies (\mathfrak{Q}_1 \mathbf{y}) [B(x, \mathbf{y})];$$
$$x \notin L \implies (\mathfrak{Q}_2 \mathbf{y}) [\neg B(x, \mathbf{y})],$$

where $\mathbf{y} = (y_1, y_2, \ldots, y_n)$ and y_i is the variable quantified by the ith quantifier in $\mathfrak{Q}_1$ and $\mathfrak{Q}_2$, respectively, and $|y_i| \leq p(|x|)$ for some suitable polynomial p.

We now introduce a new quantifier, the *majority quantifier*, that is suitable to represent probabilistic classes such as BPP and RP.

Definition 6.17 (Polynomially Length-Bounded Majority Quantifier).
Let B be a predicate, and let p be a given polynomial. For each fixed string x, define $(\exists^+ y) [B(x, y)]$ to be true if and only if at least three-quarters of all strings y with $|y| \leq p(|x|)$ satisfy $B(x, y)$.

In the notation of Definition 6.16, we have BPP $= (\exists^+ \mid \exists^+)$ and RP $= (\exists^+ \mid \forall)$. Observe that swapping the quantifier strings for acceptance and rejection yields the complementary class. The easy proof of Fact 6.18 is left to the reader as Exercise 6.6.

Fact 6.18 *For each sensible pair $(\mathfrak{Q}_1, \mathfrak{Q}_2)$ of quantifier strings,*

$$(\mathfrak{Q}_1 \mid \mathfrak{Q}_2) = \text{co}(\mathfrak{Q}_2 \mid \mathfrak{Q}_1).$$

Corollary 6.19. BPP *is closed under complementation.*

The above uniform approach to define complexity classes via quantifiers gives us a powerful tool for studying the inclusion relations between certain complexity classes and quantifier-based hierarchies such as the Arthur-Merlin hierarchy, which will be introduced and studied in Section 6.3.2. Our goal now is to give further characterizations of BPP in terms of quantifiers. This will allow us to prove that BPP is contained in the polynomial hierarchy. First, we provide some technical lemmas.

Lemma 6.20. *Let B be any predicate in* P, *let x be any string, and suppose that* $(\forall y)(\exists^+ z)[B(x, y, z)]$. *Then, the following two statements are true:*

1. $(\exists^+ Z)(\forall y)(\exists z \in Z)[B(x, y, z)]$.
2. $(\forall Y)(\exists^+ z)(\forall y \in Y)[B(x, y, z)]$.

Here, the polynomials implicitly bounding the lengths of the quantified variables depend on the length n of x. In the first statement, if $|z| \leq p(n)$ for some polynomial p, then Z is viewed as a variable ranging over sets of strings of length at most $p(n)$. To ensure that Z itself can be represented by a string of length polynomially in n, we require Z to satisfy $||Z|| = q(n)$ for some polynomial q. Furthermore, let r be some polynomial bounding the lengths of the strings y, i.e., $y \leq r(n)$. An analogous comment applies to the set variable Y in the second statement.

Proof.   Let $B \in$ P, let x be any string of length n, and suppose that

$$(\forall y)(\exists^+ z)[B(x, y, z)]. \tag{6.9}$$

We prove only the first statement of the lemma; the proof of the second statement is analogous and thus omitted; see Exercise 6.7. Let p, q, and r be polynomials bounding the variable lengths as explained in the lemma.

Let $S = \{0, 1\}^{\leq p(n)}$ be the set of all binary strings of length at most $p(n)$. Clearly, $||S|| = 2^{p(n)+1} - 1$. Our set variable Z ranges over subsets of S having exactly $q(n)$ elements. There are exactly $\binom{||S||}{q(n)}$ such subsets. We now estimate the number of subsets Z of S with exactly $q(n)$ elements that do *not* satisfy

$$(\forall y)(\exists z \in Z)[B(x, y, z)].$$

Equivalently, we may ask how many subsets Z of S with exactly $q(n)$ elements *do* satisfy

$$(\exists y)(\forall z \in Z)[\neg B(x, y, z)]. \tag{6.10}$$

Consider any fixed string $\tilde{y}$. By our supposition (6.9), at most $1/4$ of all strings z with $|z| \leq p(n)$ do not satisfy the predicate $B(x, \tilde{y}, z)$. Thus, for this fixed $\tilde{y}$, the number of subsets $Z \subseteq S$ with $||Z|| = q(n)$ satisfying $(\forall z \in Z)[\neg B(x, \tilde{y}, z)]$ is at most

$$\binom{\lceil 2^{-2}(2^{p(n)+1} - 1)\rceil}{q(n)} \leq \binom{2^{p(n)-1}}{q(n)}.$$

There are exactly $2^{r(n)+1} - 1$ strings y of length at most $r(n)$. It follows that the number of subsets $Z \subseteq S$ with $||Z|| = q(n)$ satisfying $(\exists y)(\forall z \in Z)[\neg B(x, y, z)]$ is at most

$$\left(2^{r(n)+1} - 1\right) \cdot \binom{2^{p(n)}-1}{q(n)} \leq 2^{r(n)+1} \cdot \binom{2^{p(n)}-1}{q(n)}.$$

Since there is a total of $\binom{2^{p(n)+1}-1}{q(n)}$ subsets of S with $q(n)$ elements, the proportion of such subsets $Z \subseteq S$ with $||Z|| = q(n)$ satisfying (6.10) can be estimated above by

$$\frac{2^{r(n)+1} \cdot \binom{2^{p(n)}-1}{q(n)}}{\binom{2^{p(n)+1}-1}{q(n)}} \leq \frac{2^{r(n)+1}}{2^{q(n)}} = \frac{1}{4},$$

where the latter equality can be achieved by choosing $q(n) = r(n) + 3$. It follows that

$$(\exists^+ Z)(\forall y)(\exists z \in Z)[B(x, y, z)]$$

as desired. ∎

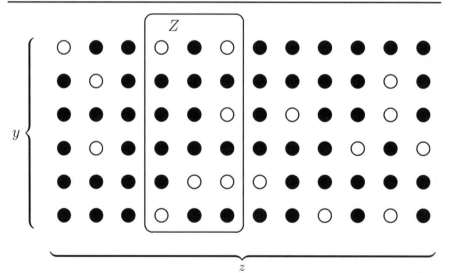

Fig. 6.4. Illustration of the first statement of Lemma 6.20

Here is an illustrative interpretation of the assertions of Lemma 6.20. As an example, consider its first statement:

$$(\forall y)(\exists^+ z)[B(x, y, z)] \implies (\exists^+ Z)(\forall y)(\exists z \in Z)[B(x, y, z)]. \qquad (6.11)$$

This implication can be seen by looking at Figure 6.4, which gives a matrix whose entries are the values of the predicate $B(x, y, z)$ for fixed x and varying y and z. A full circle means that $B(x, y, z)$ is true, and an empty circle means that $B(x, y, z)$ is false. The left-hand side of (6.11) says that every row y has many (namely, at least three-quarters) full circles. The right-hand side of (6.11) says that for many "windows" Z, every row of the window has at least one full circle.

Lemma 6.20 is applied in the proofs of Lemma 6.21 and Theorem 6.22 below. The assertion of Lemma 6.21 is "almost" the unlikely inclusion

$$\Sigma_2^p = (\exists\forall \,|\, \forall\exists) \subseteq (\forall\exists \,|\, \exists\forall) = \Pi_2^p,$$

except that the rejection conditions of Lemma 6.21 have an $\exists^+$ quantifier in place of an $\exists$ quantifier.

Lemma 6.21. $(\exists\forall \,|\, \forall\exists^+) \subseteq (\forall\exists \,|\, \exists^+\forall)$.

Proof. Let A be any set in $(\exists\forall \,|\, \forall\exists^+)$. By Definition 6.16, there exists a predicate $B \in P$ such that for each x,

$$
\begin{aligned}
x \notin A &\implies (\forall y)\,(\exists^+ z)\,[\neg B(x, y, z)] &&\text{as per Definition 6.16}\\
&\implies (\exists^+ Z)\,(\forall y)\,(\exists z \in Z)\,[\neg B(x, y, z)] &&\text{by part 1 of Lemma 6.20}\\
&\implies (\exists Z)\,(\forall y)\,(\exists z \in Z)\,[\neg B(x, y, z)]\\
&\implies (\forall y)\,(\exists z)\,[\neg B(x, y, z)]\\
&\implies x \notin A,
\end{aligned}
$$

where the last implication again follows from Definition 6.16, applying the contrapositive of $x \in A \implies (\exists y)\,(\forall z)\,[B(x, y, z)]$. Now, defining the predicate C by

$$C(x, y, Z) \equiv (\forall z \in Z)\,[B(x, y, z)],$$

it follows that

$$x \notin A \iff (\exists^+ Z)\,(\forall y)\,[\neg C(x, y, Z)]; \tag{6.12}$$
$$x \notin A \iff (\exists Z)\,(\forall y)\,[\neg C(x, y, Z)]. \tag{6.13}$$

Negating (6.13), we obtain

$$x \in A \iff (\forall Z)\,(\exists y)\,[C(x, y, Z)]. \tag{6.14}$$

Since Z contains only polynomially many elements, $B \in P$ implies $C \in P$. By Definition 6.16, it follows from (6.12) and (6.14) that A is a set in $(\forall\exists \,|\, \exists^+\forall)$. ∎

The following result is known as the "BPP Theorem," as it provides two additional useful characterizations of the class BPP in terms of quantifier-based complexity classes. Note that Theorem 6.22 holds in any (sensible) quantifier context.

Theorem 6.22 (Zachos and Heller).

$$\text{BPP} = (\exists^+ \,|\, \exists^+) = (\forall\exists^+ \,|\, \exists^+\forall) = (\exists^+\forall \,|\, \forall\exists^+).$$

Proof.   It is enough to prove the equality $(\exists^+ \,|\, \exists^+) = (\forall\exists^+ \,|\, \exists^+\forall)$. The other equality follows immediately from Fact 6.18 and Corollary 6.19, since

$$(\forall\exists^+ \,|\, \exists^+\forall) = \mathrm{co}(\exists^+\forall \,|\, \forall\exists^+).$$

To prove the inclusion $(\forall\exists^+ \,|\, \exists^+\forall) \subseteq (\exists^+ \,|\, \exists^+)$, let A be any set in $(\forall\exists^+ \,|\, \exists^+\forall)$. By Definition 6.16, there exists a set $B \in \mathrm{P}$ such that for each x,

$$x \in A \implies (\forall y)\,(\exists^+ z)\,[B(x,y,z)]$$
$$\implies (\exists^+ \langle y, z \rangle)\,[C(x, \langle y, z \rangle)],$$

where the predicate C is defined by $C(x, \langle y, z \rangle) \equiv B(x, y, z)$. Note that C is in P. Furthermore, for each x,

$$x \notin A \implies (\exists^+ y)\,(\forall z)\,[\neg B(x, y, z)]$$
$$\implies (\exists^+ \langle y, z \rangle)\,[\neg C(x, \langle y, z \rangle)].$$

Thus, A is in $(\exists^+ \,|\, \exists^+)$.

Conversely, to prove the inclusion $(\exists^+ \,|\, \exists^+) \subseteq (\forall\exists^+ \,|\, \exists^+\forall)$, let A be any set in $(\exists^+ \,|\, \exists^+)$. Thus, there exists a set $B \in \mathrm{P}$ such that for each x,

$$x \in A \implies (\exists^+ y)\,[B(x, y)]; \tag{6.15}$$
$$x \notin A \implies (\exists^+ y)\,[\neg B(x, y)]. \tag{6.16}$$

y	s_0	s_1	s_2	$\cdots$	s_{m-2}	s_{m-1}
z						
s_0	b_0	b_1	b_2	$\cdots$	b_{m-2}	b_{m-1}
s_1	b_1	b_2	b_3	$\cdots$	b_{m-1}	b_0
s_2	b_2	b_3	b_4	$\cdots$	b_0	b_1
$\vdots$	$\vdots$	$\vdots$	$\vdots$	$\ddots$	$\vdots$	$\vdots$
s_{m-2}	b_{m-2}	b_{m-1}	b_0	$\cdots$	b_{m-4}	b_{m-3}
s_{m-1}	b_{m-1}	b_0	b_1	$\cdots$	b_{m-3}	b_{m-2}

Table 6.3. Definition of predicate C in the proof of Theorem 6.22

Let p be some polynomial bounding the lengths of the variables y quantified in (6.15) and (6.16). Let x be any fixed string of length n. Let $S = \{0,1\}^{\leq p(n)}$ be the set of all binary strings of length at most $p(n)$. Suppose that the strings in S are lexicographically ordered, i.e., $S = \{s_0, s_1, \ldots, s_{m-1}\}$, where $m = 2^{p(n)+1} - 1$. For fixed x, define a predicate $C(x, y, z)$ as follows, where the variables y and z range over the strings in S:

$$C(x, s_i, s_j) \equiv B(x, s_{i+j \bmod m}),$$

where i and j are from the set $\mathbb{Z}_m = \{0, 1, \ldots, m - 1\}$, i.e., they are residues modulo m. Table 6.3 illustrates the definition of C: Letting $b_i = B(x, s_i)$ for $i \in \mathbb{Z}_m$, the ith row of Table 6.3 gives the values of $C(x, y, s_i)$ for varying y, and the jth column of Table 6.3 gives the values of $C(x, s_j, z)$ for varying z. Note that $C(x, y, z)$ is symmetric in its last two arguments. Thus, the rows are cyclically shifted by one position, and so are the columns. Consequently, every row and every column in Table 6.3 has the same number of ones and the same number of zeros.

Note that $B \in \text{P}$ implies $C \in \text{P}$. From (6.15) it follows that for each x,

$$x \in A \implies (\forall z)\,(\exists^+ y)\,[C(x, y, z)] \qquad \text{since each row has the same number of ones}$$

$$\implies (\forall y)\,(\exists^+ z)\,[C(x, y, z)] \qquad \text{since } C \text{ is symmetric in its last two arguments}$$

$$\implies (\forall Y)\,(\exists^+ z)\,\underbrace{(\forall y \in Y)\,[C(x, y, z)]}_{D(x, z, Y)} \qquad \text{by part 2 of Lemma 6.20,}$$

where the predicate D is defined by $D(x, z, Y) \equiv (\forall y \in Y)\,[C(x, y, z)]$. Since the for-all quantifier in D ranges over a domain of polynomial size, $C \in \text{P}$ implies $D \in \text{P}$.

Similarly, from (6.16) it follows that for each x,

$$x \notin A \implies (\forall z)\,(\exists^+ y)\,[\neg C(x, y, z)] \qquad \text{since each row has the same number of zeros}$$

$$\implies (\forall y)\,(\exists^+ z)\,[\neg C(x, y, z)] \qquad \text{since } C \text{ is symmetric in its last two arguments}$$

$$\implies (\exists^+ Z)\,(\forall y)\,\underbrace{(\exists z \in Z)\,[\neg C(x, y, z)]}_{\neg D(x, y, Z)} \qquad \text{by part 1 of Lemma 6.20}$$

$$\implies (\exists^+ Z)\,(\forall y)\,[\neg D(x, y, Z)].$$

Thus, A is in $(\forall \exists^+ \mid \exists^+ \forall)$. ∎

Corollary 6.23. BPP $\subseteq \Sigma_2^p \cap \Pi_2^p$.

Proof. Since BPP is closed under complementation as per Corollary 6.19, it is enough to prove the inclusion BPP $\subseteq \Sigma_2^p$. So, let A be any set in BPP. By Theorem 6.22, BPP $= (\exists^+ \forall \mid \forall \exists^+)$. Thus, there exists some $B \in \text{P}$ such that for each x,

$$x \in A \implies (\exists^+ y)\,(\forall z)\,[B(x, y, z)]$$
$$\implies (\exists y)\,(\forall z)\,[B(x, y, z)],$$

and

$$x \notin A \implies (\forall y)\,(\exists^+ z)\,[\neg B(x, y, z)]$$
$$\implies (\forall y)\,(\exists z)\,[\neg B(x, y, z)].$$

By Theorem 5.31, A is in Σ_2^p. ∎

6.3.2 Arthur-Merlin Hierarchy

Now listen to the story of King Arthur and Merlin, the mighty wizard.

Story 6.24 (Arthur-Merlin Games)   *Merlin and Arthur play the following game. The goal of the game is for them to jointly solve some problem. For example, suppose they are trying to solve the graph nonisomorphism problem. Given a pair of graphs, G and H, they thus want to decide whether or not G and H are nonisomorphic. They draw one after the other taking turns, and they gamble for every problem instance. Merlin's intention always is to convince Arthur that the given graphs indeed are nonisomorphic, even if in fact they are isomorphic. So, one move of Merlin is to present a proof that the given graphs are nonisomorphic.*

However, Arthur is suspicious and does not trust the sneaky wizard. Of course, he himself cannot come up with such powerful proofs of his own. After all, Merlin has supernatural, nondeterministic powers and spells at his disposal, and Arthur does not. Still, Arthur doubts that the proofs are valid, flips some coins and, depending on these random choices, he challenges the wizard's proofs. Such is one of Arthur's moves in this game. Again, it's Merlin's turn to move, and so on. Eventually, after a finite number of moves, they will have determined whether or not to accept the input. It is also possible that Arthur makes the first move in a game.

To be somewhat more specific, suppose that Merlin is represented by an NP machine M, and that Arthur is represented by a randomized polynomial-time bounded Turing machine A. Let x be the problem instance at stake, and let L be the problem they want to solve. One move of Merlin is a proof (or witness; cf. Example 5.22 and Definition 5.23) for "$x \in L$," and he can find such a proof by simulating $M(x, y)$, where y encodes the history of moves made as yet. That is, the string y describes all nondeterministic choices of Merlin and all random choices of Arthur previously made in this game. In order to satisfy the impatient king, Merlin must convince him with overwhelming probability. One move of Arthur is given by the computation of $A(x, y)$ that depends on Arthur's random choices, where again y encodes the previous history of the game.

Just as the polynomial hierarchy can be described by alternating (polynomially length-bounded) existential and universal quantifiers (see Theorem 5.31 in Section 5.2), the idea of Arthur-Merlin games is captured by alternating (polynomially length-bounded) existential and probabilistic quantifiers. The $\exists$ quantifier represents one of Merlin's moves, which is an NP computation, and the $\exists^+$ quantifier represents one of Arthur's moves, which is a BPP computation. According to the notation from Definition 6.16, one obtains a hierarchy of complexity classes, the so-called Arthur-Merlin hierarchy.

Definition 6.25 (Arthur-Merlin Hierarchy).
The levels of the Arthur-Merlin hierarchy *are the following classes:*

$$A = (\exists^+ \,|\, \exists^+), \quad AM = (\exists^+\exists \,|\, \exists^+\forall), \quad AMA = (\exists^+\exists\exists^+ \,|\, \exists^+\forall\exists^+),$$
$$M = (\exists \,|\, \forall), \quad MA = (\exists\exists^+ \,|\, \forall\exists^+), \quad MAM = (\exists\exists^+\exists \,|\, \forall\exists^+\forall), \ldots$$

Define the Arthur-Merlin hierarchy, AMH, *as the union of all these classes.*

Example 6.26 (Arthur-Merlin Hierarchy).   Consider the class MA, which consists of precisely those problems L for which there exist an NPTM M and a randomized polynomial-time Turing machine A such that for each input x:

- If $x \in L$, then there exists a path y of $M(x)$ such that $A(x, y)$ accepts with probability at least $3/4$. That is, Arthur cannot refute Merlin's correct proof y for "$x \in L$," and Merlin wins.
- If $x \notin L$, then for each path y of $M(x)$, $A(x, y)$ rejects with probability at least $3/4$. That is, Arthur cannot be fooled by Merlin's false proofs for "$x \in L$" and thus wins.

Analogously, the classes AM, MAM, AMA, . . . can be described, see Exercise 6.8.

Certainly, an error probability of up to $1/4$ is unacceptably large. Note, however, that the probability threshold of $3/4$ in defining the majority quantifier $\exists^+$ (see Definition 6.17), which occurs in the classes introduced in Definition 6.25, is chosen at will. Other thresholds would work as well. Using the probability amplification techniques from Section 6.2, the error probability can be made exponentially small. In other words, one might use even a probability threshold of $1/2 + \epsilon$ for an arbitrary, fixed constant $\epsilon > 0$ in the definition of the $\exists^+$ quantifier—and thus in Definition 6.25—and would still be able to amplify so as to achieve an exponentially small error probability. An error that unlikely can be considered negligible, as even hardware errors may be expected to occur with a higher probability.

The following result shows that, for a constant number of moves, the Arthur-Merlin hierarchy collapses down to AM. Whether or not any of the inclusions NP $\subseteq$ MA $\subseteq$ AM or BPP $\subseteq$ MA is proper is an open question. Moreover, it is open whether or not MA and AM are closed under complement.

Theorem 6.27. NP $\cup$ BPP $\subseteq$ MA $\subseteq$ AM $=$ AMA $=$ MAM $= \cdots =$ AMH.

Proof.   By Definition 6.25, NP $\subseteq$ MA and BPP $\subseteq$ MA. To prove the inclusion MA $\subseteq$ AM, we first characterize these classes in terms of quantifier-based classes and then apply Lemma 6.21. That is, we will prove that

$$\text{MA} = (\exists \forall \,|\, \forall \exists^+) \subseteq (\forall \exists \,|\, \exists^+ \forall) = \text{AM}. \tag{6.17}$$

In what follows, we apply Lemma 6.21 and Theorem 6.22 in certain quantifier contexts. The quantifiers to which the lemma or the BPP Theorem are applied are underlined so as to distinguish them from their quantifier context.

The first equality in (6.17) can be seen as follows:

$$
\begin{array}{lll}
\text{MA} = (\exists \underline{\exists^+} \,|\, \forall \underline{\exists^+}) & \text{by Definition 6.25} \\[4pt]
\quad = (\exists \underline{\exists^+ \forall} \,|\, \forall \underline{\forall \exists^+}) & \text{by Theorem 6.22 in quantifier context} \\[4pt]
\quad \subseteq (\exists \exists \forall \,|\, \forall \forall \exists^+) & \text{since } (\exists^+ v)\,[\cdots]\text{ implies }(\exists v)\,[\cdots] \\[4pt]
\quad = (\exists \forall \,|\, \forall \exists^+) & \text{by combining adjacent quantifiers of the same type} \\[4pt]
\quad \subseteq (\exists \exists^+ \,|\, \forall \exists^+) & \text{since } (\forall v)\,[\cdots]\text{ implies }(\exists^+ v)\,[\cdots] \\[4pt]
\quad = \text{MA} & \text{by Definition 6.25.}
\end{array}
$$

The last equality in (6.17) can be seen as follows:

$$
\begin{aligned}
\text{AM} &= (\exists^+\exists \mid \exists^+\forall) & &\text{by Definition 6.25} \\
&= (\forall\exists^+\exists \mid \exists^+\forall\forall) & &\text{by Theorem 6.22 in quantifier context} \\
&\subseteq (\forall\exists\exists \mid \exists^+\forall\forall) & &\text{since } (\exists^+v)[\cdots] \text{ implies } (\exists v)[\cdots] \\
&= (\forall\exists \mid \exists^+\forall) & &\text{by combining adjacent quantifiers of the same type} \\
&\subseteq (\exists^+\exists \mid \exists^+\forall) & &\text{since } (\forall v)[\cdots] \text{ implies } (\exists^+v)[\cdots] \\
&= \text{AM} & &\text{by Definition 6.25.}
\end{aligned}
$$

By Lemma 6.21, inclusion (6.17) is proven, so MA $\subseteq$ AM.

We now show that the entire Arthur-Merlin hierarchy collapses down to AM. It is clear that we have the inclusions AM $\subseteq$ MAM, AM $\subseteq$ AMA, etc. Conversely, applying the inclusion MA $\subseteq$ AM from (6.17) in a quantifier context implies

$$\text{AMA} \subseteq \text{AAM} \subseteq \text{AM},$$

since two adjacent $\exists^+$ quantifiers can be combined to one $\exists^+$ quantifier the same way that this can be done for the $\exists$ or the $\forall$ quantifier.[3]

The inclusion MAM $\subseteq$ AM can be seen as follows:

$$
\begin{aligned}
\text{MAM} &= (\exists\exists^+\exists \mid \forall\exists^+\forall) & &\text{by Definition 6.25} \\
&= (\exists\exists^+\forall\exists \mid \forall\forall\exists^+\forall) & &\text{by Theorem 6.22 in quantifier context} \\
&\subseteq (\exists\exists\forall\exists \mid \forall\forall\exists^+\forall) & &\text{since } (\exists^+v)[\cdots] \text{ implies } (\exists v)[\cdots] \\
&= (\exists\forall\exists \mid \forall\exists^+\forall) & &\text{by combining adjacent quantifiers of the same type} \\
&\subseteq (\forall\exists\exists \mid \exists^+\forall\forall) & &\text{by Lemma 6.21 in quantifier context} \\
&= (\forall\exists \mid \exists^+\forall) & &\text{by combining adjacent quantifiers of the same type} \\
&\subseteq (\exists^+\exists \mid \exists^+\forall) & &\text{since } (\forall v)[\cdots] \text{ implies } (\exists^+v)[\cdots] \\
&= \text{AM} & &\text{by Definition 6.25.}
\end{aligned}
$$

Thus, AM $=$ MAM $=$ AMA. The remaining equalities now follow by induction. $\blacksquare$

The following corollary states the relations between the Arthur-Merlin classes and the polynomial hierarchy. In addition, the containment of BPP in the second level of the polynomial hierarchy stated in Corollary 6.23 is strengthened.

Corollary 6.28.   *1.* MA $\subseteq \Sigma_2^p$ *and* AM $\subseteq \Pi_2^p$.
   2. If NP $\subseteq$ coAM *then* $\Sigma_2^p = \Pi_2^p = $ PH.
   3. BPP $\subseteq$ MA $\cap$ coMA.

---

[3] Note that, for example, $(\exists^+\exists^+ \mid \exists^+\exists^+) = (\exists^+ \mid \exists^+) = $ BPP. Equivalently, this can be written as $\text{BPP}^{\text{BPP}} = \text{BPP}$, see Problem 6.3(a).

Proof.   1. MA $= (\exists\exists^{+}\,|\,\forall\exists^{+}) = (\exists\forall\,|\,\forall\exists^{+}) \subseteq (\exists\forall\,|\,\forall\exists) = \Sigma_2^p$, where the second equality follows from (6.17) in the proof of Theorem 6.27. The inclusion AM $\subseteq \Pi_2^p$ can be shown analogously.

2. Suppose that NP $\subseteq$ coAM, i.e., $(\exists\,|\,\forall) \subseteq (\exists^{+}\forall\,|\,\exists^{+}\exists)$. Then,

$$\Pi_2^p = (\forall\exists\,|\,\exists\forall) \subseteq (\forall\underline{\exists^{+}\forall}\,|\,\underline{\exists\exists^{+}\exists}) = \text{coMAM} = \text{coAM} \subseteq \Sigma_2^p,$$

where the last inclusion follows from part 1 of this corollary. By Theorem 5.33, the polynomial hierarchy collapses down to its second level.

3. This follows immediately from Theorem 6.27 and the closure of BPP under complementation stated in Fact 6.14.   ∎

Theorem 6.29 (Schöning). $\Sigma_2^{p,\text{AM}\cap\text{coAM}} = \Sigma_2^p$.

Proof.   The proof is akin to the (relativized version of the) proof of Theorem 5.31. The inclusion $\Sigma_2^p \subseteq \Sigma_2^{p,\text{AM}\cap\text{coAM}}$ is straightforward. To prove the converse inclusion, $\Sigma_2^{p,\text{AM}\cap\text{coAM}} \subseteq \Sigma_2^p$, we will show the equivalent inclusion $\Pi_2^{p,\text{AM}\cap\text{coAM}} \subseteq \Pi_2^p$. So let L be any set in $\Pi_2^{p,\text{AM}\cap\text{coAM}}$. By the relativized version of Corollary 5.32, there exists a set $A \in \text{AM} \cap \text{coAM}$ and a predicate $B \in \text{P}^A$ such that for each x,

$$x \in L \iff (\forall y)\,(\exists z)\,[B(x,y,z)],$$

where all quantifiers are polynomially length-bounded as usual. Let M be some DPOTM deciding B with oracle A, i.e., $L(M^A) = B$. Define a predicate C as follows:

$$C(u,v,x,y,z) \equiv \begin{cases} M^A(x,y,z) \text{ accepts, } u = \langle u_1, u_2, \ldots, u_k \rangle, \\ \text{and } v = \langle v_1, v_2, \ldots, v_\ell \rangle, \text{ where } u \text{ and } v \\ \text{contain exactly the queries of } M^A(x,y,z), \\ \text{and exactly the queries in } u \text{ have the answer "yes"} \\ \text{and exactly the queries in } v \text{ have the answer "no."} \end{cases}$$

Define the sets

$$A_{\text{yes}} = \{\langle u_1, u_2, \ldots, u_k \rangle \mid u_1, u_2, \ldots, u_k \in A\};$$
$$A_{\text{no}} = \{\langle v_1, v_2, \ldots, v_\ell \rangle \mid v_1, v_2, \ldots, v_\ell \notin A\}.$$

Since both A and $\overline{A}$ are in AM, both A_{yes} and A_{no} are in AM. Defining a predicate D by $D(u,v) \equiv (u \in A_{\text{yes}} \land v \in A_{\text{no}})$, it follows that D also is in AM. Thus, for each x,

$$\begin{aligned} x \in L \iff & (\forall y)\,(\exists z)\,[M^A(x,y,z) \text{ accepts}] \\ \iff & (\forall y)\,(\exists z)\,(\exists u)\,(\exists v)\,[C(u,v,x,y,z) \land \\ & u_1, u_2, \ldots, u_k \in A \land v_1, v_2, \ldots, v_\ell \notin A] \\ \iff & (\forall y)\,(\exists z)\,(\exists u)\,(\exists v)\,[C(u,v,x,y,z) \land D(u,v)]. \end{aligned}$$

By (6.17) in the proof of Theorem 6.27, we have AM $= (\forall\exists \,|\, \exists^+\forall)$. Thus, there exists a predicate E in P such that

$$D(u, v) \implies (\forall r)\,(\exists s)\,[E(u, v, r, s)];$$
$$\neg D(u, v) \implies (\exists^+ r)\,(\forall s)\,[\neg E(u, v, r, s)].$$

Thus, for each x,

$$x \in L \implies (\forall y)\,(\exists z)\,(\exists u)\,(\exists v)\,[C(u, v, x, y, z) \,\wedge\, (\forall r)\,(\exists s)\,[E(u, v, r, s)]]$$
$$\implies (\forall y)\,(\exists z)\,(\exists u)\,(\exists v)\,(\forall r)\,(\exists s)\,[C(u, v, x, y, z) \,\wedge\, E(u, v, r, s)]$$

and

$$x \notin L \implies (\exists y)\,(\forall z)\,(\forall u)\,(\forall v)\,[\neg C(u, v, x, y, z) \,\vee\, (\exists^+ r)\,(\forall s)\,[\neg E(u, v, r, s)]]$$
$$\implies (\exists y)\,(\forall z)\,(\forall u)\,(\forall v)\,(\exists^+ r)\,(\forall s)\,[\neg C(u, v, x, y, z) \,\vee\, \neg E(u, v, r, s)].$$

Combining contiguous quantifiers of the same type to one quantifier, we conclude that L is a member of the class

$$(\forall\underline{\exists}\underline{\forall}\exists \,|\, \exists\underline{\forall}\underline{\exists}^+\forall) \subseteq (\forall\underline{\forall}\exists\exists \,|\, \exists\exists^+\underline{\forall}\underline{\forall}) \subseteq (\forall\exists \,|\, \exists\forall) = \Pi_2^p,$$

where the first inclusion follows from applying Lemma 6.21 in a quantifier context (again underlining the quantifiers to which the lemma is applied). The second inclusion follows from combining contiguous quantifiers of the same type to one quantifier and from weakening $\exists^+$ to $\exists$.   ∎

Problem 6.3(c) states that AM $\cap$ coAM is low for AM, i.e., $\mathrm{AM}^{\mathrm{AM} \cap \mathrm{coAM}} = \mathrm{AM}$.

As an immediate consequence, Theorem 6.29 implies that every coAM set in NP is low for the second level of the polynomial hierarchy. This result will be applied in the proof of the forthcoming Theorem 6.45, which says that the graph isomorphism problem is in Low_2.

Corollary 6.30 (Schöning).   NP $\cap$ coAM $\subseteq \mathrm{Low}_2$.

6.4 Counting Classes

In Section 6.2, probabilistic classes such as PP, RP, ZPP, and BPP were introduced based on the probability weight of accepting computations. Remark 6.3 pointed out an alternative view on these classes that is based on counting the accepting and rejecting computations of NPTMs. In this section, we develop a theory of counting-based complexity classes, which will be employed later in Section 6.5 to prove certain lowness properties of the graph isomorphism problem.

We start by defining the function classes #P and GapP and stating some of their basic properties. The proof of Proposition 6.32 is left to the reader as Exercise 6.11.

Definition 6.31 (#P and GapP). *For any NPTM M and for any input string x, let $\mathrm{acc}_M(x)$ denote the number of accepting computation paths of $M(x)$, and let $\mathrm{rej}_M(x)$ denote the number of rejecting computation paths of $M(x)$. Both acc_M and rej_M map from Σ^* to $\mathbb{N}$. Define the function $\mathrm{gap}_M : \Sigma^* \to \mathbb{Z}$ by*

$$\mathrm{gap}_M(x) = \mathrm{acc}_M(x) - \mathrm{rej}_M(x).$$

Define the following two function classes:

$$\#\mathrm{P} = \{\mathrm{acc}_M \mid M \text{ is some NPTM}\};$$
$$\mathrm{GapP} = \{\mathrm{gap}_M \mid M \text{ is some NPTM}\}.$$

Note that the NPTMs in Definition 6.31 are not required to be normalized. This is reasonable because, for example, normalized machines always have an even gap.

Proposition 6.32. *1.* $\mathrm{GapP} = \#\mathrm{P} - \#\mathrm{P} = \#\mathrm{P} - \mathrm{FP} = \mathrm{FP} - \#\mathrm{P}$, *where the minus sign refers to elementwise subtraction, not to set-theoretic difference, i.e., for function classes $\mathcal{F}$ and $\mathcal{G}$, $\mathcal{F} - \mathcal{G} = \{f - g \mid f \in \mathcal{F} \text{ and } g \in \mathcal{G}\}$.*
2. $\mathrm{FP} \subseteq \#\mathrm{P} \subseteq \mathrm{GapP}$.

#P and GapP share some useful closure properties, including closure under addition and multiplication, that will be useful later on. On the other hand, GapP is even closed under subtraction, a property #P is unlikely to possess. We summarize below some of the closure properties of GapP. The proof of Lemma 6.33 is left to the reader as Exercise 6.11, which also asks to find out which of the closure properties stated for GapP are shared by #P. Of the closure properties stated in Lemma 6.33, closure under binomial coefficients is perhaps the most useful and least obvious.

Lemma 6.33 (Closure Properties of GapP).

1. GapP *is closed under subtraction: If $f \in$ GapP then $-f \in$ GapP.*
2. If $f \in$ GapP and $p \in$ Pol, then the functions a and b defined below are in GapP:

$$a(x) = \sum_{|y| \leq p(|x|)} f(\langle x, y \rangle) \quad \text{and} \quad b(x) = \prod_{0 \leq y \leq p(|x|)} f(\langle x, y \rangle).$$

3. If $f, g \in$ GapP and $0 \leq g(x) \leq p(|x|)$ for some polynomial p, then the functions c, d, and e defined below are in GapP:

$$c(x) = f(\langle x, g(x) \rangle) \quad \text{and} \quad d(x) = \binom{f(x)}{g(x)} \quad \text{and} \quad e(x) = f(x)^{g(x)}.$$

It was noted in Remark 6.3 that PP can be characterized using #P functions. Alternatively, PP can be characterized using GapP functions; see Exercise 6.9(a). Definition 6.34 introduces the counting classes $\oplus$P, $\mathrm{C}_=$P, and SPP via GapP functions. They are examples of so-called *gap-definable* complexity classes. In light of Proposition 6.32, $\oplus$P, $\mathrm{C}_=$P, and SPP can be characterized via #P functions as well, just as PP was characterized via #P functions in Remark 6.3; see Exercise 6.9(b).

Definition 6.34 (Counting Classes).   *Define the following language classes:*

$$\text{C}_{=}\text{P} = \{A \mid (\exists f \in \text{GapP})\,(\forall x \in \Sigma^*)\,[x \in A \iff f(x) = 0]\};$$
$$\oplus\text{P} = \{A \mid (\exists f \in \text{GapP})\,(\forall x \in \Sigma^*)\,[x \in A \iff f(x) \equiv 1 \bmod 2]\};$$
$$\text{SPP} = \left\{ A \left| \begin{array}{l} (\exists f \in \text{GapP})\,(\forall x \in \Sigma^*) \\ {}[(x \in A \implies f(x) = 1) \wedge (x \notin A \implies f(x) = 0)] \end{array} \right. \right\}.$$

SPP is an acronym for *s*toic *p*robabilistic *p*olynomial time. An SPP machine is "stoic" in the sense that its "gap"—the difference between the number of accepting and the number of rejecting computation paths—takes on only two values out of the exponentially many values an NPTM can have. In this regard, SPP resembles the class UP, see Definition 3.81. Replacing "GapP" by "#P" in the definition of SPP yields UP, so SPP is the gap-analog of UP. Just like UP and unlike PP, $\oplus$P, or C$_{=}$P, the class SPP is a promise class, since an SPP machine M "promises" that $\text{gap}_M(x)$ is in $\{0, 1\}$ for all x; see also Exercise 6.10. SPP is the smallest "reasonable" gap-definable counting class, where a class is said to be reasonable if and only if it contains both the empty set and Σ^*.

The inclusions between PP, C$_{=}$P, $\oplus$P, SPP, and other classes are stated in Proposition 6.35. They are easy to prove, see Exercise 6.12. Some proofs (e.g., that of C$_{=}$P $\subseteq$ PP) are greatly simplified by the use of GapP functions. Note that, just like PP, both SPP and $\oplus$P are closed under complementation, whereas C$_{=}$P is unlikely to share this property. None of the inclusions stated in Proposition 6.35 is known to be proper.

Proposition 6.35.   *1.* SPP $\subseteq$ $\oplus$P.
2. P $\subseteq$ UP $\subseteq$ SPP $\subseteq$ C$_{=}$P *and* P $\subseteq$ coUP $\subseteq$ SPP $\subseteq$ coC$_{=}$P.
3. P $\subseteq$ coUP $\subseteq$ coNP $\subseteq$ C$_{=}$P $\subseteq$ PP *and* P $\subseteq$ UP $\subseteq$ NP $\subseteq$ coC$_{=}$P $\subseteq$ PP.

The notion of lowness, introduced in Section 5.7, can be defined for every relativizable complexity class $\mathcal{C}$. In the notation of Definition 6.36 below, the kth level Low$_k$ of the low hierarchy (see Definition 5.73) contains precisely those NP sets that are Σ_k^p-low. And Theorem 6.29 says that AM $\cap$ coAM is Σ_2^p-low.

Definition 6.36 (Lowness).   *Let $\mathcal{C}$ be any relativizable complexity class.*

- *A set A is said to be $\mathcal{C}$-low if and only if $\mathcal{C}^A = \mathcal{C}$.*
- *A class $\mathcal{A}$ of sets is said to be $\mathcal{C}$-low if and only if every A in $\mathcal{A}$ is $\mathcal{C}$-low.*

The following theorem says that SPP contains precisely the sets that are low for GapP. Consequently, all sets in SPP are low for each class definable via GapP functions, including not only SPP itself but also PP, $\oplus$P, and C$_{=}$P. Complexity classes $\mathcal{C}$ that are low for themselves—i.e., they satisfy $\mathcal{C}^{\mathcal{C}} = \mathcal{C}$—are said to be *self-low*.

Theorem 6.37. SPP $= \{A \mid \text{GapP}^A = \text{GapP}\}$.

Proof.   To prove that SPP contains all GapP-low sets, suppose that A is any set satisfying $\text{GapP}^A = \text{GapP}$. Define an NPOTM M that on input x asks its oracle about x. If the answer is "yes" (i.e., if x belongs to the oracle set), then M accepts on exactly one path; otherwise, if the answer is "no," then M generates one accepting and one rejecting path. Thus, for each oracle B, the gap of $M^B(x)$ coincides with the characteristic function of B at x, i.e., $\text{gap}_{M^B} \equiv \chi_B$. Specifically, for our oracle set A, we have

$$\text{gap}_{M^A}(x) = \begin{cases} 1 & \text{if } x \in A \\ 0 & \text{if } x \notin A. \end{cases}$$

By our assumption that $\text{GapP}^A = \text{GapP}$, there exists an NPTM N (which does not have an oracle) such that $\text{gap}_N \equiv \text{gap}_{M^A}$. Thus, N witnesses that A is in SPP.

Conversely, we have to prove that $\text{SPP} \subseteq \{A \mid \text{GapP}^A = \text{GapP}\}$. Let M be a given NPOTM, and let A be any set in SPP. Suppose that, no matter which oracle is used, M on input x makes exactly $k(|x|)$ queries on each path, for some polynomial k. Fix x, and let $k = k(|x|)$. Let S be some NPTM witnessing that $A \in \text{SPP}$, i.e., $\text{gap}_S \equiv \chi_A$.

We now define an NPTM N (without an oracle) that satisfies $\text{gap}_N \equiv \text{gap}_{M^A}$.

Step 1: On input x, N guesses a tuple $\mathbf{a} = (a_1, a_2, \ldots, a_k)$ of answer bits, where $a_i = 1$ corresponds to the answer "yes," and $a_i = 0$ corresponds to the answer "no."

Step 2: N guesses a computation path α of $M^{(\cdot)}(x)$, substituting the answers of $\mathbf{a}$ instead of querying the oracle, i.e., if q_i is the ith query of $M^{(\cdot)}(x)$ on α, then $N(x)$ continues the simulation according to the answer a_i.

Step 3: For each such path α, N extends α by creating a subtree below α that has a gap G_α, which is defined as follows: For each i with $1 \le i \le k$, let

$$g_i = \begin{cases} \text{gap}_S(q_i) & \text{if } a_i = 1 \\ 1 - \text{gap}_S(q_i) & \text{if } a_i = 0 \end{cases} \quad \text{and} \quad G_\alpha = \begin{cases} \prod_{i=1}^k g_i & \text{if } \alpha \text{ accepts} \\ -\prod_{i=1}^k g_i & \text{if } \alpha \text{ rejects.} \end{cases}$$

By the closure properties of GapP, G_α is in GapP, so N can generate the corresponding gap G_α for each path α. Note that, for each i with $1 \le i \le k$, $g_i = 1$ if and only if a_i is the correct answer, i.e., if and only if $a_i = \chi_A(q_i)$. Thus, for each path α, $G_\alpha \in \{-1, 1\}$ if all queries along α were answered correctly, and $G_\alpha = 0$ otherwise. It follows that no path with incorrect answers contributes to the gap of N, and the remaining gap corresponds to that path along which all oracle answers of $M^A(x)$ were correctly simulated. Thus, $\text{gap}_N(x) = \text{gap}_{M^A}(x)$ for each x. Hence, A satisfies $\text{GapP}^A = \text{GapP}$. ∎

Corollary 6.38.   *1.* $\text{GapP}^{\text{SPP}} = \text{GapP}$.
   2. SPP is closed under $\le_T^p$-reductions, i.e., $\text{P}^{\text{SPP}} = \text{SPP}$.
   3. SPP is PP-low, i.e., $\text{PP}^{\text{SPP}} = \text{PP}$.
   4. SPP is $\oplus$P-low, i.e., $\oplus\text{P}^{\text{SPP}} = \oplus\text{P}$.
   5. SPP is $\mathrm{C}_{=}\text{P}$-low, i.e., $\mathrm{C}_{=}\text{P}^{\text{SPP}} = \mathrm{C}_{=}\text{P}$.
   6. SPP is self-low, i.e., $\text{SPP}^{\text{SPP}} = \text{SPP}$.

The proof of Corollary 6.38 is straightforward and thus omitted, but see Exercise 6.13(a). In contrast to the first item of Corollary 6.38, it is unlikely that $\#P^{SPP} = \#P$, or even that $\#P^{UP} = \#P$; see Exercise 6.13(b).

Lemma 6.40 below states some useful properties of SPP to be applied in Section 6.5. We omit the proof of Lemma 6.40 but note that it is a straightforward consequence of the self-lowness of SPP (i.e., $SPP^{SPP} = SPP$) and the following result, Theorem 6.39. The proof of Theorem 6.39 is also omitted; it uses a technique similar to the proof of Theorem 6.37, see Exercise 6.14.

Theorem 6.39. *Let $A \in$ NP via an NPTM N, and let M be some NPOTM satisfying that for each input x, $M^A(x)$ makes only "UP-like" queries (i.e., queries q for which $\mathrm{acc}_N(q) \leq 1$). Then, the function $f(x) = \mathrm{gap}_{M^A}(x)$ is in GapP.*

Lemma 6.40.   1. *Let $A \in$ NP via an NPTM N, and let $L \in SPP^A$ via an NPOTM M satisfying that for each input x, $M^A(x)$ makes only "UP-like" queries (i.e., queries q for which $\mathrm{acc}_N(q) \leq 1$). Then, L is in SPP.*
   2. *Let $A \in$ NP via an NPTM N, and let $f \in FP^A$ via an DPOTM M satisfying that for each input x, $M^A(x)$ makes only "UP-like" queries (i.e., queries q for which $\mathrm{acc}_N(q) \leq 1$). Then, f is in FP^{SPP}.*

6.5 Graph Isomorphism and Lowness

In this section, we show the lowness properties of the graph isomorphism problem. In particular, GI is low for the second level of the polynomial hierarchy, and it is also low for probabilistic classes and counting classes, including PP, C$_{=}$P, $\oplus$P, and SPP.

6.5.1 Graph Isomorphism Is in the Low Hierarchy

We start by showing that GI is contained in Low_2. This result provides strong evidence that the graph isomorphism problem is not NP-complete. Why? Suppose GI were NP-complete. By Theorem 5.76, High_0 contains all $\leq_T^p$-complete sets in NP and thus, in particular, all $\leq_m^p$-complete NP sets . By Theorem 5.77, $\mathrm{High}_0 \subseteq \mathrm{High}_2$; so GI is in High_2. However, also by Theorem 5.77, $\mathrm{Low}_2 \cap \mathrm{High}_2$ is nonempty if and only if the polynomial hierarchy collapses down to Σ_2^p, which is considered unlikely.

In order to prove, as Theorem 6.45 below, that GI is in Low_2, we need as a technical prerequisite the so-called hashing lemma, stated as Lemma 6.42 below. Hashing is a method used in computer science for dynamic data management. Every data set is uniquely identified by some (short) key. The set of all potential keys, called the universe U, is usually very large, whereas the set $V \subseteq U$ of all keys actually used can be much smaller. A *hashing function* $h : U \to T$ maps the elements of U to the *hashing table* $T = \{0, 1, \ldots, k-1\}$. Hashing functions are many-to-one, which means that distinct keys from U can be mapped to the same address in T. If possible, however, any two distinct keys from V should be mapped to distinct addresses in T. That is, one seeks to avoid collisions on the set of actually used keys. In other words, a hashing function should, if possible, be injective on V. Hashing is also a very useful technique in cryptographic applications. Cryptographic hash functions usually map large keys to smaller keys in a "secure" manner.

Among the various hashing techniques, *universal hashing* is of particular interest for proving Theorem 6.45. Universal hashing was invented by Carter and Wegman in 1979. The idea is to not focus on a particular, concrete hashing function, but rather to *randomly* select one from a suitable family of hashing functions. This hashing technique is universal in the sense that it no longer depends on a specific set V of keys that are actually used; instead, it seeks to avoid collisions on *all* sufficiently small sets V with high probability. The probability is taken over the random choice of hashing functions. In what follows, we think of keys as strings over the alphabet $\Sigma = \{0, 1\}$, and we denote by Σ^n the set of all length n strings in Σ^*.

Definition 6.41 (Universal Hashing).   *Let $\Sigma = \{0, 1\}$, and let m and t be integers with $t > m$. A hashing function $h : \Sigma^t \to \Sigma^m$ is a linear mapping determined by a boolean $(t \times m)$ matrix $B_h = (b_{i,j})_{i,j}$, where $b_{i,j} \in \{0, 1\}$.*

For $\mathbf{x} \in \Sigma^t$ and for each j with $1 \leq j \leq m$, the jth bit of $\mathbf{y} = h(\mathbf{x}) \in \Sigma^m$ is given by

$$y_j = (b_{1,j} \wedge x_1) \oplus (b_{2,j} \wedge x_2) \oplus \cdots \oplus (b_{t,j} \wedge x_t),$$

where $\oplus$ denotes the exclusive-or *operation (a.k.a. the* parity *operation, see Definition 4.18 and Table 4.14 in Section 4.2). Note that $\oplus$ is associative. We can thus write:*

$$a_1 \oplus a_2 \oplus \cdots \oplus a_n = 1 \iff ||\{i \mid a_i = 1\}|| \equiv 1 \bmod 2.$$

Let $\mathcal{H}_{t,m} = \{h : \Sigma^t \to \Sigma^m \mid B_h \text{ is a boolean } (t \times m) \text{ matrix}\}$ be a family of hashing functions for the parameters t and m. We assume the uniform distribution on $\mathcal{H}_{t,m}$: A hashing function h is chosen from $\mathcal{H}_{t,m}$ by picking the bits $b_{i,j}$ in B_h independently according to the uniform distribution.

Let $V \subseteq \Sigma^t$. For any subfamily $\widehat{\mathcal{H}}$ of $\mathcal{H}_{t,m}$, we say there is a collision *on V if*

$$(\exists \mathbf{v} \in V)(\forall h \in \widehat{\mathcal{H}})(\exists \mathbf{x} \in V)[\mathbf{v} \neq \mathbf{x} \wedge h(\mathbf{v}) = h(\mathbf{x})].$$

Otherwise, $\widehat{\mathcal{H}}$ is collision-free *on V.*

A collision on V means that the injectivity of each hashing function from the subfamily $\widehat{\mathcal{H}}$ is destroyed on V. Lemma 6.42 says that on every sufficiently small set V, a randomly selected subfamily of $\mathcal{H}_{t,m}$ is collision-free with high probability. If V is too large, however, a collision cannot be avoided.

Lemma 6.42 (Hashing Lemma).   *Let $t, m \in \mathbb{N}$ be fixed parameters, let $V \subseteq \Sigma^t$, and let $\widehat{\mathcal{H}} = (h_1, h_2, \ldots, h_{m+1})$ be some family of hashing functions randomly selected from $\mathcal{H}_{t,m}$ under the uniform distribution. Let the collision predicate be*

$$\mathrm{Col}(V) = \{\widehat{\mathcal{H}} \mid (\exists \mathbf{v} \in V)(\forall h \in \widehat{\mathcal{H}})(\exists \mathbf{x} \in V)[\mathbf{v} \neq \mathbf{x} \wedge h(\mathbf{v}) = h(\mathbf{x})]\}.$$

That is, $\mathrm{Col}(V)$ is the event that, given $\widehat{\mathcal{H}}$, a collision occurs on V. Then, the following two statements are true:

1. *If* $||V|| \leq 2^{m-1}$, *then* $\text{Col}(V)$ *occurs with probability at most* $1/4$.
2. *If* $||V|| > (m+1)2^m$, *then* $\text{Col}(V)$ *occurs with probability* 1.

The proof of Lemma 6.42 is left to the reader as Exercise 6.15.

Definition 6.43 (Graph Nonisomorphism Problem).
Define the graph nonisomorphism problem *by*

$$\text{GNI} = \{\langle G, H \rangle \mid G \text{ and } H \text{ are nonisomorphic graphs}\}.$$

The Arthur-Merlin hierarchy is introduced in Definition 6.25, and Theorem 6.27 says that this hierarchy collapses down to AM. We now show that the graph nonisomorphism problem is contained in AM. Consequently, GI is in coAM. By Corollary 6.30, every NP set in coAM is a member of Low_2. It follows that GI is in Low_2.

Lemma 6.44. GNI *is in* AM.

Proof.   Let G and H be two graphs with n vertices each. We want to apply the hashing lemma. It seems to be reasonable to use as the set V from Lemma 6.42 the set

$$A(G, H) = \{\langle F, \varphi \rangle \mid F \cong G \wedge \varphi \in \text{Aut}(F)\} \cup \{\langle F, \varphi \rangle \mid F \cong H \wedge \varphi \in \text{Aut}(F)\}$$

defined right before Lemma 2.53 in Section 2.4.3. By Lemma 2.53, $||A(G, H)|| = n!$ if G and H are isomorphic, and $||A(G, H)|| = 2n!$ if G and H are nonisomorphic.

The AM machine for GNI to be defined below is, of course, polynomial-time bounded. This bound requires the parameters t and m from the hashing lemma to be polynomially in n. However, in order to apply this lemma, we had to choose the polynomial $m = m(n)$ such that

$$n! \leq 2^{m-1} < (m+1)2^m < 2n!, \tag{6.18}$$

since otherwise the set $V = A(G, H)$ would not be large enough to tell two isomorphic graphs G and H apart from two nonisomorphic graphs, with sufficiently high probability as per Lemma 6.42. Unfortunately, it is not possible to find a polynomial m satisfying (6.18).

That is why we choose, as our V from Lemma 6.42, a set other than $A(G, H)$, one that creates a gap between the upper and the lower bound in (6.18) that is large enough so as to tell isomorphic graphs apart from nonisomorphic graphs. Define

$$V = A(G, H)^n = \underbrace{A(G, H) \times A(G, H) \times \cdots \times A(G, H)}_{n \text{ times}}.$$

Now, (6.18) becomes

$$(n!)^n \leq 2^{m-1} < (m+1)2^m < (2n!)^n, \tag{6.19}$$

and this inequality can be satisfied by setting $m = m(n) = 1 + \lceil n \log n! \rceil$, which is polynomially in n.

Define an AM machine M for GNI as follows. Given two graphs G and H with n vertices each, M starts by computing the parameter $m = m(n)$. Note that the set $V = A(G, H)^n$ contains n-tuples of pairs of the form $\langle F, \varphi \rangle$, where F is a graph with n vertices, and φ is a permutation in the automorphism group $\text{Aut}(F)$. The elements of V can be suitably encoded as strings over the alphabet $\Sigma = \{0, 1\}$, where $t = t(n)$ is an appropriate polynomial. So far, all computations are deterministic.

Then, M performs a probabilistic move by Arthur: Randomly choose a family $\widehat{\mathcal{H}} = (h_1, h_2, \ldots, h_{m+1})$ of hashing functions under the uniform distribution. Each such hashing function $h_i \in \widehat{\mathcal{H}}$ is given by a boolean $(t \times m)$ matrix whose entries are chosen independently and uniformly distributed. The $m + 1$ hashing functions $h_i \in \widehat{\mathcal{H}}$ can thus be encoded by a string $r_{\widehat{\mathcal{H}}} \in \Sigma^*$ of length $p(n)$, for some suitable polynomial p.

Modify the collision predicate $\text{Col}(V)$ from Lemma 6.42 as follows:

$$B = \left\{ \langle G, H, r_{\widehat{\mathcal{H}}} \rangle \;\middle|\; \begin{array}{l} (\exists \mathbf{v} \in V)\, (\forall i : 1 \leq i \leq m + 1) \\ (\exists \mathbf{x} \in V)\, [\mathbf{v} \neq \mathbf{x} \wedge h_i(\mathbf{v}) = h_i(\mathbf{x})] \end{array} \right\}.$$

Since the $\forall$ quantifier in B ranges over only polynomially many i, it can be evaluated deterministically in polynomial time. Thus, the two $\exists$ quantifiers in B can be combined to just *one* polynomially length-bounded $\exists$ quantifier. By Theorem 5.31, B is a set in $\Sigma_1^p = \text{NP}$. Let N be an NPTM for B. If $r_{\widehat{\mathcal{H}}}$ is the randomly chosen string encoding $m + 1$ independently and uniformly distributed hashing functions from $\mathcal{H}_{t,m}$, then simulating the computation of $N(\langle G, H, r_{\widehat{\mathcal{H}}} \rangle)$ corresponds to Merlin's move. This completes the description of M.

Suppose that G and H are nonisomorphic. By Lemma 2.53, $\|A(G, H)\| = 2n!$. Inequality (6.19) implies $\|V\| = (2n!)^n > (m + 1)2^m$. By Lemma 6.42, the probability of $\langle G, H, r_{\widehat{\mathcal{H}}} \rangle$ being in B is 1, i.e., a collision occurs with certainty. Thus, for each choice of $r_{\widehat{\mathcal{H}}}$, there exists an accepting computation path of $N(\langle G, H, r_{\widehat{\mathcal{H}}} \rangle)$.

Now suppose that G and H are isomorphic. By Lemma 2.53, $\|A(G, H)\| = n!$. Inequality (6.19) implies $\|V\| = (n!)^n \leq 2^{m-1}$. By Lemma 6.42, the probability of $\langle G, H, r_{\widehat{\mathcal{H}}} \rangle$ being in B is at most $1/4$. Thus, for more than $3/4$ of the possible choices of $r_{\widehat{\mathcal{H}}}$, $N(\langle G, H, r_{\widehat{\mathcal{H}}} \rangle)$ has no accepting computation path. It follows that GNI is in $(\exists^+ \exists \,|\, \exists^+ \forall) = \text{AM}$, which proves the lemma. ∎

Theorem 6.45 (Schöning).   GI *is in* Low$_2$.

Proof.   By Corollary 6.30, $\text{NP} \cap \text{coAM} \subseteq \text{Low}_2$. From Lemma 6.44 it follows that GI is in $\text{NP} \cap \text{coAM}$. So GI $\in \text{Low}_2$. ∎

Corollary 6.46. GI *is not contained in any of the classes* High$_k$, *unless the polynomial hierarchy collapses down to* $\Sigma_{\max(k,2)}^p$. *In particular,* GI *is not* $\leq_m^p$-*complete in* NP, *unless* $\text{PH} = \Sigma_2^p$.

Proof.   The argument is given in the first paragraph of Section 6.5.1. ∎

6.5.2 Graph Isomorphism Is in SPP

We now prove that the graph isomorphism problem is in SPP. By Corollary 6.38, GI is low for PP, $\oplus$P, $\mathbb{C}$P, and SPP. To prove this result, stated as Theorem 6.50 below, we first show that the lexicographically least permutation in a right co-set can be efficiently computed. Recall the notions defined in Sections 2.4.2 and 2.4.3. In particular, recall that the isomorphism set, ISO(G, H), of two isomorphic graphs G and H is a right co-set of the automorphism group Aut(G) in the permutation group $\mathfrak{S}_n$. In symbols, ISO$(G, H) = \text{Aut}(G)\tau$, where $\tau \in \text{ISO}(G, H)$. Recall also the notions from Definition 2.47 in Section 2.4 and (2.13). The lexicographical order on $\mathfrak{S}_n$ is defined in Example 5.26.

Theorem 6.47. *Let $\mathfrak{G} \leq \mathfrak{S}_n$ be a permutation group represented by a generator G, i.e., $\mathfrak{G} = \langle G \rangle$, and let $\pi \in \mathfrak{S}_n$ be a permutation. There is a polynomial-time algorithm that, given G and π, determines the lexicographically least permutation in the right co-set $\mathfrak{G}\pi$ of $\mathfrak{G}$ in $\mathfrak{S}_n$.*

Proof.   Let G be a generator of the permutation group $\mathfrak{G} \leq \mathfrak{S}_n$, i.e., $\mathfrak{G} = \langle G \rangle$, and let $\pi \in \mathfrak{S}_n$ be a permutation. Figure 6.5 shows the algorithm LERC: Given G and π, LERC computes the lexicographically least permutation in the right co-set $\mathfrak{G}\pi$ of $\mathfrak{G}$ in $\mathfrak{S}_n$.

```
LERC(G, π) {
    Compute the tower 𝔊(n) ≤ 𝔊(n-1) ≤ ⋯ ≤ 𝔊(1) ≤ 𝔊(0) of stabilizers in 𝔊;
    φ₀ = π;
    for (i = 0, 1, ..., n − 1) {
        x := i + 1;
        Compute the element y in the orbit 𝔊(i)(x) for which φᵢ(y) is minimum;
        Determine a permutation τᵢ in 𝔊(i) with τᵢ(x) = y;
        φᵢ₊₁ := τᵢφᵢ;
    }
    return φₙ;
}
```

Fig. 6.5. Algorithm LERC for computing the least element in the right co-set $\mathfrak{G}\pi$

By Theorem 2.48, the tower $\mathbf{id} = \mathfrak{G}^{(n)} = \mathfrak{G}^{(n-1)} \leq \cdots \leq \mathfrak{G}^{(1)} \leq \mathfrak{G}^{(0)} = \mathfrak{G}$ of stabilizers of $\mathfrak{G}$ can be computed in polynomial time. More precisely, for each i with $1 \leq i \leq n$, the algorithm determines the complete right transversals T_i of $\mathfrak{G}^{(i)}$ in $\mathfrak{G}^{(i-1)}$ and thus a strong generator $S = \bigcup_{i=1}^{n-1} T_i$ of $\mathfrak{G}$.

Since $\varphi_0 = \pi$ and $\mathfrak{G}^{(n-1)} = \mathfrak{G}^{(n)} = \mathbf{id}$, for proving that LERC is correct, it is enough to show that for each i with $0 \leq i \leq n - 1$, the lexicographically least permutation of $\mathfrak{G}^{(i)}\varphi_i$ is contained in $\mathfrak{G}^{(i+1)}\varphi_{i+1}$. By induction, this implies that $\mathfrak{G}^{(n)}\varphi_n = \{\varphi_n\}$ contains the lexicographically least permutation of

$\mathfrak{G}\pi = \mathfrak{G}^{(0)}\varphi_0$. Thus, algorithm LERC outputs indeed the lexicographically least permutation of $\mathfrak{G}\pi$.

For any permutation group $\mathfrak{H} \leq \mathfrak{S}_n$, let $\mathfrak{H}(x)$ denote the orbit of the element $x \in [n]$ in $\mathfrak{H}$. To prove the above claim, let τ_i be the permutation in $\mathfrak{G}^{(i)}$ that maps $i+1$ onto the element y in the orbit $\mathfrak{G}^{(i)}(i+1)$ for which $\varphi_i(y) = x$ is the minimum element in the set $\{\varphi_i(z) \mid z \in \mathfrak{G}^{(i)}(i+1)\}$. By Theorem 2.48, the orbit $\mathfrak{G}^{(i)}(i+1)$ can be computed in polyomial time, and since $\mathfrak{G}^{(i)}(i + 1)$ contains at most $n - i$ elements, y can be determined efficiently. The algorithm is designed so as to satisfy $\varphi_{i+1} = \tau_i\varphi_i$. Note that every permutation in $\mathfrak{G}^{(i)}$ maps each element of $[i]$ onto itself and that $\tau_i \in \mathfrak{G}^{(i)}$. Thus, for each j with $1 \leq j \leq i$, for each $\tau \in \mathfrak{G}^{(i)}$, and for each $\sigma \in \mathfrak{G}^{(i+1)}$, we have

$$(\sigma\varphi_{i+1})(j) = \varphi_{i+1}(j) = (\tau_i\varphi_i)(j) = \varphi_i(j) = (\tau\varphi_i)(j).$$

In particular, for the lexicographically least permutation μ in $\mathfrak{G}^{(i)}\varphi_i$, it follows that every permutation from $\mathfrak{G}^{(i+1)}\varphi_{i+1}$ coincides with μ in the first i elements, i.e., it coincides with μ on $[i]$. In addition, for each $\sigma \in \mathfrak{G}^{(i+1)}$ and for the element $x = \varphi_i(y)$ defined above, we have

$$(\sigma\varphi_{i+1})(i + 1) = \varphi_{i+1}(i + 1) = (\tau_i\varphi_i)(i + 1) = x.$$

Clearly, $\mathfrak{G}^{(i+1)}\varphi_{i+1} = \{\varphi \in \mathfrak{G}^{(i)}\varphi_i \mid \varphi(i + 1) = x\}$. The claim now follows from the fact that $\mu(i + 1) = x$ for the lexicographically least permutation μ of $\mathfrak{G}^{(i)}\varphi_i$. We have thus shown that algorithm LERC works efficiently and correctly. ∎

Theorem 6.47 can easily be extended to Corollary 6.48, see Exercise 6.16.

Corollary 6.48. *Let $\mathfrak{G} \leq \mathfrak{S}_n$ be a permutation group represented by a generator G, i.e., $\mathfrak{G} = \langle G\rangle$, and let π and ψ be two permutations in $\mathfrak{S}_n$. There is a polynomial-time algorithm that, given $\langle G, \pi, \psi\rangle$, determines the lexicographically least permutation in $\psi\mathfrak{G}\pi$.*

We now define a problem that we need in the proof of Theorem 6.50; see also the notions from Section 2.4, in particular Definitions 2.47 and 2.49.

Definition 6.49. *Define the functional problem* auto *as follows: Given a graph G, compute a strong generator of the automorphism group* Aut(G).

By Mathon's [Mat79] result, the problems auto and GI are $\leq_T^P$-equivalent; see Exercise 6.17. That is, auto $\in$ FP^{GI} and GI $\in$ P^{auto}.

We now are ready to prove Theorem 6.50, the main result in this section.

Theorem 6.50 (Arvind and Kurur). GI *is in* SPP.

Proof. In order to prove the theorem, it is enough to show that auto is in FP^{SPP}. Why? Suppose that auto $\in$ FP^{SPP}. As mentioned above, auto and GI are $\leq_T^P$-equivalent, so GI is in P$^{\text{auto}} \subseteq$ P$^{\text{FP}^{\text{SPP}}} =$ P^{SPP}. By Corollary 6.38, SPP is closed under $\leq_T^P$-reductions, i.e., P$^{\text{SPP}} =$ SPP. It follows that GI is in SPP.

So, we have to design an FP^{SPP} algorithm for $\texttt{auto}$. Given any graph G, this algorihm computes a strong generator $S = \bigcup_{i=0}^{n-1} T_i$ for $\text{Aut}(G)$, where

$$\mathbf{id} = \text{Aut}(G)^{(n)} \leq \text{Aut}(G)^{(n-1)} \leq \cdots \leq \text{Aut}(G)^{(1)} \leq \text{Aut}(G)^{(0)} = \text{Aut}(G)$$

is the tower of stabilizers of $\text{Aut}(G)$, and T_i is a complete right transversal of $\text{Aut}(G)^{(i+1)}$ in $\text{Aut}(G)^{(i)}$, $0 \leq i < n$.

Starting with the trivial case of $\text{Aut}(G)^{(n)} = \mathbf{id}$, we construct, step by step, a strong generator for $\text{Aut}(G)^{(i)}$, where i is decreasing. Eventually, we thus obtain a strong generator for $\text{Aut}(G)^{(0)} = \text{Aut}(G)$. So let us assume we have already found a strong generator $S_i = \bigcup_{j=i}^{n-1} T_j$ for $\text{Aut}(G)^{(i)}$. We now describe how the FP^{SPP} algorithm will determine a complete right transversal T_{i-1} of $\text{Aut}(G)^{(i)}$ in $\text{Aut}(G)^{(i-1)}$. To this end, we define the following set:

$$A = \left\{ \langle G, S, i, j, \pi \rangle \left| \begin{array}{l} S \subseteq \text{Aut}(G) \text{ and } \langle S \rangle \text{ is a pointwise stabilizer of } [i] \\ \text{in } \text{Aut}(G), \pi \text{ is a partial permutation that pointwise} \\ \text{stabilizes } [i-1] \text{ and satisfies } \pi(i) = j, \text{ and there} \\ \text{exists a } \tau \in \text{Aut}(G)^{(i-1)} \text{ such that } \tau(i) = j \text{ and} \\ \text{LERC}(S, \tau) \text{ extends } \pi \end{array} \right. \right\}.$$

By Theorem 6.47, the lexicographically least permutation $\text{LERC}(S, \tau)$ of the right co-set $\langle S \rangle \tau$ can be computed in polynomial time by the algorithm in Figure 6.5. The partial permutation π is part of the input instance $\langle G, S, i, j, \pi \rangle$, since the set A will be used as an oracle in a prefix search for the lexicographically least permutation $\tau \in \text{Aut}(G)^{(i-1)}$ with $\tau(i) = j$. (For another prefix search algorithm, see Figure 5.9 in Example 5.26.)

$N(\langle G, S, i, j, \pi \rangle)$ {
  Verify that $S \subseteq \text{Aut}(G)^{(i)}$;
  Nondeterministically guess a permutation $\tau \in \mathfrak{S}_n$; $//$ G has n vertices
  $\texttt{if}$ ($\tau \in \text{Aut}(G)^{(i-1)}$ and $\tau(i) = j$ and τ extends π and $\tau = \text{LERC}(S, \tau)$)
    accept and halt;
  $\texttt{else}$ reject and halt;
}

Fig. 6.6. NP machine N accepting the set A

Figure 6.6 shows an NPTM N for the oracle set A. So A is in NP. Observe that if $\tau(i) = j$ then $\sigma(i) = j$ for each permutation σ in the right co-set $\langle S \rangle \tau$.

We now prove that the number of accepting computation paths of N on input $\langle G, S, i, j, \pi \rangle$ is either 0 or 1, provided that $\langle S \rangle = \text{Aut}(G)^{(i)}$. In general, regardless of whether or not $\langle S \rangle = \text{Aut}(G)^{(i)}$, we have $\text{acc}_N(\langle G, S, i, j, \pi \rangle) \in \{0, k\}$, where

$$k = \frac{||\text{Aut}(G)^{(i)}||}{||\langle S \rangle||}.$$

Suppose that $\langle G, S, i, j, \pi \rangle$ is in A and $\langle S \rangle = \mathrm{Aut}(G)^{(i)}$. If $\tau(i) = j$ for some $\tau \in \mathrm{Aut}(G)^{(i-1)}$ and $j > i$, then the right co-set $\langle S \rangle \tau$ consists of exactly those permutations in $\mathrm{Aut}(G)^{(i-1)}$ that map i to j. Hence, the only accepting computation path of $N(\langle G, S, i, j, \pi \rangle)$ corresponds to the uniquely determined lexicographically least permutation $\tau = \mathrm{LERC}(S, \tau)$. On the other hand, if $\langle S \rangle$ is a proper subgroup of $\mathrm{Aut}(G)^{(i)}$, then $\mathrm{Aut}(G)^{(i)} \tau$ can be written as the disjoint union of k right co-sets of $\langle S \rangle$. In general, $N(\langle G, S, i, j, \pi \rangle)$ thus has k accepting computation paths if $\langle G, S, i, j, \pi \rangle$ is in A, and it has no accepting path otherwise.

$M^A(G)$ {
   Set $T_i := \{\mathtt{id}\}$ for each i, $0 \leq i \leq n - 2$;   // G has n vertices
      // T_i will eventually be a complete right transversal of $\mathrm{Aut}(G)^{(i+1)}$ in $\mathrm{Aut}(G)^{(i)}$
   Set $S_i := \emptyset$ for each i, $0 \leq i \leq n - 2$;
   Set $S_{n-1} := \{\mathtt{id}\}$;   // S_i will be a strong generator for $\mathrm{Aut}(G)^{(i)}$
   for $(i = n - 1, n - 2, \ldots, 1)$ {
            // before the ith iteration, S_i is already found and S_{i-1} is to be computed
      Let $\pi : [i - 1] \rightarrow [n]$ be the partial permutation with $\pi(a) = a$ for each $a \in [i - 1]$
      // for $i = 1$, $\pi = \underbrace{* \cdots *}_{n}$ is the empty permutation, in the notation of Example 5.26

   for $(j = i + 1, i + 2, \ldots, n)$ {
      Set $\hat{\pi} := \pi j$;   // $\hat{\pi}$ extends π by the pair (i, j), i.e., $\hat{\pi}(i) = j$
      if $(\langle G, S_i, i, j, \hat{\pi} \rangle \in A)$ {
         // prefix search constructs the least permutation in $\mathrm{Aut}(G)^{(i-1)}$ mapping i to j
         for $(k = i + 1, i + 2, \ldots, n)$ {
            Find the element ℓ not in the image of $\hat{\pi}$ such that $\langle G, S_i, i, j, \hat{\pi} \ell \rangle \in A$;
            $\hat{\pi} := \hat{\pi} \ell$;
         }   // $\hat{\pi}$ now is a total permutation in $\mathfrak{S}_n$
         $T_{i-1} := T_{i-1} \cup \hat{\pi}$;
      }
   }   // T_{i-1} now is a complete right transversal of $\mathrm{Aut}(G)^{(i)}$ in $\mathrm{Aut}(G)^{(i-1)}$
   $S_{i-1} := S_i \cup T_{i-1}$;
   }
   return S_0;   // S_0 is a strong generator for $\mathrm{Aut}(G) = \mathrm{Aut}(G)^{(0)}$
}

Fig. 6.7. FP^{SPP} algorithm M^A for auto

Figure 6.7 shows the FP^A algorithm M^A for auto. Note that the DPOTM M makes only queries $q = \langle G, S_i, i, j, \pi \rangle$ to its oracle A for which $\langle S_i \rangle = \mathrm{Aut}(G)^{(i)}$. Hence, $\mathrm{acc}_N(q) \leq 1$ for each query q actually asked. By part 2 of Lemma 6.40, auto $\in$ FP^{SPP}.

That the output S_0 of $M^A(G)$ is a strong generator for $\mathrm{Aut}(G) = \mathrm{Aut}(G)^{(0)}$ can be shown by induction on n. The induction base is $n - 1$, and $S_{n-1} = \{\mathtt{id}\}$ certainly generates $\mathrm{Aut}(G)^{(n-1)} = \mathbf{id}$. For the induction step, suppose that, at the beginning of the ith iteration, a strong generator S_i for $\text{Aut}(G)^{(i)}$ has already been found. We prove that after the ith iteration, the set $S_{i-1} = S_i \cup T_{i-1}$ is a strong generator for $\text{Aut}(G)^{(i-1)}$. For each j with $i+1 \leq j \leq n$, the oracle query "$\langle G, S_i, i, j, \hat{\pi} \rangle \in A$?" checks whether or not there is a permutation in $\text{Aut}(G)^{(i-1)}$ mapping i to j.

By asking suitable oracle queries, the subsequent prefix search constructs the lexicographically least permutation $\hat{\pi}$ in $\text{Aut}(G)^{(i-1)}$ such that $\hat{\pi}(i) = j$. As mentioned above, A is asked only about queries q with $\text{acc}_N(q) \leq 1$, since S_i is a strong generator for $\text{Aut}(G)^{(i)}$, i.e., $\langle S_i \rangle = \text{Aut}(G)^{(i)}$. By construction, at the end of the ith iteration, T_{i-1} is a complete right transversal of $\text{Aut}(G)^{(i)}$ in $\text{Aut}(G)^{(i-1)}$. Hence, $S_{i-1} = S_i \cup T_{i-1}$ is a strong generator for $\text{Aut}(G)^{(i-1)}$. Eventually, after n iterations, a strong generator S_0 for $\text{Aut}(G) = \text{Aut}(G)^{(0)}$ has been determined. ∎

Corollary 6.38 and Theorem 6.50 have the following corollary.

Corollary 6.51. GI *is low for* SPP, PP, $\mathbb{C}$P, *and* $\oplus$P, *i.e.,* $\text{SPP}^{\text{GI}} = \text{SPP}$, $\text{PP}^{\text{GI}} = \text{PP}$, $\mathbb{C}\text{P}^{\text{GI}} = \mathbb{C}\text{P}$, *and* $\oplus\text{P}^{\text{GI}} = \oplus\text{P}$.

6.6 Exercises and Problems

Exercise 6.1 Run the algorithm BACKTRACKING-SAT from Figure 6.1 for the boolean formula

$$\varphi = (x \vee y \vee \neg z) \wedge (\neg x \vee \neg y \vee z) \wedge (\neg u \vee y \vee z) \wedge (u \vee \neg y \vee \neg z) \wedge (u \vee \neg y \vee z).$$

Construct a satisfying assignment of φ according to BACKTRACKING-SAT step by step, if one exists. Draw the corresponding recursion tree, and mark those subtrees that are pruned.

Exercise 6.2 Argue why choosing the number $t = \lceil (4/3)^n \rceil$ of repetitions in the algorithm RANDOM-SAT from Figure 6.2 achieves an error probability small enough.

Hint: Recall the rule of thumb mentioned in Section 6.1.2 (see also page 47 in Section 2.5): To achieve a sufficiently small error probability, the number of repetitions needed is roughly reciprocal to the success probability of one trial. More precisely, suppose that the algorithm executes t independent trials each having success probability p. Show that the error probability can then be estimated by

$$(1 - p)^t \leq e^{-t \cdot p}.$$

where $e = 2.71828 \cdots$ is the base of the natural logarithm. Suppose further that ϵ is a fixed error probability that should not be exceeded. Show that this can be achieved by choosing t large enough to satisfy $t \geq \ln(1/\epsilon)/p$.

Exercise 6.3 Prove the second part of Theorem 6.4: PP = coPP.

Exercise 6.4 Prove Corollary 6.7: RP is closed under union and intersection.

Exercise 6.5 Prove that PP, BPP, RP, and ZPP are closed under $\leq_m^P$-reductions.

Exercise 6.6 Prove Fact 6.18: For each sensible pair $(\mathfrak{Q}_1, \mathfrak{Q}_2)$ of quantifier strings, $(\mathfrak{Q}_1 \mid \mathfrak{Q}_2) = \mathrm{co}(\mathfrak{Q}_2 \mid \mathfrak{Q}_1)$.

Exercise 6.7 Prove the second statement of Lemma 6.20:

$$(\forall y)\,(\exists^+ z)\,[B(x, y, z)] \implies (\forall Y)\,(\exists^+ z)\,(\forall y \in Y)\,[B(x, y, z)].$$

Exercise 6.8 Describe the classes AM, MAM, and AMA of the Arthur-Merlin hierarchy (see Definition 6.25) analogous to the way the class MA is described in Example 6.26.

Exercise 6.9 (a) Characterize the class PP by GapP functions similar to the definition of $\oplus$P, C=P, and SPP in Definition 6.34.

(b) Characterize the classes $\oplus$P, C=P, and SPP from Definition 6.34 by #P functions similar to the characterization of PP as per Remark 6.3.

Exercise 6.10 (a) Which of the following classes are promise classes: NP, coNP, PP, RP, coRP, ZPP, BPP, AM, coAM, MA, coMA, $\mathrm{PP}_{\mathrm{path}}$, $\mathrm{BPP}_{\mathrm{path}}$, and $\mathrm{RP}_{\mathrm{path}}$? For the definition of the latter three classes, see Problem 6.1.

(b) Do promise classes have complete problems?

Exercise 6.11 (a) Prove Proposition 6.32.

(b) Prove the closure properties of GapP stated in Lemma 6.33.

   Hint: The proof can be found in [FFK94]. Here are some hints.

   • **Subtraction:** Use Proposition 6.32.
   • **Addition:** Given $f = \mathrm{gap}_M$ and x, guess all strings y of length at most $p(|x|)$ and simulate M on input $\langle x, y \rangle$ for each y guessed.
   • **Multiplication:** Given $f = \mathrm{gap}_M$ and x, NPTM N guesses a sequence of computation paths of M on the inputs $\langle x, 0 \rangle, \langle x, 1 \rangle, \ldots, \langle x, p(|x|) \rangle$ and accepts if and only if an even number of these paths are accepting. Now, the proof of
   $$b(x) = \prod_{0 \leq y \leq p(|x|)} f(\langle x, y \rangle) = \mathrm{gap}_N(x)$$
   can be completed by induction on $n = p(|x|)$.
   • **Binomial coefficients, limited composition, and exponentiation:** First, prove a weaker version of the closure property under binomial coefficients: If $f \in \mathrm{GapP}$ and $k \in \mathrm{FP}$ such that $k(x)$ is polynomially bounded in $|x|$, then $h(x) = \binom{f(x)}{k(x)}$ is a function in GapP. To this end, prove the following combinatorial lemma.

   Lemma 6.52. *For each $r, s \in \mathbb{Z}$ and for each $k \in \mathbb{N}$,*
   $$\binom{s}{k} = \sum_{i=0}^{k} (-1)^i \binom{r+i}{i} \binom{r+s+1}{k-i}.$$

The binomial coefficients are defined by

$$\binom{x}{y} = \frac{x(x-1)(x-2)(x-y+1)}{y!}$$

for all real numbers x (including negative x) and for nonnegative integers y. By convention, $\binom{x}{0} = 1$.

To prove Lemma 6.52, use Vandermonde's convolution [GKP89, p. 174], which states that for each $a, b \in \mathbb{Z}$ and for each $k \in \mathbb{N}$,

$$\binom{a+b}{k} = \sum_{i=0}^{k} \binom{a}{i}\binom{b}{k-i}. \tag{6.20}$$

The intuition behind (6.20) is that choosing a committee of k members from a set of a women and b men is nothing other than first choosing i women and then $k - i$ men independently for each i.

Next, consider the following "δ" functions that will be useful below: For all integers k and B with $0 \le k \le B$ and for each integer x, define

$$\delta_k^B(x) = \binom{x}{k}\binom{B-x}{B-k}.$$

Note that these functions are in FP (and thus in GapP) and that

$$\delta_k^B(x) = \begin{cases} 1 & \text{if } x = k \\ 0 & \text{if } 0 \le x \le B \text{ and } x \ne k. \end{cases} \tag{6.21}$$

Using the above-mentioned weaker closure property under binomial coefficients and (6.21), prove that $c(x) = f(\langle x, g(x) \rangle)$ is in GapP if f and g are in GapP. This closure of GapP under limited composition, in turn, can be used to prove the stronger version of closure under binomial coefficients and closure under exponentiation: If f and g are in GapP and $0 \le g(x) \le p(|x|)$ for some polynomial p, then d and e are in GapP, where

$$d(x) = \binom{f(x)}{g(x)} \quad \text{and} \quad e(x) = f(x)^{g(x)}.$$

(c) Which of the closure properties stated for GapP in Lemma 6.33 are shared by #P? Prove your answers.

Hint: If you doubt that #P is closed under some property π, show that π is "hard" for the closure properties of #P in the sense that #P is closed under π if and only if it is closed under *every* polynomial-time computable operation. Results of this form were established by Ogihara and L. Hemaspaandra [OH93] who developed a general theory of closure properties of #P and related classes.

Exercise 6.12 Prove Proposition 6.35.

Exercise 6.13 (a) Prove Corollary 6.38.

(b) Prove that $\#P^{UP} = \#P$ implies $UP = coUP$.   **Hint:** See [KST89].

Exercise 6.14 (a) Prove Theorem 6.39.

   Hint: Apply the technique used in the proof of Theorem 6.37. See also Theorem 4.2 in [KST92] for a slightly more general result.

(b) Show that Theorem 6.39 and the self-lowness of SPP (i.e., $SPP^{SPP} = SPP$) imply Lemma 6.40.

Exercise 6.15 Prove Lemma 6.42.

Exercise 6.16 Modify the proof of Theorem 6.47 so as to prove Corollar 6.48.

Exercise 6.17 Prove that the problems GI and auto, defined in respectively Definition 2.49 and Definition 6.49, are $\leq_T^P$-equivalent, that is, auto $\in$ FP^{GI} and GI $\in$ P^{auto}.   **Hint:** See Köbler, Schöning, and Torán [KST93].

Problem 6.1 (Threshold Classes: PP_{path}, RP_{path}, and BPP_{path})

As stated in Remark 6.3, probabilistic complexity classes such as PP and RP can be defined in terms of probability weights or, alternatively, in terms of the number of accepting paths of normalized NPTMs. Is the normalization requirement necessary for the proof to work? In particular, define the function $tot_M : \Sigma^* \to \mathbb{N}$ for any given NPTM M by

$$tot_M(x) = ||\{\alpha \mid \alpha \text{ is some path of } M(x)\}||,$$

and consider the classes:

$$PP_{path} = \left\{ A \,\middle|\, \begin{array}{l} \text{there is some NPTM } M \text{ such that for each input } x, \\ x \in A \iff acc_M(x) \geq (1/2)tot_M(x) \end{array} \right\};$$

$$RP_{path} = \left\{ A \,\middle|\, \begin{array}{l} \text{there is some NPTM } M \text{ such that for each input } x, \\ x \in A \implies acc_M(x) \geq (1/2)tot_M(x); \\ x \notin A \implies acc_M(x) = 0 \end{array} \right\};$$

$$BPP_{path} = \left\{ A \,\middle|\, \begin{array}{l} \text{there is some NPTM } M \text{ and some } \epsilon > 0 \text{ such that for each } x, \\ x \in A \implies acc_M(x) \geq (1/2 + \epsilon)tot_M(x); \\ x \notin A \implies acc_M(x) \leq (1/2 - \epsilon)tot_M(x) \end{array} \right\},$$

where the machines are not necessarily normalized. PP_{path}, RP_{path}, and BPP_{path} are sometimes dubbed *threshold complexity classes*. Prove the following claims:

(a) $PP_{path} = PP$.

(b) $RP_{path} = NP$.

(c) $NP \subseteq BPP_{path} \subseteq PP$.

(d) $P^{NP[O(\log)]} \subseteq BPP_{path}$.   **Hint:** Prove that BPP_{path} is closed under $\leq_{tt}^P$-reductions and use the equality $P^{NP[O(\log)]} = P_{tt}^{NP}$ from Corollary 5.55.

(e) BPP is low for BPP_{path}, i.e., $\text{BPP}_{\text{path}}^{\text{BPP}} = \text{BPP}_{\text{path}}$.   **Hint:** See [HHT97].

(f) $\text{BPP} \subseteq \text{NP}^{\text{BPP}} \subseteq \text{MA} \subseteq \text{BPP}_{\text{path}} \subseteq \text{BPP}^{\text{NP}}$.   **Hint:** See [HHT97].

(g) Insert the classes PP_{path}, BPP_{path}, and RP_{path} in Figure 6.8.

Problem 6.2 (Closure Properties of PP)

(a) Prove that the class PP is closed under intersection.

> **Hint:** See Beigel, Reingold, and Spielman [BRS91]. The key to this proof is to find a rational function $R_n : \mathbb{Z} \to \mathbb{Z}$ such that for each x and y with $-2^n \leq x, y \leq 2^n$, $R_n(x, y)$ is positive if and only if both x and y are positive. Here, x and y represent the gaps between the number of accepting and rejecting paths of NPTMs (i.e., the values of the given GapP functions) for the given PP languages X and Y, and $R_n(x, y)$ represents the value of the GapP function, to be constructed, for the set $Z = X \cap Y$. How to construct such a function R_n and how to prove the required properties of R_n can be found in [BRS91].

(b) Prove that the class PP is closed even under $\leq_{\text{tt}}^{\text{P}}$-reductions.

> **Hint:** See Fortnow and Reingold [FR96].

Problem 6.3 (Lowness for Probabilistic and Counting Classes)

Prove the following lowness results:

(a) BPP is self-low, i.e., $\text{BPP}^{\text{BPP}} = \text{BPP}$.   **Hint:** Use the probability amplification technique stated in Theorem 6.13. See also [Ko82, Zac82].

(b) $\oplus\text{P}$ is self-low, i.e., $\oplus\text{P}^{\oplus\text{P}} = \oplus\text{P}$.   **Hint:** See [PZ83].

(c) $\text{AM} \cap \text{coAM}$ is low for AM, i.e., $\text{AM}^{\text{AM} \cap \text{coAM}} = \text{AM}$.

> **Hint:** The proof is similar to the proof of Theorem 6.29 stating that $\text{AM} \cap \text{coAM}$ is low for Σ_2^p, i.e., $\Sigma_2^{p,\text{AM} \cap \text{coAM}} = \Sigma_2^p$. See also part 2 of Theorem 5.76 stating that $\text{NP} \cap \text{coNP}$ is low for NP, i.e., $\text{NP}^{\text{NP} \cap \text{coNP}} = \text{NP}$. See also Theorem 2.44 in [KST93].

6.7 Summary and Bibliographic Remarks

Dantsin et al. [DGH$^+$02] established the currently best upper bound for the deterministic time complexity of k-SAT for $k \geq 3$, see Table 6.1. The random walk algorithm for 3-SAT presented in Section 6.1.2 is due to Schöning [Sch99, Sch02b]. The error and running time analysis of RANDOM-SAT, which was only roughly sketched in Section 6.1.2, can be found in more detail in Schöning's book [Sch01]. For k-SAT with $k \geq 4$, the algorithm by Paturi et al. [PPSZ98] is even slightly better than Schöning's algorithm. The currently best randomized algorithm for k-SAT with $3 \leq k \leq 4$, which is due to Iwama and Tamaki [IT03], has a running time of $\tilde{\mathcal{O}}(1.324^n)$ for 3-SAT and of $\tilde{\mathcal{O}}(1.474^n)$ for 4-SAT. Their algorithm is a clever combination of the algorithm by Paturi et al. [PPSZ98] and Schöning's random walk algorithm [Sch99]. For k-SAT with $k \geq 5$, Iwama and Tamaki's algorithm is not better than the one by Paturi et al. [PPSZ98]. Comprehensive surveys on algorithmics in exponential time are due to Woeginger [Woe03] and Schöning [Sch05].

Probabilistic Turing machines and the classes PP, RP, ZPP, and BPP were introduced and studied by Gill [Gil77]. Simon [Sim75] introduced the related notion of threshold machines that are based on the portion of accepting paths rather than the probability weight of accepting paths; see Remark 6.3. Problem 6.1(a) is taken from [Sim75]. Han, L. Hemaspaandra, and Thierauf [HHT97] pursued this line of research. In particular, they carefully studied the class BPP_{path}, which is defined in Problem 6.1, with respect to its relation to other complexity classes and with respect to secure database access. Problems 6.1(b) through 6.1(f) are taken from [HHT97]. The closure of PP under intersection was proven by Beigel, Reingold, and Spielman [BRS91]. Fortnow and Reingold [FR96] improved this result by proving that PP is closed even under the $\leq_{tt}^{p}$-reducibility, as mentioned in Section 6.2.1 and in Problem 6.2.

Arthur-Merlin games were introduced by Babai and Moran [BM88, Bab85]. Independently, Goldwasser, Micali und Rackoff [GMR89] developed the theory of interactive proof systems that yields an essentially equivalent concept. One of the best and most comprehensive sources for this theory is Chapter 4 in Goldreich's book [Gol01]. Other nice introductions to this field can be found in, e.g., the books by Balcázar, Díaz, and Gabarró [BDG90], Beutelspacher [Beu02], Buchmann [Buc01], Köbler, Schöning, and Torán [KST93], Papadimitriou [Pap94], Salomaa [Sal96], Stinson [Sti02], and Wechsung [Wec00], and in the surveys [Gol88, Gol89, Rot02]. Lemmas 6.20 and 6.21 and Theorem 6.22 are due to Zachos and Heller [Zac88, ZH86]. Corollary 6.23, which shows that BPP is contained in the second level of the polynomial hierarchy, is due to Gács (in Sipser [Sip83]) and, independently, to Lautemann [Lau83]. Part 2 of Corollary 6.28 is due to Boppana, Håstad, and Zachos [BHZ87]. Theorem 6.29 and Corollary 6.30 were shown by Schöning [Sch88], who also provided results generalizing the collapse stated in part 2 of Corollary 6.28 and the lowness for probabilistic classes stated in Theorem 6.29, see [Sch89]. Vereshchagin [Ver92] proved that MA ⊆ PP.

As noted above, Arthur-Merlin games and interactive proof systems are essentially the same concept. One (notational) difference is that, in the latter model, Merlin is called the *prover* and Arthur is called the *verifier*. Prover and verifier don't play games, they communicate via a protocol similar to a cryptographic protocol, even though not for the purpose of conveying secret messages. Another, at first glance more significant, difference between Arthur-Merlin games and interactive proof systems is that, in the former model, Arthur's random bits are public (and in particular known to Merlin), whereas in the latter model the verifier's random bits are private. However, Goldwasser and Sipser [GS89] proved that this difference between the two models in fact is irrelevant: it does not matter whether or not one uses private or public coins.

If the two players (Arthur and Merlin, or verifier and prover) do not play a constant number of rounds but polynomially many rounds, one obtains a complexity class that is dubbed IP. By definition, IP contains all of NP, and in particular GI. It also contains problems from coNP suspected to not be in NP, such as the graph nonisomorphism problem, which by Theorem 6.45 is a member of AM and thus of IP. A celebrated result by A. Shamir [Sha92] says that IP equals PSPACE, thus characterizing IP by a traditional complexity class.

The class #P was introduced by Valiant [Val79a, Val79b]. Fenner, Fortnow, and Kurtz [FFK94] generalized #P to obtain the class GapP and developed a theory of gap-definable counting classes. Similar ideas were independently developed by Köbler, Schöning, Toda, and Torán [KSTT92, KST92], Gupta [Gup91], and Ogihara and Hemaspaandra [OH93]. Probabilistic complexity classes such as PP are gap-definable, and so are many other counting classes, such as $\oplus$P, C=P, and SPP. The class $\oplus$P was introduced by Papadimitriou and Zachos [PZ83] and, independently, by Goldschlager and Parberry [GP86]. The "exact counting" class C=P was introduced by Simon [Sim75], see also [Wag86]. Analogous to the polynomial hierarchy and based on operators corresponding to the classes PP and C=P, Wagner [Wag86] defined the *counting hierarchy*, which was also intensely studied by Torán [Tor91]. Papadimitriou and Zachos proved that $\oplus$P is self-low; see Problem 6.3(b). Ko [Ko82] and Zachos showed that BPP is self-low (see Problem 6.3(a)), and Köbler et al. [KSTT92] proved that BPP is PP-low.

The class SPP was introduced in [FFK94]. The first SPP-like machine was described in [KSTT92], see also [KST92]. SPP was independently introduced by Ogihara and Hemaspaandra [OH93] under the name XP, and by Gupta [Gup91] under the name ZUP. Theorem 6.37 and Corollary 6.38 are due to Fenner, Fortnow, and Kurtz [FFK94]. Theorem 6.39 and Lemma 6.40 are due to Köbler, Schöning, and Torán [KST92]. A slightly more general version of Theorem 6.39 can be found as Theorem 4.2 in [KST92]. SPP generalizes Valiant's [Val76] class UP, which is defined in Definition 3.81 of Section 3.6. The promise classes UP and SPP have been intensely studied; see, e.g., [Val76, HH88, Sel92, KST92, KSTT92, FFK94, RRW94, Rot95, HR97b, HRW97b, BHR00, RH02, AK02b, HT03b, Hom04].

The relationship between the polynomial hierarchy and the counting classes PP, C=P, $\oplus$P, and SPP is open. The highest level of the polynomial hierarchy known to be contained in PP is Θ_2^p, by Beigel, Hemaspandra, and Wechsung's result [BHW91]. In contrast, Beigel [Bei91b] proved that, relative to an oracle, PP does not contain Δ_2^p. Further relativized separation results involving the counting classes PP, C=P, and $\oplus$P and the polynomial hierarchy have been obtained by Balcázar and Russo [Bal85, BR88], Bruschi [Bru92], Green [Gre91], Ko [Ko90], Rothe [Rot99], and Torán [Tor91]. Some of these results employ lower bounds on the circuit complexity of certain boolean functions, which were obtained by, e.g., Razborov [Raz87], Smolensky [Smo87], and Furst, Saxe, and Sipser [FSS84].

In contrast, Toda [Tod91] proved that every set from the polynomial hierarchy $\leq_T^p$-reduces to some set PP, i.e., PH $\subseteq$ P^{PP}. Even better, his technique established that the entire polynomial hierarchy is low for P^{PP}, i.e., P$^{PP^{PH}}$ = P^{PP}. Generalizing a seminal result by Valiant and Vazirani [VV86], Toda and Ogihara [TO92, Tod91] and, independently, Tarui [Tar93] proved that counting classes are at least as hard as the polynomial hierarchy. More precisely, they showed that, for each $\mathcal{C} \in \{$PP, $\oplus$P, C=P$\}$, every set in $\mathcal{C}^{PH}$ reduces to some set in $\mathcal{C}$ under polynomial-time randomized many-one reductions. Rothe [Rot95] showed that, in the context of *promise problems* and *reductions between promise problems* as introduced by Even, Selman, and Yacobi [EY80, ESY84, Sel88b], every set in the polynomial hierarchy randomly reduces to a class, denoted $\mathcal{SPP}$, that generalizes SPP. The complexity-theoretic investigations in [EY80, ESY84, Sel88b, GS88] are motivated by questions arising in public-key cryptography. Further results on counting classes can be found, e.g., in the papers [Her90, BG92, Gup93, OH93, HO93, Tar93].

Köbler, Schöning, and Torán [KST93] have written a comprehensive treatise on the graph isomorphism problem, in particular regarding its complexity-theoretic properties. Hoffman [Hof82] investigates group-theoretic algorithms for GI.

Lemma 6.44 was independently proven by Goldreich, Micali, and Wigderson [GMW91] and by Goldwasser and Sipser [GS89]. Theorem 6.45 is due to Schöning [Sch88]. Arvind and Köbler [AK02a] improved Schöning's result by proving that the graph isomorphism problem is even low for the class ZPP^{NP}, which is contained in Σ_2^p. Lemma 6.42, which is applied in the proof of Theorem 6.45, is called Sipser's Coding Lemma and first appeared in [Sip83], see also [GS89]. It can be seen as an application of universal hashing due to Carter and Wegman [CW79]. Köbler et al. [KST92, KSTT92] achieved the first lowness results for GI with respect to probabilistic and counting classes such as PP and $\oplus$P. They also showed that the graph automorphism problem, GA, is in SPP and thus low for SPP, $\oplus$P, PP, and $\oplus$P. Arvind and Kurur [AK02b] showed that GI is contained in SPP as well, which implies that it is low for SPP and other counting classes, see Theorem 6.50.

Figure 6.8 gives an overview over the known inclusion relations between probabilistic classes, Arthur-Merlin classes, and counting classes and the polynomial hierarchy. This inclusion structure is shown as a Hasse diagram, that is, containment of a class $\mathcal{C}$ in a class $\mathcal{D}$ is indicated by a line going from $\mathcal{C}$ upward to $\mathcal{D}$. None of the inclusions shown is known to be strict.

Finally, we mention some interesting problems related to GI that are inspired by the *Graph Reconstruction Conjecture*, which is due to P. J. Kelly and S. M. Ulam, cf. [Har69, Har74]. Though stated already in 1942, this conjecture is still open and is considered to be very hard to solve. First, some definitions are in order. Let G be a graph with n vertices, $V(G) = \{1, 2, \ldots, n\}$. A sequence $\mathcal{G} = (G_1, G_2, \ldots, G_n)$ of graphs is said to be a *deck of G* if and only if there is a permutation $\pi \in \mathfrak{S}_n$ such that for each i with $1 \leq i \leq n$, $G_{\pi(i)}$ is isomorphic to the graph obtained from G by deleting the vertex i and all incident edges. If $\mathcal{G}$ is a deck of G, then G is called a *preimage of $\mathcal{G}$*. A sequence $\mathcal{G} = (G_1, G_2, \ldots, G_n)$ is said to be a *legitimate deck* if and only if it has some preimage. The *Graph Reconstruction Conjecture* states that for any legitimate deck, there exists only one preimage up to isomorphism. Define the following problems:

Deck-Checking $= \{\langle G, \mathcal{G} \rangle \mid G$ is a preimage of $\mathcal{G} = \langle G_1, G_2, \ldots, G_n \rangle\}$;
Legitimate-Deck $= \{\mathcal{G} \mid \mathcal{G} = \langle G_1, G_2, \ldots, G_n \rangle$ is a legitimate deck$\}$.

Kratsch and L. Hemaspaandra [KH94] proved that

Deck-Checking $\leq_m^P$ GI $\leq_m^P$ Legitimate-Deck.

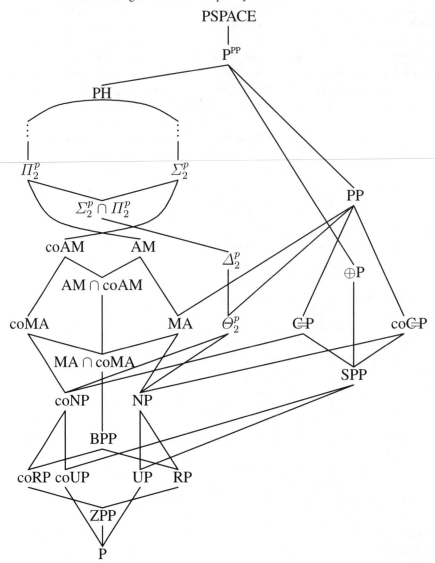

Fig. 6.8. Probabilistic, Arthur-Merlin, and counting classes and the polynomial hierarchy

The question of whether Legitimate-Deck $\leq_m^p$-reduces to GI is left open. Köbler, Schöning, and Torán [KST92] proved that if the Graph Reconstruction Conjecture holds, then Legitimate-Deck is low for certain probabilistic and counting classes, including PP and C=P. For some more recent complexity results in graph reconstruction, see E. Hemaspaandra, L. Hemaspaandra, Radziszowski, and Tripathi [HHRT04].

7

RSA Cryptosystem, Primality, and Factoring

The problem of distinguishing prime numbers from composites, and of resolving composite numbers into their prime factors, is one of the most important and useful in all of arithmetic. ... The dignity of science seems to demand that every aid to the solution of such an elegant and celebrated problem be zealously cultivated.

(Taken from "Disquisitiones Arithmeticae" by Carl Friedrich Gauß, the translation from Latin into English is taken from [Knu98])

Again turning to cryptography, the last two chapters introduce a number of fundamental cryptographic protocols. The security of such protocols usually depends on the assumption that certain problems from number theory and algebra are intractable. Thus, to describe these cryptosystems and protocols and to discuss the related security issues, we need number-theoretical, algebraic, and complexity-theoretic notions, methods, and results.

Section 7.1 presents the famous RSA cryptosystem, invented by Rivest, Shamir, and Adleman in 1978. Their result is a milestone in the history of cryptography, as RSA was the very first public-key cryptosystem (in the open literature, see the bibliographic remarks in Section 7.6). RSA is still very popular and is used in various cryptographic applications. For example, the RSA system can be modified so as to yield a digital signature scheme.

The RSA system uses large prime numbers. The primality problem, which asks whether or not a given integer is prime, has been studied since ancient times. This problem can be solved efficiently in random polynomial time, and Section 7.2 presents some of the common randomized primality tests, such as the Miller–Rabin test and the Solovay–Strassen test. The number-theoretical results on which these tests rest are presented in as much depth as needed in order to understand the tests. We also mention a celebrated result by Agrawal, Kayal, and Saxena, which says that the primality problem can even be solved in deterministic polynomial time.

The RSA system is secure only if large integers cannot be factored efficiently. Section 7.3 studies the factoring problem, which as yet has defied all attempts to design efficient algorithms for it. There are tons of literature on factoring algorithms and their applications in practice, and some of them are discussed in Section 7.3. Section 7.4 investigates the security of RSA by presenting certain potential attacks against this cryptosystem and discussing appropriate countermeasures.

7.1 RSA

We have seen in Chapter 4 that many of the symmetric cryptosystems can be broken by certain types of attacks. In particular, affine linear block ciphers are vulnerable to known-plaintext attacks. In addition to such security issues (and notwithstanding their advantages with respect to efficiency), another major disadvantage of symmetric cryptosystems is the problem of key management and key distribution. If many users participate in a large computer network or communicate over the internet, the issue of how to distribute and how to share keys for symmetric cryptosystems can be quite troublesome.

An elegant solution to this problem, the Diffie–Hellman protocol, will be presented in Section 8.1. Interestingly, their solution to the secret-key agreement problem in symmetric cryptography opened the door to a fundamentally different, new direction in cryptography in which there is no longer any need to share and to distribute any private keys. In public-key cryptography, Bob chooses both a private key, which he keeps secret, and a public key, which is made available to all other users in a public directory. If Alice wants to send him a message, she looks up his public key and uses it to encrypt her message. The idea is that Bob can easily decrypt her ciphertext using his private key, whereas any unauthorized party, such as eavesdropper Erich, fails when trying to decipher Alice's ciphertext because he lacks Bob's private key.

7.1.1 RSA Public-Key Cryptosystem

Many of the protocols presented in Chapters 7 and 8 require elementary notions from number theory, see Section 2.4. In particular, to describe the RSA cryptosystem, we need the multiplicative group

$$\mathbb{Z}_k^* = \{i \mid 1 \leq i \leq k - 1 \text{ and } \gcd(i, k) = 1\},$$

which was introduced in Example 2.35. Recall also the Euler function φ from Definition 2.36, which gives the order of $\mathbb{Z}_k^*$, and recall the arithmetics in the ring $\mathbb{Z}_k = \{0, 1, \ldots, k - 1\}$ from Problem 2.1. The notion of a public-key cryptosystem is introduced formally in Definition 4.1.

Figure 7.1 summarizes the single steps of the RSA protocol. We now describe these steps in more detail.

Step 1: Key Generation. Bob chooses two distinct large prime numbers, p and q with $p \neq q$, and computes their product $n = pq$. Then, he chooses an exponent $e \in \mathbb{N}$ satisfying

$$1 < e < \varphi(n) = (p - 1)(q - 1) \quad \text{and} \quad \gcd(e, \varphi(n)) = 1. \tag{7.1}$$

Using the extended Euclidean Algorithm from Figure 2.2, he then determines the inverse element of $e \bmod \varphi(n)$, i.e., the unique number d satisfying

$$1 < d < \varphi(n) \quad \text{and} \quad e \cdot d \equiv 1 \bmod \varphi(n). \tag{7.2}$$

The pair (n, e) is Bob's public key, and d is Bob's private key.

Step	Alice	Erich	Bob
1			chooses two large primes, p and q, at random, computes $n = pq$ and $\varphi(n) = (p-1)(q-1)$, his public key (n, e), and his private key d satisfying (7.1) and (7.2)
2		$\Leftarrow (n, e)$	
3	encrypts m as $c = m^e \bmod n$		
4		$c \Rightarrow$	
5			decrypts c as $m = c^d \bmod n$

Fig. 7.1. RSA protocol

Step 2: Communication. Bob makes his key (n, e) public.

Step 3: Encryption. As in Chapter 4, messages are strings over an alphabet Σ, which can be viewed as natural numbers in $||\Sigma||$-adic representation. Every message can be encoded block-wise with a fixed block length. Let $m < n$ be the number encoding one block of the message Alice wants to send to Bob. Alice knows Bob's public key (n, e) and encrypts m as the number $c = E_{(n,e)}(m)$, where the encryption function is defined by

$$E_{(n,e)}(m) = m^e \bmod n. \tag{7.3}$$

Step 4: Communication. Alice sends her encrypted message c to Bob.

Step 5: Decryption. Let c with $0 \leq c < n$ be the number encoding one block of the ciphertext that Bob receives. The eavesdropper Erich may also know c, but he does not know Bob's private key d. Bob decrypts c using d and the following decryption function:

$$D_d(c) = c^d \bmod n. \tag{7.4}$$

Theorem 7.1 says that the RSA scheme described above indeed is a cryptosystem as per Definition 4.1. That is, encryption and decryption are inverse to each other.

Theorem 7.1. *Let (n, e) be the public key, and let d be the private key used in the RSA protocol. Then, for each message m with $0 \leq m < n$,*

$$m = (m^e)^d \bmod n.$$

Proof. By (7.2), we have $e \cdot d \equiv 1 \bmod \varphi(n)$. Thus, there exists an integer k such that

$$e \cdot d = 1 + k(p-1)(q-1),$$

where $n = pq$. Hence, we have

$$\begin{aligned}
(m^e)^d = m^{e \cdot d} &= m^{1+k(p-1)(q-1)} \\
&= m\left(m^{k(p-1)(q-1)}\right) \\
&= m\left(m^{p-1}\right)^{k(q-1)}.
\end{aligned}$$

It follows that

$$(m^e)^d \equiv m \bmod p, \tag{7.5}$$

since if p divides m then both sides of (7.5) are congruent to $0 \bmod p$, and if p does not divide m (i.e., $\gcd(p, m) = 1$) then we have

$$m^{p-1} \equiv 1 \bmod p \tag{7.6}$$

by Fermat's Little Theorem. A symmetric argument shows that

$$(m^e)^d \equiv m \bmod q. \tag{7.7}$$

Since p and q are distinct primes, (7.6) and (7.7) imply via Theorem 2.46

$$(m^e)^d \equiv m \bmod n.$$

Since $m < n$, the proof is complete.   ∎

The RSA protocol can be executed efficiently. Note that Alice has to compute $c = m^e \bmod n$ and Bob has to compute $m = c^d \bmod n$. Performed naively, these computations would require a large number of multiplications depending on the size of the exponent. Fortunately, however, the modular exponentiation function can be computed efficiently by employing the "square-and-multiply" algorithm that is shown in Figure 7.2.

SQUARE-AND-MULTIPLY(a, b, m) {
    // a is the exponent, $b < m$ is the base, and m is the modulus
  Determine the binary expansion of the exponent $a = \sum_{i=0}^{k} a_i 2^i$, where $a_i \in \{0, 1\}$;
  Successively, compute $b^{2^0}, b^{2^1}, \ldots, b^{2^k}$ by applying the congruence

$$b^{2^{i+1}} \equiv \left(b^{2^i}\right)^2 \bmod m;$$

    // the intermediate values b^{2^i} need not be stored
  In the arithmetics modulo m, compute $b^a = \prod_{\substack{i=0 \\ a_i=1}}^{k} b^{2^i}$;
  return b^a;
}

Fig. 7.2. The "square-and-multiply" algorithm

The computation of $b^a \bmod m$ in Figure 7.2 is correct, since in the arithmetics modulo m,

$$b^a = b^{\sum_{i=0}^{k} a_i 2^i} = \prod_{i=0}^{k} \left(b^{2^i}\right)^{a_i} = \prod_{\substack{i=0 \\ a_i=1}}^{k} b^{2^i}.$$

How should one choose the prime numbers p and q in the RSA protocol from Figure 7.1? First of all, they must be large enough, since otherwise Erich could factor the number n in Bob's public key (n, e). Knowing n, he could use the extended Euclidean Algorithm from Figure 2.2 to determine Bob's private key d, which is the unique inverse of e mod $\varphi(n)$, where $\varphi(n) = (p-1)(q-1)$. That is why the primes p and q must be kept secret and thus need to be large enough to prevent this direct attack. In practice, they should be chosen so as to have at least 80 decimal digits. One generates numbers of this size randomly and then checks—using one of the common primality tests—whether or not the numbers chosen are primes indeed. By the prime number theorem, there are approximately $N/\ln N$ primes not exceeding N, see Theorem 7.3. Thus, the odds are good to hit a prime after reasonably few trials. Primality tests are described in Section 7.2. Example 7.2 gives a concrete application of the RSA system. Of course, this is just a toy example with way too small numbers and thus far from being secure.

Example 7.2 (RSA).   Bob chooses the primes $p = 67$ and $q = 11$ and computes $n = 67 \cdot 11 = 737$ and $\varphi(n) = (p-1)(q-1) = 66 \cdot 10 = 660$. If Bob now chooses the smallest possible exponent for $\varphi(n) = 660$, which is $e = 7$, then his public key is the pair $(n, e) = (737, 7)$. Using the extended Euclidean Algorithm from Figure 2.2, Bob determines his private key $d = 283$, and we have (see Exercise 7.1):

$$e \cdot d = 7 \cdot 283 = 1981 \equiv 1 \bmod 660.$$

As in Section 4.1, the alphabet $\Sigma = \{A, B, \ldots, Z\}$ is identified with the set $\mathbb{Z}_{26} = \{0, 1, \ldots, 25\}$. Messages again are strings over Σ and will be encoded blockwise, with a fixed block length, as nonnegative integers in 26-adic representation. In our example, the block length is

$$\ell = \lfloor \log_{26} n \rfloor = \lfloor \log_{26} 737 \rfloor = 2.$$

Any block $b = b_1 b_2 \cdots b_\ell$ of length ℓ with $b_i \in \mathbb{Z}_{26}$ is represented by the integer $m_b = \sum_{i=1}^{\ell} b_i \cdot 26^{\ell-i}$. From the definition of the block length $\ell = \lfloor \log_{26} n \rfloor$, we have

$$0 \leq m_b \leq 25 \cdot \sum_{i=1}^{\ell} 26^{\ell-i} = 26^\ell - 1 < n.$$

Using the RSA encryption function (7.3), the integer m_b corresponding to the block b is encrypted by $c_b = (m_b)^e \bmod n$, where $c_b = c_0 c_1 \cdots c_\ell$ with $c_i \in \mathbb{Z}_{26}$ is the ciphertext for block b. RSA thus maps blocks of length ℓ injectively to blocks of length $\ell + 1$. Table 7.1 shows how some message of length 34 is subdivided into 17 blocks of length 2, and how the single blocks written as integers are then encrypted. For example, the first block, "RS," is turned into an integer as follows: the "R" corresponds to 17 and the "S" to 18, and we have

$$17 \cdot 26^1 + 18 \cdot 26^0 = 442 + 18 = 460.$$

The resulting integer c_b is again written in 26-adic representation and may have length $\ell + 1$:

	RS	AI	ST	HE	KE	YT	OP	UB	LI	CK	EY	CR	YP	TO	GR	AP	HY
m_b	460	8	487	186	264	643	379	521	294	62	128	69	639	508	173	15	206
c_b	697	387	229	340	165	223	586	5	189	600	325	262	100	689	354	665	673

Table 7.1. Example of an RSA encryption

$$c_b = \sum_{i=0}^{\ell} c_i \cdot 26^{\ell-i},$$

where $c_i \in \mathbb{Z}_{26}$, see Exercise 7.1. In particular, the first block, $697 = 676 + 21 = 1 \cdot 26^2 + 0 \cdot 26^1 + 21 \cdot 26^0$, is turned into the ciphertext "BAV."

Decryption also works block-wise. For instance, to decrypt the first block using the private key $d = 283$, compute $697^{283} \mod 737$, again employing the fast exponentiation from Figure 7.2. It is useful to reduce modulo $n = 737$ after each multiplication to prevent the integers from becoming too large. The binary expansion of the exponent is $283 = 2^0 + 2^1 + 2^3 + 2^4 + 2^8$, and we obtain

$$697^{283} \equiv 697^{2^0} \cdot 697^{2^1} \cdot 697^{2^3} \cdot 697^{2^4} \cdot 697^{2^8} \equiv 697 \cdot 126 \cdot 9 \cdot 81 \cdot 15 \equiv 460 \mod 737$$

as desired.

7.1.2 RSA Digital Signature Scheme

The RSA public-key cryptosystem from Figure 7.1 can be modified so as to obtain a protocol for digital signatures as shown in Figure 7.3. It is easy to verify that the protocol works, see Exercise 7.2. This protocol is vulnerable to chosen-plaintext attacks, i.e., the attacker can choose plaintexts and learns the corresponding ciphertexts from which the keys used can be determined. Section 7.4 describes this attack and possible countermeasures to prevent it.

Step	Alice	Erich	Bob
1	chooses $n = pq$, her public key (n, e) and her private key d just as Bob does in the RSA protocol from Figure 7.1		
2		$(n, e) \Rightarrow$	
3	signs the message m with $\mathrm{sig}_A(m) = m^d \mod n$		
4		$\langle m, \mathrm{sig}_A(m) \rangle \Rightarrow$	
5			verifies Alice's signature by $m \equiv (\mathrm{sig}_A(m))^e \mod n$

Fig. 7.3. RSA digital signature scheme

7.2 Primality Tests

As mentioned in Section 7.1.1, many public-key cryptosystems make use of large prime numbers. In practice, they are obtained by randomly picking large numbers of the required size and then checking whether or not they indeed are prime numbers. This checking is done by means of one of the randomized primality tests to be described in this section, which also investigates the complexity of the primality problem. Both the generation of large numbers and the primality tests require a suitable source of randomness. Ideally, one would like to toss a fair coin to generate a random bit stream or a fair "dice" with n faces to randomly pick a number in the interval $\{1, 2, \ldots, n\}$ under the uniform distribution. In practice, however, one uses pseudorandom generators, which produce sequences of numbers (or bits) that "look" random in the sense that they cannot be distinguished statistically or efficiently from truly random sequences.

A natural number $n \geq 2$ is said to be a *prime number* if it has no divisors other than the trivial ones, 1 and n. Otherwise, if n is not prime, it is said to be *composite*, i.e., $n = x \cdot y$ for integers x and y with $1 < x, y < n$. The reason the method of finding primes described in the previous paragraph is likely to be successful is that the prime numbers are sufficiently dense in intervals of the form $\{1, 2, \ldots, N\}$. This fact is known as the prime number theorem, a deep result from number theory the proof of which is omitted here.

Theorem 7.3 (Prime Number Theorem).   *If $\pi(N)$ denotes the number of primes $p \leq N$ and $\ln N$ denotes the natural logarithm, then*

$$\lim_{N \to \infty} \frac{\pi(N) \ln N}{N} = 1.$$

It is often enough to consider the following weaker version of the prime number theorem, which gives (up to constants) approximate upper and lower bounds of $\pi(N)$:

$$\mathcal{O}\left(\frac{N}{\log N}\right) \leq \pi(N) \leq \mathcal{O}\left(\frac{N}{\log N}\right).$$

The primality problem asks, given an integer $n \geq 2$ in binary, whether or not n is prime. This utterly natural, intriguing problem was first studied in ancient Greece, long before its practical importance (e.g., in cryptographic applications) became evident, and it has continued to fascinate mathematicians and computer scientists ever since.

Definition 7.4 (Primality Problem).   *Define the primality problem by*

$$\texttt{Primes} = \{\texttt{bin}(n) \mid n \text{ is a prime number}\}.$$

Of course, this problem would be trivial if Primes were a finite set. However, Euclid proved that there are infinitely many prime numbers, see Exercise 7.3. A well-known method to generate a finite list of primes is the *sieve of Eratosthenes*.

Example 7.5 (Sieve of Eratosthenes). Informally stated, this ancient algorithm works as follows. Suppose you want to find out which numbers in $\{2, 3, \ldots, n\}$ are primes. Initially, none of the elements in this interval is marked. For each

$i=2$	2	3	4	5	6	7	8	9	10	11	12	13	14	15	16	17	18	19	20
	21	22	23	24	25	26	27	28	29	30	31	32	33	34	35	36	37	38	39
$i=3$	2	3	4	5	6	7	8	9	10	11	12	13	14	15	16	17	18	19	20
	21	22	23	24	25	26	27	28	29	30	31	32	33	34	35	36	37	38	39
$i=4$	2	3	4	5	6	7	8	9	10	11	12	13	14	15	16	17	18	19	20
	21	22	23	24	25	26	27	28	29	30	31	32	33	34	35	36	37	38	39
$i=5$	2	3	4	5	6	7	8	9	10	11	12	13	14	15	16	17	18	19	20
	21	22	23	24	25	26	27	28	29	30	31	32	33	34	35	36	37	38	39
$i=6$	2	3	4	5	6	7	8	9	10	11	12	13	14	15	16	17	18	19	20
	21	22	23	24	25	26	27	28	29	30	31	32	33	34	35	36	37	38	39

Table 7.2. Sieve of Eratosthenes

$i \in \{2, 3, \ldots, \lfloor\sqrt{n}\rfloor\}$ in this order, carry out the following steps: If i is unmarked, then mark all multiples of i, i.e., all numbers $j = k \cdot i$ with $i \le k \le n/i$. No prime number can ever be marked by this procedure, since only numbers with nontrivial divisors are marked. However, all composite numbers in $\{2, 3, \ldots, n\}$ will be marked. For a concrete example, look at Table 7.2 that shows which numbers from the interval $\{2, 3, \ldots, 39\}$ are marked in the course of applying the sieve of Eratosthenes.

```
TRIAL-DIVISION(n) {                    // n ∈ ℕ with n ≥ 2
    for (i = 2, 3, ..., ⌊√n⌋) {
        if (i divides n) return "n is composite" and halt;
    }
    return "n is prime" and halt;
}
```

Fig. 7.4. Trial division to solve the primality problem

Figure 7.4 shows a naive approach to solving the primality problem, the trial division algorithm. Starting with $i = 2$, this algorithm checks in each loop whether the current value of i divides n. If so, n is composite. Otherwise, i is incremented by one to check the next candidate, and so on until i is $\lfloor\sqrt{n}\rfloor$. If none of the tests reveals that i is composite, the algorithm answers that n is prime. If $\ell = \lfloor\log n\rfloor + 1$ is the length of the input n given in binary, this algorithm runs in the worst case in time $\mathcal{O}(2^{\ell/2})$ and thus is far from being efficient.

One might try to improve the TRIAL-DIVISION algorithm. For example, checking if n is divisible by 2, 3, 5, or 7 in a preparatory phase and then skipping all multiples of 2, 3, 5, and 7 in the for loop will speed this computation up. However, such tricks do not help to save an appreciable amount of computing time. In contrast, randomized algorithms employing certain number-theoretical results are much more appropriate when one seeks efficient ways of checking primality. In the following sections, randomized algorithms for the primality problem are discussed.

7.2.1 Fermat Test

Recall Fermat's Little Theorem (see Corollary 2.39), which says that if p is a prime number and $1 \leq a < p$, then $a^{p-1} \equiv 1 \bmod p$. This result provides a criterion for checking primality that we are going to employ in a randomized primality test.

Example 7.6. Let $a = 3$. Table 7.3 gives the pairs $(n, 3^{n-1} \bmod n)$ for each n with $4 \leq n \leq 23$. All composite numbers n in this table have a value $3^{n-1} \bmod n$ distinct from 1, whereas all prime numbers n satisfy $3^{n-1} \bmod n = 1$. It thus seems that Fermat's Little Theorem provides a good criterion for checking primality.

n	4	5	6	7	8	9	10	11	12	13	14	15	16	17	18	19	20	21	22	23
$3^{n-1} \bmod n$	3	1	3	1	3	0	3	1	3	1	3	9	11	1	9	1	7	9	3	1

Table 7.3. Using Fermat's Little Theorem for testing primality

We now introduce the notion of a Fermat witness and a Fermat liar. Intuitively, a Fermat witness certifies compositeness: By the contrapositive of Fermat's Little Theorem, if n and a, $1 \leq a < n$, satisfy $a^{n-1} \not\equiv 1 \bmod n$, then n must be composite. Such an a is called a Fermat witness for n. On the other hand, a Fermat liar a makes n look like a prime number in that it satisfies $a^{n-1} \equiv 1 \bmod n$, even though n in fact is composite.

Definition 7.7 (Fermat Witness and Fermat Liar).

- *For each $n \geq 2$, any number a, $1 \leq a < n$, satisfying $a^{n-1} \not\equiv 1 \bmod n$ is said to be a* Fermat witness *for n.*
- *For each odd composite number $n \geq 3$, any number a, $1 \leq a < n$, satisfying $a^{n-1} \equiv 1 \bmod n$ is said to be a* Fermat liar *for n.*

Note that a Fermat witness a for a composite number n does not provide any information about the prime factors of n. That is why the Fermat test given in Figure 7.5 below is not a factoring algorithm. Exercise 7.4 asks you to show that 2 is a Fermat witness for each $n \leq 340$, yet is a Fermat liar for $341 = 11 \cdot 31$. In contrast, 3 is a Fermat witness for 341, since $3^{340} \equiv 56 \bmod 341$.

The existence of Fermat liars shows that the converse of Fermat's Little Theorem is not true, i.e., the condition $a^{n-1} \equiv 1 \bmod n$ does not imply that n is prime. For example, as noted above, $2^{340} \equiv 1 \bmod 341$, yet 341 is composite. However, one can show a claim somewhat weaker than this converse.

Lemma 7.8. *Let $n \geq 2$ be any integer.*

1. *If a satisfies $1 \leq a < n$ and $a^k \equiv 1 \bmod n$ for some $k \geq 1$, then $a \in \mathbb{Z}_n^*$.*
2. *If n is an odd composite number, then there exists some Fermat witness a for n.*

Proof.   1. Suppose that $a^k \equiv 1 \bmod n$ for some $k \geq 1$ and a with $1 \leq a < n$. Then $a \cdot a^{k-1} \equiv 1 \bmod n$. It is easy to show that $a \in \mathbb{Z}_n^*$ if and only if there exists some $b \in \mathbb{Z}_n$ with $a \cdot b \equiv 1 \bmod n$, see Exercise 7.5. With $b = a^{k-1} \in \mathbb{Z}_n$, the claim follows.

2. We prove the contrapositive. Suppose that n has no Fermat witness. For each a with $1 \leq a < n$, we thus have $a^{n-1} \equiv 1 \bmod n$. By the first part of this lemma, $\mathbb{Z}_n^* = \{1, 2, \ldots, n-1\}$. But this means that n has no nontrivial divisors and thus is a prime number.   ∎

One can even assert a claim stronger than the second part of Lemma 7.8: For each odd composite number n, the set

$$\{1, 2, \ldots, n-1\} - \mathbb{Z}_n^* = \{a \mid 1 \leq a < n \text{ and } \gcd(a, n) \neq 1\}$$

does not contain any Fermat liar. Unfortunately, this set is very sparse for many composite numbers. In the RSA cryptosystem, for instance, one chooses two primes, p and q, and takes their product $n = pq$. A number a satisfies $\gcd(a, n) \neq 1$ if and only if a is a multiple of p or q. There are exactly $p + q - 2$ such numbers in the set $\{1, 2, \ldots, n-1\}$, very few compared with n if p and q are roughly of the same size.

Example 7.9 (Fermat Witness and Fermat Liar).   Suppose that $n = 143 = 11 \cdot 13$. Table 7.4 shows all Fermat witnesses for n and all Fermat liars for n. The Fermat witnesses are partitioned into three subsets: multiples of p, multiples of q, and Fermat witnesses in $\mathbb{Z}_{143}^*$. Observe that the latter group of Fermat witnesses is way larger than the set of multiples of p and q.

FERMAT(n) {   // $n \geq 3$ is an odd integer
    Randomly choose a number $a \in \{2, 3, \ldots, n-2\}$ under the uniform distribution;
    if $(a^{n-1} \not\equiv 1 \bmod n)$ return "n is composite" and halt;
      else return "n is prime" and halt;
}

Fig. 7.5. Fermat test for primality

Figure 7.5 describes the Fermat test, our first randomized primality test. As per Table 7.4 from Example 7.9, if the Fermat test runs on input $n = 143$, then the

Multiples of 11	11	22	33	44	55	66	77	88	99	110	121	132
Multiples of 13	13	26	39	52	65	78	91	104	117	130		
Fermat witnesses	2	3	4	5	6	7	8	9	10	14	15	16
in $\mathbb{Z}_{143}^{*}$	17	18	19	20	21	23	24	25	27	28	29	30
	31	32	34	35	36	37	38	40	41	42	43	45
	46	47	48	49	50	51	53	54	56	57	58	59
	60	61	62	63	64	67	68	69	70	71	72	73
	74	75	76	79	80	81	82	83	84	85	86	87
	89	90	92	93	94	95	96	97	98	100	101	102
	103	105	106	107	108	109	111	112	113	114	115	116
	118	119	120	122	123	124	125	126	127	128	129	133
	134	135	136	137	138	139	140	141				
Fermat liars	1	12	131	142								

Table 7.4. Fermat witnesses and Fermat liars for $n = 143$

probability that it answers "n is composite" is $138/140 \approx 0.9857$, since there are only two Fermat liars other than the trivial ones, 1 and 142. In other words, the Fermat witnesses outnumber the Fermat liars clearly in this example. If this were the case for all odd composite numbers, the Fermat test would be a no-biased Monte Carlo algorithm for the primality problem or, equivalently, a yes-biased Monte Carlo algorithm for the complementary problem of deciding whether a given number is composite.

Recall from Section 6.2.1 that if a yes-biased Monte Carlo algorithm for some decision problem L gives the answer "yes" then the input is in L; conversely, if the input is in L then the (correct) answer "yes" occurs with probability at least $1/2$, but an incorrect answer "no" can occur with probability less than $1/2$. Thus, yes-biased Monte Carlo algorithms always give correct "yes" answers but perhaps incorrect "no" answers.

If the Fermat test from Figure 7.5 gives the answer "n is composite," then a Fermat witness was picked at random, which implies that n is composite indeed. However, if n is composite, then the Fermat test does not say so with probability at least $1/2$ for each given n, and thus is not a Monte Carlo algorithm. To wit, in the extreme case, there exist composite numbers n for which all elements of $\mathbb{Z}_n^*$ are Fermat liars. Such stubborn numbers are called *Carmichael numbers*; the smallest example is $561 = 3 \cdot 11 \cdot 17$. Carmichael numbers also have Fermat witnesses in $\mathbb{Z}_n - \mathbb{Z}_n^*$, i.e., the Fermat witnesses of a Carmichael number n is not coprime to n. It is known that there are infinitely many Carmichael numbers.

Theorem 7.12 below says that the Fermat test has a sufficiently high success probability for "good" inputs. To this end, we first need some elementary group-theoretic facts. Lemma 7.10 below provides a condition sufficient to prove that a subset of a finite group in fact is a subgroup. Note that the assumption that the group be finite is crucial here. For example, although $\mathbb{N} \subseteq \mathbb{Z}$ and $\mathbb{N}$ contains 0 and is closed under addition, $(\mathbb{N}, +)$ is not a subgroup of $(\mathbb{Z}, +)$ because $\mathbb{Z}$ is not finite.

Recall from Definition 2.34 in Section 2.4.1 that $\mathfrak{H} = (H, \circ)$ is a subgroup of a group $\mathfrak{G} = (G, \circ)$ if $H \subseteq G$ and $\mathfrak{H}$ satisfies the group axioms: $\mathfrak{H}$ is closed under the group operation $\circ$, which is associative on H; $\mathfrak{H}$ inherits the neutral element e from $\mathfrak{G}$; and all elements of $\mathfrak{H}$ have inverses.

Lemma 7.10. *If* $\mathfrak{G} = (G, \circ)$ *is a finite group with neutral element* e *and* H *is a subset of* G *such that* $e \in H$ *and* H *is closed under the group operation* $\circ$, *then* $\mathfrak{H} = (H, \circ)$ *is a subgroup of* $\mathfrak{G}$.

Proof.   It is enough to show that all elements of $\mathfrak{H}$ have inverses. Given any element x of H, define the function $\sigma_x : H \to H$ by

$$\sigma_x(y) = x \circ y.$$

Since H is closed under the group operation $\circ$, every function σ_x is well-defined. Since $\mathfrak{G} = (G, \circ)$ is a group, every function σ_x is injective. Since $\mathfrak{G}$ is finite, every σ_x is a bijection on H. Since σ_x is a bijection on H and since e, the neutral element in $\mathfrak{G}$, belongs to H, there exists an element $z \in H$ such that $\sigma_x(z) = x \circ z = e$. Thus, $z = x^{-1}$ is the inverse element of x in $\mathfrak{H}$.   ∎

Recall that $\mathbb{Z}_n^*$ is a finite multiplicative group of order $\varphi(n)$. The following lemma says that the order of any finite group $\mathfrak{G}$ is divided by the order of each subgroup of $\mathfrak{G}$. The proof of Lemma 7.11 is left to the reader as Exercise 7.6.

Lemma 7.11. *If* $\mathfrak{G} = (G, \circ)$ *is a finite group and* $\mathfrak{H}$ *is a subgroup of* $\mathfrak{G}$, *then the order of* $\mathfrak{H}$ *divides the order of* $\mathfrak{G}$.

We are now ready to prove the following result that gives a good probability bound of the Fermat test for many composite numbers, namely, for all numbers that are not Carmichael numbers.

Theorem 7.12. *If* $n \geq 3$ *is an odd composite number that has at least one Fermat witness in* $\mathbb{Z}_n^*$, *then the Fermat test on input* n *gives the correct answer "n is composite" with probability at least* $1/2$.

Proof.   By the first part of Lemma 7.8, the set of Fermat liars for any number n is a subset of $\mathbb{Z}_n^*$. For each $n \geq 3$, define this set by

$$\text{F-Liars}_n = \{a \mid 1 \leq a < n \text{ and } a^{n-1} \equiv 1 \bmod n\}.$$

We now show that F-Liars$_n$ even is a subgroup of $\mathbb{Z}_n^*$. Since $\mathbb{Z}_n^*$ is a finite multiplicative group, Lemma 7.10 can be applied. Thus, it is enough to prove that F-Liars$_n$ contains the neutral element of $\mathbb{Z}_n^*$ and is closed under multiplication modulo n. The neutral element of $\mathbb{Z}_n^*$ is 1 and, as mentioned above, 1 trivially is in F-Liars$_n$, see Exercise 7.4(c). To show that the set F-Liars$_n$ is closed under multiplication modulo n, note that if $a^{n-1} \equiv 1 \bmod n$ and $b^{n-1} \equiv 1 \bmod n$, then

$$(a \cdot b)^{n-1} \equiv a^{n-1} \cdot b^{n-1} \equiv 1 \cdot 1 \equiv 1 \bmod n.$$

By Lemma 7.10, F-Liars$_n$ is a subgroup of $\mathbb{Z}_n^*$.

By assumption, there is at least one Fermat witness for n in $\mathbb{Z}_n^*$. Thus, F-Liars$_n$ even is a *proper* subgroup of $\mathbb{Z}_n^*$. This fact can be employed to establish a much better bound on the size of F-Liars$_n$ than $\varphi(n) - 1$, the size of $\mathbb{Z}_n^*$ minus the one Fermat witness in $\mathbb{Z}_n^*$. Since F-Liars$_n$ is a proper subgroup of $\mathbb{Z}_n^*$, Lemma 7.11 implies that the size of F-Liars$_n$ is a nontrivial divisor of $\varphi(n)$. Since $\varphi(n) < n - 1$, the size of F-Liars$_n$ is at most $(n - 2)/2$.

Consider the event that an integer a randomly chosen from $\{2, 3, \ldots, n - 2\}$ by the Fermat test is a Fermat liar other than the trivial ones, 1 or $n - 1$. It follows that this event occurs with probability at most

$$\frac{(n - 2)/2 - 2}{n - 3} = \frac{n - 6}{2(n - 3)} < \frac{1}{2}$$

as desired.   ∎

7.2.2 Miller–Rabin Test

As mentioned above, the reason why the Fermat test is not a Monte Carlo algorithm for `Primes` is that $\mathbb{Z}_n^*$ contains too many Fermat liars for infinitely many composite numbers n, namely, for all Carmichael numbers n. In this case, $\mathbb{Z}_n^*$ consists of nothing else than Fermat liars. Thus, given a Carmichael number n as input, the Fermat test gives the wrong answer "n is prime" with probability

$$\frac{\varphi(n) - 2}{n - 3} > \frac{\varphi(n)}{n}.$$

Since one can show that $\varphi(n)/n$ equals $\prod(1 - 1/p)$, where the product is taken over all prime factors p of n, the error probability of the Fermat test running on a Carmichael number n is annoyingly close to one. This disadvantage is avoided by the Miller–Rabin test, one of the most popular randomized primality tests, which is shown in Figure 7.6.

Theorem 7.19 below says that the Miller–Rabin test is a no-biased Monte Carlo algorithm for `Primes`, that is, its "no" answers are always reliable, whereas its "yes" answers may be erroneous. In symbols, `Primes` is in coRP. The class RP, introduced in Definition 6.2, contains precisely the problems A for which there is an NPTM M such that for each input x, if $x \in A$ then $M(x)$ accepts with a probability of at least $1/2$, and if $x \notin A$ then $M(x)$ rejects with certainty. And coRP $= \{\overline{A} \mid A \in \text{RP}\}$ is the class of complements of RP sets.

The proof of Theorem 7.19 requires some basic number-theoretical facts some of which are provided without proof here. The proof of Lemma 7.13 is left to the reader as Exercise 7.7(a).

Lemma 7.13. *Every Carmichael number is the product of at least three distinct prime factors.*

```
MILLER-RABIN(n) {                                    // n ≥ 3 is an odd integer
    Determine the representation n − 1 = 2^k m, where m is odd;
    Randomly choose a number a ∈ {1, 2, . . . , n − 1} under the uniform distribution;
    x := a^m mod n;
    if (x ≡ 1 mod n) return "n is prime" and halt;
    for (j = 0, 1, . . . , k − 1) {
        if (x ≡ −1 mod n) return "n is prime" and halt;
            else x := x^2 mod n;
    }
    return "n is composite" and halt;
}
```

Fig. 7.6. Primality test by Miller and Rabin

Definition 2.43 introduced the notion of quadratic residues modulo n. An element x is a quadratic residue modulo n if and only if there is some a, $1 \leq a < n$, such that $x \equiv a^2 \bmod n$. If $x = 1$, such an a is said to be a *square root of* 1 *modulo* n. Trivially, 1 and $n - 1$ are always square roots of 1 modulo n, since

$$1^2 \equiv 1 \bmod n \quad \text{and} \quad (n - 1)^2 \equiv (-1)^2 \equiv 1 \bmod n.$$

If n is a prime number, then it has no square roots of 1 modulo n other than the trivial ones. The proof of Lemma 7.14 is left to the reader as Exercise 7.7(b).

Lemma 7.14. *Every prime number n has only the two trivial square roots of* 1 *modulo n, namely* ± 1 mod n.

Hence, if n has a nontrivial square root of 1 modulo n, then n must be composite. Conversely, if $n = p_1 p_2 \cdots p_k$ is composite, where the p_i are odd prime numbers, then the Chinese Remainder Theorem (see Theorem 2.46) can be applied to show that n has exactly 2^k square roots of 1 modulo n. More precisely, the square roots of 1 modulo n are all numbers a, $1 \leq a < n$, that satisfy $a \bmod p_i \in \{1, p_i - 1\}$ for $1 \leq i \leq k$. Thus, trying to find nontrivial square roots of 1 modulo n by randomly picking a number a is hopeless, unless n happens to have extraordinarily many prime factors.

Example 7.15 (Nontrivial Square roots of 1 *modulo n).*   Continuing Example 7.9, consider the composite number $n = 143 = 11 \cdot 13$. Since 143 has two prime factors, there are four square roots of 1 modulo 143, namely 1, 12, 131, and 142. The nontrivial square roots of 1 modulo 143 are 12 and 131. In this example, the square roots of 1 modulo 143 happen to be just the Fermat liars for 143, see Table 7.4. In general, however, this is not the case.

The Miller–Rabin test uses a criterion that strengthens Fermat's Little Theorem. To describe this criterion, we now introduce the notion of a Miller–Rabin witness and a Miller–Rabin liar (for short, MR-witness and MR-liar). Intuitively, an MR-witness a certifies that a number n is composite, and an MR-liar a makes n look like a prime number, even though n in fact is composite.

Definition 7.16 (MR-Witness and MR-Liar).

Let $n \geq 3$ be any odd number, and let a be any number in $\mathbb{Z}_n^*$. Define $m = (n-1)/2^k$, where $k = \max\{j \in \mathbb{N} \mid 2^j \text{ divides } n - 1\}$.

- *We say that a is an MR-witness for n if and only if none of (7.8) and (7.9) is true:*

$$a^m \equiv 1 \bmod n; \tag{7.8}$$

$$(\exists j \in \{0, 1, \ldots, k - 1\})\, [a^{2^j m} \equiv -1 \bmod n]. \tag{7.9}$$

- *We say that a is an MR-liar for n if and only if n is a composite number and a is not an MR-witness.*

Example 7.17 (MR-Witness and MR-Liar). Consider $n = 561 = 3 \cdot 11 \cdot 17$, the above-mentioned smallest Carmichael number. Table 7.5 displays 22 selected MR-

a	$a^{35} \bmod 561$	$a^{70} \bmod 561$	$a^{140} \bmod 561$	$a^{280} \bmod 561$	$a^{560} \bmod 561$
1	1	1	1	1	1
2	263	166	67	1	1
3	78	474	276	441	375
4	166	67	1	1	1
5	23	529	463	67	1
6	318	144	540	441	375
7	241	298	166	67	1
8	461	463	67	1	1
9	474	276	441	375	375
10	439	298	166	67	1
11	209	484	319	220	154
12	45	342	276	441	375
13	208	67	1	1	1
14	551	100	463	67	1
15	111	540	441	375	375
16	67	1	1	1	1
17	527	34	34	34	34
18	120	375	375	375	375
19	76	166	67	1	1
20	452	100	463	67	1
30	21	441	375	375	375
40	505	331	166	67	1
50	560	1	1	1	1
101	560	1	1	1	1
452	320	298	166	67	1
460	1	1	1	1	1

Table 7.5. MR-witnesses and MR-liars for the Carmichael number $n = 561$

witnesses for 561 and four MR-liars for 561. Note that 13 of the 22 MR-witnesses for 561 are in $\mathbb{Z}_{561}^*$, while nine of them are multiples of the prime factors of 561. In contrast, no element of $\mathbb{Z}_{561}^*$ is a Fermat witness for 561, since 561 is a Carmichael number. Thus, the Fermat test is not able to detect that 561 is composite.

As per Definition 7.16, since $560 = 35 \cdot 2^4$ and no larger power of two divides 560, we have $k = 4$ and $m = 35$. In the leftmost column of Table 7.5, each of the numbers a other than those from $\{1, 50, 101, 460\}$ is an MR-witness, since neither condition (7.8) nor condition (7.9) is satisfied. However, (7.9) is true for $a = 50$:

$$50^{2^0 \cdot 35} = 50^{35} \equiv -1 \bmod 561,$$

and similarly so for 101. Thus, both 50 and 101 are MR-liars. And 1 and 460 are MR-liars as well, since they satisfy condition (7.8):

$$1^{35} \equiv 460^{35} \equiv 1 \bmod 561.$$

By definition of k and m, we have $a^{n-1} = a^{2^k m}$ for each a; the corresponding values of $a^{560} \equiv a^{2^4 \cdot 35} \bmod 561$ are in the rightmost column of Table 7.5. As mentioned above, all $a \in \mathbb{Z}_{561}^*$ in this column are Fermat liars for 561, since 561 is a Carmichael number.

The following lemma is easy to verify, see Exercise 7.7(c) and also the proof of Theorem 7.19.

Lemma 7.18. *If there exists an MR-witness for n, then n is composite.*

Theorem 7.19. `Primes` *is in* coRP.

Proof. We show that the Miller–Rabin test accepts `Primes` with a one-sided error probability. First, we prove that if the input n indeed is a prime number, then the algorithm from Figure 7.6 must answer that n is prime. For a contradiction, assume that n is prime, yet the Miller–Rabin test halts with the output: "n is composite." We show that it then must have found an MR-witness a for n, which by Lemma 7.18 certifies that n must be composite contradicting the assumption.

Since the Miller–Rabin test outputs "n is composite," we have $a^m \not\equiv 1 \bmod n$, where $a \in \{1, 2, \ldots, n-1\}$ is the number randomly picked by the Miller–Rabin test. Since x is squared in each `for` loop, the algorithm tests sequentially the values $a^m, a^{2m}, \ldots, a^{2^{k-1}m}$. For none of these values does the algorithm answer that n is a prime. It follows that for each j with $0 \le j \le k - 1$,

$$a^{2^j m} \not\equiv -1 \bmod n.$$

Since $n - 1 = 2^k m$, it follows from Fermat's Little Theorem (see Corollary 2.39) that $a^{2^k m} \equiv 1 \bmod n$. Thus, $a^{2^{k-1} m}$ is a square root of 1 modulo n. Since n is prime by our assumption, Lemma 7.14 implies that there are only the two trivial square roots of 1 modulo n, namely $\pm 1 \bmod n$, see also Exercise 7.7(b).

Since $a^{2^{k-1}m} \not\equiv -1 \bmod n$ and n is prime, it follows that $a^{2^{k-1}m} \equiv 1 \bmod n$. Thus, $a^{2^{k-2}m}$ is also a square root of 1 modulo n. Applying the same argument, we again have $a^{2^{k-2}m} \equiv 1 \bmod n$. Repeatedly applying this argument, we eventually obtain $a^m \equiv 1 \bmod n$, a contradiction. Thus, the Miller–Rabin test correctly outputs "n is prime" for each prime number n.

Conversely, if n is composite, we show that the Miller–Rabin test incorrectly outputs that n is prime with probability less than $1/2$. However, we cannot do so by applying the same argument as in the proof of Theorem 7.12: We cannot bound the number of MR-liars by showing that the set

$$\text{MR-Liars}_n = \{a \mid a \text{ is an MR-liar for } n\}$$

forms a proper subgroup of $\mathbb{Z}_n^*$, since this is not true in general; see Exercise 7.8(c) for some counterexamples. That is why we use a different argument: We specify some set containing MR-Liars$_n$ and forming a proper subgroup of $\mathbb{Z}_n^*$. Distinguish two cases.

Case 1: n is not a Carmichael number. So MR-Liars$_n \subseteq$ F-Liars$_n \neq \mathbb{Z}_n^*$, and the argument of Theorem 7.12 can be applied to prove that the probability of hitting an MR-liar when randomly picking a number in $\{1, 2, \ldots, n-1\}$ is less than $1/2$.

Case 2: n is a Carmichael number. In this case, MR-Liars$_n \subseteq$ F-Liars$_n = \mathbb{Z}_n^*$, so the set of Fermat liars is not a *proper* subgroup of $\mathbb{Z}_n^*$. In order to specify a proper subgroup of $\mathbb{Z}_n^*$ that still contains all MR-liars, let m and k be as in Definition 7.16: $m = (n-1)/2^k$ is odd, and $k = \max\{j \in \mathbb{N} \mid 2^j \text{ divides } n-1\}$. Since m is odd, $(n-1)^m \equiv (-1)^m \equiv -1 \bmod n$. Thus, there exist MR-liars a satisfying (7.9). Let $j_{\max}$ be the maximum $j \in \{0, 1, \ldots, k-1\}$ such that $a^{2^j m} \equiv -1 \bmod n$. Since n is a Carmichael number, we have

$$a^{2^k m} = a^{n-1} \equiv 1 \bmod n,$$

so $j_{\max} < k$. Define the set

$$\text{MR-LIARS}_n = \{a \mid 0 \leq a < n \text{ and } a^{m \cdot 2^{j_{\max}}} \equiv \pm 1 \bmod n\}.$$

The following proposition says that MR-LIARS$_n$ has the desired properties.

Proposition 7.20. *1.* MR-Liars$_n \subseteq$ MR-LIARS$_n$.
2. MR-LIARS$_n$ *is a proper subgroup of* $\mathbb{Z}_n^*$.

Proof of Proposition 7.20. 1. Let a be an arbitrary MR-liar. Thus, a satisfies either condition (7.8) or condition (7.9). If a satisfies condition (7.8), i.e., if $a^m \equiv 1 \bmod n$, then $a^{m \cdot 2^{j_{\max}}} \equiv 1 \bmod n$, which implies that a is in MR-LIARS$_n$.

On the other hand, if a satisfies condition (7.9), i.e., if $a^{2^j m} \equiv -1 \bmod n$ for some j with $0 \leq j < k$, then $j \leq j_{\max}$ by the definition of $j_{\max}$. If $j = j_{\max}$, then a is immediately in MR-LIARS$_n$. If $j < j_{\max}$, then

$$a^{m \cdot 2^{j_{\max}}} \equiv a^{m \cdot 2^j \cdot 2^{j_{\max}-j}} \equiv \left(a^{m \cdot 2^j}\right)^{2^{j_{\max}-j}} \equiv 1 \bmod n,$$

which implies that a is in MR-LIARS$_n$.

2. Since $\mathbb{Z}_n^*$ is a finite group, Lemma 7.10 implies that MR-LIARS$_n$ is a subgroup of $\mathbb{Z}_n^*$. Clearly, the neutral element of $\mathbb{Z}_n^*$ is in MR-LIARS$_n$, since

$$1^{m \cdot 2^{j_{\max}}} \equiv 1 \bmod n.$$

To prove that MR-LIARS$_n$ is closed under multiplication, the group operation in $\mathbb{Z}_n^*$, let a and b be arbitrary elements of MR-LIARS$_n$. Thus, both $a^{m \cdot 2^{j_{\max}}}$ and $b^{m \cdot 2^{j_{\max}}}$ are congruent to $\pm 1 \bmod n$.

Note that $1 \cdot 1 = 1$ and $1(n-1) \equiv -1 \bmod n$ and $(n-1)(n-1) \equiv 1 \bmod n$. Hence,

$$(a \cdot b)^{m \cdot 2^{j_{\max}}} \equiv a^{m \cdot 2^{j_{\max}}} \cdot b^{m \cdot 2^{j_{\max}}} \equiv \pm 1 \bmod n.$$

Thus, the product $a \cdot b$ is in MR-LIARS$_n$. By Lemma 7.10, MR-LIARS$_n$ is a subgroup of $\mathbb{Z}_n^*$.

To prove that MR-LIARS$_n$ is a *proper* subgroup of $\mathbb{Z}_n^*$, we apply Lemma 7.13, which says that every Carmichael number is the product of at least three distinct prime factors. Thus, n can be written as $n = n_1 \cdot n_2$ for odd numbers n_1 and n_2 with $\gcd(n_1, n_2) = 1$.

Let $\hat{a}$ be a fixed MR-liar satisfying $\hat{a}^{m \cdot 2^{j_{\max}}} \equiv -1 \bmod n$. Let $a_1 = \hat{a} \bmod n_1$. Since $\gcd(n_1, n_2) = 1$, the Chinese Remainder Theorem (see Theorem 2.46) implies that the system of two congruences:

$$a \equiv a_1 \bmod n_1$$
$$a \equiv 1 \bmod n_2$$

has the unique solution $a = a_1 \cdot n_2 \cdot n_2^{-1} + 1 \cdot n_1 \cdot n_1^{-1} \bmod n$, where n_1^{-1} is the inverse element of n_1 in $\mathbb{Z}_{n_2}^*$ and n_2^{-1} is the inverse element of n_2 in $\mathbb{Z}_{n_1}^*$. We show that this solution a is in $\mathbb{Z}_n^* -$ MR-LIARS$_n$.

To see that a does not belong to MR-LIARS$_n$, note that

$$a^{m \cdot 2^{j_{\max}}} \equiv \hat{a}^{m \cdot 2^{j_{\max}}} \equiv -1 \bmod n_1; \tag{7.10}$$
$$a^{m \cdot 2^{j_{\max}}} \equiv 1^{m \cdot 2^{j_{\max}}} \equiv 1 \bmod n_2. \tag{7.11}$$

where (7.10) follows from $a \equiv a_1 \equiv \hat{a} \bmod n_1$. Congruence (7.10) implies that $a^{m \cdot 2^{j_{\max}}} \not\equiv 1 \bmod n$, and congruence (7.11) implies that $a^{m \cdot 2^{j_{\max}}} \not\equiv -1 \bmod n$. Thus, $a^{m \cdot 2^{j_{\max}}} \not\equiv \pm 1 \bmod n$. It follows that a is not in MR-LIARS$_n$.

To see that a does belong to $\mathbb{Z}_n^*$, note that (7.10) and (7.11) imply:

$$a^{m \cdot 2^{j_{\max}+1}} \equiv 1 \bmod n_1;$$
$$a^{m \cdot 2^{j_{\max}+1}} \equiv 1 \bmod n_2.$$

By the Chinese Remainder Theorem, $a^{m \cdot 2^{j_{\max}+1}} \equiv 1 \bmod n$. Now, the first part of Lemma 7.8 implies that a is in $\mathbb{Z}_n^*$.   ■ Proposition 7.20

Using Proposition 7.20, an argument as in the proof of Theorem 7.12 can now be used to show that also in Case 2 the error probability of the Miller–Rabin test is less than $1/2$.

To complete the proof of Theorem 7.19, note that the Miller–Rabin test runs in polynomial time, see Exercise 7.7(d).   ■   Theorem 7.19

Remark 7.21.   1. By a more sophisticated analysis, one can show that the error probability of the Miller–Rabin test does not exceed the threshold of $1/4$, see Problem 7.1.
  2. By running sufficiently many (but still only polynomially many in $\log n$) independent trials, the error probability can be made arbitrarily close to zero, see Theorem 6.6 and its proof for details. The formal proof of this claim is left to the reader as Exercise 7.7(e).

7.2.3 Solovay–Strassen Test

Solovay and Strassen developed a primality test that is based on different number-theoretical results than the Miller–Rabin test. Their no-biased Monte Carlo algorithm for the primality problem can be used alternatively to prove Theorem 7.19. However, the Solovay–Strassen test is less popular than the Miller–Rabin test, since it is less efficient in practice and less accurate. To explain the Solovay–Strassen test, recall the following notions and facts from Section 2.4.1, see Definitions 2.43 and 2.45:

- A *quadratic residue modulo* n is any element a in $\mathbb{Z}_n^*$ satisfying $a \equiv w^2 \bmod n$ for some $w \in \mathbb{Z}_n$. Otherwise, a is a *quadratic nonresidue modulo* n.
- The *Euler criterion* (see Theorem 2.44) states that for each odd prime number p, a is a quadratic residue modulo p if and only if $a^{(p-1)/2} \equiv 1 \bmod p$.
- The *Legendre symbol* $\left(\frac{a}{p}\right)$ for $a \in \mathbb{Z}_p$ and prime number p expresses the property of being or not being a quadratic residue modulo p as follows:

$$
\left(\frac{a}{p}\right) = \begin{cases} 0 & \text{if } a \equiv 0 \bmod p \\ 1 & \text{if } a \text{ is a quadratic residue modulo } p \\ -1 & \text{if } a \text{ is a quadratic nonresidue modulo } p. \end{cases}
$$

By the Euler criterion, $a^{(p-1)/2} \equiv 1 \bmod p$ if and only if $\left(\frac{a}{p}\right) = 1$. On the other hand, if a is a multiple of p then $a^{(p-1)/2} \equiv 0 \bmod p$, and if a is a quadratic nonresidue modulo p then $a^{(p-1)/2} \equiv -1 \bmod p$, since

$$
\left(a^{(p-1)/2}\right)^2 \equiv a^{p-1} \equiv 1 \bmod p \quad \text{and} \quad a^{(p-1)/2} \not\equiv 1 \bmod p.
$$

To summarize, for each odd prime number p, we have $\left(\frac{a}{p}\right) \equiv a^{(p-1)/2} \bmod p$. Thus, the Legendre symbol can be computed efficiently.

- The *Jacobi symbol* $\left(\frac{a}{n}\right)$, which extends the Legendre symbol to composite "denominators" n with prime power factorization $n = p_1^{e_1} \cdots p_k^{e_k}$, is introduced in Definition 2.45 as follows:

$$\left(\frac{a}{n}\right) = \prod_{i=1}^{k} \left(\frac{a}{p_i}\right)^{e_i}. \tag{7.12}$$

Let $n \geq 3$ be an odd number. It follows from the above definitions and observations that if n is prime, then for each a,

$$\left(\frac{a}{n}\right) \equiv a^{(n-1)/2} \bmod n. \tag{7.13}$$

If n is composite, however, then $\left(\frac{a}{n}\right) \equiv a^{(n-1)/2} \bmod n$ may or may not be true. Thus, congruence (7.13) provides a reliable criterion for checking compositeness: If $\left(\frac{a}{n}\right) \not\equiv a^{(n-1)/2} \bmod n$ for some a, then n must be composite. On the other hand, if (7.13) is true for some randomly picked a, then n may or may not be prime. This criterion is employed by the Solovay–Strassen test shown in Figure 7.7.

SOLOVAY-STRASSEN(n) { $// \; n \geq 3$ is an odd integer
    Randomly choose a number $a \in \{1, 2, \ldots, n-1\}$ under the uniform distribution;
    $x := \left(\frac{a}{n}\right)$;
    if $(x = 0)$ **return** "n is composite" and halt;
    $y := a^{(n-1)/2} \bmod n$;
    if $(x \equiv y \bmod n)$ **return** "n is prime" and halt;
        else return "n is composite" and halt;
}

Fig. 7.7. Primality test by Solovay and Strassen

Two questions arise: First, is the Solovay–Strassen test an efficient algorithm? Second, what is its error probability? As mentioned above, by (7.13), if n is prime, then SOLOVAY-STRASSEN on input n correctly says so with certainty. So what is the probability that the Solovay–Strassen test, given a composite number n, incorrectly answers that n is prime?

Let us deal with the first question first. We have already seen that $a^{(n-1)/2} \bmod n$ can be computed efficiently by the fast exponentiation algorithm from Figure 7.2. And we know from Euler's criterion that if n is prime, computing $a^{(n-1)/2} \bmod n$ is enough to evaluate the Legendre symbol $\left(\frac{a}{n}\right)$. However, if n is composite, it is not clear yet how to evaluate the Jacobi symbol $\left(\frac{a}{n}\right)$ efficiently.

Since the Jacobi symbol is defined in terms of the prime power factorization of n, one might be tempted to think that finding the prime factors of n would be necessary to determine the value of the Jacobi symbol $\left(\frac{a}{n}\right)$. But factoring n (which itself is a hard task, see Section 7.3) would already answer the question of whether or not n

is prime and would thus render the primality test superfluous. Fortunately, however, the Jacobi symbol $\left(\frac{a}{n}\right)$ can be efficiently computed without finding the prime factors of n first. This efficient algorithm crucially draws on the following properties of the Jacobi symbol, which are stated here without proof.

Proposition 7.22 (Properties of the Jacobi Symbol).

1. Law of Quadratic Reciprocity: *If m and n are odd positive integers, then*

$$\left(\frac{m}{n}\right) = \begin{cases} -\left(\frac{n}{m}\right) & \text{if } m \equiv n \equiv 3 \bmod 4 \\ \left(\frac{n}{m}\right) & \text{otherwise.} \end{cases}$$

2. If n is an odd positive integer and $a \equiv b \bmod n$, then $\left(\frac{a}{n}\right) = \left(\frac{b}{n}\right)$.
3. Multiplicativity: *If n is an odd positive integer and a and b are integers, then*

$$\left(\frac{a \cdot b}{n}\right) = \left(\frac{a}{n}\right)\left(\frac{b}{n}\right).$$

In particular, if $m = a \cdot 2^k$ and a is odd, then $\left(\frac{m}{n}\right) = \left(\frac{a}{n}\right)\left(\frac{2}{n}\right)^k$.
4. If n is an odd positive integer, then

$$\left(\frac{2}{n}\right) = \begin{cases} 1 & \text{if } n \equiv \pm 1 \bmod 8 \\ -1 & \text{if } n \equiv \pm 3 \bmod 8. \end{cases}$$

5. If n is an odd positive integer, then $\left(\frac{1}{n}\right) = 1$ and $\left(\frac{0}{n}\right) = 0$.

Exercise 7.9(a) asks you to design an efficient algorithm for the Jacobi symbol, using its number-theoretical properties stated in Proposition 7.22. The following example illustrates the application of these properties.

Example 7.23 (Computing the Jacobi Symbol).   Suppose you want to determine the value of the Jacobi symbol $\left(\frac{5775}{6399}\right)$. Note that both $5775 = 3 \cdot 5^2 \cdot 7 \cdot 11$ and $6399 = 3^4 \cdot 79$ are composite. In particular, since 6399 is not a prime number, $\left(\frac{5775}{6399}\right)$ is not a Legendre symbol. Apply the properties of Proposition 7.22 as follows:

$$
\begin{aligned}
\left(\tfrac{5775}{6399}\right) &= -\left(\tfrac{6399}{5775}\right) && \text{by Property 1, since } 5775 \equiv 6399 \equiv 3 \bmod 4 \\
&= -\left(\tfrac{624}{5775}\right) && \text{by Property 2, since } 6399 \equiv 624 \bmod 5775 \\
&= -\left(\tfrac{39}{5775}\right)\left(\tfrac{2}{5775}\right)^4 && \text{by Property 3, since } 624 = 39 \cdot 2^4 \\
&= -\left(\tfrac{39}{5775}\right) && \text{by Property 4, since } 5775 \equiv -1 \bmod 8 \\
&= \left(\tfrac{5775}{39}\right) && \text{by Property 1, since } 39 \equiv 5775 \equiv 3 \bmod 4 \\
&= \left(\tfrac{3}{39}\right) && \text{by Property 2, since } 5775 \equiv 3 \bmod 39 \\
&= -\left(\tfrac{39}{3}\right) && \text{by Property 1, since } 3 \equiv 39 \equiv 3 \bmod 4 \\
&= -\left(\tfrac{0}{3}\right) && \text{by Property 2, since } 39 \equiv 0 \bmod 3 \\
&= 0 && \text{by Property 5.}
\end{aligned}
$$

Hence, if SOLOVAY-STRASSEN(6399) has picked the number $a = 5775$ at random, it correctly outputs: "6399 is composite," since $\left(\frac{5775}{6399}\right) = 0$.

Now consider the case that SOLOVAY-STRASSEN(6399) has picked the number $a = 1111$ at random. Again computing the Jacobi symbol gives:

$$\left(\tfrac{1111}{6399}\right) \overset{(1)}{=} -\left(\tfrac{6399}{1111}\right) \overset{(2)}{=} -\left(\tfrac{844}{1111}\right) \overset{(3)}{=} -\left(\tfrac{211}{1111}\right)\left(\tfrac{2}{1111}\right)^2 \overset{(4)}{=} -\left(\tfrac{211}{1111}\right)$$
$$\overset{(1)}{=} \left(\tfrac{1111}{211}\right) \overset{(2)}{=} \left(\tfrac{56}{211}\right) \overset{(3)}{=} \left(\tfrac{7}{211}\right)\left(\tfrac{2}{211}\right)^3 \overset{(4)}{=} -\left(\tfrac{7}{211}\right)$$
$$\overset{(1)}{=} \left(\tfrac{211}{7}\right) \overset{(2)}{=} \left(\tfrac{1}{7}\right) \overset{(5)}{=} 1,$$

where $\overset{(i)}{=}$ denotes that Property i from Proposition 7.22 is applied. On the other hand, computing $a^{(n-1)/2} \bmod n$ for $a = 1111$ and $n = 6399$ means that we have to compute $1111^{3199} \bmod 6399$ using fast exponentiation, see Figure 7.2. The binary expansion of the exponent is

$$3199 = 2^0 + 2^1 + 2^2 + 2^3 + 2^4 + 2^5 + 2^6 + 2^{10} + 2^{11},$$

and Table 7.6 shows the values $a^{2^i} \bmod n$ computed sequentially by the "square-

a^{2^0}	a^{2^1}	a^{2^2}	a^{2^3}	a^{2^4}	a^{2^5}	a^{2^6}	a^{2^7}	a^{2^8}	a^{2^9}	$a^{2^{10}}$	$a^{2^{11}}$
1111	5713	3469	3841	3586	3805	3487	1069	3739	4705	2884	5155

Table 7.6. Computing $a^{(n-1)/2} \bmod n$ for the Solovay–Strassen primality test

and-multiply" algorithm. Multiplying the values in the gray boxes of Table 7.6 and reducing modulo 6399, we obtain

$$1111^{3199} \equiv 6088 \bmod 6399.$$

Thus, $\left(\frac{1111}{6399}\right) = 1 \neq 6088 \equiv 1111^{3199} \bmod 6399$, and SOLOVAY-STRASSEN(6399) correctly outputs "6399 is composite," for the random number $a = 1111$.

On the other hand, if SOLOVAY-STRASSEN(6399) picks a number $a \in \{1, 6398\}$ at random, then it incorrectly outputs "6399 is prime," since

$$\left(\tfrac{1}{6399}\right) \overset{(5)}{=} 1 = 1^{3199} \bmod 6399, \quad \text{and} \tag{7.14}$$
$$\left(\tfrac{6398}{6399}\right) \overset{(3)}{=} \left(\tfrac{3199}{6399}\right)\left(\tfrac{2}{6399}\right) \overset{(4)}{=} \left(\tfrac{3199}{6399}\right) \overset{(1)}{=} -\left(\tfrac{6399}{3199}\right) \overset{(2)}{=} -\left(\tfrac{1}{3199}\right)$$
$$\overset{(5)}{=} -1 = (-1)^{3199} \bmod 6399. \tag{7.15}$$

Note that the behavior shown in (7.14) and (7.15) is not a coincidence. Given a composite number n, the Solovay–Strassen algorithm from Figure 7.7 always gives the wrong answer "n is prime" when it has picked some number $a \in \{1, n-1\}$, see Exercise 7.9(b). That is why the Solovay–Strassen test can as well be implemented so as to pick random numbers a only in the range $\{2, 3, \ldots, n-2\}$.

We now turn to the second question raised above: What is the probability that the Solovay–Strassen test, given a composite number n, incorrectly answers that n is prime? In Example 7.23, we have seen that the Solovay–Strassen test, running on a composite number n, may or may not give the correct answer, depending on the random number a it picks. We now introduce the notion of a Solovay–Strassen witness and a Solovay–Strassen liar (for short, SS-witness and SS-liar), based on the criterion (7.13). Intuitively, an SS-witness a certifies that a number n is composite, and an SS-liar a makes n look like a prime number, even though n in fact is composite.

Definition 7.24 (SS-Witness and SS-Liar).   *Let $n \geq 3$ be an odd number.*

- *We say that a is an* SS-witness *for n if and only if a does not satisfy (7.13):*

$$\left(\frac{a}{n}\right) \not\equiv a^{(n-1)/2} \bmod n.$$

- *We say that a is an* SS-liar *for n if and only if n is a composite number and a is not an SS-witness, i.e., a does satisfy (7.13):*

$$\left(\frac{a}{n}\right) \equiv a^{(n-1)/2} \bmod n.$$

Define the set SS-Liars$_n = \{a \mid a \text{ is an SS-liar for } n\}$.

The following theorem says that the error probability of the Solovay–Strassen test is at most $1/2$. In other words, at most one half of the elements in $\mathbb{Z}_n^*$ are SS-liars for n. Theorem 7.25 follows from Lemma 7.26 by the argument given in the proof of Theorem 7.12.

Theorem 7.25. *The Solovay–Strassen test is an efficient no-biased Monte Carlo algorithm for* Primes *with error probability of at most $1/2$.*

Lemma 7.26. *For each odd composite number $n \geq 3$, SS-Liars$_n$ is a proper subgroup of $\mathbb{Z}_n^*$.*

Proof.   It is easy to see that SS-Liars$_n \subseteq$ F-Liars$_n$, see Exercise 7.9(d). Thus, SS-Liars$_n \subseteq \mathbb{Z}_n^*$. We again apply Lemma 7.10 to show that SS-Liars$_n$ is a subgroup of $\mathbb{Z}_n^*$.

As noted in Example 7.23, the neutral element 1 of $\mathbb{Z}_n^*$ is in SS-Liars$_n$, see also Exercise 7.9(b). To show that SS-Liars$_n$ is closed under multiplication, let a and b be any elements of SS-Liars$_n$, so $\left(\frac{a}{n}\right) \equiv a^{(n-1)/2} \bmod n$ and $\left(\frac{b}{n}\right) \equiv b^{(n-1)/2} \bmod n$. By the multiplicativity of the Jacobi symbol (see Property 3 of Proposition 7.22), it follows that

$$\left(\frac{a \cdot b}{n}\right) = \left(\frac{a}{n}\right)\left(\frac{b}{n}\right) \equiv \left(a^{(n-1)/2}\right)\left(b^{(n-1)/2}\right) \equiv (a \cdot b)^{(n-1)/2} \bmod n.$$

Thus, $a \cdot b$ is in SS-Liars$_n$. By Lemma 7.10, SS-Liars$_n$ is a subgroup of $\mathbb{Z}_n^*$.

To show that SS-Liars$_n$ is a *proper* subgroup of $\mathbb{Z}_n^*$, we prove that $\mathbb{Z}_n^*$ contains at least one SS-witness. Distinguish the following two cases.

Case 1: There exists some odd prime number p such that p^2 divides n. In this case, we construct a Fermat witness $a \in \mathbb{Z}_n^*$ for n. Since SS-Liars$_n \subseteq$ F-Liars$_n$ (see Exercise 7.9(d)), it follows that a is an SS-witness for n as well. Thus, SS-Liars$_n \neq \mathbb{Z}_n^*$.

Since p^2 divides n, we have $n = k \cdot p^i$ for some $i \geq 2$ and some odd k with $\gcd(p, k) = 1$. Thus $\gcd(p^2, k) = 1$. Define

$$a = \begin{cases} p + 1 & \text{if } k = 1 \\ (p+1) \cdot k \cdot k^{-1} + 1 \cdot p^2 \cdot (p^2)^{-1} \bmod k \cdot p^2 & \text{if } k \geq 3, \end{cases}$$

where $(p^2)^{-1}$ is the inverse element of p^2 in $\mathbb{Z}_k^*$ and k^{-1} is the inverse element of k in $\mathbb{Z}_{p^2}^*$. Note that, if $k \geq 3$, then by the Chinese Remainder Theorem (see Theorem 2.46), a is the unique solution of the system

$$a \equiv p + 1 \bmod p^2$$
$$a \equiv 1 \bmod k.$$

Since $a - (p+1) \equiv 0 \bmod p^2$, we have $\gcd(p, a) = 1$. Since $a - 1 \equiv 0 \bmod k$, we have $\gcd(k, a) = 1$. It follows that $\gcd(n, a) = 1$. Thus, $a \in \mathbb{Z}_n^*$.

To prove that a is a Fermat witness for n, suppose $a^{n-1} \equiv 1 \bmod n$ for a contradiction. Since p^2 divides n, this assumption implies $a^{n-1} \equiv 1 \bmod p^2$. By the Binomial Theorem,

$$a^{n-1} \equiv (p+1)^{n-1} \equiv 1 + (n-1)p + \sum_{2 \leq i \leq n-1} \binom{n-1}{i} p^i$$

$$\equiv 1 + (n-1)p \bmod p^2.$$

Since $a^{n-1} \equiv 1 \bmod p^2$, p^2 divides $(n-1)p$, which is a contradiction because p does not divide $n - 1 = k \cdot p^i - 1$.

Case 2: All prime factors of n are distinct. In this case, we have $n = k \cdot p$ for some odd numbers k and p such that p is prime and $\gcd(p, k) = 1$. Let $x \in \mathbb{Z}_p^*$ be some quadratic nonresidue modulo p. Thus, $\left(\frac{x}{p}\right) = -1$, by the definition of the Legendre symbol. By the Chinese Remainder Theorem, the system of congruences

$$a \equiv x \bmod p$$
$$a \equiv 1 \bmod k$$

has a unique solution a. Clearly, since p does not divide a and $\gcd(a, k) = 1$, we have that a is in $\mathbb{Z}_n^*$.

We now show that this solution a is an SS-witness for n. By Proposition 7.22,

$$\left(\frac{a}{n}\right) = \left(\frac{a}{k}\right)\left(\frac{a}{p}\right) = \left(\frac{1}{k}\right)\left(\frac{x}{p}\right) = (-1) \cdot 1 = -1. \qquad (7.16)$$

If a were in SS-Liars$_n$, then (7.16) would imply that

$$a^{(n-1)/2} \equiv -1 \bmod n.$$

Since k divides n, it follows that $a^{(n-1)/2} \equiv -1 \bmod k$, which contradicts $a \equiv 1 \bmod k$. Thus, a is an SS-witness for n.

The proof of Lemma 7.26 is complete.   ∎

7.2.4 Primality Is in P

All efficient primality tests introduced so far are randomized algorithms. Can the primality problem be solved even in *deterministic* polynomial time? This intriguing question had been open in complexity theory for many decades. Eventually, Agrawal, Kayal, and Saxena achieved a decisive breakthrough and solved this problem in their "Primes is in P" paper [AKS02].

Their celebrated result that primality can be decided in deterministic polynomial time created much sensation, not only in complexity theory but also in number theory, cryptology, and even in the daily press such as in *The New York Times*. Immediately after the authors had published this result on their website on August 6, 2002, the news spread faster than a bushfire. Why is this result so important and spectacular? Just as the graph isomorphism problem, the primality problem had been considered one of the rare candidates of a problem that is neither in P nor NP-complete, see Sections 3.6.1 and 5.7 and, in particular, Section 6.5.

Primes now has lost its status as a good candidate, but in return has won the status of being an efficiently solvable problem. We state this result without proof, referring the reader to the original source [AKS02] and to Dietzfelbinger's excellent presentation [Die04]. Surprisingly enough, Agrawal, Kayal, and Saxena's elegant proof of Theorem 7.27 applies number-theoretical results that are rather elementary.

Theorem 7.27 (Agrawal, Kayal, and Saxena).   Primes *is in* P.

The importance of Theorem 7.27 notwithstanding, it seems unlikely that this deterministic algorithm for the primality problem will soon replace the randomized primality tests such as the Miller–Rabin test. The original paper [AKS02] obtains a running time of $\mathcal{O}(n^{12})$, where n is the length of the input. Using a more careful analysis, this bound has been improved to $\mathcal{O}(n^6)$ meanwhile. Nonetheless, the common randomized primality tests are still more efficient. And for practical purposes, the error probabilities of these randomized algorithms can be made small enough so as to be negligible.

7.3 Factoring

As mentioned in Section 7.1, RSA is secure only if large numbers cannot be factored efficiently. Traditionally, the factoring problem is a functional problem: Given an integer $n \geq 2$, determine the prime factorization of n, where the factors are listed in increasing order.

Definition 7.28 (Factoring Problem).   *Define the* factoring problem *as a functional problem by*

$$\text{factoring}(n) = \langle p_1, p_2, \ldots, p_k \rangle,$$

where $n = \prod_{i=1}^{k} p_i$ *is the prime factorization of* n *and* $p_i \leq p_j$ *for* $i < j$. *As usual, all numbers are represented in binary over the alphabet* $\Sigma = \{0, 1\}$.

For example, $\text{factoring}(1453452) = \langle 2, 2, 3, 7, 11, 11, 11, 13 \rangle$ means that $1453452 = 2 \cdot 2 \cdot 3 \cdot 7 \cdot 11 \cdot 11 \cdot 11 \cdot 13$. Equivalently, the factoring problem can be formulated as a decision problem, see Exercises 7.10(a) and (b).

No efficient algorithm for the factoring problem is known, despite considerable effort in the past to design such algorithms. Thus, factoring is not known to be in FP. That is to say that the factoring problem, suitably formalized as a decision problem, is not known to be in P. On the other hand, the factoring problem is easily seen to be in NP, see Exercise 7.10(c). It is even known to be in UP ∩ coUP, see Fellows and Koblitz [FK92]. This result can be viewed as evidence that the factoring problem is unlikely to be NP-complete, just as the graph isomorphism problem. Thus, it is yet another candidate of a problem that seems to be neither in P nor NP-complete. Unlike GI, however, the factoring problem is not known to be low or to have any similar properties; cf. Sections 5.7, 6.5, and Section 7.6.

The hypothesis that factoring is a hard problem—on which the security of RSA largely rests—is supported merely by the persistent inability of designing an efficient algorithm for it. This is rather weak evidence for the hardness of factoring, of course. As noted in Section 7.2.4, the primality problem had been considered to be a hard problem as well, merely due to the persistent inability to find efficient algorithms for it. Eventually, however, it turned out that primality can be checked efficiently by some clever deterministic algorithm that applies profound number theory.

And even if someone would find a rigorous proof of the above hypothesis that factoring is hard, this proof would not guarantee security of the RSA cryptosystem. Breaking RSA is at most as hard as factoring integers, yet it is not known whether these two problems are equally hard. It might well be the case that one can break RSA without factoring the RSA modulus n in the public key (n, e). Potential attacks on the RSA system and suitable countermeasures against these attacks are discussed in Section 7.4. In the current section, we survey some of the known algorithms for the factoring problem.

7.3.1 Trial Division

The first observation is that the trial division algorithm from Figure 7.4 can be used for factoring as well. More precisely, to find the prime factors of a given integer $n \geq 2$, do the following.

Step 1: Compute all primes less than or equal to some prespecified bound b. This can be done using the sieve of Eratosthenes from Example 7.5.

Step 2: For each prime p in this list, determine the maximum power of p dividing n, i.e., the maximum exponent e_p such that p^{e_p} divides n, and output the corresponding prime factors of n in increasing order.

A typical bound would be $b = 1\,000\,000$, and a typical RSA modulus n would have at least 768 bits. In our toy example below, however, we are content with a much smaller bound and a much smaller integer to be factored.

Example 7.29 (Factoring by Trial Division).   Suppose you want to factor the integer $n = 1404$. In Step 1, choosing the bound $b = 39$, determine all primes not exceeding 39 using the sieve of Eratosthenes. Table 7.2 shows the resulting list. Step 2 now gives the following prime power factorization: $1404 = 2^2 \cdot 3^3 \cdot 13$. Thus, the output is $\langle 2, 2, 3, 3, 3, 13 \rangle$.

7.3.2 Pollard's Algorithm

Some factoring algorithms work especially well for numbers n having certain properties. Thus, such numbers must be avoided when choosing the modulus n in the public key of the RSA cryptosystem. For example, Pollard's $p - 1$ method for factoring works well for composite numbers n having a prime factor p such that the prime factors of $p - 1$ are small. Figure 7.8 presents the algorithm, which runs on input n and a prespecified bound B.

```
POLLARD(n, B) {              // n ≥ 3 is an odd integer and B is a prespecified bound
    x := 2;
    for (i = 2, 3 ..., B) { x := x^i mod n; }
    d := gcd(n, x − 1);
    if (1 < d < n) {
        return d;
        Recurse by calling POLLARD(d, B) and POLLARD(n/d, B); }
    else return "failure" and restart with a new bound B̃ > B;
}
```

Fig. 7.8. Pollard's $p - 1$ factoring algorithm

Let p be a prime factor of n, and let B be an upper bound of every prime power dividing $p - 1$. That is, $q^k \leq B$ for each prime q and $k \geq 1$ such that q^k divides $p - 1$. Then, $B!$ is a multiple of $p - 1$. After the `for` loop in Figure 7.8, the value of the variable x satisfies $x \equiv 2^{B!} \bmod n$. Since p is a prime factor of n, it follows that $x \equiv 2^{B!} \bmod p$ as well. By Fermat's Little Theorem (see Corollary 2.39),

$$2^{p-1} \equiv 1 \bmod p.$$

And since $B!$ is a multiple of $p - 1$, we have

$$x \equiv 2^{B!} \equiv 2^{p-1} \equiv 1 \bmod p.$$

Thus, p divides $x - 1$. Since p also divides n, p divides $d = \gcd(n, x - 1)$. It follows that, unless $x = 1$, d is a nontrivial factor of n, and we can recursively apply this procedure to factor d and n/d. If no nontrivial divisor of n is found, the algorithm restarts with a new bound $\tilde{B} > B$. Provided that the bound chosen is large enough, this method eventually finds all prime factors of n.

Example 7.30 (Pollard's $p - 1$ Method).   Let $n = 56291$. Choosing the bound $B = 10$ and starting with $x = 2$, Table 7.7 shows the values of $x = x^i \bmod 56291$ for $2 \le i \le 10$, which are obtained during the `for` loop in Figure 7.8.

i	2	3	4	5	6	7	8	9	10
x	4	64	2498	29092	49595	2535	5793	25522	1268

Table 7.7. Computing $x^i \bmod n$ for Pollard's $p - 1$ factoring algorithm

At the end of the `for` loop, we have $x = 1268 \equiv 2^{10!} \bmod 56291$. Then, $\gcd(56291, 1267) = 181$ can be determined by the Euclidean Algorithm from Figure 2.1. Indeed, $p = 181$ is a prime factor of $n = 56291$, and the other prime factor of n is $q = 311$. Note that all prime powers dividing $180 = 2^2 \cdot 3^2 \cdot 5$ are smaller than $B = 10$. Thus, $p - 1 = 180$ does divide $10! = 3628800 = 180 \cdot 20160$ as desired.

If N is the length of the integer n to be factored and if B is the bound chosen, then it is easy to see that the running time of one execution of Pollard's $p-1$ method from Figure 7.8 is in $\mathcal{O}(B \log B N^2 + N^3)$, not taking account of the recursion or the restart with a new bound. The proof of this claim is left to the reader as Exercise 7.11(c). It follows that if B is polynomially in N, i.e., $B \in \mathcal{O}(N^k)$ for some fixed constant k, then Pollard's $p - 1$ algorithm runs in polynomial time. Unfortunately, for such a small bound B, the probability that all prime powers dividing $p - 1$ are below B is rather small. Thus, the algorithm is unlikely to be successful in this case. On the other hand, if we choose a large bound B, say $B \in \mathcal{O}(\sqrt{n})$, the method is guaranteed to work, yet it runs no faster than trial division.

7.3.3 Quadratic Sieve

Some of the currently best factoring methods are based on the following quite simple idea. Suppose you want to factor an odd integer $n \ge 3$. Using an appropriate *sieving method*, which will be described in more detail below, determine integers a and b satisfying

$$a^2 \equiv b^2 \bmod n \quad \text{and} \quad a \not\equiv \pm b \bmod n. \tag{7.17}$$

Hence, n divides $a^2 - b^2 = (a - b)(a + b)$ but neither $a - b$ nor $a + b$. Thus, both $\gcd(n, a - b)$ and $\gcd(n, a + b)$ are nontrivial factors of n.

Example 7.31 (Quadratic Sieve Idea).   Let $n = 561$, $a = 322$, and $b = 256$. Then, $a^2 = 103684 \equiv 460 \bmod 561$ and $b^2 = 65536 \equiv 460 \bmod 561$, so $a^2 \equiv b^2 \bmod n$. On the other hand, $a \equiv -239 \bmod 561$ and $b \equiv -305 \bmod 561$, so $a \not\equiv \pm b \bmod n$, and (7.17) is satisfied. Hence, 561 divides

$$103684 - 65536 = (322 - 256)(322 + 256) = 66 \cdot 578 = 38148 = 68 \cdot 561,$$

but 561 does not divide either of 66 or 578. Thus, both $\gcd(561, 66) = 33$ and $\gcd(561, 578) = 17$ are nontrivial factors of 561.

To give yet another example, let $n = 1269$, $a = 213$, and $b = 210$. Then, we have $a^2 = 45369 \equiv 954 \bmod 1269$ and $b^2 = 44100 \equiv 954 \bmod 1269$, so $a^2 \equiv b^2 \bmod n$. Since $a \equiv -1056 \bmod 1269$ and $b \equiv -1059 \bmod 1269$, we further have $a \not\equiv \pm b \bmod n$, and (7.17) is satisfied. Hence, 1269 divides

$$45369 - 44100 = (213 - 210)(213 + 210) = 3 \cdot 423 = 1269,$$

but 1269 does not divide either of 3 or 423. Thus, both $\gcd(1269, 3) = 3$ and $\gcd(1269, 423) = 3$ are nontrivial factors of 1269.

There are various such sieving methods that differ in the specific way of how to determine the numbers a and b satisfying (7.17). An example of a very successful sieving method is the "number field sieve." This section introduces the *quadratic sieve*, which is older but still widely used in practice and may be somewhat easier to comprehend.

How were the numbers a and b satisfying (7.17) found in Example 7.31? Well, to be honest, the numbers $a = 322$ and $b = 256$ in the first example (for $n = 561$) were determined simply by trial and error. The second example (where $n = 1269$) was more carefully contrived, though, as will be shown below.

Example 7.32 (Quadratic Sieve—Continued).   As in Example 7.31, suppose you want to factor $n = 1269$. Let $s = \lfloor \sqrt{n} \rfloor = 35$. Define a function $\sigma : \mathbb{Z} \to \mathbb{Z}$ by

$$\sigma(x) = (x + s)^2 - n.$$

So, in our example, we have $\sigma(x) = (x + 35)^2 - 1269$. Table 7.8 shows the values of $\sigma(x)$ for $-5 \le x \le 5$.

x	-5	-4	-3	-2	-1	0	1	2	3	4	5
$\sigma(x)$	-369	-308	-245	-180	-113	-44	27	100	175	252	331

Table 7.8. Computing $\sigma(x)$ for the quadratic sieve factoring algorithm

In particular, for $x \in \{3, 4\}$, we have:

$$\sigma(3) = 38^2 - 1269 = 175 = 5^2 \cdot 7 \tag{7.18}$$
$$\sigma(4) = 39^2 - 1269 = 252 = 2^2 \cdot 3^2 \cdot 7. \tag{7.19}$$

Equations (7.18) and (7.19) imply

$$38^2 \equiv 5^2 \cdot 7 \bmod 1269 \tag{7.20}$$
$$39^2 \equiv 2^2 \cdot 3^2 \cdot 7 \bmod 1269. \tag{7.21}$$

Now, multiplying (7.20) and (7.21), we obtain

$$(38 \cdot 39)^2 \equiv (2 \cdot 3 \cdot 5 \cdot 7)^2 \bmod 1269. \tag{7.22}$$

Thus, on both sides of (7.22), we have a square number, where the square on the right-hand side consists of small primes. Setting

$$a = 38 \cdot 39 \bmod 1269 = 213 \quad \text{and} \quad b = 2 \cdot 3 \cdot 5 \cdot 7 \bmod 1269 = 210$$

now gives the values of a and b from Example 7.31.

In (7.18) and (7.19) and in Table 7.8 from Example 7.32, we determined $\sigma(x)$ for certain arguments x such that $\sigma(x)$ has only small prime factors and

$$(x + s)^2 \equiv \sigma(x) \bmod n. \tag{7.23}$$

We then selected suitable congruences of the form (7.23) such that their product yields a square on both sides. The left-hand side of (7.23) is a square, so taking the product of left-hand sides always yields a square again. The problem is to find congruences of the form (7.23) such that the right-hand sides yield a square as well when multiplied. Obviously, this will be the case if the sum of the exponents of -1 and of the prime factors of $\sigma(x)$ is even. Thus, to select suitable congruences of the form (7.23), we simply have to solve a linear system of equations over the field $\mathbb{Z}_2$. This is shown in the following example, which continues Example 7.32.

Example 7.33 (Quadratic Sieve—Continued).   We show how to select suitable congruences of the form (7.23) such that their product yields a square on both sides. For illustration, suppose that we are given not only the equations (7.18) and (7.19) for $\sigma(x)$ with $x \in \{3, 4\}$, which imply the congruences (7.20) and (7.21), but we are given two more equations for $\sigma(x)$, where $x \in \{-4, -2\}$. Thus, we are faced with the problem of selecting the suitable ones among the following four congruences of the form (7.23):

$$31^2 \equiv -1 \cdot 2^2 \cdot 7 \cdot 11 \bmod 1269$$
$$33^2 \equiv -1 \cdot 2^2 \cdot 3^2 \cdot 5 \bmod 1269$$
$$38^2 \equiv 5^2 \cdot 7 \bmod 1269$$
$$39^2 \equiv 2^2 \cdot 3^2 \cdot 7 \bmod 1269.$$

In order to select those congruences whose right-hand side product is a square, one has to find coefficients $\alpha_i \in \{0, 1\}$, where $1 \leq i \leq 4$, such that

$$(-1 \cdot 2^2 \cdot 7 \cdot 11)^{\alpha_1}(-1 \cdot 2^2 \cdot 3^2 \cdot 5)^{\alpha_2}(5^2 \cdot 7)^{\alpha_3}(2^2 \cdot 3^2 \cdot 7)^{\alpha_4} \tag{7.24}$$
$$= (-1)^{\alpha_1+\alpha_2} \cdot 2^{2\alpha_1+2\alpha_2+2\alpha_4} \cdot 3^{2\alpha_2+2\alpha_4} \cdot 5^{\alpha_2+2\alpha_3} \cdot 7^{\alpha_1+\alpha_3+\alpha_4} \cdot 11^{\alpha_1}.$$

The coefficient α_i corresponds to the exponent of the ith congruence. The number in (7.24) is a square if and only if the exponents of -1 and of all prime factors are even numbers. In other words, one has to solve the following system of congruences:

$$\alpha_1 + \alpha_2 \equiv 0 \bmod 2$$
$$2\alpha_1 + 2\alpha_2 + 2\alpha_4 \equiv 0 \bmod 2$$
$$2\alpha_2 + 2\alpha_4 \equiv 0 \bmod 2$$
$$\alpha_2 + 2\alpha_3 \equiv 0 \bmod 2$$
$$\alpha_1 + \alpha_3 + \alpha_4 \equiv 0 \bmod 2$$
$$\alpha_1 \equiv 0 \bmod 2.$$

Reducing modulo 2, we can eliminate two of these six congruences and obtain the following simplified system of four congruences:

$$\alpha_1 + \alpha_2 \equiv 0 \bmod 2$$
$$\alpha_2 \equiv 0 \bmod 2$$
$$\alpha_1 + \alpha_3 + \alpha_4 \equiv 0 \bmod 2$$
$$\alpha_1 \equiv 0 \bmod 2,$$

which has the nontrivial (i.e., distinct from the zero vector) solution $\alpha_1 = \alpha_2 = 0$ and $\alpha_3 = \alpha_4 = 1$. Thus, exactly the equations (7.18) and (7.19) for $\sigma(x)$ with $x \in \{3, 4\}$ are selected, just as in Example 7.32.

How does the quadratic sieve determine congruences of the form (7.23)? In practical applications, the integer n to be factored is likely to be much larger than the $n = 1269$ in our example above; it will not have four digits but more than one hundred digits. Here is a rough sketch of how the principle described above works in general, omitting numerous tricks and mathematical refinements used so as to speed up the computation in practice.

Step 1: Let n be the number to be factored. Choose a *factor base* $\mathfrak{B}$ consisting of -1 and prime numbers small enough to be allowed as factors in $\sigma(x)$. More precisely, let B be some "small" prespecified bound and define

$$\mathfrak{B} = \{-1\} \cup \{p \mid p \text{ is a prime number less than or equal to } B\}.$$

Step 2: Let $s = \lfloor \sqrt{n} \rfloor$. A function value $\sigma(x) = (x+s)^2 - n$ is said to be $\mathfrak{B}$-*smooth* if and only if all its prime factors are contained in $\mathfrak{B}$.

Step 3: Determine $\|\mathfrak{B}\|$ integers x such that $\sigma(x)$ is $\mathfrak{B}$-smooth.[1]

Step 4: Solve the corresponding system of $\|\mathfrak{B}\|$ congruences to select suitable congruences of the form (7.23) such that their product yields a square on both sides, as is shown in Example 7.33. This can be done using either standard methods such as Gaussian elimination or specialized methods that are more efficient.

---

[1] In Example 7.33, the four equations corresponding to the integers $x \in \{-4, -2, 3, 4\}$ are actually too few for a reasonable factor base such as $\mathfrak{B} = \{-1, 2, 3, 5, 7, 11\}$. However, it should be clear from that example how the method works in principle.

Step 5: Determine the values of a and b satisfying (7.17) by taking the product of the congruences selected, as is shown in Example 7.32.

Step 6: Determine the nontrivial factors $d_1 = \gcd(n, a-b)$ and $d_2 = \gcd(n, a+b)$ of n, as is shown in Example 7.31. (Note that $n = d_1 \cdot d_2$.)

Step 7: Recursively apply this procedure to d_1 and d_2 until the prime factorization of n has been found.

It remains to specify the details of Step 3: How are the integers $x_1, x_2, \ldots, x_{||\mathfrak{B}||}$ to be determined such that each $\sigma(x_i)$ is $\mathfrak{B}$-smooth? This step is the actual sieving procedure and is again explained by an illustrating example.

Example 7.34 (Quadratic Sieve—Continued).   We continue Examples 7.31, 7.32, and 7.33. Recall that $n = 1269$ is the number to be factored, that $s = \lfloor \sqrt{n} \rfloor = 35$, and that $\sigma(x) = (x + 35)^2 - 1269$. Choose the factor base $\mathfrak{B} = \{-1, 2, 3, 5, 7, 11\}$.

For these small numbers, one might take the naive approach of evaluating $\sigma(x)$ for each $x \in \{0, \pm 1, \pm 2, \ldots\}$ and then checking whether $\sigma(x)$ is $\mathfrak{B}$-smooth by trial division. However, this approach would take too long in practical applications. For example, if n has 120 digits, then the factor base has roughly 245000 elements, and all these elements have to be tested in order to check just one value $\sigma(x)$. It is much smarter to use a sieve instead.

Fix some sieve interval, $S = \{-D, -D+1, \ldots, -1, 0, 1, \ldots, D-1, D\}$, where D is a prespecified constant. For each $x \in S$, compute $\sigma(x)$. For each prime p in $\mathfrak{B}$ and for each x in S, divide $\sigma(x)$ by the maximum power of p. Note that $\sigma(x)$ is $\mathfrak{B}$-smooth if and only if this procedure eventually leaves the quotient ± 1.

Given a prime p in $\mathfrak{B}$ and an x in S, it can be checked whether p divides $\sigma(x)$ as follows. First, determine all $x \in \mathbb{Z}_p$ for which p divides $\sigma(x)$, i.e., $\sigma(x) \equiv 0 \bmod p$. Since $\sigma(x)$ is a polynomial of degree 2, there are at most two such integers x in $\mathbb{Z}_p$. Now, starting from these x and passing through the sieve interval to the left and to the right in steps of distance p will reveal all $x \in S$ for which p divides $\sigma(x)$. This procedure is called a *sieve with p*. The advantage is that a sieve with p considers only those values $\sigma(x)$ that are multiples of p, skipping any unsuccessful trial divisions.

x	-5	-4	-3	-2	-1	0	1	2	3	4	5
$\sigma(x)$	-369	-308	-245	-180	-113	-44	27	100	175	252	331
sieve with 2		-77		-45		-11		25		63	
sieve with 3	-41			-5			1				7
sieve with 5			-49		-1			1	7		
sieve with 7		-11	-1						1	1	
sieve with 11		-1				-1					

Table 7.9. Determining $\mathfrak{B}$-smooth values $\sigma(x)$ using sieves with p

Specifically, let $S = \{-5, -4, \ldots, -1, 0, 1, \ldots, 4, 5\}$ be our sieve interval. Table 7.9 extends Table 7.8 from Example 7.32 by showing the sieve with p for each prime p in $\mathfrak{B}$. Thus, $\sigma(x)$ is $\mathfrak{B}$-smooth for each $x \in \{-4, -3, -2, 0, 1, 2, 3, 4\}$.

7.3.4 Other Factoring Methods

In this section, some further factoring methods and their running times are mentioned without going into detail. In many cases, the running times of factoring algorithms depend on certain assumptions and parameters, such as the choice of the size of the factor base for the quadratic sieve, and thus allow only a heuristic analysis.

Usually, there is a trade-off between the success probability of some factoring method and its running time. For example, choosing a large factor base $\mathfrak{B}$ for the quadratic sieve increases the probability of finding $\mathfrak{B}$-smooth values $\sigma(x)$ and thus the probability of successfully factoring n. On the other hand, the larger the factor base is, the more congruences of the form (7.23) are obtained, which implies that solving the corresponding system of congruences takes more time.

Applying certain number-theoretical results and making certain useful assumptions, one can show that the quadratic sieve runs on input n in time

$$\mathcal{O}\left(e^{(1+o(1))\sqrt{\ln n \ln \ln n}}\right),$$

where $\ln n$ denotes the natural logarithm of n, i.e., the logarithm base $e = 2.71\cdots$. In particular, one uses the prime number theorem (see Theorem 7.3) to estimate the size of the factor base by $||\mathfrak{B}|| = 1 + \pi(B) \approx B/\ln B$, where B is the prespecified bound and $\pi(B)$ denotes the number of primes $p \leq B$.

Table 7.10 summarizes the best running times of selected factoring algorithms running on input n currently known. Here, p denotes the smallest prime factor of n, and the other notations are explained in the previous paragraph.

Algorithm	Running time
Pollard's $p - 1$ algorithm	$\mathcal{O}(B \log B (\log n)^2 + (\log n)^3)$
Quadratic sieve	$\mathcal{O}\left(e^{(1+o(1))\sqrt{\ln n \ln \ln n}}\right)$
Number field sieve	$\mathcal{O}\left(e^{(1.92+o(1))\sqrt[3]{\ln n}\sqrt[3]{(\ln \ln n)^2}}\right)$
Elliptic curve method	$\mathcal{O}\left(e^{(1+o(1))\sqrt{2 \ln p \ln \ln p}}\right)$

Table 7.10. Running times of selected factoring algorithms

Pollard's $p - 1$ algorithm is presented and analyzed in Section 7.3.2, and Section 7.3.3 explains how the quadratic sieve works. Dixon's *random squares method* uses the same principle as the quadratic sieve, see Stinson [Sti02]. A difference is that the congruences are determined by factoring $z^2 \bmod n$, where z is a variable randomly chosen in $\mathbb{Z}_n$ under the uniform distribution. Again, all prime factors are in the factor base $\mathfrak{B}$, and the product of $z^2 \bmod n$ is taken for some of these z so as to find a congruence of the form (7.17).

The *number field sieve* also generalizes the quadratic sieve and factors n using congruences of the form (7.17). A difference is that all computations are performed in rings over algebraic integers, see A. Lenstra and H. Lenstra, Jr. [LL93]. Asymptotically, the number field sieve has the best running time of the factoring methods currently known, see Table 7.10.

The *elliptic curve method*, a randomized algorithm developed by H. Lenstra in the 1980s, is a generalization of Pollard's $p - 1$ algorithm. Here, the computations are done in groups defined on elliptic curves modulo p instead of the ring $\mathbb{Z}_p$. Its running time depends on the size of the smallest prime factor of n. In the worst case, all prime factors of n are of roughly the same size. In particular, if n has two prime factors as in the case of the RSA cryptosystem, their size is approximately $\sqrt{n}$, so the running times of the quadratic sieve and the elliptic curve method are essentially equal asymptotically. If the prime factors of n are of differing sizes, however, the elliptic curve method is more efficient. For example, a very large number that could be factored by Brent using the elliptic curve method is $2^{2^{11}} - 1$.

Numbers of the form $F_m = 2^{2^m} + 1$ are called *Fermat numbers*. Fermat believed that all F_m were prime numbers, which indeed is the case for $F_0 = 3$, $F_1 = 5$, $F_2 = 17$, $F_3 = 257$, and $F_4 = 65537$. However, $F_5 = 641 \cdot 6700417$ is a composite number, as proven by Euler in 1732. F_6 could be factored by Landry and Le Lasseur in 1880. Brillhart and Morrison factored F_7 in 1970, almost a century later. In 1980, Brent and Pollard found the factorization of F_8; A. Lenstra, H. Lenstra, Manasse, and Pollard factored F_9 in 1990; and Brent factored F_{10} in 1995:

$$F_{10} = 45592577 \cdot 6487031809 \cdot 4659775785220018543264560743076778192897 \cdot P_{252},$$

where P_{252} denotes the 252th prime number; see also Exercise 7.12(c). Note that it is crucial here to specify the input representation. If the input $F_m = 2^{2^m} + 1$ is given in binary, it has the form $\text{bin}(F_m) = 10^{2^m-1}1$. Even prior to Agrawal, Kayal, and Saxena's algorithm [AKS02] was it known that it can be checked in time polynomial in the input length, $2^m + 1$, whether or not F_m is prime or composite. It is thus common to measure the time for algorithms deciding primality of F_m in the length of m written in binary.

Challenge	Factoring method	Year
RSA-129	quadratic sieve	1994
RSA-130	number field sieve	1996
RSA-140	number field sieve	1999
RSA-155	number field sieve	1999

Table 7.11. Factoring RSA-d numbers

The RSA-d numbers are a similar challenge to factoring algorithms as the Fermat numbers. Each such number is a d-digit RSA modulus n having two prime factors of roughly the same size. The numbers RSA-100, RSA-110, ..., RSA-500 were made public on the internet, and factoring specialists around the world have been trying to factor them. They often distribute the necessary computations to hundreds of computers and workstations in order to jointly tackle one such challenge number. This approach, sometimes dubbed "factoring by e-mail," often proved successful. Some of these milestones in the history of factoring are listed in Table 7.11.

7.4 Security of RSA: Possible Attacks and Countermeasures

The RSA protocol and the RSA digital signature scheme are presented in Section 7.1, see Figures 7.1 and 7.3. As mentioned there, the security of the RSA cryptosystem strongly depends on the assumption that factoring large integers is an intractable task. Section 7.3 shows that the best factoring algorithms known run in superpolynomial time and thus are not efficient, although some are subexponential-time algorithms. Further, it is not known whether the factoring problem and the problem of cracking the RSA system are equally hard.

In this section, we list various potential attacks on the RSA system, among which the factoring attacks are the most obvious. To prevent these direct attacks, some care must be taken in choosing the primes p and q, the modulus n, the exponent e, and the private key d from Figure 7.1. There is an abbundance of literature on the security of RSA, and the list of attacks presented here is far from being complete. For each attack on RSA that has been proposed in the literature to date, some practical countermeasures are known, rules of thumb that prevent the success of those attacks or make their likelihood of success negligibly small.

Factoring Attacks

Attacker Erich aims at using the public key (n, e) to recover the private key d by factoring n, i.e., by computing the prime factors p and q of $n = pq$. Knowing p and q, he can compute $\varphi(n) = (p - 1)(q - 1)$ and, just like Bob, he can find the inverse d of e modulo $\varphi(n)$, using the extended algorithm of Euclid; see Figure 2.1. There are various ways in which factoring attacks on RSA can be mounted. We distinguish the following types of factoring attacks.

Brute-force attack: By exhaustive search, Erich tries to factor n simply by trial division, see Section 7.3.1. Choosing n sufficiently large will prevent this type of attack. Currently, it is recommended to use a modulus n with at least 1024 bits, or better yet 1024 bits. That is, the size of 512 bits formerly in use no longer provides adequate protection today. Note that the number RSA-155, which was successfully factored in 1999 (see Table 7.11), is roughly of the same size as a 512 bit number. On the other hand, a recommendation such as 1024 bits has to be taken with care, since the progress in algorithmics and in hardware developments is hard to predict. If it turns out that factoring is an efficiently solvable problem, all cryptosystems based on it, including RSA, are no longer secure.

Of course, the time complexity of modular exponentiation grows rapidly with the size of the modulus, and thus there is a trade-off between increasing the security of RSA and decreasing its efficiency. Further, it is widely recognized that those n whose prime factors p and q are of roughly the same size are the hardest to factor.

Special-purpose factoring methods: Pollard's $p - 1$ method is an example of this type of attack. As shown in Section 7.3.2, this factoring method seeks to exploit a weakness of the prime factors of n chosen: If $n = pq$ and $p - 1$ has only small prime factors, then Pollard's $p - 1$ algorithm can efficiently factor the RSA modulus n. This potential threat led to the introduction of "strong primes," which are required to satisfy certain conditions. For example, for p to be a *strong* prime factor of n, the number $p - 1$ should have a large factor r to prevent the $p - 1$ method from working efficiently. Similarly, $r - 1$ should also have a large factor, etc.

Another example of a special-purpose factoring method is Lenstra's *elliptic curve method*, which generalizes Pollard's $p - 1$ method as noted in Section 7.3.4. It is the more effective for breaking RSA, the smaller the smallest prime factor of n is.

Special-purpose factoring methods, which exploit certain properties of the prime factors p and q of n, may be more effective and more successful than the general-purpose factoring methods described below. However, since they depend on special properties of the RSA parameters chosen, these types of attack are easier to avoid.

General-purpose factoring methods: Examples are the *quadratic sieve* and the *number field sieve* discussed in Sections 7.3.3 and 7.3.4. Regardless of the form of the prime factors of n, these factoring algorithms have a certain success probability. Therefore, the most effective countermeasure against these methods is to use primes of very large size. This countermeasure simultaneously provides, with high probability, protection against all types of special-purpose factoring methods. In short, size does matter, and large primes are more important than strong primes.

Using the Euler Function to Factor n

Suppose that Erich can determine $\varphi(n)$, where φ is the Euler function. Knowing both n and $\varphi(n)$, he could then determine the prime factors of $n = pq$ by solving the following two equations for the unknowns p and q:

$$n = p \cdot q$$
$$\varphi(n) = (p - 1)(q - 1).$$

Substituting $q = n/p$ into the second equation gives a quadratic equation in p:

$$p^2 - (n - \varphi(n) + 1)p + n = 0. \tag{7.25}$$

By Vieta's Theorem, p and q are the solutions of a quadratic equation of the form $p^2 + ap + b = 0$ if and only if $p + q = -a$ and $pq = b$. Since the prime factors p and q of n satisfy both $pq = n$ and

$$p + q = pq - pq + p + q - 1 + 1 = pq - (p - 1)(q - 1) + 1 = n - \varphi(n) + 1,$$

(7.25) has the roots p and q. It follows that a cryptanalyst who knows $\varphi(n)$ can easily break RSA. In other words, computing $\varphi(n)$ is at least as hard as factoring n, and vice versa. That is, computing $\varphi(n)$ and factoring n are equally hard tasks.

Example 7.35. Let $n = 60477719$. Suppose that Erich was able to determine the value $\varphi(n) = 60462000$. By (7.25), he can determine the prime factors of n simply by solving the quadratic equation

$$p^2 - 15720p + 60477719 = 0$$

as follows:

$$p = \frac{15720}{2} + \sqrt{\left(\frac{15720}{2}\right)^2 - 60477719} = 9001 \quad \text{and}$$

$$q = \frac{15720}{2} - \sqrt{\left(\frac{15720}{2}\right)^2 - 60477719} = 6719.$$

Superencryption

Simmons and Norris proposed an attack on RSA as early as 1977, shortly after the invention of RSA. Their attack, called superencryption, is based on the observation that a sufficient number of encryptions, cycling through $\mathbb{Z}_n$, may eventually recover the original message m. This attack is a threat to the security of RSA, provided that the number of encryptions required to recover m is small. Fortunately, if the primes p and q are large and are chosen at random, then superencryption is not a practical attack.

Example 7.36 (Superencryption).   Let $n = 5 \cdot 7 = 35$, so $\varphi(n) = 4 \cdot 6 = 24$. Choose the encryption exponent $e = 5$; note that $\gcd(24, 5) = 1$. Encrypting the message $m = 11$ yields

$$11^5 \bmod 35 = 16.$$

Now, encrypting the message $m' = 16$ recovers the original message:

$$16^5 \bmod 35 = 11,$$

which is not suprising, since the decryption key d happens to be equal to e in this case: $5^2 \bmod 24 = 1$, so $d = 5 = e$. In fact, every number e with $\gcd(24, e) = 1$ equals its inverse modulo 24, see Exercise 7.13.

So, let us now choose $n = 11 \cdot 13 = 143$. Then $\varphi(n) = 10 \cdot 12 = 120$. The encryption exponent $e = 7$ has the inverse $d = 103$ modulo 120, so $e \neq d$ in this case. Still, encrypting the message $m = 11$ now yields

$$11^7 \bmod 143 = 132 \quad \text{and} \quad 132^7 \bmod 143 = 11.$$

Thus, without knowing the private key $d = 103$, a cryptanalyst can recover the original message simply by a double encryption.

Small-Message Attack

If both the message m to be encrypted and the encryption exponent e are small relative to the modulus n, then the RSA encryption is not effective. In particular, if the ciphertext $c = m^e$ is smaller than n, then m can be recovered from c by ordinary root extraction. To prevent this from happening, the public exponent should be large or the messages to be encrypted should always be large. It is this latter suggestion that is more useful, since a small public exponent is often preferred in order to speed up encryption and to preclude Wiener's attack.

Wiener's Attack

Wiener proposed an attack on the RSA system that uses a continued fraction approximation and the public key (n, e) so as to compute the private key d. This attack is efficient and practical, and thus is a concern only if the private key d is chosen to be small relative to the modulus n. More precisely, Wiener's attack works if and only if

$$3d < \sqrt[4]{n} \quad \text{and} \quad q < p < 2q, \tag{7.26}$$

where $n = pq$.

Here is a rough sketch of the idea. By (7.2), since the encryption and decryption exponent satisfy $ed \equiv 1 \bmod \varphi(n)$, there is some integer $k < d$ such that

$$ed - k\varphi(n) = 1,$$

which implies

$$\left| \frac{e}{\varphi(n)} - \frac{k}{d} \right| = \frac{1}{d\varphi(n)}. \tag{7.27}$$

Since $n = pq > q^2$, we have $q < \sqrt{n}$. Since $q < p < 2q$ by (7.26), Equation (7.27) implies that

$$0 < n - \varphi(n) = p + q - 1 < 2q + q - 1 < 3q < 3\sqrt{n}.$$

Hence,

$$\left| \frac{e}{n} - \frac{k}{d} \right| = \left| \frac{ed - kn}{dn} \right| = \left| \frac{1 + k(\varphi(n) - n)}{dn} \right| < \frac{3k\sqrt{n}}{dn} = \frac{3k}{d\sqrt{n}} < \frac{1}{d\sqrt[4]{n}}, \tag{7.28}$$

where the latter inequality follows from $3k < 3d < \sqrt[4]{n}$, which is implied by $k < d$ and (7.26). Again, since $3d < \sqrt[4]{n}$, we have

$$\left| \frac{e}{n} - \frac{k}{d} \right| < \frac{1}{3d^2}. \tag{7.29}$$

Note that the encryption key (n, e) is public. Inequality (7.29) says that the fraction k/d is a very close approximation to the fraction e/n. Hence, to recover the private key d from the public key (n, e), an attacker might employ the following fact known from the theory of continued fractions: Every approximation of e/n that is as close as shown in (7.29) must be one of the convergents of the continued fraction expansion of e/n. A (finite) *continued fraction* is the rational number

$$c_1 + \cfrac{1}{c_2 + \cfrac{1}{c_3 + \cdots + \frac{1}{c_t}}}, \tag{7.30}$$

which is represented as the t-tuple $(c_1, c_2, \ldots, c_t)$ of nonnegative integers, where $c_t \neq 0$.

Suppose that a and b are positive integers satisfying $\gcd(a, b) = 1$, and let $r_0, r_1, \ldots, r_t$ be the sequence of integers generated by running EUCLID(a, b), see Figure 2.1. That is, $r_0 = a$, $r_1 = b$, and $r_{i+1} \equiv r_{i-1} \bmod r_i$ for $1 \le i < t$, see the left column of Table 2.1 for an example. Let $c_i = \lfloor r_{i-1}/r_i \rfloor$ for $1 \le i \le t$. Then, a/b equals the continued fraction from (7.30), and $(c_1, c_2, \ldots, c_t)$ is said to be the *continued fraction expansion of a/b*. For each i with $1 \le i \le t$, $\mathbf{C}_i = (c_1, c_2, \ldots, c_i)$ is said to be the ith *convergent of* $(c_1, c_2, \ldots, c_t)$, which can be written as the rational number $\mathbf{C}_i = x_i/y_i$, where x_i and y_i are defined to be the solutions of the following recurrences:

$$x_i = \begin{cases} 1 & \text{if } i = 0 \\ c_1 & \text{if } i = 1 \\ c_i x_{i-1} + x_{i-2} & \text{if } i \ge 2 \end{cases} \quad \text{and} \quad y_i = \begin{cases} 0 & \text{if } i = 0 \\ 1 & \text{if } i = 1 \\ c_i y_{i-1} + y_{i-2} & \text{if } i \ge 2. \end{cases} \tag{7.31}$$

Example 7.37 (Continued Fraction Expansion). To compute the continued fraction expansion of $a/b = 101/37$, run EUCLID$(101, 37)$. Table 7.12 shows the resulting values. Thus, the continued fraction expansion of $101/37$ is $(2, 1, 2, 1, 2, 3)$, which means that

$$\frac{101}{37} = 2 + \cfrac{1}{1 + \cfrac{1}{2 + \cfrac{1}{1 + \cfrac{1}{2 + \frac{1}{3}}}}}.$$

i	0	1	2	3	4	5	6
r_i	101	37	27	10	7	3	1
c_i		2	1	2	1	2	3
$\mathbf{C}_i = \frac{x_i}{y_i}$		$\frac{2}{1}$	$\frac{3}{1}$	$\frac{8}{3}$	$\frac{11}{4}$	$\frac{30}{11}$	$\frac{101}{37}$

Table 7.12. Computing the continued fraction expansion of $101/37$ and its convergents

Table 7.12 also lists the convergents $\mathbf{C}_i = x_i/y_i$ of $(2, 1, 2, 1, 2, 3)$, $1 \le i \le 6$. It can be verified that the x_i and y_i satisfy the recurrences (7.31).

The crucial property of convergents of a continued fraction expansion that can be used to break RSA is stated in the following result without proof.

Theorem 7.38. *If a, b, c, and d are positive integers such that $|a/b - c/d| < 1/(2d^2)$ and $\gcd(a, b) = \gcd(c, d) = 1$, then c/d is one of the convergents of the continued fraction expansion of a/b.*

By Theorem 7.38, (7.29) implies that k/d is one of the convergents of the continued fraction expansion of e/n. Since e/n is known, all one has to do to determine k/d is to compute all convergents of e/n and to check if one of them is the correct one. To this end, if some convergent $\mathbf{C}_i = x_i/y_i$ of e/n is suspected to be equal to k/d, one computes the value of $\varphi(n)$ by

$$\varphi(n) = \frac{e \cdot d - 1}{k} = \frac{e \cdot y_i - 1}{x_i}.$$

Once both n and $\varphi(n)$ are known, n can be factored by solving the quadratic equation (7.25), whose roots will be the prime factors of n. If this test fails, then $\mathbf{C}_i$ was not the correct convergent, and one proceeds to check the next suspect. If none of the convergents of e/n was tested successfully, one concludes that the assumptions made in (7.26) do not apply. For a concrete implementation of Wiener's attack, see Exercise 7.14(a).

Example 7.39 (Wiener's Attack).   Let $n = 60477719$. Note that this is the same n as in Example 7.35. Suppose that the public exponent is $e = 47318087$, so the public key is $(n, e) = (60477719, 47318087)$. Thus, a cryptanalyst knows the value

$$\frac{e}{n} = \frac{47318087}{60477719} = 0.78240528549.$$

Running EUCLID$(47318087, 60477719)$ and computing the values r_i and c_i as above gives the following continued fraction expansion of e/n:

$$(0, 1, 3, 1, 1, 2, 8, 1, 9, 4, 1, 4, 1, 1, 4, 2, 1, 1, 2, 2, 3). \tag{7.32}$$

Now, using the recurrences (7.31) to compute the x_i and y_i, one can determine the 21 convergents $\mathbf{C}_i = x_i/y_i$ of this continued fraction expansion of e/n. Table 7.13 shows the first 10 convergents; see also Exercise 7.14(c).

i		1	2	3	4	5	6	7	8	9	10	$\cdots$
c_i		0	1	3	1	1	2	8	1	9	4	$\cdots$
$\mathbf{C}_i = \frac{x_i}{y_i}$		0	1	$\frac{3}{4}$	$\frac{4}{5}$	$\frac{7}{9}$	$\frac{18}{23}$	$\frac{151}{193}$	$\frac{169}{216}$	$\frac{1672}{2137}$	$\frac{6857}{8764}$	$\cdots$

Table 7.13. Computing the convergents of the continued fraction expansion in Wiener's attack

Each convergent is a suspect of being equal to k/d, and one after the other is to be checked. The first five tests will fail. However, when checking $C_6 = 18/23$, one obtains

$$\varphi(n) = \frac{e \cdot y_6 - 1}{x_6} = \frac{47318087 \cdot 23 - 1}{18} = 60462000,$$

which is precisely the value of $\varphi(n)$ from Example 7.35. As in this example, the cryptanalyst proceeds to compute the prime factors 6719 and 9001 of $n = 60477719$. Note that Wiener's attack works in this example, since the prime factors of n are of roughly the same size and $3 \cdot 23 = 69 < 88 = \lfloor \sqrt[4]{60477719} \rfloor$, so (7.26) is satisfied.

As noted above, Wiener's attack is a real threat only if the hypotheses in (7.26) are satisfied, in particular, only if $3d < \sqrt[4]{n}$. However, since the encryption exponent e is chosen first and is usually chosen to be small to speed up encryption, it is unlikely that a small d will be generated. That is, if e is small enough, then d is likely to be large enough to resist Wiener's attack. One should keep in mind, though, that it might be dangerous if one seeks to speed up decryption by using a small private key d.

Another interesting observation is that if an attacker knows the decryption exponent d, be it small or large, it is possible to factor n using a randomized algorithm. That is to say that computing d is no easier than factoring n, see Problem 7.3.

Low-Exponent Attack

A recommended value of the encryption exponent e that is commonly used today is $e = 2^{16} + 1$. One advantage of this value for e is that its binary expansion has only two ones, which implies that the "square-and-multiply" algorithm from Figure 7.2 requires very few operations.[2] Thus, encryption is very efficient.

However, one should be cautious not to choose the public encryption exponent too small. A preferred value of e that has been used often in the past is $e = 3$. Suppose that three parties participating in the same system encrypt the same message m using the same public exponent $e = 3$, yet distinct RSA moduli, say n_1, n_2, and n_3. Then, a cryptanalyst can easily compute m from the three ciphertexts:

$$c_1 \equiv m^3 \bmod n_1$$
$$c_2 \equiv m^3 \bmod n_2$$
$$c_3 \equiv m^3 \bmod n_3.$$

Since the message m must be smaller than each of the moduli n_i, it follows that m^3 must be smaller than $n_1 n_2 n_3$. Using the Chinese Remainder Theorem (see Theorem 2.46), one can compute the unique solution

$$c \equiv m^3 \bmod n_1 n_2 n_3 = m^3.$$

Hence, one can recover m from c by ordinary root extraction.

---

[2] How many exactly?

More generally, suppose that k related plaintexts are encrypted with the same exponent e:

$$c_1 \equiv (a_1 m + b_1)^e \bmod n_1$$
$$c_2 \equiv (a_2 m + b_2)^e \bmod n_2$$
$$\vdots$$
$$c_k \equiv (a_k m + b_k)^e \bmod n_k,$$

where a_i and b_i, $1 \leq i \leq k$, are known constants, $k > e(e + 1)/2$, and we have $\min(n_i) > 2^{e^2}$. Then, an attacker can solve the above system of k congruences for m in polynomial time using so-called lattice reduction techniques, see Micciancio and Goldwasser [MG02]. This observation was made by Håstad in the late 1980s. This attack is a concern if the messages are related in a known way. In this case, they should not be encrypted with many RSA keys of the form (n_i, e). A recommended countermeasure, which prevents mounting this attack in practice, is to pad the messages with pseudorandom strings prior to encryption, see, e.g., [KR95].

Forging RSA Signatures

We present a chosen-plaintext attack that is based on the fact that the RSA encryption function is a homomorphism: If (n, e) is the public key and m_1 and m_2 are two messages, then

$$m_1^e \cdot m_2^e \equiv (m_1 \cdot m_2)^e \bmod n. \tag{7.33}$$

Another congruence that can easily be verified is

$$(m \cdot r^e)^d \equiv m^d \cdot r \bmod n. \tag{7.34}$$

The congruences (7.33) and (7.34) can be used to mount an attack on the RSA digital signature scheme, see Figure 7.3 in Section 7.1.2. Given previous message-signature pairs $\langle m_1, \mathrm{sig}_A(m_1) \rangle, \langle m_2, \mathrm{sig}_A(m_2) \rangle, \ldots, \langle m_k, \mathrm{sig}_A(m_k) \rangle$, Erich can use the congruences (7.33) and (7.34) to compute a new message-signature pair $\langle m, \mathrm{sig}_A(m) \rangle$ by

$$m = r^e \prod_{i=1}^{k} m_i^{e_i} \bmod n;$$

$$\mathrm{sig}_A(m) = r \prod_{i=1}^{k} (\mathrm{sig}_A(m_i))^{e_i} \bmod n,$$

where r and the e_i are arbitrary. Hence, Erich can forge Alice's signature without knowing her private key, and Bob will not detect the forgery, since

$$m \equiv (\mathrm{sig}_A(m))^e \bmod n.$$

The above attack looks like a known-plaintext attack at first glance. However, note that, in (7.33), even if m_1 and m_2 are meaningful plaintexts, $m_1 \cdot m_2$ usually is not. Thus, Erich can forge Alice's signature only for messages that may or may not be useful. However, he might choose the messages m_i so as to generate a meaningful message m with a forged digital signature. This chosen-plaintext attack can again be avoided by pseudorandom padding techniques that destroy the algebraic relations between messages.

Pseudorandom padding is also a useful countermeasure against the following chosen-ciphertext attack: Erich intercepts some ciphertext c, chooses $r \in \mathbb{N}$ at random, and computes $c \cdot r^e \bmod n$, which he sends to the legitimate receiver Bob. By (7.34), Bob will decrypt the string $\hat{c} = c^d \cdot r \bmod n$, which is likely to look like a random string. Erich, however, if he were to get his hands on $\hat{c}$, could obtain the original message m by computing

$$ m = r^{-1} \cdot c^d \cdot r \bmod n, $$

i.e., he multiplies by r^{-1}, the inverse of r modulo n.

7.5 Exercises and Problems

Exercise 7.1 (a) Prove that for the values of $\varphi(n) = 660$ and $e = 7$ in Example 7.2, the extended Euclidean Algorithm from Figure 2.2 yields indeed the private key $d = 283$, which is the inverse to 7 mod 660.

(b) For the cleartext from Table 7.1 in Example 7.2, determine the encoding of the ciphertext by letters from $\Sigma = \{A, B, \ldots, Z\}$ for each of the 17 blocks.

(c) Decipher all 17 blocks of the ciphertext from Table 7.1 using (7.4), and show that the original cleartext is obtained.

Exercise 7.2 Prove that the RSA digital signature protocol from Figure 7.3 works.

Exercise 7.3 Prove that there exist infinitely many prime numbers.

Hint: First, show that every integer $n \geq 2$ has a prime divisor. Use this result to show that the assumption that there are only finitely many prime numbers leads to a contradiction.

Exercise 7.4 (a) Show that 2 is a Fermat witness for each $n \leq 340$.

   Hint: Write a program to check this property on a computer.

(b) Show that 2 is a Fermat liar for 341.

(c) Prove that for each odd composite number n, the numbers 1 and $n - 1$ trivially are Fermat liars for n.

(d) What is the running time of the Fermat test from Figure 7.5? Prove your answer.

Exercise 7.5 Look at the proof of Lemma 7.8, which uses the following assertion: $a \in \mathbb{Z}_n^*$ if and only if there exists some $b \in \mathbb{Z}_n$ with $a \cdot b \equiv 1 \bmod n$. Prove this assertion.   **Hint:** By definition, $a \in \mathbb{Z}_n^*$ means that $\gcd(n, a) = 1$. Recall that the extended Euclidean Algorithm computes a linear combination of the given two numbers, a and n, by determining numbers x and y with $\gcd(n, a) = x \cdot n + y \cdot a$.

Exercise 7.6 Prove Lemma 7.11: The order of any finite group is divided by the order of each of its subgroups.

Hint: Given a subgroup $\mathfrak{H} = (H, \circ)$ of a finite group $\mathfrak{G} = (G, \circ)$, define $x \cong_H y$ if and only if $y^{-1} \circ x \in H$. Prove that:

(a) $\cong_H$ is an equivalence relation, and

(b) for each $x \in G$, there exists a bijection between H and the equivalence class of x with respect to $\cong_H$.

Using (a) and (b), show that the order of $\mathfrak{G}$ equals the number of equivalence classes of $\cong_H$ times the order of $\mathfrak{H}$.

Exercise 7.7 The proof of Theorem 7.19 in particular requires certain basic number-theoretical facts and lemmas, some of which are listed below.

(a) Prove Lemma 7.13: Every Carmichael number is the product of at least three distinct prime factors.

   Hint: The proof of this lemma is not quite easy. Among other arguments, it involves applications of the Chinese Remainder Theorem and of the Binomial Theorem, similar to the proof of Lemma 7.26. Lemma 7.13 can be found, for example, as Lemma 5.1.8 in Dietzfelbinger's book [Die04].

(b) Prove Lemma 7.14: Every prime number n has only two square roots of 1 modulo n, namely $\pm 1 \bmod n$.   **Hint:** Use the fact that an integer a is a square root of 1 modulo n if and only if n divides $(a - 1)(a + 1)$.

(c) Prove Lemma 7.18: If there exists an MR-witness for n, then n is composite. **Hint:** Look at the proof of Theorem 7.19.

(d) Show that the Miller–Rabin test from Figure 7.6 runs in time $\mathcal{O}(N^3)$ on inputs of length N.

(e) Amplify the success probability of the Miller–Rabin test so as to achieve an error arbitrarily close to zero. In particular, letting q be a nondecreasing polynomial such that $q(n) \geq 2$ for each n, show that Primes is in coRP$_q$, where the class RP$_q$ is defined in Definition 6.5.

Hint: See the proof of Theorem 6.6.

Exercise 7.8 (a) Show that each of the following numbers is an MR-witness for 561:

$$52, \ 59, \ 62, \ 65, \ 70, \ 71, \ 74, \ 80, \ 83, \ 86, \ 89, \ 92, \ 95, \ 98, \ 100, \ 325, \ 556.$$

(b) Show that each of the following numbers is an MR-liar for 561:

$$103, \ 256, \ 305, \ 458, \ 511.$$

(c) Create a table similar to Table 7.5 for the composite number $325 = 5^2 \cdot 13$. Show that both 32 and 318 are MR-liars for 325, yet their product $32 \cdot 318 \equiv 101 \bmod 325$ is an MR-witness for 325. Similarly, show that also 293 is an

MR-liar for 325, yet the product $293 \cdot 318 \equiv 224 \bmod 325$ is an MR-witness for 325. Can you find further counterexamples to the (incorrect) claim that the set MR-Liars$_{325}$ is a subgroup of $\mathbb{Z}^*_{325}$?

Hint: Another example for $n = 325$ can be found in Table 5.3 of [Die04].

(d) Can you find similar counterexamples as in (c) for the Carmichael number 561?

Exercise 7.9 **(a)** Use the properties of the Jacobi symbol stated in Proposition 7.22 to design a polynomial-time algorithm for computing the Jacobi symbol.

(b) Prove that for each odd positive integer n,

$$\left(\frac{n-1}{n}\right) = (-1)^{(n-1)/2}.$$

(c) Evaluate the following Jacobi symbols:

$$\left(\frac{4335}{6399}\right), \quad \left(\frac{2222}{1111}\right), \quad \left(\frac{1234}{9876}\right), \quad \left(\frac{2365}{7882}\right), \quad \left(\frac{9275}{6273}\right), \quad \text{and} \quad \left(\frac{4367}{5932}\right).$$

(d) Prove that every SS-liar for $n \geq 3$ is also a Fermat liar for n.

Exercise 7.10 The factoring problem can be defined both as a functional problem, as in Definition 7.28, and as a decision problem. There are different ways of doing so. For example, define the *factoring problem as a decision problem* by

$$\text{Factoring} = \{\langle n, k\rangle \mid n \text{ has no prime factor that is less than or equal to } k\},$$

where n and k are again represented in binary.

(a) Prove that the functional version `factoring` from Definition 7.28 and the above language version `Factoring` of this problem are polynomial-time Turing-reducible to one another:

$$\text{Factoring} \in \text{P}^{\text{factoring}} \quad \text{and} \quad \text{factoring} \in \text{FP}^{\text{Factoring}}.$$

(b) How many queries suffice in these reductions?

(c) Prove that the factoring problem, suitably formalized as a language problem, is in NP.

Exercise 7.11 **(a)** Factor $n = 3^{21} + 1 = 10460353204$ by trial division.

(b) Use Pollard's $p - 1$ method from Figure 7.8 to factor $n = 1241143$.

(c) Prove that one execution of Pollard's $p - 1$ method from Figure 7.8 (not taking account of the recursion or of the restart with a new bound) runs in time $\mathcal{O}(B \log B N^2 + N^3)$, where B is the bound chosen and N is the length of the integer n to be factored.

Hint: Consider the algorithms invoked in one run of Pollard's $p - 1$ method. In particular, how often is the "square-and-multiply" algorithm invoked? What is its running time? What time is needed to compute the greatest common divisor?

Exercise 7.12 (a) Factor $n = 7429$ by the quadratic sieve method. **Hint:** Use the factor base $\mathfrak{B} = \{-1, 2, 3, 5, 7\}$ and apply the method from Section 7.3.3.

(b) Let $n = 106$, so $s = \lfloor \sqrt{n} \rfloor = 10$. Choose the factor base $\mathfrak{B} = \{-1, 2, 3, 5, 7\}$, and let $\sigma(x) = (x + 10)^2 - 106$. As in Table 7.9, for each prime p in $\mathfrak{B}$, apply the sieve with p to the sieve interval $S = \{-10, -9, \ldots, -1, 0, 1, \ldots, 9, 10\}$.

In particular, show that we obtain equations for $\sigma(6)$ and $\sigma(10)$ that, when multiplied, yield a congruence of the form (7.23), which has squares on both sides. Why are the resulting numbers a and b not suitable to factor n?

(c) Make bibliographic inquiries to find out the prime factors of the Fermat number $F_{11} = 2^{2^{11}} + 1$. Who was the first to discover this factorization and when?

Exercise 7.13 Let $n = 35$ be the RSA modulus from Example 7.36, so $\varphi(n) = 24$. Prove that every possible choice e of the encryption exponent equals the inverse of e modulo 24. Thus, the encryption exponent and the decryption exponent are identical in this case, and RSA with these parameters in fact is a symmetric cryptosystem.

Exercise 7.14 (a) Write a program in pseudocode that implements Wiener's attack presented in Section 7.4. **Hint:** See Wiener [Wie90] or Stinson [Sti02].

(b) Verify that the continued fraction expansion of $e/n = 0.78240528549$ stated in (7.32) from Example 7.39 is correct.

(c) Compute the remaining 11 convergents, $\mathbf{C}_{11}$ through $\mathbf{C}_{21}$, of the continued fraction expansion of $e/n = 47318087/60477719$, which were omitted in Table 7.13 from Example 7.39.

Problem 7.1 (Decreasing the Error of the Miller–Rabin Test)

Prove that the Miller–Rabin test from Figure 7.6 has an error probability of at most $1/4$, by doing a more careful analysis.

Hint: It is enough to prove that if $n \geq 3$ is an odd composite number, then there are at most $(n - 1)/4$ MR-liars for n in $\mathbb{Z}_n^*$. So assume that a is an MR-liar for n, i.e., a satisfies condition (7.8): $a^m \equiv 1 \bmod n$, or it satisfies condition (7.9): for some $j \in \{0, 1, \ldots, k - 1\}$, $a^{2^j m} \equiv -1 \bmod n$.

If a satisfies (7.8), then $-a$ satisfies (7.9). So, let $j_{\max}$ be the largest j for which there exists an $a \in \mathbb{Z}_n^*$ satisfying (7.9). Let $k = 2^{m \cdot j_{\max}}$. Consider the prime power factorization of $n = \prod p^{e_p}$, where $e_p \geq 1$ and the product is taken over all prime factors p of n. Define the following four subsets of $\mathbb{Z}_n^*$:

$$A = \{a \in \mathbb{Z}_n^* \mid a^{n-1} \equiv 1 \bmod n\};$$
$$B = \{a \in \mathbb{Z}_n^* \mid a^k \equiv \pm 1 \bmod p^{e_p} \text{ for each prime factor } p \text{ of } n\};$$
$$C = \{a \in \mathbb{Z}_n^* \mid a^k \equiv \pm 1 \bmod n\};$$
$$D = \{a \in \mathbb{Z}_n^* \mid a^k \equiv 1 \bmod n\}.$$

Note that $A \subset B \subset C \subset D \subset \mathbb{Z}_n^*$. In particular, every MR-liar a belongs to C. Show that each of A, B, C, and D is a subgroup of $\mathbb{Z}_n^*$. By Lemma 7.11, the group order of C divides $\varphi(n)$. To show that there are at most $(n-1)/4$ MR-liars for n in $\mathbb{Z}_n^*$, prove that $\varphi(n)/\|C\| \geq 4$.

Problem 7.2 (Primality Problem)

Prove that Primes is in P. **Hint:** See Section 7.2.4 and [AKS02]. Another recommended source for this proof is [Die04]. This problem is very difficult to solve.

Problem 7.3 (Factoring n Using a Known RSA Decryption Exponent)

Let (n, e) be a public RSA key, and let d be the corresponding private RSA key. Design an efficient (randomized) Las Vegas algorithm that factors n with probability at least $1/2$, provided that the input $\langle n, e, d \rangle$ satisfies $ed \equiv 1 \mod \varphi(n)$.

Hint: See Stinson [Sti02].

7.6 Summary and Bibliographic Remarks

General Remarks: For their fundamental contributions to public-key cryptography, Rivest, Shamir, and Adleman received the Turing Award in 2002. The importance of RSA can be seen from the fact that probably no cryptography textbook written since the late 1970s has omitted presenting RSA. Primality tests and factoring methods are also presented in many books on cryptography; see, e.g., Stinson [Sti02], Salomaa [Sal96], Goldreich [Gol01], and Buchmann [Buc01]. Koblitz [Kob97] focuses on the algebraic aspects of cryptography. One of the most profound and up-to-date sources on primality testing is Dietzfelbinger's book [Die04], which provides both randomized primality tests, such as the Miller–Rabin test, and a comprehensive presentation of Agrawal, Kayal, and Saxena's proof that Primes is in P [AKS02]. D. Bernstein [Ber04] gives a comprehensive taxonomy of the currently best primality tests.

Specific Remarks: The idea of public-key cryptography was first published by Diffie and Hellman in their pathbreaking paper [DH76]. The very first concrete public-key cryptosystem that appeared in the open literature is RSA. Both the RSA cryptosystem and the related digital signature scheme, presented in Section 7.1, are due to Rivest, Shamir, and Adleman [RSA78]. Decades later, in December of 1997, the British Government Communications Headquarters (GCHQ) revealed that Ellis, Cocks, and Williamson, employed at the Communications Electronics Security Group of the GCHQ, had independently and even earlier discovered the principle of public-key cryptography, the cryptosystem now called RSA, and the secret-key agreement protocol now called Diffie–Hellman, which will be presented in Section 8.1.

Ellis came up with the principal idea for public-key cryptosystems as early as 1969. Cocks invented the system now called RSA in 1973, about four years before Rivest, Shamir, and Adleman found it independently in 1977. And Williamson discovered the mathematical principles on which the Diffie–Hellman protocol rests at about the same time as Diffie and Hellman [DH76]. Strangely enough, while Diffie–Hellman predates RSA, the corresponding findings were obtained in reverse order at the GCHQ. The interesting story of these secret developments in the nonpublic sector is told in more detail by Singh [Sin99] and others.

Based on Miller's [Mil76] ideas for a deterministic algorithm for the primality problem, Rabin [Rab80] developed the randomized algorithm now known as the Miller–Rabin test, which is shown in Figure 7.6. Independently, Solovay and Strassen [SS77] developed their Monte Carlo primality test, see Figure 7.7. For more information on the primality problem and primality testing, see, e.g., Adleman and Huang [AH87, AH92a], D. Bernstein [Ber04], and Dietzfelbinger [Die04].

Pollard's $p-1$ method can be found in [Pol74]. The quadratic sieve, which is presented in Section 7.3, is due to Pomerance. Dixon's random squares method [Dix81] is presented in Stinson [Sti02], for example. The number field sieve, a more recent and even more successful sieving method for factoring, was developed in the late 1980s based on an idea of Pollard, see Lenstra and Lenstra [LL93]. The elliptic curve method for factoring integers is due to H. Lenstra [Len87]. Exercises 7.11(a), 7.11(b), and 7.12(a) are taken from Buchmann [Buc01].

It was mentioned in Section 7.3 that the factoring problem is a candidate of a problem that seems to be neither in P nor NP-complete, just as the graph isomorphism problem. However, the current evidence against NP-completeness for the factoring problem is different from that against NP-completeness for the graph isomorphism problem. The currently strongest results suggesting that Factoring is unlikely to be NP-complete are due to Fellows and Koblitz [FK92] and to Kayal and Saxena [KS04]. Fellows and Koblitz show that the factoring problem is in UP∩coUP. Cai and Threlfall [CT04] show that also the quadratic residue problem introduced in Definition 2.43 is in UP ∩ coUP.

Kayal and Saxena prove that the factoring problem reduces to the problem of counting the automorphisms in rings (and various related problems) under polynomial-time randomized Turing reductions with zero error probability. In particular, denoting the counting problem for ring automorphisms by #RA, they prove that Factoring is in ZPP$^{\#RA}$, and they also show that #RA is in FP$^{AM∩coAM}$. It follows that Factoring is in ZPP$^{AM∩coAM}$.

The superencryption attack is due to Simmons and Norris [SN77]. Wiener's attack can be found in [Wie90]; the sketch of its idea presented in Section 7.4 is based on Stinson's presentation in [Sti02]. A solution to Problem 7.3 can also be found in [Sti02]. Boneh and Durfee [BD00] improved Wiener's attack to be effective for each private key $d < n^{0.292}$. A generalized Wiener attack on RSA is due to Blömer and May [BM04]. Their method of factoring the RSA modulus n is successful whenever the public key (n, e) satisfies $ex + y \equiv 0 \bmod \varphi(n)$ for $3x < \sqrt[4]{n}$ and $|y| \in \mathcal{O}(n^{-3/4}ex)$. The generalization of the low-exponent attack presented in Section 7.4 is due to Håstad [Hås88]. This attack was later improved by Coppersmith [Cop97]. Bleichenbacher [Ble98] proposed an adaptive chosen-ciphertext attack against protocols based on RSA. May [May04] showed that computing the secret RSA key is equivalent to factoring under polynomial-time deterministic Turing reductions. More precisely, he designed a deterministic polynomial-time algorithm for factoring a given RSA modulus n, provided that the prime factors p and q of n are of the same bit size and that the public RSA exponent e and the private RSA key d are known, where $e, d < \varphi(n)$. Previously, the equivalence of factoring and computing the secret RSA key was known to hold only for polynomial-time *randomized* Turing reductions [RSA78].

For further background on the security of the RSA system, on potential attacks proposed to break this system, and on effective countermeasures to prevent these attacks, the reader is referred to the survey papers by Moore [Moo92], Shamir [Sha95], Kaliski and Robshaw [KR95], Boneh [Bon99], and Rothe [Rot02].

8

Other Public-Key Cryptosystems and Protocols

This chapter presents various important cryptosystems and cryptographic protocols. Most of these cryptosystems are public-key, though we start in Section 8.1 by introducing the Diffie–Hellman secret-key agreement protocol that is very useful in symmetric cryptography. Diffie and Hellman's protocol solves the problem of sharing a joint secret key in a symmetric cryptosystem via an insecure channel. It is the first such protocol in the open literature, see the bibliographic remarks in Section 7.6. As already mentioned, Diffie and Hellman's work also opened the door to public-key cryptography, which no longer requires that Alice and Bob agree on a joint secret key before exchanging encrypted messages.

The security of the Diffie–Hellman protocol is based on the assumption that computing discrete logarithms is a hard problem. Many other protocols and cryptosystems use the same assumption as well. In particular, Section 8.2 presents the ElGamal public-key cryptosystem and the ElGamal digital signature protocol whose security is likewise based on the hardness of the discrete logarithm problem.

In Section 8.3, Rabin's cryptosystem is presented. This public-key cryptosystem assumes that factoring large integers n and computing square roots modulo n are both computationally hard tasks. Unlike the RSA or ElGamal systems, Rabin's cryptosystem is provably secure under the assumption that the factoring problem is computationally intractable.

In Section 8.4, we return to the notion of Arthur-Merlin games introduced in Section 6.3. As noted there, Arthur-Merlin games are closely related to the theory of interactive proof systems, which is important both in complexity theory and for cryptographic applications. In particular, zero-knowledge protocols are interactive proof systems that can be used for authentication. Section 8.4 presents a zero-knowledge protocol for the graph isomorphism problem, which is also studied in Section 6.5.

Section 8.5 discusses a public-key cryptosystem due to Merkle and Hellman, which is based on an NP-complete problem. Finally, Section 8.6 presents Rabi, Rivest, and Sherman's secret-key agreement and digital signature protocols. The security of their protocols is based on complexity-theoretic (i.e., worst-case) one-way functions with certain useful algebraic and security properties. In particular, these protocols require two-argument one-way functions that are commutative, associative, and "strongly noninvertible." We also discuss the issue of constructing such functions under appropriate complexity-theoretic assumptions.

8.1 Diffie–Hellman and the Discrete Logarithm Problem

Public-key cryptosystems are usually less efficient than symmetric cryptosystems. Suppose that, for the sake of efficiency, Alice and Bob want to use a symmetric cryptosystem, so encryption and decryption is done using the same key. How can Alice and Bob agree on such a joint secret key, without meeting in private prior to exchanging encrypted messages and without using an expensive secure channel for key distribution? If they were to agree on a shared secret key to be used in future communications by first sending it over an insecure channel, properly encrypted by means of their symmetric cryptosystem, then which secret key could they use in order to encrypt *this* message? This paradoxical situation is known as the *secret-key agreement problem*.

Key distribution for symmetric systems is an issue, and it is the more demanding, the more users are participating in the same system. It often happens in cryptographic applications that one party wants to send the same message to several other parties, sometimes to several hundred or even more parties. Just think of a military scenario in which the message "ATTACK AT SIX A.M. SKIPPING BREAKFAST" is to be sent to the soldiers of the Sixth Infantry Regiment. Or think of a scenario in which all CIA agents worldwide are to be informed about the details of a terroristic assassination plan that could be uncovered, in order to coordinate appropriate countermeasures to prevent it on time.

The secret-key agreement problem has been considered unsolvable since the beginnings of cryptography. Thus, it caused much surprise when Diffie and Hellman came up with an ingenious, simple idea to solve it. Using their secret-key agreement protocol, Alice and Bob can agree on a joint secret key by exchanging some messages. Eavesdropper Erich, however, does not have a clue about their key, even though he knows every single bit exchanged, provided that he cannot solve the discrete logarithm problem.

8.1.1 Diffie and Hellman's Secret-Key Agreement Protocol

Figure 8.1 shows the Diffie–Hellman secret-key agreement protocol. It is based on the following number-theoretical notions and facts introduced in Section 2.4.1:

- A *primitive element* γ of n is defined to be a generator of the multiplicative group $\mathbb{Z}_n^*$ of order $\varphi(n)$, see Definition 2.40. That is,

$$\langle \gamma \rangle = \{ \gamma^i \mid 0 \leq i < \varphi(n) \} = \mathbb{Z}_n^*.$$

Recall that for each prime number p, $\mathbb{Z}_p^*$ is a group of order $\varphi(p) = p - 1$ and has exactly $\varphi(p - 1)$ primitive elements; see Example 2.41.

- Let p be a prime number, and let γ be a primitive element modulo p. The *modular exponential function with base γ and modulus p* is introduced in Definition 2.42 by

$$\exp_{\gamma,p}(a) = \gamma^a \bmod p,$$

and its inverse function is called the *discrete logarithm*. For $\alpha = \exp_{\gamma,p}(a)$, we write $a = \log_\gamma \alpha \bmod p$.

Step	Alice	Erich	Bob
1	Alice and Bob agree on a large prime p and a primitive element γ of p; p and γ are public		
2	chooses a large random number a, keeps it secret, and computes $\alpha = \gamma^a \bmod p$		chooses a large random number b, keeps it secret, and computes $\beta = \gamma^b \bmod p$
3		$\alpha \Rightarrow$ $\Leftarrow \beta$	
4	computes her key $k_A = \beta^a \bmod p$		computes his key $k_B = \alpha^b \bmod p$

Fig. 8.1. Diffie–Hellman secret-key agreement protocol

The Diffie–Hellman protocol from Figure 8.1 works, since

$$k_A = \beta^a = \gamma^{ba} = \gamma^{ab} = \alpha^b = k_B$$

in the arithmetics modulo p. Thus, Alice and Bob indeed compute the same key. Using the "square-and-multiply" algorithm from Figure 7.2 in Section 7.1 so as to perform exponentiation fast, both Alice and Bob can efficiently determine this key. Recall that $\beta^a \bmod p$ requires $a-1$ multiplications if performed naively, yet no more than $2 \log a$ multiplications if "square-and-multiply" is used.

Example 8.1 (Diffie–Hellman Protocol).   Suppose that Alice und Bob have chosen the prime number $p = 17$ and now want to choose a primitive element of 17. Recall that γ is a primitive element of p if and only if γ generates $\mathbb{Z}_p^*$, i.e.,

$$\mathbb{Z}_p^* = \{\gamma^i \mid 0 \leq i < p - 1\}.$$

Every element $x \in \mathbb{Z}_p^*$ can be uniquely written as $x = \gamma^i$ for some i, $0 \leq i < p - 1$. Recall from Definition 2.34 that the order of an element x of the group $\mathbb{Z}_p^*$ is the smallest positive integer k such that $x^k = 1$. Thus, the order of $x = \gamma^i$ is

$$\frac{p-1}{\gcd(p-1, i)}. \tag{8.1}$$

It follows that x itself is a primitive element of p if and only if $\gcd(p - 1, i) = 1$, and hence there are exactly $\varphi(p - 1)$ primitive elements of p.

Note that $\mathbb{Z}_{16}^* = \{1, 3, 5, 7, 9, 11, 13, 15\}$, so $\varphi(16) = 8$ is the number of primitive elements modulo 17. It can be verified that 3 is a primitive element of 17, since 3 generates $\mathbb{Z}_{17}^* = \{1, 3, 9, 10, 13, 5, 15, 11, 16, 14, 8, 7, 4, 12, 2, 6\}$. The remaining primitive elements modulo 17 can be determined as follows. First, compute all successive powers of 3 modulo 17, as shown in Table 8.1. By (8.1), an element $3^i \bmod 17$ is primitive if and only if $\gcd(16, i) = 1$. Table 8.1 shows these primitive elements in gray boxes.

i	0	1	2	3	4	5	6	7	8	9	10	11	12	13	14	15
$3^i \bmod 17$	1	3	9	10	13	5	15	11	16	14	8	7	4	12	2	6

Table 8.1. Computing the primitive elements modulo 17

Suppose that Alice and Bob choose the primitive element $\gamma = 12$ of 17, see Exercise 8.1(a). Further, Alice chooses the secret number $a = 10$ at random. She wants to send the number $\alpha = 12^{10} \bmod 17$ to Bob. Applying the "square-and-multiply" algorithm from Figure 7.2, she first computes the binary expansion of the exponent, $10 = 2^1 + 2^3$, and then the values $12^{2^i} \bmod 17$ for $0 \le i \le 3$, see Table 8.2.

$12^{2^0} \bmod 17$	$12^{2^1} \bmod 17$	$12^{2^2} \bmod 17$	$12^{2^3} \bmod 17$	$\alpha = 12^{10} \bmod 17$
12	8	13	16	9

Table 8.2. Computing $\alpha = 12^{10} \bmod 17$ for the Diffie–Hellman protocol

Multiplying the values in the gray boxes of Table 8.2, she obtains

$$\alpha = 12^{10} \equiv 9 \bmod 17$$

and sends $\alpha = 9$ to Bob. Meanwhile, Bob has chosen his secret exponent $b = 15$ and has computed his value $\beta = 12^{15} \equiv 10 \bmod 17$ by the same procedure, see Exercise 8.1(b). Bob sends $\beta = 10$ to Alice. Now, Alice and Bob compute

$$k_A = 10^{10} \equiv 2 \bmod 17 \quad \text{and} \quad k_B = 9^{15} \equiv 2 \bmod 17$$

to determine their joint secret key, $k_A = 2 = k_B$.

Erich, however, encounters difficulties when trying to determine Alice and Bob's secret key, provided that their numbers are chosen large enough. (Needless to say, the numbers in the above toy example are much too small to resist a brute-force attack.) If he was eavesdropping carefully on their communication—and Erich is infamous for being an alert eavesdropper—then all he knows are the public values p and γ and the communicated values α and β. In order to compute the secret values a and b from α and β, it seems that he has to solve the discrete logarithm. However, the discrete logarithm is considered to be a hard problem, see Section 8.1.2. That is why $\exp_{\gamma,p}$, the modular exponential function, is considered to be a candidate of a one-way function, a function that is easy to compute but hard to invert.

To avoid confusion, we mention that Definition 3.78 in Section 3.6.2 introduces the notion of (complexity-theoretic) one-way functions in the worst-case complexity model. In contrast, $\exp_{\gamma,p}$ is suspected to be hard to invert even on average, a more challenging and more appealing feature of one-way-ness required in cryptographic applications. Things are bad. To this day, it is not known whether or not one-way functions do exist, not even in the less challenging worst-case model. Things are worse. Although we do not know if there is any one-way function, many cryptosystems and protocols use presumed one-way functions as their cryptographic primitives, and thus their security is based merely on the assumption, or the hope, that these functions indeed are one-way.

Since the discrete logarithm problem seems to be hard, the above direct attack on the Diffie–Hellman secret-key agreement protocol is not a real concern currently, provided that the prime p and the private exponents a and b are chosen large enough. In particular, these exponents should be at least 2^{160}. The next section will present algorithms for computing the discrete logarithm and will discuss the above direct attack, which is related to the so-called "Diffie–Hellman problem."

In addition to this most obvious attack, there are other, indirect attacks on Diffie–Hellman in which the cryptanalyst is not just a passive eavesdropper who tries to break the protocol by determining the secret key from the values α and β. For example, Diffie–Hellman is vulnerable to the "*man-in-the-middle*" attack, an *active* attack in which the attacker tries to modify the protocol to his advantage. Suppose that Erich, the man in the middle, intercepts Alice's number $\alpha = \gamma^a \bmod p$ sent to Bob, and he intercepts Bob's number $\beta = \gamma^b \bmod p$ sent to Alice. Erich then replaces α and β by his own values and forwards $\alpha_E = \gamma^e \bmod p$ to Bob and $\beta_E = \gamma^e \bmod p$ to Alice, where e is Erich's private exponent. According to the protocol, Alice and Bob now compute the keys

$$k_A = (\beta_E)^a \bmod p \quad \text{and} \quad k_B = (\alpha_E)^b \bmod p,$$

which they presume to share with their respective partners. However, k_A in fact is a key that Alice shares with Erich, who will use the same key in future communications with her, pretending to be Bob. He can determine this key by computing

$$k_E = \alpha^e = \gamma^{ae} = \gamma^{ea} = (\beta_E)^a = k_A$$

in the arithmetics modulo p. Similarly, Erich can determine the key k_B to be used in future communications with Bob, where Erich pretends to be Alice. The man-in-the-middle attack is related to the issue of *authentication*, which will be discussed later in Section 8.4.

8.1.2 Discrete Logarithm and the Diffie–Hellman Problem

Consider the Diffie–Hellman protocol, and suppose that Erich knows the values p, γ, α, and β as defined in Figure 8.1, yet he does not know the secret exponents a and b. His aim is to determine Alice and Bob's joint secret key,

$$k_A = k_B \equiv \gamma^{ab} \bmod p.$$

This problem, called the *Diffie–Hellman problem*, is formally defined below as a functional problem. Equivalently, it can be formalized as a decision problem, Diffie-Hellman, which is equivalent to the functional version diffie-hellman (to be defined below) under polynomial-time Turing reductions, see Exercise 8.2(a). However, the functional version is more important for cryptographic applications.

Similarly, the *discrete logarithm problem* from Definition 2.42 can be formalized equivalently as a decision problem, see Exercise 8.2(b). Again, the functional version is cryptographically more relevant. We define the functional discrete logarithm problem below for arbitrary multiplicative groups, thus generalizing Definition 2.42. We assume that groups are suitably represented by a generator, see Section 2.4.2.

Definition 8.2 (Discrete Logarithm and Diffie–Hellman Problem).

- *The* functional discrete logarithm problem, *denoted by* dlog, *is defined as follows: Given a multiplicative group* $(G, \cdot)$, *an element* $\gamma \in G$ *of order* n, *and an element* $\alpha \in \langle \gamma \rangle$, *compute the unique element* a *with* $0 \leq a \leq n - 1$ *such that*

$$a = \log_\gamma \alpha.$$

  (Equivalently, given γ *and* α, *compute the unique element* a *with* $\gamma^a = \alpha$.)
- *The* functional Diffie–Hellman problem, *denoted by* diffie-hellman, *is defined as follows: Given a multiplicative group* $(G, \cdot)$, *an element* $\gamma \in G$ *of order* n, *and two elements* α *and* β *in* $\langle \gamma \rangle$, *compute an element* $\delta \in \langle \gamma \rangle$ *such that*

$$\log_\gamma \delta \equiv (\log_\gamma \alpha)(\log_\gamma \beta) \bmod n.$$

  (Equivalently, given $\gamma^a \bmod n$ *and* $\gamma^b \bmod n$, *compute* $\gamma^{ab} \bmod n$.)

If Erich were able to compute discrete logarithms efficiently, he would be able to solve the Diffie–Hellman problem, since he could determine Alice's private exponent $a = \log_\gamma \alpha \bmod p$ from p, γ, and α, and he could determine Bob's private exponent $b = \log_\gamma \beta \bmod p$ from p, γ, and β. Thus, computing discrete logarithms is no easier than solving the Diffie–Hellman problem. This argument can easily be generalized from $\mathbb{Z}_p^*$ to arbitrary multiplicative groups and thus proves the following fact.

Fact 8.3 *The Diffie–Hellman problem reduces to the discrete logarithm problem under polynomial-time Turing reductions. That is,* diffie-hellman $\in$ FP^{dlog}.

The converse question of whether the discrete logarithm problem is at least as hard as the Diffie–Hellman problem remains an unproven conjecture. The Diffie–Hellman protocol currently has no proof of security, not even in the sense that it is as hard as the discrete logarithm, which itself is a problem whose precise complexity is an open issue. The remainder of this section briefly discusses some algorithms for the discrete logarithm problem.

Exhaustive Search Algorithm

The first observation is that the discrete logarithm problem can be solved by exhaustive search: Given γ and α as in Definition 8.2, successively compute

$$\gamma, \gamma^2, \gamma^3, \ldots,$$

until the unique exponent a with $\gamma^a = \alpha$ is found. This can be done by computing $\gamma^i = \gamma \cdot \gamma^{i-1}$ for $1 < i < n$. Hence, assuming that executing one group operation costs constant time, this naive brute-force algorithm requires time $\mathcal{O}(n)$, which is exponential in the length of n and thus exponential in the input length.

Shanks' Baby-Step Giant-Step Algorithm

Figure 8.2 presents Shanks' baby-step giant-step algorithm, which is more efficient than the above exhaustive search algorithm for the discrete logarithm problem. However, Shanks' algorithm gains this speed-up only at the cost of using more memory.

SHANKS(G, n, γ, α) {
    // G is a multiplicative group, $\gamma \in G$ is a primitive element of order n, and $\alpha \in \langle \gamma \rangle$
    $s := \lceil \sqrt{n} \rceil$;
    for $(i = 0, 1, \ldots, s - 1)$ { add (γ^{is}, i) to a list $\mathcal{L}_1$; }
    Sort the elements of $\mathcal{L}_1$ with respect to their first coordinates;
    for $(j = 0, 1, \ldots, s - 1)$ { add $(\alpha\gamma^{-j}, j)$ to a list $\mathcal{L}_2$; }
    Sort the elements of $\mathcal{L}_2$ with respect to their first coordinates;
    Find a pair $(\delta, i) \in \mathcal{L}_1$ and a pair $(\delta, j) \in \mathcal{L}_2$, i.e., find two pairs with identical first
        coordinates;
    return "$\log_\gamma \alpha = is + j$" and halt;
}

Fig. 8.2. Shanks' baby-step giant-step algorithm

In order to compute $\log_\gamma \alpha$ for given values α and γ, where γ is a primitive element of order n, Shanks' algorithm first determines $s = \lceil \sqrt{n} \rceil$. If we now set

$$a = is + j, \quad 0 \leq j < s,$$

we have

$$\alpha = \gamma^a = \gamma^{is+j}. \tag{8.2}$$

We want to determine $a = \log_\gamma \alpha$. Equation (8.2) implies $\alpha\gamma^{-j} = (\gamma^s)^i$. The pairs $(\alpha\gamma^{-j}, j)$ with $0 \leq j < s$ are the elements of the list $\mathcal{L}_2$, sorted with respect to the first coordinates, which represent the "baby steps." If the pair $(1, j)$ is in $\mathcal{L}_2$ for some j, we are done, since $\alpha\gamma^{-j} = 1$ implies $\alpha = \gamma^j$, so setting $a = j$ solves the discrete logarithm problem in this case. Otherwise, we determine

$$\delta = \gamma^s$$

and search for a group element δ^i, $1 \leq i < s$, occurring as the first coordinate of some element in $\mathcal{L}_2$. The elements $(\gamma^s)^i = \gamma^{is}$ are collected in the list $\mathcal{L}_1$, again sorted with respect to the first coordinates, and represent the "giant steps." Once a pair (γ^{is}, i) is found in $\mathcal{L}_1$ such that (γ^{is}, j) occurs in the list $\mathcal{L}_2$ of baby steps, we have solved the discrete logarithm problem, since

$$\alpha\gamma^{-j} = \delta^i = \gamma^{is}$$

implies $\alpha = \gamma^{is+j}$, so $a = \log_\gamma \alpha = is + j$.

Example 8.4 (Shanks' Algorithm).   Suppose we want to find $a = \log_2 47 \bmod 101$ in the group $\mathbb{Z}_{101}^*$, using Shanks' algorithm. That is, $p = 101$, $\gamma = 2$, and $\alpha = 47$ are given. Note that 101 is a prime number and 2 is a primitive element of 101, see Exercise 8.3(a). Since $n = p - 1 = 100$ is the order of 2, we have $s = \lceil \sqrt{100} \rceil = 10$. It follows that $\gamma^s \bmod p = 2^{10} \bmod p = 14$. Now, the sorted lists $\mathcal{L}_1$ and $\mathcal{L}_2$ can be determined as shown in Table 8.3.

$\mathcal{L}_1$	$(1,0)$	$(14,1)$	$(95,2)$	$(17,3)$	$(36,4)$	$(100,5)$	$(87,6)$	$(6,7)$	$(84,8)$	$(65,9)$
$\mathcal{L}_1$ sorted	$(1,0)$	$(6,7)$	$(14,1)$	$(17,3)$	$(36,4)$	$(65,9)$	$(84,8)$	$(87,6)$	$(95,2)$	$(100,5)$
$\mathcal{L}_2$	$(47,0)$	$(74,1)$	$(37,2)$	$(69,3)$	$(85,4)$	$(93,5)$	$(97,6)$	$(99,7)$	$(100,8)$	$(50,9)$
$\mathcal{L}_2$ sorted	$(37,2)$	$(47,0)$	$(50,9)$	$(69,3)$	$(74,1)$	$(85,4)$	$(93,5)$	$(97,6)$	$(99,7)$	$(100,8)$

Table 8.3. Computing the sorted lists $\mathcal{L}_1$ and $\mathcal{L}_2$ for Shanks' algorithm

Since $(100,5)$ is in $\mathcal{L}_1$ and $(100,8)$ is in $\mathcal{L}_2$, we obtain $a = 5 \cdot 10 + 8 = 58$. It can be verified that $2^{58} \bmod 101 = 47$, as desired.

The first **for** loop in Figure 8.2 can be implemented so as to first compute γ^s and then raising its powers by multiplying by γ^s. Similarly, the second **for** loop in Figure 8.2 is performed by first computing the inverse element γ^{-1} of γ in the group and then computing its powers. Both **for** loops require time $\mathcal{O}(s)$. Using an efficient sorting algorithm such as quicksort, the lists $\mathcal{L}_1$ and $\mathcal{L}_2$ can be sorted in time $\mathcal{O}(s \log s)$. Finally, the two pairs whose first coordinate occurs in both lists can be found in time $\mathcal{O}(s)$ by simultaneously passing through both lists. Summing up, Shanks' algorithm can be implemented to run in time $\mathcal{O}(s) = \mathcal{O}(\sqrt{n})$ and to require the same amount of space, where logarithmic factors are neglected as is usually done in the analysis of discrete logarithm algorithms.

Although Shanks' algorithm is more efficient than the exhaustive search algorithm, it is not an efficient algorithm. There are many other algorithms for the discrete algorithm problem, some of which are better than Shanks' algorithm. Among the most popular such algorithms are Pollard's ρ algorithm, the Pohlig–Hellman algorithm, the index calculus method, and variants thereof. The index calculus method is particularly suitable for computing the discrete logarithm in $\mathbb{Z}_p^*$ for primes p and is closely related to factoring methods such as the quadratic sieve or the number field sieve, see Sections 7.3.3 and 7.3.4. For a detailed description and analysis of these alternative discrete logarithm algorithms, the reader is referred to, e.g., Stinson [Sti02] and Buchmann [Buc01]. None of the known discrete logarithm algorithms is efficient. The precise complexity of dlog remains an open research question.

8.2 ElGamal's Protocols

The Diffie–Hellman protocol can be modified so as to yield either a public-key cryptosystem or a digital signature protocol. These modifications are due to ElGamal [ElG85]. The security of ElGamal's protocols is again based on the presumed hardness of computing discrete logarithms. The number-theoretical notions needed for these protocols are explained in Section 8.1.

8.2.1 ElGamal's Public-Key Cryptosystem

Figure 8.3 shows the single steps of the ElGamal public-key cryptosystem. A more detailed description and explanation of these steps is in order.

Step	Alice	Erich	Bob
1	Alice and Bob agree upon a large prime p and a primitive element γ of p; p and γ are public		
2			chooses a large random number b as his private key and computes $$\beta = \gamma^b \bmod p$$
3		$\Leftarrow \beta$	
4	chooses a large random number a and encrypts the message m by: $$\alpha_1 = \gamma^a \bmod p$$ $$\alpha_2 = m\beta^a \bmod p$$		
5		$(\alpha_1, \alpha_2) \Rightarrow$	
6			decrypts by computing $$\alpha_2 (\alpha_1)^{-b} \bmod p$$

Fig. 8.3. ElGamal's public-key cryptosystem

Step 1: Preparation. As in the Diffie–Hellman protocol, Alice and Bob agree upon a large prime number p such that the discrete logarithm problem is intractable in $\mathbb{Z}_p^*$. They also agree upon a primitive element γ of p. Both p and γ are public.

Step 2: Key Generation. Bob generates his private key b at random and computes his public key by $\beta = \gamma^b \bmod p$.

Step 3: Communication. Bob's public key β is now known to Alice.

Step 4: Encryption. As usual, messages are encoded block-wise, where any block is represented by an element of the plaintext space $\mathbb{Z}_p^*$. Suppose that Alice wants to send the message block $m \in \mathbb{Z}_p^*$ to Bob. The ciphertext space is $\mathbb{Z}_p^* \times \mathbb{Z}_p^*$, and the two components of the ciphertext $c = (\alpha_1, \alpha_2)$ encrypting m are computed by:

$$\alpha_1 = \gamma^a \bmod p \tag{8.3}$$
$$\alpha_2 = m\beta^a \bmod p. \tag{8.4}$$

The encryption function $E_{(p,\gamma,\beta,a)}(m) = (\alpha_1, \alpha_2)$ is defined according to (8.3) and (8.4). Alice "masks" her plaintext m by multiplying it by her "Diffie–Hellman key" $\beta^a \equiv \gamma^{ba} \bmod p$. The value of $\alpha_1 = \gamma^a \bmod p$ is also part of the ciphertext in order to allow decryption by the legitimate receiver Bob.

Step 5: Communication. Alice sends the ciphertext $c = (\alpha_1, \alpha_2)$ to Bob.

Step 6: Decryption. The decryption function is given by

$$D_{(p,\gamma,b)}(\alpha_1, \alpha_2) = \alpha_2 \left(\alpha_1\right)^{-b} \bmod p. \tag{8.5}$$

According to (8.5), Bob uses his private key b to first compute $\gamma^{-ab} \bmod p$ from $\alpha_1 = \gamma^a \bmod p$. Then, multiplying α_2 by γ^{-ab}, he removes the "mask" β^a from the plaintext. Summing up, Bob decrypts the ciphertext c by computing

$$\alpha_2 \left(\alpha_1\right)^{-b} \equiv m\beta^a \left(\gamma^a\right)^{-b} \equiv m\gamma^{ba}\gamma^{-ab} \equiv m \bmod p$$

and thus obtains the original plaintext m.

Example 8.5 (ElGamal's Public-Key Cryptosystem).   Suppose that Alice and Bob agree on the prime number $p = 101$ and on the primitive element $\gamma = 8$ of 101. Bob chooses his private key to be $b = 12$ and computes his public key

$$\beta = 8^{12} \bmod 101 = 78.$$

Then, Alices chooses her private exponent to be $a = 33$ and computes

$$\beta^a = 78^{33} \bmod 101 = 92.$$

Suppose that Alice wishes to send the message $m = 53$. To encrypt m, she computes

$$\alpha_1 = \gamma^a \bmod p = 8^{33} \bmod 101 = 51$$
$$\alpha_2 = m\beta^a \bmod p = 53 \cdot 92 \bmod 101 = 28$$

and sends the ciphertext $c = (51, 28)$ to Bob. On the other side of town, Bob receives c and decrypts it by computing

$$\alpha_2 \left(\alpha_1\right)^{-b} \equiv 28 \left(51\right)^{-12} \equiv 28 \left(51^{-1}\right)^{12} \equiv 28 \cdot 2^{12} \equiv 28 \cdot 56 \equiv 53 \bmod 101,$$

yielding the original plaintext $m = 53$ as desired.

ElGamal's system modifies the Diffie–Hellman protocol in the following way. While in the Diffie–Hellman scheme Alice and Bob *simultaneously* compute and send their "partial keys" α and β, respectively, they do so *sequentially* in the ElGamal protocol. That is, Alice must wait for Bob's value β to be able to compute her second component of the ciphertext, α_2, in which her message m is "masked" by β^a.

Another difference between the two protocols is that Bob generates his public key β once and for all in the ElGamal protocol. Thus, he can use β for more than one communication with Alice, and also for users other than Alice who might want to send him encrypted messages. However, Alice (or any other user who wants to send a message to Bob) has to generate her secret exponent a and thus her $\alpha_1 = \gamma^a \bmod p$ anew again and again every time she communicates with Bob, just as in the Diffie–Hellman protocol.

Before discussing security issues related to ElGamal's cryptosystem in the forthcoming Section 8.2.3, we now introduce the ElGamal digital signature scheme.

8.2.2 ElGamal's Digital Signature Scheme

The ElGamal public-key cryptosystem from Figure 8.3 can be modified so as to yield a digital signature scheme, which is presented in Figure 8.4. A particularly efficient variant of this protocol, due to an ingenious idea of Schnorr [Sch90], is now the United States *Digital Signature Standard*, see [Nat91, Nat92]. The single steps of the ElGamal digital signature protocol are now described in detail.

Step 1: Preparation. Alice and Bob agree on a large prime number p, chosen so that the discrete logarithm problem is infeasible in $\mathbb{Z}_p^*$, and on a primitive element γ of p. Both p and γ are public.

Step 2: Signing the message. Suppose that Bob wants to send Alice some message m. As in the ElGamal cryptosystem, Bob chooses his private exponent b and computes $\beta = \gamma^b \bmod p$. In addition, he now chooses a secret number s coprime with $p - 1$, keeping b and s secret. To sign m, Bob first computes $\sigma = \gamma^s \bmod p$ and a solution ρ to the congruence

$$b\sigma + s\rho \equiv m \bmod p - 1 \tag{8.6}$$

using the extended algorithm of Euclid, see Figure 2.1. Then, his signature for m is defined by $\mathrm{sig}_B(m) = (\sigma, \rho)$.

Step 3: Communication. Along with his message m, Bob sends his digital signature $\mathrm{sig}_B(m) = (\sigma, \rho)$ and the value β to Alice.

Step	Alice	Erich	Bob
1	Alice and Bob agree upon a large prime p and a primitive element γ of p; p and γ are public		
2			chooses two large random numbers b and s with $\gcd(s, p-1) = 1$, and computes his signature for message m by $\text{sig}_B(m) = (\sigma, \rho)$, where $$\beta = \gamma^b \bmod p$$ $$\sigma = \gamma^s \bmod p$$ $$\rho = (m - b\sigma)s^{-1} \bmod (p-1)$$
3		$\Leftarrow \langle m, \beta, \text{sig}_B(m)\rangle$	
4	verifies Bob's signature by checking $$\gamma^m \equiv \beta^\sigma \sigma^\rho \bmod p$$		

Fig. 8.4. ElGamal's digital signature scheme

Step 4: Verifying the signature. Alice checks the validity of the signature by verifying the congruence

$$\gamma^m \equiv \beta^\sigma \sigma^\rho \bmod p. \qquad (8.7)$$

By Fermat's Little Theorem (see Corollary 2.39) and by (8.6), we have that

$$\gamma^m \equiv \gamma^{b\sigma+s\rho} \equiv \beta^\sigma \sigma^\rho \bmod p.$$

Thus, as desired, (8.7) verifies correctly that Bob's signature is valid, which shows that the ElGamal digital signature protocol works. Let us look at a small example.

Example 8.6 (ElGamal's Digital Signature Protocol). Let $p = 1367$ be a given prime number, and let $\gamma = 2$ be a given primitive element of 1367. Suppose that Bob chooses the private exponents $b = 513$ and $s = 129$; note that $\gcd(129, 1366) = 1$. First, Bob computes

$$\beta = 2^{513} \bmod 1367 = 307 \quad \text{and} \quad \sigma = 2^{129} \bmod 1367 = 652.$$

Suppose that Bob wants to sign the message $m = 457$. Bob has to solve the congruence

$$513 \cdot 652 + 129\rho \equiv 457 \bmod 1366$$

for ρ. Using the extended algorithm of Euclid from Figure 2.1, he determines the inverse element $s^{-1} = 593$ of $s = 129$ modulo 1366, and thus he obtains the solution

$$\rho = (457 - 513 \cdot 652)593 \bmod 1366 = 831.$$

Now, Bob's signature for $m = 457$ is given by $\text{sig}_B(457) = (652, 831)$, and he transfers the triple $\langle 457, 307, (652, 831)\rangle$ to Alice. On the other side of town, Alice checks whether the signature is valid by verifying the congruence

$$2^{457} \equiv 386 \equiv 231 \cdot 1345 \equiv 307^{652} \cdot 652^{831} \bmod 1367. \qquad (8.8)$$

As usual, Alice employs the "square-and-multiply" algorithm from Figure 7.2 to compute the values γ^m, β^σ, and σ^ρ in the arithmetics modulo p, see Table 8.4.

2^0	2^1	2^2	2^3	2^4	2^5	2^6	2^7	2^8	2^9	
2	4	16	256	1287	932	579	326	1017		$\gamma^m \equiv 386 \bmod p$
307	1239	8	64	1362	25	625	1030	108	728	$\beta^\sigma \equiv 231 \bmod p$
652	1334	1089	732	1327	233	976	1144	517	724	$\sigma^\rho \equiv 1345 \bmod p$

Table 8.4. Verifying Bob's signature in ElGamal's digital signature protocol

The gray boxes of this table contain the values to be multiplied according to the binary expansion of the exponents:

$$m = 457 = 2^0 + 2^3 + 2^6 + 2^7 + 2^8;$$
$$\sigma = 652 = 2^2 + 2^3 + 2^7 + 2^9;$$
$$\rho = 831 = 2^0 + 2^1 + 2^2 + 2^3 + 2^4 + 2^5 + 2^8 + 2^9.$$

8.2.3 Security of ElGamal's Protocols

In this section, we discuss security issues related to ElGamal's protocols. Just as with the Diffie–Hellman protocol, the security of the ElGamal cryptosystem from Figure 8.3 and of the ElGamal digital signature scheme from Figure 8.4 relies on the hardness of the discrete logarithm problem. In other words, if Erich can compute discrete logarithms efficiently, then he can break the ElGamal protocols. All he has to do to break, for example, the ElGamal system from Figure 8.3 is to compute Bob's private key

$$b = \log_\gamma \beta \bmod p$$

from Bob's public key β and the public prime p with its public primitive element γ.

On the other hand, it is not known if computing discrete logarithms and breaking either of the ElGamal protocols are equally hard problems. However, it can be shown that breaking the ElGamal public-key cryptosystem is computationally equivalent to the Diffie–Hellman problem `diffie-hellman` introduced in Definition 8.2.

Breaking ElGamal and the Diffie–Hellman Problem

Definition 8.7 (Problem of Breaking ElGamal).   *Define the* functional problem of breaking ElGamal, *denoted by* `break-elgamal` *as follows: Given* $\langle p, \gamma, \beta, \alpha_1, \alpha_2\rangle$, *where p is a prime number, γ is a primitive element of p, and β, α_1, and α_2 are defined as in Figure 8.3 for any message m, compute m.*

Theorem 8.8. *The problem of breaking ElGamal and the Diffie–Hellman problem are equivalent under polynomial-time Turing reductions. That is,*

$$\texttt{diffie-hellman} \in \text{FP}^{\text{break-elgamal}} \quad \textit{and} \quad \texttt{break-elgamal} \in \text{FP}^{\texttt{diffie-hellman}}.$$

Proof.   Suppose that eavesdropper Erich has an algorithm, D, for solving the Diffie–Hellman problem. He wants to use D to break ElGamal's cryptosystem. Let p be a prime number, and let γ be a primitive element of p. As in Figure 8.3, for any message m, let β, α_1, and α_2 be the transmitted values, which Erich knows. On input $\langle p, \gamma, \beta, \alpha_1, \alpha_2 \rangle$, he wishes to compute the corresponding message m. Looking at Figure 8.3, note that $\alpha_1 = \gamma^a \bmod p$ and $\beta = \gamma^b \bmod p$. Using his algorithm D, Erich can compute $\gamma^{ab} \bmod p$ from α_1 and β. Note further that

$$\alpha_2 = m\beta^a \equiv m\gamma^{ab} \bmod p.$$

Hence, using the extended algorithm of Euclid from Figure 2.1, Erich can recover the message m by computing $\alpha_2 \gamma^{-ab} \bmod p = m$.

Conversely, suppose that Erich has an algorithm, E, for breaking the ElGamal cryptosystem. Let p, γ, β, α_1, and α_2 be given as in Figure 8.3, for an arbitrary message m. Using E, Erich can determine m from $\langle p, \gamma, \beta, \alpha_1, \alpha_2 \rangle$. To solve the Diffie–Hellman problem, given $\alpha_1 = \gamma^a \bmod p$ and $\beta = \gamma^b \bmod p$, he runs E on input $\langle p, \gamma, \beta, \alpha_1, 1 \rangle$ for the specific value of $\alpha_2 = 1$, obtaining some corresponding message m. It follows that

$$m\beta^a \equiv m\gamma^{ab} \equiv 1 \bmod p.$$

Thus, in order to determine $\gamma^{ab} = m^{-1} \bmod p$, it is enough to compute the inverse element of m modulo p, using the extended algorithm of Euclid from Figure 2.1.   ∎

Bit Security of Discrete Logarithms

We have seen that both the Diffie–Hellman protocol and ElGamal's protocols are secure only if it is computationally hard to compute discrete logarithms. We have also noted that the discrete logarithm problem is widely considered to be hard, even though an actual proof of its hardness remains elusive. In this section, we consider restricted variants of the discrete logarithm problem, which ask to determine individual bits of a discrete logarithm. Specifically, we consider the following problem and study the question of whether it is easy or hard.

Definition 8.9 (Discrete Logarithm Bit Problem).   *Define the (functional) discrete logarithm bit problem, denoted by* dlogbit *as follows: Given* $\langle p, \gamma, \alpha, i \rangle$, *where p is a prime number, γ is a primitive element of p, $\alpha \in \mathbb{Z}_p^*$, and i is an integer with $1 \leq i \leq \lceil \log(p-1) \rceil$, compute the ith least significant bit in the binary representation of* $\log_\gamma \alpha \bmod p$.

Example 8.10 (Discrete Logarithm Bit Problem).   In Example 8.4, Shanks' algorithm was used to compute $\log_2 47 \bmod 101 = 58$. Every element of $\mathbb{Z}_{101}^*$ can be represented in binary using no more than $\lceil \log 100 \rceil = 7$ bits. In particular, since $58 = 2^5 + 2^4 + 2^3 + 2^1$, the binary representation of 58 is $\mathtt{bin}(58) = 111010$ and has six bits, dropping leading zeros. The least significant bit of $\mathtt{bin}(58)$ is the rightmost zero. In general, the least significant bit of $\mathtt{bin}(n)$ is the coefficient of 2^0 in the binary expansion of n. This bit determines the parity of n: it is one if n is odd, and it is zero if n is even. Suppose that an instance $\langle 101, 2, 47, i \rangle$ of $\mathtt{dlogbit}$ is given for $1 \leq i \leq 7$. Table 8.5 shows the function values of $\mathtt{dlogbit}(\langle 101, 2, 47, i \rangle)$ for the possible values of i, where leading zeros are not being dropped.

i	1	2	3	4	5	6	7
$\mathtt{dlogbit}(\langle 101, 2, 47, i \rangle)$	0	1	0	1	1	1	0

Table 8.5. An instance of the discrete logarithm bit problem

We now show that the discrete logarithm bit problem can be efficiently solved for instances with $i = 1$. In other words, computing the parity of discrete logarithms is easy. Recall the notion of quadratic residues modulo a prime number and Euler's criterion from Definition 2.43 and Theorem 2.44 in Section 2.4.1.

Theorem 8.11. *If $\langle p, \gamma, \alpha, 1 \rangle$ is an instance of the discrete logarithm bit problem, then $\mathtt{dlogbit}(\langle p, \gamma, \alpha, 1 \rangle)$ can be evaluated in polynomial time.*

Proof.   Let $\langle p, \gamma, \alpha, 1 \rangle$ be a given instance of the discrete logarithm bit problem, i.e., p is prime, γ is a primitive element of p, $\alpha \in \mathbb{Z}_p^*$, and the least significant bit of the binary representation of $\log_\gamma \alpha \bmod p$ is to be evaluated.
Define the function $s : \mathbb{Z}_p^* \to \mathbb{Z}_p^*$ by

$$s(w) = w^2 \bmod p.$$

Recall from Definition 2.43 that QR is the set of quadratic residues modulo an integer, i.e., $\mathtt{QR} = \{(x, n) \mid x \in \mathbb{Z}_n^*, n \in \mathbb{N}, \text{ and } x \equiv w^2 \bmod n\}$. Define

$$\mathtt{QR}_p = \{w^2 \bmod p \mid w \in \mathbb{Z}_p^*\}.$$

Note that $s(w) = s(p - w)$, since $p \equiv 0 \bmod p$. Note further that

$$x^2 \equiv w^2 \bmod p \iff p \text{ divides } (x - w)(x + w)$$
$$\iff x \equiv \pm w \bmod p.$$

Hence, every $z \in \mathtt{QR}_p$ has exactly two preimages with respect to s. It follows that

$$\|\mathtt{QR}_p\| = \frac{p - 1}{2}.$$

In other words, exactly half of the elements of $\mathbb{Z}_p^*$ are quadratic residues modulo p and the remaining half of the elements of $\mathbb{Z}_p^*$ are quadratic nonresidues modulo p.

Since γ is a primitive element of p, $\gamma^a \in QR_p$ if the exponent a is even. Since the $(p-1)/2$ elements $\gamma^0, \gamma^2, \ldots, \gamma^{p-3}$ are pairwise distinct, they are precisely the elements of QR_p, i.e.,

$$QR_p = \{\gamma^{2i} \bmod p \mid 0 \leq i \leq (p-3)/2\}.$$

It follows that an element α is a quadratic residue modulo p if and only if $\log_\gamma \alpha$ is even. That is, the least significant bit of the binary representation of $\log_\gamma \alpha$ is zero if and only if $\alpha \in QR_p$, which by Euler's criterion is equivalent to $\alpha^{(p-1)/2} \equiv 1 \bmod p$. Hence, we have

$$\texttt{dlogbit}(\langle p, \gamma, \alpha, 1 \rangle) = 0 \iff \alpha^{(p-1)/2} \equiv 1 \bmod p.$$

Since $\alpha^{(p-1)/2} \equiv 1 \bmod p$ can be efficiently computed using fast exponentiation (see Figure 7.2), Euler's criterion provides an efficient algorithm for evaluating $\texttt{dlogbit}(\langle p, \gamma, \alpha, 1 \rangle)$. ∎

Now, consider the problem of computing $\texttt{dlogbit}(\langle p, \gamma, \alpha, i \rangle)$ for values $i > 0$. Writing $p - 1 = r2^q$, where r is odd, it can be shown that $\texttt{dlogbit}(\langle p, \gamma, \alpha, i \rangle)$ is easy to compute for all $i \leq q$. In contrast, computing $\texttt{dlogbit}(\langle p, \gamma, \alpha, q + 1 \rangle)$ presumably is a hard task: it is at least as hard as solving the general discrete logarithm problem in $\mathbb{Z}_p^*$. The proof of Theorem 8.12 is left to the reader as Problem 8.1.

Theorem 8.12. *Let $\langle p, \gamma, \alpha, i \rangle$ be an instance of the discrete logarithm bit problem, and let $p - 1 = r2^q$ for some odd number r. Then,*

- *for each $i \leq q$, $\texttt{dlogbit}(\langle p, \gamma, \alpha, i \rangle)$ can be evaluated in polynomial time, and*
- *$\log_\gamma \alpha \bmod p$ can be computed in $\text{FP}^{\texttt{dlogbit}(\langle p, \gamma, \alpha, q+1 \rangle)}$.*

Breaking the ElGamal Digital Signature Scheme

In Section 4.1, several types of attacks on a cryptosystem were introduced in order to characterize different levels of security (or vulnerability) of the cryptosystem. In particular, we distinguish ciphertext-only attacks, known-plaintext attacks, chosen-plaintext attacks, chosen-ciphertext attacks, and key-only attacks. Examples of these types of attacks are provided in Chapters 4 and 7.

When breaking a cryptosystem, a cryptanalyst usually aims at determining the private key used and the plaintext encrypted. When trying to break a digital signature scheme, however, a cryptanalyst usually pursues a different goal, namely, forging signatures of signed messages. The following specific types of forgery are commonly distinguished:

- **Total break:** The cryptanalyst is able to determine the private key of the sender in a digital signature scheme; e.g., Bob's secret numbers b and s in the ElGamal digital signature scheme presented in Figure 8.4, or Alice's secret key d in the RSA digital signature scheme presented in Figure 7.3. Using this private key, cryptanalyst Erich can create a valid signature for any message of his choice.

- **Selective forgery:** The cryptanalyst is able to create, with nonnegligible probability of success, a valid signature for some message chosen by somebody else. That is, if Erich intercepts a message m that was previously not signed by Bob, he is able to create a valid signature for m with a certain success probability.
- **Existential forgery:** The cryptanalyst is able to create a valid signature for at least one message that was previously not signed by Bob. Here, no specified probability of success is required.

Again, one can distinguish several levels of security for a digital signature scheme, depending on what information is available to the cryptanalyst during the attack. In particular, the following types of attacks are commonly considered:

- **Key-only attack:** Cryptanalyst Erich only knows Bob's public key.
- **Known-message attack:** Erich knows some pairs of messages and corresponding signatures in addition to the public key.
- **Chosen-message attack:** Erich knows the public key and obtains a list of Bob's signatures corresponding to a list of messages he has chosen at will.

The terms "known-plaintext attack" and "chosen-plaintext attack" are sometimes used in place of "known-message attack" and "chosen-message attack," respectively. An example of a chosen-plaintext attack on the RSA digital signature scheme can be found in Section 7.4.

Turning now to the security of the ElGamal digital signature scheme, what possibilities does an attacker like Erich have to forge Bob's signature under this scheme, without knowing Bob's private exponents b and s? Of course, Erich knows Bob's public key $\beta = \gamma^b \bmod p$, where γ is a primitive element of the prime number p. Suppose that m is the message Erich wants to sign with a forged signature that looks like Bob's signature. According to the protocol from Figure 8.4, Erich has to choose some elements σ and ρ satisfying

$$\sigma = \gamma^s \bmod p$$
$$\rho = (m - b\sigma)s^{-1} \bmod (p-1).$$

The order in which σ and ρ are chosen does matter here. Suppose that Erich chooses σ first and then the corresponding ρ. By (8.7), he must solve the discrete logarithm $\log_\sigma \beta^{-\sigma}\gamma^m \bmod p$ in this case.

On the other hand, if Erich prefers to choose ρ first and then the corresponding σ, he faces the problem of solving the ElGamal verification condition (8.7)

$$\gamma^m \equiv \beta^\sigma \sigma^\rho \bmod p$$

for the unknown σ. This problem is not known to have an efficient algorithm either. However, it does not seem to be closely related to other thoroughly investigated problems such as the discrete logarithm problem. Thus, it might well be that there exists such an efficient solution to this problem that just eluded us so far. It might also be the case that there is some clever way of determining σ and ρ simultaneously so that (σ, ρ) is a valid signature for m that Alice would have to accept when verifying it using Bob's public key β.

Finally, Erich might try to choose σ and ρ simultaneously and then try to solve (8.7) for the unknown value m. In this case, he again faces the problem of computing a discrete logarithm, namely $\log_\gamma \beta^\sigma \sigma^\rho \bmod p$. This approach has the disadvantage that, depending on the choice of σ and ρ, the message signed may not be meaningful. Again, since solving discrete logarithms is considered to be hard, this is not a practical attack.

However, Erich is able to create a valid ElGamal signature for a random message m, by choosing σ, ρ, and m simultaneously. Thus, this key-only attack allows an existential forgery. This attack works as follows. Let x and y be integers with $0 \le x \le p - 2$ and $0 \le y \le p - 2$. Writing σ as $\sigma = \gamma^x \beta^y \bmod p$ implies that the ElGamal verification condition (8.7) is of the form

$$\gamma^m \equiv \beta^\sigma \, (\gamma^x \beta^y)^\rho \bmod p,$$

which is equivalent to

$$\gamma^{m-x\rho} \equiv \beta^{\sigma+y\rho} \bmod p. \tag{8.9}$$

Now, (8.9) is true if and only if the following two congruences are satisfied:

$$m - x\rho \equiv 0 \bmod (p - 1); \tag{8.10}$$
$$\sigma + y\rho \equiv 0 \bmod (p - 1). \tag{8.11}$$

Given x and y and assuming that $\gcd(y, p - 1) = 1$, the congruences (8.10) and (8.11) can easily be solved for ρ and m, and we obtain:

$$\sigma = \gamma^x \beta^y \bmod p;$$
$$\rho = -\sigma y^{-1} \bmod (p - 1);$$
$$m = -x\sigma y^{-1} \bmod (p - 1).$$

By way of construction, (σ, ρ) is a valid signature for the message m.

Example 8.13 (Key-Only Attack on ElGamal's Digital Signature Protocol). As in Example 8.6, let $p = 1367$ be a given prime number, and let $\gamma = 2$ be a given primitive element of 1367. Bob's private exponents are $b = 513$ and $s = 129$, which Erich does not know. However, Erich does know Bob's public value $\beta = 307$. Suppose he chooses $x = 33$ and $y = 77$. Using the extended Euclidean algorithm from Figure 2.2, he checks that $\gcd(77, 1366) = 1$ and determines the inverse element $y^{-1} = 479$ of y modulo $p - 1$. Then, Erich computes:

$$\sigma = 2^{33} \cdot 307^{77} \equiv 497 \cdot 545 \equiv 199 \bmod 1367;$$
$$\rho = -199 \cdot 479 \equiv 299 \bmod 1366;$$
$$m = -33 \cdot 199 \cdot 479 \equiv 305 \bmod 1366.$$

Hence, $(199, 299)$ is a valid signature for the message 305. As a check, note that Alice will verify it using the condition (8.7):

$$2^{305} \equiv 1307 \equiv 1033 \cdot 786 \equiv 307^{199} \cdot 199^{299} \bmod 1367,$$

and will thus accept Erich's forgery. It is not certain, though, that 305 indeed is a message that Erich would wish to send to Alice with Bob's forged signature.

Another existential forgery of ElGamal signatures can be achieved using a known-message attack. Suppose that Erich knows a previous signature $(\hat{\sigma}, \hat{\rho})$ for some message $\hat{m}$. He can then sign new messages forging Bob's signature. As usual, let p be a prime number with primitive element γ, and let β be Bob's public key. Let $x, y, z \in \mathbb{Z}_{p-1}$ be chosen such that $\gcd(x\hat{\sigma} - z\hat{\rho}, p-1) = 1$. Erich computes:

$$
\begin{aligned}
\sigma &= \hat{\sigma}^x \gamma^y \beta^z \bmod p; \\
\rho &= \hat{\rho}\sigma(x\hat{\sigma} - z\hat{\rho})^{-1} \bmod (p-1); \\
m &= \sigma(x\hat{m} + y\hat{\rho})(x\hat{\sigma} - z\hat{\rho})^{-1} \bmod (p-1).
\end{aligned}
\tag{8.12}
$$

The reader should check that the ElGamal verification condition (8.7),

$$\gamma^m \equiv \beta^\sigma \sigma^\rho \bmod p,$$

is satisfied, see Exercise 8.7(a). Hence, (σ, ρ) is a valid signature for the message m. Here is a small example to illustrate.

Example 8.14 (Known-Message Attack on ElGamal's Digital Signature Protocol). As in Examples 8.6 and 8.13, Bob chooses the prime number $p = 1367$, the primitive element $\gamma = 2$ of 1367, and the public key $\beta = 307$. Suppose that Erich knows Bob's signature $(\hat{\sigma}, \hat{\rho}) = (652, 831)$ for the message $\hat{m} = 457$, see Example 8.6. Erich chooses the integers $x = 17$, $y = 65$, and $z = 29$. Using the extended Euclidean Algorithm from Figure 2.2, he checks that

$$\gcd(x\hat{\sigma} - z\hat{\rho}, p-1) = \gcd(645, 1366) = 1,$$

and he computes the inverse element $645^{-1} \bmod 1366 = 665$. Using (8.12), Erich now computes:

$$
\begin{aligned}
\sigma &= 652^{17} \cdot 2^{65} \cdot 307^{29} \equiv 1260 \cdot 1158 \cdot 105 \equiv 976 \bmod 1367; \\
\rho &= 831 \cdot 976 \cdot 645^{-1} \equiv 800 \bmod 1366; \\
m &= 976 \cdot (17 \cdot 457 + 65 \cdot 831) \cdot 645^{-1} \equiv 976 \cdot 314 \cdot 665 \equiv 922 \bmod 1366.
\end{aligned}
$$

Hence, $(976, 800)$ is a valid signature for the message 922, as can be checked by the ElGamal verification condition (8.7):

$$2^{922} \equiv 942 \equiv 1250 \cdot 27 \equiv 307^{976} \cdot 976^{800} \bmod 1367.$$

Thus, Alice accepts Erich's forged signature.

Both of the above attacks on the ElGamal signature scheme yield an existential forgery. It is currently not known whether these attacks can be strengthened to yield even selective forgeries. Therefore, mounting these attacks is not a practical threat for the ElGamal digital signature scheme. As a countermeasure to prevent these attacks, one can make use of a cryptographic hash function as sketched below.

The principle of hashing has already been explained in Section 6.5, in a completely different context. In cryptography, a hashing function $h : \Sigma^* \to T$ can be used to produce a "message digest" of prespecified length from any given message of arbitrary length. A common choice of the length of the hash values in T is 160 bits. If Bob wishes to sign a message m, he first computes the message digest $t = h(m)$, which is an element of the hashing table T. Then, he computes his signature $s = \mathrm{sig}_B(t)$ for t, using a digital signature scheme such as ElGamal, and sends (m, s) to Alice. To verify the signature, she first reconstructs the message digest $t = h(m)$, using the public hashing function h, and then checks the validity of the signature s for t.

To prevent existential forgeries by key-only or known-message attacks, hashing functions are required to have certain properties so as to be considered cryptographically secure. For example, suppose that Erich mounts a known-message attack. Thus, he already knows some pair (m, s), where m is a message previously signed by Bob and s is the signature for the message digest $t = h(m)$ generated from m by some hashing function h. Since h is public, Erich can determine t. He might then try to find some other mesage $\tilde{m} \neq m$ such that $h(\tilde{m}) = h(m)$. This would enable him to forge Bob's signature for the message $\tilde{m}$, since the pair $(\tilde{m}, s)$ contains a valid signature s for $\tilde{m}$. This type of attack can be prevented by requiring the hashing function used to be "collision-free" on the relevant domain in the sense that it is computationally infeasible to determine, given m, some message $\tilde{m}$ with $\tilde{m} \neq m$ and $h(\tilde{m}) = h(m)$.

We conclude this section by remarking that, in order to avoid Erich totally breaking the ElGamal digital signature scheme, some care must be taken in choosing the parameters of this scheme. In particular, Bob's secret exponent s (see Figure 8.4) must never be revealed. If Erich knows s, then it is a matter of routine for him to compute, using (8.6), Bob's secret exponent b from m and the signature (σ, ρ) by

$$b \equiv (m - s\rho)\sigma^{-1} \bmod p - 1.$$

This known-message attack results in a total break of the ElGamal digital signature scheme, and Erich can henceforth forge Bob's signature at will. Similarly, a known-message attack can be mounted so as to totally break the ElGamal scheme if the same value s is used twice for signing distinct messages, see Exercise 8.8.

8.3 Rabin's Public-Key Cryptosystem

In 1979, Rabin developed a public-key cryptosystem that is based on the difficulty of computing square roots modulo some integer n. His cryptosystem is provably secure against chosen-plaintext attacks, assuming that the factoring problem is computationally intractable, i.e., assuming that it is hard to find the prime factors of $n = pq$.

8.3.1 Rabin's Cryptosystem

Figure 8.5 presents the single steps of Rabin's cryptosystem, which are now explained in more detail.

Step	Alice	Erich	Bob
1			chooses two large random primes, p and q with $p \equiv q \equiv 3 \bmod 4$, keeps them secret, and computes his public key $n = pq$
2		$\Leftarrow n$	
3	encrypts the message m by $$c = m^2 \bmod n$$		
4		$c \Rightarrow$	
5			decrypts c by computing $$m = \sqrt{c} \bmod n$$

Fig. 8.5. Rabin's public-key cryptosystem

Step 1: Key Generation. Bob randomly chooses two large prime numbers p and q, which satisfy $p \equiv q \equiv 3 \bmod 4$. The pair (p, q) is his private key. He then computes the modulus $n = pq$, his public key.

Step 2: Communication. Bob's public key n is now known to Alice.

Step 3: Encryption. Given the public key n, Alice computes her ciphertext c by squaring her message m modulo n, i.e., the encryption function $E_n : \mathbb{Z}_n^* \to \mathbb{Z}_n^*$ is defined by

$$E_n(m) = c = m^2 \bmod n.$$

Step 4: Communication. Alice sends the ciphertext c to Bob.

Step 5: Decryption. The decryption function is given by

$$D_{(p,q)}(c) = \sqrt{c} \bmod n. \tag{8.13}$$

It is not clear yet how the private key (p, q) is used for decryption. Note that, in general, computing square roots modulo some integer with unknown prime factors is considered to be a hard problem. However, since Bob knows the prime factors p and q of n, he can make use of the fact that determining m by (8.13) is equivalent to solving the following two congruences for the values m_p and m_q:

$$(m_p)^2 \equiv c \bmod p; \tag{8.14}$$
$$(m_q)^2 \equiv c \bmod q. \tag{8.15}$$

By Euler's criterion (see Theorem 2.44), Bob can efficiently decide whether or not c is a quadratic residue modulo p, and also whether or not c is a quadratic residue modulo q. However, Euler's criterion does not actually find these square roots. Fortunately, using the assumption that $p \equiv q \equiv 3 \bmod 4$, Bob can do the following. First, he computes

$$m_p = c^{(p+1)/4} \bmod p \quad \text{and} \quad m_q = c^{(q+1)/4} \bmod q.$$

Note that c must be a square root modulo p, provided that c is a valid ciphertext, i.e., provided that c was created by proper encryption of some message. Again by Euler's criterion, c is a square root modulo p if and only if $c^{(p-1)/2} \equiv 1 \bmod p$. Hence,

$$(\pm m_p)^2 \equiv \left(\pm c^{(p+1)/4} \right)^2 \equiv c^{(p+1)/2} \equiv c^{(p-1)/2}c \bmod p \equiv c \bmod p,$$

which proves (8.14). Thus, $\pm m_p$ are the two square roots of c modulo p. Analogously, $\pm m_q$ are the two square roots of c modulo q, which proves (8.15). Then, using the Chinese Remainder Theorem, Bob determines the four square roots of c modulo n. To this end, he first uses the extended Euclidean Algorithm from Figure 2.2 to compute integer coefficients z_p and z_q such that

$$z_p p + z_q q = 1.$$

Finally, applying Theorem 2.46, he computes

$$s = (z_p p m_q + z_q q m_p) \bmod n \quad \text{and} \quad t = (z_p p m_q - z_q q m_p) \bmod n.$$

It can be checked that $\pm s$ and $\pm t$ are the four square roots of c modulo n. Which one yields the "right" plaintext, is not immediately clear, see Remark 8.15.1.

Remark 8.15. 1. Note that encryption in Rabin's system is not injective. That is, since n is the product of two prime numbers, every ciphertext c has four square roots modulo n; cf. Lemma 7.14 and the subsequent paragraph. Thus, Rabin's system has the disadvantage, that decryption recovers not only the original plaintext, but also three other square roots of c that hopefully are "sufficiently meaningless" so as to be eliminated. Other than that, one way for Bob to tell the "right" decryption apart from these three "wrong" decryptions is to give the plaintext a special structure identifying the original plaintext. For example, one might repeat one specified block of plaintext, e.g., attach to m the last 64 bits of m. However, in this case the proof that breaking the Rabin system is computationally equivalent to the factoring problem is no longer valid, see Theorem 8.18.
2. Rabin's system also works for prime factors that are not so-called *Blum numbers*, i.e., if one does not require that $p \equiv q \equiv 3 \bmod 4$. However, the usage of Blum numbers simplifies the analysis of this system. For example, if $p \equiv 1 \bmod 4$, then there is no known *deterministic* polynomial-time algorithm for computing the square roots modulo p, which is needed for efficient decryption, even though there is an efficient randomized Las Vegas algorithm for this problem. Finally, note that in Rabin's system it would also be possible to use $\mathbb{Z}_n$ instead of $\mathbb{Z}_n^*$ as the message and ciphertext space.

Example 8.16 (Rabin's Public-Key Cryptosystem).   Suppose that Bob chooses the prime numbers $p = 43$ and $q = 47$. Note that $43 \equiv 47 \equiv 3 \bmod 4$. He then computes the Rabin modulus $n = pq = 2021$. To encrypt the message $m = 741$, Alice computes

$$c = 741^2 = 549081 \equiv 1390 \bmod 2021$$

and sends $c = 1390$ to Bob. To decrypt the ciphertext c, Bob first determines the following values:

$$m_p = 1390^{(43+1)/4} = 1390^{11} \equiv 10 \bmod 43;$$
$$m_q = 1390^{(47+1)/4} = 1390^{12} \equiv 36 \bmod 47,$$

using fast exponentiation from Figure 7.2. Now, using the extended Euclidean Algorithm from Figure 2.2, he computes the integer coefficients $z_p = -12$ and $z_q = 11$ satisfying $z_p p + z_q q = -12 \cdot 43 + 11 \cdot 47 = 1$. Finally, by Theorem 2.46, he computes

$$s = z_p p m_q + z_q q m_p = -12 \cdot 43 \cdot 36 + 11 \cdot 47 \cdot 10 \equiv 741 \bmod 2021;$$
$$t = z_p p m_q - z_q q m_p = -12 \cdot 43 \cdot 36 - 11 \cdot 47 \cdot 10 \equiv 506 \bmod 2021.$$

As can easily be checked, the four plaintexts that are encrypted to the same ciphertext $c = 1390$ are $\pm s$ and $\pm t$, i.e., 741, 1280, 506, and 1515.

8.3.2 Security of Rabin's System

Suppose Erich is able to factor the Rabin modulus n. He thus obtains Bob's private key and can decipher any message sent to Bob. That is, breaking the Rabin system is computationally no harder than solving the factoring problem. Conversely, we show that factoring large integers is no harder than breaking the Rabin system, so these are equally hard problems. Thus, Rabin's cryptosystem has a proof of security that is based on the assumption that factoring is computationally intractable. In this regard, Rabin's system is superiour to other public-key systems such as RSA or ElGamal.

This result is proven by a polynomial-time *randomized* Turing reduction from the factoring problem to the (functional) problem of breaking Rabin's system. The latter problem is formally defined in Definition 8.17, where

$$QR_n = \{x^2 \bmod n \mid x \in \mathbb{Z}_n^*\}$$

denotes the set of quadratic residues modulo n as in Section 8.2.3.

Definition 8.17 (Problem of Breaking Rabin).   *Define the functional problem of breaking Rabin, denoted by* `break-rabin` *as follows: Given* $\langle n, c \rangle$, *where n is the product of two (unknown) prime numbers in $3 + 4\mathbb{Z}$ and $c \in QR_n$, compute some $m \in \mathbb{Z}_n^*$ such that $c = m^2 \bmod n$.*

Randomized algorithms, including Las Vegas algorithms, were introduced in Section 6.2.1. In particular, the class ZPP contains precisely those decision problems solvable by polynomial-time randomized algorithms with zero error probability, a.k.a. Las Vegas algorithms; see Definition 6.8. The randomized Turing reduction we are about to construct in Theorem 8.18 is such a Las Vegas algorithm. However, it does not concern decision problems but functions: it reduces the functional factoring problem to the functional problem break-rabin. For simplicity, we restrict ourselves to the case that the integer n to be factored in fact is a Rabin modulus. Note that this restriction of the factoring problem is no easier than the general factoring problem.

Theorem 8.18. *There is a polynomial-time Las Vegas algorithm* RANDOM-FACTOR *that, given any integer* $n = pq$ *with* $p \equiv q \equiv 3 \bmod 4$, *uses its function oracle* break-rabin *to find the prime factors of* n *with probability at least* $1/2$.

Proof.   Let $n = pq$ be the Rabin modulus to be factored, where $p \equiv q \equiv 3 \bmod 4$. Figure 8.6 presents the algorithm RANDOM-FACTOR with oracle break-rabin.

RANDOM-FACTOR$^{\text{break-rabin}}(n)$ {   // Rabin modulus $n = pq$ with $p \equiv q \equiv 3 \bmod 4$
    Randomly choose a number $x \in \mathbb{Z}_n^*$ under the uniform distribution;
    $c := x^2 \bmod n$;
    $m :=$ break-rabin$(\langle n, c \rangle)$;
         // query the oracle about $\langle n, c \rangle$ to obtain an answer m with $c := m^2 \bmod n$
    if $(m \equiv \pm x \bmod n)$ return "failure" and halt;
      else
        $p := \gcd(m - x, n)$;
        $q := n/p$;
        return "p and q are the prime factors of n" and halt;
}

Fig. 8.6. Factoring a Rabin modulus using an oracle to break Rabin's system

---

On input n, RANDOM-FACTOR with oracle break-rabin randomly picks an element $x \in \mathbb{Z}_n^*$ and squares it modulo n to obtain $c \in QR_n$. Then, the algorithm queries its oracle break-rabin about the pair $\langle n, c \rangle$ and obtains the answer m, which is one of the square roots of c modulo n. The two square roots m and x of c modulo n need not be identical. However, m and x must satisfy either one of the following two cases.

Case 1: $m \equiv \pm x \bmod n$.   Then, we have either $m = x$ or $m + x = n$. Thus, $\gcd(m - x, n)$ is either n or 1. In both cases, the algorithm does not find a prime factor of n and returns "failure."

Case 2: $m \equiv \pm \alpha x \bmod n$, where α is a nontrivial square root of 1 mod n. In this case, $m^2 \equiv x^2 \bmod n$ and $m \not\equiv \pm x \bmod n$. Thus, $\gcd(m - x, n)$ is either p or q, which yields the factorization of n.

To estimate the success probability of RANDOM-FACTOR, let x be any element randomly chosen in $\mathbb{Z}_n^*$ under the uniform distribution. Let α be a nontrivial square root of 1 mod n. Consider the set

$$R_x = \{\pm x \bmod n\} \cup \{\pm \alpha x \bmod n\}.$$

Squaring any element r of R_x yields the same $c = r^2 = x^2 \bmod n$. In particular, the oracle answer $m = \texttt{break-rabin}(\langle n, c\rangle)$ is an element of R_x, and is independent of which of the four elements of R_x in fact was chosen to yield c. In Case 2 above, we noted that the algorithm finds the prime factors of n if and only if $m \equiv \pm \alpha x \bmod n$. For fixed m, the probability that an $x \in R_x$ with $m \equiv \pm \alpha x \bmod n$ was chosen is $1/2$. Hence, the success probability of RANDOM-FACTOR is $1/2$.   ∎

By the techniques of Section 6.2, the success probability of RANDOM-FACTOR can be amplified so as to be arbitrarily close to one.

Theorem 8.18 has two interesting consequences. On the one hand, it says that Rabin's cryptosystem cannot be broken by a chosen-plaintext attack if factoring is computationally infeasible. This can be seen as an advantage of the Rabin system.

Corollary 8.19. *Assuming that large integers cannot be factored by an efficient randomized algorithm with nonnegligible probability of success, Rabin's cryptosystem is secure against chosen-plaintext attacks.*

On the other hand, it follows from Theorem 8.18 that the Rabin system is insecure against chosen-ciphertext attacks. The scenario of a chosen-ciphertext attack is that a cryptanalyst has temporary access to the decryption device. Thus, choosing some ciphertext c at will, he learns the corresponding plaintext m. This can be seen as having an efficient algorithm (as opposed to a hypothetical oracle) for computing $\texttt{break-rabin}$. By Theorem 8.18, the attacker can take advantage of this fact as follows. He chooses some plaintext x at random, computes $c = x^2 \bmod n$, and decrypts c to obtain a square root m of c modulo n. As in the proof of Theorem 8.18, he can factor the Rabin modulus n with high probability, and obtains the private key.

Corollary 8.20. *Rabin's cryptosystem is insecure against chosen-ciphertext attacks.*

The following toy example illustrates Theorem 8.18 and its corollaries.

Example 8.21 (Factoring by Breaking Rabin's System).   Let $n = 23 \cdot 7 = 161$ be the given Rabin modulus. Suppose Erich does not know the prime factors 7 and 23. However, he has the oracle $\texttt{break-rabin}$ (alternatively, he has an efficient algorithm for computing $\texttt{break-rabin}$) and can thus determine square roots modulo 161. Using the algorithm RANDOM-FACTOR from Figure 8.6, Erich randomly picks $x = 13$; note that $\gcd(161, 13) = 1$, so $13 \in \mathbb{Z}_{161}^*$. He then computes $c = 13^2 \bmod 161 = 8$. The four square roots of 8 mod 161 are $R_{13} = \{13, 36, 125, 148\}$. Let m be the oracle answer for the query $\langle 161, 8\rangle$, i.e., $m = \texttt{break-rabin}(\langle 161, 8\rangle)$. For each possible answer $m \in R_{13}$, we determine $\gcd(m - x, n)$.

If $m = 13$ then $\gcd(m - x, n) = \gcd(0, 161) = 161$. And if $m = 148$ then $\gcd(m - x, n) = \gcd(135, 161) = 1$. In both cases, RANDOM-FACTOR fails to find the prime factors of 161. But if $m = 36$ then $\gcd(m - x, n) = \gcd(23, 161) = 23$, and if $m = 125$ then $\gcd(m - x, n) = \gcd(112, 161) = 7$. In these two cases, RANDOM-FACTOR succeeds and provides Erich with the prime factors of 161. Thus, Erich has a fifty percent chance of factoring n.

8.4 Arthur-Merlin Games and Zero-Knowledge

"There are known knowns. These are things we know that we know. There are known unknowns. That is to say, there are things we know we don't know. But, there are also unknown unknowns. These are things we don't know we don't know," a U.S. Secretary of Defense is quoted as saying. One might add, *"And there is zero-knowledge. These are things we know that somebody else knows, and we provably cannot know what they are."* In this section, we introduce this notion that concerns the issue of proving knowledge of a secret, without revealing it. Zero-knowledge is closely related to authentication, a central task in cryptography as noted in Section 4.1.

Consider, for example, the man-in-the-middle attack against the Diffie–Hellman protocol mentioned in Section 8.1. This attack is possible because Alice did not prove her identity to Bob before executing the protocol and Bob did not verify that Alice indeed is the person she claims to be. That is why Erich, the malicious man in the middle, can pretend to be Alice when communicating with Bob. Similarly, he can pretend to be Bob in the communication with Alice who did not verify Bob's authenticity either. This section presents a zero-knowledge protocol that Alice and Bob can use to avoid Erich's trap.

To authenticate her identity, Alice might wish to use some private information—some personal *secret*—that no one knows but her. Suppose that a trusted third party certifies that Alice alone knows her secret. For example, she uses her PIN (her personal identification number) at the cash machine of her bank for authentication. But here is the catch: If she proves her identity to Bob by telling him her secret, she has given it away! It is no longer a secret! Using Alice's secret, Bob would be able to pretend to be Alice when communicating with Charlie, a third party. How can Alice prove she has a secret without conveying any bit of information about it? This is what zero-knowledge is all about.

The question just raised is this: How can Alice use her secret to *prove* her identity beyond any doubt, in such a way that Bob can *verify* her authenticity but does not learn her secret? Prover and verifier are the adversaries in an interactive proof system, a notion introduced in Section 6.3 in the specific form of Arthur-Merlin games. Comparing both terminologies, Merlin corresponds to the prover and is represented by an NP machine, and Arthur corresponds to the verifier and is represented by a BPP machine. The idea of zero-knowledge is illustrated by the following short story.

Story 8.22 (Zero-Knowledge Protocol)   *Arthur and Merlin again play one of their games. This time, Arthur wishes to verify Merlin's identity, as he is uncertain of whether he is talking with Merlin or with some other wizard who merely pretends to be Merlin. To verify Merlin's identity, Arthur challenges him for a proof of his secret, a magic spell that puts a dangerous, fire-breathing dragon to sleep. Merlin alone knows this spell. The dragon lives in a secret, subterranean labyrinth, shown in Figure 8.7, that may be entered only by Arthur's permission. The dragon sits there right in the middle between the Holy Grail and the One Ring That Rules Them All. So, if the labyrinth is entered through the left entrance and the dragon is awake, one can get only the Holy Grail and not the Ruling Ring. If the labyrinth is entered through* *the right entrance and the dragon is awake, one can get only the Ruling Ring and not the Holy Grail. The only way from the Holy Grail to the Ruling Ring or vice versa passes by the dragon and can be used only if the dragon sleeps. (As you may know, dragons never sleep, except when they are compelled to by a magic spell.)*

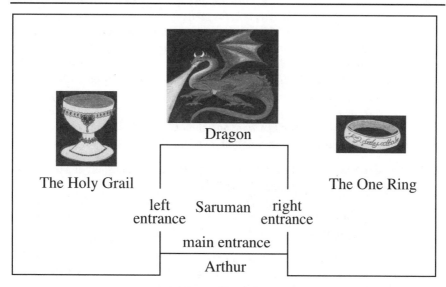

Fig. 8.7. Arthur's labyrinth

The Arthur-Merlin game is as follows. First, Merlin enters through the main entrance, closes this door, and chooses either the left or the right entrance to the labyrinth. Arthur now follows him through the main entrance and does not know whether Merlin has used the left or the right entrance. He challenges Merlin by requesting to see either the Holy Grail or the Ruling Ring. If Merlin has used the left entrance and Arthur wishes to see the Holy Grail, Merlin just takes it and leaves the labyrinth. Similarly, Merlin has no problem to authenticate himself if he has used the right entrance and Arthur requests to see the Ruling Ring. On the other hand, if Merlin has used the left entrance and Arthur requests to see the Ruling Ring, or if Merlin has entered through the right entrance and Arthur wishes to see the Holy grail, Merlin (and Merlin alone) is able to authenticate himself by using his magic spell to put the dragon to sleep.

Meanwhile, Saruman the White, the malicious wizard of Orthanc, has also reached Camelot. He has had a hard time in Orthanc lately, but he managed to escape from there. Now, after having suffered defeat by Gandalf, he is out for revenge and needs the power of the Ruling Ring more than ever. He has heard rumors that Arthur keeps it in his secret labyrinth. Using his magic, Saruman therefore appears disguised as Merlin in Camelot and requests entry to the hidden labyrinth.

He is much less powerful a wizard than Merlin and, sure enough, he does not know his secret spells. In fact, Saruman's magic power can bring about no more than the computing power of a polynomial-time randomized Turing machine. Still, he wishes to steal the Ruling Ring and therefore he pretends to know Merlin's secret.

When Saruman chooses the left or the right entrance to the labyrinth, he does not know Arthur's challenge in advance. Thus, all he can do is toss a coin. If the outcome (heads for left and tails for right, say) is in his favor, he uses the entrance corresponding to Arthur's subsequent request and succeeds. In this case, Arthur is taken in by him. However, if Saruman's random choice is unlucky, he cannot fool Arthur. For example, if Saruman enters the labyrinth through the right entrance but Arthur requests to see the Holy Grail, then Saruman loses. He cannot pass the dragon, since he does not know Merlin's secret spell for putting the dragon to sleep. By repeatedly challenging Saruman for a proof of Merlin's secret, Arthur will detect the attempted fraud with high probability. The first time Saruman fails to present the Holy Grail or the Ruling Ring, Arthur knows for sure that he is not Merlin.

The authentication procedure described in the story above has nothing to do with zero-knowledge as yet; it is just an ordinary "*challenge-and-response*" authentication protocol. Before formally defining zero-knowledge, we provide Goldreich, Micali, and Wigderson's zero-knowledge protocol for GI, the graph isomorphism problem, as an example. Recall that GI is in NP ∩ coAM, see Lemma 6.44.

Example 8.23 (Zero-Knowledge Protocol for Graph Isomorphism).
As in Story 8.22, Merlin wants to authenticate himself by proving knowledge of his secret. Merlin has the power of an NP machine, and his secret is the isomorphism between two large isomorphic graphs. Since GI is not known to be polynomial-time solvable, not even via randomized algorithms, it may be assumed that neither Arthur nor the fraudulent wizard Saruman are able to discover Merlin's secret.

Merlin can easily create his secret, and he does not even need his full NP power. He first chooses a large graph G_0 with n vertices and a permutation $\pi \in \mathfrak{S}_n$ at random. Then, he computes the graph $G_1 = \pi(G_0)$. That is, G_0 and G_1 are isomorphic graphs and π is an isomorphism between them. Merlin makes the pair (G_0, G_1) public, and he keeps the isomorphism $\pi \in \mathrm{ISO}(G_0, G_1)$ secret. Suppose that Gandalf, a trusted third party, certifies that (G_0, G_1) indeed was created by Merlin. Figure 8.8 presents a challenge-and-response authentication protocol between Arthur and Merlin. We will show later that this protocol has the zero-knowledge property in addition.

Sure enough, Merlin cannot just send π to Arthur because then he would have given his secret away. Rather, to prove that G_0 and G_1 indeed are isomorphic, Merlin randomly chooses a permutation $\mu \in \mathfrak{S}_n$ and a bit $m \in \{0, 1\}$ under the uniform distribution, and he computes the graph $H = \mu(G_m)$. That is, m determines which of G_0 or G_1 is to be permuted by μ to yield H, a graph isomorphic to G_m via μ. Merlin sends H to Arthur, who chooses a random bit $a \in \{0, 1\}$ under the uniform distribution. Arthur then sends a to Merlin as his challenge, requesting Merlin to respond with an isomorphism α between G_a and H. Arthur accepts Merlin's response α if and only if $\alpha(G_a) = H$. This protocol works, since Merlin knows his secret isomorphism $\pi \in \mathrm{ISO}(G_0, G_1)$, his random bit $m \in \{0, 1\}$, and his random permutation

Step	Merlin	Saruman	Arthur
1	chooses a large graph G_0 with n vertices and a permutation $\pi \in \mathfrak{S}_n$ at random, and computes $G_1 = \pi(G_0)$; (G_0, G_1) is public and π is secret		
2		$(G_0, G_1) \Rightarrow$	
3	chooses a permutation $\mu \in \mathfrak{S}_n$ and a bit $m \in \{0,1\}$ at random, and computes $H = \mu(G_m)$		
4		$H \Rightarrow$	
5			chooses a bit $a \in \{0,1\}$ at random and requests an isomorphism in $\mathrm{ISO}(G_a, H)$
6		$\Leftarrow a$	
7	computes $\alpha \in \mathrm{ISO}(G_a, H)$ by: if $a = m$ then $\alpha = \mu$; if $0 = a \neq m = 1$ then $\alpha = \pi\mu$; if $1 = a \neq m = 0$ then $\alpha = \pi^{-1}\mu$		
8		$\alpha \Rightarrow$	
9			verifies that $\alpha(G_a) = H$ and accepts accordingly

Fig. 8.8. Zero-knowledge protocol for graph isomorphism

$\mu \in \mathrm{ISO}(G_m, H)$. Thus, he can easily determine an isomorphism $\alpha \in \mathrm{ISO}(G_a, H)$, which he uses for authentication; see Figure 8.8 and Exercise 8.10. Since G_0 and G_1 are isomorphic, Arthur accepts with probability one.[1]

Now, suppose that Saruman, disguised as Merlin, executes the protocol from Figure 8.8 with Arthur. Saruman knows the public pair (G_0, G_1) of isomorphic graphs but not Merlin's isomorphism π, which is kept secret during the protocol. Still, he wishes to pretend to be Merlin. He randomly chooses a permutation $\sigma \in \mathfrak{S}_n$ and his bit $s \in \{0,1\}$, and computes the graph $H_S = \sigma(G_s)$. Then, Saruman sends H_S to Arthur and receives Arthur's challenge a. If he is lucky and $s = a$, then Saruman wins. However, if $s \neq a$, the computation of $\alpha = \pi\sigma$ or $\alpha = \pi^{-1}\sigma$ would require knowledge of π. Since computing an isomorphism is too hard even for randomized polynomial-time algorithms, Saruman cannot determine π if the graphs G_0 and G_1 are chosen large enough.

Without knowing π, he can only guess. His chances of hitting a bit s with $s = a$ are at most $1/2$. Of course, Saruman can always guess and thus his probability of success is exactly $1/2$. If Arthur challenges him sufficiently often, say in k independent rounds of this protocol, the cheating probability can be made as small as 2^{-k}.

---

[1] The case of nonisomorphic graphs does not occur in this protocol. On the other hand, the protocol from Figure 8.8 can be modified such that Arthur and Merlin decide the problem GI, cf. Lemma 6.44. The pair (G_0, G_1) is their input then and is not chosen by Merlin. If G_0 and G_1 are nonisomorphic, Arthur rejects Merlin's false proof with probability $1/2$.

Already for $k = 20$, this probability is negligible: Saruman's probability of success is then less than one in one million.

Unlike other challenge-and-response authentication protocols, zero-knowledge protocols have an important additional property: One can prove with mathematical rigor that the protocol does not leak any information about the secret. In other words, even though the verifier Arthur will eventually be convinced that the prover Merlin knows his secret, neither Arthur nor an eavesdropper can learn anything about Merlin's secret. We now formally define the zero-knowledge property. Recall from Section 6.3 the notion of Arthur-Merlin games and the Arthur-Merlin hierarchy, denoted by AMH. In the context of cryptographic authentication, an Arthur-Merlin game is dubbed an Arthur-Merlin protocol.

Definition 8.24 (Zero-Knowledge Protocol).   *Let $L \in$ AMH be accepted by some Arthur-Merlin protocol (M, A), where M represents an NP machine and A represents a polynomial-time randomized Turing machine. We say that (M, A) is a zero-knowledge protocol for L if and only if there exists a polynomial-time randomized Turing machine S, called the simulator, such that*

* *(S, A) simulates the original protocol (M, A), and*
* *for each $x \in L$, the tuples $(m_1, m_2, \ldots, m_k)$ and $(s_1, s_2, \ldots, s_k)$ that describe the information conveyed in (M, A) and in (S, A), respectively, are identically distributed over the coin tosses in (M, A) and in (S, A), respectively.*

Regarding Definition 8.24, note that Merlin's nondeterministic choices can also be viewed as random choices or "coin tosses." Note further that the notion defined above is called "*honest-verifier perfect zero-knowledge*" in the literature. That is, (a) it is assumed that the verifier Arthur is *honest* and does not try to tamper with the protocol in order to change it to his advantage, and (b) the definition requires that the information conveyed in the simulated protocol *perfectly* coincides with the information conveyed in the original protocol. Assumption (a) may be somewhat too idealistic in real-world cryptographic applications. Requirement (b) may be somewhat too strict; weaker requirements might work as well. That is why there also exist other, less restrictive, types of zero-knowledge, see the remarks in Section 8.8.

Continuing Story 8.22, we now show that Arthur and Merlin's challenge-and-response authentication protocol indeed has the zero-knowledge property.

Story 8.25 (Zero-Knowledge Protocol—Continued)   *It took Arthur three challenges to eventually detect Saruman's fraud and to uncover his true identity. The king was filled with anger at the way he had almost been tricked. Enraged, he nearly decapitated the whining wizard. But then he calmed down, and decided to use Saruman to prove that the protocol he used to execute with Merlin has the zero-knowledge property. Saruman agreed submissively and gratefully.*

Thus, Arthur and Saruman again execute several rounds of the protocol. Arthur carefully records this simulated protocol. His record of the protocol shows Saruman entering through the main entrance and closing the door—thus, Arthur does not see whether he uses the left or the right entrance to the labyrinth. Next, his record shows Arthur's challenge requesting either the Holy Grail or the Ruling Ring, and Saruman's response yielding either success or failure. If Saruman is lucky and meets Arthur's challenge, then this round of the protocol looks just like the original protocol with Merlin, who never fails. If Saruman has bad luck and fails, this round of their protocol looks different from the original protocol. However, whenever the wizard fails, they simply omit this round of the protocol in the record.

Then, Arthur goes to Lancelot to show him this record of the simulated protocol and a record of a previous original protocol between him and Merlin. He asks Lancelot to look at both records and to tell which was the original protocol with Merlin and which was the faked one with Saruman. Of course, Lancelot cannot tell them apart; all he can see in the records is Arthur's challenge and the wizard's successful response in each round, since Saruman's failures have been carefully deleted.

But if Saruman is able to generate a faked Arthur-Merlin protocol that cannot be distinguished from the original one, Arthur concludes, then the protocol has leaked no information whatsoever about Merlin's secret. Remember that Saruman does not know Merlin's secret. That is, he could not put any information about Merlin's secret into the simulated protocol. If there is nothing to put in, there can be nothing to take out.

Continuing Example 8.23, we now show that Goldreich, Micali, and Wigderson's protocol for the graph isomorphism problem has the zero-knowledge property.

Example 8.26 (Zero-Knowledge Protocol for Graph Isomorphism—Continued).
Look at Figure 8.8, which shows the original protocol between Arthur and Merlin. Saruman is just an eavesdropper there who seeks to impersonate Merlin, and we have seen that his chances of successfully deceiving Arthur are small.

Step	Saruman		Arthur
1 & 2	Merlin's pair (G_0, G_1) of isomorphic graphs is public information		
3	chooses a permutation $\sigma \in \mathfrak{S}_n$ and a bit $s \in \{0, 1\}$ at random, and computes $H = \sigma(G_s)$		
4		$H \Rightarrow$	
5			chooses a bit $a \in \{0, 1\}$ at random and requests an isomorphism in $\text{ISO}(G_a, H)$
6		$\Leftarrow a$	
7	if $a = s$, Saruman sends $\alpha = \sigma$; if $a \neq s$, he deletes this round		
8		$\alpha \Rightarrow$	
9			$a = s$ implies $\alpha(G_a) = H$, thus Arthur accepts Saruman's false identity

Fig. 8.9. Simulation of the zero-knowledge protocol for graph isomorphism

In order to show that the protocol from Figure 8.8 has the zero-knowledge property, consider the protocol shown in Figure 8.9. This protocol simulates the original protocol between Arthur and Merlin, where Saruman takes Merlin's position. Note that this simulated protocol is not executed for the purpose of authentication but is used merely to prove that the original protocol is zero-knowledge.

In the simulated protocol, Saruman does not know Merlin's secret isomorphism π, but he pretends to know it. Let us assume that Arthur and Saruman execute a number of rounds of the protocol, always using the same pair (G_0, G_1) of isomorphic graphs, which is Merlin's public information. That is, steps 1 and 2 are skipped. Thus, the information conveyed in one round of the protocol has the form of a triple, (H, a, α). Whenever Saruman happens to choose a random bit s with $s = a$, he simply sends $\alpha = \sigma$ to Arthur and wins: Arthur must accept him as Merlin. On the other hand, if $s \neq a$ then Saruman cannot fool Arthur and fails. However, that is no problem for them. They simply delete this round from the protocol and restart. In this way, they can produce a sequence of triples of the form (H, a, α) that are indistinguishable from the corresponding sequence of triples in the original protocol. It follows that the protocol from Figure 8.8 has the zero-knowledge property.

Theorem 8.27 (Goldreich, Micali, and Wigderson).
The protocol from Figure 8.8 is a zero-knowledge protocol.

Step	Merlin	Saruman	Arthur
1	chooses two large primes p and q and a secret $s \in \mathbb{Z}_n^*$, and computes $n = pq$ and $v = s^2 \mod n$		
2		$(n, v) \Rightarrow$	
3	chooses $r \in \mathbb{Z}_n^*$ at random and computes $x = r^2 \mod n$		
4		$x \Rightarrow$	
5			chooses a bit $a \in \{0, 1\}$ at random
6		$\Leftarrow a$	
7	computes $y = r \cdot s^a \mod n$		
8		$y \Rightarrow$	
9			verifies $y^2 \equiv x \cdot v^a \mod n$ and accepts accordingly

Fig. 8.10. Fiat–Shamir zero-knowledge identification scheme

We conclude this section by presenting a zero-knowledge protocol, shown in Figure 8.10, that was developed by Fiat and Shamir in 1986. It is based on the number-theoretical problem QR defined in Definition 2.43 from Section 2.4. The security of this protocol rests on the assumption that computing square roots in $\mathbb{Z}_n^*$ and factoring the modulus n are both infeasible tasks.

Theorem 8.28 (Fiat and Shamir).   *The Fiat–Shamir identification scheme shown in Figure 8.10 is a zero-knowledge protocol.*

Exercise 8.11 asks the reader to prove that this protocol works correctly, that impersonation by an eavesdropper can occur with probability 2^{-k} only (under reasonable assumptions), and that it has the zero-knowledge property.

Remark 8.29. Unlike digital signatures, which certify the authenticity of electronically transmitted *documents* such as emails or digital contracts, the authentication protocols presented in this section can be used to authenticate *individuals* participating in a computer network or as parties in a cryptographic protocol. As mentioned in Section 4.1, "individuals" here are not meant to be human beings only, but are to be understood in a wider sense, including computers that automatically execute protocols with other computers in a network.

8.5 Merkle and Hellman's Public-Key Cryptosystem

This section presents a public-key cryptosystem that was proposed by Merkle and Hellman in 1978. Although it was broken by Shamir in the early 1980s,[2] it is still worth studying it, since it is simple and elegant and particularly suitable for illustrating the basic design principles of public-key cryptography.

All public-key cryptosystems considered so far are based on the idea of *trapdoor one-way functions*. For example, the RSA public-key cryptosystem introduced in Figure 7.1 of Section 7.1 employs the fact that modular exponentiation can be performed efficiently using the "square-and-multiply" algorithm from Figure 7.2. Thus, both encryption and authorized decryption are easy. In contrast, unauthorized decryption seems to be hard, since computing m from e, n, and $c = m^e \bmod n$ (i.e., extracting the eth root of c modulo n) and factoring the RSA modulus n both are considered to be computationally infeasible tasks.

For efficient authorized decryption, it is important that Bob knows the prime factors p and q of the RSA modulus n from which he can determine his private decryption key. In other words, Bob has some *trapdoor information* that gives him an advantage over the eavesdropper, who lacks this information.

Another example is the ElGamal public-key cryptosystem introduced in Figure 8.3 of Section 8.2. Again, encryption and authorized decryption are easy, where the latter uses Bob's private key b as trapdoor information. In contrast, unauthorized decryption appears to be hard, since computing discrete logarithms is considered infeasible. Both computing discrete logarithms and extracting roots modulo an integer can be viewed as inverses of the modular exponentiation function. The difference between these two inverse functions is that root extraction for $\alpha = \beta^a \bmod n$ means computing the base β from α, a, and n, whereas the discrete logarithm of α requires computing the exponent a given α, β, and n.

---

[2] However, there are variants of this cryptosystem that are still unbroken to this date, see the remarks in Section 8.8.

The Merkle–Hellman cryptosystem is also based on the idea of trapdoor one-way functions. In particular, its security rests on the hardness of the subset-of-sums problem, denoted SOS and introduced in Definition 3.66 of Section 3.5.3. Recall that SOS is a restricted variant of the knapsack problem, and we have seen in Theorem 3.67 that SOS is NP-complete. Thus, there is no known deterministic or randomized polynomial-time algorithm solving this problem. The trapdoor information used here is that certain instances of SOS are nonetheless easy to solve.

Definition 8.30. *Let* $\langle s, T \rangle$ *be a given* SOS *instance, i.e.,* $s = (s_1, s_2, \ldots, s_n)$ *is a sequence of positive integers (called the* sizes*) and* T *is a positive integer (called the* target sum*). The sequence* s *of sizes is said to be* superincreasing *if and only if for each* i *with* $2 \leq i \leq n$,

$$s_i > \sum_{j=1}^{i-1} s_j.$$

Proposition 8.31 says that the subset-of-sums problem is efficiently solvable, provided that the given sequence of sizes is superincreasing. The easy proof of Proposition 8.31 is left to the reader as Exercise 8.12(a).

Proposition 8.31. *For instances* $\langle s, T \rangle$ *with a superincreasing sequence* s *of sizes, the problem* SOS *can be solved in deterministic polynomial time.*

Step	Alice	Erich	Bob
1			chooses a superincreasing sequence of sizes, $s = (s_1, s_2, \ldots, s_n)$, a prime $p > \sum_{i=1}^{n} s_i$, and a multiplier $b \in \mathbb{Z}_p$, and computes the vector $t = (t_1, t_2, \ldots, t_n)$ by the linear modular transformation $$t_i = bs_i \bmod p;$$ t is public and s, p, and b are private
2		$\Leftarrow t$	
3	encrypts the message $m = (m_1, m_2, \ldots, m_n)$ as $c = \sum_{i=1}^{n} m_i t_i$		
4		$c \Rightarrow$	
5			decrypts c by defining $T = b^{-1} c \bmod p$ and solving the SOS problem for the instance $\langle s, T \rangle$

Fig. 8.11. Merkle and Hellman's public-key cryptosystem

Figure 8.11 shows the Merkle–Hellman system. To make unauthorized decryption even harder, one can apply a random permutation on the vector t in addition. This public-key cryptosystem makes use of Proposition 8.31 as follows.

Step 1: Key Generation. The legitimate receiver Bob chooses a superincreasing sequence $\mathbf{s}$ of sizes, a multiplier b, and a prime number p. These values are his private key, i.e., his trapdoor information. He then determines his public key, which is a new vector $\mathbf{t} = (t_1, t_2, \ldots, t_n)$ obtained by the following linear modular transformation:

$$t_i = b s_i \bmod p.$$

Step 2: Communication. Bob's public key $\mathbf{t}$ is now known to Alice.

Step 3: Encryption. If $\mathbf{m} = (m_1, m_2, \ldots, m_n) \in \{0,1\}^n$ is the message Alice wishes to encrypt, she computes

$$c = \sum_{i=1}^{n} m_i t_i.$$

Step 4: Communication. Alice sends the ciphertext c to Bob.

Step 5: Decryption. When Bob receives the ciphertext c, $0 \le c \le n(p-1)$, he uses his trapdoor information to invert the linear modular transformation previously applied. In particular, he computes the target sum

$$T = b^{-1} c \bmod p,$$

which can be used to recover the original message. Since $\mathbf{s}$ is a superincreasing sequence of sizes, Bob can apply the algorithm from Proposition 8.31 to efficiently solve the SOS problem for the instance $\langle \mathbf{s}, T \rangle$. Thus, he can easily decrypt Alice's message.

On the other hand, unauthorized decryption seems to be hard. An eavesdropper—who lacks Bob's trapdoor information and thus does not know how to invert the linear modular transformation—is faced with an instance of the general SOS problem, which is NP-complete. However, as mentioned previously, there do exist ways to break the Merkle–Hellman system nonetheless, see Problem 8.2.

Example 8.32 (Merkle–Hellman Cryptosystem).   Suppose that Bob chooses the superincreasing sequence

$$\mathbf{s} = (2, 3, 6, 12, 25, 51, 101, 203, 415),$$

the prime number $p = 821$, which satisfies $p > \sum_{i=1}^{n} s_i$, and the multiplier $b = 444$. He then computes his public key

$$\mathbf{t} = (67, 511, 201, 402, 427, 477, 510, 643, 356),$$

which is not superincreasing. Let $\mathbf{m} = (1, 0, 1, 1, 0, 1, 0, 0, 1)$ be the message Alice wishes to encrypt. Knowing $\mathbf{t}$, she computes the ciphertext

$$c = 67 + 201 + 402 + 477 + 356 = 1503$$

and sends c to Bob. To decrypt c, he first applies the extended Euclidean Algorithm from Figure 2.2 to compute the inverse of 444 modulo 821, which is $b^{-1} = 723$. He then computes the target sum

$$T = 723 \cdot 1503 \bmod 821 = 486.$$

Finally, using the algorithm from Proposition 8.31 (see Exercise 8.12(a)), Bob recovers the original message by solving the SOS instance $\langle s, T \rangle$. Since his private sequence s of sizes is superincreasing, he can do so efficiently.

8.6 Rabi, Rivest, and Sherman's Protocols

Figure 8.12 presents another protocol for secret-key agreement, which was proposed by Rivest and Sherman in 1984. It can be modified so as to yield a protocol for digital signatures, see Exercise 8.13(a). This digital signature scheme was developed by Rabi and Sherman [RS97]. The differences between the Diffie–Hellman and the Rivest–Sherman secret-key agreement protocols are discussed in Section 8.8.

Step	Alice	Erich	Bob
1	chooses two large random strings, x and y, keeps x secret and computes $x\sigma y$		
2		$\langle y, x\sigma y \rangle \Rightarrow$	
3			chooses a large random string, z, keeps z secret and computes $y\sigma z$
4		$\Leftarrow y\sigma z$	
5	computes her key $$k_A = x\sigma(y\sigma z)$$		computes his key $$k_B = (x\sigma y)\sigma z$$

Fig. 8.12. Rivest–Sherman secret-key agreement protocol

The Rivest–Sherman protocol in Figure 8.12 uses a "strongly noninvertible, associative one-way function," σ. Before providing formal definitions of these properties, let us briefly give an intuitive idea and discuss the complexity model used. First, recall that a function is *one-way* if it is honest and easy to compute, but hard to invert. To capture the notion of "noninvertibility," various models have been proposed to date.[3] Depending on the model used, there are various candidates for one-way functions some of which were mentioned in Section 8.5.

Definition 3.78 in Section 3.6.2 introduced the notion of a *complexity-theoretic one-way function in the worst-case model*, and the present section focuses completely on this notion of one-way-ness. The average-case model is very important

---

[3] In this section, "noninvertibility" usually refers to non-FP-invertibility, see Definition 3.78.

in cryptographic applications as well as in complexity theory; for example, in relation to derandomization via pseudorandom generators. Nonetheless, the challenge
of proving that one-way functions exist remains an open problem even in the "less
challenging" worst-case model. Thus, it is reasonable to study which complexity-
theoretic assumptions are required to create various types of complexity-theoretic
one-way functions, as a first, modest step towards the creation of one-way functions
in the more demanding average-case model under appropriate assumptions.

Properties such as associativity make sense only for functions with two argu-
ments; let us assume that they map from $\Sigma^* \times \Sigma^*$ to Σ^*.[4] We further assume that
one-way functions may be partial and may be many-to-one. That is, they are not
required to be total functions on $\Sigma^* \times \Sigma^*$, and they are not required to be injec-
tions. For two-argument functions, we use the infix notation (e.g., $x\sigma y$) instead of
the prefix notation (e.g., $\sigma(x, y)$). Intuitively, a two-argument function σ is said to
be *strongly noninvertible* if, given some function value and one of the corresponding
arguments, it is hard to determine the other argument. This property is required of
the function σ used in Figure 8.12 in order to prevent the most obvious direct attack
that works as follows: If σ were not strongly noninvertible, an eavesdropper could
easily determine the secret strings x and z (and thus the secret keys k_A and k_B) from
the transmitted values y, $x\sigma y$, and $y\sigma z$.

Recall that the notion of honesty in Definition 3.78 is needed to prevent functions from being trivially noninvertible. That is, a dishonest function like $\delta(x) =
0^{\lceil \log \log \max(|x|,2) \rceil}$ shrinks its input more than polynomially and is thus trivially non-
invertible. However, this artificial length-trick noninvertibility is of no help in cryptography or complexity theory and is thus precluded in the definition of one-way
functions. The formal definition of strong noninvertibility requires an appropriate
variant of honesty called *s-honesty*. Intuitively, a strong inverter for a function σ
takes as inputs both a function value of σ and an argument of σ and computes the
corresponding other argument. Thus, to prevent σ from being trivially strongly noninvertible, s-honesty requires that σ shrinks no argument more than polynomially in
relation to the length of the function value *and* to the length of the corresponding
other argument. Note that there exist dishonest functions that are s-honest, and there
exist honest functions that are not s-honest; see Exercise 8.13(b).

Definition 8.33 (Strong One-Way Function).   *Let* $\sigma : \Sigma^* \times \Sigma^* \to \Sigma^*$ *be any
partial function.* D_σ *denotes the domain of* σ*, and* R_σ *denotes the range of* σ*.*

1. *We say that* σ *is s-honest if and only if there exists a polynomial* p *such that
   both (a) and (b) are true:*
   (a) *For each* $x, z \in \Sigma^*$ *with* $x\sigma y = z$ *for some* $y \in \Sigma^*$*, there exists some string*
       $\tilde{y} \in \Sigma^*$ *such that* $x\sigma\tilde{y} = z$ *and* $|\tilde{y}| \leq p(|x| + |z|)$*.*
   (b) *For each* $y, z \in \Sigma^*$ *with* $x\sigma y = z$ *for some* $x \in \Sigma^*$*, there exists some string*
       $\tilde{x} \in \Sigma^*$ *such that* $\tilde{x}\sigma y = z$ *and* $|\tilde{x}| \leq p(|y| + |z|)$*.*

---

[4] The strings x, y, and z in Figure 8.12 can also be viewed as integers represented in binary.

2. *We say that σ is* (polynomial-time) invertible with respect to the first argument *if and only if there exists an inverter $g_1 \in$ FP such that for each $z \in R_\sigma$ and for all $x, y \in \Sigma^*$ with $(x, y) \in D_\sigma$ and $x\sigma y = z$, we have $x\sigma g_1(\langle x, z \rangle) = z$.*

3. *We say that σ is* (polynomial-time) invertible with respect to the second argument *if and only if there exists an inverter $g_2 \in$ FP such that for each $z \in R_\sigma$ and for all $x, y \in \Sigma^*$ with $(x, y) \in D_\sigma$ and $x\sigma y = z$, we have $g_2(\langle y, z \rangle)\sigma y = z$.*

4. *We say that σ is* strongly noninvertible *if and only if σ is neither invertible with respect to the first argument nor invertible with respect to the second argument.*

5. *We say σ is* strong *if and only if σ is polynomial-time computable, s-honest, and strongly noninvertible.*

Associativity ensures that the Rivest–Sherman protocol works. Suppose for the moment that the function σ from Figure 8.12 is total. Then, associativity of σ means $(x\sigma y)\sigma z = x\sigma(y\sigma z)$ for all $x, y, z \in \Sigma^*$. This property guarantees that Alice and Bob indeed compute the same secret key:

$$k_A = x\sigma(y\sigma z) = (x\sigma y)\sigma z = k_B.$$

The above notion of associativity is meaningful for total functions, yet it is not meaningful for nontotal two-argument functions. Consider the following attempt to capture associativity for nontotal functions: σ is *weakly associative* if and only if

$$(x\sigma y)\sigma z = x\sigma(y\sigma z) \tag{8.16}$$

for all $x, y, z \in \Sigma^*$ such that $x\sigma y$, $y\sigma z$, $(x\sigma y)\sigma z$, and $x\sigma(y\sigma z)$ each are defined. However, this definition attempt fails to do the job for nontotal functions. What is wrong with it? Consider, for example, a function σ such that $0\sigma 1 = 0$ and $1\sigma 0 = 1$, yet σ is not defined on the pair $(0, 0)$. Then $0\sigma(1\sigma 0) = 0\sigma 1 = 0$, yet σ is not defined on $((0\sigma 1), 0) = (0, 0)$. Thus, (8.16) has the form "undefined = 0." But the weak associativity above fails to evaluate (8.16) as being false for these values of $x = 0$, $y = 1$, and $z = 0$.

When defining associativity for partial (including both total and nontotal) functions, it seems more natural to require that both sides of (8.16) stand or fall together. That is, either both sides of (8.16) should be defined and equal, or each side should be undefined. This observation is related to Kleene's careful distinction between "complete equality" and "weak equality" of partial functions [Kle52, pp. 327–328]. This natural behavior is achieved by the following definition of associativity and commutativity, which both are based on Kleene's "complete equality." Commutativity is needed to ensure that the Rivest–Sherman protocol from Figure 8.12 works for more than two parties as well, see Exercise 8.13(c).

Definition 8.34 (Associativity). *Let $\sigma : \Sigma^* \times \Sigma^* \to \Sigma^*$ be any partial function. Let $\perp$ be a symbol indicating, in the usage "$x\sigma y = \perp$," that σ is undefined on (x, y). Let $\Gamma = \Sigma^* \cup \{\perp\}$ be an extension of Σ^*, and define an extension $\widehat{\sigma} : \Gamma \times \Gamma \to \Gamma$ of σ by*

$$x\widehat{\sigma}y = \begin{cases} x\sigma y & \text{if } x \neq \perp \neq y \text{ and } (x, y) \in D_\sigma \\ \perp & \text{otherwise.} \end{cases} \tag{8.17}$$

We say that σ is associative *if and only if for each* $x, y, z \in \Sigma^*$,

$$(x\widehat{\sigma}y)\widehat{\sigma}z = x\widehat{\sigma}(y\widehat{\sigma}z).$$

We say that σ is commutative *if and only if for each* $x, y \in \Sigma^*$,

$$x\widehat{\sigma}y = y\widehat{\sigma}x.$$

Now that all technical prerequisites are provided, we turn to the most natural question arising from the protocol in Figure 8.12: Does there *exist* any total one-way function σ that is strong and associative? No unconditional answer to this question is known. After all, it is not known either whether or not any plain one-way function exists, dropping all the nice additional properties σ is required to have. However, we will now show that such a function σ with all the properties desired exists exactly if a plain one-way function exists. That is, one can construct σ from any given complexity-theoretic one-way function. First, recall the first two items of Theorem 3.82: One-to-one one-way functions exist if and only if P $\neq$ UP. It is straightforward to analogously characterize many-to-one one-way functions by the condition P $\neq$ NP, as stated in Proposition 8.35. In the remainder of this section, the term "many-to-one" is being dropped, i.e., whenever we speak of a one-way function, we mean a one-way function that is allowed to be many-to-one.

Proposition 8.35. *There exist one-way functions if and only if* P $\neq$ NP.

We now characterize the type of one-way functions needed for the Rivest–Sherman protocol.

Theorem 8.36. *There exist total, strong, commutative, associative one-way functions if and only if* P $\neq$ NP.

Proof.   By Proposition 8.35, the existence of total, strong, commutative, associative one-way functions immediately implies P $\neq$ NP. It remains to prove the converse. So assume that P $\neq$ NP. Let L be some set in NP such that $L \notin$ P, and let M be some given NPTM accepting L. For example, assuming P $\neq$ NP, any NP-complete set can be chosen as L. Recall from Definition 5.23 in Section 5.2 that a witness for "$x \in L$" is any string $w \in \Sigma^*$ encoding an accepting path of M on input x. For each $x \in L$, the set of witnesses for "$x \in L$" is defined by

$$\text{Wit}_M(x) = \{w \in \Sigma^* \mid w \text{ is a witness for ``}x \in L\text{''}\}.$$

For instance, the witnesses for elements in the NP-complete set SOS are shown in Example 5.22 in Section 5.2. Note that $\text{Wit}_M(x)$ is empty if and only if $x \notin L$.

As a technical detail, we assume that, for each $x \in L$, any witness w for "$x \in L$" is of length $p(|x|)$ for some strictly increasing polynomial p, and the length of w is strictly larger than the length of x. This assumption allows us to tell input strings in L apart from their witnesses, a property that will be useful in our construction of the total, strong, commutative, associative one-way function.

The construction proceeds in two stages. First, we show how to construct a nontotal, strong, commutative, associative one-way function σ from L. Then, we claim that σ can be extended to a total function that inherits all the other properties of σ. The proof of this claim in the second stage of the construction is left to the reader as Exercise 8.13(e). Before providing the formal details of the first stage of the construction, which defines σ from L, we illustrate the idea by the following short story.

Story 8.37 *At the police department of this small town, Officer Sigma is on duty today. On her desk, there is a list L of the usual suspects and there are many reports about crimes that happened recently. Some of the reports contain the description of one of the usual suspects, say x, from the list L. Officer Sigma attaches a file copy to it, so the report now has the form $\langle x, x \rangle$. Some reports contain the testimony w of an eye witness who has seen this suspect x on the scene of a crime. Officer Sigma attaches w to x, so the report now has the form $\langle x, w \rangle$. There are also many other reports that contain neither the description of a suspect nor the testimony of a witness.*

Officer Sigma is more than qualified for her job. Two years ago, she graduated from the Police Academy with distinction. That is why she can easily tell the description of a suspect from the testimony of a witness.[5] That is, she can immediately tell whether the report at hand is of the form $\langle x, x \rangle$ or $\langle x, w \rangle$. Better yet, Officer Sigma can easily check how reliable a witness is. Before filing her report, she verifies each witness testimony using a lie detector.

Every once in a while, Officer Sigma takes two reports from the desk, say a and b. Holding a with her left hand and b with her right hand, she reads them both carefully. She then chooses one of a and b to pass on to her boss, Sergeant Omega, and tosses the other one. Occasionally, she tosses them both. How does Officer Sigma decide which reports to pass on and which to throw out?

Whenever report a has the form $\langle x, w_1 \rangle$ and report b has the form $\langle x, w_2 \rangle$, Officer Sigma chooses one of a and b to give to Sergeant Omega, tossing the other one. In this case, both reports describe the same suspect x and there are two testimonies attached to them, which may be identical. Officer Sigma always hands over the report containing the shorter testimony.

Whenever one of the reports a and b has the form $\langle x, x \rangle$ and the other one has the form $\langle x, w \rangle$ for the same suspect x and for a testimony w of a witness who has seen x on the crime scene, Officer Sigma passes report $\langle x, x \rangle$ on to Sergeant Omega, distractedly tossing $\langle x, w \rangle$ into the trashbin.[6]

Whenever the reports a and b are not of the form described in the above two cases, Officer Sigma rigorously tosses them both.

Turning back to the formal proof of Theorem 8.36, let $a, b \in \Sigma^*$ be any two given input strings for our function σ. Define σ by

---

[5] Some of her colleagues at the police department keep confusing suspect descriptions and witness testimonies, which explains in part why so few crimes can be solved in this town.

[6] No wonder so few crimes are solved in this town.

$$a\sigma b = \begin{cases} \langle x, \min(w_1, w_2) \rangle & \text{if } a = \langle x, w_1 \rangle \text{ and } b = \langle x, w_2 \rangle \\ & \text{for some } x \in \Sigma^* \text{ and } w_1, w_2 \in \text{Wit}_M(x) \\ \langle x, x \rangle & \text{if } (a = \langle x, x \rangle \text{ and } b = \langle x, w \rangle) \\ & \text{or } (a = \langle x, w \rangle \text{ and } b = \langle x, x \rangle) \\ & \text{for some } x \in \Sigma^* \text{ and } w \in \text{Wit}_M(x) \\ \text{undefined} & \text{otherwise,} \end{cases} \qquad (8.18)$$

where $\min(w_1, w_2)$ denotes the lexicographical minimum of w_1 and w_2. It remains to show that σ has the desired properties. It is a matter of routine to check that σ is commutative, honest, s-honest, polynomial-time computable, and noninvertible, see Exercise 8.13(d). In particular, σ is thus a one-way function.

We now prove that σ is strong. For a contradiction, suppose that there is a polynomial-time inverter i with respect to the first argument of σ. That is, for each string z in the range of σ and for each fixed first argument $a \in \Sigma^*$ for which there exists a corresponding second argument $b \in \Sigma^*$ with $a\sigma b = z$, we have that $a\sigma i(\langle a, z \rangle) = z$. The inverter i can be used to decide the set L in polynomial time as follows:

Step 1: Given any input string x, to decide whether or not x is in L, compute the string $u = i(\langle \langle x, x \rangle, \langle x, x \rangle \rangle)$.
Step 2: Compute the unique strings v and w for which $\langle v, w \rangle = u$, i.e., v and w are the projections of our pairing function at u.
Step 3: Accept x if and only if $v = x$ and $w \in \text{Wit}_M(x)$.

The above algorithm runs in polynomial time and thus shows that L is in P, which contradicts our assumption that $L \notin$ P. Thus, σ is not invertible with respect to the first argument. An analogous argument shows that σ is not invertible with respect to the second argument either. It follows that σ is strongly noninvertible.

Finally, we prove that σ is associative. Let $a, b, c \in \Sigma^*$ be any fixed arguments for σ. Consider the projections of our pairing function at a, b, and c, respectively: $a = \langle a_1, a_2 \rangle$, $b = \langle b_1, b_2 \rangle$, and $c = \langle c_1, c_2 \rangle$. Let $k \in \{0, 1, 2, 3\}$ be the number that counts how many of a_2, b_2, and c_2 are elements of $\text{Wit}_M(a_1)$. For example, if $a_2 = b_2 \in \text{Wit}_M(a_1)$, but $c_2 \notin \text{Wit}_M(a_1)$, then $k = 2$. As per Definition 8.34, we have to show that

$$(a\widehat{\sigma}b)\widehat{\sigma}c = a\widehat{\sigma}(b\widehat{\sigma}c), \qquad (8.19)$$

where $\widehat{\sigma}$ is the extension of σ from that definition. There are two cases to distinguish.

Case 1: $a_1 = b_1 = c_1$ and $\{a_2, b_2, c_2\} \subseteq \{a_1\} \cup \text{Wit}_M(a_1)$. The intuition in this case is that the number of witnesses occurring in the arguments of σ are decreased by one as follows:

- If none of σ's arguments contains a witness for "$a_1 \in A$," then σ is undefined, so $\widehat{\sigma}$ outputs $\bot$.
- If exactly one of σ's arguments contains a witness for "$a_1 \in A$," then σ—and thus $\widehat{\sigma}$ as well—has the value $\langle a_1, a_1 \rangle$.

- If both of σ's arguments contain a witness for "$a_1 \in A$," then $\hat{\sigma}$ outputs $\langle a_1, w \rangle$, where $w \in \{a_2, b_2, c_2\}$ is the lexicographically smaller of the two witnesses.

From the above three subcases, we conclude the following:

- If $k \in \{0, 1\}$ then $(a\hat{\sigma}b)\hat{\sigma}c = \perp = a\hat{\sigma}(b\hat{\sigma}c)$.
- If $k = 2$ then $(a\hat{\sigma}b)\hat{\sigma}c = \langle a_1, a_1 \rangle = a\hat{\sigma}(b\hat{\sigma}c)$.
- If $k = 3$ then $(a\hat{\sigma}b)\hat{\sigma}c = \langle a_1, \min(a_2, b_2, c_2) \rangle = a\hat{\sigma}(b\hat{\sigma}c)$, where again $\min(a_2, b_2, c_2)$ denotes the lexicographically smallest of a_2, b_2, and c_2.

Case 2: Either $(a_1 \neq b_1 \text{ or } a_1 \neq c_1 \text{ or } b_1 \neq c_1)$ **or** $(a_1 = b_1 = c_1$ **and** $\{a_2, b_2, c_2\} \not\subseteq \{a_1\} \cup \mathrm{Wit}_M(a_1))$. In either of these two subcases of Case 2, one can verify that

$$(a\hat{\sigma}b)\hat{\sigma}c = \perp = a\hat{\sigma}(b\hat{\sigma}c).$$

In each of the above cases, (8.19) is satisfied. Hence, σ is associative. To complete the proof of Theorem 8.36, it remains to show that σ can be extended to a total function without destroying any of the other properties of σ, see Exercise 8.13(e). ∎

Note that even if it were known that P $\neq$ NP—and thus total, strong, commutative, associative one-way functions would exist by Theorem 8.36—it would not follow that the Rivest–Sherman protocol from Figure 8.12 is secure. Exercise 8.13(f) asks the reader to discuss the issue of security for this protocol.

8.7 Exercises and Problems

Exercise 8.1 Figure 8.1 presents the Diffie–Hellman protocol, see also Example 8.1.

(a) Verify that 12 is a primitive element of 17 by showing that $\langle 12 \rangle = \mathbb{Z}_{17}^*$.

(b) Verify Bob's secret number $\beta = 12^{15} \equiv 10 \bmod 17$ from Example 8.1 using the "square-and-multiply" algorithm from Figure 7.2.

(c) Execute the Diffie–Hellman protocol from Figure 8.1 for $p = 17$ and $\gamma = 11$, where Alice chooses the secret exponent $a = 5$ and Bob chooses $b = 7$.

(d) Determine all primitive elements of the prime number 101 and execute the Diffie–Hellman protocol from Figure 8.1 for some primitive element γ of 101, and some private exponents a and b of your choice.

Exercise 8.2 (a) Define the Diffie–Hellman problem from Definition 8.2 as a decision problem, say `Diffie-Hellman`, and show that the two versions are equivalent under polynomial-time Turing reductions:

- `Diffie-Hellman` $\in \mathrm{P}^{\mathtt{diffie-hellman}}$ and
- `diffie-hellman` $\in \mathrm{FP}^{\mathtt{Diffie-Hellman}}$.

(b) Define the discrete logarithm problem from Definition 2.42 as a decision problem, say `DLog`, and show that the two versions are equivalent under polynomial-time Turing reductions: `DLog` $\in \mathrm{P}^{\mathtt{dlog}}$ and `dlog` $\in \mathrm{FP}^{\mathtt{DLog}}$.

Exercise 8.3 (a) Verify that 2 is a primitive element of 101, as claimed in Example 8.4, and determine all other primitive elements of 101.

(b) Compute $a = \log_{27} 89 \bmod 101$, using Shanks' algorithm from Figure 8.2.

(c) Compute $a = \log_{569} 413 \bmod 809$, using Shanks' algorithm from Figure 8.2.

Exercise 8.4 Consider the ElGamal public-key cryptosystem from Figure 8.3.

(a) Let $p = 101$ be the prime number chosen, and suppose that Alice and Bob have agreed on the primitive element $\gamma = 27$ of 101. Alice chooses the private exponent $a = 23$ and Bob chooses the private exponent $b = 87$. Using ElGamal's cryptosystem, encrypt the message $m = 89$ and show that decryption according to (8.5) yields the original plaintext.

(b) Do the same as in (a) with the parameters $p = 809$, $\gamma = 569$, $a = 227$, $b = 781$, and $m = 801$.

Exercise 8.5 Consider the ElGamal digital signature scheme from Figure 8.4.

(a) Choose the parameters $p = 1367$ and $\gamma = 2$ as in Example 8.6. Suppose that Bob chooses his private exponents to be $b = 711$ and $s = 117$. Check that $\gcd(s, p - 1) = 1$. What is Bob's signature for the message $m = 828$? Verify that this signature is valid by checking (8.7).

(b) Execute the ElGamal digital signature scheme from Figure 8.4 with different parameters of your choice.

Exercise 8.6 Look at the key-only attack on the ElGamal digital signature scheme presented in Section 8.2.3.

(a) As in Example 8.13, choose the parameters $p = 1367$ and $\gamma = 2$. Suppose that Erich does not know Bob's private exponents $b = 711$ and $s = 117$ from Exercise 8.5(a). However, he does know the corresponding public value β. Suppose further that Erich chooses the values $x = 67$ and $y = 99$ in order to mount the key-only attack from Example 8.13. Determine his signature and the corresponding message.

(b) Execute the key-only attack from (a) with different parameters of your choice.

Exercise 8.7 Look at the known-message attack on the ElGamal digital signature scheme presented in Section 8.2.3.

(a) Verify that the values σ, ρ, and m constructed in (8.12) indeed satisfy the ElGamal verification condition (8.7): $\gamma^m \equiv \beta^\sigma \sigma^\rho \bmod p$.

(b) Mount this known-message attack on the ElGamal digital signature scheme with parameters of your choice.

Exercise 8.8 Mount a known-message attack so as to yield a total break of the ElGamal scheme, provided that the same value s (see Figure 8.4) is used twice for signing distinct messages, m_1 and m_2.

Hint: Let γ be the primitive element of the prime number p used in the protocol, and let β be Bob's public key. Suppose that (σ, ρ_1) is Bob's signature for m_1 and (σ, ρ_2) is Bob's signature for m_2. Writing $\sigma = \gamma^s$, we have

$$\beta^\sigma \sigma^{p_1} \equiv \gamma^{m_1} \bmod p \quad \text{and} \quad \beta^\sigma \sigma^{p_2} \equiv \gamma^{m_2} \bmod p.$$

Find a way to determine the unknown value s, using the above congruences. Once s is known, it can be used to determine Bob's other private exponent, b, as explained at the end of Section 8.2.3.

Exercise 8.9 Consider Rabin's cryptosystem from Figure 8.5 in Section 8.3.

(a) Using the parameters from Example 8.16, suppose that Bob chooses the prime numbers $p = 43$ and $q = 47$, so $n = 2021$ is the Rabin modulus. Determine the Rabin encryptions of the following messages: $m_1 = 234, m_2 = 1789$, and $m_3 = 1989$. For each of the corresponding ciphertexts c_i, $i \in \{1, 2, 3\}$, determine all plaintexts that are mapped to c_i by the Rabin encryption function.

(b) Suppose you are Bob. Repeat (a) with different parameters of your choice.

(c) Suppose that Erich knows the Rabin modulus $n = 13081$. Apply the method of Theorem 8.18 to determine the prime factors of n by a chosen-ciphertext attack; see also Example 8.21.

Exercise 8.10 Look at Figure 8.8 in Example 8.23, which shows the zero-knowledge protocol for GI.

(a) Prove that the isomorphism σ computed in Figure 8.8 indeed is in $\text{ISO}(G_a, H)$, as requested by Arthur.

(b) Execute this protocol for the graphs $G_0 = G$ and $G_1 = H$ and the isomorphism $\pi = \left(\begin{smallmatrix} 1 & 2 & 3 & 4 & 5 \\ 2 & 5 & 4 & 5 & 3 \end{smallmatrix}\right)$ in $\text{ISO}(G, H)$, where G and H are the graphs from Example 2.50 in Section 2.4. Use an isomorphism μ of your choice and consider every possible combinations of the random bits $m \in \{0, 1\}$ and $a \in \{0, 1\}$.

(c) Suppose you are Saruman and you do not know Merlin's secret isomorphism π. Ask somebody else to play Arthur's role and execute this protocol with him.

(d) Repeat (b) using different graphs with 10 vertices of your choice.

(e) Modify the protocol from Figure 8.8 such that Saruman's cheating probability in *one round* of the protocol is at most 2^{-10}.

Exercise 8.11 Look at Figure 8.10 in Section 8.4, which shows the Fiat–Shamir zero-knowledge protocol for QR.

(a) Prove that this protocol works correctly.

(b) Assuming that it is infeasible to compute square roots modulo n and to factor the modulus n, prove that an eavesdropper can impersonate as Merlin in this protocol with probability 2^{-k} only, for some fixed k.

(c) Prove that this protocol has the zero-knowledge property.

(d) Suppose that Merlin has chosen the prime numbers $p = 43$ and $q = 47$, so $n = 2021$. His secret number is $s = 97$; note that $\gcd(2021, 97) = 1$. According to Figure 8.10, execute the Fiat–Shamir protocol for various values of r and a of your choice.

Exercise 8.12 Consider the Merkle–Hellman cryptosystem in Section 8.5.

(a) Prove Proposition 8.31. That is, design a deterministic polynomial-time algorithm that solves the problem SOS for instances $\langle \mathbf{s}, T \rangle$ with a superincreasing sequence $\mathbf{s}$ of sizes. As a check, verify that your algorithm, when applied to the instance $\langle \mathbf{s}, T \rangle$ with $\mathbf{s} = (2, 3, 6, 12, 25, 51, 101, 203, 415)$ and $T = 486$, recovers the original message $\mathbf{m} = (1, 0, 1, 1, 0, 1, 0, 0, 1)$, as claimed in Example 8.32.

(b) Modify the Merkle-Hellman cryptosystem as follows: The public key is a superincreasing sequence $\mathbf{s} = (s_1, s_2, \ldots, s_n)$ of sizes, and encryption is done via the encryption function

$$E_{\mathbf{s}}(\mathbf{m}) = \sum_{i=1}^{n} m_i s_i$$

mapping from $\{0, 1\}^n$ to $\{0, 1, \ldots \sum_{i=1}^{n} s_i\}$. Since $E_{\mathbf{s}}$ is injective, the algorithm from Proposition 8.31 can be used for authorized decryption. What is wrong with this simplification of the Merkle-Hellman cryptosystem?

(c) Suppose that Bob chooses the superincreasing sequence

$$\mathbf{s} = (1, 3, 7, 15, 29, 57, 117, 235, 475, 940),$$

the prime number $p = 1889$, and the mulitplier $b = 666$. Encrypt the message $\mathbf{m} = (1, 0, 1, 1, 0, 0, 1, 1, 0, 1)$. As a check, decrypt your ciphertext to see if the original message can be recovered.

Exercise 8.13 Consider Rivest und Sherman's protocol for secret-key agreement shown in Figure 8.12.

(a) Modify this protocol so as to create a protocol for digital signatures.

Hint: See Rabi and Sherman [RS97].

(b) Construct a dishonest, polynomial-time computable, two-argument function that is s-honest, and construct an honest, polynomial-time computable, two-argument function that is not s-honest.

Hint: See L. Hemaspaandra, Pasanen, and Rothe [HPR01].

(c) Suppose that the total, strongly noninvertible, associative one-way function σ on which the protocol in Figure 8.12 is based in addition is commutative, i.e., for each $x, y \in \Sigma^*$, $x\sigma y = y\sigma x$. Modify both the secret-key agreement protocol from Figure 8.12 and the digital signature protocol from (a) to multi-party protocols, i.e., to protocols for $k \geq 2$ parties, not only for Alice and Bob.

Hint: See Rabi and Sherman [RS97].

(d) Look at the proof of Theorem 8.36. Prove that the function σ defined in (8.18) is commutative, honest, s-honest, polynomial-time computable, and noninvertible.

Hint: See L. Hemaspaandra and Rothe [HR99].

(e) Show that the nontotal function σ defined in (8.18) can be extended to a total function σ_t without destroying any of the other properties of σ. Specifically, consider the following construction of $\sigma_t : \Sigma^* \times \Sigma^* \to \Sigma^*$. Let $\hat{x}$ be a fixed string not in L (and argue why such a string must exist). Let $\hat{a} = \langle \hat{x}, 1\hat{x} \rangle$. Argue why $\hat{a}$ is neither of the form $\langle x, x \rangle$ for any $x \in \Sigma^*$, nor of the form $\langle x, w \rangle$ for any $x \in \Sigma^*$ and any witness $w \in W_M(x)$. By (8.18), σ is defined neither on $(\hat{a}, b)$ nor on $(b, \hat{a})$ for any $b \in \Sigma^*$. Define the total extension σ_t to coincide with σ on D_σ, and to map all pairs $(a, b) \notin D_\sigma$ to the "garbage" element $\hat{a}$. Prove that σ_t is a strong, commutative, associative one-way function.

Hint: See L. Hemaspaandra and Rothe [HR99].

(f) Discuss the security of the Rivest–Sherman protocol from Figure 8.12 under all necessary aspects.

Hint: See L. Hemaspaandra and Rothe [HR99].

(g) Prove that no total, associative function can be injective.

Hint: See Rabi and Sherman [RS97].

Problem 8.1 (Bit Security of Discrete Logarithms)

Prove Theorem 8.12: Let $\langle p, \gamma, \alpha, 1 \rangle$ be an instance of the discrete logarithm bit problem, and let $p - 1 = r2^q$ for some odd number r. Then,

(a) for each $i \leq q$, $\mathtt{dlogbit}(\langle p, \gamma, \alpha, i \rangle)$ can be evaluated in polynomial time, and

(b) $\log_\gamma \alpha \bmod p$ can be computed in $\mathrm{FP}^{\mathtt{dlogbit}(\langle p, \gamma, \alpha, q+1 \rangle)}$.

Hint for (b): Consider the case $q = 1$, i.e., $p - 1 = 2r$ for some odd number r. Thus, $p \equiv 3 \bmod 4$. Show that if p is prime and $p \equiv 3 \bmod 4$, then every $\alpha \in \mathrm{QR}_p$ has the two square roots $\pm \alpha^{(p+1)/4}$. Moreover, show that if $p \equiv 3 \bmod 4$, then

$$\mathtt{dlogbit}(\langle p, \gamma, \alpha, 1 \rangle) \neq \mathtt{dlogbit}(\langle p, \gamma, p - \alpha, 1 \rangle).$$

It follows that if $\alpha \equiv \gamma^a \bmod p$ for some unknown even exponent a, then either

$$\alpha^{(p+1)/4} \equiv \gamma^{a/2} \bmod p, \quad \text{or} \tag{8.20}$$

$$-\alpha^{(p+1)/4} \equiv \gamma^{a/2} \bmod p. \tag{8.21}$$

Which of (8.20) or (8.21) is true can be tested efficiently by Theorem 8.11, provided that the value of $\mathtt{dlogbit}(\langle p, \gamma, \alpha, 2 \rangle)$ is known, since

$$\mathtt{dlogbit}(\langle p, \gamma, \alpha, 2 \rangle) = \mathtt{dlogbit}(\langle p, \gamma, \gamma^{a/2}, 1 \rangle).$$

Exploit this property to design a polynomial-time algorithm that uses the oracle $\mathtt{dlogbit}(\langle p, \gamma, \alpha, 2 \rangle)$ to compute the binary representation of $a = \log_\gamma \alpha \bmod p$. The details of this proof can be found in Stinson [Sti02].

Problem 8.2 (Breaking the Merkle–Hellman Cryptosystem)

Break the basic Merkle–Hellman Cryptosystem from Figure 8.11 in Section 8.5.

Hint: See A. Shamir [Sha84] and also A. Shamir and Zippel [SZ80]. The crucial idea of breaking the Merkle–Hellman cryptosystem is to apply H. Lenstra's efficient algorithm for integer programming with a fixed number of variables [Len83].

Problem 8.3 (A Protocol Without Keys)

Your task in solving this problem is best understood by carefully reading the following story.

Story 8.38 *As is common among children of their age, Paula and Ella love to share secrets.*[7] *When Paula had to go to the hospital to be treated for severe pneumonia, the two otherwise inseparable sisters were very unhappy. Fortunately, Paula recovered quickly from her illness, but she had to stay in the hospital for another week. Ella was not allowed to visit her sister—that's the rule in the hospital's intensive care unit. Only her parents had permission to see Paula there. Still, Paula and Ella were eager to communicate and to keep sharing secrets. The problem was that they had to rely on their parents to pass them on, and it is common knowledge among children that parents are never trustworthy when it comes to keeping a secret.*

Step	Ella	Parents	Paula
1	Ella buys a box B and two padlocks, x and y, asks her parents to hand y over to Paula in the hospital, and keeps x for herself		
2	locks the message m in the box B using her padlock x		
3		$B_x \Rightarrow$	
4			puts her padlock y on the box
5		$\Leftarrow B_x^y$	
6	removes her padlock x		
7		$B^y \Rightarrow$	
8			removes her padlock y and reads the message m

Fig. 8.13. Paula and Ella's no-key protocol

Here is their clever plan for how to share a secret while keeping it from their parents. Look at Figure 8.13, which shows Paula and Ella's protocol: Ella buys a box B and two padlocks, x and y, asks her parents to hand y over to Paula in the hospital, and keeps x for herself. Then, she writes the message m containing the secret she wishes to share with Paula.[8] *She puts m into the box B, and locks the box with her padlock x. The locked box is denoted by B_x. Her parents now take B_x along to the hospital and hand it over to Paula, who doesn't open it (well, she can't, as she doesn't have a key for x), but locks it again using her padlock y. The double-locked box is denoted by B_x^y, and the parents take it back home and hand it over to Ella, who removes her lock x. Now, the box, B^y, is still locked with Paula's padlock. At the parents' next visit in the hospital, Paula receives B^y from them, waits until they have left, and*

---

[7] I must admit that these secrets were kept from me and I have no knowledge of their content.

[8] Again, I unfortunately have no clue what this secret might be.

then she removes her lock y, opens the box, and—bursting with anticipation—starts reading Ella's message.

Here is your task: Design a protocol based on Paula and Ella's protocol from Figure 8.13. Unlike theirs, your protocol should not need boxes and padlocks, but should use suitable mathematical notions and functions.

Hint: Note that whenever the parents had access to the box, it was locked, sadly enough. Your protocol should also have the feature that whenever some information is conveyed, the eavesdropper should not have a way to decipher it, under reasonable complexity-theoretic assumptions. Note further that to execute this protocol, there is no need for Ella and Paula to share a joint secret key. That is why this protocol, which is based on an unpublished work of A. Shamir, is sometimes dubbed the "no-key protocol." It is enough for Paula and Ella each to have a private key, for locking and unlocking just their own padlock. Finally, note that the order of locking and removing the two padlocks does not matter here: Padlock x can be removed from the box even though the box is still locked by y, which was put on *after* x. In other words, these are *symmetric* operations in some sense. The function on which your protocol should be based must include this feature as well. As a more specific hint, recall the modular exponentiation function used in the Diffie–Hellman protocol from Figure 8.1, which is symmetric in the exponents as well: $\gamma^{ab} \equiv \gamma^{ba} \bmod p$.

Oh... and if you happen to learn Ella and Paula's secret in Story 8.38 somehow, please let me know. I'm their father.

8.8 Summary and Bibliographic Remarks

General Remarks: As noted in Section 7.6, Diffie and Hellman laid the foundations for public-key cryptography. Their path-breaking work [DH76] is a milestone in the history of cryptography, not only since they were the first to discover a solution to the secret-key agreement problem that is central to symmetric cryptography, but also since they were the first to propose the idea of public-key cryptography. As mentioned in Section 7.6, similar findings were obtained independently and even earlier in the nonpublic sector. Most of the public-key cryptosystems and protocols presented in this chapter can also be found in other textbooks on cryptography; see, e.g., Stinson [Sti02], Buchmann [Buc01], Salomaa [Sal96], and Goldreich [Gol01].

Specific Remarks: The Diffie–Hellman secret-key agreement protocol presented in Figure 8.1 can be found in [DH76]. ElGamal's cryptosystem from Figure 8.3 and the related digital signature scheme from Figure 8.4 are presented in [ElG85]. The baby-step giant-step algorithm from Figure 8.2 for computing discrete logarithms is due to Shanks [Sha54]. For more background and details on the discrete logarithm problem, the reader is referred to the surveys by Odlyzko and LaMacchia [Odl85, LO91, Odl00].

Schnorr [Sch90] proposed a modification of the ElGamal digital signature scheme that led to the United States *Digital Signature Standard*, see [Nat91, Nat92]. Let p

and q be primes with $p \equiv 1 \bmod q$; typically, p is represented in binary by a 1024 bit string and q is represented in binary by a 160 bit string. In this modification of the ElGamal signature scheme, Bob signs a message of length $\log q$ by a signature of length roughly $2 \log q$. Schnorr's idea was to speed the computation up by working in a subgroup of $\mathbb{Z}_p^*$ that has size q and for which computing discrete logarithms is assumed to be hard.

Rabin's cryptosystem was presented in [Rab79]. Williams [Wil80] and Kurosawa, Ito, and Takeuchi [KIT88] proposed public-key cryptosystems that like Rabin's system are provably secure in the sense that breaking them is as hard as factoring. Unlike Rabin's system, however, decryption is unambiguous in their systems.

The notions of interactive proof systems and zero-knowledge protocols were introduced by Goldwasser, Micali, and Rackoff [GMR89]. The related notion of Arthur-Merlin games is due to Babai and Moran [Bab85, BM88]. Zachos and Heller [Zac88, ZH86] and Boppana, Håstad, and Zachos [BHZ87] investigated these notions early on.

Interactive proof systems, zero-knowledge, Arthur-Merlin games, and related notions are studied in many research papers and textbooks, both in relation to cryptography and to complexity theory. For example, a celebrated complexity-theoretic result is due to A. Shamir [Sha92]: Interactive proof systems have precisely the same computational power as polynomial-space Turing machines. Regarding cryptographic applications of these notions, one of the most profound and comprehensive sources is Chapter 4 in Goldreich's book [Gol01]. These important notions are also presented in an abundance of survey papers and book chapters, for example in those by Balcázar, Díaz, and Gabarró [BDG90], Beutelspacher et al. [Beu94, BSW01, Beu02], Bovet and Crescenzi [BC93], Buchmann [Buc01], Du and Ko [DK00], Feigenbaum [Fei92], Goldreich [Gol88], Goldwasser [Gol89], Köbler, Schöning, and Torán [KST93], Papadimitriou [Pap94], Rothe [Rot02, Rot04c], Stinson [Sti95], Schöning [Sch95b], Wechsung [Wec00], and Wegener [Weg03].

The particular notion of zero-knowledge introduced in Definition 8.24 is called "*honest-verifier perfect zero-knowledge*," which assumes (a) the verifier to be honest, and (b) the probability distributions in the original and in the simulated protocol to be perfectly identical. As mentioned immediately after this definition, assumption (a) may be not realistic enough for most cryptographic applications, since a dishonest verifier might alter the protocol to his own advantage. To avoid such behavior, one can modify the definition of zero-knowledge by requiring that for *each* potential verifier A there exists a simulator S such that the simulated protocol they jointly generate cannot be distinguished from the original protocol. However, if the random bits are public, then honest-verifier zero-knowledge protocols can always be transformed to protocols that are zero-knowledge even in the presence of dishonest verifiers.

We further mentioned that assumption (b) may be too strict, and requirements weaker than perfect zero-knowledge might work as well. Such weaker notions include "*statistical zero-knowledge*" (a.k.a. *almost-perfect zero-knowledge*) and "*computational zero-knowledge*." The former model requires that the information conveyed in the original and in the simulated protocol be indistinguishable by suitable statistical tests. The latter model merely requires that the information conveyed in the original and in the simulated protocol be computationally indistinguishable, i.e., for each randomized polynomial-time Turing machine, the probability of detecting differences in the corresponding distributions is negligibly small.

The zero-knowledge protocol for GI from Example 8.23 is due to Goldreich, Micali, and Wigderson [GMW91]. They also proved one of the most important results on zero-knowledge: Every problem in NP has a computational zero-knowledge protocol under the plausible assumption that there exist cryptographically secure bit-commitment schemes. One of the key ideas in their proof is the design of a computational zero-knowledge protocol for a well-known NP-complete problem, 3-Colorability, see Theorem 3.56. In contrast, Brassard and Crépeau [BC89] provided evidence that such a strong claim is unlikely to hold in the perfect zero-knowledge model of Definition 8.24.

The zero-knowledge protocol for QR from Figure 8.10 was proposed by Fiat and Shamir [FS86]. The Fiat–Shamir protocol is particularly suitable for authentication in large computer networks. It is a public-key protocol but more efficient than many other public-key protocols. It can be implemented on a chip card. And it has the zero-knowledge property. These advantages led to a rapid deployment of this protocol in practical applications. For example, it is integrated in the "videocrypt" pay-TV system [CH91]. Feige, Fiat, and Shamir [FFS88] improved the original Fiat–Shamir zero-knowledge identification scheme to a zero-knowledge protocol in which not only the secret square roots modulo n are not revealed, but also the information of whether or not there *exists* a square root modulo n is not leaked.

The basic Merkle–Hellman cryptosystem from Figure 8.11 is due to Merkle and Hellman [MH78]. As mentioned in the hint to solving Problem 8.2, their system was broken in the early 1980s by A. Shamir [Sha84], see also A. Shamir and Zippel [SZ80]. The iterated variant of the Merkle–Hellman system was broken by Brickell [Bri85], see also Adleman [Adl83] and Brickell, Lagarias, and Odlyzko [BLO83, Bri83, Lag83].

Another variant of a knapsack-based public-key cryptosystem, proposed by Chor and Rivest [CR88], resisted all attempts of breaking it for about a decade. For example, Schnorr and Hörner's attack [SH95] was partially successful; they broke the Chor–Rivest cryptosystem in the dimensions 103 and 151. Their attack and various other attacks on knapsack-based cryptosystems use lattice reduction algorithms that improve the LLL algorithm by Lenstra, Lenstra, and Lovász [LLL82]. Lattice-based techniques are particularly useful for breaking systems that are based on knapsacks (or subsets of sums) of *low density*. In contrast, the Chor–Rivest cryptosystem is based on high-density knapsacks. Eventually, this system was broken by Vaudenay [Vau01] using algebraic methods. Among the knapsack-based and lattice-based cryptosystems, the NTRU cryptosystem developed by Hoffstein, Pipher, and Silverman [HPS98] and related protocols [HPS01, HHGP$^+$03] are currently still unbroken, see also Coppersmith and A. Shamir [CS97].

Kellerer, Pferschy, and D. Pisinger have written an in-depth, very comprehensive treatise on knapsack problems [KPP04], focusing on their algorithmic properties and computational complexity. For more background and details on cryptosystems based on subset of sums and knapsack problems, the reader is referred to Chapter 3 of

Salomaa [Sal96]. In particular, it presents Shamir's cryptanalytic attack on the basic Merkle–Hellman cryptosystem, see also the survey by Brickell and Odlyzko [BO92]. Lagarias and Odlyzko [LO85] were among the first to solve subset sum problems via lattice reduction techniques. For more background and details on the complexity of lattice problems in general and in particular on their applications in cryptology, the interested reader is referred to the book by Micciancio and Goldwasser [MG02] and to the surveys by Cai [Cai99], Kumar and Sivakumar [KS01], and Nguyen and Stern [NS01].

Different public-key cryptosystems whose security is based on NP-complete problems were proposed by, e.g., Shamir [Sha83], Impagliazzo and Naor [IN96], and Ajtai and Dwork [AD97]. Even, Selman, and Yacobi [ESY84, EY80] also studied cryptosystems that are NP-hard to break. Relatedly, they developed the theory of "promise problems," focusing on their applications in public-key cryptography, see also Grollmann and Selman [GS88].

The secret-key agreement protocol from Figure 8.12 is attributed to Rivest and Sherman in [RS97]. Rabi and Sherman proposed the related digital signature scheme [RS97], see Exercise 8.13(a). Both protocols use a function σ that is specified merely by its properties: σ is supposed to be a total, strongly noninvertible, commutative, associative one-way function. It is not known whether such functions exist. Rabi and Sherman [RS97] proved that commutative, associative one-way functions exist if and only if P $\neq$ NP. However, the functions they construct are neither total[9] nor strongly noninvertible, not even if one assumes P $\neq$ NP. They left open the question of whether P $\neq$ NP is also sufficient for functions σ to exist that possess all the properties required by the Rivest–Sherman and Rabi–Sherman protocols.

This question was solved by L. Hemaspaandra and Rothe [HR99], who proved Theorem 8.36: Total, strongly noninvertible, commutative, associative one-way functions exist in the worst-case model under the (unproven, yet plausible) assumption that P $\neq$ NP. One-way functions with these properties have been thoroughly studied since, in a variety of contexts; see, e.g., the work by L. Hemaspaandra, Pasanen, and Rothe [HPR01] and Homan [Hom04], and the survey by Beygelzimer et al. [BHHR99]. It is important to note, however, that Theorem 8.36 is far from proving the Rivest–Sherman and Rabi–Sherman protocols secure. That is, these protocols lack a proof of security, even if it were known that P $\neq$ NP, i.e., even if a function σ with the desired properties were known to exist.

The security issues of the Rivest–Sherman and Rabi–Sherman protocols are discussed in more detail in [HR99], see also Exercise 8.13(f). In a nutshell, strong noninvertibility merely precludes the obvious direct attack mentioned in Section 8.6 but does not preclude other potential types of attack. Further, noninvertibility and strong noninvertibility are defined in the worst-case model, which is not suitable in applied cryptography. For cryptographic applications, one would need to construct

---

[9] Rabi and Sherman [RS97] propose a construction that they claim can be used to obtain a total, associative one-way function from any given nontotal, (weakly) associative one-way function. However, the proof of their claim is flawed: If their claim were true then the unlikely collapse UP $=$ NP would follow immediately [HR99].

functions that are noninvertible and strongly noninvertible in the average-case complexity model, under plausible assumptions. There do exist interesting results in complexity theory that provide potential candidates for achieving this goal. In particular, Ajtai [Ajt96] proved that certain variants of the NP-complete shortest lattice vector problem are equally hard in the worst-case model and in the average-case model. The public-key cryptosystem designed by Ajtai and Dwork [AD97] is based on this worst-case/average-case equivalence.

Neither of the two secret-key agreement protocols presented in this chapter has a proof of security to date, neither the Diffie–Hellman protocol from Figure 8.1 nor the Rivest–Sherman protocol from Figure 8.12. One major difference between these two protocols is that, unlike the Rivest–Sherman protocol that is based on an unspecified function σ, the Diffie–Hellman scheme uses a concrete, specific function as its key building block. Its security rests on the (unproven, yet plausible) assumption that computing discrete logarithms is computationally intractable. However, breaking Diffie–Hellman is not known to be as hard as computing discrete logarithms. Some progress has been made by Maurer and Wolf [MW99, MW00], who established conditions for relating the hardness of breaking Diffie–Hellman to that of computing discrete logarithms. Again, their results rest on unproven, yet plausible assumptions: Breaking Diffie–Hellman and computing the discrete logarithm are polynomial-time equivalent tasks in the underlying cyclic group $\mathfrak{G}$, assuming that $\nu(p)$ is polynomial in $\log p$, where $\nu(p)$ denotes the minimum of the largest prime factors of d, taken over all numbers d in the interval $[p - 2\sqrt{p} + 1, \, p + 2\sqrt{p} + 1]$.

The notion of complexity-theoretic (i.e., worst-case) one-way functions was introduced by Grollmann and Selman [GS88]; see also Berman [Ber77], Brassard, Fortune, and Hopcroft [BFH78, Bra79], and Ko [Ko85]. Complexity-theoretic one-way functions of different sorts, and related notions, have been intensely studied ever since; see, e.g., [AR88, Wat88, HH91, Sel92, RS93, HRW97b, RS97, HR99, BHHR99, HR00, HPR01, RH02, FFNR03, HT03b, Hom04, HRS04]. For example, worst-case one-way functions are closely related to the isomorphism conjecture, see Conjectures 3.73, 3.79, and 3.80 in Section 3.6.2.

In another line of research, the existence of certain types of worst-case one-way functions has been characterized in terms of suitable complexity class separations. For example, the question of whether or not there exist one-way permutations (i.e., total, one-to-one, onto one-way functions) was raised by Grollmann and Selman [GS88], studied by L. Hemaspaandra and Rothe [HR00, RH02], and finally solved by Homan and Thakur [HT03b]: One-way permutations exist if and only if $P \neq UP \cap coUP$. Fenner, Fortnow, Naik, and J. Rogers [FFNR03] proved that partial, many-to-one, onto one-way functions exist if and only if $P \neq NP$; related results were independently obtained by L. Hemaspaandra, Rothe, and Wechsung [HRW97a].

As a final remark, Story 8.37 is inspired by a story told in [BHHR99], and Story 8.38 is based on a true story.

List of Figures

1.1 A typical cryptographic scenario (the design of Alice and Bob is due to Crépeau) 1

2.1 Euclidian Algorithm 10
2.2 Extended Euclidean Algorithm 12
2.3 Syntax tree for the grammar G_2 from Example 2.8 19
2.4 A deterministic and a nondeterministic finite automaton 21
2.5 A Turing machine 23
2.6 Three graphs: G is isomorphic to H, but not to F 44

3.1 2-SAT is NL-complete 84
3.2 Cook reduction 89
3.3 3-SAT $\leq_m^P$ IS 94
3.4 3-SAT $\leq_m^P$ 3-Colorability 96
3.5 3-Colorability $\leq_m^P$ DNP 98
3.6 3-SAT $\leq_m^P$ 3-DM 101

4.1 A linear feedback shift register 151

5.1 Boolean hierarchy over NP (Hasse diagram) 176
5.2 Boolean hierarchy over NP (Venn diagram) 177
5.3 Exact-5-DNP is DP-complete 181
5.4 Tree-like structure S_i in the Guruswami–Khanna reduction 185
5.5 Basic template 186
5.6 Connection pattern between the templates of a tree-like structure 186
5.7 Gadget connecting two "leaves" of the "same row" kind 187
5.8 Gadget connecting two "leaves" of the "different rows" kind 188
5.9 Prefix search to find the smallest graph isomorphism 192
5.10 Polynomial hierarchy (Hasse diagram) 195
5.11 Polynomial hierarchy (Venn diagram) 196
5.12 Easy-hard technique: Prefix search for the smallest hard string 220

5.13   An accepting alternating subtree of an ATM 222
5.14   ATMs as a model of parallel computation 223
5.15   ATIME(t) $\subseteq$ DSPACE(t): Initializing the $(k+1)^{\text{st}}$ tape of DTM N 225
5.16   ATIME(t) $\subseteq$ DSPACE(t): Simulating ATM M 226
5.17   ATIME(t) $\subseteq$ DSPACE(t): Evaluating ATM M 226
5.18   DTIME($2^{\mathbf{Lin}(s)}$) $\subseteq$ ASPACE(s): Head movement of DTM M 229
5.19   DTIME($2^{\mathbf{Lin}(s)}$) $\subseteq$ ASPACE(s): Computation tree of ATM N 230
5.20   The low and the high hierarchy within NP 234

6.1   Backtracking algorithm for 3-SAT 264
6.2   Algorithm RANDOM-SAT 266
6.3   Transition graph of a stochastic automaton for RANDOM-SAT 266
6.4   Illustration of the first statement of Lemma 6.20 282
6.5   Algorithm LERC for computing the least element in a right co-set .. 298
6.6   NP machine N accepting the set A 300
6.7   FP^{SPP} algorithm M^A for auto 301
6.8   Probabilistic, Arthur-Merlin, and counting classes and the
       polynomial hierarchy 310

7.1   RSA protocol 313
7.2   The "square-and-multiply" algorithm 314
7.3   RSA digital signature scheme 316
7.4   Trial division to solve the primality problem 318
7.5   Fermat test for primality 320
7.6   Primality test by Miller and Rabin 324
7.7   Primality test by Solovay and Strassen 330
7.8   Pollard's $p-1$ factoring algorithm 337

8.1   Diffie–Hellman secret-key agreement protocol 363
8.2   Shanks' baby-step giant-step algorithm 367
8.3   ElGamal's public-key cryptosystem 369
8.4   ElGamal's digital signature scheme 372
8.5   Rabin's public-key cryptosystem 381
8.6   Factoring a Rabin modulus using an oracle to break Rabin's system . 384
8.7   Arthur's labyrinth 387
8.8   Zero-knowledge protocol for graph isomorphism 389
8.9   Simulation of the zero-knowledge protocol for graph isomorphism .. 391
8.10   Fiat–Shamir zero-knowledge identification scheme 392
8.11   Merkle and Hellman's public-key cryptosystem 394
8.12   Rivest–Sherman secret-key agreement protocol 396
8.13   Paula and Ella's no-key protocol 407

List of Tables

2.1 Test run of the Euclidean Algorithm 11
2.2 Test run of the extended Euclidean Algorithm 12
2.3 The first twenty Fibonacci numbers 13
2.4 The Fibonacci numbers proliferate like rabbits and vice versa 14
2.5 Transition functions of the DFA and the NFA from Figure 2.4 21
2.6 M's transition function δ for $L = \{a^n b^n c^n \mid n \geq 1\}$ 26
2.7 Interpretation of the states of M 26
2.8 Truth tables for various boolean operations 29
2.9 Equivalences between boolean formulas 31

3.1 Some central worst-case complexity classes 61
3.2 Comparing some polynomial and exponential functions 62
3.3 What if the computers get faster? 62
3.4 Cook reduction 89

4.1 Example of an encryption by the shift cipher with key $k = 17$ 132
4.2 Example of an encryption by the affine cipher with key $k = (5, 7)$ .. 133
4.3 Frequencies of letters in long, typical English texts 134
4.4 Frequencies of letters in the ciphertext from Example 4.7 135
4.5 Guessing in the frequency counts method 135
4.6 Vigenère square 136
4.7 Example of an encryption by the Vigenère cipher with key ELLA .. 137
4.8 Example of an encryption by the Hill cipher 139
4.9 Cryptanalysis of a polyalphabetic system with period 7 140
4.10 Kasiski's method: ciphertext obtained by the Vigenère cipher 141
4.11 Kasiski's method: second column of the ciphertext rearranged 142
4.12 Kasiski's method: Vigenère ciphertext decrypted 143
4.13 Breaking the Hill cipher with a known-plaintext attack 144
4.14 Truth table for the exclusive-or operation 147
4.15 Block encryption in the CFB mode 148
4.16 Block encryption in the OFB mode 149

4.17 A ciphertext obtained by the affine cipher for Exercise 4.2(a) 162
4.18 Two ciphertexts encrypting the same plaintext for Exercise 4.3 162
4.19 A ciphertext obtained by the Hill cipher for Exercise 4.4(d) 163
4.20 A ciphertext obtained by the Vigenère cipher for Exercise 4.5 163
4.21 Beaufort square 164

5.1   Example of a $\leq_{tt}^{P}$-reduction from IN-Odd to IS 203

6.1   Running times of selected algorithms for the satisfiability problem .. 263
6.2   A ZPP computation 274
6.3   Definition of predicate C in the proof of Theorem 6.22 284

7.1   Example of an RSA encryption 316
7.2   Sieve of Eratosthenes 318
7.3   Using Fermat's Little Theorem for testing primality 319
7.4   Fermat witnesses and Fermat liars for $n = 143$ 321
7.5   MR-witnesses and MR-liars for the Carmichael number $n = 561$ ... 325
7.6   Computing $a^{(n-1)/2} \bmod n$ for the Solovay–Strassen primality test 332
7.7   Computing $x^i \bmod n$ for Pollard's $p - 1$ factoring algorithm 338
7.8   Computing $\sigma(x)$ for the quadratic sieve factoring algorithm 339
7.9   Determining $\mathfrak{B}$-smooth values $\sigma(x)$ using sieves with p 342
7.10 Running times of selected factoring algorithms 343
7.11 Factoring RSA-d numbers 344
7.12 Computing the continued fraction expansion of $101/37$............ 349
7.13 Computing the convergents in Wiener's attack 350

8.1   Computing the primitive elements modulo 17 364
8.2   Computing $\alpha = 12^{10} \bmod 17$ for the Diffie–Hellman protocol 364
8.3   Computing the sorted lists $\mathcal{L}_1$ and $\mathcal{L}_2$ for Shanks' algorithm 368
8.4   Verifying Bob's signature in ElGamal's digital signature protocol ... 373
8.5   An instance of the discrete logarithm bit problem 375

References

[ACG+03] G. Ausiello, P. Crescenzi, G. Gambosi, V. Kann, M. Marchetti-Spaccamela, and M. Protasi. *Complexity and Approximation.* Springer-Verlag, second edition, 2003.

[AD97] M. Ajtai and C. Dwork. A public-key cryptosystem with worst-case/average-case equivalence. In *Proceedings of the 29th ACM Symposium on Theory of Computing*, pages 284–293. ACM Press, 1997.

[Adl83] L. Adleman. On breaking the iterated Merkle-Hellman public key cryptosystem. In *Proceedings of the 15th ACM Symposium on Theory of Computing*, pages 402–412. ACM Press, 1983.

[AH87] L. Adleman and M. Huang. Recognizing primes in random polynomial time. In *Proceedings of the 19th ACM Symposium on Theory of Computing*, pages 462–469. ACM Press, May 1987.

[AH92a] L. Adleman and M. Huang. *Primality Testing and Abelian Varieties over Finite Fields.* Springer-Verlag *Lecture Notes in Mathematics #1512*, Berlin, Heidelberg, New York, 1992.

[AH92b] E. Allender and L. Hemachandra. Lower bounds for the low hierarchy. *Journal of the ACM*, 39(1):234–251, 1992.

[AHH+93] V. Arvind, Y. Han, L. Hemachandra, J. Köbler, A. Lozano, M. Mundhenk, M. Ogiwara, U. Schöning, R. Silvestri, and T. Thierauf. Reductions to sets of low information content. In K. Ambos-Spies, S. Homer, and U. Schöning, editors, *Complexity Theory*, pages 1–45. Cambridge University Press, 1993.

[AHS93] K. Ambos-Spies, S. Homer, and U. Schöning, editors. *Complexity Theory: Current Research.* Cambridge University Press, 1993.

[Ajt96] M. Ajtai. Generating hard instances of lattice problems. In *Proceedings of the 28th ACM Symposium on Theory of Computing*, pages 99–108. ACM Press, 1996.

[AK02a] V. Arvind and J. Köbler. New lowness results for ZPP(NP) and other complexity classes. *Journal of Computer and System Sciences*, 65(2):257–277, 2002.

[AK02b] V. Arvind and P. Kurur. Graph isomorphism is in SPP. In *Proceedings of the 43rd IEEE Symposium on Foundations of Computer Science*, pages 743–750. IEEE Computer Society Press, November 2002.

[AKS02] M. Agrawal, N. Kayal, and N. Saxena. PRIMES is in P. Unpublished manuscript, August 2002.

[All85]   E. Allender. Invertible functions, 1985. PhD thesis, Georgia Institute of Technology.

[All86]   E. Allender. The complexity of sparse sets in P. In *Proceedings of the 1st Structure in Complexity Theory Conference*, pages 1–11. Springer-Verlag *Lecture Notes in Computer Science #223*, June 1986.

[All88]   E. Allender. Isomorphisms and 1-L reductions. *Journal of Computer and System Sciences*, 36(6):336–350, 1988.

[All91]   E. Allender. Limitations of the upward separation technique. *Mathematical Systems Theory*, 24(1):53–67, 1991.

[ALM⁺98]   S. Arora, C. Lund, R. Motwani, M. Sudan, and M. Szegedy. Proof verification and intractability of approximation problems. *Journal of the ACM*, 45(3):501–555, May 1998.

[AM77]   L. Adleman and K. Manders. Reducibility, randomness, and intractibility. In *Proceedings of the 9th ACM Symposium on Theory of Computing*, pages 151–153. ACM Press, 1977.

[Ant00]   H. Anton. *Elementary Linear Algebra*. John Wiley and Sons, New York, eighth edition, 2000.

[AR88]   E. Allender and R. Rubinstein. P-printable sets. *SIAM Journal on Computing*, 17(6):1193–1202, 1988.

[Aro94]   S. Arora. *Probabilistic Checking of Proofs and Hardness of Approximation Problems*. PhD thesis, University of California at Berkeley, November 1994. Revised version available as Princeton University Technical Report CS-TR-476-94.

[Arr63]   K. Arrow. *Social Choice and Individual Values*. John Wiley and Sons, 1951 (revised editon 1963).

[AS92]   S. Arora and S. Safra. Probabilistic checking of proofs: A new characterization of NP. In *Proceedings of the 33rd IEEE Symposium on Foundations of Computer Science*, pages 2–11, 1992.

[AS98]   S. Arora and S. Safra. Probabilistic checking of proofs: A new characterization of NP. *Journal of the ACM*, 45(1):70–122, January 1998. Preliminary version appears as [AS92].

[AT99]   V. Arvind and J. Torán. Sparse sets, approximable sets, and parallel queries to NP. *Information Processing Letters*, 69:181–188, February 1999.

[AT01]   M. Agrawal and T. Thierauf. The formula isomorphism problem. *SIAM Journal on Computing*, 30(3):990–1009, June 2001.

[Bab85]   L. Babai. Trading group theory for randomness. In *Proceedings of the 17th ACM Symposium on Theory of Computing*, pages 421–429. ACM Press, April 1985.

[Bal85]   J. Balcázar. Simplicity, relativizations and nondeterminism. *SIAM Journal on Computing*, 14(1):148–157, 1985.

[Bal90]   J. Balcázar. Self-reducibility. *Journal of Computer and System Sciences*, 41(3):367–388, 1990.

[Bau00a]   F. Bauer. *Decrypted Secrets: Methods and Maxims of Cryptology*. Springer-Verlag, second edition, 2000.

[Bau00b]   F. Bauer. *Entzifferte Geheimnisse: Methoden und Maximen der Kryptologie*. Springer-Verlag, third edition, 2000. In German.

[BBJ⁺89]   A. Bertoni, D. Bruschi, D. Joseph, M. Sitharam, and P. Young. Generalized boolean hierarchies and boolean hierarchies over RP. In *Proceedings of the 7th Conference on Fundamentals of Computation Theory*, pages 35–46. Springer-Verlag *Lecture Notes in Computer Science #380*, August 1989.

[BBS86a]   J. Balcázar, R. Book, and U. Schöning. The polynomial-time hierarchy and sparse oracles. *Journal of the ACM*, 33(3):603–617, 1986.

[BBS86b]   J. Balcázar, R. Book, and U. Schöning. Sparse sets, lowness and highness. *SIAM Journal on Computing*, 15(3):739–746, 1986.

[BC89]   G. Brassard and C. Crépeau. Sorting out zero-knowledge. In *Advances in Cryptology – EUROCRYPT '89*, pages 181–191. Springer-Verlag *Lecture Notes in Computer Science #434*, April 1989.

[BC93]   D. Bovet and P. Crescenzi. *Introduction to the Theory of Complexity*. Prentice Hall, 1993.

[BCKT94]   N. Bshouty, R. Cleve, S. Kannan, and C. Tamon. Oracles and queries that are sufficient for exact learning. In *Proceedings of the 7th ACM Conference on Computational Learning Theory*, pages 130–139. ACM Press, 1994.

[BCO93]   R. Beigel, R. Chang, and M. Ogiwara. A relationship between difference hierarchies and relativized polynomial hierarchies. *Mathematical Systems Theory*, 26(3):293–310, 1993.

[BCS92]   D. Bovet, P. Crescenzi, and R. Silvestri. A uniform approach to define complexity classes. *Theoretical Computer Science*, 104(2):263–283, 1992.

[BD76]   A. Borodin and A. Demers. Some comments on functional self-reducibility and the NP hierarchy. Technical Report TR 76-284, Cornell Department of Computer Science, Ithaca, NY, July 1976.

[BD00]   D. Boneh and G. Durfee. Cryptanalysis of RSA with private key d less than $N^{0.292}$. *IEEE Transactions on Information Theory*, IT-46, 2000.

[BDG90]   J. Balcázar, J. Díaz, and J. Gabarró. *Structural Complexity II*. EATCS Monographs on Theoretical Computer Science. Springer-Verlag, 1990.

[BDG95]   J. Balcázar, J. Díaz, and J. Gabarró. *Structural Complexity I*. EATCS Monographs on Theoretical Computer Science. Springer-Verlag, second edition, 1995.

[Bei91a]   R. Beigel. Bounded queries to SAT and the boolean hierarchy. *Theoretical Computer Science*, 84(2):199–223, 1991.

[Bei91b]   R. Beigel. Relativized counting classes: Relations among thresholds, parity, and mods. *Journal of Computer and System Sciences*, 42(1):76–96, 1991.

[Ber77]   L. Berman. *Polynomial Reducibilities and Complete Sets*. PhD thesis, Cornell University, Ithaca, NY, 1977.

[Ber78]   P. Berman. Relationship between density and deterministic complexity of NP-complete languages. In *Proceedings of the 5th International Colloquium on Automata, Languages, and Programming*, pages 63–71. Springer-Verlag *Lecture Notes in Computer Science #62*, 1978.

[Ber04]   D. Bernstein. Distinguishing prime numbers from composite numbers: The state of the art in 2004. Manuscript at http://cr.yp.to/primetests.html, 2004.

[Beu94]   A. Beutelspacher. *Cryptology*. Spectrum series. Mathematical Association of America, 1994.

[Beu02]   A. Beutelspacher. *Kryptologie*. Vieweg, 6th edition, 2002. In German.

[BF98]   H. Buhrman and L. Fortnow. Two queries. In *Proceedings of the 13th Annual IEEE Conference on Computational Complexity*, pages 13–19. IEEE Computer Society Press, May 1998.

[BFH78]   G. Brassard, S. Fortune, and J. Hopcroft. A note on cryptography and NP ∩ coNP − P. Technical Report TR-338, Department of Computer Science, Cornell University, Ithaca, NY, April 1978.

[BG70]   R. Book and S. Greibach. Quasi-realtime languages. *Mathematical Systems Theory*, 4:97–111, 1970.

[BG82]   A. Blass and Y. Gurevich. On the unique satisfiability problem. *Information and Control*, 55(1–3):80–88, 1982.

420   References

[BG92]   R. Beigel and J. Gill. Counting classes: Thresholds, parity, mods, and fewness. *Theoretical Computer Science*, 103(1):3–23, 1992.

[BGS75]   T. Baker, J. Gill, and R. Solovay. Relativizations of the P=?NP question. *SIAM Journal on Computing*, 4(4):431–442, 1975.

[BH77]   L. Berman and J. Hartmanis. On isomorphisms and density of NP and other complete sets. *SIAM Journal on Computing*, 6(2):305–322, 1977.

[BH88]   S. Buss and L. Hay. On truth-table reducibility to SAT and the difference hierarchy over NP. In *Proceedings of the 3rd Structure in Complexity Theory Conference*, pages 224–233. IEEE Computer Society Press, June 1988.

[BH91]   S. Buss and L. Hay. On truth-table reducibility to SAT. *Information and Computation*, 91(1):86–102, March 1991.

[BHHR99] A. Beygelzimer, L. Hemaspaandra, C. Homan, and J. Rothe. One-way functions in worst-case cryptography: Algebraic and security properties are on the house. *SIGACT News*, 30(4):25–40, December 1999.

[BHL95]   H. Buhrman, E. Hemaspaandra, and L. Longpré. SPARSE reduces conjunctively to TALLY. *SIAM Journal on Computing*, 24(3):673–681, June 1995.

[BHR00]   B. Borchert, L. Hemaspaandra, and J. Rothe. Restrictive acceptance suffices for equivalence problems. *London Mathematical Society Journal of Computation and Mathematics*, 3:86–95, March 2000.

[BHW91]   R. Beigel, L. Hemachandra, and G. Wechsung. Probabilistic polynomial time is closed under parity reductions. *Information Processing Letters*, 37(2):91–94, 1991.

[BHZ87]   R. Boppana, J. Håstad, and S. Zachos. Does co-NP have short interactive proofs? *Information Processing Letters*, 25(2):127–132, 1987.

[BJY90]   D. Bruschi, D. Joseph, and P. Young. Strong separations for the boolean hierarchy over RP. *International Journal of Foundations of Computer Science*, 1(3):201–218, 1990.

[Bla58]   D. Black. *The Theory of Committees and Elections*. Cambridge University Press, 1958.

[Ble98]   D. Bleichenbacher. Chosen ciphertext attacks against protocols based on the RSA encryption standard PKCS #1. In *Advances in Cryptology – CRYPTO '98*, pages 1–12. Springer-Verlag *Lecture Notes in Computer Science #1462*, August 1998.

[BLO83]   E. Brickell, J. Lagarias, and A. Odlyzko. Evaluation of the Adleman attack on multiply iterated knapsack cryptosystems. In *Advances in Cryptology – CRYPTO '83*, pages 39–42, New York, 1983. Plenum Press.

[BLS99]   A. Brandstädt, V. Le, and J. Spinrad. *Graph Classes: A Survey*. SIAM Monographs on Discrete Mathematics and Applications. Society for Industrial and Applied Mathematics, Philadelphia, PA, 1999.

[Blu67]   M. Blum. A machine-independent theory of the complexity of recursive functions. *Journal of the ACM*, 14(2):322–336, April 1967.

[BM88]   L. Babai and S. Moran. Arthur-Merlin games: A randomized proof system, and a hierarchy of complexity classes. *Journal of Computer and System Sciences*, 36(2):254–276, 1988.

[BM04]   J. Blömer and A. May. A generalized Wiener attack on RSA. In *Seventh International Workshop on Practice and Theory in Public-Key Cryptography*, pages 1–13. Springer-Verlag *Lecture Notes in Computer Science #2947*, 2004.

[BO92]   E. Brickell and A. Odlyzko. Cryptanalysis, a survey of recent results. In G. Simmons, editor, *Contemporary Cryptology: The Science of Information Integrity*, pages 501–540. IEEE Computer Society Press, 1992.

[Bon85]   M. Bonuccelli. Dominating sets and dominating number of circular arc graphs. *Discrete Applied Mathematics*, 12:203–213, 1985.

[Bon99]   D. Boneh. Twenty years of attacks on the RSA cryptosystem. *Notices of the AMS*, 46(2):203–213, February 1999.

[Boo74]   R. Book. Tally languages and complexity classes. *Information and Control*, 26(2):186–193, 1974.

[Bor89]   J. Borges. The library of babel. In J. Borges and A. Kerrigan, editors, *Ficciones*, pages 79–88. Grove Press, 1989.

[BORW88] R. Book, P. Orponen, D. Russo, and O. Watanabe. Lowness properties of sets in the exponential-time hierarchy. *SIAM Journal on Computing*, 17(3):504–516, 1988.

[BR88]   J. Balcázar and D. Russo. Immunity and simplicity in relativizations of probabilistic complexity classes. *R.A.I.R.O. Theoretical Informatics and Applications*, 22(2):227–244, 1988.

[BR93]   B. Borchert and D. Ranjan. The subfunction relations are Σ_2^p-complete. Technical Report MPI-I-93-121, Max-Planck Institut Saarbrücken, Saarbrücken, Germany, 1993.

[Bra79]   G. Brassard. A note on the complexity of cryptography. *IEEE Transactions on Information Theory*, 25(2):232–233, 1979.

[Bri83]   E. Brickell. Solving low density knapsacks. In *Advances in Cryptology – CRYPTO '83*, pages 25–37, New York, 1983. Plenum Press.

[Bri85]   E. Brickell. Breaking iterated knapsacks. In *Advances in Cryptology – CRYPTO '84*, pages 342–358. Springer-Verlag *Lecture Notes in Computer Science #196*, 1985.

[BRS91]   R. Beigel, N. Reingold, and D. Spielman. PP is closed under intersection. In *Proceedings of the 23rd ACM Symposium on Theory of Computing*, pages 1–9. ACM Press, May 1991.

[BRS98]   B. Borchert, D. Ranjan, and F. Stephan. On the computational complexity of some classical equivalence relations on boolean functions. *Mathematical Systems Theory*, 31(6):679–693, 1998.

[Bru92]   D. Bruschi. Strong separations of the polynomial hierarchy with oracles: Constructive separations by immune and simple sets. *Theoretical Computer Science*, 102(2):215–252, 1992.

[BST93a]   H. Buhrman, E. Spaan, and L. Torenvliet. Bounded reductions. In K. Ambos-Spies, S. Homer, and U. Schöning, editors, *Complexity Theory*, pages 83–99. Cambridge University Press, 1993.

[BST93b]   H. Buhrmann, E. Spaan, and L. Torenvliet. The relative power of logspace and polynomial time reductions. *Computational Complexity*, 3(3):231–244, 1993.

[BSW01]   A. Beutelspacher, J. Schwenk, and K. Wolfenstetter. *Moderne Verfahren der Kryptographie*. Vieweg, 4th edition, 2001. In German.

[BT96]   H. Buhrman and L. Torenvliet. P-selective self-reducible sets: A new characterization of P. *Journal of Computer and System Sciences*, 53(2):210–217, 1996.

[BTT89a]   J. Bartholdi III, C. Tovey, and M. Trick. The computational difficulty of manipulating an election. *Social Choice and Welfare*, 6:227–241, 1989.

[BTT89b]   J. Bartholdi III, C. Tovey, and M. Trick. Voting schemes for which it can be difficult to tell who won the election. *Social Choice and Welfare*, 6:157–165, 1989.

[BTT92]   J. Bartholdi III, C. Tovey, and M. Trick. How hard is it to control an election? *Mathematical Comput. Modelling*, 16(8/9):27–40, 1992.

[Buc01]   J. Buchmann. *Introduction to Cryptography*. Undergraduate Texts in Mathematics. Springer-Verlag, 2001.

[BvHT93]   H. Buhrman, P. van Helden, and L. Torenvliet. P-selective self-reducible sets: A new characterization of P. In *Proceedings of the 8th Structure in Complexity Theory Conference*, pages 44–51. IEEE Computer Society Press, May 1993.

[Cai99]   J. Cai. Some recent progress on the complexity of lattice problems. In *Proceedings of the 14th Annual IEEE Conference on Computational Complexity*, pages 158–179. IEEE Computer Society Press, May 1999.

[Cai01]   J. Cai. $S_2^p \subseteq ZPP^{NP}$. In *Proceedings of the 42nd IEEE Symposium on Foundations of Computer Science*, pages 620–629. IEEE Computer Society Press, October 2001.

[Can96]   R. Canetti. More on BPP and the polynomial-time hierarchy. *Information Processing Letters*, 57(5):237–241, 1996.

[CCHO03]   J. Cai, V. Chakaravarthy, L. Hemaspaandra, and M. Ogihara. Competing provers yield improved Karp–Lipton collapse results. In *Proceedings of the 20th Annual Symposium on Theoretical Aspects of Computer Science*, pages 535–546. Springer-Verlag *Lecture Notes in Computer Science #2607*, 2003.

[CGH$^+$88]   J. Cai, T. Gundermann, J. Hartmanis, L. Hemachandra, V. Sewelson, K. Wagner, and G. Wechsung. The boolean hierarchy I: Structural properties. *SIAM Journal on Computing*, 17(6):1232–1252, 1988.

[CGH$^+$89]   J. Cai, T. Gundermann, J. Hartmanis, L. Hemachandra, V. Sewelson, K. Wagner, and G. Wechsung. The boolean hierarchy II: Applications. *SIAM Journal on Computing*, 18(1):95–111, 1989.

[CH86]   J. Cai and L. Hemachandra. The boolean hierarchy: Hardware over NP. In *Proceedings of the 1st Structure in Complexity Theory Conference*, pages 105–124. Springer-Verlag *Lecture Notes in Computer Science #223*, June 1986.

[CH91]   M. Cohen and J. Hashkes. A system for controlling access to broadcast transmissions. European Patent Application 0 428252 A2, May 1991.

[Cha91]   R. Chang. *On the Structure of NP Computations under Boolean Operators*. PhD thesis, Cornell University, Ithaca, NY, 1991.

[CHV92]   J. Cai, L. Hemachandra, and J. Vyskoč. Promise problems and access to unambiguous computation. In *Proceedings of the 17th Symposium on Mathematical Foundations of Computer Science*, pages 162–171. Springer-Verlag *Lecture Notes in Computer Science #629*, August 1992.

[CHV93]   J. Cai, L. Hemachandra, and J. Vyskoč. Promises and fault-tolerant database access. In K. Ambos-Spies, S. Homer, and U. Schöning, editors, *Complexity Theory*, pages 101–146. Cambridge University Press, 1993.

[CK96]   R. Chang and J. Kadin. The boolean hierarchy and the polynomial hierarchy: A closer connection. *SIAM Journal on Computing*, 25(2):340–354, April 1996.

[CKR95]   R. Chang, J. Kadin, and P. Rohatgi. On unique satisfiability and the threshold behavior of randomized reductions. *Journal of Computer and System Sciences*, 50(3):359–373, 1995.

[CKS81]   A. Chandra, D. Kozen, and L. Stockmeyer. Alternation. *Journal of the ACM*, 26(1), 1981.

[CLRS01]   T. Cormen, C. Leiserson, R. Rivest, and C. Stein. *Introduction to Algorithms*. MIT Press and McGraw-Hill, second edition, 2001.

[CLS03]   V. Conitzer, J. Lang, and T. Sandholm. How many candidates are needed to make elections hard to manipulate? In *Proceedings of the 9th Conference on Theoretical Aspects of Rationality and Knowledge*, pages 201–214. ACM Press, 2003.

[CM87]   J. Cai and G. Meyer.   Graph minimal uncolorability is D^P-complete.   *SIAM Journal on Computing*, 16(2):259–277, April 1987.

[Cob64]   A. Cobham. The intrinsic computational difficulty of functions. In *Proceedings of the 1964 International Congress for Logic Methodology and Philosophy of Science*, pages 24–30. North Holland, 1964.

[Con85]   M. J. A. N. de Caritat, Marquis de Condorcet. Essai sur l'application de l'analyse à la probabilité des décisions rendues à la pluralité des voix. 1785. Facsimile reprint of original published in Paris, 1972, by the Imprimerie Royale. English translation appears in I. McLean and A. Urken, *Classics of Social Choice*, University of Michigan Press, 1995, pages 91–112.

[Coo71]   S. Cook. The complexity of theorem-proving procedures. In *Proceedings of the 3rd ACM Symposium on Theory of Computing*, pages 151–158. ACM Press, 1971.

[Coo74]   S. Cook. An observation on time-storage trade off. *Journal of Computer and System Sciences*, 9:308–316, 1974.

[Cop97]   D. Coppersmith.   Small solutions to polynomial equations, and low exponent RSA vulnerabilities. *Journal of Cryptology*, 10(4):233–260, 1997.

[CPS99]   J. Cai, A. Pavan, and D. Sivakumar. On the hardness of permanent. In *Proceedings of the 16th Annual Symposium on Theoretical Aspects of Computer Science*, pages 90–99. Springer-Verlag *Lecture Notes in Computer Science #1563*, 1999.

[CR88]   B. Chor and R. Rivest. A knapsack-type public key cryptosystem based on arithmetic in finite fields. *IEEE Transactions on Information Theory*, IT-45(5):901–909, 1988.

[CS92]   J. Castro and C. Seara. Characterizations of some complexity classes between Θ_2^p and Δ_2^p. In *Proceedings of the 9th Annual Symposium on Theoretical Aspects of Computer Science*, pages 305–317. Springer-Verlag *Lecture Notes in Computer Science #577*, February 1992.

[CS97]   D. Coppersmith and A. Shamir. Lattice attacks on NTRU. In *Advances in Cryptology – EUROCRYPT '97*, pages 52–61. Springer-Verlag *Lecture Notes in Computer Science #1233*, 1997.

[CS99]   J. Cai and D. Sivakumar. Sparse hard sets for P: Resolution of a conjecture of Hartmanis. *Journal of Computer and System Sciences*, 58(2):280–296, April 1999.

[CS00]   J. Cai and D. Sivakumar. Resolution of Hartmanis' conjecture for NL-hard sparse sets. *Theoretical Computer Science*, 240(2):257–269, 2000.

[CS02]   V. Conitzer and T. Sandholm. Complexity of manipulating elections with few candidates. In *Proceedings of the 18th National Conference on Artificial Intelligence*, pages 314–319. AAAI Press, 2002.

[CT95]   Z. Chen and S. Toda. The complexity of selecting maximal solutions. *Information and Computation*, 119:231–239, 1995.

[CT04]   J. Cai and R. Threlfall. A note on quadratic residuosity and UP. *Information Processing Letters*, 92(3):127–131, 2004.

[CW79]   J. Carter and M. Wegman. Universal classes of hash functions. *Journal of Computer and System Sciences*, 18:143–154, 1979.

[CW04]   J. Cai and O. Watanabe. Relativized collapsing between BPP and PH under stringent oracle access. *Information Processing Letters*, 90(3):147–154, 2004.

[DGH$^+$02]   E. Dantsin, A. Goerdt, E. Hirsch, R. Kannan, J. Kleinberg, C. Papadimitriou, P. Raghavan, and U. Schöning. A deterministic $(2 - 2/(k + 1))^n$ algorithm for k-SAT based on local search. *Theoretical Computer Science*, 289(1):69–83, October 2002.

424   References

[DH76]   W. Diffie and M. Hellman. New directions in cryptography. *IEEE Transactions on Information Theory*, IT-22(6):644–654, 1976.

[Die04]   M. Dietzfelbinger. *Primality Testing in Polynomial Time: From Randomized Algorithms to "PRIMES is in P"*. Tutuorial. Springer-Verlag *Lecture Notes in Computer Science #3000*, Berlin, Heidelberg, New York, 2004.

[Dix81]   J. Dixon. Asymptotically fast factorization of integers. *Mathematics of Computation*, 36:255–260, 1981.

[DK00]   D. Du and K. Ko. *Theory of Computational Complexity*. John Wiley and Sons, 2000.

[DKNS01]   C. Dwork, R. Kumar, M. Naor, and D. Sivakumar. Rank aggregation methods for the web. In *Proceedings of the 10th International World Wide Web Conference*, pages 613–622. ACM Press, 2001.

[Dod76]   C. Dodgson. A method of taking votes on more than two issues. Pamphlet printed by the Clarendon Press, Oxford, and headed "not yet published" (see the discussions in [MU95, Bla58], both of which reprint this paper), 1876.

[DR01]   J. Daemen and V. Rijmen. *The Design of Rijndael*. Springer-Verlag, 2001.

[Edm65]   J. Edmonds. Paths, trees and flowers. *Canadian Journal of Mathematics*, 17:449–467, 1965.

[EG93]   T. Eiter and G. Gottlob. Propositional circumscription and extended closed-world reasoning are Π_2^p-complete. *Theoretical Computer Science*, 114(2):231–245, 1993. Addendum appears in the same journal, 118(2):315, 1993.

[EG97]   T. Eiter and G. Gottlob. The complexity class Θ_2^p: Recent results and applications. In *Proceedings of the 11th Conference on Fundamentals of Computation Theory*, pages 1–18. Springer-Verlag *Lecture Notes in Computer Science #1279*, September 1997.

[EHTY92]   D. Eppstein, L. Hemachandra, J. Tisdall, and B. Yener. Simultaneous strong separations of probabilistic and unambiguous complexity classes. *Mathematical Systems Theory*, 25(1):23–36, 1992.

[ElG85]   T. ElGamal. A public key cryptosystem and a signature scheme based on discrete logarithms. *IEEE Transactions on Information Theory*, IT-31(4):469–472, 1985.

[Esp01]   W. Espelage. *Bewegungsminimierung in der Förderband-Flow-Shop-Verarbeitung*. PhD thesis, Heinrich-Heine-Universität Düsseldorf, Düsseldorf, Germany, 2001. In German.

[ESY84]   S. Even, A. Selman, and Y. Yacobi. The complexity of promise problems with applications to public-key cryptography. *Information and Control*, 61(2):159–173, 1984.

[EW00]   W. Espelage and E. Wanke. Movement optimization in flow shop processing with buffers. *Mathematical Methods of Operations Research*, 51(3):495–513, 2000.

[EW01]   W. Espelage and E. Wanke. A 3-approximation algorithmus for movement minimization in conveyor flow shop processing. In *Proceedings of the 26th International Symposium on Mathematical Foundations of Computer Science*, pages 363–374. Springer-Verlag *Lecture Notes in Computer Science #2136*, 2001.

[EW03]   W. Espelage and E. Wanke. Movement minimization for unit distances in conveyor flow shop processing. *Mathematical Methods of Operations Research*, 57(2):172–206, 2003.

[EY80]   S. Even and Y. Yacobi. Cryptocomplexity and NP-completeness. In *Proceedings of the 7th International Colloquium on Automata, Languages, and Programming*, pages 195–207. Springer-Verlag *Lecture Notes in Computer Science*, 1980.

[Far84]   M. Farber. Domination, independent domination, and duality in strongly chordal graphs. *Discrete Applied Mathematics*, 7:115–130, 1984.

[Fei92]   J. Feigenbaum. Overview of interactive proof systems and zero-knowledge. In G. Simmons, editor, *Contemporary Cryptology: The Science of Information Integrity*, pages 423–439. IEEE Computer Society Press, 1992.

[Fel68]   W. Feller. *Introduction to Probability Theory and its Applications*, volume 1. John Wiley and Sons, 1968.

[FFK92]   S. Fenner, L. Fortnow, and S. Kurtz. An oracle relative to which the isomorphism conjecture holds. In *Proceedings of the 33rd IEEE Symposium on Foundations of Computer Science*, pages 30–39. IEEE Computer Society Press, October 1992.

[FFK94]   S. Fenner, L. Fortnow, and S. Kurtz. Gap-definable counting classes. *Journal of Computer and System Sciences*, 48(1):116–148, 1994.

[FFNR96]   S. Fenner, L. Fortnow, A. Naik, and J. Rogers. Inverting onto functions. In *Proceedings of the 11th Annual IEEE Conference on Computational Complexity*, pages 213–222. IEEE Computer Society Press, May 1996.

[FFNR03]   S. Fenner, L. Fortnow, A. Naik, and J. Rogers. Inverting onto functions. *Information and Computation*, 186(1):90–103, 2003.

[FFS88]   U. Feige, A. Fiat, and A. Shamir. Zero-knowledge proofs of identity. *Journal of Cryptology*, 1(2):77–94, 1988.

[FHKS02]   U. Feige, M. Halldórsson, G. Kortsarz, and A. Srinivasan. Approximating the domatic number. *SIAM Journal on Computing*, 32(1):172–195, 2002.

[Fis77]   P. Fishburn. Condorcet social choice functions. *SIAM Journal on Applied Mathematics*, 33:469–489, 1977.

[FK92]   M. Fellows and N. Koblitz. Self-witnessing polynomial-time complexity and prime factorization. *Designs, Codes and Cryptography*, 2(3):231–235, 1992.

[For79]   S. Fortune. A note on sparse complete sets. *SIAM Journal on Computing*, 8(3):431–433, 1979.

[For97]   L. Fortnow. Counting complexity. In L. Hemaspaandra and A. Selman, editors, *Complexity Theory Retrospective II*, pages 81–107. Springer-Verlag, 1997.

[FR96]   L. Fortnow and N. Reingold. PP is closed under truth-table reductions. *Information and Computation*, 124(1):1–6, 1996.

[FS86]   A. Fiat and A. Shamir. How to prove yourself: Practical solutions to identification and signature problems. In *Advances in Cryptology – CRYPTO '86*, pages 186–194. Springer-Verlag *Lecture Notes in Computer Science #263*, 1986.

[FSS84]   M. Furst, J. Saxe, and M. Sipser. Parity, circuits, and the polynomial-time hierarchy. *Mathematical Systems Theory*, 17(1):13–27, 1984.

[FY96]   L. Fortnow and T. Yamakami. Generic separations. *Journal of Computer and System Sciences*, 52(1):191–197, 1996.

[Gai39]   H. Gaines. *Cryptoanalysis*. Dover Publications, New York, 1939.

[Gas02]   W. Gasarch. The P =? NP poll. *SIGACT News*, 33(2):34–47, 2002.

[GH92]   K. Ganesan and S. Homer. Complete problems and strong polynomial reducibilities. *SIAM Journal on Computing*, 21(4):733–742, August 1992.

[GH96]   J. Goldsmith and S. Homer. Scalability and the isomorphism problem. *Information Processing Letters*, 57(3):137–143, 1996.

[GHLP99]   A. Gál, S. Halevi, R. Lipton, and E. Petrank. Computing from partial solutions. In *Proceedings of the 14th Annual IEEE Conference on Computational Complexity*, pages 34–45. IEEE Computer Society Press, May 1999.

[Gil77]   J. Gill. Computational complexity of probabilistic Turing machines. *SIAM Journal on Computing*, 6(4):675–695, 1977.

[GJ79]   M. Garey and D. Johnson. *Computers and Intractability: A Guide to the Theory of NP-Completeness*. W. H. Freeman and Company, New York, 1979.

[GJ86]   J. Goldsmith and D. Joseph. Three results on the polynomial isomorphism of complete sets. In *Proceedings of the 27th IEEE Symposium on Foundations of Computer Science*, pages 390–397, 1986.

[GJS76]   M. Garey, D. Johnson, and L. Stockmeyer. Some simplified NP-complete graph problems. *Theoretical Computer Science*, 1:237–267, 1976.

[GJY87]   J. Goldsmith, D. Joseph, and P. Young. Self-reducible, P-selective, near-testable, and P-cheatable sets: The effect of internal structure on the complexity of a set. In *Proceedings of the 2nd Structure in Complexity Theory Conference*, pages 50–59, 1987.

[GK00]   V. Guruswami and S. Khanna. On the hardness of 4-coloring a 3-colorable graph. In *Proceedings of the 15th Annual IEEE Conference on Computational Complexity*, pages 188–197. IEEE Computer Society Press, May 2000.

[GKP89]   R. Graham, D. Knuth, and O. Patashnik. *Concrete Mathematics*. Addison-Wesley, 1989.

[GMR89]   S. Goldwasser, S. Micali, and C. Rackoff. The knowledge complexity of interactive proof systems. *SIAM Journal on Computing*, 18(1):186–208, February 1989.

[GMW91]   O. Goldreich, S. Micali, and A. Wigderson. Proofs that yield nothing but their validity or all languages in NP have zero-knowledge proof systems. *Journal of the ACM*, 38(3):691–729, July 1991.

[GNW90]   T. Gundermann, N. Nasser, and G. Wechsung. A survey on counting classes. In *Proceedings of the 5th Structure in Complexity Theory Conference*, pages 140–153. IEEE Computer Society Press, July 1990.

[Gol80]   M. Golumbic. *Algorithmic Graph Theory and Perfect Graphs*. Academic Press, 1980.

[Gol88]   O. Goldreich. Randomness, interactive proofs, and zero-knowledge—A survey. In R. Herken, editor, *The Universal Turing Machine: A Half-Century Survey*, pages 377–405. Oxford University Press, Oxford, 1988.

[Gol89]   S. Goldwasser. Interactive proof systems. In J. Hartmanis, editor, *Computational Complexity Theory*, pages 108–128. AMS Short Course Lecture Notes: Introductory Survey Lectures, Proceedings of Symposia in Applied Mathematics, Volume 38, American Mathematical Society, 1989.

[Gol97]   O. Goldreich. A taxonomy of proof systems. In L. Hemaspaandra and A. Selman, editors, *Complexity Theory Retrospective II*, pages 109–134. Springer-Verlag, 1997.

[Gol99]   O. Goldreich. *Modern cryptography, probabilistic proofs, and pseudorandomness*, volume 17 of *Algorithms and Combinatorics*. Springer-Verlag, 1999.

[Gol01]   O. Goldreich. *Foundations of Cryptography*. Cambridge University Press, 2001.

[GOR98]   J. Goldsmith, M. Ogihara, and J. Rothe. Tally NP sets and easy census functions. In *Proceedings of the 23rd International Symposium on Mathematical Foundations of Computer Science*, pages 483–492. Springer-Verlag *Lecture Notes in Computer Science #1450*, August 1998.

[GOR00]   J. Goldsmith, M. Ogihara, and J. Rothe. Tally NP sets and easy census functions. *Information and Computation*, 158(1):29–52, April 2000.

[GP86]   L. Goldschlager and I. Parberry. On the construction of parallel computers from various bases of boolean functions. *Theoretical Computer Science*, 43(1):43–58, 1986.

[Gre91]   F. Green. An oracle separating $\oplus P$ from PP^{PH}. *Information Processing Letters*, 37(3):149–153, 1991.

[GRW01]   A. Große, J. Rothe, and G. Wechsung. Relating partial and complete solutions and the complexity of computing smallest solutions. In *Proceedings of the Seventh Italian Conference on Theoretical Computer Science*, pages 339–356. Springer-Verlag *Lecture Notes in Computer Science #2202*, October 2001.

[GRW02]   A. Große, J. Rothe, and G. Wechsung. Computing complete graph isomorphisms and hamiltonian cycles from partial ones. *Theory of Computing Systems*, 35(1):81–93, February 2002.

[GS88]   J. Grollmann and A. Selman. Complexity measures for public-key cryptosystems. *SIAM Journal on Computing*, 17(2):309–335, 1988.

[GS89]   S. Goldwasser and M. Sipser. Private coins versus public coins in interactive proof systems. In S. Micali, editor, *Randomness and Computation,* volume 5 of *Advances in Computing Research*, pages 73–90. JAI Press, Greenwich, 1989. A preliminary version appeared in *Proc. 18th Ann. ACM Symp. on Theory of Computing*, 1986, pp. 59–68.

[Gup91]   S. Gupta. The power of witness reduction. In *Proceedings of the 6th Structure in Complexity Theory Conference*, pages 43–59. IEEE Computer Society Press, June/July 1991.

[Gup93]   S. Gupta. On bounded-probability operators and ⊕P. *Information Processing Letters*, 48:93–98, 1993.

[GW87]   T. Gundermann and G. Wechsung. Counting classes with finite acceptance types. *Computers and Artificial Intelligence*, 6(5):395–409, 1987.

[Hač79]   L. Hačijan. A polynomial algorithm in linear programming. *Soviet Math. Dokl.*, 20:191–194, 1979.

[Har69]   F. Harary. *Graph Theory*. Addison-Wesley, 1969.

[Har74]   F. Harary. A survey of the reconstruction conjecture. In *Graphs and Combinatorics*, pages 18–28. Springer-Verlag *Lecture Notes in Mathematics #406*, 1974.

[Har78]   J. Hartmanis. On log-tape isomorphisms of complete sets. *Theoretical Computer Science*, 7(3):273–286, 1978.

[Har83a]   J. Hartmanis. Generalized Kolmogorov complexity and the structure of feasible computations. In *Proceedings of the 24th IEEE Symposium on Foundations of Computer Science*, pages 439–445. IEEE Computer Society Press, 1983.

[Har83b]   J. Hartmanis. On sparse sets in NP−P. *Information Processing Letters*, 16(2):55–60, 1983.

[Har89]   J. Hartmanis. Gödel, von Neumann, and the P =? NP problem. *Bulletin of the EATCS*, 38:101–107, 1989.

[Hås88]   J. Håstad. Solving simultaneous modular equations of low degree. *SIAM Journal on Computing*, 17(2):336–341, April 1988. Special issue on cryptography.

[Hau14]   F. Hausdorff. *Grundzüge der Mengenlehre*. Walter de Gruyter and Co., 1914.

[Hem87]   L. Hemachandra. The strong exponential hierarchy collapses. In *Proceedings of the 19th ACM Symposium on Theory of Computing*, pages 110–122. ACM Press, May 1987.

[Hem89]   L. Hemachandra. The strong exponential hierarchy collapses. *Journal of Computer and System Sciences*, 39(3):299–322, 1989.

[Hem93]   L. Hemaspaandra. Lowness: A yardstick for NP-P. *SIGACT News*, 24 (Spring)(2):10–14, 1993.

[Hem98]   H. Hempel. *Boolean Hierarchies – On Collapse Properties and Query Order*. PhD thesis, Friedrich-Schiller-Universität Jena, Jena, Germany, October 1998.

[Her90]   U. Hertrampf. Relations among MOD-classes. *Theoretical Computer Science*, 74(3):325–328, 1990.

[HH88]   J. Hartmanis and L. Hemachandra. Complexity classes without machines: On complete languages for UP. *Theoretical Computer Science*, 58(1–3):129–142, 1988.

[HH91]   J. Hartmanis and L. Hemachandra. One-way functions and the nonisomorphism of NP-complete sets. *Theoretical Computer Science*, 81(1):155–163, 1991.

[HH00]   E. Hemaspaandra and L. Hemaspaandra. Computational politics: Electoral systems. In *Proceedings of the 25th International Symposium on Mathematical Foundations of Computer Science*, pages 64–83. Springer-Verlag *Lecture Notes in Computer Science #1893*, 2000.

[HHGP⁺03]   J. Hoffstein, N. Howgrave-Graham, J. Pipher, J. Silverman, and W. Whyte. NTRUSIGN: Digital signatures using the NTRU lattice. In *Topics in Cryptology – CT-RSA 2003, The Cryptographers' Track at the RSA Conference*, pages 122–140. Springer-Verlag *Lecture Notes in Computer Science #2612*, 2003.

[HHH98a]   E. Hemaspaandra, L. Hemaspaandra, and H. Hempel. Query order in the polynomial hierarchy. *Journal of Universal Computer Science*, 4(6):574–588, June 1998.

[HHH98b]   E. Hemaspaandra, L. Hemaspaandra, and H. Hempel. What's up with downward collapse: Using the easy-hard technique to link boolean and polynomial hierarchy collapses. *SIGACT News*, 29(3):10–22, 1998.

[HHH99]   E. Hemaspaandra, L. Hemaspaandra, and H. Hempel. A downward collapse within the polynomial hierarchy. *SIAM Journal on Computing*, 28(2):383–393, 1999.

[HHH01]   E. Hemaspaandra, L. Hemaspaandra, and H. Hempel. Using the no-search easy-hard technique for downward collapse. Technical Report TR-752, University of Rochester, Department of Computer Science, Rochester, NY, June 2001. Earlier versions or parts of this paper appeared in the Proceedings of the *Sixth Italian Conference on Theoretical Computer Science* (ICTCS'98) and of the *16th Annual Symposium on Theoretical Aspects of Computer Science* (STACS'99).

[HHR97a]   E. Hemaspaandra, L. Hemaspaandra, and J. Rothe. Exact analysis of Dodgson elections: Lewis Carroll's 1876 voting system is complete for parallel access to NP. *Journal of the ACM*, 44(6):806–825, November 1997.

[HHR97b]   E. Hemaspaandra, L. Hemaspaandra, and J. Rothe. Raising NP lower bounds to parallel NP lower bounds. *SIGACT News*, 28(2):2–13, June 1997.

[HHR05]   E. Hemaspaandra, L. Hemaspaandra, and J. Rothe. Anyone but him: The complexity of precluding an alternative. In *Proceedings of the 20th National Conference on Artificial Intelligence*. AAAI Press, 2005. To appear.

[HHRT04]   E. Hemaspaandra, L. Hemaspaandra, S. Radziszowski, and R. Tripathi. Complexity results in graph reconstruction. In *Proceedings of the 29th International Symposium on Mathematical Foundations of Computer Science*, pages 287–297. Springer-Verlag *Lecture Notes in Computer Science #3153*, 2004.

[HHT97]   Y. Han, L. Hemaspaandra, and T. Thierauf. Threshold computation and cryptographic security. *SIAM Journal on Computing*, 26(1):59–78, February 1997.

[HHW99]   L. Hemaspaandra, H. Hempel, and G. Wechsung. Query order. *SIAM Journal on Computing*, 28(2):637–651, 1999.

[HIS85]   J. Hartmanis, N. Immerman, and V. Sewelson. Sparse sets in NP−P: EXPTIME versus NEXPTIME. *Information and Control*, 65(2/3):159–181, 1985.

[HJ95]   L. Hemaspaandra and S. Jha. Defying upward and downward separation. *Information and Computation*, 121:1–13, 1995.

[HJRW97]   L. Hemaspaandra, Z. Jiang, J. Rothe, and O. Watanabe. Polynomial-time multiselectivity. *Journal of Universal Computer Science*, 3(3):197–229, March 1997.

[HJRW98] L. Hemaspaandra, Z. Jiang, J. Rothe, and O. Watanabe. Boolean operations, joins, and the extended low hierarchy. *Theoretical Computer Science*, 205(1–2):317–327, September 1998.

[HK73]   J. Hopcroft and R. Karp. An $n^{5/2}$ algorithm for maximum matching in bipartite graphs. *SIAM Journal on Computing*, 2:225–231, 1973.

[HL94]   S. Homer and L. Longpré. On reductions of NP sets to sparse sets. *Journal of Computer and System Sciences*, 48(2):324–336, April 1994.

[HLS65]   J. Hartmanis, P. Lewis, and R. Stearns. Classification of computations by time and memory requirements. In *Proc. IFIP Congress 65*, pages 31–35, Washington, D.C., 1965. International Federation for Information Processing, Spartan Books.

[HM80]   J. Hartmanis and S. Mahaney. An essay about research on sparse NP complete sets. In *Proceedings of the 9th Symposium on Mathematical Foundations of Computer Science*, pages 40–57. Springer-Verlag *Lecture Notes in Computer Science #88*, September 1980.

[HM83]   S. Homer and W. Maass. Oracle dependent properties of the lattice of NP sets. *Theoretical Computer Science*, 24(3):279–289, 1983.

[HMU01]   J. Hopcroft, R. Motwani, and J. Ullman. *Introduction to Automata Theory, Languages, and Computation*. Addison-Wesley, second edition, 2001.

[HNOS96] E. Hemaspaandra, A. Naik, M. Ogihara, and A. Selman. P-selective sets and reducing search to decision vs. self-reducibility. *Journal of Computer and System Sciences*, 53(2):194–209, 1996.

[HO93]   L. Hemachandra and M. Ogiwara. Is #P closed under subtraction? In G. Rozenberg and A. Salomaa, editors, *Current Trends in Theoretical Computer Science: Essays and Tutorials*, pages 523–536. World Scientific Press, 1993.

[HO02]   L. Hemaspaandra and M. Ogihara. *The Complexity Theory Companion*. EATCS Texts in Theoretical Computer Science. Springer-Verlag, Berlin, Heidelberg, New York, 2002.

[Hof82]   C. Hoffman. *Group-Theoretic Algorithms and Graph Isomorphism. Lecture Notes in Computer Science #136*. Springer-Verlag, 1982.

[Hom04]   C. Homan. Tight lower bounds on the ambiguity in strong, total, associative, one-way functions. *Journal of Computer and System Sciences*, 68(3):657–674, 2004.

[HOW92]   L. Hemachandra, M. Ogiwara, and O. Watanabe. How hard are sparse sets? In *Proceedings of the 7th Structure in Complexity Theory Conference*, pages 222–238. IEEE Computer Society Press, June 1992.

[HPR01]   L. Hemaspaandra, K. Pasanen, and J. Rothe. If P $\neq$ NP then some strongly noninvertible functions are invertible. In *Proceedings of the 13th International Symposium on Fundamentals of Computation Theory*, pages 162–171. Springer-Verlag *Lecture Notes in Computer Science #2138*, August 2001.

[HPS98]   J. Hoffstein, J. Pipher, and J. Silverman. NTRU: A ring-based public key cryptosystem. In *Proceedings of the Third International Symposium on Algorithmic Number Theory*, pages 267–288, 1998.

[HPS01]   J. Hoffstein, J. Pipher, and J. Silverman. NSS: An NTRU lattice-based signature scheme. In *Advances in Cryptology – EUROCRYPT '01*, pages 211–228. Springer-Verlag *Lecture Notes in Computer Science #2045*, 2001.

[HR95]   L. Hemaspaandra and J. Rothe. Intersection suffices for boolean hierarchy equivalence. In *Proceedings of the First Annual International Computing and Combinatorics Conference*, pages 430–435. Springer-Verlag *Lecture Notes in Computer Science #959*, August 1995.

430   References

[HR97a]   E. Hemaspaandra and J. Rothe. Recognizing when greed can approximate maximum independent sets is complete for parallel access to NP. Technical Report Math/Inf/97/14, Friedrich-Schiller-Universität Jena, Jena, Germany, May 1997.

[HR97b]   L. Hemaspaandra and J. Rothe. Unambiguous computation: Boolean hierarchies and sparse Turing-complete sets. *SIAM Journal on Computing*, 26(3):634–653, June 1997.

[HR98]   E. Hemaspaandra and J. Rothe. Recognizing when greed can approximate maximum independent sets is complete for parallel access to NP. *Information Processing Letters*, 65(3):151–156, February 1998.

[HR99]   L. Hemaspaandra and J. Rothe. Creating strong, total, commutative, associative one-way functions from any one-way function in complexity theory. *Journal of Computer and System Sciences*, 58(3):648–659, June 1999.

[HR00]   L. Hemaspaandra and J. Rothe. Characterizing the existence of one-way permutations. *Theoretical Computer Science*, 244(1–2):257–261, August 2000.

[HRS]   E. Hemaspaandra, J. Rothe, and H. Spakowski. Recognizing when heuristics can approximate minimum vertex covers is complete for parallel access to NP. *R.A.I.R.O. Theoretical Informatics and Applications*. To appear.

[HRS04]   L. Hemaspaandra, J. Rothe, and A. Saxena. Enforcing and defying associativity, commutativity, totality, and strong noninvertibility for one-way functions in complexity theory. Technical Report TR-854, Department of Computer Science, University of Rochester, Rochester, NY, December 2004. Revised in April, 2005. Also appears as ACM Computing Research Repository (CoRR) Technical Report cs.CC/050304, April 2005.

[HRSZ98]   L. Hemaspaandra, K. Rajasethupathy, P. Sethupathy, and M. Zimand. Power balance and apportionment algorithms for the United States Congress. *The ACM Journal of Experimental Algorithmics*, 3(1):article 1, 16 pp., 1998.

[HRW97a]   L. Hemaspaandra, J. Rothe, and G. Wechsung. Easy sets and hard certificate schemes. *Acta Informatica*, 34(11):859–879, November 1997.

[HRW97b]   L. Hemaspaandra, J. Rothe, and G. Wechsung. On sets with easy certificates and the existence of one-way permutations. In *Proceedings of the Third Italian Conference on Algorithms and Complexity*, pages 264–275. Springer-Verlag *Lecture Notes in Computer Science #1203*, March 1997.

[HS65]   J. Hartmanis and R. Stearns. On the computational complexity of algorithms. *Transactions of the American Mathematical Society*, 117:285–306, 1965.

[HS66]   F. Hennie and R. Stearns. Two-tape simulation of multitape Turing machines. *Journal of the ACM*, 13:533–546, 1966.

[HS89]   S. Homer and A. Selman. Oracles for structural properties: the isomorphism problem and public-key cryptography. In *Proceedings of the 4th Structure in Complexity Theory Conference*, pages 3–14. IEEE Computer Society Press, June 1989.

[HS97]   L. Hemaspaandra and A. Selman, editors. *Complexity Theory Retrospective II*. Springer-Verlag, 1997.

[HS01]   S. Homer and A. Selman. *Computability and Complexity Theory*. Texts in Computer Science. Springer-Verlag, 2001.

[HSV]   E. Hemaspaandra, H. Spakowski, and J. Vogel. The complexity of Kemeny elections. *Theoretical Computer Science*. Accepted subject to minor revision.

[HT98]   P. Heggernes and J. Telle. Partitioning graphs into generalized dominating sets. *Nordic Journal of Computing*, 5(2):128–142, 1998.

[HT02]   C. Homan and M. Thakur. One-way permutations and self-witnessing languages. In R. Baeza-Yates, U. Montanari, and N. Santoro, editors, *Foundations of Information Technology in the Era of Network and Mobile Computing*, pages 243–254. Kluwer Academic Publishers, August 2002. Proceedings of the Second IFIP International Conference on Theoretical Computer Science, Stream 1 of the 17th IFIP World Computer Congress.

[HT03a]   L. Hemaspaandra and L. Torenvliet. *Theory of Semi-Feasible Algorithms*. EATCS Monographs in Theoretical Computer Science. Springer-Verlag, 2003.

[HT03b]   C. Homan and M. Thakur. One-way permutations and self-witnessing languages. *Journal of Computer and System Sciences*, 67(3):608–622, 2003.

[HW79]   G. Hardy and E. Wright. *An Introduction to the Theory of Numbers*. Clarendon Press, Oxford, 5th edition, 1979.

[HW97]   E. Hemaspaandra and G. Wechsung. The minimization problem for boolean formulas. In *Proceedings of the 38th IEEE Symposium on Foundations of Computer Science*, pages 575–584. IEEE Computer Society Press, October 1997.

[HW02]   E. Hemaspaandra and G. Wechsung. The minimization problem for boolean formulas. *SIAM Journal on Computing*, 31(6):1948–1958, 2002.

[HY84]   J. Hartmanis and Y. Yesha. Computation times of NP sets of different densities. *Theoretical Computer Science*, 34(1–2):17–32, 1984.

[HZ96]   L. Hemaspaandra and M. Zimand. Strong self-reducibility precludes strong immunity. *Mathematical Systems Theory*, 29(5):535–548, 1996.

[Imm88]   N. Immerman. Nondeterministic space is closed under complementation. *SIAM Journal on Computing*, 17:935–938, 1988.

[IN96]   R. Impagliazzo and M. Naor. Efficient cryptographic schemes provably as secure as subset sum. *Journal of Cryptology*, 9(4):199–216, 1996.

[IT03]   K. Iwama and S. Tamaki. Improved upper bounds for 3-SAT. Technical Report TR03-053, Electronic Colloquium on Computational Complexity, July 2003. 3 pages.

[Jac74]   N. Jacobson. *Basic Algebra I*. W. H. Freeman, 1974.

[JL76]   N. Jones and W. Laaser. Problems complete for deterministic polynomial time. *Theoretical Computer Science*, 3(1):105–117, October 1976.

[JLL76]   N. Jones, Y. Lien, and W. Laaser. New problems complete for nondeterministic log space. *Mathematical Systems Theory*, 10(1):1–17, 1976.

[Joh81]   D. Johnson. The NP-completeness column: An ongoing guide. *Journal of Algorithms*, 2(4):393–405, December 1981. First column in a series of columns on NP-completeness appearing in the same journal.

[Jon75]   N. Jones. Space-bounded reducibility among combinatorial problems. *Journal of Computer and System Sciences*, 11:68–75, 1975.

[JY85]   D. Joseph and P. Young. Some remarks on witness functions for nonpolynomial and noncomplete sets in NP. *Theoretical Computer Science*, 39(2–3):225–237, August 1985.

[JY90]   D. Joseph and P. Young. Self-reducibility: Effects of internal structure on computational complexity. In A. Selman, editor, *Complexity Theory Retrospective*, pages 82–107. Springer-Verlag, 1990.

[Kad88]   J. Kadin. The polynomial time hierarchy collapses if the boolean hierarchy collapses. *SIAM Journal on Computing*, 17(6):1263–1282, 1988. Erratum appears in the same journal, 20(2):404, 1991.

[Kad89]   J. Kadin. $P^{NP[\log n]}$ and sparse Turing-complete sets for NP. *Journal of Computer and System Sciences*, 39(3):282–298, 1989.

[Kah67]   D. Kahn. *The Codebreakers: The Story of Secret Writing*. MacMillan Publishing Company, 1967.

[Kar72]   R. Karp. Reducibilities among combinatorial problems. In R. Miller and J. Thatcher, editors, *Complexity of Computer Computations*, pages 85–103, 1972.

[KH94]   D. Kratsch and L. Hemaspaandra. On the complexity of graph reconstruction. *Mathematical Systems Theory*, 27(3):257–273, 1994.

[KIT88]   K. Kurosawa, T. Ito, and M. Takeuchi. Preliminary comments on the MIT public-key cryptosystem. *Cryptologia*, 12(4):225–233, 1988.

[KL80]   R. Karp and R. Lipton. Some connections between nonuniform and uniform complexity classes. In *Proceedings of the 12th ACM Symposium on Theory of Computing*, pages 302–309. ACM Press, April 1980. An extended version has also appeared as: Turing machines that take advice, *L'Enseignement Mathématique*, 2nd series 28, 1982, pages 191–209.

[KLD86]   K. Ko, T. Long, and D. Du. On one-way functions and polynomial-time isomorphisms. *Theoretical Computer Science*, 47:263–276, 1986.

[Kle52]   S. Kleene. *Introduction to Metamathematics*. D. van Nostrand Company, Inc., New York and Toronto, 1952.

[KLS00]   S. Khanna, N. Linial, and S. Safra. On the hardness of approximating the chromatic number. *Combinatorica*, 20(3):393–415, 2000.

[KMR87]   S. Kurtz, S. Mahaney, and J. Royer. Progress on collapsing degrees. In *Proceedings of the 2nd Structure in Complexity Theory Conference*, pages 126–131. IEEE Computer Society Press, June 1987.

[KMR88]   S. Kurtz, S. Mahaney, and J. Royer. Collapsing degrees. *Journal of Computer and System Sciences*, 37:247–268, 1988.

[KMR89]   S. Kurtz, S. Mahaney, and J. Royer. The isomorphism conjecture fails relative to a random oracle. In *Proceedings of the 21st ACM Symposium on Theory of Computing*, pages 157–166. ACM Press, May 1989.

[KMR90]   S. Kurtz, S. Mahaney, and J. Royer. The structure of complete degrees. In A. Selman, editor, *Complexity Theory Retrospective*, pages 108–146. Springer-Verlag, 1990.

[Knu98]   D. Knuth. *The Art of Computer Programming: Seminumerical Algorithms*, volume 2 of *Computer Science and Information*. Addison-Wesley, third edition, 1998.

[Ko82]   K. Ko. Some observations on the probabilistic algorithms and NP-hard problems. *Information Processing Letters*, 14(1):39–43, 1982.

[Ko85]   K. Ko. On some natural complete operators. *Theoretical Computer Science*, 37(1):1–30, 1985.

[Ko90]   K. Ko. A note on separating the relativized polynomial time hierarchy by immune sets. *R.A.I.R.O. Theoretical Informatics and Applications*, 24(3):229–240, 1990.

[Köb89]   J. Köbler. *Strukturelle Komplexität von Anzahlproblemen*. PhD thesis, University of Stuttgart, Stuttgart, Germany, 1989. In German.

[Köb94]   J. Köbler. Locating P/poly optimally in the extended low hierarchy. *Theoretical Computer Science*, 134:263–285, 1994.

[Köb95]   J. Köbler. On the structure of low sets. In *Proceedings of the 10th Structure in Complexity Theory Conference*, pages 246–261. IEEE Computer Society Press, 1995.

[Kob97]   N. Koblitz. *Algebraic Aspects of Cryptography*, volume 3 of *Algorithms and Computation in Mathematics*. Springer-Verlag, 1997.

[KPP04]   H. Kellerer, U. Pferschy, and D. Pisinger. *Knapsack Problems*. Springer-Verlag, Berlin, Heidelberg, New York, 2004.

[KR95]   B. Kaliski Jr. and M. Robshaw. The secure use of RSA. *CryptoBytes*, 1(3):7–13, 1995.

[Kre88]   M. Krentel. The complexity of optimization problems. *Journal of Computer and System Sciences*, 36:490–509, 1988.

[KRS88]   B. Kaliski Jr., R. Rivest, and A. Sherman. Is the data encryption standard a group? (Results of cycling experiments on DES). *Journal of Cryptology*, 1(1):3–36, 1988.

[KS85]   K. Ko and U. Schöning. On circuit-size complexity and the low hierarchy in NP. *SIAM Journal on Computing*, 14(1):41–51, 1985.

[KS94]   H. Kaplan and R. Shamir. The domatic number problem on some perfect graph families. *Information Processing Letters*, 49(1):51–56, January 1994.

[KS01]   R. Kumar and D. Sivakumar. Complexity of SVP—A reader's digest. *SIGACT News*, 32(3):40–52, June 2001.

[KS04]   N. Kayal and N. Saxena. On the ring isomorphism & automorphism problems. Technical Report TR04-109, Electronic Colloquium on Computational Complexity, October 2004.

[KST89]   J. Köbler, U. Schöning, and J. Torán. On counting and approximation. *Acta Informatica*, 26(4):363–379, 1989.

[KST92]   J. Köbler, U. Schöning, and J. Torán. Graph isomorphism is low for PP. *Computational Complexity*, 2:301–330, 1992.

[KST93]   J. Köbler, U. Schöning, and J. Torán. *The Graph Isomorphism Problem: Its Structural Complexity*. Birkhäuser, 1993.

[KSTT92]   J. Köbler, U. Schöning, S. Toda, and J. Torán. Turing machines with few accepting computations and low sets for PP. *Journal of Computer and System Sciences*, 44(2):272–286, 1992.

[KSW87]   J. Köbler, U. Schöning, and K. Wagner. The difference and truth-table hierarchies for NP. *R.A.I.R.O. Informatique théorique et Applications*, 21:419–435, 1987.

[Kur64]   S. Kuroda. Classes of languages and linear-bounded automata. *Information and Control*, 7(2):207–223, June 1964.

[KV91]   S. Khuller and V. Vazirani. Planar graph coloring is not self-reducible, assuming $P \neq NP$. *Theoretical Computer Science*, 88(1):183–189, 1991.

[KW98]   J. Köbler and O. Watanabe. New collapse consequences of NP having small circuits. *SIAM Journal on Computing*, 28(1):311–324, 1998.

[Lad75]   R. Ladner. On the structure of polynomial time reducibility. *Journal of the ACM*, 22(1):155–171, 1975.

[Lag83]   J. Lagarias. Knapsack public key cryptosystems and diophantine approximation. In *Advances in Cryptology – CRYPTO '83*, pages 3–23, New York, 1983. Plenum Press.

[Lau83]   C. Lautemann. BPP and the polynomial hierarchy. *Information Processing Letters*, 17(4):215–217, 1983.

[Len83]   H. Lenstra Jr. Integer programming with a fixed number of variables. *Mathematics of Operations Research*, 8:538–548, 1983.

[Len87]   H. Lenstra Jr. Factoring integers with elliptic curves. *Annals of Mathematics*, 126:649–673, 1987.

[Lev73]   L. Levin. Universal sorting problems. *Problemy Peredaci Informacii*, 9:115–116, 1973. In Russian. English translation in *Problems of Information Transmission*, 9:265–266, 1973.

[Lis86]   G. Lischke. Oracle constructions to prove all possible relationships between relativizations of P, NP, NEL, EP, and NEP. *Zeitsch. f. math. Logik und Grundlagen d. Math.*, 32:257–270, 1986.

[Lis99]   G. Lischke. Towards the actual relationship between NP and exponential time. *Mathematical Logic Quarterly*, 45(1):31–49, 1999. A preliminary version has appeared as: Impossibilities and possibilities of weak separation between NP and exponential time. In *Proceedings of the 5th Structure in Complexity Theory Conference*, pages 245–253. IEEE Computer Society Press, 1990.

[LL76]   R. Ladner and N. Lynch. Relativization of questions about log space computability. *Mathematical Systems Theory*, 10(1):19–32, 1976.

[LL93]   A. Lenstra and H. Lenstra, Jr. *The Development of the Number Field Sieve*, volume 1554 of *Lecture Notes in Mathematics*. Springer-Verlag, 1993.

[LLL82]   A. Lenstra, H. Lenstra, Jr., and L. Lovász. Factoring polynomials with rational coefficients. *Mathematische Annalen*, 261:513–534, 1982.

[LLS75]   R. Ladner, N. Lynch, and A. Selman. A comparison of polynomial time reducibilities. *Theoretical Computer Science*, 1(2):103–124, 1975.

[LO85]   J. Lagarias and A. Odlyzko. Solving low-density subset sum problems. *Journal of the ACM*, 32(1):229–246, 1985.

[LO91]   B. LaMacchia and A. Odlyzko. Computation of discrete logarithms in prime fields. *Designs, Codes and Cryptography*, 1(1):47–62, 1991.

[Lon82a]   T. Long. A note on sparse oracles for NP. *Journal of Computer and System Sciences*, 24:224–232, 1982.

[Lon82b]   T. Long. Strong nondeterministic polynomial-time reducibilities. *Theoretical Computer Science*, 21:1–25, 1982.

[Lon85]   T. Long. On restricting the size of oracles compared with restricting access to oracles. *SIAM Journal on Computing*, 14(3):585–597, 1985. Erratum appears in the same journal, 17(3):628, 1988.

[LOT03]   M. Liśkiewicz, M. Ogiwara, and S. Toda. The complexity of counting self-avoiding walks in subgraphs of two-dimensional grids and hypercubes. *Theoretical Computer Science*, 304(1–3):129–156, July 2003.

[LR94]   K.-J. Lange and P. Rossmanith. Unambiguous polynomial hierarchies and exponential size. In *Proceedings of the 9th Structure in Complexity Theory Conference*, pages 106–115. IEEE Computer Society Press, June/July 1994.

[LS86]   T. Long and A. Selman. Relativizing complexity classes with sparse oracles. *Journal of the ACM*, 33(3):618–627, 1986.

[LSH65]   P. Lewis, R. Stearns, and J. Hartmanis. Memory bounds for recognition of context-free and context-sensitive languages. In *Proceedings of the 6th IEEE Symposium on Switching Circuit Theory and Logical Design*, pages 191–202, 1965.

[Lub96]   M. Luby. *Pseudorandomness and Cryptographic Applications*. Princeton Computer Science Notes. Princeton University Press, Princeton, New Jersey, 1996.

[Mah82]   S. Mahaney. Sparse complete sets for NP: Solution of a conjecture of Berman and Hartmanis. *Journal of Computer and System Sciences*, 25(2):130–143, 1982.

[Mah86]   S. Mahaney. Sparse sets and reducibilities. In R. Book, editor, *Studies in Complexity Theory*, pages 63–118. John Wiley and Sons, 1986.

[Mah89]   S. Mahaney. The isomorphism conjecture and sparse sets. In J. Hartmanis, editor, *Computational Complexity Theory*, pages 18–46. American Mathematical Society, 1989. Proceedings of Symposia in Applied Mathematics #38.

[Mat79]   R. Mathon. A note on the graph isomorphism counting problem. *Information Processing Letters*, 8(3):131–132, 1979.

[May04]   A. May. Computing the RSA secret key is deterministic polynomial time equivalent to factoring. In *Advances in Cryptology – CRYPTO '04*, pages 213–219. Springer-Verlag *Lecture Notes in Computer Science #3152*, 2004.

[MG02]   D. Micciancio and S. Goldwasser. *Complexity of Lattice Problems: A Cryptographic Perspective*, volume 671 of *The Kluwer International Series in Engineering and Computer Science*. Kluwer Academic Publishers, Boston, Massachusetts, March 2002.

[MH78]   R. Merkle and M. Hellman. Hiding information and signatures in trapdoor knapsacks. *IEEE Transactions on Information Theory*, IT-24(5):525–530, 1978.

[Mil76]   G. Miller. Riemann's hypothesis and tests for primality. *Journal of Computer and System Sciences*, 13:300–317, 1976.

[Moo92]   J. Moore. Protocol failures in cryptosystems. In G. Simmons, editor, *Contemporary Cryptology: The Science of Information Integrity*, pages 541–558. IEEE Computer Society Press, 1992.

[MP79]   A. Meyer and M. Paterson. With what frequency are apparently intractable problems difficult? Technical Report MIT/LCS/TM-126, MIT Laboratory for Computer Science, Cambridge, MA, 1979.

[MS72]   A. Meyer and L. Stockmeyer. The equivalence problem for regular expressions with squaring requires exponential space. In *Proceedings of the 13th IEEE Symposium on Switching and Automata Theory*, pages 125–129, 1972.

[MS85]   B. Monien and E. Speckenmeyer. Solving satisfiability in less than 2^n steps. *Discrete Applied Mathematics*, 10:287–295, 1985.

[MU95]   I. McLean and A. Urken. *Classics of Social Choice*. University of Michigan Press, Ann Arbor, Michigan, 1995.

[Mül93]   H. Müller. A note on balanced immunity. *Mathematical Systems Theory*, 26(2):157–167, 1993.

[MW99]   U. Maurer and S. Wolf. The relationship between breaking the Diffie-Hellman protocol and computing discrete logarithms. *SIAM Journal on Computing*, 28(5):1689–1721, 1999.

[MW00]   U. Maurer and S. Wolf. The Diffie–Hellman protocol. *Designs, Codes and Cryptography*, 19(2/3):147–171, 2000.

[MY85]   S. Mahaney and P. Young. Reductions among polynomial isomorphism types. *Theoretical Computer Science*, 39:207–224, 1985.

[Nat91]   National Institute of Standards and Technology (NIST). Digital signature standard (DSS). *Federal Register*, 56(169), August 1991.

[Nat92]   National Institute of Standards and Technology (NIST). The Digital Signature Standard, proposed by NIST. *Communications of the Association for Computing Machinery*, 35(7):36–40, July 1992.

[NR98]   R. Niedermeier and P. Rossmanith. Unambiguous computations and locally definable acceptance types. *Theoretical Computer Science*, 194:137–161, 1998.

[NS01]   P. Nguyen and J. Stern. The two faces of lattices in cryptology. In *Proceedings of the International Conference on Cryptography and Lattices*, pages 146–180. Springer-Verlag *Lecture Notes in Computer Science #2146*, 2001.

[Odi89]   P. Odifreddi. *Classical Recursion Theory*. North-Holland, 1989.

[Odl85]   A. Odlyzko. *Discrete Logarithms in Finite Fields and Their Cryptographic Significance*. Springer-Verlag *Lecture Notes in Computer Science #209*, Berlin, Heidelberg, New York, 1985.

[Odl00]   A. Odlyzko. Discrete logarithms: The past and the future. *Designs, Codes and Cryptography*, 19(2/3):129–145, 2000.

[Ogi95]   M. Ogihara. Sparse hard sets for P yield space-efficient algorithms. In *Proceedings of the 36th IEEE Symposium on Foundations of Computer Science*, pages 354–361. IEEE Computer Society Press, 1995.

436   References

[OH93]   M. Ogiwara and L. Hemachandra. A complexity theory for feasible closure properties. *Journal of Computer and System Sciences*, 46(3):295–325, 1993.

[OT01]   M. Ogihara and S. Toda. The complexity of computing the number of self-avoiding walks in two-dimensional grid graphs and in hypercube graphs. In *Proceedings of the 26th International Symposium on Mathematical Foundations of Computer Science*, pages 585–597. Springer-Verlag *Lecture Notes in Computer Science #2136*, 2001.

[OW91]   M. Ogiwara and O. Watanabe. On polynomial-time bounded truth-table reducibility of NP sets to sparse sets. *SIAM Journal on Computing*, 20(3):471–483, June 1991.

[OW02]   T. Ottmann and P. Widmayer. *Algorithmen und Datenstrukturen*. Spektrum Akademischer Verlag, Heidelberg, Berlin, fourth edition, 2002. In German.

[Pap84]   C. Papadimitriou. On the complexity of unique solutions. *Journal of the ACM*, 31(2):392–400, 1984.

[Pap94]   C. Papadimitriou. *Computational Complexity*. Addison-Wesley, 1994.

[Pol74]   J. Pollard. Theorems on factorization and primality testing. *Proc. Cambridge Philos. Soc.*, 76:521–528, 1974.

[PPSZ98]   R. Paturi, P. Pudlák, M. Saks, and F. Zane. An improved exponential-time algorithm for k-SAT. In *Proceedings of the 39th IEEE Symposium on Foundations of Computer Science*, pages 628–637. IEEE Computer Society Press, November 1998.

[Pra75]   V. Pratt. Every prime has a succinct certificate. *SIAM Journal on Computing*, 4(3):214–220, 1975.

[PS82]   C. Papadimitriou and K. Steiglitz. *Combinatorial Optimization: Algorithms and Complexity*. Prentice-Hall, 1982.

[PW88]   C. Papadimitriou and D. Wolfe. The complexity of facets resolved. *Journal of Computer and System Sciences*, 37(1):2–13, 1988.

[PY84]   C. Papadimitriou and M. Yannakakis. The complexity of facets (and some facets of complexity). *Journal of Computer and System Sciences*, 28(2):244–259, 1984.

[PZ83]   C. Papadimitriou and S. Zachos. Two remarks on the power of counting. In *Proceedings of the 6th GI Conference on Theoretical Computer Science*, pages 269–276. Springer-Verlag *Lecture Notes in Computer Science #145*, 1983.

[Rab60]   M. Rabin. Degree of difficulty of computing a function and a partial ordering of recursive sets. Technical Report Technical Report 2, The Hebrew University, Jerusalem, Israel, 1960.

[Rab79]   M. Rabin. Digitalized signatures and public-key functions as intractable as factorization. Technical Report LCS/TR-212, Massachussetts Institute of Technology, Laboratory for Computer Science, 1979.

[Rab80]   M. Rabin. Probabilistic algorithms for testing primality. *Journal of Number Theory*, 12:128–138, 1980.

[Rac82]   C. Rackoff. Relativized questions involving probabilistic algorithms. *Journal of the ACM*, 29(1):261–268, 1982.

[Raz87]   A. Razborov. Lower bounds on the size of bounded depth circuits over a complete basis with logical addition. *Mat. Zametki*, 41(4):598–607, 1987. In Russian. English Translation in *Mathematical Notes of the Academy of Sciences of the USSR*, 41(4):333–338, 1987.

[Rei90]   R. Reischuk. *Einführung in die Komplexitätstheorie*. Teubner, Stuttgart, 1990. In German.

[RH02]   J. Rothe and L. Hemaspaandra. On characterizing the existence of partial one-way permutations. *Information Processing Letters*, 82(3):165–171, May 2002.

[Rog67]   H. Rogers, Jr. *The Theory of Recursive Functions and Effective Computability.* McGraw-Hill, 1967.

[Rog97]   J. Rogers. The Isomorphism Conjecture holds and one-way functions exist relative to an oracle. *Journal of Computer and System Sciences*, 54(3):412–423, June 1997.

[Roh95]   P. Rohatgi. Saving queries with randomness. *Journal of Computer and System Sciences*, 50(3):476–492, 1995.

[Ros67]   A. Rosenberg. Real-time definable languages. *Journal of the ACM*, 14:645–662, 1967.

[Ros99]   K. Rosen. *Elementary Number Theory and its Applications.* Addison-Wesley, 1999.

[Rot95]   J. Rothe. A promise class at least as hard as the polynomial hierarchy. *Journal of Computing and Information*, 1(1):92–107, April 1995. Special Issue: *Proceedings of the Sixth International Conference on Computing and Information*, CD-ROM ISSN 1201-8511, Trent University Press.

[Rot99]   J. Rothe. Immunity and simplicity for exact counting and other counting classes. *R.A.I.R.O. Theoretical Informatics and Applications*, 33(2):159–176, March/April 1999.

[Rot02]   J. Rothe. Some facets of complexity theory and cryptography: A five-lecture tutorial. *ACM Computing Surveys*, 34(4):504–549, December 2002.

[Rot03]   J. Rothe. Exact complexity of Exact-Four-Colorability. *Information Processing Letters*, 87(1):7–12, July 2003.

[Rot04a]   J. Rothe. Bonyolultságelmélet (Complexity Theory). In A. Iványi, editor, *Informatikai Algoritmusok I (Algorithms of Computer Science I)*, pages 125–160. ELTE Eötvös Kiadó, 2004. In Hungarian. German version available on-line at http://www.cs.uni-duesseldorf.de/~rothe/TONY/main.pdf.

[Rot04b]   J. Rothe. Erlkönig. In H. Hempel, editor, *Wechsung in Jena. Ein Sammelband mit Erinnerungen an das Wirken von Gerd Wechsung an der alma mater jenensis*, page 114, Jena, Germany, February 2004. Appeared also in *Informatik Spektrum*, 27(1):80, Springer-Verlag, February 2004.

[Rot04c]   J. Rothe. Kriptográfia (Cryptography). In A. Iványi, editor, *Informatikai Algoritmusok I (Algorithms of Computer Science I)*, pages 94–124. ELTE Eötvös Kiadó, 2004. In Hungarian. German version available on-line at http://www.cs.uni-duesseldorf.de/~rothe/TONY/main.pdf.

[RR04]   T. Riege and J. Rothe. Complexity of the exact domatic number problem and of the exact conveyor flow shop problem. *Theory of Computing Systems*, December 2004. On-line publication DOI 10.1007/s00224-004-1209-8. Paper publication to appear.

[RRW94]   R. Rao, J. Rothe, and O. Watanabe. Upward separation for FewP and related classes. *Information Processing Letters*, 52(4):175–180, April 1994. Corrigendum appears in the same journal, 74(1–2):89, 2000.

[RS59]   M. Rabin and D. Scott. Finite automata and their decision problems. *IBM Journal of Research and Development*, 3:114–125, 1959.

[RS93]   M. Rabi and A. Sherman. Associative one-way functions: A new paradigm for secret-key agreement and digital signatures. Technical Report CS-TR-3183/UMIACS-TR-93-124, Department of Computer Science, University of Maryland, College Park, Maryland, 1993.

[RS97]   M. Rabi and A. Sherman. An observation on associative one-way functions in complexity theory. *Information Processing Letters*, 64(5):239–244, 1997.

[RS98]   A. Russell and R. Sundaram. Symmetric alternation captures BPP. *Computational Complexity*, 7(2):152–162, 1998.

[RSA78]   R. Rivest, A. Shamir, and L. Adleman. A method for obtaining digital signature and public-key cryptosystems. *Communications of the ACM*, 21(2):120–126, 1978.

[RSV02]   J. Rothe, H. Spakowski, and J. Vogel. Exact complexity of Exact-Four-Colorability and of the winner problem for Young elections. In R. Baeza-Yates, U. Montanari, and N. Santoro, editors, *Foundations of Information Technology in the Era of Network and Mobile Computing*, pages 310–322. Kluwer Academic Publishers, August 2002. Proceedings of the Second IFIP International Conference on Theoretical Computer Science, Stream 1 of the 17th IFIP World Computer Congress.

[RSV03]   J. Rothe, H. Spakowski, and J. Vogel. Exact complexity of the winner problem for Young elections. *Theory of Computing Systems*, 36(4):375–386, June 2003.

[Rue86]   R. Rueppel. *Analysis and Design of Stream Ciphers*. Springer-Verlag, Berlin, Heidelberg, New York, 1986.

[RW01]   S. Reith and K. Wagner. On boolean lowness and boolean highness. *Theoretical Computer Science*, 261(2):305–321, June 2001.

[Saa95]   D. Saari. *Basic Geometry of Voting*. Springer-Verlag, Berlin, Germany, 1995.

[Saa01]   D. Saari. *Chaotic Elections! A Mathematician Looks at Voting*. American Mathematical Society, 2001.

[Sal73]   A. Salomaa. *Formal Languages*. Academic Press, 1973.

[Sal96]   A. Salomaa. *Public-Key Cryptography*, volume 23 of *EATCS Monographs on Theoretical Computer Science*. Springer-Verlag, second edition, 1996.

[Sav70]   W. Savitch. Relationships between nondeterministic and deterministic tape complexities. *Journal of Computer and System Sciences*, 4(2):177–192, 1970.

[Sav73]   W. Savitch. Maze recognizing automata and nondeterministic tape complexity. *Journal of Computer and System Sciences*, 7(4):389–403, August 1973.

[SB84]   U. Schöning and R. Book. Immunity, relativization, and nondeterminism. *SIAM Journal on Computing*, 13(2):329–337, 1984.

[Sch76]   C. Schnorr. Optimal algorithms for self-reducible problems. In S. Michaelson and R. Milner, editors, *Proceedings of the 3rd International Colloquium on Automata, Languages, and Programming*, pages 322–337, University of Edinburgh, July 1976. Edinburgh University Press.

[Sch79]   C. Schnorr. On self-transformable combinatorial problems, 1979. Presented at *IEEE Symposium on Information Theory*, Udine, and *Symposium über Mathematische Optimierung*, Oberwolfach.

[Sch81]   U. Schöning. A note on complete sets for the polynomial hierarchy. *SIGACT News*, 13:30–34, 1981.

[Sch82]   U. Schöning. A uniform approach to obtain diagonal sets in complexity classes. *Theoretical Computer Science*, 18:95–103, 1982.

[Sch83]   U. Schöning. A low and a high hierarchy within NP. *Journal of Computer and System Sciences*, 27:14–28, 1983.

[Sch87]   U. Schöning. Probabilistic complexity classes and lowness. In *Proceedings of the 2nd Structure in Complexity Theory Conference*, pages 2–8. IEEE Computer Society Press, June 1987.

[Sch88]   U. Schöning. Graph isomorphism is in the low hierarchy. *Journal of Computer and System Sciences*, 37(3):312–323, 1988.

[Sch89]   U. Schöning. Probabilistic complexity classes and lowness. *Journal of Computer and System Sciences*, 39(1):84–100, 1989.

[Sch90]   C. Schnorr. Efficient identification and signature schemes for smart cards. In *Advances in Cryptology – CRYPTO '89*, pages 239–251. Springer-Verlag *Lecture Notes in Computer Science #435*, February 1990.

[Sch95a]   U. Schöning. *Logik für Informatiker*. Spektrum Akademischer Verlag, Heidelberg, Berlin, 1995. In German.

[Sch95b]   U. Schöning. *Perlen der Theoretischen Informatik*. BI Wissenschaftsverlag, Mannheim, 1995. In German.

[Sch96]   B. Schneier. *Applied Cryptography: Protocols, Algorithms, and Source Code in C*. John Wiley and Sons, New York, second edition, 1996.

[Sch99]   U. Schöning. A probabilistic algorithm for k-SAT and constraint satisfaction problems. In *Proceedings of the 40th IEEE Symposium on Foundations of Computer Science*, pages 410–414. IEEE Computer Society Press, October 1999.

[Sch01]   U. Schöning. *Algorithmik*. Spektrum Akademischer Verlag, Heidelberg, Berlin, 2001. In German.

[Sch02a]   U. Schöning. *Ideen der Informatik*. Oldenbourg Verlag, München, Wien, 2002. In German.

[Sch02b]   U. Schöning. A probabilistic algorithm for k-SAT based on limited local search and restart. *Algorithmica*, 32(4):615–623, 2002.

[Sch05]   U. Schöning. Algorithmics in exponential time. In *Proceedings of the 22nd Annual Symposium on Theoretical Aspects of Computer Science*, pages 36–43. Springer-Verlag *Lecture Notes in Computer Science #3404*, 2005.

[Sel78]   A. Selman. Polynomial time enumeration reducibility. *SIAM Journal on Computing*, 7(4):440–457, 1978.

[Sel79]   A. Selman. P-selective sets, tally languages, and the behavior of polynomial time reducibilities on NP. *Mathematical Systems Theory*, 13:55–65, 1979.

[Sel82a]   A. Selman. Analogues of semirecursive sets and effective reducibilities to the study of NP complexity. *Information and Control*, 52:36–51, 1982.

[Sel82b]   A. Selman. Reductions on NP and P-selective sets. *Theoretical Computer Science*, 19:287–304, 1982.

[Sel88a]   A. Selman. Natural self-reducible sets. *SIAM Journal on Computing*, 17(5):989–996, 1988.

[Sel88b]   A. Selman. Promise problems complete for complexity classes. *Information and Computation*, 78:87–98, 1988.

[Sel90]   A. Selman, editor. *Complexity Theory Retrospective*. Springer-Verlag, 1990.

[Sel92]   A. Selman. A survey of one-way functions in complexity theory. *Mathematical Systems Theory*, 25(3):203–221, 1992.

[Sel94]   A. Selman. A taxonomy of complexity classes of functions. *Journal of Computer and System Sciences*, 48(2):357–381, 1994.

[SH95]   C. Schnorr and H. Hörner. Attacking the Chor–Rivest cryptosystem by improved lattice reduction. In *Advances in Cryptology – EUROCRYPT '89*, pages 1–12. Springer-Verlag *Lecture Notes in Computer Science #921*, May 1995.

[Sha49]   C. Shannon. Communication theory of secrecy systems. *Bell System Technical Journal*, 28(4):657–715, 1949.

[Sha54]   D. Shanks. A logarithm algorithm. *Math. Tables and Other Aids to Computation*, 8:60–64, 1954.

[Sha83]   A. Shamir. Embedding cryptographic trapdoors in arbitrary knapsack systems. *Information Processing Letters*, 17(2):77–79, 1983.

[Sha84]   A. Shamir. A polynomial-time algorithm for breaking the basic Merkle-Hellman cryptosystem. *IEEE Transactions on Information Theory*, IT-30(5):699–704, 1984.

[Sha92]   A. Shamir. IP = PSPACE. *Journal of the ACM*, 39(4):869–877, 1992.

[Sha95]   A. Shamir. RSA for paranoids. *CryptoBytes*, 1(3):1–4, 1995.

[SHL65]   R. Stearns, J. Hartmanis, and P. Lewis. Hierarchies of memory limited computations. In *Proceedings of the 6th IEEE Symposium on Switching Circuit Theory and Logical Design*, pages 179–190, 1965.

[Sho67]   J. Shoenfield. *Mathematical Logic*. Addison-Wesley, 1967.

[Sim75]   J. Simon. *On Some Central Problems in Computational Complexity*. PhD thesis, Cornell University, Ithaca, NY, January 1975. Available as Cornell Department of Computer Science Technical Report TR75-224.

[Sim79]   G. Simmons. Symmetric and asymmetric encryption. *ACM Computing Surveys*, 11(4):305–330, 1979.

[Sin99]   S. Singh. *The Code Book. The Science of Secrecy from Ancient Egypt to Quantum Cryptography*. Fourth Estate, London, 1999.

[Sip80]   M. Sipser. Halting space-bounded computations. *Theoretical Computer Science*, 10(3):335–338, March 1980.

[Sip83]   M. Sipser. A complexity theoretic approach to randomness. In *Proceedings of the 15th ACM Symposium on Theory of Computing*, pages 330–335. ACM Press, 1983.

[Sip92]   M. Sipser. The history and status of the P versus NP question. In *Proceedings of the 24th ACM Symposium on Theory of Computing*, pages 603–618. ACM Press, 1992.

[SL94]   M. Sheu and T. Long. The extended low hierarchy is an infinite hierarchy. *SIAM Journal on Computing*, 23(3):488–509, 1994.

[Smo87]   R. Smolensky. Algebraic methods in the theory of lower bounds for boolean circuit complexity. In *Proceedings of the 19th ACM Symposium on Theory of Computing*, pages 77–82. ACM Press, May 1987.

[SN77]   G. Simmons and M. Norris. Preliminary comments on the MIT public-key cryptosystem. *Cryptologia*, 1(4):406–414, 1977.

[Soa77]   R. Soare. Computational complexity, speedability, and levelable sets. *Journal of Symbolic Logic*, 42:545–563, 1977.

[Soa87]   R. Soare. *Recursively Enumerable Sets and Degrees: A Study of Computable Functions and Computably Generated Sets*. Perspectives in Mathematical Logic. Springer-Verlag, 1987.

[SS77]   R. Solovay and V. Strassen. A fast Monte Carlo test for primality. *SIAM Journal on Computing*, 6:84–85, 1977. Erratum appears in the same journal, 7(1):118, 1978.

[Ste90]   R. Stearns. Juris Hartmanis: The beginnings of computational complexity. In A. Selman, editor, *Complexity Theory Retrospective*, pages 1–18. Springer-Verlag, 1990.

[Sti95]   D. Stinson. *Cryptography: Theory and Practice*. CRC Press, Boca Raton, 1995.

[Sti02]   D. Stinson. *Cryptography: Theory and Practice*. CRC Press, Boca Raton, second edition, 2002.

[Sto73]   L. Stockmeyer. Planar 3-colorability is NP-complete. *SIGACT News*, 5(3):19–25, 1973.

[Sto77]   L. Stockmeyer. The polynomial-time hierarchy. *Theoretical Computer Science*, 3(1):1–22, 1977.

[SU02a]   M. Schaefer and C. Umans. Completeness in the polynomial-time hierarchy: Part I: A compendium. *SIGACT News*, 33(3):32–49, September 2002.

[SU02b]   M. Schaefer and C. Umans. Completeness in the polynomial-time hierarchy: Part II. *SIGACT News*, 33(4):22–36, December 2002.

[Sud95]   M. Sudan. *Efficient Checking of Polynomials and Proofs and the Hardness of Approximation Problems*. Springer-Verlag *Lecture Notes in Computer Science #1001*, 1995. ACM Distinguished Thesis. Based on the author's Ph.D. thesis, UC Berkeley, 1992.

[SV00]   H. Spakowski and J. Vogel. Θ_2^p-completeness: A classical approach for new results. In *Proceedings of the 20th Conference on Foundations of Software Technology and Theoretical Computer Science*, pages 348–360. Springer-Verlag *Lecture Notes in Computer Science #1974*, December 2000.

[SZ80]   A. Shamir and R. Zippel. On the security of the Merkle-Hellman cryptographic scheme. *IEEE Transactions on Information Theory*, IT-26(3):339–340, 1980.

[Sze88]   R. Szelepcsényi. The method of forced enumeration for nondeterministic automata. *Acta Informatica*, 26:279–284, 1988.

[Tar93]   J. Tarui. Probabilistic polynomials, AC^0 functions and the polynomial-time hierarchy. *Theoretical Computer Science*, 113:167–183, 1993.

[Thi00]   T. Thierauf. *The Computational Complexity of Equivalence and Isomorphism Problems*. Springer-Verlag *Lecture Notes in Computer Science #1852*, New York, NY, USA, 2000.

[TO92]   S. Toda and M. Ogiwara. Counting classes are at least as hard as the polynomial-time hierarchy. *SIAM Journal on Computing*, 21(2):316–328, 1992.

[Tod91]   S. Toda. PP is as hard as the polynomial-time hierarchy. *SIAM Journal on Computing*, 20(5):865–877, 1991.

[Tor91]   J. Torán. Complexity classes defined by counting quantifiers. *Journal of the ACM*, 38(3):753–774, 1991.

[Tur36]   A. Turing. On computable numbers, with an application to the Entscheidungsproblem. *Proceedings of the London Mathematical Society, ser. 2*, 42:230–265, 1936. Correction, *ibid*, vol. 43, pp. 544–546, 1937.

[TvEB89]   L. Torenvliet and P. van Emde Boas. Simplicity, immunity, relativizations and nondeterminism. *Information and Computation*, 80(1):1–17, 1989.

[Uma98]   C. Umans. The Minimum Equivalent DNF problem and shortest implicants. In *Proceedings of the 39th IEEE Symposium on Foundations of Computer Science*, pages 556–563. IEEE Computer Society Press, November 1998.

[Val76]   L. Valiant. The relative complexity of checking and evaluating. *Information Processing Letters*, 5(1):20–23, 1976.

[Val79a]   L. Valiant. The complexity of computing the permanent. *Theoretical Computer Science*, 8(2):189–201, 1979.

[Val79b]   L. Valiant. The complexity of enumeration and reliability problems. *SIAM Journal on Computing*, 8(3):410–421, 1979.

[Vau01]   S. Vaudenay. Cryptanalysis of the Chor–Rivest cryptosystem. *Journal of Cryptology*, 14(2):87–100, 2001.

[Vaz03]   V. Vazirani. *Approximation Algorithms*. Springer-Verlag, second edition, 2003.

[Ver92]   N. Vereshchagin. On the power of PP. In *Proceedings of the 7th Structure in Complexity Theory Conference*, pages 138–143. IEEE Computer Society Press, June 1992.

[Vol99]   H. Vollmer. *Introduction to Circuit Theory*. EATCS Texts in Theoretical Computer Science. Springer-Verlag, 1999.

[VV86]   L. Valiant and V. Vazirani. NP is as easy as detecting unique solutions. *Theoretical Computer Science*, 47:85–93, 1986.

[Wag86]   K. Wagner. The complexity of combinatorial problems with succinct input representations. *Acta Informatica*, 23:325–356, 1986.

[Wag87a] K. Wagner. More complicated questions about maxima and minima, and some closures of NP. *Theoretical Computer Science*, 51:53–80, 1987.

[Wag87b] K. Wagner. Number-of-query hierarchies. Institut für Mathematik 158, Universität Augsburg, Augsurg, Germany, October 1987.

[Wag89] K. Wagner. Number-of-query hierarchies. Institut für Informatik 4, Universität Würzburg, Würzburg, Germany, February 1989.

[Wag90] K. Wagner. Bounded query classes. *SIAM Journal on Computing*, 19(5):833–846, 1990.

[Wan97] J. Wang. Average-case computational complexity theory. In L. Hemaspaandra and A. Selman, editors, *Complexity Theory Retrospective II*, pages 295–328. Springer-Verlag, 1997.

[Wat88] O. Watanabe. On hardness of one-way functions. *Information Processing Letters*, 27(3):151–157, 1988.

[Wat91] O. Watanabe. On the P-isomorphism conjecture. *Theoretical Computer Science*, 83(2):337–343, June 1991.

[Wec85] G. Wechsung. On the boolean closure of NP. In *Proceedings of the 5th Conference on Fundamentals of Computation Theory*, pages 485–493. Springer-Verlag *Lecture Notes in Computer Science #199* , 1985. (An unpublished precursor of this paper was coauthored by K. Wagner).

[Wec00] G. Wechsung. *Vorlesungen zur Komplexitätstheorie*, volume 32 of *Teubner-Texte zur Informatik*. Teubner, Stuttgart, 2000. In German.

[Weg87] I. Wegener. *The Complexity of Boolean Functions*. Wiley Teubner Series in Computer Science. John Wiley and Sons, New York, 1987.

[Weg03] I. Wegener. *Komplexitätstheorie. Grenzen der Effizienz von Algorithmen*. Springer-Verlag, Berlin, Heidelberg, New York, 2003. In German.

[Wel93] D. Welsh. *Complexity: Knots, Colourings and Counting*. Cambridge University Press, 1993.

[Wel98] D. Welsh. *Codes and Cryptography*. Oxford science publications. Clarendon Press, Oxford, 6th edition, 1998. Reprinted with corrections.

[Wie90] M. Wiener. Cryptanalysis of short RSA secret exponents. *IEEE Transactions on Information Theory*, IT-36(3):553–558, 1990.

[Wil80] H. Williams. A modification of the RSA public-key encryption procedure. *IEEE Transactions on Information Theory*, IT-26(6):726–729, 1980.

[Woe03] G. Woeginger. Exact algorithms for NP-hard problems. In M. Jünger, G. Reinelt, and G. Rinaldi, editors, *Combinatorical Optimization: "Eureka, you shrink!"*, pages 185–207. Springer-Verlag *Lecture Notes in Computer Science #2570*, 2003.

[Wra77] C. Wrathall. Complete sets and the polynomial-time hierarchy. *Theoretical Computer Science*, 3:23–33, 1977.

[WW86] K. Wagner and G. Wechsung. *Computational Complexity*. D. Reidel Publishing Company, 1986. Distributors for the U.S.A. and Canada: Kluwer Academic Publishers.

[Yap83] C. Yap. Some consequences of non-uniform conditions on uniform classes. *Theoretical Computer Science*, 26:287–300, 1983.

[You77] H. Young. Extending Condorcet's rule. *Journal of Economic Theory*, 16:335–353, 1977.

[You83] P. Young. Some structural properties of polynomial reducibilities and sets in NP. In *Proceedings of the 15th ACM Symposium on Theory of Computing*, pages 392–401. ACM Press, April 1983.

[You90]   P. Young. Juris Hartmanis: Fundamental contributions to isomorphism problems. In A. Selman, editor, *Complexity Theory Retrospective*, pages 28–58. Springer-Verlag, 1990.

[You92]   P. Young. How reductions to sparse sets collapse the polynomial-time hierarchy: A primer. *SIGACT News*, 1992. Part I (#3, pages 107–117), Part II (#4, pages 83–94), and Corrigendum to Part I (#4, page 94).

[Zac82]   S. Zachos. Robustness of probabilistic complexity classes under definitional perturbations. *Information and Computation*, 54(3):143–154, 1982.

[Zac88]   S. Zachos. Probabilistic quantifiers and games. *Journal of Computer and System Sciences*, 36:433–451, 1988.

[ZH86]   S. Zachos and H. Heller. A decisive characterization of BPP. *Information and Control*, 69:125–135, 1986.

[Zim04]   M. Zimand. *Computational Complexity: A Quantitative Perspective*, volume 196 of *North-Holland Mathematics Studies*. Elsevier, 2004.

Index

□   **23**
⌊·⌋   **11**, 65
⌈·⌉   **11**, 66
|·| **16**
‖·‖   **16**
*   **17**
+   **17**
⁻   **17**
∪   **17**
∩   **17**
⊢   **18**
⊢*   **18**
¬   **29**, 30
∨   **29**, 30
∧   **29**, 30
⟹   **29**, 30
⟺   **29**, 30
⊕   **147, 258**
Δ   **239**
⋁   see ∃
⋀   see ∀
∃   **32**
∃^{p} 190, **191**, 196, 198
∃$^+$ **280**, 281–297, 303
∀   **32**

∀^{p} 190, **191**, 196, 198
∨   **174**, 241
∧   **174**, 241
Δ **256**
⋈   **189**, 243
≡   **31, 36, 50**
≅   **43**
≅$_p$ **117**
∘   **37, 59, 273**
≤   **38**
≤$_{ae}$, <$_{ae}$, ≥$_{ae}$, >$_{ae}$ **59**
≤$_{io}$, <$_{io}$, ≥$_{io}$, >$_{io}$ **59**
≼, ≺, ≽, ≻   **60**
≼$_{io}$, ≺$_{io}$, ≽$_{io}$, ≻$_{io}$ **60**
≤$_m^{log}$ **79**, 81, 82, 84, 86, 87, 121, 122, 193, 231, 232 , 244
≤$_m^{log}$-completeness   **79**, 82, 84, 121, 122, 231, 232
≤$_m^{log}$-hardness   **79**
≤$_m^p$ **77**, 78, 116, 185, 193, 194, 236–239, 244, 246, 255, 274, 278, 294, 297, 303, 309, 310
≤$_m^p$-completeness   **77**, 109, 110, 112, 213, 236–239, 246, 255, 274, 278, 294, 297

$\leq^{P}_{m}$-hardness   **77**
$\leq^{NP}_{T}$ **193**, 244, 252
$\leq^{NP}_{T}$-hardness   218
$\leq^{NP}_{sT}$ **233**, 236, 245, 246, 257
$\leq^{NP}_{sT}$-completeness   **233**
$\leq^{NP}_{sT}$-hardness   **233**
$\leq^{P}_{pos\text{-}T}$ 194, **244**, 252
$\leq^{P}_{T}$ 125, **193**, 194, 238, 244, 246, 252, 254, 293, 308
$\leq^{P}_{T}$-completeness   **193**, 233, 255
$\leq^{P}_{T}$-hardness   125, **193**, 244, 254
$\leq^{P}_{tt}$ **202**, 203, 252, 255
$\leq^{P}_{tt}$-completeness   **202**
$\leq^{P}_{tt}$-hardness   **202**
$\left(\frac{m}{n}\right)$ **40**
#P   124, 262, 290, **291**, 303–305, 308
  – closure properties of,
      see function class, closure of a
#P-completeness   **124**
#P$_1$ **124**, 125
#P$_1$-completeness   124
#RA   358
$\oplus$P   125, 291, **292**, 293, 294, 298, 302, 303, 306, 308–310
$\oplus$P-low   293, 308
$\oplus$P^{SPP} 293
2-Colorability   **95**, 116
2$^{\mathbf{Lin}}$ **59**
2$^{\mathbf{Lin}(\cdot)}$ **59**
2$^{\mathbf{Pol}}$ **59**
2$^{\mathbf{Pol}(\cdot)}$ **59**
2-SAT   55, **83**, 84, 87, 121
3-Colorability   5, 55, **95**, 116, 172, 185, 250
3-DM   **99**, 100, 117, 190
3-SAT   55, **83**, 92, 185, 120, 250, 262–265, 306
4-SAT   263, 306
5-SAT   263, 306
6-SAT   263, 306

A
$\alpha(\cdot)$ **202**
absorption   **31**

accepting computation
      see Turing machine, computation of a, accepting
  – number of —s   *see* acc$_M$
acc$_M$ **270**
adjoint matrix   **138**
Adleman, L.   257, 311, 312, 357, 358, 410
Advanced Encryption Standard,   *see also* AES   170
AES   170
affine cipher   *see* cipher, affine
affine linear cipher   *see* cipher, affine linear
AGAP   **232**
Agrawal, M.   106, 118, 252, 311, 335, 344, 357
Ajtai, M.   411, 412
Alberti, B.   168
AL   **231**
algebra   **37–41**, 51
al Choresmi, M.   9
algorithm, *see also* Turing machine 9
  – baby-step giant-step
      see SHANKS
  – *see* BACKTRACKING-SAT
  – *see* EUCLID
  – execution time of an   61
  – *see* EXTENDED-EUCLID
  – *see* FERMAT
  – Monte Carlo   6, 261, 268, **271**, 323
    no-biased,   *see also* RP   **271**, 273, 321, 323, 329, 333, 358
    yes-biased, *see also* coRP   **271**, 273, 321
  – Las Vegas,   *see also* ZPP   6, 261, 268, **273**, 357, 382–384
  – *see* LERC
  – *see* LLL
  – *see* MILLER-RABIN
  – *see* POLLARD
  – randomized   6, 7, 46, 110, 241, **261–310**, 382, 383
  – *see* RANDOM-FACTOR

– *see* RANDOM-SAT
– random walk   266
– *see* SHANKS
– *see* SOLOVAY-STRASSEN
– *see* SQUARE-AND-MULTIPLY
– *see* TRIAL-DIVISION
algorithmic device   54
algorithmics   **9–16**, 51
Alice   1
Al-Khowarizmi, A. *see* al Choresmi, M.
Allen, W.   142, 163
Allender, E.   119, 123, 258
ALOGTIME   **224**
alphabet   **16**
– set of strings over an,
    see also Σ^* **16**
alternating logarithmic space,
    see also AL   6, **231**
alternating logarithmic time,
    see also ALOGTIME   53, **224**
alternating polynomial time,
    see also AP   6, **228**
alternating sums hierarchy   250
– *see also* boolean hierarchy, normal form
alternating Turing machine *see* ATM;
    see Turing machine, alternating
alternation   221–232
alternative   *see* candidate
AM   **286**, 287, 288, 290, 292, 296, 303, 310
– *see also* Arthur-Merlin games
$AM^{AM\cap coAM}$ 290
AMA   **286**, 287, 288, 303
– *see also* Arthur-Merlin games
AMH   **286**, 287, 390
– *see also* Arthur-Merlin games
Ambos-Spies, K.   VIII, 8
Anton, H.   51
AP   **228**
approximability   8, 121, 251, 254
arithmetics modulo an integer
    see $\mathbb{Z}_n$, arithmetics in
Arora, S.   251

Arrow, K.   206
Arthur   *see* Arthur-Merlin games
Arthur's labyrinth   387
Arthur-Merlin games   7, 251, 261, 262, **279–290**, 296, 303, 307, 310, 361, **386–393**, 409
Arthur-Merlin hierarchy   *see* AMH;
    see Arthur-Merlin games
artificial intelligence   251, 254
Arvind, V.   122, 255, 299, 309
ASPACE($\cdot$)   **223**, 228–231, 245
Assing, S.   VIII
associativity   **31**, **37**, **398**
– weak   **398**, 411
asymmetric cryptography
    see cryptography, asymmetric;
    see cryptography, public-key
asymmetric cryptosystem
    see cryptosystem, asymmetric;
    see cryptosystem, public-key
ATIME($\cdot$)   **223**, 225–228, 245
ATM   53, 54, 58, 171, **221**, 222, 223
attack,   *see also* cryptanalytic attack
– active   129, 365
– chosen-ciphertext   **128**, 316, 353, 358, 385, 404
– chosen-message
    see attack, chosen-plaintext
– chosen-plaintext   **128**, 142, 316, 352, 353, 377, 385
– ciphertext-only   **128**, 132, 133, 155, 167
– impersonation   129
– key-only   **128**, 377
– known-message
    see attack, known-plaintext
– known-plaintext   **128**, 142, 144, 155, 162, 165, 377
– man-in-the-middle   129, 365, 386
– passive   129
– substitution   129
Aurich, V.   VIII
Ausiello, G.   8, 251
Aut($\cdot$)   **43**

authentication   2, 7, 129, 361, 365, 386–393, 410
authentication code   129
authentication problem   129
  – *see* message authentication
  – *see* message integrity
  – *see* user authentication
authentication protocol   386–393
  – *see* challenge-and-response protocol
  – *see* zero-knowledge protocol
auto   **299**, 301, 305
automorphism of a graph,   *see also* Aut($\cdot$)   **43**
axe   *see* tools, axe

B
Babai, L.   7, 307, 409
Babbage, C.   140, 151, 168
baby cloning   4, 100
baby-step giant-step algorithm
    see SHANKS
BACKTRACKING-SAT **264**, 265, 302
Baker, T.   258
balanced immunity   258, 259
Balcázar, J.   8, 118, 121, 257, 307, 308, 409
Bartholdi III, J.   253
Bauer, F.   2, 168, 169
Bayes, T.   46
Bayes's Theorem
    see Theorem, Bayes's
BC($\mathcal{C}$)   **174**, 175, 242
BC(NP)   **174**, 176, 216, 241
Beatles   162
Beaufort, F.   164
Beaufort cipher
    see cipher, Beaufort
Beaufort square   **164**
Beckwith, J.   VII
Beigel, R.   218, 250, 254, 256, 307, 308
Berman, L.   6, 108–110, 122, 123, 125, 255, 412

Berman–Hartmanis conjecture
    see isomorphism conjecture
Bernstein, D.   357, 358
Bernstein, F.   108
Bertoni, A.   250
Beutelspacher, A.   168, 307, 409
Beygelzimer, A.   VII, 168, 411
BH($\mathcal{C}$)   **175**, 242
BH$_k$($\mathcal{C}$)   **175**, 242, 256
BH(NP)   **174**, 176, 177, 216, 242, 254
BH$_2$(NP)   **173**, 174, 176, 177, 180, 184, 188, 243, 247, 248
BH$_k$(NP)   **174**, 176, 177, 179, 180, 188, 213, 217, 242, 245, 250, 256
BH$_k$(NP)-complete   179, 180, 188, 213, 242, 245
BH$_k$(NP)-hard   179, 250
BHT   **217**
bi-immunity   258
bin($\cdot$)   **17**
Bin($\cdot$)   **71**
binary search   191, 201, 215
Blass, A.   249
Bletchley Park   2, 169
block cipher   *see* cipher, block
Bleichenbacher, D.   358
Blömer, J.   358
Blum, M.   57, 114, 119, 382
Blum complexity measure   **57**, 114, 119
Blum number   *see* number, Blum
Blum's axioms   **57**
Bob   1
Boneh, D.   358
Book, R.   66, 70, 119, 124, 217, 257
boolean algebra   **175**
boolean closure,   *see also* set class, closure of a, boolean
  – of $\mathcal{C}$,   *see also* BC($\mathcal{C}$)   **174**, 175, 242
  – of NP,   *see also* BC(NP)   **174**, 176, 216, 241
boolean constant   **30**

boolean expression
  see boolean formula
boolean formula   29, **30**, 34, 83
  – conjunctive normal form of a,
    see also CNF   **30**
  – disjunctive normal form of a,
    see also DNF   **48**
  – in predicate logic   **34**
    see also structure
    see also term
  – in propositional logic   **29**
  – isomorphic —s   **252**
  – satisfiable   **31**
  – truth assignment of a   **31**
  – quantified
    see quantified boolean formula
  – semantically equivalent —s,   *see*
    also ≡   **31**, **36**
boolean hierarchy
  – extended   250
  – normal form
    alternating sums
      see alternating sums hierarchy
    Hausdorff
      see Hausdorff hierarchy
    nested difference
      see nested difference hierarchy
    symmetric difference   *see* sym-
      metric difference hierarchy
    union-of-differences
      see Hausdorff hierarchy
  – over $\mathcal{C}$, *see also* BH($\mathcal{C}$)   **175**, 242
    kth level of the   *see* BH$_k(\mathcal{C})$
  – over NP,   *see also* BH(NP)   6,
    171, **174**, 176, 177, 216, 217,
    242, 249, 250, 254, 256
    collapse of the   177, 217, 249
    kth level of the   *see* BH$_k$(NP)
    second level of the
      see BH$_2$(NP);   *see also* DP
  – over RP   250
  – over UP   250
Boolean Hierarchy Tower,   *see also*
    BHT   177, 217
boolean operation

  – *see* conjunction,   *see also* ∧
  – *see* disjunction,   *see also* ∨
  – *see* equivalence,   *see also* ⟺
  – *see* exclusive-or,   *see also* ⊕
  – *see* implication,   *see also* ⟹
  – *see* negation,   *see also* ¬
boolean variable   **30**
  – bound   **32**
  – free   **32**
  – quantified   *see* boolean variable,
    bound
Boppana, R.   307, 409
Borchert, B.   VII, 252
Borges, J.   4
Borodin, A.   123
Borodin–Demers Theorem
    see Theorem, Borodin–Demers
Bovet, D.   8, 118, 409
BPP   6, 125, 261, 275, **276**, 277–
    281, 283, 285–288, 290, 303,
    305–308, 310
BPP^{BPP} 288
BPP$_{\text{path}}$ 303, **305**, 306, 307
Brandstädt, A.   51, 118, 120
Brassard, G.   410, 412
Brauer, W.   VIII
break-elgamal   **373**, 374
break-rabin   **383**, 384, 385
Brent, R.   344
Brickell, E.   410, 411
Brillhart, J.   344
Bruschi, D.   308
Bshouty, N.   252
$\mathfrak{B}$-smooth   **341**, 342, 343
Buchmann, J.   4, 168, 307, 357, 358,
    369, 408, 409
Buhrman, H.   119, 121, 252, 256
Bush, G. W.   206
Buss, S.   216, 254

C
Caesar cipher   *see* cipher, Caesar
Caesar, J.   2, 132, 168
Cai, J.   122, 124, 168, 248, 249,
    254–258, 358, 411

candidate   207
Canetti, R.   255
Cantor, G.   108
Cantor–Bernstein Theorem
    see Theorem, Cantor–Bernstein
Carmichael number   *see* number, Carmichael
Carroll, L.   *see* Dodgson, C.
Carter, J.   295, 309
Castro, J.   254
CBC   **146**, **147**, 148–150, 165
census$_L$ **109**, 110
certificate   *see* witness
CF   **19**, 20, 50
CFB   **148**, **149**, 165
chain-saw   *see* tools, chain-saw
challenge-and-response protocol 388,
    390
Chandra, A.   257
Chang, R.   218, 249, 250, 256
Chakaravarthy, V.   255
characteristic function   *see* function,
    characteristic
Chen, Z.   252
Chinese Remainder Theorem   *see* The-
    orem, Chinese Remainder
choice set   **207**
Chomsky hierarchy   **19**
Chomsky, N.   19
Chor, B.   410
Chor–Rivest cryptosystem   410
chosen-ciphertext attack   *see* attack,
    chosen-ciphertext
chosen-plaintext attack   *see* attack,
    chosen-plaintext
Cicero, Q.   168
cipher,   *see also* cryptosystem;
    see also cryptanalytic attack
 – affine   6, **132**
 – affine linear block   6, 135, 137,
    138, 139, 142, 165
 – Beaufort   **164**
 – block   6, **130**, 135–149
 – Caesar   **132**
 – Hill   6, **139**, 144, 150, 162, 163,
    165

 – linear block   **138**
 – permutation   6, 130, **131**, 139,
    146, 148, 161, 165, 168
 – shift   **131**, 132, 133, 135, 162,
    166
 – stream   6, 145, **150**, 165, 166,
    168, 169
 – substitution   6, **130**
 – transposition
    see cipher, permutation
 – Vigenère   6, **136**, 137, 139–141,
    143, 145, 150, 151, 162, 163,
    165, 168, 169
cipherblock chaining mode   *see* CBC
cipher feedback mode   *see* CFB
ciphertext   **127**
ciphertext-only attack
    see attack, ciphertext-only
ciphertext space   **127**
circuit complexity   118,
    – *see also* polynomial-size circuit
Clique   **93**, 116
Clique-Facet   **249**, 243
clique polytope,
    see also Polytope($\cdot$)   249
clique problem   **93**, 116, 190, 248
    see also Clique
CNF,   *see also* k-CNF   **30**
coAM   289, 290, 292, 296, 310, 388
coBPP   277
Cobham, A.   120
co$\mathcal{C}$ *see* set class, co operator, ap-
    plied to a
Cocks, C.   357
co$\mathcal{C}$P   292, 310
codebreakers   2
coDP   **174**, 176, 177, 249
co-graph   **93**
Cohen, S.   VII
colorability problem   55, **95**
    see 2-Colorability;
    see 3-Colorability;
    see k-Colorability

– exact,   *see also*
   Exact-i-Colorability   **184**,
   188, 251
– generalized exact,   *see also*
   Exact-M_k-Colorability   **184**,
   184, 188
coMA   288, 303, 310
coMAM   289
communication network
   see network, communication
commutativity   **31, 399**
completeness
   see $\leq_{\mathrm{m}}^{\log}$-completeness;
   see $\leq_{\mathrm{m}}^{\mathrm{P}}$-completeness;
   see $\leq_{\mathrm{T}}^{\mathrm{P}}$-completeness;
   see $\leq_{\mathrm{tt}}^{\mathrm{P}}$-completeness;
   see #P-completeness;
   see #P$_1$-completeness;
   see BH$_k$(NP)-complete;
   see coNP-complete;
   see Δ_2^p-complete;
   see DP-complete;
   see NL-complete;
   see NP-complete;
   see Π_2^p-complete;
   see Π_i^p-complete;
   see P-complete;
   see PP-complete;
   see PSPACE-complete;
   see Σ_2^p-complete;
   see Σ_i^p-complete;
   see Θ_2^p-complete
complete right transversal   **42**, 301
complete search reducing to partial
   search   122
complex intersection   *see* set class,
   complex intersection of —es
complexity class   5
– alternating time and space   **223**
– average-case   5
– $\leq_{\mathrm{m}}^{\log}$-closure of a   **79**, 81, 116
– $\leq_{\mathrm{m}}^{\mathrm{P}}$-closure of a   **78**, 116, 194,
   258, 303
– $\leq_{\mathrm{T}}^{\mathrm{NP}}$-closure of a,   *see also* NP$^{\mathcal{C}}$
   193

– $\leq_{\mathrm{T}}^{\mathrm{P}}$-closure of a,   *see also* P$^{\mathcal{C}}$
   193, 194, 244, 293
– $\leq_{\mathrm{tt}}^{\mathrm{P}}$-closure of a,   *see also* P$_{\mathrm{tt}}^{\mathcal{C}}$
   203
– deterministic time and space   **57**
– name of a   *see* complexity
   class, resource function of a
– nondeterministic time and space
   58
– probabilistic   6, 257
– resource function of a   57, 59
– worst-case   5, **56–62**
complexity measure   5, 54
– alternating time and space   **222**
– average-case   5
– deterministic time and space   **56**
– nondeterministic time and space
   58
– worst-case   5, **56–62**
complexity theory
   see theory, complexity
complex symmetric difference   *see*
   set class, complex symmetric difference of —es
complex union   *see* set class, complex union of —es
computability   **25**
computability theory
   see theory, recursive function
computable function
   see function, partial recursive;
   see function, total recursive
computation   *see* Turing machine,
   computation of a
– efficient   5, **61**, 120
– feasible
   see computation, efficient
– inefficient   5, **61**
– intractable
   see computation, inefficient
– parallel   223, 228
– threshold   **270**, 307
computational model
   see algorithmic device;
   see Turing machine

computational paradigm   *see* Turing
   machine, acceptance mode of a
computational politics   206, 254
computer network
   see network, computer
Condorcet, the Marquis de,
   M. de Caritat   207
Condorcet Paradox   **207**
Condorcet Principle   **207**, 253, 254
Condorcet SCF   **207**
Condorcet winner   **207**, 253
congruence modulo an integer,   *see*
   also ≡   **50**
conjunction,   *see also* ∧   **29**, 30
coNL   **77**, 121
coNLINSPACE   **77**
coNP   **110**, 118, 123, 173, **174**, 176,
   177, 195, 196, 218, 233, 241–
   243, 245, 249, 251, 252, 254–
   256, 280, 292, 280, 292, 303,
   306, 308, 310
coNP-complete   117, 218, 242, 245,
   251, 252, 255
coNP-hard   122, 184, 218, 243, 245,
   249, 251
$coNP^{NP}$,   *see also* Π_2^p 195, 196
Conrad, S.   VIII
coNSPACE($\cdot$)   **77**
constructible in time   **67**
continued fraction expansion   **349**
   – convergent of a   **349**
conveyor flow shop problem   250
Cook, S.   6, 55, 88, 112, 113, 120,
   120, 116, 252
Cook–Levin Theorem
   see Theorem, Cook's
Cook's criterion   6 228
Cook reduction   *see* Theorem, Cook's
Cook's Theorem   *see* Theorem, Cook's
co operator   *see* set class, co operator, applied to a
Coppersmith, D.   358, 410
Cormen, T.   51
coRP   271, 273, 310, 323, 326, 354
$coRP_q$ 354

counting classes   290–294
counting hierarchy   308
coUP   113, 117, 123, 305, 310, 336,
   358, 399, 412
C⃥P   125, 291, **292**, 293, 294, 298,
   302, 303, 306, 308–310
C⃥P-low   293, 310
C⃥P^{SPP} 293
Crépeau, C.   VIII, 1, 410
Crescenzi, P.   8, 118, 251, 409
Critical-Clique   **248**, 249
critical problem   6, 171, 248
   – *see* Critical-Clique
   – *see* Minimal-3-Uncolorability
   – *see* Minimal-3-UNSAT
   – *see* MDNHC
   – *see* MNHC
cryptanalysis   2, 6, 7, 127–170, 345–
   353, 361–412
cryptanalytic attack
   see also cryptanalysis
   – on affine ciphers 6, **133**, **134**, 162
   – on affine linear block ciphers
      142–145, 162–164
   – on Diffie–Hellman   361, **365–
      369**
   – by frequency counts   **134**, 162
   – on ElGamal   **373–380**, 403, 404
      see also break-elgamal
   – on the Hill cipher   6, **144**, 162,
      163
   – on Merkle–Hellman   **406**, 410
   – on permutation ciphers   6, 161
   – on Rabin   **383–385**, 404
      see also break-rabin
   – on RSA   7, 335–337, 344, **345–
      353**, 356–358
      see low-exponent attack
      see RSA superencryption
      see small-message attack
      see Wiener's attack
   – on the shift cipher   162
   – on stream ciphers   165, 166
   – on substitution ciphers   6, 133,
      134, 162

– on triple encryption   161
– on the Vigenère cipher   6, **140–
    143**, 162, 163
cryptography   1–8, 127–170, 312–
    316, 361–412
– asymmetric
    see cryptosystem, public-key
– lattice-based   352, 410, 412
– private-key
    see cryptosystem, private-key
– public-key
    see cryptosystem, public-key
– symmetric
    see cryptosystem, private-key
– worst-case   5, 365, 396, 411,
    412
cryptology   1–8
cryptosystem
– asymmetric
    see cryptosystem, public-key
– Chor–Rivest
    see Chor–Rivest cryptosystem
– ElGamal
    see ElGamal cryptosystem
– entropy of a   157
– monoalphabetic
    see monoalphabetic cryptosys-
    tem
– NTRU *see* NTRU cryptosystem
– polyalphabetic
    see polyalphabetic cryptosystem
– private-key   6, **128**
– public-key   5, 7, **128**
– Rabin *see* Rabin cryptosystem
– Merkle–Hellman   *see*
    Merkle–Hellman cryptosystem
– RSA   *see* RSA cryptosystem
– security of a   2
– symmetric,
    see cryptosystem, private-key
CS   **19**, 20, 77
$cs(\cdot|\cdot)$ **118**

D
$\delta(\cdot)$ **97**, 172

Δ_2^p,   *see also* P^{NP} **194**, 195, 196,
    252, 254, 308, 310
Δ_2^p-complete   252
Δ_2^p-hard   252
Δ_3^p,   *see also* $P^{NP^{NP}}$ **194**, 195, 196,
    256
Δ_i^p **194**, 194–196, 198, 244, 257
$D_{(\cdot)}$ **28**, 57
DAAD   VIII
Dantsin, E.   263, 265, 306
Daemen, J.   170
Data Encryption Standard,   *see also*
    DES   169
decidability   **25**
deck   *see* graph, deck of a
– legitimate   **309**
– preimage of a   **309**
Deck-Checking   **309**
Demers, A.   123
deMorgan, A.   31
deMorgan's rule   **31**
DES   169
det   124, **138**, 167
determinant of a matrix
    see matrix, determinant of a
deterministic polynomial time *see* P
Deutsche Wehrmacht   2, 166
DFA   **21**, 22, 48
DFG   VIII
Díaz, J.   8, 118, 307, 409
Dietzfelbinger, M. 335, 354, 357, 358
diffie-hellman **366**, 373, 402
Diffie-Hellman   366, 402
Diffie–Hellman protocol 7, 312, 357–
    361, **362–369**, 370, 371, 373,
    374, 386, 396, 402, 408, 412
– security of the   *see* cryptana-
    lytic attack, on Diffie–Hellman
Diffie–Hellman problem   **366**, 373,
    402, 412
– as a decision problem
    see Diffie-Hellman
– as a functional problem
    see diffie-hellman

Diffie, W.   7, 357, 358, 362, 408
digital signature   7, **129**
  – forgery of a   *see* forgery
  – *see* protocol, digital signature
digital signature scheme
      see protocol, digital signature
digital signature standard *see* United
      States Digital Signature Standard
discrete logarithm   **39**, 363
  – bit security of the   374, 406
  – *see* function, logarithm, discrete
      — with modulus p and base r
discrete logarithm bit problem,   *see*
      also dlogbit   **374**, 375, 376
discrete logarithm problem   7, 361–
      363, 365, **366**, 367, 369, 371,
      373, 377, 393, 402, 408, 409,
      412
  – as a decision problem
      see DLog
  – as a functional problem
      see dlog
disjunction,   *see also* ∨   **29**, 30
distance map   **248**
distributivity   **31**
divide-and-conquer   **11**, 265
Dixon, J.   358
dlog   **366**, 402
DLog   **402**
dlogbit   **374**, 375, 376
DNA tests   4, 100, 101
DNF   **48**
DNF-SAT   **48**
DNP   **97**, 172
Dodgson, C.   253
Dodgson election system   253
  – homogeneous variant of the   253
  – ranking problem for the   253
  – winner problem for the   253
Dodgson score   **253**
Dodgson voting scheme
      see Dodgson election system
Dodgson winner   **253**
dogma   4, **61**, 62

domatic number problem,   *see also*
      DNP   **96**, 97, 120, 172
  – approximation of the   121
  – exact, *see also* Exact-i-DNP   **172**,
      180, 184, 241, 242
  – generalized exact,   *see also*
      Exact-M_k-DNP   **173**, 180
DOTM   **28**
double negation   **31**
downward collapse
      see upward separation
downward separation
      see upward collapse
DP   **173**, 174, 176, 177, 180, 184,
      188, 241, 243, 247–249, 251,
      252
DP-complete   173, 180, 188, 241,
      243, 247–249, 251, 252
DPOTM   **28**, 193
dragon   4, 387
DSPACE($\cdot$)   **57**, 60, 67, 69, 74, 114,
      115, 225–228, 245
DTM   56, **24**
DTIME($\cdot$)   **57**, 60, 63, 64, 70, 74,
      114, 228–231, 245
Du, D.   8, 118, 123, 409
Durfee, G.   358
Dwork, C.   254, 411, 412

E
ε **16**
e   273, 302
E   **61**, 70, 71, 116, 124
E($\cdot$)   **47**
$E(\cdot)$ **81**
EASY$_\forall^\forall$ **123**
easy-hard technique   218, **219**
eavesdropper   *see* Erich
ECB   **145**, **146**, 147, 165
edge   *see* graph, edge set of a
Edmonds, J.   120
Eiter, T.   251, 254
election system   206, **207**, 253
  – homogeneity of an   **253**
  – manipulation of an   253

– monotonicity of an   206
– properties of an   253
  see Condorcet Principle;
  see election system, homogeneity
    of an;
  see independence of irrelevant al-
    ternatives;
  see election system, monotonicity
    of an;
  see nondictatorship;
  see Pareto Principle;
– *see also* Dodgson election system
– *see also* Kemeny election system
– *see also* majority rule
– *see also* Young election system
electronic codebook mode *see* ECB
ElGamal, T.   7, 361, 369, 371, 373
ElGamal digital signature   7, **371–373**, 403, 408
  – security of the   *see* cryptana-
    lytic attack, on ElGamal
ElGamal cryptosystem 361, **369–371**,
    383, 393, 403, 408
  – security of the   *see* cryptana-
    lytic attack, on ElGamal
Ella   *see* Rothe, E.
Ellis, J.   357
ELow$_2$ **257**
ELow$_k$ **257**
Enigma   2, 166
entropy   6, 151, 155, **156**, 157, 167,
    169, 268
  – conditional   **159**, 160, 166
  – grouping property of   **158**
  – properties of   **158**, 160, 166
  – subadditivity of   **158**
equivalence,   *see also* $\Longleftrightarrow$ **29**, 30
equivalence relation   **117**
Eratosthenes   318
  – sieve of
    see sieve of Eratosthenes
Erdélyi, G.   VIII
Erich   1
Erlkönig   171
Espelage, W.   250

Euclid   10
  – algorithm of   *see* Euclid
  – extended algorithm of
    see Extended-Euclid
Euclid   **10**, 15, 16, 349, 350
Euclidean Algorithm   *see* Euclid
Euler function,   *see also* $\varphi(\cdot)$ **38**,
    39, 49, 133, 312, 346
Euler, L.   38–41, 49, 133, 312, 329,
    330, 344, 346, 375, 376, 382
Euler's criterion   **40**, 41, 329, 330,
    375, 376, 382
Euler's Theorem
    see Theorem, Euler's
eval($\cdot$)   **221**
Even, S.   309, 411
event   **46**
exact conveyor flow shop problem 250
exact cover by 3-sets problem   98,
    103
  – *see also* X-3-Cover
exact domatic number problem   *see*
    domatic number problem, exact
  – generalized   *see* domatic num-
    ber problem, generalized exact
Exact-i-Clique   243
Exact-M_k-Clique   243
Exact-3-Colorability   184, 251
Exact-4-Colorability   188, 251
Exact-7-Colorability   242
Exact-i-Colorability   **184**
Exact-M_k-Colorability   **184**, 188,
    242
Exact-2-DNP   184, 242
Exact-3-DNP   184
Exact-4-DNP   184
Exact-5-DNP   180
Exact-i-DNP   **172**
Exact-M_k-DNP   **173**, 180
Exact-i-Favorite   243
Exact-M_k-Favorite   243
Exact-i-IS   243
Exact-M_k-IS   243
exclusive-or,   *see also* $\oplus$ **147**

existential forgery
   see forgery, existential
existential quantifier   *see* quantifier,
   existential
  – polynomially length-bounded
    see $\exists^p$
EXP   **61**, 70
expectation value,   *see also* $E(\cdot)$ **47**
exponential space
  – deterministic   *see* EXPSPACE
  – nondeterministic *see* NEXPSPACE
exponential time   **61**
  – deterministic   *see* E;   *see* EXP
  – nondeterministic
    see NE;   *see* NEXP
$\exp_{r,p}(\cdot)$ **39**, 363
EXPSPACE   **61**, 69, 115
EXTENDED-EUCLID   11, **12**
extended lowness
  – *see* ELow$_2$
  – *see* ELow$_k$
  – *see* low hierarchy, extended

F
$\varphi(\cdot)$ **38**
F_m **344**, 356
f_n **12**
facet   *see* clique polytope
facet problem   6, **248**
  – *see* Clique-Facet
  – *see* TSP-Facet
factor base   341
factoring   **336**, 355
Factoring   **355**, 358
factoring algorithm   7, 311, **335–345**
  346, 356, 358
  – elliptic curve   343, 344, 346,
    358
  – general-purpose   **346**
  – number field sieve   343, 344,
    346, 358
  – Pollard's $p-1$ *see* Pollard's $p-1$
    factoring algorithm
  – quadratic sieve   7, **338–343**, 346,
    356, 358

  – special-purpose   **346**
  – trial division   **337**, 253
    see also TRIAL-DIVISION
factoring attack   345
  – brute force   **345**
  – elliptic curve   346
  – general-purpose   **346**
  – special-purpose   **346**
factoring method
    see factoring algorithm
factoring problem   5, 7, 106, 335,
  336, 345, 357
  – as a decision problem
    see Factoring
  – as a functional problem
    see factoring
Favorite   206, 243
Favorite-Equ   206
Favorite-Geq   206
Favorite-Odd   206
Feige, U.   121, 410
Feigenbaum, J.   168, 409
Feller, W.   51
Fellows, M.   336, 358
Fenner, S.   123, 308, 412
Fermat, P. de   39, 344
FERMAT   **320**
Fermat liar   **319**, 321
Fermat number   *see* number, Fermat
Fermat's Little Theorem
    see Theorem, Fermat's Little
Fermat test
    see primality test, Fermat
Fermat witness   **319**, 321
FewE   119
FewP   119, **123**, 124, 255, 257, 271
FI   **252**
Fiat, A.   392, 393, 410
Fiat–Shamir identification scheme
  392, 404, 410
    see also zero-knowledge
Fibonacci number
    see number, Fibonacci
field   **38**
finite automaton

– deterministic, *see also* DFA **20**,
    21, 22, 48, 53
– extended transition function of a
    20, 21
– final state of a **20, 21**
– Gödelization of 48
– initial state of a **20, 21**
– language accepted by a **20, 21**
– nondeterministic, *see also* NFA
    21, 22, 48, 52, 53
– state of a **20, 21**
– stochastic **265**, 266
    absorbing state of a **265**
    transition graph of a
    see Markov chain
– transition function of a **20, 21**
Fishburn, P. 207, 253
FL **79**
F-Liars$_n$ **322**, 323, 327, 333
forgery
– existential **376**
– selective **376**
– *see also* total break
formula isomorphism problem,
    see also FI **252**
Forstinger, C. VIII
Fortnow, L. 123, 124, 256, 258, 306–
    308, 412
Fortune, S. 109, 412
FP **77**, 124
FP^{NP} 192, 252
FP-invertibility **110**
frequency counts method *see* cryptana-
    lytic attack, by frequency counts
Friedberg, R. 121
Friedberg–Muchnik Theorem
    see Theorem, Friedberg–Muchnik
function
– associative **398**
– census, *see also* census$_L$ **109**,
    124, 125
– characteristic, *see also* χ_B **202**
– commutative **399**
– composition of —s, *see also* ○
    59

– computable
    see function, partial recursive
– domain of a, *see also* $D_{(\cdot)}$ **28**,
    57
– Euler   *see* Euler function
– exponential
    modular — with modulus p and
    base r, *see also* $\exp_{r,p}$ **39**,
    363
    with linear exponent,
    see also 2^{Lin} 59
    with polynomial exponent,
    see also 2^{Pol} 59
– FP-invertible *see* FP-invertibility
– growth rate of a **59**, 61, 62
– honest **110**, 397, 405
– linear, *see also* Lin 59
– logarithm, *see also* log 16
    discrete — with modulus p and
    base r, *see also* $\log_r \alpha$ mod
    p **39**, 363
– log-space computable,
    see also FL **79**
– one-way *see* one-way function
– partial recursive, *see also* P
    25
    Gödelization of —s 57
    effective enumeration of —s
    see function, partial recursive,
    Gödelization of —s
– polynomial, *see also* Pol 59
– polynomial-time computable,
    see also FP **77**
– productive **110**
– range of a, *see also* $R_{(\cdot)}$ **28**
– s-honest **397**, 405
– social choice *see* social choice
    function; *see* SCF
– space, *see also* Space$_M(\cdot)$ **56**
– space-constructible **67**, 115
– time, *see also* Time$_M(\cdot)$ **56**
– time-constructible **67**, 115
– total 25
– total recursive, *see also* R **25**,
    57

function class,   *see also* complexity
    class
  – closure of a
    under addition   **291**, **303**
    under binomial coefficients   **291**,
      303, **304**
    under exponentiation   **291**, **303**,
      304
    under limited composition   **291**,
      303, **304**
    under multiplication   **291**, **303**
    under subtraction   **291**, **303**
function symbol   **34**
Furst, M.   308

G
γ-reducibility   257
GA   **43**
Gabarró, J.   8, 118, 307, 409
Gács, P.   307
Gál, A.   122, 247
Gandalf   387, 388
Ganesan, K.   123
GAP   55, **82**, 121
GAP$_{acyclic}$ **86**, 87, 116
gap$_M$ **291**
GapP   262, 290, **291**, 293, 294, 303,
      304, 306, 308
  – closure properties of,
      see function class, closure of a
GapP-low   292, 293
Garey, M.   8, 62, 88, 99, 118, 120,
      250
Gasarch, W.   106
Gauß, C.   124
Gaussian elimination   124
$\gcd(\cdot, \cdot)$ **10**
GCHQ   *see* Government Communi-
    cations Head Quarters
GI   **43**
Gibb's Lemma,   *see also* entropy,
    properties of   **158**
Gill, J.   258, 307
GNI   **296**
Gödel, K.   27, 120

Gödelization
  – *see* finite automata, Gödelization
    of
  – *see* function, partial recursive,
    Gödelization of —s
  – *see* Turing machine, Gödelization
    of —s
Gödel number   *see* number, Gödel
Goethe, J. W. von   171
golden cut   14, **47**
Goldreich–Micali–Wigderson protocol
      388–392, 404, 410
Goldreich, O.   8, 168, 251, 307, 309,
      357, 388, 391, 392, 408–410
Goldschlager, L.   308
Goldsmith, J.   VII, 122–124
Goldwasser, S.   8, 168, 307, 309,
      352, 409, 411
Golumbic, M.   51, 118, 120
Gottlob, G.   251, 254
Government Communications Head
      Quarters   357
grammar   **17**
  – context-free   **19**
  – context-sensitive   **19**
  – derivation relation with respect to
    a,   *see also* $\vdash$ **18**
    reflexive, transitive closure of $\vdash$,
    see also $\vdash^*$ **18**
  – language of a   **17**
  – productions of a
    see grammar, rules of a
  – rules of a   **17**
  – start symbol of a   **17**
  – terminals of a   **17**
  – nonterminals of a   **17**
  – regular   **19**
  – type 0   **19**
  – type of a   **19**
  – variables of a
    see grammar, nonterminals of a
  – words of a   **18**
graph   **43**, 81
  – alternating   **231**
    reachability in an   **231**

– bipartite   **98**, 121
– critical   **248**
– deck of a   **309**
– directed   **81**
  acyclic   **86**
  cycle in a   **86**
  hamiltonian circuit in a   **246**
  path in a   **82**
– edge set of a,   *see also* $E(\cdot)$
  81
– isomorphic —s,   *see also* $\cong$ **43**
– join of —s,   *see also* $\bowtie$ **189**,
  243
– minimum degree of a,   *see also*
  min-deg$(\cdot)$ **97**, 181
– network   172
– planar   248
– simple   43
– undirected   **93**
  automorphism of an
    see automorphism of a graph
  chromatic number of an
    see number, chromatic
  clique of an   **93**
  coloring of an   **95**
  domatic number of an
    see number, domatic
  dominating set of an   **96**, 172
  hamiltonian circuit in an   **246**
  independence number of an
    see number, independence
  independent set of an   **93**
  isomorphism between —s
    see isomorphism between graphs
  k-colorable   **95**
  vertex cover of an   **93**
– vertex set of a,   *see also* $V(\cdot)$
  81
graph accessibility problem,   *see*
  also GAP   55, **82**, 82, 121
– alternating,   *see also* AGAP   **231**
– restricted to acyclic graphs,
  see also GAP$_{acyclic}$ **86**, 86, 87,
  116

graph automorphism problem,
  see also GA   **43**, 309
graph isomorphism problem,
  see also GI   5, 7, 55, **43**, 106,
    107, 117, 121, 122, 171, 241,
    252, 257, 294–302, 305, 308–
    310, 336, 388–392, 404, 410
– smallest solution of the   192
graph nonisomorphism problem,
  see also GNI   **296**
Graph Reconstruction Conjecture 309,
  310
graph three-colorability problem
  see 3-Colorability
greatest common divisor,   *see also*
  gcd$(\cdot, \cdot)$ **10**
Green, F.   308
Greibach, S.   66
Grollmann, J.   123, 411, 412
Große, A.   VII, VIII, 122, 247, 252
group   **37**
– abelian   **38**
– commutative   **38**
– closure property of a   **37**
– inverse element in a   **37**
– neutral element of a   **37**
– order of a finite —   **38**
– order of a — element   **37**
– operation,   *see also* ∘   **37**
– permutation
    see permutation group
– subgroup of a,   *see also* $\leq$ **38**
group axioms   **37**
Gundermann, T.   249, 250
Gupta, S.   308
Gurevich, Y.   249
Guruswami, V.   185, 188, 250
Guruswami–Khanna reduction
  185, 189, 250

H
Halevi, S.   122, 247
Halldórsson, M.   8, 121, 251
halting problem   235
Han, Y.   307

hamiltonian circuit problem **246**
- for directed graphs **246**
- for undirected graphs **246**
Harary, J.   51
hardness   *see* $\leq^{\log}_m$-hardness;
    see $\leq^P_m$-hardness;
    see $\leq^P_T$-hardness;
    see $\leq^P_{tt}$-hardness;
    see $BH_k(NP)$-hard;
    see Δ^p_2-hard;
    see coNP-hard;
    see NP-hard;
    see Θ^p_2-hard
Hardy, G.   51
Hartmanis, J.   6, 108–111, 119, 122,
    123, 125, 255
hashing
- universal **295**, 309
hashing function **295**
- family of —s **295**
    collision-free **295**
Hassan, N.   VII
Håstad, J.   307, 352, 358, 409
Hausdorff, F.   175, 249
Hausdorff hierarchy **175**, 250
- *see also* boolean hierarchy , nor-
    mal form
Hay, L.   216, 254
Heggernes, P.   250
Heller, H.   283, 307, 409
Hellman, M.   7, 357–362, 393, 408,
    410, 411
Hemachandra, L.
    see Hemaspaandra, L.
Hemaspaandra, E.   VII, 119, 121,
    218, 251–254, 256, 257, 310
Hemaspaandra, L.   VII, 8, 62, 111,
    118, 119, 122–125, 175, 216,
    218, 249, 250, 252–258, 304,
    307–310, 405, 406, 411, 412
Hempel, H.   VIII, 218, 256, 257
Hennie, F.   70, 119
HH   **232**, 234, 235, 239, 240, 246
hierarchy

- alternating sums
    see alternating sums hierarchy
- Arthur-Merlin
    see Arthur-Merlin games
- boolean   *see* boolean hierarchy
    normal form   *see* boolean hier-
    archy normal form
- Chomsky
    see Chomsky hierarchy
- counting
    see counting hierarchy
- Hausdorff
    see Hausdorff hierarchy
- high   *see* high hierarchy
- low   *see* low hierarchy
- nested difference
    see nested difference hierarchy
- parallel query   *see* query hierar-
    chy over NP, parallel
- polynomial
    see polynomial hierarchy
- query *see* query hierarchy over NP
- space   *see* space hierarchy
- symmetric difference   *see*
    symmetric difference hierarchy
- time   *see* time hierarchy
- truth-table query   *see* query hi-
    erarchy over NP, parallel
- union-of-differences
    see Hausdorff hierarchy
$High_0$ 233, 294
$High_1$ 233
$High_2$ 294
high hierarchy,   *see also* HH   6,
    232, 234, 235, 239, 240, 246,
    257
- first level of the   *see* $High_1$
- kth level of the   *see* $High_k$
- second level of the   *see* $High_2$
- zeroth level of the   *see* $High_0$
$High_k$ **232**, 234, 235, 238, 240, 246
highness   232, 238, 257
    see also high hierarchy
Hill cipher   *see* cipher, Hill
Hinrichs, M.   VIII

Hoffman, C.   309
Hoffstein, J.   410
Hofmann, A.   VIII
Holy Grail   4, 387
Homan, C.   VII, 411, 412
Homer, S.   8, 118, 51, 123, 123, 255
honesty   *see* function, honest
Hopcroft, J.   51, 99, 412
Hörner, H.   410
Huang, M.   358

I
IBM   169
id   **41**
id   41
idempotence   **31**
Immerman, N.   77, 119, 121
immunity   **258**
Impagliazzo, R.   411
impersonation attack   *see* attack, impersonation
implication,   *see also* $\Longrightarrow$ **29**, 30
impossibility theorem   **206**
independence number problems   **202**
  – IN-Equ   **202**, 204, 245
  – IN-Geq   **202**, 204, 245, 253
  – IN-Odd   **202**, 204, 245, 253
independence of irrelevant alternatives   206
independent set problem,   *see also*
    IS   **93**, 94, 116
  – approximation heuristics for the   254
information and coding theory   *see* theory, information and coding
integer linear programming
    see linear programming problem, integer
integer   *see* number, integer
interactive proof system
    see proof system, interactive
intruder-in-the-middle attack
    see attack, man-in-the-middle
IP   244, **307**, 308
  – *see also* proof system, interactive

IS   **93**, 94, 116
ISO$(\cdot, \cdot)$ **43**
isomorphism
  – between boolean formulas   **252**
  – between graphs,
    see also ISO$(\cdot, \cdot)$ **43**
  – between sets   **108**
isomorphism conjecture   6, **108**, 109, 110, 122, 125, 255, 412
Ito, T.   409
Iwama, K.   263, 306

J
Jacobi symbol,   *see also* $\left(\frac{m}{n}\right)$ **40**
Jacobson, N.   51
Jensen's inequality   **157**, 158
Jerschow, Y.   4
Jha, S.   119
Jiang, Z.   VII, 258
Johnson, D.   8, 62, 88, 99, 118, 120, 250
Jones, N.   121
Joseph, D.   110, 111, 122, 123
jump operator   **235**

K
$\kappa(\cdot)$ **103**, **208**
K   **235**, 236, 246
K$(\cdot)$ **236**, 238, 246
K^n **236**, 237, 238, 246
K$^n(\cdot)$ **236**, 237, 238, 246
K-operator   *see* K$(\cdot)$;   *see* K
  – iterated   *see* K$^n(\cdot)$;   *see* K^n
Kadin, J.   217, 218, 249, 254–256
Kahn, D.   168
Kann, V.   8, 251
Kaplan, H.   120
Karp, R.   99, 120, 254
Karp–Lipton Theorem
    see Theorem, Karp–Lipton
Karpinski, M.   8, 251
Kaliski, B.   169, 359
Kasiski, F.   140, 141, 143, 145, 151, 163, 168

Kasiski's method **140**, 141, 143, 145,
 163
  see also cryptanalytic attack, on
  the Vigenère cipher
Kayal, N.   106, 118, 311, 335, 344,
 357, 358
k-CNF   **31**
k-Colorability   **95**
Kellerer, H.   410
Kelly, P.   309
Kemenization
 – local   254
Kemeny election system   253, 254
Kerckhoffs von Nieuwenhof, J.   129
Kerckhoffs's Principle   **129**
key   **127**
 – spurious   **167**
key equivocation   151, 155, **159**, 160
key-only attack   *see* attack, key-only
key space   **127**
key stream   *see* cipher, stream
Khanna, S.   185, 188, 250, 251
Khuller, S.   252
Kiometzis, C.   VIII
Kleene, S.   17, 51, 398
knapsack problem   5, 98, **104**
 – high-density   410
 – low-density   410
known-plaintext attack   *see* attack,
  known-plaintext
Ko, K.   8, 118, 123, 257, 308, 409,
 412
Köbler, J.   121, 216, 250, 254, 255,
 257, 258, 305, 307–310, 409
Koblitz, N.   336, 357, 358
Königstein, G.   VIII
Kortsarz, G.   121
Kozen, D.   257
Kratsch, D.   VIII, 309
Krentel, M.   252, 254
k-SAT   **83**, 306
Kumar, R.   168, 254, 411
Kuroda, S.   77
Kurosawa, K.   409
Kurtz, S.   111, 122, 123, 308

Kurur, P.   299, 309

L
L   **61**, 69, 72, 81, 122, 193, 116, 244
$L(\cdot)$ 56, **25**
$\mathcal{L}_0$ **19**, 20, 28
$\mathcal{L}_1$ *see* CS
$\mathcal{L}_2$ *see* CF
$\mathcal{L}_3$ *see* REG
Laaser, W.   121
Ladner, R.   106, 106, 121, 121, 241,
 252
Lagarias, J.   410, 411
Lagrange, J.   39
Lagrange's Theorem
  see Theorem, Lagrange's
LaMacchia, B.   408
Landers-Appell, C.   VII
Landers-Appell, K.   VII
Landry, F.   344
Lange, K.   257
language   **16**
 – cardinality of a   **16**
 – complement of a, *see also* $^-$ **17**
 – concatenation of —es   **17**
 – context-free, *see also* CF; $\mathcal{L}_2$ **19**,
  20, 50
 – context-sensitive, *see also* CS; $\mathcal{L}_1$
  19, 20, 77
 – ε-free iteration, *see also* $^+$ **17**
 – formal   **16**
 – intersection of —es, *see also* $\cap$
  17
 – iteration of a, *see also* * **17**
 – Kleene closure of a
  see language, iteration of a
 – nontrivial   **78**
 – operation on —es   **17**
 – recursively enumerable, *see also*
  RE   **27**, 28
 – reduction to a   254, 255
 – redundancy of a   167, 169
 – regular, *see also* REG; $\mathcal{L}_3$ **19**,
  20, 50

– sparse   109, 110, 119, 122, 123, 125, **218**, 254, 257
– tally   **71**, 124, 125
    binary representation of a,   *see also* Bin($\cdot$)   **71**
– tally encoding of a,   *see also* Tally($\cdot$)   **71**
– type 0, *see also* $\mathfrak{L}_0$ **19**, 20, 28
– type of a   **19**
– union of —es, *see also* $\cup$ **17**
Las Vegas algorithm   *see* algorithm, Las Vegas
lattice problem   352, 410, 412
– average-case hardness of —s   412
– worst-case hardness of —s   412
lattice reduction   352, 410, 412
lattice-based cryptography
    see cryptography, lattice-based
Lautemann, C.   307
Legendre symbol, *see also* $\left(\frac{m}{n}\right)$ **40**
legitimate deck   *see* deck, legitimate
Legitimate-Deck   **309**, 310
Leibert, M.   VII
Leiserson, C.   51
Le Lasseur, H.   344
Lenstra, A.   344, 358, 410
Lenstra Jr., H.   104, 344, 346, 358, 406, 410
LERC   **298**, 299–301
Levin, L.   88, 120
Lewis, P.   119
LH   **232**, 234, 235, 239, 240, 246
Lien, Y.   121
Lin   **59**
Lin($\cdot$)   **59**
Lindner, C.   4
linear bounded automaton   **26**
linear feedback shift register   **151**
linear programming problem   **104**, 249, 253, 253
– integer   104, 253
linear space
– deterministic   *see* LINSPACE
– nondeterministic *see* NLINSPACE

linear speed-up theorem
    see theorem, linear speed-up
linear tape-compression theorem
    see theorem, linear tape-compression
linear time   *see* LINTIME
Linial, N.   251
LINSPACE   **61**, 69, 115
LINTIME   **61**, 66
Lipton, R.   122, 247, 254
Lischke, G.   VIII, 258
Liśkiewicz, M.   124
LLL algorithm   410
log   16
logarithm function
    see function, logarithm
logarithmic space
– alternating   *see* AL
– deterministic   *see* L
– nondeterministic   *see* NL
logic   4, **29–37**, 51
– modal   254
– nonmonotonic   252
– predicate   **34–37**
    first-order   37
    second-order   37
– propositional   **29–33**
$\log_r \alpha \bmod p$ **39**
Long, T.   123, 255, 257, 258
Longpré, L.   119, 255
Lovász, L.   249, 410
Low$_0$ 233
Low$_1$ 233
Low$_2$ 290, 292, 294, 296, 297
low-exponent attack   **351**, 358
low hierarchy, *see also* LH   6, 7, 171, **232**, 234, 235, 239, 240, 246, 257, 258
– extended, *see also* ELow$_k$ 257,
– first level of the   *see* Low$_1$
– kth level of the   *see* Low$_k$
– second level of the   *see* Low$_2$; *see also* Σ_2^p-low
– zeroth level of the   *see* Low$_0$

Low_k **232**, 234, 235, 238, 240, 246, 292

lowness   232, 238, 257, 262, 290, **292**, 294–302, 306, 307, 309
  see also low hierarchy;
  see also self-lowness

Luby, M.   8, 168

Lund, C.   251

Lutz, D.   VII

Lynch, N.   121, 252

M

MA   **286**, 287–290, 292, 303, 306, 307, 310
  – *see also* Arthur-Merlin games

Mahaney, S.   109, 111, 122, 123, 255

majority quantifier
  – *see* quantifier, polynomially length-bounded, majority
  – *see* $\exists^+$

majority rule   **207**
  – defeat according to the   **207**
  – win according to the   **207**
  – winner according to the
    see Condorcet winner

Majority-SAT   **274**

MAM   **286**, 287, 288, 303
  – *see also* Arthur-Merlin games

Manasse, M.   344

Manders, K.   257

man-in-the-middle attack
  see attack, man-in-the-middle

many-one reducibility
  see reducibility, many-one;
  see $\leq_m^{\log}$;
  see $\leq_m^p$

Markov chain   **265**, 266

marriage problem   *see* matching problem, bipartite

matching
  – bipartite   98
  – tripartite   99, 117

matching problem   **98**
  – bipartite   98

– three-dimensional
    see 3-DM
  – tripartite   *see* matching problem, three-dimensional
  – two-dimensional
    see matching problem, bipartite

matrix
  – adjoint   *see* adjoint matrix
  – determinant of a,   *see also* det
    124, **138**, 167
  – inverse of a   **138**
  – permanent of a,
    see also perm$(\cdot)$ **124**

Maurer, U.   412

Mauve, M.   VIII

maximal non-hamiltonian circuit
    problem   **246**, 249
  – for directed graphs,
    see also MNHC **246**,   249
  – for undirected graphs,
    see also MDNHC   **246**

Max-SetPacking-Geq   **208**, 245

May, A.   358

Mayer, I.   VIII

MEE-DNF   245, **251**

Merkle–Hellman cryptosystem   361, **393–396**, 405, 406, 410, 411
  – iterated   410
  – security of the   *see* cryptanalytic attack, on Merkle–Hellman

Merkle, R.   361, 393, 410, 411

Merlin,   *see also*
    Arthur-Merlin games   4

Merz, J.   VIII

message   *see* plaintext

message authentication   **130**

message integrity   **130**

message space   *see* plaintext space

Meyer, A.   107, 121, 251, 254

Meyer, G.   248

Micali, S.   307, 309, 388, 391, 392, 409, 410

Micciancio, D.   8, 168

Miller, G.   7, 311, 323–329, 335, 354, 356–358

MILLER-RABIN **324**
Miller–Rabin liar   *see* MR-liar
Miller–Rabin test   *see* primality test,
    Miller–Rabin
Miller–Rabin witness
    see MR-witness
mind-change technique **214**
$min\text{-}deg(\cdot)$ **97**, 181
Minimal-3-Uncolorability **248**,
  – restricted to planar graphs   248
Minimal-3-UNSAT **248**, 247
minimum equivalent expression prob-
    lem,   *see also* MEE-DNF   171,
    245, **251**
MDNHC **246**
MNHC **246**, 249
mod   *see* congruence modulo an
    integer
modular *see also* function, logarithm,
    discrete — with modulus p and
    base r
Monien, B.   263, 265
monoalphabetic cryptosystem   131,
    132, **134**, 135, 140, 142, 167–
    169
monoid **37**
  – abelian **38**
  – commutative **38**
Monte Carlo algorithm
    see algorithm, Monte Carlo
Moore, J.   359
Moran, S.   7, 307, 409
Morgenstern, C.   161
Morrison, M.   344
Mothers of Invention   163
Muchnik, A.   121
Motwani, R.   51, 251
MR-liar **325**
MR-Liars$_n$ **327**, 355
MR-LIARS$_n$ **327**, 328
MR-witness **325**
Müller, H.   VIII, 258
multiset **207**

N
$\mathbb{N}$ **10**
Nader, R.   206
Naik, A.   121, 123, 412
nail file   *see* tools, nail file
Naor, M.   254, 411
Nasser, N.   250
natural   *see* number, natural
Navajo code   169
NE **61**, 71, 116, 124
negation,   *see also* ¬   **29**, 30
nested difference hierarchy 175, **176**,
    250, 250
  – *see also* boolean hierarchy, nor-
    mal form
network
  – communication   **172**
  – computer   172, **172**
NEXP **61**
NEXPSPACE **61**
NFA **21**, 22, 48
Nguyen, P.   168, 411
Niedermeier, R.   257
NIST   170, 408
NL   5, **61**, 72, 76, 77, 81, 82, 84, 86,
    116, 121, 122
NL-complete   82, 84, 86, 116, 121,
    122
    see also $\leq_{\mathrm{m}}^{\log}$-completeness
NLINSPACE   **61**, 77, 115
Nöckel, B.   VIII
nonapproximability 8, 121, 251, 254
nondeterministic polynomial time
    see NP
nondictatorship   206
nonresidue
  – quadratic,   *see also* QNR   **40**
Norris, M.   347, 358
NOTM **28**
NP   5, **61**, 71, 72, 78, 106–110, 116,
    118, 120, 122, 123, 125, 174,
    176, 177, 179, 184, 191, 193–
    196, 218, 232–236, 238, 241,
    248, 253–256, 241, 243, 244,
    246, 247, 271, 278–280, 292,

294, 287, 290, 310, 355, 388, 399, 402, 410–412
- certificate of an problem
  see witness
- P versus NP question   5, **106–108**, 120
- solution of an problem
  see witness
- $\leq_{tt}^{p}$-closure of,
  see also P_{tt}^{NP} **213**, 254
NP$^{\mathcal{C}}$ **193**, 244
NP-complete   5, 6, 7, 88, 92, 93, 95, 97, 100, 103, 105, 106, 108, 109, 116, 120, 121, 236, 241, 243, 246–248, 253, 255, 335, 336, 358, 361
  see also $\leq_{m}^{\log}$-completeness;
  see also $\leq_{m}^{p}$-completeness
- exact variant of — problems   6, 171, 173, 248
- *see also* theory of NP-completeness
NP-hard   172, 185, 241, 249, 251–253
NP^{NP},   *see also* Σ_{2}^{p} 194, 195, 196, 245
NPOTM   **28**, 193
NP^{P} 193, 244
NP^{PSPACE} 193, 244
NPSPACE   **61**, 76
NSF   VIII
NSpace$_{M}(\cdot)$ **58**
NSPACE$(\cdot)$ **59**, 66, 74, 77, 114, 228, 231
NTM   **23**, 56
NTime$_{M}(\cdot)$ **58**
NTIME$(\cdot)$ **59**, 66, 74, 114, 225, 228
NTRU cryptosystem   410
Nugent, R.   VIII
number
- Blum   **382**
- Carmichael   **321**, 322, 323, 325, 327, 328, 354, 355
- chromatic,   *see also* $\chi(\cdot)$ **95**

- domatic,   *see also* $\delta(\cdot)$ **97**, 121, 172
- Fermat, *see also* F_{m} **344**, 356
- Fibonacci,   *see also* f_{n} **12**
- Gödel   **27**
- independence, *see also* $\alpha(\cdot)$ **202**
- integer,   *see also* $\mathbb{Z}$ 10
- natural,   *see also* $\mathbb{N}$ **10**
  binary representation of a,
  see also bin$(\cdot)$ 17
- prime   38, **317**
- primitive element of a   **7**, 362
- rational,   *see also* $\mathbb{Q}$ 49
- real,   *see also* $\mathbb{R}$ 49
- RSA-d 344, 345
number theory   *see* theory, number

O
$o(\cdot)$ **60**
$\mathcal{O}(\cdot)$ 16, 34, **59**
$\tilde{\mathcal{O}}(\cdot)$ **262**
Odd-k-SAT   **213**
Odd-Max-SAT   **252**
Odd-SAT   **245**
Odifreddi, P.   51
Odlyzko, A.   408, 410, 411
OFB   **149**, 165
Ogihara, M.   VII, 8, 62, 109, 118, 121, 122, 124, 218, 250, 255, 256, 304, 307, 308
Ogiwara, M. *see* Ogihara, M.
one-time pad
  see Vernam's one-time pad
one-way conjecture   **111**
one-way function   2, 5, 8, 108, **110**, 111, 123, 123,
- associative   **398**
- commutative   **399**
- polynomial-to-one   123
- one-to-one   123
- onto   113, 117
- strong   **397**, **398**, 399, 405
- trapdoor   8, **393**, 394
- worst-case   361, 365, 396, 411, 412

one-way/isomorphism conjecture   **111**
one-way permutation   **124**
Orponen, P.   257
Ottmann, T.   51
output feedback mode   *see* OFB

P

Π_2^p,   *see also* coNP^{NP} **194**, 195,
    196, 251, 252, 256, 283, 285,
    288–290, 310
$\Pi_2^{p,AM\cap coAM}$ 289
Π_2^p-complete   251, 252
Π_3^p 280
Π_i^p **194**, 195, 196, 198, 200, 256
Π_i^p-complete   200, 217, 218
Π_iSAT   **200**, 244
Π_iSAT formula   **200**
P   5, 6, **61**, 70–72, 78, 106, 108,
    109, 111–113, 116, 120–122, 174,
    176, 177, 191, 193–196, 198,
    231–233, 241, 244, 262, 271,
    281, 292, 310, 335, 357, 358,
    411, 412
    – P versus NP question   5, **106–**
    108, 120
$\mathbb{P}$ **25**
$\mathfrak{P}(\cdot)$ **103**
P$^{\mathcal{C}}$ **193**, 244
P^{NP},   *see also* Δ_2^p 194–196
P$^{A[k]}$ **213**
P$^{\mathcal{C}[k]}$ **213**
P$^{NP[k]}$ **212**, 213
P$^{NP[\mathcal{O}(1)]}$ **212**, 216
P$^{NP[\mathcal{O}(\log)]}$,   *see also* Θ_2^p **202**, **212**,
    216, 254, 255
P$^{\Sigma_{i-1}^p[\mathcal{O}(\log)]}$ **202**
P$_{k\text{-tt}}^A$ **213**
P$_{k\text{-tt}}^{\mathcal{C}}$ **213**
P$_{bf}^{NP}$ 253
P$_{btt}^{NP}$ **213**, 216, 254
P$_{k\text{-tt}}^{NP}$ **213**
P$_{k\text{-tt}}^{\Sigma_i^p}$ 256
P$_{tt}^{\mathcal{C}}$ **203**
P$_{tt}^{NP}$ **213**, 216, 253, 254

P$^{NP^{NP}}$,   *see also* Δ_3^p 195, 256
P^P 193, 244
P^{PP} 308, 310
P$^{PP^{PH}}$ 308
P^{PSPACE} 193, 244
P^{SPP} 293
Papadimitriou, C.   8, 51, 118, 173,
    202, 248, 249, 252, 307, 308,
    409
parallel access to NP,   *see also* Θ_2^p;
    P$^{NP[\mathcal{O}(\log)]}$; P$_{tt}^{NP}$ 201, **203**, 206,
    208, 254
parallel oracle access   203
parallel time   228
Parberry, I.   308
Pareto Principle   206
partial order
    – polynomially length-related   **107**
    – polynomially well-founded   **107**
partial recursive function
    see function, partial recursive
Pasanen, K.   VII, 405, 411
Paterson, M.   107, 121
Paturi, R.   263, 306
Paula   *see* Rothe, P.
Pavan, A.   124
P-complete   121, 122, 231, 232, 238,
    239
PCP   **251**
PCP theorem   *see* theorem, PCP
perfect secrecy   6, **151–155**, 166
perm$(\cdot)$ **124**
permanent of a matrix
    see matrix, permanent of a
permutation,   *see also* $\mathfrak{S}_n$ **41**
    – composition of —s   **41**
permutation group   **41**
    – complete right transversal in a
      42
    – generator of a   **42**
    – identity of a,   *see also* id   **41**
    – (pointwise) stabilizer in a   **42**
    – right co-set of a   **42**
    – strong generator of a   **42**
    – tower of stabilizers in a   **42**

Petrank, E.   122, 247
Pferschy, U.   410
PH   125, 171, **194**, 195, 196, 198, 200, 217, 218, 234, 244, 249, 252, 254–256, 310
PHT   **217**
Pipher, J.   410
Pisinger, D.   410
p-isomorphism,   *see also* $\cong_p$ **108**, 117
plaintext   **127**
plaintext space   **127**
Poe, Edgar A.   127, 167
Pollard, J.   337, 338, 343, 344, 346, 355, 358
POLLARD   **337**
Pollard's $p - 1$ factoring algorithm, *see also* POLLARD   **337**, 338, 343, 344, 346, 355, 358
$\mathbb{P}$ol   **59**
$\mathbb{P}$ol$(\cdot)$ **59**
polyalphabetic cryptosystem **135**, 136, 140, 163
polygamy   4, 99
POLYLOGSPACE   **69**, 115
polymer chemistry   124
polynomial hierarchy,   *see also* PH   6, 125, 171, **194**, 195, 196, 198, 200, 217, 218, 232, 234, 235, 240, 251, 252, 254, 257, 261, 277, 281, 286, 288, 294, 297, 307–309
– collapse of the   198, 217, 218, 234, 235, 240, 249, 252, 255–257, 297
– downward collapse within the 256
– ith level of the,   *see also* Σ_i^p; Π_i^p; Δ_i^p; Θ_i^p **194**, 195, 196, 198, 200, 201, 217, 218, 232, 234, 237, 238, 240, 246, 256, 257
– second level of the,   *see also* Σ_2^p; NP^{NP}; Π_2^p; coNP^{NP}; Δ_2^p; P^{NP}; Θ_2^p; P$^{NP[\mathcal{O}(\log)]}$ **194**, 195,

196, 212, 245, 251, 252, 256, 257
Polynomial Hierarchy Tower,   *see also* PHT   217
polynomial-size   254, 257
polynomial space
– deterministic   *see* PSPACE
– nondeterministic   *see* NPSPACE
polynomial time   **61**
– alternating   *see* AP
– deterministic   *see* P
– nondeterministic   *see* NP
– probabilistic   *see* PP
   bounded-error —   *see* BPP
   one-sided error —   *see* RP;
      see coRP
   stoic —   *see* SPP
   zero-error —   *see* ZPP
– random   *see* RP
– unambiguous   *see* UP
Polytope$(\cdot)$ 249
Pomerance, C.   358
Porta, G.   168
Post, E.   121
Post's problem   121
Potthoff, M.   VIII
PP   6, 7, 124, 257, 261, **270**, 271, 274, 277, 290–294, 298, 302, 303, 305–308, 310
PP-complete   7, 274
PP-low   293, 308, 310
PP$_{path}$ 303, **305**, 306
P-printability   **123**, 125
PP^{SPP} 293
Pr$(\cdot)$ **46**
Pr$(\cdot \mid \cdot)$ **46**
Pratt, V.   118
predicate symbol   **34**
preference order   **207**
preference profile   **207**
prefix search   191, 220
primality problem, see also Primes   7, 62, 106, 118, 311, **317**, 318–321, 324, 326, 330, 333, 335, 336, 354, 357, 358

primality test   7, **317–335**
– Fermat,   *see also* FERMAT   7,
     319–323, 326, 353
– Miller–Rabin,
     see also MILLER-RABIN   7,
     311, **323–329**, 354, 356, 358
– Solovay–Strassen,
     see also SOLOVAY-STRASSEN
          7, 311, **329–335**, 358
prime number   *see* number, prime
prime number theorem
     see theorem, prime number
Primes   317
primitive element   *see* number, prim-
     itive element of a
private-key cryptography
     see crytography, private-key
private-key cryptosystem
     see cryptosystem, private-key
probabilistically checkable proof sys-
          tem   *see* proof system, proba-
          bilistically checkable
probabilistic polynomial time *see* PP
– bounded-error   *see* BPP
– one-sided error *see* RP; *see* coRP
– stoic   *see* SPP
– zero-error   *see* ZPP
probability,   *see also* Pr(·)   **46**
– conditional, *see also* Pr(· | ·)   **46**
probability amplification 7, 272, 276
probability distribution   **46**
– uniform   **46**
probability space   **46**
probability theory
     see theory, probability
problem of breaking ElGamal
     see break-elgamal
problem of breaking Rabin
     see break-rabin
projection theorem
     see theorem, projection
promise class   55, **271**, 273, 276,
     292, 303, 308
promise problem   308, 309, 411
proof system

– interactive   2, 7, 251, 252, 256
     see also Arthur-Merlin games
– probabilistically checkable,
     see also PCP   251
prover   307
– *see also* proof system, interactive
– *see also* zero-knowledge protocol
proof verification   251
     see also PCP
protocol
– authentication
     see authentication protocol
– challenge-and-response   *see*
     challenge-and-response protocol
– digital signature
     ElGamal   *see* ElGamal digital
          signature
     Rabi–Sherman   *see* Rabi–Sher-
          man digital signature
     RSA   *see* RSA digital signature
– ElGamal
     see ElGamal cryptosystem
– Merkle–Hellman   *see* Merkle–
     Hellman cryptosystem
– Rabin *see* Rabin cryptosystem
– RSA   *see* RSA cryptosystem
– secret-key agreement
     Diffie–Hellman
          see Diffie–Hellman protocol
     Rivest–Sherman
          see Rivest–Sherman protocol
– Shamir's no-key
     see Shamir's no-key protocol
– zero-knowledge
     see zero-knowledge protocol
p-selectivity   *see* set, p-selective
PSPACE   6, **61**, 69, 72, 76, 78, 115,
     193, 194, 200, 201, 228, 241,
     244, 271, 308, 310
PSPACE-complete   200, 228, 244
public-key cryptography
     see cryptography, public-key
public-key cryptosystem
     see cryptosystem, public-key
Pumping Lemma

– for context-free languages **50**
– for regular languages **50**

Q
$\mathbb{Q}$ **49**
QBF **32**
QBF **199**, 200, 201, 228, 244
QBF$_{\text{simple}}$ **244**
$(\mathfrak{Q}_1 \mid \mathfrak{Q}_2)$ **280**
quadratic nonresidue
    see nonresidue, quadratic
quadratic residue
    see residue, quadratic
quadratic sieve   *see* factoring
    algorithm, quadratic sieve
QNR **40**
QR **40**, 375
QR$_p$ **375**
quantified boolean formula,
    see also QBF **32**
– closed **32**
– open **32**
– in prenex form **33**
– satisfiable **36**
– simple, *see also* QBF$_{\text{simple}}$ **244**
– valid **36**
quantified boolean formula problem
    199
– with a bounded number of alter-
    nations, *see also* Σ_iSAT;
    Π_iSAT 6, **200**, 244
– with an unbounded number of al-
    ternations, *see also* QBF 6,
    199, 200, 201
quantifier
– existential, *see also* $\exists$; $\bigvee$ **32**
– polynomially length-bounded
    existential, *see also* $\exists^p$ 190,
    191, 196, 198
    majority, *see also* $\exists^+$ **280**,
    281–297, 303
    universal, *see also* $\forall^p$ 190,
    191, 196, 198
– universal, *see also* $\forall$; $\bigwedge$ **32**
quantifier string 280

– sensible pair of —s **280**
– complexity class defined by —s,
    see also $(\mathfrak{Q}_1 \mid \mathfrak{Q}_2)$ **280**
query hierarchy over NP,   *see also*
    P$^{\text{NP}[\mathcal{O}(1)]}$; P$^{\text{NP}[\mathcal{O}(\log)]}$ 6, **212**,
    254
– kth level of the,   *see also* P$^{\text{NP}[k]}$
    212, 213
– parallel, *see also* P$^{\text{NP}}_{\text{btt}}$; P$^{\text{NP}}_{\text{tt}}$ 212,
    213, 254, 256
    kth level of the,
    see also P$^{\text{NP}}_{k\text{-tt}}$ **213**
– truth-table   *see* query hierarchy
    over NP, parallel
query order 257

R
$\mathbb{R}$ **25**, 57
$\mathbb{R}$ **49**
$R_{(\cdot)}$ **28**
Rabi, M. 361, 396, 405, 406, 411
Rabin cryptosystem 361, **380–385**,
    404, 409
Rabin, M. 7, 22, 52, 63, 311, 323–
    329, 335, 354, 356–361, 380–
    385, 404, 409
Rabin's Theorem
    see Theorem, Rabin's
Rabi–Sherman digital signature 405
– security of the 411, 412
Rackoff, C. 123, 307, 409
Radziszowski, S. 310
Rajasethupathy, K. 254
RANDOM-FACTOR **384**, 385
randomized algorithm
    see algorithm, randomized
random polynomial time *see* RP
RANDOM-SAT 262, **266**, 267, 268,
    302, 306
random walk algorithm
    see algorithm, random walk
random variable **47**
Ranjan, D. 252
Rao, R. VII, 119

rate of growth
  see function, growth rate of a
rationals   *see* number, rational
Razborov, A.   308
RE   **27**, 28, 121, 191, 235
real   *see* number, real
real-time, *see also* REALTIME   **53**,
    66, 117
REALTIME   **61**, 66
recursive enumerability *see* language,
    recursively enumerable;
    see also RE
recursive function theory
    see theory, recursive function
recursively presentable **239**, 240, 246
reducibility   5
  – many-one
    log-space   *see also* $\leq_m^{\log}$ 55,
    79, 81, 82, 84, 86, 87, 121, 122,
    193, 231, 232, 244, 252
    polynomial-time,   *see also* $\leq_m^P$
    55, **77**, 78, 116, 120, 185, 193,
    194, 236, 238, 239, 244, 246,
    252, 255, 274, 278, 294, 297,
    303, 309
  – polynomial-time randomized
    249, 254
  – polynomial-time truth-table,
    see also $\leq_{tt}^P$ **202**, 203, 252,
    255
    disjunctive   **255**
  – polynomial-time Turing
    deterministic, *see also* $\leq_T^P$ 125,
    193, 194, 238, 244, 246, 252,
    254, 255, 308, 366, 374
    nondeterministic,   *see also* $\leq_T^{NP}$
    193, 193, 252, 244
    positive,   *see also* $\leq_{pos-T}^P$ 194,
    252, **244**
    randomized   355, 358, 383
    strong nondeterministic, *see also*
    $\leq_{sT}^{NP}$ **233**, 236, 245, 246, 257
  – *see also* γ-reducibility
  – *see also* self-reducibility
reflexivity   **50**, 117

REG   **19**, 20, 50
Reingold, N.   306, 307
Reischuk, R.   8, 118
Reith, S.   256
rejecting computation
    see Turing machine, computa-
    tion of a, rejecting
  – number of —s   *see* rej_M
rej_M **291**
relativization   258
relativized world
  – *see* relativization
  – *see* set, oracle
remainder class   **50**
residue
  – quadratic, *see also* QR   **40**
  – class of —s   *see* remainder class
resource   *see* complexity measure
resource function   *see* complexity
    class, resource function of a
Riege, T.   VII, VIII, 4, 250
right co-set   *see* permutation group,
    right co-set of a
  – *see also* LERC   **42**
Rijmen, V.   170
ring   **38**
  – commutative   **38**
  – invertibility in a   **38**
  – one element of a   **38**
  – zero element of a   **38**
ring automorphism   358
  – counting problem for —s,
    see also #RA   358
ring with one   **38**
Rivest, R.   51, 169, 311, 312, 357,
    361, 396–399, 402, 405, 406,
    410–412
Rivest–Sherman protocol   361, **396–
    402**
  – security of the   411, 412
Robshaw, M.   359
Rogers, J.   111, 123, 412
Rogers Jr., H.   51, 108, 235, 257
Rohatgi, P.   249, 254
Rosen, A.   51

Rosenberg, A.   66
Rossmanith, P.   257
Rothe, E.   V, VIII, 70, 137, 165, 217, 407, 408
Rothe, I.   V, VIII
Rothe, J.   119, 122–124, 168, 175, 206, 247, 250–254, 257, 258, 308, 359, 405, 406, 411, 412
Rothe, P.   V, VIII, 70, 142, 165, 217, 407, 408
Royer, J.   111, 122, 123
Rozenberg, G.   VIII
RP   6, 250, 255, 261, 268, **270**, 271–273, 277, 278, 290, 302, 303, 305, 307, 310, 323
RP_{path} 271, 303, **305**, 306
RP_q **272**, 354
RSA cryptosystem   5, 7, 106, 311, **312–316**, 320, 335–337, 344, 357, 361, 383, 393
– security of the   *see* cryptanalytic attack, on RSA
RSA digital signature   7, **316**, 353, 376
– forging —s   **343**
– security of —s   *see* cryptanalytic attack, on RSA
RSA-d number   *see* number, RSA-d
RSA superencryption   **347**, 356, 358
Rubinstein, R.   123
Rueppel, R.   168
Ruling Ring   4, 387
Russel, A.   255
Russo, D.   257, 308

S
Σ^* **16**
Σ_2^p,   *see also* NP^{NP} **194**, 195, 196, 245, 251, 252, 256, 257, 283, 285, 288, 289, 294, 297, 306, 309, 310
$\Sigma_2^{p,AM \cap coAM}$ 289, 292
Σ_2^p-complete   200, 245, 251, 252
Σ_2^p-low,   *see also* Low$_2$ 289, 292
Σ_3^p 280

Σ_i^p **194**, 195, 196, 198, 200, 201, 217, 218, 232, 234, 237, 238, 240, 246, 256, 257
Σ_i^p-complete   200, 237, 238, 246
Σ_iSAT   **200**, 244
Σ_iSAT formula   **200**
$\mathfrak{S}_n$ **41**
$S^{\leq n}$ 109, **218**
S_2^p **255**
Saari, D.   206
Safra, S.   251
Salomaa, A.   VIII, 8, 51, 134, 168, 307, 357, 408, 411
Saruman   387–392, 404
SAT   55, **83**, 88, 107, 111–113, 218, 249, 261–268, 278
satisfiability problem   5, 55, **83**, 88, 101, 109, 190, 199, 228, 236, 261–268, 278
– *see* 2-SAT
– *see* 3-SAT
– *see* 4-SAT
– *see* 5-SAT
– *see* 6-SAT
– *see* DNF-SAT
– *see* k-SAT
– *see* Majority-SAT
– *see* Minimal-3-UNSAT
– *see* Odd-k-SAT
– *see* Odd-Max-SAT
– *see* Odd-SAT
– *see* SAT
– *see* SAT-UNSAT
– *see* Threshold-SAT
– *see* Unique-SAT
SAT-UNSAT   **218**, 241, 241
Savitch, W.   74, 120, 121, 200, 227, 244
Savitch's Theorem
    see Theorem, Savitch's
Saxe, J.   308
Saxena, A.   VII
Saxena, N.   106, 118, 311, 335, 344, 357, 358
SCF   **207**

Schaefer, M.   252
Schlüter, T.   4
Schneider, D.   4
Schneier, B.   8, 168
Schnorr, C.   121, 252, 371, 408–410
Schöning, U.   VIII, 8, 51, 106, 121, 216, 232, 235, 236, 238, 240, 250, 254, 257, 263, 265, 289, 290, 297, 305–308, 409
Scott, D.   22, 52
Seara, C.   254
search engine   254
search reducing to decision   122
secret-key agreement   7, 8, 312, 357, 361, **362**   *see also* protocol, secret-key agreement
secret-key agreement problem   312, **362**
selective forgery
        see forgery, selective
self-avoiding walk problem   **124**
self-lowness   **292**, 293, 294, 305, 306, 308
self-reducibility   **107**, 109, 114, 121, 252
    – disjunctive   **108**
self-reducibility tree   **107**
Selman, A.   8, 51, 118, 168, 121, 123, 124, 233, 252, 257, 258, 309, 411, 412
separation   258
    – by immune sets   *see* separation, strong
    – strong   258
    – downward   *see* upward collapse
    – upward   *see* upward separation
sequential space   228
set,   *see also* language
    – balanced-immune   *see* balanced immunity
    – bi-immune   *see* bi-immunity
    – choice   *see* choice set
    – cofinite   240
    – creative   **110**
    – decidable   **25**, 191

    – finite   108, 240
    – immune   *see* immunity
    – isomorphic —s   **108**
    – join of —s,   *see also* $\oplus$ **258**
    – k-creative   **110**
    – non-p-isomorphic —s   **111**
    – nonsparse   **109**
    – oracle   **28**, 190, 191
        generic   258
        random   258
    – of strings up to length n,
        see also $S^{\leq n}$ **109**, 218
    – p-isomorphic —s
        see p-isomorphism
    – P-printable   *see* P-printability
    – p-selective   252, 257, 258
    – power set of a,   *see also* $\mathfrak{P}(\cdot)$ **103**
    – recursively enumerable   **27**, 28, 191, 235, 239
    – self-reducible   *see* self-reducibility
    – sparse   *see* language, sparse
    – symmetric difference of —s,
        see also Δ **239**
set class,   *see also* complexity class
    – closure of a
        boolean   **174**, 258
        under complement   **174**
        under finite variations   **239**, 240, 246
        under intersection   **174**, 241, 258
        under union   **174**, 241, 258
    – complex intersection of —es,
        see also $\wedge$ **174**, 241
    – complex symmetric difference of
        —es,   *see also* Δ **256**
    – complex union of —es,
        see also $\vee$ **174**, 241
    – co operator, applied to a,
        see also co$\mathcal{C}$ **77**, **174**
SetCovering   **103**
set covering problem   98, **103**
Sethupathy, P.   254,
SetPacking   **103**, 117
set packing problem   98, **103**

set ring   **175**, 241

Sewelson, V.   119

Shamir, A.   244, 308, 311, 312, 357, 359, 392, 393, 406, 408–411

Shamir, R.   120

Shamir's no-key protocol   **407**, 408

SHANKS   **367**, 368, 375, 403

Shanks, D.   367, 368, 375, 403, 408

Shannon, C.   6, 151, 153–155, 169

Shannon's Theorem
  see Theorem, Shannon's

Sherman, A.   169, 361, 396, 398, 399, 405, 406, 411, 412,

Sheu, M.   258

shift cipher   *see* cipher, shift

s-honesty   *see* function, s-honest

shortest lattice vector problem   412

Shoenfield, J.   51

sieve of Eratosthenes   **318**, 336, 337

Silverman, J.   410

Simmons, G.   347, 358

Simon, J.   307, 308

simulated annealing   254

Singh, S.   2, 168, 169, 358

Sipser, M.   67, 120, 254, 307–309

Sipser's Coding Lemma   309

Sivakumar, D.   168, 122, 124, 254, 411

small-message attack   **348**

Smolensky, R.   308

Soare, R.   257

social choice function,   *see also* SCF   **207**

– Condorcet   *see* Condorcet SCF

social choice theory   *see* theory, social choice

Solovay, R.   258, 311, 329–335, 358

SOLOVAY-STRASSEN   **330**, 332

Solovay–Strassen liar   *see* SS-liar

Solovay–Strassen test   *see* primality test, Solovay–Strassen

Solovay–Strassen witness
  see SS-witness

SOS   **104**, 105, 117, 394, 395, 399, 405

– sizes of an — instance   **104**

– target sum of an — instance   **104**

– *see also* superincreasing sequence

Spaan, E.   *see* Hemaspaandra, E.

Spielman, D.   307

space-constructible   *see* function, space-constructible

space function   *see* function, space

$space_M(\cdot)$ **56**, 114

$Space_M(\cdot)$ **56**

space hierarchy   5, **67**, 119

space hierarchy theorem
  see theorem, space hierarchy

Spakowski, H.   VII, VIII, 206, 251, 253, 254

spamming   254

sparse set   *see* language, sparse

Speckenmeyer, E.   263, 265

SPP   125, 291, **292**, 293, 294, 298, 302, 303, 306, 308–310

$\mathcal{SPP}$ 309

SPP^{SPP} 293

SQUARE-AND-MULTIPLY   **314**

Srinivasan, A.   121

SS-liar   **333**

$SS\text{-}Liars_n$ **333**, 334

SS-witness   **333**

statistical physics   124

Stearns, R.   70, 119

Steiglitz, K.   118

Stein, C.   51

Stelzer, A.   VIII, 4

Stephan, F.   252

Stern, J.   168, 411

Stinson, D.   8, 168, 169, 307, 343, 356–358, 369, 406, 408, 409

stochastic automaton
  see finite automaton, stochastic

Stöcker, P.   4

Stockmeyer, L.   120, 250, 251, 257

Stoyan, D.   VIII

Strassen, V.   311, 329–335, 358

strategic voting   *see* election system, manipulation of an

stream cipher   *see* cipher, stream

string **16**
– easy **219**
– empty, *see also* ε **16**
– hard **219**
– length of a, *see also* $|\cdot|$ **16**
– operation on —s **17**
  concatenation of —s **17**
Stromnes, M. VII
strong exponential-time hierarchy
– collapse of the 125
strong noninvertibility *see* one-way
  function, strong
structure *35*
subset-of-sums problem, *see also*
  SOS **104**, 105, 117, 394, 395,
  399, 405
substitution attack
  see attack, substitution
Sudan, M. 251
Sundaram, R. 255
superincreasing sequence **394**, 395,
  405
symmetric alternation, *see also* S_2^p
  255
symmetric cryptography
– *see* cryptography, private-key
– *see* cryptography, symmetric
symmetric cryptosystem
– *see* cryptosystem, private-key
– *see* cryptosystem, symmetric
symmetric difference hierarchy 250
– *see also* boolean hierarchy, normal form
symmetry **50**, 117
Szegedy, M. 251
Szelepcsényi, R. 77, 121

T
Θ_2^p, *see also* $P^{NP[\mathcal{O}(\log)]}$ **202**, 204,
  208, 211, 212, 216, 245, 251,
  253–255, 308, 310
Θ_2^p-complete 204, 208, 211, 245,
  253, 254
Θ_2^p-hard 204, 208, 245, 251
Θ_i^p, *see also* $P^{\Sigma_{i-1}^p[\mathcal{O}(\log)]}$ **202**

Takeuchi, M. 409
Tally$(\cdot)$ **71**, 116
TALLY **71**
tally set *see* language, tally
Tamaki, S. 263, 306
Tarjan, R. 120
Tarui, J. 308
tautology 30, **31**, 49
tautology problem **245**
tautology rule **31**
Tchernin, A. 4
technique
– easy-hard
  see easy-hard technique
– mind-change
  see mind-change
  technique
– Wagner *see* Wagner technique
Telle, J. 250
Tenenbaum, P. 4
term *35*
Thakur, M. 412
theorem
– impossibility **206**
– linear speed-up 5, 54, 59, 63,
  64, 119
  for nondeterministic classes **66**
– linear tape-compression 5, 54,
  63, 119
  for nondeterministic classes **66**
– PCP 251
– prime number 315, **317**, 343
– projection **191**
– space hierarchy 5, **67**, 119
– time hierarchy 5, **70**, 119
– uniform diagonalization **240**
Theorem
– Bayes's **46**
– Borodin–Demers 123
– Cantor–Bernstein 108
– Chinese Remainder **41**
– Cook–Levin *see* Theorem, Cook's
– Cook's 55, **88**, 112, 113, 116,
  120
– Euler's **39**

– Fermat's Little   **39**, 40, 314, 319, 320, 325, 326, 337, 372
– Friedberg–Muchnik   121
– Karp–Lipton   254, 255
– Lagrange's   39
– Rabin's   **63**
– Savitch's   **74**, 200, 227, 244
– Shannon's   **153**, 154
– Vieta's   346
theory
– complexity   1–8, 53–125, 171–259, 261–310, 317–345, 386–402
– computability
    see theory, recursive function
– graph   4, 9, **37–41**, 51
– information and coding   6, 155
– learning   252
– number   4, 9, **37–41**, 51
– probability   5, 9, **46–47**, 51
– recursive function   2, 4, 9, **16–28**, 51, 108, 110, 191, 235, 252, 257, 258
– social choice   206, 253, 254
– of data compression   155
– of formal languages   9, **16–28**, 51
– of NP-completeness   **88–106**, 120, 99, 116
thermodynamics   155
– second principle of   155
Thierauf, T.   252, 307
Threlfall, R.   358
Threshold-SAT   **274**
time-constructible   *see* function, time-constructible
time function   *see* function, time
time$_M(\cdot)$ **56**, 63, 114
Time$_M(\cdot)$ **56**
time hierarchy   5, **70**, 119
time hierarchy theorem
    see theorem, time hierarchy
Toda, S.   124, 252, 257, 308
Tomaschewski, J.   VIII
tools

– axe   54
– chain-saw   4, 54
– nail file   54
– *see* Turing machine
Torán, J.   121, 255, 257, 305, 307–310, 409
Torenvliet, T.   121, 252, 253
total break   **376**
total function   *see* function, total
total recursive function
    see function, total recursive
Tovey, C.   253
transducer   **239**
transitivity   **50**, 117
transmitting group   **172**
trapdoor information   **393**, 394, 395
trapdoor one-way function
    see one-way function, trapdoor
traveling salesperson problem,   *see also* TSP   **248**
traveling salesperson tour   **248**
– unique optimal   252
TRIAL-DIVISION   **318**, 319
Trick, M.   253
tripartite matching problem   *see* matching problem, three-dimensional
Tripathi, R.   310
Triple-DES   170
triple encryption   **145**
Trithemius, J.   168
truth-table reducibility
    – *see* reducibility, polynomial-time truth-table
    – *see* $\leq_{tt}^{p}$
truth-table closure of NP   *see* NP, $\leq_{tt}^{p}$-closure of;   *see* P$_{tt}^{NP}$
TSP   **248**
TSP-Facet   247, 249
Turing, A.   2, 9, 22, 51
Turing Award   52, 119, 120, 357
Turing closure
    – *see* complexity class, $\leq_{T}^{p}$-closure of a
    – *see* P^{C}

Turing degree   121
Turing machine   2, 9, 22, **23**, **24**,
        26–28, 48, 51, 53
    – acceptance mode of a   54, 224
    – alphabet of a
        input   **23**
        working   **23**
    – alternating,   see also ATM   6,
        53, 54, 58, 106, 171, **221**, 222,
        223, 228, 257
        accepting alternating subtree of an
            221, **222**
        address register of an   see Tur-
            ing machine, alternating, index
            tape of an
        evaluation function of an,   see
            also eval($\cdot$)   **221**
        index tape of an   **224**
        language of an   **222**
        semantics of an   **221**
        syntax of an   **221**
    – blank symbol of a,
        see also □   **23**
    – categorical   see Turing machine,
        unambiguous
    – composition of —s, see also ∘
        273
    – computation of a   56
        accepting   **25**
        rejecting   **25**
    – configuration of a   **24**, 56
        accepting   **221**, 262
        existential   **221**
        final   **24**, 56
        halting   see Turing machine,
            configuration of a, final
        initial   **24**, 56
        rejecting   **221**, 262
        universal   **221**
    – crossing sequence of a,   see also
        cs($\cdot|\cdot$)   **118**
    – deterministic,   see also DTM
        24, 54, 56
        computation of a   56

    – effective enumeration of —s   see
        Turing machine, Gödelization of
        —s
    – Gödelization of —s   **27**, 63, 68,
        70, 239
    – language of a,   see also $L(\cdot)$
        25, 56
    – multitape   54
    – nondeterministic,   see also NTM
        23, 54, 56
        computation of a   56
    – normalized   **270**, 305
    – one-way   53
    – oracle   **28**, 190, 191
        see also DOTM; NOTM
        deterministic polynomial-time,
            see also DPOTM   **193**
        nondeterministic polynomial-time,
            see also NPOTM   **193**
        positive   **244**
    – probabilistic   54, **269**, 307
    – randomized   388
        see also Turing machine, prob-
            abilistic
    – semantics of a   **24**
    – state of a   **23**
        accepting   **25**, 221
        existential   221
        final   **23**
        halting   see Turing machine,
            state of a, final
        initial   **23**
        rejecting   **25**, 221
        universal   221
    – syntax of a   **23**
    – threshold   **270**, 307
    – transition function of a   **23**
    – two-way   54
    – unambiguous   54, **111**
Turing reducibility
    – see reducibility, Turing
    – see $\leq^P_T$

U
Ulam, S.   309

Ullman, J.   51
Umans, C.   251, 252
Umanski, O.   4
unambiguous polynomial time   *see* UP
unicity distance   167, 169
uniform diagonalization theorem   *see*
        theorem, uniform diagonalization
unique solution problem   248, 249
Unique-SAT   243, **249**
United States Digital Signature Stan-
        dard   7, 371, 408
universal quantifier   *see* quantifier,
        universal
    – polynomially length-bounded
        see $\forall^p$
unsatisfiability rule   **31**
UP   5, **111**, 112, 113, 117, 119, 123,
        124, 175, 242, 250, 271, 292,
        294, 305, 308, 310, 336, 358,
        399, 411, 412
upward collapse   **177**, 198
upward separation   **70**, 71, 119, 124
    – limitations of   119
U.S. Congress   254
user authentication   **130**
U.S. Presidential Election   206
U.S. Secretary of Defense   386

V
$V(\cdot)$ **47**
$V(\cdot)$ **81**
Valiant, L.   111, 123, 124, 249, 308
van Helden, P.   121
variance, *see also* $V(\cdot)$ **47**
Vaudenay, S.   410
Vazirani, V.   8, 248, 249, 251, 252,
        308
VC   **93**, 116
Vereshchagin, N.   307
verifier   307, 409
    – dishonest   409
    – honest   409
    – *see also* proof system, interactive
    – *see also* zero-knowledge protocol
Vernam, G.   151, 154

Vernam's one-time pad   151, **154**,
        155
vertex   *see* graph, vertex set of a
    – degree of a   **181**
vertex cover problem,   *see also* VC
        93, 116
    – approximation heuristics for the
        254
Vieta, F.   346
Vieta's Theorem
        see Theorem, Vieta's
Vigenère, B. de   135
Vigenère cipher
        see cipher, Vigenère
Vigenère square   **136**, 163
Vogel, J.   VII, VIII, 206, 251, 253
Voigt, L.   VIII
Vollmer, H.   8, 79, 118
von Haeseler, A.   VIII
von Neumann, J.   120
voter   207
voting scheme   *see* election system
voting system   *see* election system
Vyskoč, J.   257

W
Wagner, K.   VIII, 8, 76, 118, 179,
        180, 204, 216, 218, 249, 250,
        253, 254, 256, 308
Wagner technique   **179**, 184, 188,
        189, **203**, 206, 251
Wang, J.   5
Wanke, E.   VIII, 250
Watanabe, O.   VII, 109, 119, 122,
        123, 255, 257, 258
weakly associative
        see associativity, weak
website ranking   254
    – manipulation of a   254
Wechsung, G.   VII, VIII, 8, 76, 118,
        119, 122–124, 171, 247, 249–
        254, 256, 307, 308, 409, 412
Wegener, I.   8, 118
Wegman, M.   295, 309
Welsh, D.   8, 124, 168

Widmayer, P.   51
Wigderson, M.   309, 388, 391, 392, 410
Wiener, M.   348, 350, 356, 358
Wiener's attack   348, **350**, 356, 358
Williams, H.   409
Williamson, M.   357
witness   **190**, 214
  – number of —es   *see* accepting computation, number of —s;
    see acc$_M$;
    see also #P
  – set of —es   *see* witness set
Wit$_M(\cdot)$ **191**
witness set,   *see also* Wit$_M(\cdot)$ **191**
Woeginger, G.   8, 251, 306
Wolf, S.   412
Wolfe, D.   248, 249
Wollermann, O.   4
Wolters, I.   4
World War II   2, 166, 169
worst-case cryptography
    see cryptography, worst-case
Wrathall, C.   251
Wright, E.   51

X
$\chi(\cdot)$ 95
χ_B **202**
X-3-Cover   **103**
  – *see also* exact cover by 3-sets problem
XP   308

Y
Yacobi, Y.   309, 411
Yamakami, T.   258
Yannakakis, M.   173, 248, 249
Yap, C.   218, 254
Young election system   206, 207, **208**, 253
  – homogeneous variant of the   253
  – ranking problem for the,   *see also* YoungRanking   **208**, 245

  – winner problem for the,   *see also* YoungWinner   206, **208**, 211, 245
Young, H.   206–208, 253
Young, P.   110, 111, 122, 123
YoungRanking   **208**, 245
Young score,   *see also* YScore$(\cdot, \cdot, \cdot)$ **208**
Young voting scheme
    see Young election system
Young winner   **208**
YoungWinner   206, **208**, 211, 245
YScore$(\cdot, \cdot, \cdot)$ **208**

Z
$\mathbb{Z}$ **10**
$\mathbb{Z}^+$ **248**
$\mathbb{Z}_n$ **38**
  – arithmetics in   **50**
$\mathbb{Z}_n^*$ **38**
Zachos, S.   283, 307, 308, 409
Zappa, F.   163
zero-knowledge   **386–393**, 409
  – almost-perfect   409
  – computational   409
  – honest-verifier   390, 409
  – perfect   390, 409
  – statistical   409
zero-knowledge property   388, **390**, 404
zero-knowledge protocol 2, 7, 41, 262, 361, **386–393**, 409
  – *see* Goldreich–Micali–Wigderson protocol
  – *see* Fiat–Shamir identification scheme
Zimand, M.   251, 254, 258
Zippel, R.   406, 410
ZPP   6, 255, 261, 268, **273**, 274, 290, 303, 307, 310
ZPP$^{\text{AM}\cap\text{coAM}}$ 358
ZPP^{NP} 255, 256, 309
ZUP   308

Monographs in Theoretical Computer Science · An EATCS Series

K. Jensen
Coloured Petri Nets
Basic Concepts, Analysis Methods
and Practical Use, Vol. 1
2nd ed.

K. Jensen
Coloured Petri Nets
Basic Concepts, *Analysis Methods*
and Practical Use, Vol. 2

K. Jensen
Coloured Petri Nets
Basic Concepts, Analysis Methods
and *Practical Use,* Vol. 3

A. Nait Abdallah
The Logic of Partial Information

Z. Fülöp, H. Vogler
Syntax-Directed Semantics
Formal Models Based
on Tree Transducers

A. de Luca, S. Varricchio
**Finiteness and Regularity
in Semigroups and Formal Languages**

E. Best, R. Devillers, M. Koutny
Petri Net Algebra

S. P. Demri, E. S. Orlowska
**Incomplete Information:
Structure, Inference, Complexity**

J. C. M. Baeten, C. A. Middelburg
Process Algebra with Timing

L. A. Hemaspaandra, L. Torenvliet
Theory of Semi-Feasible Algorithms

E. Fink, D. Wood
Restricted-Orientation Convexity

Zhou Chaochen, M. R. Hansen
Duration Calculus
A Formal Approach to Real-Time
Systems

M. Große-Rhode
**Semantic Integration
of Heterogeneous Software
Specifications**

Texts in Theoretical Computer Science · An EATCS Series

J. L. Balcázar, J. Díaz, J. Gabarró
Structural Complexity I

M. Garzon
Models of Massive Parallelism
Analysis of Cellular Automata
and Neural Networks

J. Hromkovič
**Communication Complexity
and Parallel Computing**

A. Leitsch
The Resolution Calculus

A. Salomaa
Public-Key Cryptography
2nd ed.

K. Sikkel
Parsing Schemata
A Framework for Specification
and Analysis of Parsing Algorithms

H. Vollmer
Introduction to Circuit Complexity
A Uniform Approach

W. Fokkink
Introduction to Process Algebra

K. Weihrauch
Computable Analysis
An Introduction

J. Hromkovič
Algorithmics for Hard Problems
Introduction to Combinatorial
Optimization, Randomization,
Approximation, and Heuristics
2nd ed.

S. Jukna
Extremal Combinatorics
With Applications
in Computer Science

C. S. Calude
Information and Randomness
An Algorithmic Perspective, 2nd ed.

J. Hromkovič
Theoretical Computer Science
Introduction to Automata,
Computability, Complexity,
Algorithmics, Randomization,
Communication and Cryptography

K. Schneider
Verification of Reactive Systems
Formal Methods and Algorithms

S. Ronchi Della Rocca, L. Paolini
The Parametric Lambda Calculus
A Metamodel for Computation

Y. Bertot, P. Castéran
**Interactive Theorem Proving
and Program Development**
Coq'Art: The Calculus
of Inductive Constructions

L. Libkin
Elements of Finite Model Theory

M. Hutter
Universal Artificial Intelligence
Sequential Decisions
Based on Algorithmic Probability

G. Păun, G. Rozenberg, A. Salomaa
DNA Computing
New Computing Paradigms
2nd corr. printing

J. Hromkovič, R. Klasing, A. Pelc,
P. Ružička[†], W. Unger
**Dissemination of Information
in Communication Networks**
Broadcasting, Gossiping, Leader
Election, and Fault-Tolerance

Texts in Theoretical Computer Science · An EATCS Series

P. Clote, E. Kranakis
**Boolean Functions
and Computation Models**

L. A. Hemaspaandra, M. Ogihara
The Complexity Theory Companion

W. Kluge
Abstract Computing Machines
A Lambda Calculus Perspective

R. Kurki-Suonio
**A Practical Theory
of Reactive Systems**
Incremental Modeling
of Dynamic Behaviors

J. Hromkovič
**Design and Analysis of Randomized
Algorithms**
Introduction to Design Paradigms

J. Rothe
Complexity Theory and Cryptology
An Introduction to Cryptocomplexity